Lecture Notes in Computer Science 2575

Edited by G. Goos, J. Hartmanis, and J. van Leeuwen

Springer
Berlin
Heidelberg
New York
Hong Kong
London
Milan
Paris
Tokyo

Lenore D. Zuck
Paul C. Attie
Agostino Cortesi
Supratik Mukhopadhyay (Eds.)

Verification, Model Checking, and Abstract Interpretation

4th International Conference, VMCAI 2003
New York, NY, USA, January 9-11, 2003
Proceedings

 Springer

Volume Editor

QM LIBRARY
(MILE END)

Lenore D. Zuck
Department of Computer Science, New York University
715 Broadway (7th floor), New York, NY 10003, USA
E-mail: zuck@cs.nyu.edu

Paul C. Attie
Northeastern University, College of Computer Science
360 Huntington Ave., Boston, MA 02115, USA
E-mail: attie@ccs.neu.edu

Agostino Cortesi
Venice University C'Foscari, Computer Science Department
Via Torino 155, 30170 Mestre-Venezia, Italy
E-mail: cortesi@dsi.unive.it

Supratik Mukhopadhyay
West Virginia University, Department of Computer Science and
Electrical Engineering, Morgantown, WV 26505, USA
E-mail: supratik@saul.cis.upenn.edu

Cataloging-in-Publication Data applied for

A catalog record for this book is available from the Library of Congress.
Bibliographic information published by Die Deutsche Bibliothek

Die Deutsche Bibliothek lists this publication in the Deutsche Nationalbibliografie;
detailed bibliographic data is available in the Internet at <http://dnb.ddb.de>.

CR Subject Classification (1998): F.3.1-2, D.3.1, D.2.4

ISSN 0302-9743
ISBN 3-540-00348-7 Springer-Verlag Berlin Heidelberg New York

Springer-Verlag Berlin Heidelberg New York
a member of BertelsmannSpringer Science+Business Media GmbH

http://www.springer.de

© Springer-Verlag Berlin Heidelberg 2003
Printed in Germany

Typesetting: Camera-ready by author, data conversion by PTP Berlin, Stefan Sossna e. K.
Printed on acid-free paper   SPIN: 10872328   06/3142   5 4 3 2 1 0

Preface

This volume contains the proceedings of the 4th International Conference on Verification, Model Checking, and Abstract Interpretation (VMCAI 2003), held in New York city, January 9–11, 2003. The purpose of VMCAI was to provide a forum for researchers from three communities—Verification, Model Checking, and Abstract Interpretation—that will facilitate interaction, cross-fertilization, and the advance of hybrid methods that combine the three areas. With the growing need for formal tools to reason about complex, infinite-state, and embedded systems, such hybrid methods are bound to be of great importance.

Topics covered by VMCAI include program verification, static analysis techniques, model checking, program certification, type systems, abstract domains, debugging techniques, compiler optimization, embedded systems, and formal analysis of security protocols.

VMCAI 2003 was the fourth VMCAI meeting. The previous three were held as workshops (Port Jefferson 1997, Pisa 1998, and Venice 2002). It is the success of the last meeting, and the wide response it generated, that made it clear the time had come to make it an annual conference.

The program committee selected 20 papers out of 43 submitted, on the basis of at least four reviews. The principal criteria were relevance and quality. The program of VMCAI 2003 included, in addition to the research papers, two invited talks, by Amir Pnueli (Weizmann and NYU) on *Model-Checking and Abstraction to the Aid of Parameterized Systems*, and Andreas Podelski (MPI) on *Software Model Checking with Abstraction Refinement*, and three tutorials, by Patrick Cousot (ENS) on *Automatic Verification by Abstract Interpretation*, A. Prasad Sistla (UIC) on *Symmetry Reductions in Model-Checking*, and Bernhard Steffen (Dortmund) on *Behaviour-Based Model Construction*. We would like to thank the Program Committee members and the reviewers, without whose dedicated effort the conference would not have been possible. Our thanks also to the Steering Committee members for helpful advice. Thanks to Radu Grosu, the local arrangement chair. Special thanks are due to Ittai Balaban for installing, managing, and taking care of the START software and to Yi Fang for handling the website. Alfred Hofmann and his team at Springer-Verlag were very helpful in preparing the proceedings. We remain extremely grateful to Supratik Mukhopadhyay for help in the initial stages of this conference, and to Paul Attie and Agostino Cortesi for assistance in editing this volume.

Special thanks are due to the institutions that helped sponsor this event: the National Science Foundation (NSF), the Office of Naval Research (ONR), New York University, Ca'Foscari University of Venice, the Max Planck Institute, and the State University of New York at Stony Brook. We would like to thank Marcia Saito Eckel, Lourdes Santana, and Daisy Calderon for their administrative assistance.

January 2003   Lenore Zuck

Organization

Conference Chair

Lenore D. Zuck (New York University)

Program Committee

Rajeev Alur (University of Pennsylvania)
Paul C. Attie (Northeastern University)
Annalisa Bossi (Università Ca' Foscari di Venezia)
Agostino Cortesi (Università Ca' Foscari di Venezia)
Radhia Cousot (École Polytechnique)
Javier Esparza (University of Edinburgh)
Andrew D. Gordon (Microsoft Research Cambridge)
Radu Grosu (SUNY Stony Brook)
Joshua D. Guttman (Mitre)
Barbara König (Technische Universität München)
Salvatore LaTorre (Università di Salerno)
Giorgio Levi (Università di Pisa)
Michael Lowry (NASA Ames)
Supratik Mukhopadhyay (University of West Virginia)
Doron A. Peled (University of Warwick)
Colin P. Sterling (University of Edinburgh)
Lenore D. Zuck (New York University)

Local Arrangement Chair

Radu Grosu (SUNY Stony Brook)

Steering Committee

Agostino Cortesi (Università Ca' Foscari di Venezia)
Allen E. Emerson (University of Texas at Austin)
Giorgio Levi (Università di Pisa)
Andreas Podelski (Max-Planck-Institut für Informatik)
Thomas W. Reps (University of Wisconsin-Madison)
David A. Schmidt (Kansas State University)

Reviewers

Tuomas Aura	Jérôme Feret	Laurent Mauborgne
Roberto Barbuti	Gianluigi Ferrari	Antoine Miné
Clark Barrett	Gilberto Filé	David Monniaux
Massimo Benerecetti	Riccardo Focardi	Aniello Murano
Stefan Berghofer	Cédric Fournet	Jan Obdrzalek
Bruno Blanchet	Roberto Giacobazzi	Paritosh Pandya
Chiara Bodei	Roberta Gori	Carla Piazza
Chiara Braghin	David Harel	Amir Pnueli
Luca Cardelli	Sara Kalvala	Antonino Salibra
Witold Charatonik	Ruggero Lanotte	Francesco Tapparo
Stelvio Cimato	Martin Lange	C.R. Ramakrishnan
Patrick Cousot	Ranko Lazik	Jean-Francois Raskin
Bojan Cukic	Martin Leucker	Stefan Roemer
Thao Dang	Francesca Levi	Alessandro Roncato
Roberto De Prisco	Annie Liu	Sabina Rossi
Pierpaolo Degano	Monika Maidl	Abhik Roychoudhury
Giorgio Delzanno	Rupak Majumdar	Stefan Schwoon
Catalin Dima	Matthieu Martel	Scott Stoller
Allen Emerson	Moreno Marzolla	Enea Zaffanella
Kousha Etessami	Andrea Masini	
Marco Faella	Damien Masse	
Yi Fang	Barbara Masucci	

Sponsoring Institutions

National Science Foundation (NSF)
Office of Naval Research (ONR)
New York University (NYU)
Università Ca' Foscari di Venezia
Max Planck Institute (MPI)
State University of New York at Stony Brook

Table of Contents

Invited Talks

Invited Tutorials

Static Analysis

Dynamic Systems

Model Checking II

Software Model Checking with Abstraction Refinement

Andreas Podelski

Max-Planck-Institut für Informatik
66123 Saarbrücken, Germany
podelski@mpi-sb.mpg.de

Abstract of Invited Talk

Automated verification of programs is a topic of increasing interest [1,2,3,4,5,6, 7,8,9,10,11,12,13]. In a recent approach known as *software model checking*, one tries to prove a safety property of a program by iterating three steps: (1) the construction of an abstract system for an abstraction given by *predicates* over sets of states, (2) the model checking (in fact, a reachability analysis) of the abstract system, and (3) the refinement of the abstraction. The third step is done by generating additional predicates from the spurious counterexamples of the abstract system, if there are any; if not, the program property is either proven or disproven, and the method terminates.

We will investigate the theory behind the approach and try to identify its potential interest. In principle, finding an abstraction is as hard as finding the proof itself [3]. However, using abstraction refinement (in the third step) for the search of an abstraction buys a triple-exponential saving over the direct search of a proof.

The idea that underlied the approach initially is to extend model checking to software by mapping an infinite-state transition system homomorphically to a finite one. We go beyond that idea, following the framework of abstract interpretation. We present a spectrum of three abstractions with different precision/cost trade-off's. We characterize each abstraction by different orderings over formulas, namely logical, local and syntactic entailment, respectively. Logical entailment corresponds to the above-mentioned homomorphic abstraction, that can be implemented in exponential time in the number of predicates. In *convex* theories or *independent* constraint systems, logical and local entailment coincide by definition; the ordering corresponds to the *Cartesian* abstraction formalized in [1]; it can be implemented in linear time. Syntact entailment is the ordering of the free distributive lattice and corresponds to an abstraction that can be implemented in constant time.

We qualify software model checking methods (using one of the three abstractions) in terms of relative completeness wrt. to idealized verification methods. Each idealized method is a fixpoint iteration over the domain of formulas with one of the three entailment orderings. The method is idealized in that an oracle guides the *widening*, i.e. guesses each extrapolation step during the reachability analysis.

L. Zuck et al. (Eds.): VMCAI 2003, LNCS 2575, pp. 1–3, 2003.

For relative completeness, the abstraction refinement procedure involved must amount to the extrapolation possibilities of the oracle. Thus, each widening operator represents a new quality criterion for abstraction refinement procedures. In [2], we considered 'syntactic widening' which can only extrapolate single atomic formulas in a formula by the formula *true*. It can not, for example, extrapolate the disjunction of $x = 100$, $y = -200$ with $x = 99$, $y = -198$ by the formula $2x + y = 0$. As noted in [4], this extrapolation is used to verify the following example.

```
x := 100; y := -200;
while x <> 0 do x := (x-1); y := (y+2) od;
always {y = 0 }
```

We show that every widening operator can be accommodated by a corresponding abstraction refinement procedure. This means that software model checking with abstraction refinement can achieve the precision of every widening-based method (the iterated abstraction refinement replaces the oracle needed for guessing the extrapolation steps). In particular, it can achieve sufficient precision to verify the above example.

The talk is in part based on joint work with Tom Ball and Sriram Rajamani, Microsoft Research and Andrey Rybalchenko, MPI. The paper underlying the talk is available under http://www.mpi-sb.mpg.de/~podelski.

References

1. T. Ball, A. Podelski, and S. K. Rajamani. Boolean and Cartesian abstraction for model checking C programs. In T. Margaria and W. Yi, editors, *Tools and Algorithms for the Construction and Analysis of Systems, 7th International Conference, TACAS 2001, Genova, Italy, April 2-6, 2001, Proceedings*, volume 2031 of *LNCS*, pages 268–283. Springer-Verlag, 2001.
2. T. Ball, A. Podelski, and S. K. Rajamani. Relative completeness of abstraction refinement for software model checking. In J.-P. Kaoen and P. Stevens, editors, *Tools and Algorithms for the Construction and Analysis of Systems, 8th International Conference, TACAS 2002, Grenoble, France, April 8-12, 2002, Proceedings*, volume 2280 of *LNCS*, pages 158–172. Springer-Verlag, 2002.
3. P. Cousot. Partial completeness of abstract fixpoint checking. In B. Y. Choueiry and T. Walsh, editors, *Abstraction, Reformulation, and Approximation, 4th International Symposium, SARA 2000, Horseshoe Bay, Texas, USA, July 26-29, 2000, Proceedings*, volume 1864 of *LNCS*, pages 1–15. Springer, 2000.
4. P. Cousot and R. Cousot. On abstraction in software verification. In E. Brinksma and K. G. Larsen, editors, *Computer Aided Verification, 14th International Conference, CAV 2002, Copenhagen, Denmark, July 27-31, 2002, Proceedings*, volume 2404 of *LNCS*, pages 37–56. Springer, 2002.
5. R. Giacobazzi, F. Ranzato, and F. Scozzari. Making abstract interpretations complete. *Journal of the ACM (JACM)*, 47(2):361–416, 2000.

6. J. Hatcliff and M. B. Dwyer. Using the Bandera tool set to model-check properties of concurrent Java software. In K. G. Larsen and M. Nielsen, editors, *CONCUR 2001 - Concurrency Theory, 12th International Conference, Aalborg, Denmark, August 20-25, 2001, Proceedings*, volume 2154 of *LNCS*, pages 39–58. Springer, 2001.

7. T. A. Henzinger, R. Jhala, R. Majumdar, G. C. Necula, G. Sutre, and W. Weimer. Temporal-safety proofs for systems code. In E. Brinksma and K. G. Larsen, editors, *Computer Aided Verification, 14th International Conference, CAV 2002, Copenhagen, Denmark, July 27-31, 2002, Proceedings*, volume 2404 of *LNCS*, pages 526–538. Springer, 2002.

8. G. J. Holzmann. Software analysis and model checking. In E. Brinksma and K. G. Larsen, editors, *Computer Aided Verification, 14th International Conference, CAV 2002, Copenhagen, Denmark, July 27-31, 2002, Proceedings*, volume 2404 of *LNCS*, pages 1–16. Springer, 2002.

9. Y. Lakhnech, S. Bensalem, S. Berezin, and S. Owre. Incremental verification by abstraction. In T. Margaria and W. Yi, editors, *Tools and Algorithms for the Construction and Analysis of Systems, 7th International Conference, TACAS 2001, Genova, Italy, April 2-6, 2001, Proceedings*, volume 2031 of *LNCS*, pages 98–112. Springer-Verlag, 2001.

10. A. Podelski. Model checking as constraint solving. In J. Palsberg, editor, *Static Analysis, 7th International Symposium, SAS 2000, Santa Barbara, CA, USA, June 29 - July 1, 2000, Proceedings*, volume 1824 of *LNCS*, pages 22–37. Springer-Verlag, 2000.

11. G. Ramalingam, A. Warshavsky, J. Field, D. Goyal, and M. Sagiv. Deriving specialized program analyses for certifying component-client conformance. In *Proceeding of the ACM SIGPLAN 2002 Conference on Programming language design and implementation*, pages 83–94. ACM Press, 2002.

12. M. Sagiv, T. Reps, and R. Wilhelm. Parametric shape analysis via 3-valued logic. *ACM Transactions on Programming Languages and Systems (TOPLAS)*, 24(3):217–298, 2002.

13. E. Yahav. Verifying safety properties of concurrent Java programs using 3-valued logic. In H. R. Nielsen, editor, *Proceedings of the 28th ACM SIGPLAN-SIGACT Symposium on Principles of Programming Languages*, pages 27–40. ACM Press, 2001.

Model-Checking and Abstraction to the Aid of Parameterized Systems

Amir Pnueli[1] and Lenore Zuck[2]

[1] Weizmann Institute of Science and New York University, amir@cs.nyu.edu
[2] New York University, zuck@cs.nyu.edu

Abstract. Parameterized systems are systems that involve numerous instantiations of the same finite-state module. Examples of parameterized systems include tele-communication protocols, bus protocols, cache coherence protocols, and many other protocols that underly current state-of-the-art systems. Formal verification of parameterized systems is known to be undecidable [AK86] and thus cannot be automated. Recent research has shown that in many cases it is possible to use *abstraction methods* to generate a finite-state systems from a parameterized systems. The finite-state system can then be model-checked. If successful, it is possible to conclude that the original parameterized system satisfies its requirements. Otherwise, it is often the case that the counter-example produced by the model checker can indicate an error in the original parameterized system. This combined technique allows for automatic verification of parameterized systems.

This presentation describes our recent approaches that combine abstraction and model-checking to verify safety as well we liveness properties of parameterized systems. We start with the method of *invisible invariants* [APR+01] that combines a small-model theorem with an heuristics to generate proofs of correctness of parameterized systems. We also describe the method of *network invariants* [ZPK02,KPSZ02] which allows to explicitly describe a finite-system that, in a precise sense, has the same external behavior as an infinite-state one, and can be used for model-checking properties.

References

[AK86]   K. R. Apt and D. Kozen. Limits for automatic program verification of finite-state concurrent systems. *Information Processing Letters*, 22(6), 1986.

[APR+01]   T. Arons, A. Pnueli, S. Ruah, J. Xu, and L. Zuck. Parameterized verification with automatically computed inductive assertions. In *Proc. 13th Intl. Conference on Computer Aided Verification (CAV'01), volume 2102 of* Lect. Notes in Comp. Sci., *Springer-Verlag*, pages 221–234, 2001.

[KPSZ02]   Y. Kesten, A. Pnueli, E. Shahar, and L. Zuck. Network invariants in action. In *Proceedings of Concur'02*, volume 2421 of *LNCS*. Springer-Verlag, 2002.

[ZPK02]   L. Zuck, A. Pnueli, and Y. Kesten. Automatic verification of free choice. In *Proc. of the 3rd workshop on Verification, Model Checking, and Abstract Interpretation*, volume 2294 of *LNCS*, 2002.

L. Zuck et al. (Eds.): VMCAI 2003, LNCS 2575, p. 4, 2003.
© Springer-Verlag Berlin Heidelberg 2003

Behavior-Based Model Construction

Bernhard Steffen and Hardi Hungar

Computer Science Department, University of Dortmund, Germany

Abstract. In this paper, we review behavior-based model construction from a point of view characterized by *verification, model checking* and *abstract interpretation*. It turns out that *abstract interpretation* is the key for scaling known learning techniques for practical applications, *model checking* may serve as a teaching aid in the learning process underlying the model construction, and that there are also synergies with other validation and *verification* techniques. We will illustrate our discussion by means of a realistic telecommunication scenario, where the underlying system has grown over the last two decades, the available system documentation consists of not much more than user manuals and protocol standards, and the revision cycle times are extremely short. In this situation, behavior-based model construction provides a sound basis e.g. for test-suite design and maintenance, test organization, and test evaluation.

1 Introduction

Most systems in use today lack adequate specifications or make use of un(der) specified components. In fact, the much propagated component-based software design style naturally leads to under specified systems, as most libraries only provide very partial specifications of their components. Moreover, typically, revisions and last minute changes hardly enter the system specification. We observed this dilemma in the telecommunication area: the revision cycle times are extremely short, which make the maintenance of specifications unrealistic, and at the same time the short revision cycles necessitate extensive testing effort. More generally, the lack of documentation is felt in many places of which quality control is one of the most outstanding. Moderated regular extrapolation [5] has been proposed to overcome this situation: techniques known from automata learning have been adapted to cope with structures adequate for modelling reactive systems (like telecommunication systems), and to faithfully incorporate expert knowledge for guiding the learning process.

In this paper, we review the process of moderated regular extrapolation from a point of view characterized by *verification, model checking* and *abstract interpretation*. It turns out that *abstraction* is the key for adapting known learning techniques for our application scenario, *model checking* is a good means for guiding the learning process, and that there are also synergies with other validation and *verification* techniques. The paper will focus on the abstraction point of view, which is in the heart of the whole learning procedure, while it will only sketch the aspects of model checking and verification.

L. Zuck et al. (Eds.): VMCAI 2003, LNCS 2575, pp. 5–19, 2003.

Abstract Interpretation

Regular extrapolation is a process of iterated abstraction and refinement. While abstract interpretation is necessary to achieve regular models (extended finite state machines) at all, refinement is a means for a tailored compensation of too rigid abstraction steps, i.e. for an aspect-specific enhancement of an abstract interpretation. Technically, we can distinguish three kinds of abstraction, which all naturally arise during the model construction process:

Complete Abstract Interpretations. Given an observation level, many details may be hidden in the concrete system without affecting the learning process. In our application scenario, we focus on the protocol level which is the essential one (not only) for telecommunication systems. This allows us to completely ignore the message contents. The same would be true for the timing information, as long as the qualitative system behavior is time insensitive.

Safe Approximations. Complete abstract interpretations are insufficient for arriving at a regular model as we typically deal with complex observational properties which are undecidable or at least not yet captured by current abstraction techniques. Thus we must deal with a loss of expressive power. Safe approximations, although typically being imprecise, guarantee the preservation of properties in one direction: either properties proved at the abstract level are guaranteed to be true also at the concrete level (under approximation) or vice versa (over approximation).

Faithful Hypotheses. Observation-based model construction starts by collecting finite behavioral traces which are then *extrapolated* into regular models by means of automata learning techniques: automata learning builds model structures which distinguish states only on the basis of witnesses: states are identified until a distinguishing trace is found. As state identification increases the number of possible runs, learning leads to a behavioral *over approximation* of the observed portion of the system. On the other hand, currently unobserved behavior is not modelled at all. Thus safety cannot be guaranteed in any direction. Rather, automata learning techniques iteratively construct minimal hypothesis automata consistent with all the observations. This is inherited by our regular extrapolation technique, which, additionally, comprises expert knowledge.

Our discussion will focus on:

- actor abstraction, which abstracts individual objects to roles,
- the (for our purposes adapted) L*-learning algorithm which iteratively constructs the minimal hypothesis automaton, and
- partial order reduction, based on an externally given causality relation.

Model Checking

We use temporal logic formulas to specify the expert knowledge about the considered system, concerning constraints about the protocol, security policies or functional requirements. These formulas can then be verified on each hypothesis model. Discrepancies leading to counterexamples are used to guide the learning process.

However, and perhaps more importantly, regular extrapolation can and should be regarded as an aid for verification techniques like model checking to extend their applicability, similar to the approach of black-box checking from [14]. Even legacy systems may now be model checked once a behavioral model has been constructed.

Verification/Validation

Besides model checking, we employ various verification and validation techniques. Answering membership queries, the central activity of most automata learning techniques, essentially requires 'classical' system tests, and constructed hypothesis models may well be used for monitoring the running system (online verification). Revealed discrepancies between the system and the model may then be analyzed in order to determine whether the system or the model should be modified. This analysis typically requires a manual effort, a fact which is reflected in calling our approach *moderated* regular extrapolation.

The considered class of systems are complex, reactive systems, as can be found e.g. in telecommunication systems. These systems normally consist of several subcomponents which communicate with and affect each other, typically via standardized protocols.

In the following section, we present the application scenario before we develop the methodology of model construction in more detail in Section 3.

2   Application Scenario

2.1   Complex Reactive Systems

We developed the methodology with the aim of applying it to complex reactive systems like those found in the telecommunication area. Such systems consist of several subcomponents, either hardware or software, communicating with and affecting each other. Typical examples for this kind of systems are *Computer Telephony Integrated (CTI) systems*, like complex *call-center solutions*, embedded systems, or web-based applications. One such system is depicted in Fig. 1.

Many CTI systems employ instances of the *Computer-Supported Telephony Applications (CSTA)* protocol for the communication between their components. A typical CSTA record contains several components. Some of them convey essential information relevant to modeling, others can be safely ignored. An example record (`field, value, meaning`) may look as follows:

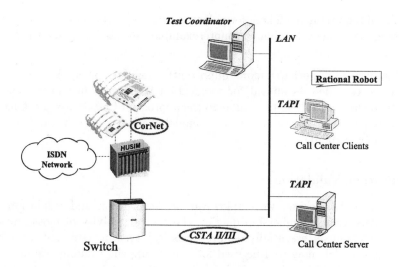

Fig. 1. Overview of the CTI system to be learned

invokeID: 58391 — a number to identify the protocol frame

operation-value: 21 — indicating the reporting of some external event (this is introduced by the observer functionality used by us to get information about internal actions in the telephone system)

event-specific info: hookswitch — name of the external event

device dialing number: 500 — number of the device which issued the event

hookswitchOnHook TRUE — reporting about the state of the external device

timestamp: 20001010095551

For most modelling purposes, projecting this record (which, in fact, contains even more components in practice) to something as abstract as (hookswitchOnHook,500).

As an example system we take a telephone switch from a call-center installation as sketched in Fig. 1. The telephone switch is connected to the ISDN telephone network and acts as a 'normal' telephone switch to the phones. Additionally, it communicates directly via a LAN or indirectly via an application server with CTI applications that are executed on PCs. Like the phones, CTI applications are active components: they may stimulate the switch (e.g. initiate calls), and they also react to stimuli sent by the switch (e.g. notify incoming calls).

2.2   Modeling

Systems as described above operate in real time in an environment exhibiting much parallelism. An interaction between components sometimes consists of several records sent back and forth. So when observing a CTI system in operation, interactions belonging to different interactions will often overlap.

We decided (for complexity reasons) not to model the real-time aspects. Additionally, just as it is done in current test practice, we do not try to capture erroneous behavior in stress situations where interactions happen quickly and reactions to different stimuli may occur interleaved. Instead, we collect all the system's reactions to each single stimulus by waiting until the system has reached a stable state. Usually, this can be realized with timeouts. By neglecting timing issues in this way, we arrive at a view of reactive systems as input-deterministic I/O transition systems.

According to the following definition, an I/O-transition system is a device which reacts on inputs by producing outputs and possibly changing its internal state. It may also be assumed that the system is *input enabled*, i.e. that it accepts all inputs regardless of its internal state. Input determinism means that the system's behavior is completely determined by its inputs, which is a very important property when one tries to capture the behavior spectrum of a given system by systematically applying stimuli and observing its reactions.

Definition 1.
An input/output transition system *is a structure* $\mathcal{S} = (\Sigma, A_I, A_O, \rightarrow, s_0)$, *consisting of*

- *a countable, non-empty set Σ of states,*
- *countable sets A_I and A_O of input, resp. output, actions,*
- *a transition relation $\rightarrow \subseteq \Sigma \times A_I \times A_O^* \times \Sigma$, and*
- *a unique start state s_0.*

It is called input deterministic *if at each state s there is at most one transition for each input starting from that state. It is* input enabled *if there is at least one transition for each input.*

Another property indispensable for our approach is finiteness of the model. There are two obstacles to viewing a given system as a finite entity:

1. Usually, the number of components connected to a system like the telephone switch might be rather large. Modelling a system with the maximal number of components (if known) would be impractical. Also, a new release might increase this parameter, thus invalidating the model. And last but not least such a large model would not reveal much additional information about the system. In fact, both protocol specifications and practical tests usually work with small, finite instantiations of a system environment. We do the same, and thereby arrive at a manageable system size where address spaces can be represented by discrete symbols.[1]

---

[1] It may be argued that in some cases (of protocol verification) it can even be proved to be safe to restrict attention to some small instantiation. These arguments, however, all require quite some elaborate side conditions which cannot be established in our real-life application domain, at least not without some very substantial work.

2. Protocols may contain items like time stamps and tags. While we can easily abstract from time stamps when modelling on the functional level, tags in general might constitute a more severe problem. Tags are e.g. used in protocols to reference some previous record (or incomplete exchange) unambiguously. Our answer to this problem is to restrict stimulation to use at most a finite number of tags, and to reuse tags whenever some exchange is completed. For this to work, it must be specified when exchanges (referenced by tags) terminate. In many cases, this can be done by either temporal-logic formulas or automata. Then, the restriction to finitely many tags is similar to the restriction to finite address spaces: It is natural and mirrors common practice. For our example application, tags appear only when CTI-components enter the modelling focus. If only telephones are connected to the switch, they do no show up.

3 Behavior-Oriented Model Construction

Fig. 2 sketches briefly our iterative approach. It starts with a model (initially empty) and a set of observations. The observations are gathered from a reference system in the form of traces. The notion *reference system* is due to the regression testing scenario: there a previous system version is available and we want to generate a cor-

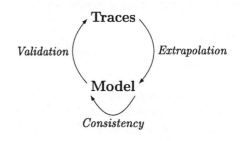

Fig. 2. Generation of Models

responding model as a means to check a new version for consistency with the previous one.

The observations can be obtained either *passively*, i.e. by observing a running reference system, or, better, *actively*, i.e. by stimulating a reference system through test cases. The set of traces (i.e. the observations) is then preprocessed, extrapolated and used to extend the current model. After extension, the model is completed through several techniques, including adjusting to expert specifications. Finally, the current hypothesis for the model is validated, which can lead to new observations.

The realization of this approach heavily uses automata operations and related techniques. The basis is given by standard automata operations like homomorphisms and boolean operations like *meet, join* and *complement* [7]. These are complemented by some specific operations for extrapolation. In particular, these are abstraction mappings more general than language homomorphisms, together with a particular folding operation, which introduces cycles in the finite traces by identifying similar states. This borrows from automata learning techniques as discussed in [1] but is quite different in several aspects.

The adequate incorporation of expert knowledge requires further techniques. Here temporal logic [3] serves to formulate specifications which limit the model from above. I.e., experts formulate properties which they believe to be true of the system, and extrapolation results should be limited by them. Temporal-logic model checking is employed to check adherence of the model to these constraints. Counter examples generated by the model checker in case of a violation are studied to pinpoint the source of the discrepancy.

Another way in which expert knowledge enters the method concerns specifying independence relations between events. This, by employing ideas of partial order approaches [11,16], leads to a generalization from (randomly) sequential observations to parallel patterns.

Finally, the validation of models draws on testing theory (cf. e.g. [10] for a survey) to generate stimuli sequences that help discovering wrongly identified states and missed behavior. On a technical level, the ingredients of our method are

Testing, for stimulating the system to be modelled to collect behavior sequences.

Automata learning, to guide the testing and to combine the results into an approximate model.

Model checking, to make use of expert knowledge for model validation.

Manual interaction, for conflict resolution.

Change management, to cope with revisions.

In the following, we explain the individual steps of the model construction process.

4   Automata Learning

4.1   Background

Let us assume that a regular language is given, so that we can test arbitrary strings for membership in the language, and that we want to construct a (minimal) acceptor.

The worst-case complexity of this learning problem is exponential in the number of states of the automaton to be learned [12]. The argument which proves the difficulty of exact learning relies on *combination-lock automata*. A combination lock within a finite automaton is a set of states linked by a sequence of transitions so that the last state can only be reached by exactly one sequence of symbols — any deviation will leave the combination lock and lead to other states. Whether an automaton to be learned contains such a lock can only be detected by testing all sequences of the length of the longest combination lock potentially contained in the automaton at hand, which results in an exponential number of tests.

In practice, however, such locks are not very common, and that an arbitrary automaton contains one has a low probability. So, approximate learning (PAC learning, [15]), which means that with high probability the learned automaton will accept a language very close to the given one, does not suffer from the combination-lock effect. And indeed, it is known that PAC learning can be done in polynomial time [8]. Experiments have even provided evidence that this theoretical result is relevant for practice, see for instance [9]: random automata can be learned pretty well.

In our scenario, the system models to be learned are not random. One might even argue that some protocols are in some way similar to combination locks in that they impose sequences to be enacted in some prescribed order, yet the combination-lock argument does not apply here: these sequences tend to be of bounded length and they are also known from manuals and protocol descriptions, they can be found in test sequences and they can be observed on systems in operation. So there is well-founded evidence that combinatorial reasons will not turn out to be harmful in our application scenario.

One way to perform the learning of automata is via the algorithm L* [1]. To factor out insecurities from approximation, L* relies on an *equivalence oracle* in addition to the *membership oracle* which is used by in most automata learning techniques. The equivalence oracle provides counter examples if an automaton constructed from the information available so far does not match the given language. With this additional resource, finite automata can be learned exactly in polynomial time in the (assumed to be known) number of states of the original system.

We use L* as the basis of our learning procedure. To make it work, it has to be adapted in several ways, as it solves learning in an idealized setting. Neither the membership oracle nor the equivalence oracle are available in practice and therefore have to be substituted by other means.

Membership queries have to be solved by testing. In the presence of nontrivial abstractions, this is not an easy task. An important ingredient in solving this problem is a tool called *Integrated Test Environment (ITE)* [6,13] which has been applied to a number of different tasks in research and in industrial practice. From a sequence of stimuli, the *ITE* generates a test program, using predefined code blocks for stimuli and additional glue code. Glue code and code blocks solve the problems connected with generating, checking and identifying non-propositional protocol elements like tags, time stamps and identifiers. In essence, the *ITE* bridges the gap between the abstract model and the concrete system. The generated test program is interfaced to the system to be learned with the help of additional test hardware.

The equivalence oracle is more difficult to substitute. If no additional information about the system is available, there is of course no reliable equivalence check – one can never be sure whether the whole behavior spectrum of a system has been explored. But there are approximations of the equivalence oracle which cover the majority of systems pretty well. This is at the basis of the theoretical result that PAC learning can be done in polynomial time with membership queries alone. The basic idea is to scan the system in the vicinity of the explored part looking for discrepancies with respect to the expected behavior.

A particularly good approximation is achieved by performing a test in the spirit of [2,17]. In essence, this test checks each transition in the hypothesis/conjecture automaton by validating that the target state behaves properly along a sequence which distinguishes it from all other states of the conjecture automaton. This test has polynomial complexity. – We have additional means at our disposal in the form of formalized expert knowledge. This is described in more detail in Sec. 4.4.

In addition to oracle substitutions we have to adapt the algorithm itself from its original application domain – deterministic acceptors – to input/output transition systems.

4.2   Learning I/O Transition Systems

The basic idea behind Angluin's algorithm is to systematically explore the system's behavior using the membership oracle and trying to build the transition table of a deterministic finite automaton with a minimal number of states. The required information is organized in the central data structure of the algorithm called *observation table* $\mathcal{OT}$, which comprises the results of the membership queries and represents the intermediate conjectures.

Definition 2 (Observation Table). *Given an alphabet A, a finite, prefix-closed set $S \subset A^*$ and a finite set $E \subset A^*$, an observation table $\mathcal{OT}$ is a two-dimensional array with rows for each string in $S \cup S \cdot A$ and columns for strings in E and entries in $\{0, 1\}$. An entry $\mathcal{OT}(s, e) = 1$ is interpreted in the context of the algorithm L^* that the sequence $s; e$ is a member of the regular set, while 0 means that it is not.*

1. *$\mathcal{OT}$ is called **closed**, if $\forall t \in S \cdot A. \exists s \in S. row(t) = row(s)$.*

2. *$\mathcal{OT}$ is called **consistent**, if $\forall s_1, s_2 \in S. row(s_1) = row(s_2) \Rightarrow \forall a \in A. row(s_1; a) = row(s_2; a)$.*

The algorithm starts with the initial state, which is reached by the empty string. It keeps a set of strings S which lead from the initial state to all the states discovered so far. S may, and in fact usually will, contain for several states more than one string leading to it. A set E of strings distinguishes between states accessed by S in that some e is accepted after one element of S but not after the other. With membership queries, the algorithm tests whether all states reachable in one step from the states so far behave like known states (*closed* table in the following definition). This provides a guess for the transition table of the automaton. Also, it is checked whether all strings which lead to states thought to be equivalent so far have the same one-step behavior (*consistent*). If not, S or E are extended according to the observed discrepancy. Otherwise (if everything seems ok), an equivalence query is raised with an automaton constructed from the available information, i.e. the actual observation table. If the query is not successful, a counterexample is returned in form of a string which serves to distinguish further states and another iteration will be started. The algorithm itself is given below in a high-level notation. The reader may note that L* identifies all states for which there has not been any witness trace so far distinguishing them. In that way, L* performs the maximal possible abstraction.

Alphabet A, Observation Table $\mathcal{OT}$ initialized to $(S, E) = (\{\lambda\}, \{\lambda\})$

repeat
   Extend $\mathcal{OT}$ to $(S \cup S \cdot A) \times E$ using membership queries
   while $(\neg isClosed(\mathcal{OT}) \vee \neg isConsistent(\mathcal{OT}))$ **do**
     if $(\neg isClosed(\mathcal{OT}))$ **then**
       $\exists s_1 \in S, a \in A. \forall s \in S. row(s_1; a) \neq row(s)$
       $S \leftarrow S \cup \{s_1; a\}$
       Extend $\mathcal{OT}$ to $(S \cup S \cdot A) \times E$ using membership queries
     end if
     if $(\neg isConsistent(\mathcal{OT}))$ **then**
       $\exists s_1, s_2 \in S, a \in A, e \in E. row(s_1) = row(s_2) \wedge \mathcal{OT}(s_1; a; e) \neq \mathcal{OT}(s_2; a; e)$
       $E \leftarrow E \cup \{a; e\}$
       Extend $\mathcal{OT}$ to $(S \cup S \cdot A) \times E$ using membership queries
     end if
   end while
   $M \leftarrow Conjecture(\mathcal{OT})$
   $\sigma'_c \leftarrow EO(M)$
   if $(\sigma'_c \neq \bot)$ **then**
     $S \leftarrow S \cup Prefix(\sigma_c)$
   end if
until $(\sigma'_c = \bot)$

Algorithm 1.1: L*

In turns out that it is not too difficult to adapt L* to produce I/O transition systems instead of deterministic finite automata. I/O systems differ from ordinary automata in that their edges are labelled with inputs and outputs instead of just one symbol, and that there are no accepting or rejecting states. Since we can assume input-determinism, to explore the system it is sufficient to provide sequences of inputs and to collect the outputs as the answer of the system. Thus, output (sequences) replace the single bit outputs an ordinary automaton provides as response to a stimulus. Accordingly, the input alphabet A_I of the transition system is used instead of A in the observation table, and its entries are elements of A_O^*. All definitions and notations can remain as they are, including the notion of a closed and consistent observation table (which now yields an I/O transition system as approximate model).

4.3   Realizing the Membership Oracle

Membership queries can be answered by testing the system we want to learn. This is not quite as easy as it sounds, simply because the sequence to be tested is an abstract, propositional string, and the system on the other hand is a physical entity whose interface follows a real-time protocol for the exchange of digital (non-propositional) data. Thus we have to drive the system with real data, which requires to reverse the abstraction and produce a concrete stimulation string.

In practice, the inversion of abstraction is a concretization function. Things abstracted from the observations have to be filled in dynamically, taking the reactions of the system into account. For instance, time stamps have to increase, and instead of symbolic addresses and symbolic tags their concrete counterparts have to be used consistently. And, finally, these data have to be transformed into signals and fed to the system.

In the case of our example telephone switch, all this is done by our testing environment, the already mentioned *ITE*. It performs this task using predefined code blocks for generating stimuli and for capturing responses and glue code, which together solve the problems connected with generating, checking and identifying the non-propositional protocol elements. Thus much of the work of putting our approach into practice relies on the *ITE* system and its diverse components.

4.4 Equivalence Oracle

Besides the approximations to the equivalence oracle by testing (mentioned above), we propose to use formalizations of expert knowledge. An expert – this could be an implementor, a system designer, or an application specialist – provides a specification of an invariant of the system, i.e. a property which all system runs must meet. This specification could be given in some universal temporal logic. We use linear-time temporal logic (LTL, [3]) to formulate such constraints. These constraints can be model checked in a hypothesis automaton.[2]

Preferably, a constraint expresses a safety property. Then, a failure yields a finite counter example. Just as a sequence of input stimuli is used to generate a test, the subsequence of input elements of the counter example can be fed to the system. Now, there are two possibilities for the output of the system test corresponding to the counter example:

1. If the observed behavior on the system is consistent with the hypothesis automaton, a discrepancy between the specified invariant and the system has been detected. Either the system itself has an error, or the specification is wrong. This has to be resolved manually, i.e. by consulting the system or application experts. If the error can be attributed to the specification, its correction is easy: The specification is corrected (or dropped), and the learning process can continue. If it is a system error, the consequences will depend on the purpose of the model (for instance, whether it makes sense to construct a model of an erroneous system, or whether one would try to correct the error in the model.)

---

[2] To be able to do so, either a temporal logic dialect for I/O transition systems has to be used, or we have to translate the transition system into a standard finite automaton.

2. If the observed behavior deviates from that predicted by the hypothesis automaton, this trace is a counter example as desired from an equivalence oracle. So, the learning procedure will take the appropriate actions.

If a liveness property is violated, the model checker will return a cycle in the hypothesis and a path leading to it so that the infinite sequence resulting from following the path and iterating the cycle contradicts the liveness requirement. It is impossible to test the infinite sequence in the system, but each finite prefix of the sequence yields a test. If some prefix of limited length provides a discrepancy, we have a counter example as in the second case above. If not, one must again consult experts who can provide information on whether the constraint or the system is wrong.

5   Speeding Up the Learning Process

The learning procedure so far does not take the peculiarities of the system into account.

5.1   Symmetries

In our telecommunication example application, the environment may contain several ordinary phones. For several protocol properties, three phones are to be modelled. Though the phones will in real life be connected to different lines, all those lines are supposed to show the same behavior. Therefore, we can abstract from concrete line identifications to, say, three symbolic names, A, B and C. These three lines are symmetric. So, if a system trace has been observed where A calls B, we know that there are also five other legal traces (A calls C, B calls A, ...). Simply, all non-identical permutations of (A, B, C) give rise to a new valid observation. Adding them, it is assured that only symmetrical models are constructed by the learning algorithm, and also all hypothesis automata will be symmetrical.

Such symmetries are already pretty useful, but they do not cover all available reduction possibilities. If A initiates and then terminates a call, the corresponding line has returned to its initial state. A second call from A could equally well originate at any other line which is in its initial state. Thus, a sequence "A calls B; A calls C" would permit the renaming "B calls C; C calls A", which is not a simple renaming of the original sequence. This kind of symmetry exploitation depends on the ability of identifying that a line is in its initial (idle) state. For the telephone switch application, this was possible by utilizing diagnosis features.

5.2   Partial-Order Methods

Another formalism to specify expert knowledge is inspired from the *partial-order reduction* methods for communicating processes [11,16]. Normally these methods help to avoid having to examine all possible interleavings among processes. However these methods can also be used as a specification formalism for generalization in the following way:

1. An expert specifies explicitly an **independence relation**, e.g. *Two independent calls can be shuffled in any order.*
2. A trace is inspected for independent subparts.
3. Instead of the explicitly observed trace, a whole equivalence class of traces (of which the observed trace is a representative) can be added to the model.

In this way, partial-order methods speed up the model construction and help to keep the model consistent.

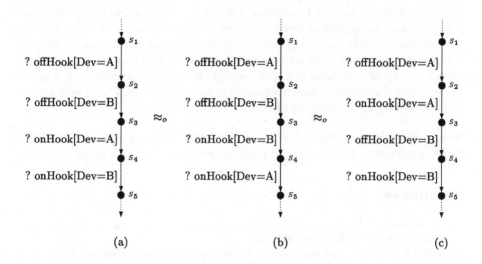

(a)   (b)   (c)

Fig. 3. Examples for reordering

Fig. 3 shows how an independence relation between stable states can be used for a further generalization of the model. When actions are independent from each other, then it is possible to change the order. The example Fig. 3(a) shows two independent *offHook/onHook* sequences: the permutations Fig. 3(b) and Fig. 3(c) are equivalent to Fig. 3(a) from the behavioral point of view.

6   Conclusion and Future Work

We have discussed behavior-based model construction from a point of view characterized by verification, model checking and abstract interpretation. Here, it turned out that *abstract interpretation* is the key for scaling known learning techniques for practical applications, *model checking* may serve as a teaching aid in the learning process underlying the model construction, and that there are also synergies with other validation and *verification* techniques. From the practical perspective, the main issue was to make automata learning, testing, and abstraction compatible. Although these are each very active research areas, they have hardly been considered in combination. At the theoretical level, a notable exception is the work of [14,4], which proposes a learning-based method for system refinement. Our focus on practicality differs from this work by looking at more rigid abstractions and by exploiting expert knowledge for steering the learning process. This has been illustrated by looking at a realistic telecommunication scenario.

A major problem in behavioral model construction is the growth of the system size and the corresponding complexity of the learning procedures. Thus methods are required to support the construction of aspect-specific models together with the possibility to suppress redundant information. We are therefore investigating various abstraction techniques and the possibility to construct concise models by exploiting additional structural information e.g. concerning the independence of events. We are convinced that we will be able to scale our techniques to capture essential parts of industrially relevant systems, in order to support test-suite design and maintenance, test organization, and test evaluation, as well as the monitoring of running applications.

Acknowledgement. We are very grateful to the ITE team, in particular Oliver Niese, as well as to Tiziana Margaria for discussions and their fruitful comments.

References

1. D. Angluin. Learning regular sets from queries and counterexamples. *Information and Computation*, 2(75):87–106, 1987.
2. T.S. Chow. Testing software design modeled by finite-state machines. *IEEE Transactions on Software Engineering*, 4(3):178–187, 1978.
3. E.A. Emerson. Temporal and modal logic. In J. van Leeuwen, editor, *Handbook of theoretical computer science*. Elsevier, 1990.
4. A. Groce, D. Peled, and M. Yannakakis. Adaptive model checking. In J.-P. Katoen and P. Stevens, editors, *Proc. of the 8th Int. Conference for Tools and Algorithms for the Construction and Analysis of Systems*, volume 2280 of *Lecture Notes in Computer Science*, pages 357–370. Springer Verlag, 2002.
5. A. Hagerer, H. Hungar, O. Niese, and B. Steffen. Model generation by moderated regular extrapolation. In R. Kutsche and H. Weber, editors, *Proc. of the 5th Int. Conference on Fundamental Approaches to Software Engineering (FASE '02)*, volume 2306 of *Lecture Notes in Computer Science*, pages 80–95. Springer Verlag, 2002.
6. A. Hagerer, T. Margaria, O. Niese, B. Steffen, G. Brune, and H. Ide. Efficient regression testing of CTI-systems: Testing a complex call-center solution. In *Annual Review of Communication*, volume 55. Int. Engineering Consortium (IEC), 2001.
7. J.E. Hopcroft and J.D. Ullman. *Introduction to Automata Theory, Languages, and Computation*. Addison-Wesley, 1979.
8. M.J. Kearns and U.V. Vazirani. *An Introduction to Computational Learning Theory*. MIT Press, 1994.
9. K. J. Lang, B. A. Pearlmutter, and R. A. Price. Results of the Abbadingo one DFA learning competition and a new evidence-driven state merging algorithm. In *Proc. 4th International Colloquium on Grammatical Inference - ICGI '98*, LNAI 1433, pages 1–12. Springer, 1998.

10. D. Lee and M. Yannakakis. Principles and methods of testing finite state machines - A survey. In *Proc. of the IEEE*, volume 84, pages 1090–1123, 1996.
11. A. Mazurkiewicz. Trace theory. In W. Brauer et al., editors, *Petri Nets, Applications and Relationship to other Models of Concurrency*, volume 255 of *Lecture Notes in Computer Science*, pages 279–324. Springer Verlag, 1987.
12. E.F. Moore. Gedanken-experiments on sequential machines. *Annals of Mathematics Studies (34), Automata Studies*, pages 129–153, 1956.
13. O. Niese, B. Steffen, T. Margaria, A. Hagerer, G. Brune, and H. Ide. Library-based design and consistency checks of system-level industrial test cases. In H. Hußmann, editor, *Proc. of the 4th Int. Conference on Fundamental Approaches to Software Engineering (FASE '01)*, volume 2029 of *Lecture Notes in Computer Science*, pages 233–248. Springer Verlag, 2001.
14. D. Peled, M.Y. Vardi, and M. Yannakakis. Black box checking. In Jianping Wu, Samuel T. Chanson, and Qiang Gao, editors, *Proc. of the Joint Int. Conference on Formal Description Techniques for Distributed System and Communication/Protocols and Protocol Specification, Testing and Verification (FORTE/PSTV '99)*, pages 225–240. Kluwer Academic Publishers, 1999.
15. L.G. Valiant. A theory of the learnable. *Communications of the ACM*, 27(11):1134–1142, 1984.
16. A. Valmari. On-the-fly verification with stubborn sets. In *Proc. of the 5th Int. Conference on Computer Aided Verification (CAV '93)*, volume 697 of *Lecture Notes in Computer Science*, pages 397–408. Springer Verlag, 1993.
17. M.P. Vasilevskii. Failure diagnosis of automata. *Kibernetika*, 4:98–108, 1973.

Automatic Verification by Abstract Interpretation

(Invited Tutorial)

Patrick Cousot

École normale supérieure, Département d'informatique,
45 rue d'Ulm, 75230 Paris cedex 05, France
Patrick.Cousot@ens.fr http://www.di.ens.fr/~cousot/

Abstract. We discuss the use of abstract interpretation in the context of automatic program verification requiring precise abstractions. We compare entirely manual versus user-guided abstractions ranging from program-specific abstractions including predicate abstraction to the systematic design of abstract domains and iteration strategies.

1 Abstract Interpretation Theory

Abstract interpretation theory [1,2,3,4,5,6] formalizes the notion of abstraction for mathematical constructs involved in the specification of computer systems. Applications range from *static program analysis* [2,3,4,6] (including data-flow analysis [3], set-based analysis [7], etc), *typing* [8], *model-checking* [9], *parsing* [10] to the *design of semantics* [11] and *program transformations* [12]. In this invited tutorial we discuss applications to *automatic program verification*.

2 Requirements

When dealing with undecidable questions on program execution, the automatic verification problem must conciliate *correctness* (which excludes non exhaustive methods such as simulation or test), *automation* (as opposed to the manual production of a program model for model-checking or to the human assistance for provers in deductive methods), *precision* (which excludes rudimentary general-purpose static program analyzers which would produce too many false alarms), *scaling up* (for software of a few hundred thousand lines), and *efficiency* (with minimal space and time requirements allowing for rapid verification during the software production process which excludes a costly iterative refinement process). Note that we consider automatic verification for proving the absence of errors, not their presence that is verification is considered in the sense of proof, not as debugging.

L. Zuck et al. (Eds.): VMCAI 2003, LNCS 2575, pp. 20–24, 2003.

3   Efficiency versus Precision

Among applications of abstract interpretation there have been many where somewhat imprecise answers to undecidable questions are tolerable provided all answers are sound and the imprecision rate remains low (typically 5 to 15%). This is the case for static program analysis when applied to *program optimization* (such as static elimination of run-time array bound checks where imprecision means delaying few array bound checks at run-time [13]), typing (where some programs which cannot go wrong are not typable) [8] or to *program transformation* (such as *partial evaluation* where any static value can always be considered dynamic, the transformed program being simply less efficient) [12], etc. In that case the analysis must be more efficient than precise. So coarse abstractions can be used which allow for the design of time and memory efficient static analyzers scaling up for very large programs.

4   Precision versus Efficiency

In the context of automatic program verification where human interaction must be reduced to a strict minimum, false alarms are undesirable. A 5% rate of false alarms on a program of a few hundred thousand lines would require several person-years effort to manually prove that no error is possible.

Fortunately, the abstract interpretation theory shows that for any program (or finite set of programs), it is possible to achieve full precision and great efficiency [14] by discovering an appropriate abstract domain. In the following we discuss the user-guided design of such abstract domains leading to precise and efficient analyzes.

5   Program-Specific Finite Abstraction

The use of a specific abstraction for a given hardware or software computer system (often called a model [15]) explains the popularity of *abstract model checking* [16]: it is always possible to provide an appropriate model of a given computer system which will model-check for the given property to be verified. The difficulty is how to get this appropriate model from a formal specification of the computer system such as a program. Most fully automatic methods, such as *software model-checking* [17,18], do not proceed directly on the software but on a user-provided finite and small model, which is difficult to design when e.g. sharp data properties must be taken into account. Moreover models for one program are hardly reusable for another program so efforts to design different models for different programs can hardly be cumulated.

6   Foundations of Predicate Abstraction

Predicate abstraction, which consists in specifying a boolean abstraction of software by providing the atomic elements of the abstract domain in logical form

[19], is certainly the most studied alternative [20,21,22]. Using a theorem prover, it is possible to automatically generate the abstract model in boolean form from the user-provided basic predicates and then to reuse existing model checkers. Moreover most implementations incorporate an automatic refinement process by success and failure [20,23] so that the abstraction can be partly automated.

We will first recall that predicate abstraction is an abstract interpretation and show why.

7   Predicate Abstraction in the Large

Then we will discuss a number of difficulties which in light of a recent experience in software verification [24] seem insurmountable to automate this design process in the present state of the art of deductive methods:

Problems of Semantics: for C programs, the prover which is used to automatically design abstract transfer functions has to take the machine-level semantics into account (e.g. floating-point arithmetic with rounding errors as opposed to real numbers). For example ESC is simply unsound with respect to modulo arithmetics [25].

State Explosion Problem: for large programs, the number of needed basic predicates can be huge. One difficulty is that model checking algorithms have worst-case behavior that is exponential in the number of predicates in the model which leads to state explosion. Another difficulty is to anticipate *a priori* which set of predicates introduced in the abstraction will be ultimately useful in the program analysis. The main successes seem to be when the full program can be abstracted very roughly into a small skeleton [15].

Refinement Problem: predicate abstraction *per se* uses a finite domain and is therefore of limited expressive power in comparison with the use of infinite abstract domains [6]. Therefore predicate abstraction is often accompanied by a refinement process to cope with false alarms [20,23]. Under specific conditions, this refinement can be proved equivalent to the use of an infinite abstract domain with widening [26]. This result is of limited scope since these specific conditions (essentially that the widening is by constraint elimination) are not satisfied e.g. by the staged widening with thresholds of [24]. Formally this counterexample-based refinement is a fixpoint computation [14,27] at the concrete semantics level, whence introduces new elements in the abstract domain state by state. In general, this process is very costly so that the needed predicates have to be provided by hand which introduces prohibitive human and computational costs for end-users.

8   Generic Abstractions

Finally we discuss a more synthetic general point of view based on the use of adequate parameterized abstract domains and iteration strategies with efficient implementations. This can be used to generate abstractions for specific classes of programs and properties to get efficient generic analyzers producing few or none false alarms [24].

References

1. Cousot, P.: Méthodes itératives de construction et d'approximation de points fixes d'opérateurs monotones sur un treillis, analyse sémantique de programmes. Thèse d'État ès sciences mathématiques, Université scientifique et médicale de Grenoble, Grenoble, FR (1978)
2. Cousot, P., Cousot, R.: Abstract interpretation: a unified lattice model for static analysis of programs by construction or approximation of fixpoints. In: 4th POPL, Los Angeles, CA, ACM Press (1977) 238–252
3. Cousot, P., Cousot, R.: Systematic design of program analysis frameworks. In: 6th POPL, San Antonio, TX, ACM Press (1979) 269–282
4. Cousot, P.: Semantic foundations of program analysis. In Muchnick, S., Jones, N., eds.: Program Flow Analysis: Theory and Applications. Prentice-Hall (1981) 303–342
5. Cousot, P., Cousot, R.: Abstract interpretation frameworks. J. Logic and Comp. **2** (1992) 511–547
6. Cousot, P., Cousot, R.: Comparing the Galois connection and widening/narrowing approaches to abstract interpretation, invited paper. In Bruynooghe, M., Wirsing, M., eds.: Proc. 4th Int. Symp. PLILP '92. Leuven, BE, 26–28 Aug. 1992, LNCS 631, Springer-Verlag (1992) 269–295
7. Cousot, P., Cousot, R.: Formal language, grammar and set-constraint-based program analysis by abstract interpretation. In: Proc. 7th FPCA, La Jolla, CA, ACM Press (1995) 170–181
8. Cousot, P.: Types as abstract interpretations, invited paper. In: 24th POPL, Paris, FR, ACM Press (1997) 316–331
9. Cousot, P., Cousot, R.: Temporal abstract interpretation. In: 27th POPL, Boston, MA, ACM Press (2000) 12–25
10. Cousot, P., Cousot, R.: Parsing as abstract interpretation of grammar semantics. Theoret. Comput. Sci. **290** (2002) 531–544
11. Cousot, P.: Constructive design of a hierarchy of semantics of a transition system by abstract interpretation. Theoret. Comput. Sci. **277** (2002) 47–103
12. Cousot, P., Cousot, R.: Systematic design of program transformation frameworks. In: 29th POPL, Portland, OR, ACM Press (2002) 178–190
13. Cousot, P., Cousot, R.: Static determination of dynamic properties of programs. In: Proc. 2nd Int. Symp. on Programming, Dunod (1976) 106–130
14. Cousot, P.: Partial completeness of abstract fixpoint checking, invited paper. In Choueiry, B., Walsh, T., eds.: Proc. 4th Int. Symp. SARA '2000. Horseshoe Bay, TX, US, LNAI 1864. Springer-Verlag (2000) 1–25
15. Clarke, E., Emerson, E.: Synthesis of synchronization skeletons for branching time temporal logic. In: IBM Workshop on Logics of Programs. Yorktown Heights, NY, US, LNCS 131, Springer-Verlag (1981)
16. Clarke, E., Grumberg, O., Long, D.: Model checking and abstraction. TOPLAS **16** (1994) 1512–1542
17. Holzmann, G.: The model checker SPIN. IEEE Trans. Software Engrg. **23** (1997) 279–295
18. Holzmann, G.: Software analysis and model checking. In Brinksma, E., Larsen, K., eds.: Proc. 14th Int. Conf. CAV '2002. Copenhagen, DK, LNCS 2404, Springer-Verlag (2002) 1–16
19. Graf, S., Saïdi, H.: Construction of abstract state graphs with PVS. In Grumberg, O., ed.: Proc. 9th Int. Conf. CAV '97. Haifa, IL, LNCS 1254, Springer-Verlag (1997) 72–83

20. Ball, T., Majumdar, R., Millstein, T., Rajamani, S.: Automatic predicate abstraction of C programs. In: Proc. ACM SIGPLAN 2001 Conf. PLDI. ACM SIGPLAN Not. 36(5), ACM Press (2001) 203–213
21. Das, S., Dill, D., Park, S.: Experience with predicate abstraction. In Halbwachs, N., Peled, D., eds.: Proc. 11th Int. Conf. CAV '99. Trento, IT, LNCS 1633, Springer-Verlag (1999) 160–171
22. Henzinger, T., Jhala, R., Majumdar, R., G.Sutre: Lazy abstraction. In: 29th POPL, Portland, OR, US, ACM Press (2002) 58–70
23. Das, S., Dill, D.: Counter-example based predicate discovery in predicate abstraction. In Aagaard, M., O'Leary, J., eds.: Proc. 4th Int. Conf. on Formal Methods in Computer-Aided Design, FMCAD 2002. Portland,, OR, US, LNCS 1633, SPRINGER (2002) 19–32
24. Blanchet, B., Cousot, P., Cousot, R., Feret, J., Mauborgne, L., Miné, A., Monniaux, D., Rival, X.: Design and implementation of a special-purpose static program analyzer for safety-critical real-time embedded software, invited chapter. In Mogensen, T., Schmidt, D., Sudborough, I., eds.: The Essence of Computation: Complexity, Analysis, Transformation. Essays Dedicated to Neil D. Jones. LNCS 2566. Springer-Verlag (2002) 85–108
25. Flanagan, C., Leino, K.R.M., Lillibridge, M., Nelson, G., Saxe, J., Stata, R.: Extended static checking for Java. In: Proc. ACM SIGPLAN 2002 Conf. PLDI. ACM SIGPLAN Not. 37(5), ACM Press (2002) 234–245
26. Katoen, J.P., Stevens, P., eds.: Relative Completeness of Abstraction Refinement for Software Model Checking. In Katoen, J.P., Stevens, P., eds.: Proc. 8th Int. Conf. TACAS '2002. Grenoble, FR, LNCS 2280, Springer-Verlag (2002)
27. Giacobazzi, R., Quintarelli, E.: Incompleteness, counterexamples and refinements in abstract model-checking. In Cousot, P., ed.: Proc. 8th Int. Symp. SAS '01. Paris, FR, LNCS 2126, Springer-Verlag (2001) 356–373

Symmetry Reductions in Model-Checking

Aravinda Prasad Sistla

Univeristy of Illinois at Chicago
sistla@cs.uic.edu

Abstract. Symmetries occur in different forms in concurrent programs. Such symmetries are induced by processes that behave similarly, and also by data items which are treated similarly by the processes. The talk will present three different methods, based on symmetry reductions, in containing the state explosion problem in model checking. The first method considers the symmetries in the program as well the formula. In this method we first construct a quotient structure, corresponding to the reachable part of the global state graph, and then check the satisfaction of the formula in the quotient structure using the traditional model checking algorithms. This method is primarily useful in checking safety properties. The second method considers only the symmetries in the program and is based on the construction of Annotated Quotient Structure (AQS). The AQS is like the quotient structure excepting that the edges carry additional information. This additional information is used for checking correctness under fairness. This method allows checking of both safety and liveness properties.

The third method employs Guarded Quotient Structures (GQS). This method can be employed for employing symmetry reductions in systems that are almost symmetric. In this method, we expand the asymmetric system by adding new edges. We construct the AQS of the expanded reachability graph, and add guards to the edges of the AQS to obtain the GQS. In order to check for correctness, we unwind the GQS. The guards on the edges are used to only consider the edges in the original graph. The method employs formula decomposition and sub-formula tracking to further speed up the model-checking process.

The talk will also present a Symmetry based Model Checker, called SMC. It is an on-the-fly model checker that employs symmetry reductions and checks for correctness under a variety of fairness conditions. SMC permits the user to invoke two different types of symmetry reductions— process symmetry and state symmetry. It also allows the user to specify the type of fairness that needs to be invoked— weak fairness, strong fairness. It also allows the user to specify different types of on-the-fly options that need to be invoked.

L. Zuck et al. (Eds.): VMCAI 2003, LNCS 2575, p. 25, 2003.

CHASE: A Static Checker for JML's *Assignable* Clause

Néstor Cataño and Marieke Huisman

INRIA Sophia-Antipolis, France
{Nestor.Catano, Marieke.Huisman}@sophia.inria.fr

Abstract. This paper presents a syntactic method to check so-called *assignable* clauses of annotated JAVA programs. Assignable clauses describe which variables may be assigned by a method. Their correctness is crucial for reasoning about class specifications. The method that we propose is incomplete, as it only makes a syntactic check and it does not take aliasing or expression evaluation into account, but it provides efficient means to find the most common errors in assignable clauses. This is demonstrated by applying the method to the specification of an industrial case study.

1 Introduction

Recently, several lightweight approaches to formal methods have demonstrated that the use of formal methods in practice is actually feasible. Up to now, formal methods merely were considered as a theoretical issue, which could not be applied to "real" problems: the complicated logical notations and the minimal tool support could not compete with the software development methods and tools used in industry. But recently, specification languages have been proposed that closer resemble programming languages, and powerful tools have been developed which are tailored to these specification languages, while at the same time, industry has started to feel the need for certified software, in particular after the discovery of bugs such as in the INTEL PENTIUM II chips.

Traditional techniques for program verification are model checking and theorem proving. Drawbacks of both are that they require a good insight in the particular verification techniques and tools and that they are often time and memory consuming. Recent tools try to overcome these drawbacks, by using efficient checking techniques that work directly on the level of the program and its specification. Two of such techniques are run-time checking and static checking. These are what could be called lightweight formal techniques, which do not result in a full correctness proof, but which are able to find the most common errors efficiently. Such techniques are useful to increase the trust in the correctness of an implementation *w.r.t.* a specification.

Run-time checking is a technique where safety conditions are checked while running the program, *e.g.* when making a method call it is checked that the precondition of the method is not violated for this particular call, otherwise an

L. Zuck et al. (Eds.): VMCAI 2003, LNCS 2575, pp. 26–40, 2003.

error message is returned. Typically, run-time checking is implemented by transforming the program into one that explicitly executes all these tests. Examples of run-time checkers are the EIFFEL-compiler [16] and JML [9] and JASS [1] (both working on JAVA programs). JML is not only a run-time checker, but it also provides a full-fledged specification language for JAVA.

Complementary to run-time checking is static checking, where one tries to find problems in a program by applying standard program verification techniques automatically. Static checking can be considered as an extended form of type checking, because it finds potential run-time problems already at compile-time. Typically, static checking gives quick feedback on a program and can find many common errors, so more expensive formal verification techniques can concentrate on the essential parts of the program. An example of a static checker for JAVA is ESC/JAVA (EXTENDED STATIC CHECKER/JAVA) [12], which generates proof obligations from an annotated program and sends these proof obligations to an automatic, dedicated theorem prover. ESC/JAVA is especially tuned to find errors such as indexing an array out of bounds, null pointer dereferencing, deadlocks and race conditions, but it also can check arbitrary functional specifications (given in a simplified version of the JML specification language). If it cannot establish a certain specification, it issues a warning. As ESC/JAVA is neither sound nor complete, a warning does not necessarily mean that the program is incorrect, and when it produces no warnings this does not necessarily mean that the program is correct.

The checking of methods in ESC/JAVA is done in a modular way, on a method per method basis. When one encounters a method call in the body that one is checking, it is not known which method implementation actually will be used – due to dynamic binding. Therefore, following the behavioral subtype approach [13], the method specification in the static class type of the receiver of the method call is used[1]. When reasoning in such a way, pre- and postconditions of methods alone are not sufficient, one also needs to know which variables may have been changed by a method. Consider for example the following annotated program fragment.

```
public class C {
   int[] arr;

   //@ ensures arr.length >= 4;
   public void m(){arr = new int[5]; n();}

   //@ ensures true;
   public void n(){arr = new int[2];}
}
```

To establish whether m satisfies its postcondition, the functional specification of n alone does not give enough information, one also needs to know whether n

---

[1] Additionally, one has to show that for each overriding method in a subclass, it satisfies the specification of the superclass.

might change the variable `arr`. Therefore, JML and ESC/JAVA allow the user to specify a so-called assignable clause – using the keyword `modifies`[2] – specifying a set of locations that may be modified by a method. An assignable clause can contain variable names, but also more complicated expressions, *e.g.* denoting all the elements in an array or all the fields of an object. By default, when a method specification does not contain an assignable clause, the method is supposed to leave all variables unchanged.

The current version of ESC/JAVA does not check assignable clauses [12,11], it only uses them when checking method calls. As specifying assignable clauses is error-prone and the information in the assignable clause is crucial in the verification of other methods, we think this is a significant omission. When specifying a real-life application it is easy to forget a variable in the assignable clause – see for example our experiences with the specification and static checking of an industrial case study [5] in Sect. 5.2. Therefore, in this paper we propose a method for static checking of assignable clauses (implemented in our tool CHASE).

As ESC/JAVA, our method is neither sound nor complete, since it does not handle aliasing and it does not keep track of variable updates (see Sect. 4.3). However, our experiments show that in practice our method is very useful, because it finds immediately the most common mistakes in an assignable clause: simply forgetting to mention that a variable may be modified. We feel that when specifying a method in which variables are modified in a complicated way, a specifier will be careful when writing the assignable clause and will be more willing to do full verification. However, for simple methods it is easy to forget to mention a variable and preferably this is detected without using full verification.

Related work. The term *frame condition* finds its origins in the field of Artificial Intelligence [15]. Borgida *et al.* [3] revealed the relationship with formal specifications, where one needs to know which part of the state may be modified. They discuss several approaches, and finally propose to use so-called change axioms which can describe the possible changes of the state under a certain condition. They also give a syntactic method which can be used to generate a first attempt for the change axioms. A limitation of their approach is that they only look at single variables, while we can also handle expressions describing a set of memory locations.

Recently, Poll and Spoto [18] have proposed a correct static analysis method for assignable clauses. However, their method is not supported by a tool.

Leino [10] and Müller [17] both studied how to specify and verify assignable clauses in subclasses and/or using abstract variables. In this paper we only look at assignable clauses containing concrete variables. When extending our work to abstract variables, their work would form the basis to deal with dependencies.

Within the JASS project [8] the non-violation of assignable clauses can be checked at run-time, but this is restricted to simple variables only, more complex expressions are not allowed in the assignable clauses.

---

[2] JML also allows the alternative keywords `assignable` and `modifiable`.

Finally, within the LOOP project [14,2] a *semantic* definition for assignable clauses is defined. When verifying a method body, one has to show that each variable not mentioned in the assignable clause is unchanged. This is a heavy proof burden, because it involves quantifications over the whole state. Therefore, it is useful to first check automatically whether the assignable clause is likely to be correct, before diving into the full verification.

Organization. The rest of this paper is organized as follows. Section 2 briefly presents the most important assertion constructs of JML and ESC/JAVA. Section 3 discusses the meaning of the assignable clause. Section 4 presents the rules to check assignable clauses, and Sect. 5 presents the implementation of CHASE on top of the JML parser and discusses practical experiences. Finally, Sect. 6 gives conclusions and presents future work.

2   JML and ESC/Java Specifications

The JML specification language is designed to be easily usable for JAVA programmers. In particular, JML expressions are side-effect-free boolean JAVA expressions, extended with specification-specific constructs. The specification language for ESC/JAVA uses the same design principles. Initially there were several differences between the two languages, but to enable the use of different tools on the same specification, effort has been put in making the two languages converge [6]. In this paper, we do not really distinguish between the two languages[3], although we take the more general JML format for assignable clauses.

We briefly present the main JML and ESC/JAVA constructs, followed by a method specification example. A complete description can be found in [9,12]. Method behaviors can be specified using preconditions (**requires** P), postconditions (**ensures** Q), and exceptional postconditions (**exsures** (E) R), describing under which conditions a certain exception can occur. Also frame conditions (**modifies** L) can be part of a method specification, denoting which modifications may be made by a method (see Sect. 3). The behavior of a class can be restricted by an **invariant** clause.

There are several specification-specific constructs, *e.g.* logical implication ==>, universal and existential quantifiers ("**forall** T V; E and "**exists** T V; E), \old(E), to denote the value of expression E in pre-state of method, and \result to denote a method return value.

As an example of a method specification, we give the specification of a method addCurrency from an electronic purse case study [5]. This specification has been checked with ESC/JAVA.

```
/*@ modifies nb, data[nb];
    ensures (\old(nb) >= MAX_DATA) ? (nb == \old(nb)) :
               (nb == \old(nb) + 1 && data[\old(nb)] == cur); */
void addCurrency(byte cur){if(nb<MAX_DATA){data[nb]=cur; nb++;}}
```

---

[3] In particular, we do not consider JML's model variables.

```
<Assignable-exp> ::= <Identifier>
                   | <Identifier>[Exp]
                   | <Identifier>[Exp ... Exp]
                   | <Identifier>[*]
                   | \fields_of(<Field-exp>)
                   | \nothing
                   | \everything

    <Field-exp> ::= <Point-identif>
                  | this
                  | \reach(<Point-identif>)
                  | \reach(this)

<Point-identif> ::= <Identifier>.<Point-identif>
                  | <Identifier>
```

Fig. 1. Syntax for assignable expressions

The method `addCurrency` belongs to a class `Currencies`, storing all currencies supported by this purse application. It adds a new currency to the list of valid currencies (the array `data`). The `modifies` clause specifies that this method may modify only `nb` and `data` in the position `nb`. The postcondition of the method `addCurrency` expresses that if `nb` has not yet reached the threshold value `MAX_DATA`, `nb` increases its value by one and the value of the formal parameter `cur` is assigned to `data[\old(nb)]`, otherwise `nb` is unchanged. In the postcondition, the expression `\old(nb)` refers to the value of `nb` before the method invocation.

3   JML's Assignable Clauses

An assignable clause specifies which variables may be modified by a method; all other variables *should* remain unchanged. Within an assignable clause, a list of so-called assignable expressions is specified, describing which memory locations may be modified.

An assignable expression can be an identifier or an array indexing expression denoting a single location, but it can also denote a set of locations. An expression `a[i ... j]` denotes the set of locations $\{a[k] \mid i \leq k \leq j\}$, while `a[*]` denotes the same set as `a[0 ... a.length-1]`. An assignable expression `\fields_of(e)` denotes the set of *all fields* of the objects represented by the expression e. The expression e can be a single object (possibly `this`), an array, or the `\reach` of an object or array f (again possibly `this`). The fields of an array are its elements. The expression `\reach(f)` denotes the minimal set containing f, the fields of f and all objects reachable from the fields of f. Finally, there are special keywords `\nothing` and `\everything`, denoting the empty set of locations and the full set of locations, respectively. Figure 1 lists the complete grammar of assignable expressions.

Given the set of locations characterized by the assignable expressions, the semantics of a JML assignable clause is defined as follows[4].

Definition 1 (Assignable clause). *An* assignable clause *only allows a method to modify a location* loc *if:*

- loc *is mentioned in the method's assignable clause;*
- loc *is not allocated when the method starts execution; or*
- loc *is local to the method (i.e., a local variable or a formal parameter).*

Notice that this is a syntactic definition, thus an assignment x = x; only is permitted if the variable x is mentioned in the appropriate assignable clause or if x is a local variable.

For a normal, non-overriding, method the assignable clause is exactly the assignable clause as given in the method specification. When overriding a method in a subclass, JML and ESC/JAVA allow one only to extend the assignable clause of the overridden method[5]. Therefore, the *complete assignable clause* of a method that is overriding a method in a superclass is the union of its specified assignable clause and the complete assignable clause of the method it is overriding. To reduce the possibilities of unsoundness in modular verification, the assignable clause in the subclass preferably only adds variables (or expressions) that are not visible in the scope of the overridden method [12,10]. Finally, for a constructor, its body may freely modify (the reach of) all instance fields of the newly created object – as they were not allocated before method execution. Therefore, for a constructor body one has to check whether it obeys the union of the assignable clause as specified and the assignable expression \fields_of(\reach(this)).

4   A Syntactical Method to Check Assignable Clauses

This section presents a syntactic method to decide for each method whether it violates its complete assignable clause. For every method we check its assignable clause by checking for every assignment and for every method call encountered in the body, whether it agrees with the assignable clause of the method that is checked. For each language construct s we define a rule which allows us to derive $s \bmod A$, with the intuitive meaning: statement s only assigns to variables which are mentioned in assignable clause A. Together, these rules define mod. In some cases we need to lift mod over a set of instructions, defined as:

$$S \overrightarrow{\bmod} A \; \hat{=} \; \forall s.\, s \in S \Rightarrow s \bmod A.$$

As mentioned in the previous section, the assignable clause can contain expressions as \fields_of(this), thus checking syntactically whether a variable

---

[4] This definition differs from [9] in that it does not consider dependencies, as we do not consider model variables.

[5] Both in JML and in ESC/JAVA such method specifications can be recognized by the keyword also.

<Full-exp> ::= <Full-exp>[<Exp>$^+$]   <Suf-exp> ::= <Identifier>
        | <Full-exp>(<Exp>*) | this
        | <Full-exp>.<Suf-exp> | super
        | <Suf-exp> | Literal
                                                     | new <Type>[<Exp>]
                                                     | new <Type>(<Exp>*)

Fig. 2. Syntax for full expressions and suffix expressions

occurs in the assignable clause cannot be done by using the standard set membership $\in$. Therefore, we use an extended notion of set membership, subsuming the standard $\in$, denoted by $\underline{\in}$. Below, in Sect. 4.2, this notion is defined formally. Intuitively, $e \underline{\in} A$ means that the expression e appears literally in A, or A contains an expression such as \fields_of(f), and the set that is described by the expression \fields_of(f) contains e.

We lift the notion of extended set membership to extended subsets:

$$A_1 \sqsubseteq A_2 \mathrel{\hat{=}} \forall v.\ v \underline{\in} A_1 \Rightarrow v \underline{\in} A_2.$$

We also use variant notions modFE and modSuf, with a similar intuitive meaning, but defined only on so-called *full expressions* and *suffix expressions*, respectively, whose syntax is defined in Fig. 2. A full expression is an array indexing expression, a method call, a qualified expression or a suffix expression. A suffix expression can be an identifier, a reference to super or this, a literal or an initialization of an object or array. This syntax is a simplified version of the JML and JAVA grammar [9,7], because we assume that the program is accepted by the JAVA compiler and/or the JML tool. We assume that we have predicates full? and suffix? to decide whether an expression is a full expression or a suffix expression, respectively.

4.1   The Rules Defining mod, modFE, and modSuf

For each language construct, appropriate rules are given to define mod, modFE and modSuf in a compositional way. In several cases, the JAVA and JML syntax prescribe that a certain subexpression of an arbitrary expression is a so-called full expression or that a subexpression of a full expression is a suffix expression. Therefore, mod is defined in terms of modFE, and modFE is defined in terms of modSuf.

Method declaration rules. The first rule that we define deals with method and constructor declarations. For each method and constructor we check that the complete assignable clause is respected by its body – assuming that the assignable clauses for all methods called within this body are correct. Following Def. 1, it is sufficient to check that a body only modifies the formal parameters or the variables in the complete assignable clause A.

$$(\text{Meth-Dec})\ \frac{body \text{ mod } (A \cup \{\overrightarrow{par}\})}{m(\overrightarrow{par})\,\{body\} \text{ mod } A}$$

Local variable declarations. Note that in the rule for method declarations the method's local variables are not added to the assignable clause. This is done because local variables are only visible in the program text below their declaration. For example, a method fragment {x = 3; int x; x = 4;} actually changes variable x (assuming that x is *e.g.* an instance variable) to 3. To handle this appropriately, we decompose statement compositions into a single statement and a composed statement, and we have a special rule for when this single statement is a local variable declaration (of some type T). In this case we add the local variable to the assignable clause of the composed statement. In addition, we also check that the initialization expression e (if present) does not have unwanted side-effects.

$$(\text{Var-Decl}) \quad \frac{e \bmod A \quad t \bmod (A \cup x)}{T \; x \; = \; e; t \bmod A}$$

Assignment rules. For assignments $e_1 = e_2$ we must check that e_1 belongs to the set of locations that the method may modify ($e_1 \subseteq A$). Also we must check that e_1 and e_2 do not have unwanted side-effects. Following the JAVA syntax, we know that e_1 must be a full expression, thus we check e_1 modFE A.

$$(\text{Assg}) \quad \frac{e_1 \subseteq A \quad e_1 \bmod\text{FE } A \quad e_2 \bmod A}{e_1 = e_2 \bmod A}$$

This rule generalizes to all JAVA's assignment operators (+=, *= *etc.*) and to JAVA's pre- and postfix operators (*e.g.* e++ and ++e) in the obvious way.

Statement rules. For all JAVA statements, *e.g.* $s;t$, if$(c)\{s\}$ and while$(c)\{s\}$ the rules pass on the check for side-effects to the components of the statement. Remember that statement compositions $s;t$ we decompose so that s is a single statement, and if s is a local variable declaration the rule Var-Decl above applies.

$$(\text{Comp}) \quad \frac{s \bmod A \quad t \bmod A}{s;t \bmod A} s \neq T \; x \; = \; e \qquad (\text{If-Then}) \quad \frac{c \bmod A \quad s \bmod A}{\text{if}(c)\{s\} \bmod A}$$

Expression rules. For most expressions the same applies as for statements: the rules pass on the check for side-effects to the arguments of the expressions. We present the rule BinOp, which applies to all binary operators. Similar rules are defined for *e.g.* the unary operators, the instanceof expression, the casting operator, and the conditional expression.

$$(\text{BinOp}) \quad \frac{e_1 \bmod A \quad e_2 \bmod A}{e_1 \oplus e_2 \bmod A} \oplus \in \left\{ \begin{array}{l} <, <=, >, >=, ==, !=, \mid\mid, \\ \&\&, +, -, *, /, \backslash, \&, \char`^, \mid \end{array} \right\}$$

If none of these rules apply to an expression, it means that the expression is a full expression and we should check for side-effects using modFE.

$$(\text{To-Fe}) \quad \frac{e \bmod\text{FE } A}{e \bmod A} \text{full?}(e)$$

Full expression rules. Following the grammar for full expressions, we define modFE. Full expressions can be method invocations, array indexing expressions, qualified expressions or suffix expressions.

The assignable clause of a method invocation should be an extended subset of the assignable clause A of the method body that is currently checked – with appropriate substitutions – to ensure that no other variables than the ones mentioned in A are changed. A method invocation is of the form $fe(\overrightarrow{par})$ where fe is a full expression again. Given that the expression is accepted by the JAVA compiler, fe is a qualified expression <Full-exp>.<Suf-exp>, or it is a suffix expression only. The suffix expression must be a method name, this or super. The appropriate assignable clause can be found by looking at the static type of the receiving object of the method call (possibly this). This is sufficient, provided that additional assignable clauses in overriding methods do not name locations that are visible in the scope of the overridden method [12,10]. Additionally it should be checked that the full expression fe and the actual parameters do not violate the assignable clause A.

$$(\text{Meth-Inv}) \quad \frac{fe(\overrightarrow{par}).\text{assignable}\,[\overrightarrow{act}/\overrightarrow{par}, fe/\text{this}] \sqsubseteq A \quad fe\;\text{modFE}\;A \quad \overrightarrow{act}\;\overrightarrow{\text{mod}}\;A}{fe(\overrightarrow{act})\;\text{modFE}\;A}$$

Otherwise, if the full expression is not a method invocation, it must be an array indexing expression, a qualified expression or a suffix expression. Both for array indexing expressions and for qualified expressions, the rules pass on the check for side-effects to the components of the expression. In case the full expression is a suffix expression, modSuf is used to check for side-effects.

$$(\text{Array}) \quad \frac{fe\;\text{modFE}\;A \quad \overrightarrow{e}\;\overrightarrow{\text{mod}}\;A}{fe[\overrightarrow{e}]\;\text{modFE}\;A} \qquad (\text{Qualified}) \quad \frac{fe\;\text{modFE}\;A \quad s\;\text{modSuf}\;A}{fe.s\;\text{modFE}\;A}$$

$$(\text{To-Suf}) \quad \frac{fe\;\text{modSuf}\;A}{fe\;\text{modFE}\;A}\;\text{suffix?}(fe)$$

Suffix expression rules. Most suffix expressions are constant values (*e.g.* this and all the literals) which do not have side-effects, thus the rules for these constructs are straightforward. Also the access to an identifier does not modify the state – if the identifier is the target of an assignment, the rule Assg takes care that it is mentioned in the assignable clause. Thus, the only suffix expressions which are of interest are the new expressions. Here, the possible arguments have to be checked for unwanted side-effects. The creation of a new object or array does not violate the rules for the assignable clause (*cf.* Def. 1).

$$(\text{This}) \quad \frac{\text{true}}{\text{this mod}\;A} \qquad (\text{New-Exp}) \quad \frac{\overrightarrow{e}\;\overrightarrow{\text{mod}}\;A}{\text{new T}(\overrightarrow{e})\;\text{modSuf}\;A}$$

4.2   The Extended Membership Relation

Finally, we define the extended membership relation. For all assignable clause expressions we give appropriate syntactic rules. First we consider the assignable expressions \nothing and \everything. In the first case the assignable clause is the empty set, in the second case it is the complete set of locations. The rules for these constructs are straightforward.

$$(\text{In-Nothing}) \; \frac{\text{false}}{e \in \backslash\texttt{nothing}} \qquad (\text{In-Everything}) \; \frac{\text{true}}{e \in \backslash\texttt{everything}}$$

For non-trivial assignable clauses, the basic case is where a variable or array index expression is mentioned literally[6]. In this case, we fall back directly on the standard definition of set membership to check whether an assignment target occurs in A. Here we give the rules for unqualified expressions, we have similar rules for qualified expressions.

$$(\text{In-Var}) \; \frac{\texttt{x} \in A}{\texttt{x} \in A} \qquad (\text{In-Arr}) \; \frac{\texttt{a[e]} \in A}{\texttt{a[e]} \in A}$$

Also expressions a[*] or a[i..j] can occur in A. These expressions allow array index expressions to be the assignment target[7]. Again, there are similar rules for qualified expressions.

$$(\text{Global-Arr}) \; \frac{\texttt{a[*]} \in A}{\texttt{a[e]} \in A} \qquad (\text{Interv-Arr}) \; \frac{\texttt{a[i..j]} \in A \quad \texttt{i} \leq e \leq \texttt{j}}{\texttt{a[e]} \in A}$$

Finally, expressions of the form \fields_of(e) might occur in A. Now we have to distinguish between two cases: e is a single object (possibly this) or array[8], or it is a \reach expression. In the first case, any field of the object e or any array index expression of the array e is allowed as assignment target.

$$(\text{In-Fld-Exp-Var}) \; \frac{\backslash\texttt{fields\_of}(e) \in A}{e.\texttt{x} \in A} \qquad (\text{In-Fld-Arr}) \; \frac{\backslash\texttt{fields\_of}(\texttt{a}) \in A}{\texttt{a[}e'\texttt{]} \in A}$$

When e is a reach expression \reach(e'), any variable access or array index expression is allowed as assignment target for which the receiving object (possibly this) or the array is an element of the set determined by the \reach expression.

$$(\text{In-Reach-Exp}) \; \frac{\backslash\texttt{fields\_of}(\backslash\texttt{reach}(e')) \in A \quad f \in \backslash\texttt{reach}(e')}{f.\texttt{x} \in A}$$

$$(\text{In-Reach-Arr}) \; \frac{\backslash\texttt{fields\_of}(\backslash\texttt{reach}(e')) \in A \quad \texttt{a} \in \backslash\texttt{reach}(e')}{\texttt{a[}f\texttt{]} \in A}$$

---

[6] We do not distinguish between this.x and x.

[7] Provided that $i \leq e \leq j$ can be checked syntactically, which is not always the case.

[8] For arrays, \fields_of(e) is equivalent to e[*] [9].

As explained in Sect. 3, the expression \reach(e') denotes the minimal set containing e', the fields of e' and all objects reachable from the fields of e'. To determine whether an object or array is part of \reach(e'), we state the two following rules: an element e is in the reach of an object, if it is the object itself (Reach-Base), or if it is in the reach of one of the fields of this object (Reach-Rec).

$$\text{(Reach-Base)} \ \frac{e = e'}{e \in \text{\reach}(e')}$$

$$\text{(Reach-Rec)} \ \frac{e'' \in \text{\fields\_of}(e') \quad e \in \text{\reach}(e'')}{e \in \text{\reach}(e')}$$

4.3 Limitations of the Method

Using our method, many specification mistakes in assignable clauses can be found (see the next section for experimental results). Nevertheless it has important limitations, because it works purely on a syntactical basis.

Firstly, our method does not handle aliasing. When two references point to the same object and a field of such an object is changed via one reference, the tool does not require that the assignable clause also reflects the changes via the other reference. For example, given a class O with an integer field i, we do not detect any problem in the specification of method p – although implicitly y.i also will be changed within p.

```
public class C {
   O y = new O();
   O x = new O();

   //@ modifies x, x.i;
   public void p(){x = y; x.i = 7;}
}
```

Secondly, our method does not take earlier variable updates into account. For example, for a program fragment {i++; a[i] = 3;}, it accepts an assignable clause containing the expression a[i] (and it rejects a[i+1]). Similarly, it will reject changes to the fields of a newly allocated object.

Overall, we think that these limitations do not severely restrict the usability of our method. Our method should be considered as a quick check to get a reasonable trust in the correctness of the specified assignable clauses. In our experience, when specifying the assignable clause of a method, it is more likely that one forgets a variable than to overlook complicated modification structures. Finding these small specification mistakes before doing formal verification significantly can help to improve the verification speed. In particular, our method is a good purity checker, because it always issue a warning if a method can have side-effects, but has an empty assignable clause.

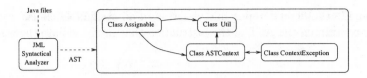

Fig. 3. Overall structure of CHASE

5   Chase: A Checker for Assignable Expressions

As mentioned above, we have implemented our method in a tool called CHASE, which is freely available [4]. This section presents its implementation and discusses our experiences using CHASE on an earlier specification case study [5]. When applying CHASE to this case study, it found several incorrect assignable clauses. Further, CHASE enables us to determine the set of side-effect free methods of this application.

5.1   The Implementation of Chase

CHASE is constructed by reusing the syntactical analyzer of JML [9] and by implementing – as static methods – the rules presented in Sect. 4. Figure 3 presents the overall structure of CHASE. The input for CHASE is an annotated JAVA file. First the JML syntactical analyzer constructs the corresponding abstract syntax tree (AST) for this file. The class `Util` then transforms the AST to make it usable for the class `Assignable`, which implements the rules presented in Sect. 4, in methods `_mod`, `_modFE`, *etc.*. Each method is parameterized by an instruction and a context. The context of an instruction is the set of locations it may modify: the union of its parameters and its assignable locations. Class `Util` also calculates these contexts, such that whenever it cannot establish the context of an instruction, it throws a `ContextException`.

As an example, the rule (Assg) is implemented as a fragment of method `_mod`.

```
public static boolean _mod(AST e, ASTContext currentContext)
    throws assignable.exception.ContextException
    { if(e.getType() == JavaTokenTypes.ASSIGN)
          return in_PRIME(e.getFirstChild(),currentContext) &&
                 _modFE(e.getFirstChild(),currentContext) &&
                 _mod(e.getFirstChild().getNextSibling(),
                      currentContext);
    ... // other cases
}
```

Whenever `e` is a `JavaTokenTypes.ASSIGN` expression, CHASE checks that its left expression appears in the list of assignable locations, (method `in_PRIME`) and recursively calls the methods `_modFE` and `_mod`, with the left and right trees of `e`, respectively.

When CHASE detects a possible violation of an assignable clause, it issues a warning containing the AST of the instruction that might violate the assignable clause.

5.2 Experiences Using Chase

In an earlier case study [5] we specified a JAVACARD purse application, describing class invariants and the functional behavior (pre- and postconditions) and frame conditions of each method. We used ESC/JAVA to check the specifications, but naturally we could not check the assignable clauses. Therefore, we applied CHASE to this case study. We checked the 3 packages of the purse application, containing 27 classes and ± 800 methods, finding 43 incorrect assignable clauses (see the CHASE web site [4] for a full compendium).

We present one example of a missing assignable clause. The method setValue sets the fields of the class Decimal, which represents a decimal number by means of an integer part, intPart, and a decimal part, decPart. Initially, our assignable clause only included the variables intPart and decPart, which are directly assigned in the body of the method.

```
//@ modifies intPart, decPart;
public Decimal setValue(short i, short d) throws DecimalException{
  if(i<0 || d<0 || d>=PRECISION || (i==MAX_DEC_NUMBER && d!=0))
    decimal_exception.throwIt(decimal_exception.DEC_OVERFLOW);
  intPart = i; decPart = d; return this;
}
```

When CHASE is applied to this method, it issues a warning that the expression decimal_exception.throwIt(decimal_exception.DEC_OVERFLOW) may cause a problem. Inspection of the method throwIt reveals that the instance variables decimal_exception.instance and decimal_exception.instance.type also may be modified, and thus that these must be mentioned in the assignable clause of setValue.

6 Conclusion and Future Work

This paper presents a method to do an efficient check on assignable clauses. It has been implemented in a tool called CHASE, which is freely available [4]. In particular, CHASE can be used to do a quick check on side-effect-freeness.

The method works on a syntactic basis: for each JAVA construct a rule is defined which checks that every assignment or method call only modifies variables that are declared as *assignable*. This approach is neither sound nor complete, but experiences have shown that it is useful in practice: it efficiently finds common specification mistakes – such as forgetting to mention a variable that may be modified. Before completely verifying an annotated JAVA program, it is good practice to use CHASE to check the assignable clauses, so that simple specification mistakes do not disturb the verification process.

There are limitations to our approach, in particular it does not work in a context with aliasing. In these cases, full formal verification is necessary. However, as said, applying our method first, one finds the simpler mistakes quickly, thus allowing to concentrate on the essentials when verifying.

As future work, we plan to improve the tool to overcome (at least partly) the limitations of the tool, *e.g.* better handling of updates and newly allocated memory, and returning a warning if a possibly aliased variable has changed.

It is also future work to extend the tool to appropriately handle so-called model variables, which allow to define specification-only variables and relate them to concrete variables by using `represents` or `depends` clauses, following [10].

References

1. D. Bartetzko, C. Fischer, M. Möller, and H. Wehrheim. Jass – Java with Assertions. In K. Havelund and G. Roşu, editors, *ENTCS*, volume 55(2). Elsevier Publishing, 2001.
2. J. van den Berg and B. Jacobs. The LOOP compiler for Java and JML. In T. Margaria and W. Yi, editors, *Tools and Algorithms for the Construction and Analysis of Systems (TACAS 2001)*, number 2031 in LNCS, pages 299–312. Springer, 2001.
3. A. Borgida, J. Mylopoulos, and R. Reiter. On the frame problem in procedure specifications. *IEEE Transactions on Software Engineering*, 21(10):785–798, 1995.
4. N. Cataño and M. Huisman. Assignable specifications for the Electronic Purse case study, 2002. http://www-sop.inria.fr/lemme/verificard/modifSpec.
5. N. Cataño and M. Huisman. Formal specification and static checking of Gemplus's electronic purse using ESC/Java. In L.-H. Eriksson and P.A. Lindsay, editors, *Formal Methods Europe (FME '02)*, number 2391 in LNCS, pages 272–289. Springer, 2002.
6. Differences between Esc/Java and JML, 2000. Comes with JML distribution, in file `esc-jml-diffs.txt`.
7. J. Gosling, B. Joy, G. Steele, and G. Bracha. *The Java Language Specification Second Edition*. The Java Series. Addison-Wesley, 2000.
8. The JASS project. http://semantik.informatik.uni-oldenburg.de/~jass/.
9. G.T. Leavens, A.L. Baker, and C. Ruby. Preliminary Design of JML: a Behavioral Interface Specification Language for Java. Technical Report 98-06, Iowa State University, Department of Computer Science, 1998. http://www.cs.iastate.edu/~leavens/JML/prelimdesign/.
10. K.R.M. Leino. Data groups: specifying the modification of extended state. In *Object-Oriented Programming, Systems, Languages and Applications (OOPSLA '98)*, pages 144–153. ACM Press, 1998.
11. K.R.M. Leino. Applications of Extended Static Checking. In P. Cousot, editor, *Static Analysis (SAS 2001)*, number 2126 in LNCS, pages 185–193. Springer, 2001.
12. K.R.M. Leino, G. Nelson, and J.B. Saxe. ESC/Java user's manual. Technical Report SRC 2000-002, Compaq System Research Center, 2000.
13. B.H. Liskov and J.M. Wing. A behavioral notion of subtyping. *ACM Trans. on Progr. Lang. and Systems*, 16(1):1811–1841, 1994.
14. The LOOP project. http://www.cs.kun.nl/~bart/LOOP/.

15. J. McCarthy and P. Hayes. Some philosophical problems from the standpoint of artificial intelligence. In B. Meltzer and D. Michie, editors, *Machine Intelligence 4*, pages 463–502. Edinburgh Univ. Press, 1969.
16. B. Meyer. *Object-Oriented Software Construction*. Prentice Hall, 2nd rev. edition, 1997.
17. P. Müller. *Modular Specification and Verification of Object Oriented Programs*. PhD thesis, FernUniversität Hagen, 2001.
18. E. Poll and F. Spoto. Static analysis for JML's assignable clauses, 2002. Manuscript.

Abstract Interpretation-Based Certification of Assembly Code

Xavier Rival

École Normale Supérieure
45, rue d'Ulm, 75230, Paris cedex 5, France*
rival@di.ens.fr

Abstract. We present a method for analyzing assembly programs based on source program analysis and invariant translation. It is generic in the choice of an abstract domain for representing stores. This method is adapted to the design of certification tools for assembly programs generated by compiling programs written in an imperative language, without writing a specific compiler or modifying an existing one since invariant translation only uses standard debugging information. A prototype was developed for a procedural subset of the C language.

Keywords: Static program analysis; compilation; Abstract Interpretation.

1 Introduction

Critical software is concerned with safety and analyzing source programs may not be considered a sufficient guarantee. Indeed, compilers are complex pieces of software and may contain bugs. Therefore, there is a need for extending the certification to the assembly code itself, especially when dealing with highly critical software (as in aeronautics).

Moreover, the safety properties usually checked concern the actual execution of the program, that is, the assembly code. For instance, checking that a C program does not contain any out-of-bound array access is useful to know that the compiled program will not access a wrong part of the memory. Furthermore, the definition of the undesirable behaviors could also be architecture or compiler dependent, as is often the case for overflows. Indeed, the specification of languages like C often leaves these behaviors unspecified, for the sake of execution speed (this avoids handling what could be considered errors and may simplify the design of compilers). Therefore, certifying the assembly code provides much a better confidence in the code as it allows to make no more assumption on the semantics of the source language and on the correctness of the compiler.

Nevertheless, certifying assembly code is quite a hard task. It requires analyzing high-level properties (like state reachability) which is rather involved at the assembly level, since part of the structure of the program is lost at compile

---

* This work was supported by the RTD project IST-1999-20527 "DAEDALUS" of the European FP5 program.

L. Zuck et al. (Eds.): VMCAI 2003, LNCS 2575, pp. 41–55, 2003.

time: the control structure is rather terse (branching to program points stored in registers), the data structure is difficult to reconstruct (various addressing modes like relative addressing). Proving the compiler formally and relying on the analysis of the source code would be a satisfactory solution but it would be too expensive since proving a compiler like in [2] is a huge amount of work and modifying the compiler forces to adapt the proof.

The solution proposed in this paper is to use the results of an analysis of the source code and the debugging information (information about the way the compilation is done, about the correspondence between source and assembly variables, program points) in order to reduce the task to handle at the assembly code level to the checking of a translated invariant. This process should not depend on the compiler itself but on the debugging information which is standard. We can imagine designing a certifying tool for a given language and a given architecture but generic in the compiler. This tool would prove the correctness of an assembly program P_a obtained by compiling a program P_s as follows: it would infer an invariant I_s for P_s, translate it into an invariant I_a, verify that I_a actually is an invariant for P_a and check that I_a entails correctness of P_a. The compiler itself is never proved which is a source of flexibility. The method presented here was formalized inside the Abstract Interpretation framework [5, 6], that provides an integrated view in a single framework of both static analysis [4,3] and program transformations [7] (hence, compilation).

The implementation of a prototype gave encouraging results.

Related works: As an example of translation of invariants at compile time we can cite the Proof Carrying Code approach [13]: in this case the translation is handled by the compiler itself which has therefore to be adapted. Moreover the target language is also modified so as to be type-safe [12]. So, this approach is restricted to type-safe programming languages (excluding C, used in many critical systems). The VOC approach [18] generates proof obligations at compile time and then solves it, so as to prove each instance of compilation: the generated proof obligations entail the correctness of the transformation. This approach also requires the compiler to be instrumented. The method proposed in [14] is similar. Among direct analyses of assembly code we can cite some works that aim at determining low level execution properties like memory usage, cache behavior or worst case execution time [1,8,16,17].

Section 2 formalizes compilation. Section 3 states the soundness of the invariant translation method. Section 4 details aspects of invariant checking. Section 5 presents implementation results ; Section 6 concludes.

2   Compilation as a Program Transformation

2.1   Abstract Interpretation and Program Transformations

Cousot and Cousot developed Abstract Interpretation [5,6] as a way of deriving relationships between different semantics so as to provide approximate but computable answers to undecidable (or costly) problems. Note that approximations are always sound: if an abstract analyzer claims that a program satisfies a property, then it actually satisfies it.

Practically, the *concrete semantics* $[\![P]\!] \in D$ (for instance the *collecting semantics* of all the states of a transition system) of a program P provides the most precise description of the behavior of P. It can be expressed as the least fixpoint of a monotone semantic function F in a lattice D. Given a Galois connection $D \xleftrightarrow[\alpha]{\gamma} D^\sharp$, the *abstract semantics* of P is $[\![P]\!]^\sharp = \alpha([\![P]\!])$. Provided there exists a monotone abstract semantic function $F^\sharp$ such that $F^\sharp \circ \alpha = \alpha \circ F$ the abstract semantics is also a least fixpoint $\mathrm{lfp}F^\sharp$ in the lattice $D^\sharp$ (thanks to the fixpoint transfer theorem of [15]). Most of the time the abstract semantics itself is not computable, so a computable and sound approximation of $[\![P]\!]^\sharp$ is derived by computing the least fixpoint of a function $F^\sharp$ such that $\alpha \circ F \sqsubseteq F^\sharp \circ \alpha$ and by using a widening operator [5] to enforce convergence.

Program transformations can also be handled in this framework [7]. A program transformation is a process that inputs a program P and outputs a program P' whose semantics can be expressed as a transformation of the semantics of P. A convenient semantics for defining the semantic transformation t_s (which may be an isomorphism) associated to the syntactic transformation t can be obtained by abstract interpretation of the standard semantics as shown below:

$$
\begin{array}{ccccc}
P & \xrightarrow{\text{semantics}} & [\![P]\!] & \overset{\gamma}{\underset{\alpha'}{\leftrightarrows}} & [\![P]\!]^\sharp \\
{\scriptstyle t}\big\downarrow & & & & \big\downarrow{\scriptstyle t_s} \\
P' & \xrightarrow[\text{semantics}]{} & [\![P']\!] & \overset{\gamma'}{\underset{\alpha'}{\leftrightarrows}} & [\![P']\!]^\sharp
\end{array}
$$

Formalizing compilation and some class of program analyses in this same framework will enable us to make them commute in some sense.

2.2   Source and Assembly Programs

A (source or assembly) program P is defined by the data of:

- its *store*: S_P is the set of the possible values for the store of P. We write R for the range of values for variables and V_P for the set of *store locations* (that is *variables* or *memory locations*) of P. In this setting, $S_P = V_P \to R$.
- its *control structure* (L_P, i_P, τ_P) where L_P is a set of *program points*, $i_P \in L_P$ is the *entry program point* and $\tau_P \subseteq (L_P \times S_P) \times (L_P \times S_P)$ is the *transition relation* of P: $((x, s), (y, t)) \in \tau_P$ if and only if, the execution of P after having reached program point x with store s, may continue at program point y, with store t. Non-determinism is allowed since τ_P is a relation.

Note that the notion of program point does not necessarily correspond to syntactic program points: a program point may be defined by a pair (l, s) where l is a syntactic point and a s is a stack in the case of procedural programs).

In the following, if $\mathcal{E}$ is a set, we note $\mathcal{E}^\star$ for the set of sequences of elements of $\mathcal{E}$ and $\mathbb{P}(\mathcal{E})$ for the powerset of $\mathcal{E}$. The concrete semantics $[\![P]\!]$ of a program P is the set of the partial execution traces of P. It can be defined as a least fixpoint in the lattice $(\mathbb{P}((L_P \times S_P)^\star), \subseteq)$ by: $[\![P]\!] = \mathrm{lfp}_\emptyset^\subseteq F_P$ where $F_P : \mathbb{P}((L_P \times S_P)^\star) \to$

$\mathbb{P}((L_P \times S_P)^\star)$ is the semantic function:

$$F_P(X) = \{\langle(i_P, s)\rangle \mid s \in S_P\}$$
$$\cup \{\langle(x_0, s_0), \ldots, (x_n, s_n), (x_{n+1}, s_{n+1})\rangle \mid \langle(x_0, s_0), \ldots, (x_n, s_n)\rangle \in X$$
$$\wedge((x_n, s_n), (x_{n+1}, s_{n+1})) \in \tau_P\}$$

The two following sections present a simple imperative source language and a simple assembly language that can be described in this setting.

2.3   A Simple Imperative Language

The syntax of the simple source language $\mathcal{L}$ is shown in Fig. 1. Variables ($v \in \mathbb{V}$) are all supposed to be globals. Statements (S) are affectations, conditionals and loops. Blocks (B) are lists of statements. Expressions (E) all have integer type. Conditions (C) represent conditional expressions and have type boolean. A store (or *environment*) maps the variables of a program to integer values.

Since this is a model, overflows are not taken into account. An erroneous execution of a program is a trace that is stopped at a non-exit program point (typically because of a division by 0). An erroneous state Ω is introduced for that purpose. The initial value of variables is not determined.

$$
\begin{array}{ll}
\text{E} ::= n & (n \in \mathbb{Z}) \\
\phantom{\text{E} ::=} \mid v & (v \in \mathbb{V}) \\
\phantom{\text{E} ::=} \mid -\text{E} \mid \text{E} + \text{E} \mid \text{E} - \text{E} \mid \text{E} \star \text{E} \mid \text{E}/\text{E} & \\
\text{C} ::= \textbf{true} \mid \textbf{false} \mid \neg\text{C} & \\
\phantom{\text{C} ::=} \mid \text{E} == \text{E} \mid \text{E} < \text{E} \mid \text{C} \wedge \text{C} \mid \text{C} \vee \text{C} &
\end{array}
$$

$$
\begin{array}{ll}
\text{S} ::= v := \text{E} & (v \in \mathbb{V}) \\
\phantom{\text{S} ::=} \mid \textbf{skip} \mid \textbf{if } \text{C} \textbf{ then } \text{B} \textbf{ else } \text{B} & \\
\phantom{\text{S} ::=} \mid \textbf{while } \text{C} \textbf{ do } \text{B} & \\
\text{B} ::= \text{S} \mid \text{S; B} &
\end{array}
$$

Fig. 1. The simple language $\mathcal{L}$.

2.4   A Simple Assembly Language

Since we restrict to the compilation of a simple language without arrays or procedures we consider a simplified assembly language $\mathcal{A}$, without relative addressing. The abstract machine provides the following store locations:

- registers: R_i ($0 \le i \le r - 1$);
- memory cells (which are indexed by integers): $M[i]$ ($i \in \mathbb{N}$);
- a condition register CR: when a test is handled this flag is set. Branching may occur later, according to the value of the condition register (LT for less than, EQ for equal, GT for greater than).

An assembly program is defined by a set of instructions labeled by distinct integers. A label l is intuitively the value of the program counter when the instruction I_l is executed. The instructions and their semantics are detailed in Fig. 2. After the execution of a non branching instruction I_l the execution flows to I_{l+1}. As above an erroneous state Ω is introduced to handle blocking error case (division by 0).

Syntax	Instruction	Semantics (sketched)
li R, n	load integer	stores integer n in register R
load R, n	load from mem.	stores $M[n]$ in register R
store R, n	store in the memory	stores the value contained in register R in the memory location $M[n]$
add R_0, R_1, R_2 (mul, div...)	addition (and other arith. ops.)	adds the values contained in R_1 and R_2 and stores the result in register R_0
cmp R_0, R_1	comparison	reads n_0 in R_0, n_1 in R_1 and compares them: if $n_0 < n_1$, then CR is set to LT if $n_0 = n_1$, then CR is set to EQ if $n_0 > n_1$, then CR is set to GT
b l	branching	branches to label l
bc(C) l (C is =, <...)	condit. branch.	branches to l if the content of CR corresponds to condition C

Fig. 2. Assembly instructions

2.5 Compilation

The compilation of the source program P_s into the assembly program P_a is correct if the semantics of these two programs are somewhat tied: the execution of a statement of P_s should be simulated by the execution of one or several steps of P_a and conversely, a step of execution of P_a should lead to a state s, such that an assembly state s' related to a state of the source code P_s should be reachable in zero or several execution steps from s. This relation between source and assembly programs semantics is defined by relations between subsets of source and assembly program points and memory locations. Not all the program points of a compiled program correspond to a point in the source since one source statement might be compiled into a sequence of assembly statements. Similarly not all the store locations of the assembly program correspond to a store location of the source program: for instance a register may correspond to no variable. Reciprocally, a source program point may correspond to no assembly program point in case of dead-code elimination (and the same for store locations in case of variable elimination).

Most compilers provide debugging information that contain the mapping between subsets of source and assembly locations and program points.

Fig. 3 shows a very simple example of compilation without any optimization of a small piece of code. Variable x is associated to $M[0]$; point 1 of P_s is mapped to point 2 of P_a... The correctness of the compilation expresses that execution traces of P_s correspond to execution traces of P_a: if x has value v at point 1 for some run r of P_s, then there exists a "corresponding" run r' of P_a that reaches point 2, and such that at that point, $M[0]$ contains value v. Note that registers are excluded from this mapping: information about equalities between the content of assembly memory locations will be needed for the invariant checking step (in Sect. 4.2).

The relation between the semantics of the source and the compiled program is built in two steps: we first restrict both semantics and then we assume a

$$\mathbb{V}_{P_s} = \{x\}$$

```
0 : x := 0;
1 : while x < 100
2 : {
3 :        x := x + 1;
4 : }
5 : exit
```

(a) source code P_s.

```
0 :   li      R_0, 0
1 :   store   R_0, 0
2 :   load    R_0, 0
3 :   li      R_1, 100
4 :   cmp     R_0, R_1
5 :   bc(<)   7
6 :   exit
7 :   load    R_0, 0
8 :   li      R_1, 1
9 :   add     R_2, R_0, R_1
10 :  store   R_2, 0
11 :  b       2
```

(b) compiled code P_a.

source	asm. prog.
Store locations	
x	$M[0]$
Program points	
0	0
1	2
3	7
4	11
5	6

(c) translation information.

Fig. 3. An example of compilation.

bijection between the restricted semantics. Let P_s be a source program and P_a an assembly program, defined by their sets of store locations V_s and V_a (as above we note $S_s = V_s \to R$ and $S_a = V_a \to R$ for the corresponding sets of stores) and their control structures (L_s, i_s, τ_s) and (L_a, i_a, τ_a). We first consider the case of the assembly program. Let $L_a^r \subseteq L_a$ and $V_a^r \subseteq V_a$ be subsets of the program points and of the store locations of P_a. We write S_a^r for the set of restricted stores $V_a^r \to R$. The store projection operator $\rho_a : S_a \to S_a^r$ is defined by $\forall s \in (V_a \to R)$, $\rho_a(s) = s \mid_{V_a^r}$ where $s \mid_{V_a^r}$ denotes the restriction of the function s to V_a^r. The trace restriction operator Φ_a is defined as follows:

$$\Phi_a(\langle (x_0, s_0), \dots, (x_n, s_n) \rangle) = \langle (x_{k_0}, \rho_a(s_{k_0})), \dots, (x_{k_l}, \rho_a(s_{k_l})) \rangle$$

where $x_{k_0}, \dots, x_{k_l}$ are exactly the program points belonging to L_a^r in the sequence $x_0, \dots, x_n$ in the same order as they appear in $\langle (x_0, s_0), \dots, (x_n, s_n) \rangle$.

Trace restriction defines an abstraction of the semantics of programs. We define the *restricted semantics* of P_a as the set of traces $[\![P_a]\!]_r = \alpha_a^r([\![P_a]\!])$ where $\alpha_a^r(\mathcal{E}) = \{\Phi_a(t) \mid t \in \mathcal{E}\}$. The function α_a^r defines a Galois connection:

$$(\mathbb{P}((L_a \times S_a)^\star), \subseteq) \xleftrightarrow[\alpha_a^r]{\gamma_a^r} (\mathbb{P}((L_a^r \times S_a^r)^\star), \subseteq) .$$

In the same way, a restricted semantics can be defined for the source program P_s as an abstraction of the concrete trace semantics $[\![P_s]\!]$, by choosing $V_s^r \subseteq V_s$ and $L_s^r \subseteq L_s$. In most cases we do not wish to abstract away any variable of the source program and therefore $V_s^r = V_s$ (except in case of dead variable elimination). For generality, this abstraction α_s^r is defined as for the assembly code (we note as above $S_s^r = V_s^r \to R$):

$$[\![P_s]\!]_r = \alpha_s^r([\![P_s]\!]) \quad \text{where} \quad (\mathbb{P}((L_s \times S_s)^\star), \subseteq) \xleftrightarrow[\alpha_s^r]{\gamma_s^r} (\mathbb{P}((L_s^r \times S_s^r)^\star), \subseteq) .$$

In the following, if f is a function $f : A \rightarrow B$, we note $\widehat{f}$ for the function $\mathbb{P}(A) \rightarrow \mathbb{P}(B)$, $[(\mathcal{E} \subseteq A) \mapsto \{f(x) \mid x \in \mathcal{E}\}]$.

The correctness of the compilation is defined as a correspondence between some source program points and some assembly program points (that is between L_s^r and L_a^r) and a correspondence between part of the store locations (that is between V_s^r and V_a^r). Generally, the relation between store locations depends on the program point. For the sake of simplicity, we consider it does not.

Definition 1 (Correctness of compilation). *With the same notations as above, let* $\pi_l : L_s^r \rightarrow L_a^r$ *a bijection between source and assembly restricted program points and* $\pi_s : S_s^r \rightarrow S_a^r$ *a bijection between source and assembly restricted stores (usually given by a bijection* $\pi_v : V_s^r \rightarrow V_a^r$ *between store locations).*

Let π *be the function defined by:*

$$
\begin{aligned}
\pi : \quad & (L_s^r \times S_s^r)^\star && \rightarrow (L_a^r \times S_a^r)^\star \\
& \langle (x_0, s_0), \dots, (x_n, s_n) \rangle && \mapsto \langle (\pi_l(x_0), \pi_s(s_0)), \dots, (\pi_l(x_n), \pi_s(s_n)) \rangle \ .
\end{aligned}
$$

Then the compilation $\mathfrak{c}$ *of* P_s *into* P_a *is correct with respect to the translation information* (π_l, π_s) *if and only if* $\widehat{\pi}$ *is a bijection between* $[\![P_s]\!]_r$ *and* $[\![P_a]\!]_r$.

$$
\begin{array}{ccccc}
P_s & \longrightarrow & [\![P_s]\!] & \underset{\alpha_s^r}{\overset{\gamma_s^r}{\longleftrightarrow}} & [\![P_s]\!]_r \\
\mathfrak{c} \downarrow & & & & \| \| \widehat{\pi} \\
P_a & \longrightarrow & [\![P_a]\!] & \underset{\alpha_a^r}{\overset{\gamma_a^r}{\longleftrightarrow}} & [\![P_a]\!]_r
\end{array}
\qquad .
$$

Remark 1 (Optimizations). As mentioned above, code or variable elimination based optimizations are handled by choosing π_s and π_l so as to get rid with the removed entities.

Many optimizations that change the structure can also be handled in this framework by defining program points in a non syntactic way. For instance in case of an unrolling of a loop L, a syntactic program point x of the source program in the loop L is mapped to two points in the assembly program: one for odd numbers of iterations and one for even numbers of iterations. Handling the optimization reduces to split x into two program points x_{odd} and x_{even}.

The formalization of compilation presented above is comparable to the transition systems of [18]. The advantage of formalizing compilation inside the Abstract Interpretation framework is to bring both static analysis and compilation (and possibly optimizations) into a single framework, which makes reasoning about the process more simple.

3   Analysis, Compilation, and Invariant Translation

3.1   Static Program Analysis and Program Transformation

This subsection introduces a class of static program analyses, practically large enough to answer many questions such as run-time errors detection. Roughly speaking a program analysis will be defined by an abstraction of the trace semantics of programs (in practice an over-approximation of the abstract semantics is computed). We also prove that the abstraction defining such a static analysis is orthogonal to the "restriction" abstraction done in the previous section.

Let us consider a program P whose store ranges in $S = V \to R$ and of control flow graph (L, i, τ). We keep the previous notations: we note L^r and V^r for the restricted sets of program points and variables, ρ for the store projection, α^r for the restriction abstraction. We suppose we are given an abstraction on the store, that is a Galois connection $(\mathbb{P}(S), \subseteq) \xleftarrow[\alpha^s]{\gamma^s} (D^\sharp, \sqsubseteq)$.

The *abstract semantics* $[\![P]\!]^\sharp$ of the program P is obtained by partitioning $[\![P]\!]$ by the program points L and abstracting the sets of stores at each program point using α^s. Formally, this amounts to computing the abstraction α^t:

$$[\![P]\!]^\sharp = \alpha^t([\![P]\!]) \quad \text{where} \quad (\mathbb{P}((L \times S)^\star), \subseteq) \xleftarrow[\alpha^t]{\gamma^t} (L \to D^\sharp, \dot{\sqsubseteq})$$

$$\text{and} \quad \alpha^t(\mathcal{E}) = [(x \in L) \mapsto \alpha^s(\{s \mid \langle \dots, (x, s), \dots \rangle \in \mathcal{E}\})] \ .$$

In some cases, the abstract semantics $[\![P]\!]^\sharp$ may also be computed directly as a least fixpoint of an abstract semantic function $F_P^\sharp$. However a static analyzer usually computes a sound approximation of $[\![P]\!]^\sharp$ by iterating a sound monotonic function $\overline{F}_P^\sharp$ and using widening to enforce convergence. Fig. 4(a) presents the result of a classical interval analysis [5] of the program of Fig. 3(a).

program point	x
0	$\top$
1	[0 ; 100]
3	[0 ; 99]
4	[1 ; 100]
5	[100 ; 100]

program point	$M[0]$
0	$\top$
2	[0 ; 100]
7	[0 ; 99]
11	[1 ; 100]
6	[100 ; 100]

(a) Source analysis.   (b) Translated invariant.

Fig. 4. Source analysis and invariant translation.

We now come to the second point of this subsection: the trace restriction abstraction used to define correctness of the compilation and the abstraction α^t corresponding to the program analysis are independent and can be commuted.

The first step to reach that goal is to design a *restricted abstract domain* $D^{r\sharp}$ for $S^r = V^r \to R$ and a projection $\rho^\sharp$ of $D^\sharp$ on $D^{r\sharp}$ such that the abstraction and the projection commute, that is a Galois connection

$$(\mathbb{P}(S^r), \subseteq) \xleftarrow[\alpha^{sr}]{\gamma^{sr}} (D^{r\sharp}, \dot{\sqsubseteq}) \quad \text{such that} \quad \alpha^{sr} \circ \rho = \rho^\sharp \circ \alpha^s$$

This is in general easy. In the case of non relational domains, α^s is the pointwise abstraction of functions in $V \to R$ to functions in $V \to R^\sharp$. The same pointwise abstraction of functions in $V^r \to R$ to functions in $V^r \to R^\sharp$ commutes with domain restriction of functions. The case of most relational domains (like the octagons of [11] or the linear inequalities of [10]) is similar: forgetting the information about the variables of $V \setminus V^r$ is sufficient.

Then an abstraction on restricted traces can be defined as above by partitioning $[\![P]\!]_r$ by L^r and abstracting the sets of stores at each program point:

$$[\![P]\!]_r^\sharp = \alpha^{tc}([\![P]\!]_r) \quad \text{where} \quad (\mathbb{P}((L^r \times S^r)^\star), \subseteq) \xrightleftharpoons[\alpha^{tc}]{\gamma^{tc}} (L^r \to D^{r\sharp}, \dot{\sqsubseteq})$$

$$\text{and } \alpha^{tc}(\mathcal{E}) = [(x \in L^r) \mapsto \alpha^{sr}(\{s \mid \langle \ldots, (x,s), \ldots \rangle \in \mathcal{E}\})] .$$

Moreover a program invariant $I \in (L \to D^\sharp)$ can be abstracted to an invariant $I^r = \alpha^{rc}(I) \in (L^r \to D^{r\sharp})$, α^{rc} being the abstract counterpart of α^r:

$$\forall x \in L^r, \ I^r(x) = \alpha^{rc}(I)(x) = \rho^\sharp(I(x))$$

$$(L \to D^\sharp, \dot{\sqsubseteq}) \xrightleftharpoons[\alpha^{rc}]{\gamma^{rc}} (L^r \to D^{r\sharp}, \dot{\sqsubseteq}) .$$

The relationship between the program analysis and the trace restriction used for formalizing the correctness of the compilation is stated by the theorem:

Theorem 1. *With the above notations (α^r denotes the restriction abstraction and α^t the program analysis abstraction), $\alpha^{tc} \circ \alpha^r = \alpha^{rc} \circ \alpha^t$. In other words, the restricted semantics $[\![P]\!]_r^\sharp$ satisfies: $[\![P]\!]_r^\sharp = \alpha^{tc} \circ \alpha^r([\![P]\!]) = \alpha^{rc} \circ \alpha^t([\![P]\!])$.*

In other words analyzing the program and then restricting the results of the analysis by forgetting the abstract store at some program points and the information about some store locations amounts to first restricting the sets of program points and of locations and then abstracting traces.

3.2   Invariant Translation

We stated above the abstractions corresponding to the compilation and to the program analysis. We now define sound invariant translation procedures and show that they output sound invariants in presence of sound compilers and analyzers.

We instantiate the notations and results of Sect. 3.1 on a source program P_s and on an assembly program P_a. For $i \in \{s, a\}$,

- α_i^r is the restriction abstraction in the sense of Sect. 2.5,
- α_i^t is the abstraction corresponding to the static analysis as in Sect. 3.1,
- α_i^{rc} is the invariant restriction abstraction (introduced in Sect. 3.1),
- α_i^{tc} corresponds to static analysis from restricted semantics (Sect. 3.1).

Let (π_l, π_s) be translation information in the sense of Def. 1. An invariant translation procedure is a function $\pi_s^\sharp : D_s^{r\sharp} \to D_a^{r\sharp}$. It is sound if and only if it is the abstract counterpart of the concrete $\widehat{\pi}_s$:

Definition 2 (Sound invariant translation procedure). *The invariant translation function $\pi_s^\sharp$ is sound with respect to π_s if and only if:*

$$\forall S \subseteq S_a^r, \ \pi_s^\sharp \circ \alpha_s^{sr}(S) = \alpha_a^{sr} \circ \widehat{\pi}_s(S) .$$

For instance, in case of non relational domains the pointwise invariant translation (guided by the memory locations mapping π_v) is sound. Fig. 4(b) presents the translated invariant corresponding to the invariant of Fig. 4(a) (example of Fig. 3(a)).

Theorem 2 (Soundness of invariant translation). *If I_s is a sound abstract invariant for the source program P_s (i.e. $[\![P_s]\!]^\sharp \sqsubseteq I_s$), if the compilation of P_s into P_a is correct with respect to (π_l, π_s) and if the invariant translation function $\pi_s^\sharp$ is correct, then the translated invariant $I_a = \pi_s^\sharp \circ \alpha_s^{rc}(I_s)$ is sound, that is: $[\![P_a]\!]_r^\sharp \sqsubseteq I_a$.*

The proof of this result is done by composing the diagrams and applying straightforwardly the definitions, and twice Theorem 1. We first fix $I_s = [\![P_s]\!]^\sharp$:

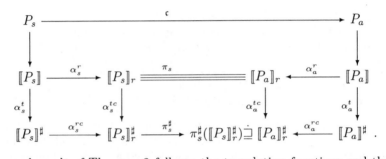

The general result of Theorem 2 follows: the translation functions and the abstraction functions are monotone ; soundness of I_s entails $[\![P_s]\!]^\sharp \sqsubseteq I_s$.

The inequality $[\![P_a]\!]^\sharp \sqsubseteq \gamma_a^{rc} \circ \pi_s^\sharp \circ \alpha_s^{rc}(I_s)$ is a direct consequence of the theorem (same hypotheses). Nevertheless the resulting approximation of $[\![P_a]\!]^\sharp$ is not precise enough, given $\forall x \in L_a \setminus L_a^r, \gamma_a^{rc} \circ \pi_s^\sharp \circ \alpha_s^{rc}(I_s) = \top$.

Sect. 4 addresses the problem of refining $I_a' = \gamma_a^{rc} \circ \pi_s^\sharp \circ \alpha_s^{rc}(I_s) = \gamma_a^{rc}(I_a)$ into an invariant I_a'' by invariant propagation and of checking that I_a'' is sound apart from any hypothesis about the correctness of the compiler or of the translator or even of the analyzer used for the source program.

4   Invariant Checking

4.1   Invariant Propagation and Checking

We suppose here that an approximate abstract semantic function $\overline{F}_a^\sharp$ for the assembly program can be computed. Such a function defines an analyzer for the assembly program: iterating it starting from $\perp$ (using widening to enforce convergence) would lead to a sound invariant (which may be imprecise since direct analyses of assembly code are made difficult by the absence of a control structure adapted to efficient iteration). Anyway this function being monotone, it has a least fixpoint, which is also an approximation of $[\![P_a]\!]^\sharp$: $[\![P_a]\!]^\sharp \sqsubseteq \mathrm{lfp}\overline{F}_a^\sharp$.

Invariant checking. Checking that the translated invariant is sound reduces to verifying that I'_a is a post-fixpoint of $\overline{F}^{\sharp}_a : (L_a \to D^{\sharp}_a) \to (L_a \to D^{\sharp}_a)$. The choice of the abstract domain for assembly programs may be crucial (as in Sect. 4.2), to tackle the specificities of the assembly language and make sure $\overline{F}^{\sharp}_a$ can be defined so that I'_a indeed is a post-fixpoint. The checking could fail even if I'_a is sound, for instance if the verifier $\overline{F}^{\sharp}_a$ was too imprecise or if the assembly code contained some statement that would be very difficult to analyze precisely.

Invariant propagation. A common technique to refine a sound invariant is to iterate the semantic function starting from it: if it is a post-fixpoint then we get a decreasing sequence (which means we improve precision).

If the invariant I'_a computed in Sect. 3.2. is a post-fixpoint of $\overline{F}^{\sharp}_a$ then, the iterates of $\overline{F}^{\sharp}_a$ starting from I'_a form a decreasing sequence. Therefore computing a given number of iterates of this sequence leads to a more precise invariant.

Practical solution. The way of propagating the invariant and checking it we adopted is slightly different. The translated invariant I_a provides precise information for the points contained in L^r_a. In practice every branch of the assembly control flow graph contains at least one point x such that $x \in L^r_a$; in particular every cycle contains such a point. Therefore we define an element J_a of the abstract domain $L_a \to D^{\sharp}_a$ by

$$J_a : \begin{cases} x \in L^r_a \mapsto I_a(x) \\ x \notin L^r_a \mapsto \bot \end{cases} ,$$

and then we compute in one iteration a post-fixpoint of Φ starting from J_a, where Φ is defined by $\Phi(X) = X \mathbin{\dot{\cup}} \overline{F}^{\sharp}_a(X)$. In practice, we compute a local invariant for each node in the graph, by propagating local invariants forwards, using a work-list algorithm: the set of nodes a local invariant is known for (the so-called treated nodes) is initialized to L^r_a; then a local invariant can be computed for a node when a local invariant has already been determined for all its predecessors. When the process finishes a local invariant has been determined for any point in L_a since every cycle of the assembly control flow graph contains at least one point belonging to L^r_a. When all nodes got a local invariant, checking that the invariant is sound reduces to checking that for every node x, the local invariant of x is "implied" by the local invariants of the predecessors of x. This property should only be checked for the nodes of L^r_a since local invariants at the other nodes have been computed so as to achieve this property.

Theorem 2 shows that invariant translation yields a sound "restricted" invariant under some soundness hypotheses (that should be realized). This subsection showed how an invariant for the assembly program is reconstructed from the "restricted" one and how it is finally checked. Checking allows this invariant to be considered safe apart from any other hypothesis than the correctness of the checker, which is much a stronger guarantee. Indeed if the invariant checker is correct and claims the invariant is stable then the invariant is sound even if the compilation is not correct.

Note that the checking may fail (for instance if some aspects of the assembly language are not analyzed precisely), which would not mean the restricted translated invariant would be incorrect.

4.2   Practical Aspects of Invariant Propagation and Checking

As mentioned above, invariant checking may require the use of a refined domain so as to handle the assembly language specificities. This section shows two of these together with their application to the example of Fig. 3.

Partitioning by the values of the CR: Conditional branching is commonly done in two steps in assembly languages (as in the language of Fig. 2): testing with modification of the condition register value according to the result of the comparison and branching according to the value of the condition register at branching time. Therefore the checker should propagate information about the condition register. In particular the local invariant at a point x should describe for any possible value $c \in \mathbb{C}$ of the condition register (where $\mathbb{C} = \{\text{LT}, \text{EQ}, \text{GT}\}$) a precise over-approximation of the set S_c of stores that can be encountered at program point x and that map the condition register to the value c. With the notations of Sect. 3, this amounts to choosing $D_a^{\sharp}$ of the form $\mathbb{C} \to D_a'^{\sharp}$: an abstract value is a function that associates to each possible CR value v an abstract representation of a set of assembly stores whose CR is positioned to v. The abstract transition functions for testing and branching are given below:

- testing: we suppose a guard operator $\textbf{guard} : D_a^{\sharp} \times \text{E} \to D_a^{\sharp}$ is provided. If P_a contains the instruction $l : \texttt{cmp } R_O, R_1$, $I \in L_a \to D_a^{\sharp}$ and $\mathcal{I}$ is the contribution of the other predecessors of $l+1$:

$$\overline{F}_a^{\sharp}(I)(l+1) = \mathcal{I} \stackrel{\cup}{} \begin{cases} \text{LT} \mapsto \textbf{guard}(I(l), R_0 < R_1) \\ \text{EQ} \mapsto \textbf{guard}(I(l), R_0 = R_1) \\ \text{GT} \mapsto \textbf{guard}(I(l), R_0 > R_1) \end{cases}$$

- branching: we suppose that P_a contains the instruction $l : \texttt{b}(\leq)l'$ and that $I \in L_a \to D_a^{\sharp}$. Then, if we define $\mathcal{I}$ and $\mathcal{I}'$ as other contributions as above,

$$\overline{F}_a^{\sharp}(I)(l+1) = \mathcal{I} \stackrel{\cup}{} \begin{cases} \text{LT} \mapsto \bot \\ \text{EQ} \mapsto \bot \\ \text{GT} \mapsto I(l)(\text{GT}) \end{cases} \qquad \overline{F}_a^{\sharp}(I)(l') = \mathcal{I}' \stackrel{\cup}{} \begin{cases} \text{LT} \mapsto I(l)(\text{LT}) \\ \text{EQ} \mapsto I(l)(\text{EQ}) \\ \text{GT} \mapsto \bot \end{cases} .$$

Partitioning by the condition register value at each program point is not necessary (and would be prohibitively costly since common architectures provide several condition registers): information about the condition register (that is partitioning over condition register values) is only necessary "between" tests and branching nodes.

Equalities between assembly locations: A test on the value of a variable x stored in $M[i]$ is done in two steps: the value of the variable is copied into a register R_j and then the test is done on the register. Checking the invariant requires to take into consideration the fact that the value contained in $M[i]$ should be affected by the test. This can be done either by doing backwards iteration (which would be costly) or by using a domain precise enough to provide information of the form $a = b$ where a and b are memory locations. When implementing, we chose the last solution and implemented a domain whose abstract elements are the partitions of $\mathbb{P}(\mathbb{V})$ as in Sect. 5.1 of [9], where an element of a partition is a set of variables that store the same value for any execution at a given point.

Results: Fig. 5 displays the final stable invariant produced for the example of Fig. 3.

Beginning of line	Equalities	CR	R_0	R_1	R_2	$M[0]$
0	none	$\top$	$\top$	$\top$	$\top$	$\top$
1	none	$\top$	$[0;0]$	$\top$	$\top$	$\top$
2	none	$\top$	$[0;99]$	$\top$	$\top$	$[0;100]$
3	$R_0 = M[0]$	$\top$	$[0;100]$	$\top$	$\top$	$[0;100]$
4	$R_0 = M[0]$	$\top$	$[0;100]$	$[100;100]$	$\top$	$[0;100]$
5	$R_0 = M[0]$	LT	$[0;99]$	$[100;100]$	$\top$	$[0;99]$
5	$R_0 = M[0]$	EQ	$[100;100]$	$[100;100]$	$\top$	$[100;100]$
5	$R_0 = M[0]$	GT	$\bot$	$\bot$	$\bot$	$\bot$
6	$R_0 = M[0]$	$\top$	$[100;100]$	$[100;100]$	$\top$	$[100;100]$
7	$R_0 = M[0]$	$\top$	$[0;99]$	$[100;100]$	$\top$	$[0;99]$
8	$R_0 = M[0]$	$\top$	$[0;99]$	$[100;100]$	$\top$	$[0;99]$
9	$R_0 = M[0]$	$\top$	$[0;99]$	$[1;1]$	$\top$	$[0;99]$
10	$R_0 = M[0]$	$\top$	$[0;99]$	$[1;1]$	$[1;100]$	$[0;99]$
11	$R_2 = M[0]$	$\top$	$[0;99]$	$[1;1]$	$[1;100]$	$[1;100]$

Fig. 5. Reconstructed and checked invariant.

5 Implementation

A prototype was implemented for certifying Motorola PowerPC assembly code obtained by compiling C programs. Most features of the C language are handled (excluding pointers and recursion which should not be used in highly critical software), including functions, procedures, structures and arrays, standard integer and floating point data types (a restricted form of alias is permitted for arrays passed by reference to functions).

The analyzer is similar to the analyzer presented in [3]. The basic abstract domain is non relational (based on the domains of intervals for the floating point numbers and the integers and on the domain of constants for the booleans) but the expressiveness of the domain is notably improved by partitioning (by the values of variables as is the case of the condition register in assembly programs or by control paths-based criteria). At the assembly code level, various addressing modes are handled (absolute, relative) thanks to a symbolic representation of addresses and to the representation of the stack in the assembly abstract domain.

After an invariant has been proved to be sound at the assembly program level by the checker, the prototype attempts to certify the code by checking it cannot cause any of the following "runtime errors": division by 0, integer or floating point overflow, erroneous memory access (dereferencing of a wrong address). This prototype successfully certified assembly programs of thousands of instructions issued from the compilation of C programs of hundreds of lines including representative fragments of embedded systems. We can expect to certify much larger programs (the current version of the prototype stores one abstract store at each program point for the sake of programming simplicity and testing; this causes a huge memory requirement and is not necessary in a certifying tool, given propagation and safety checking could be done in one pass).

6   Conclusion and Future Work

We proposed a method for certifying assembly code produced by compilation from a language we have an analyzer for. The method is generic with respect to the compiler and to the choice of an abstract domain. Invariant propagation and checking may require a precise treatment of some assembly language aspects.

The approach proved to be successful in practice. Note that the final checking of the invariant is a strong guarantee: analyzing programs is a complex task, and checking the result at the end apart from any hypothesis on the correctness of the rest of the process is a good point. Moreover the distinct steps of the process are independent: the source analysis, the translation of the invariants and their checking can be done separately. Existing tools can be used which reduces the cost of the analysis of assembly programs.

A first extension of this work would be to turn the existing prototype into a true certifying tool, for instance by extending the abstract domain to relational domains. Another more challenging goal would be to define a class of transformations (optimizations...) the method would work for. A last direction would be to use similar methods to analyze programs generated automatically from a specification: the specification could be used to compute an invariant on the program; checking the invariant on the program being simpler than inferring an invariant from the generated program alone.

Acknowledgments. We would like to thank Bruno Blanchet, Patrick and Radhia Cousot, Jérôme Feret, Charles Hymans, Laurent Mauborgne, Antoine Miné, and David Monniaux for comments, suggestions and stimulating discussions.

References

1. M. Alt, C. Ferdinand, F. Martin, and R. Wilhelm. Cache Behavior Prediction by Abstract Interpretation. In *Static Analysis Symposium*, LNCS, 1996.
2. Y. Bertot. A certified compiler for an imperative language. Technical Report RR-3488, INRIA, 1998.

3. B. Blanchet, P. Cousot, R. Cousot, J. Feret, L. Mauborgne, A. Miné, D. Monni-aux, and X. Rival. Design and implementation of a special-purpose static program analyzer for safety-critical real-time embedded software, invited chapter. In T. Mogensen, D. Schmidt, and I. Sudborough, editors, *The Essence of Computation: Complexity, Analysis, Transformation*, LNCS. Springer-Verlag, 2002. To appear.
4. P. Cousot. Semantic foundations of program analysis. In S. Muchnick and N. Jones, editors, *Program Flow Analysis: Theory and Applications*, chapter 10. Prentice-Hall, Inc., Englewood Cliffs, New Jersey, 1981.
5. P. Cousot and R. Cousot. Abstract interpretation: a unified lattice model for static analysis of programs by construction or approximation of fixpoints. In *Conference Record of the 4th Symposium on Principles of Programming Languages*, 1977.
6. P. Cousot and R. Cousot. Systematic design of program analysis frameworks. In *Conference Record of the 6th Symposium on Principles of Programming Languages*. ACM Press, New York, NY, 1979.
7. P. Cousot and R. Cousot. Systematic design of program transformation frameworks by abstract interpretation. In *Conference Record of the 29th Symposium on Principles of Programming Languages*. ACM Press, New York, NY, 2002.
8. C. Ferdinand, F. Martin, and R. Wilhelm. Applying Compiler Techniques to Cache Behavior Prediction. In *Workshop on Languages, Compilers and Tools for Real-Time Systems (LCT-RTS)*, 1997.
9. J. Feret. Dependency analysis of mobile systems. In *European Symposium on Programming (ESOP'02)*, 2002.
10. M. Karr. Affine relationships among variables of a program. *Acta Informatica*, pages 133–151, 1976.
11. A. Miné. The octagon abstract domain. In *AST 2001 in WCRE 2001*, IEEE, 2001.
12. G. Morrisett, D. Tarditi, P. Cheng, C. Stone, R. Harper, and P. Lee. The TIL/ML Compiler: Performance and Safety Through Types. In *Workshop on Compiler Support for Systems Software*, 1996.
13. G. C. Necula. Proof-Carrying Code. In *Proceedings of the 24th ACM SIGPLAN-SIGACT Symposium on Principles of Programming Langauges (POPL '97)*, 1997.
14. G. C. Necula. Translation validation for an optimizing compiler. *ACM SIGPLAN Notices*, 35(5):83–94, 2000.
15. A. Tarski. A lattice-theoretical fixpoint theorem and its applications. *Pacific Journal of Mathematics*, 1955.
16. H. Theiling and C. Ferdinand. Combining Abstract Interpretation and ILP for Microarchitecture Modelling and Program Path Analysis. In *Proceedings of the 19th IEEE Real-Time Systems Symposium*, 1998.
17. H. Theiling, C. Ferdinand, and R. Wilhelm. Fast and Precise WCET Prediction by Seperate Cache and Path Analyses. *Real-Time Systems*, 2000.
18. L. Zuck, A. Pnuelli, Y. Fang, and B. Goldberg. VOC: A translation validator for optimizing compilers. In J. Knoop and W. Zimmermann, editors, *Electronic Notes in Theoretical Computer Science*, volume 65. Elsevier Science Publishers, 2002.

Property Checking Driven Abstract Interpretation-Based Static Analysis*

Damien Massé

LIX, École Polytechnique, Palaiseau, France,
`masse@lix.polytechnique.fr`,
`http://www.lix.polytechnique.fr/~masse/`

Abstract. Concrete semantics used for abstract interpretation analyses are generally expressed as fixpoints. Checking a property on this kind of semantics can be done by intersecting the fixpoint with a specification related to the property. In this paper, we show how to produce a new, "reverse" analysis from this specification. The result of this analysis, expressed as a lower closure operator, is then used to guide the initial analysis. With this approach, we can refine the result given by the direct abstract analysis. We show that this method enables to deduce forward analyses from backward analyses (and *vice-versa*), and to combine them iteratively in a way similar to the forward-backward combination of analyses.

1 Introduction

The main idea of abstract interpretation [1,2,3] is to derive an abstract semantics of a program from its concrete semantics. When the goal is to prove a property (e.g. temporal property), the abstraction must be precise enough to express this property. However, the computation of the abstract semantics often induces losses of information, and gives only an approximation of the concrete semantics, which may not be sufficient to prove the property.

Refining the abstract domain to a complete one, as presented by Ranzato and *al.* [6], is a method to reduce the loss of information. But the refined abstract domain may be not representable (or very complex), moreover this method is not applicable when widenings [3] are required.

This paper exposes a different approach, based on the property we want to check. In general, the fixpoint defining the concrete semantics is a description of the "behaviors" of the program. This fixpoint computed (or approximated), the property is checked by "intersecting" the result with the specification of the property. From this operation, described as a lower closure operator, we construct another lower closure operator which can be included in the concrete semantics. The derived abstract semantics is then more precise than the initial

---

* This work was supported in part by the RTD project IST-1999-20527 DAEDALUS of the European IST FP5 program.

L. Zuck et al. (Eds.): VMCAI 2003, LNCS 2575, pp. 56–69, 2003.

abstract semantics. We prove that we can abstract this construction (which is then seen as a new analysis) while preserving the correctness of the method.

To complete the approach, we show how the result of this new abstract analysis can be used to refine the (approximated) lower closure operator, from which we derive another abstract semantics, and so on.

This approach gives results which are similar to the combination of backward and forward analysis used in abstract interpretation [1,8], but we start from only one analysis: the second analysis is derived from the first. As an example, we show that, by applying this approach, we can obtain constructions similar to previous such examples of combination.

This paper remains mainly theoretical. Though it is not very hard to implement analyzers based on this approach, getting the full advantage of it requires efficient abstractions on the set of lower closure operators on a lattice (and efficient abstract operators). We present in this paper a non-trivial class of abstractions on this set as a starting point for such abstractions, but more work is needed to make real analyzers.

2   Preliminaries

In order to present the new approach, we need to define some notations, and recall some known results on lower closure operators.

2.1   Notations

Let $\mathbb{Z}$ be the set of integers, and $\mathbb{Z}^\infty = \mathbb{Z} \cup \{-\infty, +\infty\}$.

Let τ be a transition relation on the set Σ, we recall the four predicate transformers in $\wp(\Sigma) \to \wp(\Sigma)$:

$$\mathrm{post}(X) = \{\sigma' \in \Sigma \mid \exists \sigma \in X, (\sigma, \sigma') \in \tau\}$$
$$\widetilde{\mathrm{post}}(X) = \{\sigma' \in \Sigma \mid \forall \sigma \in \Sigma, (\sigma, \sigma') \in \tau \Rightarrow \sigma \in X\}$$
$$\mathrm{pre}(Y) = \{\sigma \in \Sigma \mid \exists \sigma' \in Y, (\sigma, \sigma') \in \tau\}$$
$$\widetilde{\mathrm{pre}}(Y) = \{\sigma \in \Sigma \mid \forall \sigma' \in \Sigma, (\sigma, \sigma') \in \tau \Rightarrow \sigma' \in Y\}$$

If $(D, \leq)$ is a partially ordered set and $a \in D$, the principal ideal generated by a is denoted $(\uparrow_\leq a) = \{b \in D \mid a \leq b\}$. When there is no ambiguity, we will note $(\uparrow a)$ instead of $(\uparrow_\leq a)$. We let $D \xrightarrow{m} D$ be the set of monotone operators from D into D.

ϕ being a monotone operator on a complete lattice $\langle D, \leq, \vee, \wedge, \bot, \top \rangle$, we denote by $\mathrm{lfp}\,\phi$ (resp. $\mathrm{gfp}\,\phi$) the least fixpoint (resp. the greatest fixpoint) of ϕ. $\mathrm{lgfp}\,\phi$ will denote either $\mathrm{lfp}\,\phi$ or $\mathrm{gfp}\,\phi$.

We recall that ϕ is continuous (resp. co-continuous) iff for all increasing (resp. decreasing) chain A in D, $\phi(\bigvee A) = \bigvee_{a \in A} \phi(a)$ (resp. $\phi(\bigwedge A) = \bigwedge_{a \in A} \phi(a)$).

When ϕ is extensive and a is an element of D, we denote by $\mathrm{luis}\,(\phi, a)$ the limit of the upper iteration sequence of ϕ starting by a.

2.2   (Lower) Closure Operators

Closure operators and Moore families are widely used in abstract interpretation [1,3], to represent abstractions without the use of an abstract domain. Here, we will use lower closure operators to "restrict" the functions of the analysis independantly of the abstractions, which will be represented as upper closure operators.

In this section, we recall the results on lower closure operators.

General results. In the following section, $\langle D, \leq, \vee, \wedge, \bot, \top \rangle$ is a complete lattice.

We recall that an operator ρ on D is a lower (resp. upper) closure operator if it is monotone, idempotent and reductive (resp. extensive).

Proposition 1. *The set* $lco\,(D)$ *of lower closure operators on* D *is a complete lattice* $\langle lco\,(D), \sqsubseteq, \sqcup, \sqcap, \lambda x.x, \lambda x.\bot \rangle$, *with:*

$$\rho \sqsubseteq \rho' \iff \forall x \in D, \rho(x) \leq \rho'(x),$$
$$\bigsqcup\nolimits_{i \in \Delta} \rho_i = \lambda x. \bigvee\nolimits_{i \in \Delta} \rho_i(x),$$
$$\bigsqcap\nolimits_{i \in \Delta} \rho_i = \lambda x.\text{lfp}\,\lambda y.(x \wedge \bigwedge\nolimits_{i \in \Delta} \rho_i(y)).$$

For upper closure operators, we will denote by $\langle uco\,(D), \sqsubseteq, \sqcup, \sqcap, \lambda x.\top, \lambda x.x \rangle$ the complete lattice of upper closure operators on D.

Proposition 2 (Moore families). *Any lower closure operator* ρ *is uniquely determined by the set of its fixpoints* $\rho(D)$, *which is an (upper) Moore family (i.e.* $\rho(D) = \mathcal{M}\,(\rho(D)) = \{\vee X \mid X \subseteq \rho(D)\}$*). The correspondence between* $lco\,(D)$ *and the set of upper Moore families in* D *is described by the following equations:*

$$\rho \sqsubseteq \rho' \iff \rho(D) \subseteq \rho'(D)$$
$$\bigsqcup\nolimits_{i \in \Delta} \rho_i = \mathcal{M}\left(\bigcup\nolimits_{i \in \Delta} \rho(D)\right)$$
$$\bigsqcap\nolimits_{i \in \Delta} \rho_i = \bigcap\nolimits_{i \in \Delta} \rho(D)$$

We will use indifferently lower closure operators and upper Moore families. When there is no ambiguity, we will denote $\rho(D)$ by ρ itself (e.g. $\rho \sqsubseteq \rho' \iff \rho \subseteq \rho'$). An example of upper Moore family is given Fig. (3a).

Proposition 3 (Soundness [3]). *For all* $\phi \in D \xrightarrow{m} D$ *and* $\rho \in lco\,(D)$, *we have:*

$$\rho \circ \phi \circ \rho \leq \rho \circ \phi$$
$$\rho(\text{lfp}\,\phi) \geq \text{lfp}\,(\rho \circ \phi)$$
$$\rho(\text{gfp}\,\phi) \geq \text{gfp}\,(\rho \circ \phi).$$

Completeness. *Completeness* (or *exactness*) is the inverse property of soundness:

Definition 1 (Completeness [3]). *$\rho \in lco\,(D)$ is said to be* complete *for a monotone operator ϕ iff $\rho \circ \phi \circ \rho \geq \rho \circ \phi$ (and so $\rho \circ \phi \circ \rho = \rho \circ \phi$).*

Whereas the soundness is always satisfied for all monotone operator ϕ, completeness is always relative to an operator (or a set of operators). When we do not state the operator, completeness will be for ϕ.

The following proposition gives the relation between *completeness* and *fixpoint completeness*.

Proposition 4 (Fixpoint completeness).

1. *If ρ is complete, then ρ is gfp-complete (i.e. $\rho(\mathrm{gfp}\,\phi) = \mathrm{gfp}\,\rho \circ \phi$).*
2. *If ρ is complete and continuous, then ρ is lfp-complete (i.e. $\rho(\mathrm{lfp}\,\phi) = \mathrm{lfp}\,\rho \circ \phi$).*

For upper closures, it is well-known that completeness implies lfp-completeness (called *fixpoint completeness* in [6]). This result was first presented by Cousot and Cousot [3]. However, completeness (for upper closures) does *not* imply gfp-completeness. By duality, for lower closure operators, completeness ensures gfp-completeness but not lfp-completeness.

Example 1. We choose $D = \wp\,(\mathbb{Z})$ and $\phi = \lambda X.\{0\} \cup \{x + 1 \mid x \in X\}$. We know that lfp $\phi = [0, +\infty[$. Let $\rho = \{\emptyset, [0, +\infty[\}$. Since ρ is an upper Moore family, ρ defines a lower closure operator[1], and one can check easily that ρ is complete for ϕ. However, lfp $\rho \circ \phi = \emptyset$, and ρ is not lfp-complete.

Construction of complete closures. The construction of complete closure operators was studied by Giacobazzi, Ranzato and Scozzari [6]. Here is the result we will use in this paper:

Theorem 1 (Complete closures (dual of [6, Thm. 5.10])). *Let ρ_0 be a lower closure operator on D. If ϕ is co-continuous, then:*

$$R_\phi = \lambda\eta.\ \mathcal{M}(\cup_{a\in\eta}\ \min(\phi^{-1}(\uparrow a)))$$
$$and\ \mathcal{R}_\phi(\rho_0) = \mathrm{lfp}_{\sqsubseteq}\ \lambda\eta.(\rho_0 \sqcup R_\phi(\rho_0)) \tag{1}$$

are well defined and $\mathcal{R}_\phi(\rho_0)$ is the lowest complete lower closure operator greater than ρ_0[2].

---
[1]

$$\rho(X) = \begin{cases} [0, +infty[& \text{if } X \supseteq [0, +infty[, \\ \emptyset & \text{otherwise.} \end{cases}$$

[2] $\mathcal{R}_\phi(\rho_0)$ is called as the complete shell of ρ_0.

When ϕ is not co-continuous, this theorem does not hold because the min operator does not satisfy $\forall(a,x),\ x \in \phi^{-1}(\uparrow a) \Rightarrow (\exists y \in \min(\phi^{-1}(\uparrow a)), x \geq y)$. However, with $\min' : \wp(D) \to \wp(D)$ satisfying:

- $\forall X \subseteq D, \min'(X) \subseteq X,$
- $\forall X \subseteq D, \forall a \in X, \exists a' \in \min'(X)$ s.t. $a' \leq a,$

we can defined R_ϕ and $\mathcal{R}_\phi$ as:

$$R_\phi = \lambda\eta.\ \mathcal{M}(\cup_{a\in\eta} \min'(\phi^{-1}(\uparrow a)))$$
$$\text{and } \mathcal{R}_\phi(\rho_0) = \mathrm{lfp}_{\sqsubseteq} \lambda\eta.(\rho_0 \sqcup R_\phi(\rho_0)) \tag{2}$$

Then $\mathcal{R}_\phi(\rho_0)$ is a complete lower closure operator greater than ρ_0 (though it may not be minimal).

From this result, we can construct gfp-complete operators. To construct lfp-complete operator, we need a complete and continuous operator. We can achieve this goal by using an extensive operator C on $lco\,(D)$ such that $C(lco\,(D))$ includes only continuous operators.

Proposition 5. *Let C be an extensive operator on $lco\,(D)$ such that, for all lower closure operator η, $C(\eta)$ is $\leq$-continuous. Then $C \circ \mathcal{R}_\phi$ (with $\mathcal{R}_\phi$ defined either by equation (1) or by equation (2) is an extensive operator, and $luis(C \circ \mathcal{R}_\phi, \rho_0)$ is a continuous complete lower closure operator greater than ρ_0 (thus, it is lfp-continuous).*

Example 2. We give here two simple examples for C.

1. As $\lambda a.a$ is continuous, $C = \lambda\eta.(\lambda a.a)$ satisfies the conditions of the proposition. This examples is worthless, but it proves the existence of at least one possible operator.
2. When $D = \wp(\Sigma)$, $\lambda a.(a \cap X)$ for $X \subseteq \Sigma$ is a continuous lower closure operator. Therefore, $C = \lambda\eta.(\lambda a.a \cap (\eta(\Sigma)))$ satisfies the conditions. This example is interesting, as C is an upper closure operator and all elements of $C(lco\,(D))$ can be defined by a subset of Σ. Thus, we will be able to use abstractions of $\wp(\Sigma)$ to abstract lower closure operators.

3   Using Lower Closure Operators

In the abstract interpretation framework, lower closure operators are seen as lower approximations. However, this usage is hardly seen in practice[3], and does not present any additional theoretical interest, as a lower analysis is merely the dual of an upper analysis.

Our approach does not intend to use lower approximations. On the contrary, all abstractions will be upper abstractions. Lower closure operators are used to "reduce" the "range" of the analysis, to restrict it to significant parts. In this section we formalize this approach.

---

[3] It seems that useful lower abstractions are harder to find than upper abstractions.

3.1   Concrete Description

The first step of static analyses is the description of the concrete semantics of a program. The semantics is often described as a fixpoint $S = \text{lgfp}\,\phi$ on a *cpo* D. We suppose that D is a complete lattice, and, for simplicity, that $D = \wp(\Sigma)$, e.g. Σ is a set of states, traces, trees, etc.

Our main hypothesis is that the property we want to prove is expressed by the inclusion of S in a subset $\mathcal{P}$ of Σ. This hypothesis may seem too strong, but we can modify the concrete semantics in order to satisfy it.

Example 3. We can describe the program as a transition system τ, Σ being the set of states. I are the initial states of the program.

1. To express that the program will never reach error states E, we can write either:

$$(\text{lfp}\lambda X.I \cup \text{post}(X)) \subseteq \Sigma \backslash E,$$

   or

$$(\text{lfp}\lambda X.E \cup \text{pre}(X)) \subseteq \Sigma \backslash I.$$

2. To express that for all initial state, the program may not go wrong (with the CTL formalism, $\forall i \in I, i \models \mathbf{EG}(\neg error)$), we can only use a backward approach:

$$(\text{lfp}\lambda X.E \cup \widetilde{\text{pre}}(X)) \subseteq \Sigma \backslash I \qquad \text{where } E \text{ are the error states.}$$

3. For complex CTL properties, with more than one fixpoint, we may need to change the concrete domain in order to keep one general fixpoint for the computation. The backward semantics expressed in [9] is an example.

Proving $S \subseteq \mathcal{P}$ is equivalent to prove $S \cap (\Sigma \backslash \mathcal{P}) = \emptyset$. This kind of property may be checked in the framework of abstract interpretation: an upper approximation of $S \cap \mathcal{Q}$ (with $\mathcal{Q} = \Sigma \backslash \mathcal{P}$) is computed and compared with $\emptyset$.

The main idea of the approach is to consider $\rho_0 = \lambda X.X \cap \mathcal{Q}$ as a *lower closure operator* on $\wp(\Sigma)$, and to exploit the results on the construction of fixpoint complete lower closure operators. With the constructions described in section 2.2, we can construct a lower closure ρ greater than ρ_0 which is lgfp-complete for ϕ. Then:

$$\rho_0\,(\text{lgfp}\,\rho \circ \phi) = \rho_0 \circ \rho\,(\text{lgfp}\,\phi) = S \cap \mathcal{Q}$$

The figure (1) is an illustration of this result.

Thus, instead of computing an over-approximation of $\text{lgfp}\,\phi$, we can compute an over-approximation of $\text{lgfp}\,\rho \circ \phi$.

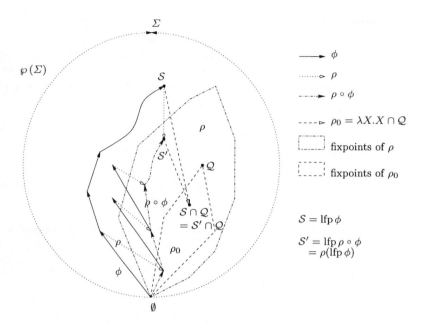

Fig. 1. Description of the combination, without abstractions. We want to compute $\mathcal{Q} \cap \operatorname{lfp} \phi = \rho_0(\operatorname{lfp} \phi)$. We design $\rho \sqsupseteq \rho_0$ such that ρ is lfp-complete for ϕ. Then $\mathcal{Q} \cap \operatorname{lfp} \rho \circ \phi = \mathcal{Q} \cap \operatorname{lfp} \phi$.

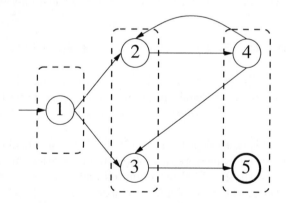

Fig. 2. Transition system described in example 4. $\{1\}$, $\{2,3\}$ and $\{4,5\}$ generates $\mathcal{R}_\phi(\rho_0)$

Example 4. With $\phi = \lambda X. F \cup \widetilde{\operatorname{pre}}(X)$, we can use the equation (1) since ϕ is co-continuous. With $a \subseteq \Sigma$, we have:

$$min(\phi^{-1}(\uparrow a)) = \{\operatorname{post}(a \backslash F)\}$$

For example, we can choose $\Sigma = \{1, 2, 3, 4, 5\}$, $\mathcal{Q} = \{1\}$, $F = \{5\}$ and $\tau = \{(1, 2), (1, 3), (2, 4), (3, 5), (4, 3), (4, 2)\}$.

Then $\mathcal{R}_\phi(\rho_0) = \mathcal{M}(\{\{1\}, \{2, 3\}, \{4, 5\}\})$ (cf. Fig. 2). The derived analysis $\mathrm{lfp}\,(\mathcal{R}_\phi(\rho_0)) \circ \phi$ gives $\emptyset$ at the first iteration. Therefore, the computation of $\mathcal{R}_\phi(\rho_0)$ is a kind of "forward analysis" which carry informations to prove the property we want to check.

3.2   Results with Abstractions

The results given until now were on the concrete domain, without abstractions. Of course, the lfp-complete lower closure operator is, in general, not computable. However, the goal of our approach is to get a new, computable analysis. Thus we need abstractions.

In this section, we introduce them, both in $\wp(\Sigma)$ (to compute sound approximations in the first analysis) and in $lco\,(\wp(\Sigma))$ (to compute sound approximations of the complete lower closure operators). We will show that the previous results are still correct with these abstractions, thanks to the usage of lower closure operators[4]. This will prove the correctness of our method.

In the following propositions, R_ϕ is defined with the equation (1) if ϕ is co-continuous or with the equation (2) otherwise.

The case of a greatest fixpoint is easier, so we present it first.

Proposition 6 (gfp **analysis**). *Let ϕ be a monotone operator on $\wp(\Sigma)$, and $\mathcal{Q}$ be a subset of Σ. We define $\rho_0 = \lambda X. X \cap \mathcal{Q}$. Let $\nu \in uco\,(\wp(\Sigma))$ and $\Upsilon \in uco\,(lco\,(\wp(\Sigma)))$ be (upper) abstractions of $\wp(\Sigma)$ and $lco\,(\wp(\Sigma))$, respectively. Then, with:*

$$\rho = \mathrm{lfp}\,\lambda\eta.\Upsilon(\rho_0 \sqcup R_\phi(\eta)),$$

we have $\mathcal{Q} \cap \mathrm{gfp}\,\phi \subseteq \mathrm{gfp}\,\nu \circ \rho \circ \phi$.

For lfp analysis, we need to construct a continuous operator. We use the method presented in proposition 5.

Proposition 7 (lfp **analysis**). *Let ϕ be a monotone operator on $\wp(\Sigma)$, and $\mathcal{Q}$ be a subset of Σ. We define $\rho_0 = \lambda X. X \cap \mathcal{Q}$. Let C be an extensive operator on $lco\,(\wp(\Sigma))$ such that for all η, $C(\eta)$ is continuous. Let $\nu \in uco\,(\wp(\Sigma))$ and $\Upsilon \in uco\,(lco\,(\wp(\Sigma)))$ be (upper) abstractions of $\wp(\Sigma)$ and $lco\,(\wp(\Sigma))$, respectively. Then, with:*

$$R = \lambda\eta.\Upsilon \circ C(\mathrm{lfp}\,\lambda\eta'.\Upsilon(\eta \sqcup R_\phi(\eta')))$$
$$\rho = luis(R, \rho_0),$$

we have $\mathcal{Q} \cap \mathrm{lfp}\,\phi \subseteq \mathrm{lfp}\,\nu \circ \rho \circ \phi$.

---

[4] Specifying the property with upper closures would require to use a lower abstraction on the closure domain *and* on the initial concrete domain.

It may seem that ρ would be long to compute, as there are two imbricated fixpoints. In practical applications, however, it is probable that we do not need to apply C many times.

These theorems give a method to define a new, "reverse" analysis (since R_ϕ depends on ϕ^{-1}) which can be used to "guide" the first analysis, and thus to enhance its result.

Expressing $R_\phi(\eta)$ is not so hard in practice. When η is generated by a set $\mathcal{A}$ of subsets of Σ (that is, $\eta = \mathcal{M}(\mathcal{A})$), we need only to know that $R_\phi(\eta)$ is generated by $\cup_{X \in \mathcal{A}} \min^?(\phi^{-1}(\uparrow X))$ ($\min^?$ being either min or min'). Therefore, we do not need to keep a representation of the whole Moore family, just of a set of generators.

Example 5. Starting from an abstraction ν of $\wp(\Sigma)$, we can use $\Upsilon = C = \lambda\eta.(\lambda X.X \cap \nu \circ \eta(\Sigma))$ (which can be represented as an element of ν). Then the result is the same for lfp and gfp analysis. To examine the result of this abstraction, we take $\nu = \lambda x.x$.

Then, for all $\eta \in \Upsilon(lco\,(\wp(\Sigma)))$, η satisfies $\eta = \mathcal{M}(\{\{x\} \mid x \in \eta(\Sigma)\})$, so we only have to express $\min'(\phi^{-1}(\uparrow \{x\}))$ to get $R_\phi(\eta)$.

With Σ being a set of states and $\phi = \lambda X.A \cap (F \cup \text{pre}(X))$ (that is, lgfp ϕ are the states which can go to F or, for the gfp, loop indefinitely in A), we can use:

$$\min'(\phi^{-1}(\uparrow \{x\})) = \begin{cases} \emptyset & \text{if } x \notin A \\ \{\emptyset\} & \text{if } x \in F \\ \{\{y\} \mid y \in \text{post}(\{x\})\} & \text{otherwise} \end{cases}$$

Then, with $\eta = \lambda X.X \cap Y$ and $\rho_0 = \lambda X.X \cap \mathcal{Q}$,

$$\Upsilon(\rho_0 \sqcup R_\phi(\eta)) = \lambda X.X \cap Y'$$
$$\text{with } Y' = \mathcal{Q} \cup \text{post}(Y \cap (A \backslash F))$$

Thus $\rho = \lambda X.X \cap (\text{lfp}\,\lambda Y.\mathcal{Q} \cup \text{post}(Y \cap (A \backslash F)))$. We got the reachability analysis in A (with a slight modification due to F). Using it before the backward analysis is a well-known idea both in abstract interpretation and in model-checking [4].

With this abstraction, this is also the best result we can get with $\phi = \lambda X.A \cap (F \cup \widetilde{\text{pre}}(X))$.

3.3   The Combination

Until now, we just show how to construct a reverse analysis from an initial one, and with this reverse analysis restrict the range of the first analysis. However, the backward-forward combination used in abstract interpretation works in both ways: the result of the first analysis is used to get a better reverse result, which we can use in the first analysis, and so on.

Our approach is not symmetrical: the first analysis is on $\wp(\Sigma)$, whereas the second one is on $lco\,(\wp(\Sigma))$. But we can still use the result of the initial analysis, even restricted, in the reverse analysis. This property is given by the following proposition for lfp analysis (the same result holds for gfp analysis):

Proposition 8. *Let ϕ be a monotone operator on $\wp(\Sigma)$, and Q be a subset of Σ. Let ρ_1 be a lfp-complete lower closure operator for ϕ such that $Q \cap \text{lfp}\,\phi \subseteq \text{lfp}\,\rho_1 \circ \phi$, and T be a subset of Σ such that $T \supseteq \text{lfp}\,\rho_1 \circ \phi$. We define $\varrho_T \in lco\,(\wp(\Sigma))$ as $\varrho_T = \lambda X.X \cap T$.*

Let C be an extensive and monotone operator on $lco\,(\wp(\Sigma))$ such that for all η, $C(\eta)$ is continuous.

Let $\nu \in uco\,(\wp(\Sigma))$ and $\Upsilon \in uco\,(lco\,(\wp(\Sigma)))$ be (upper) abstractions of $\wp(\Sigma)$ and $lco\,(\wp(\Sigma))$, respectively. Then, with:

$$R^T = \lambda\eta.\Upsilon \circ C(\text{lfp}\,\lambda\eta'.\Upsilon(\varrho_T \sqcap (\eta \sqcup R_\phi(\eta'))))$$
$$\rho^T = \text{lfp}\,\lambda\eta.(\varrho_T \sqcap (\rho_0 \sqcup R^T(\eta)))$$

then it exists $\rho_2 \in lco\,(\wp(D))$ such that ρ_2 is lfp-complete for ϕ, $\rho^T \sqsupseteq \rho_2$ and $Q \cap \text{lfp}\,\phi \subseteq \text{lfp}\,\rho_2 \circ \phi$ (hence, $Q \cap \text{lfp}\,\phi \subseteq \text{lfp}\,\nu \circ \rho^T \circ \phi$).

With this proposition, we can construct a decreasing sequence (T_n) of elements of $\wp(\Sigma)$ greater than $\text{lfp}\,\phi \cap Q$ (along with a decreasing sequence of lower closure operators (ρ^{T_n}), each ρ^{T_n} being greater than a lfp-complete closure operator ρ_n which satisfies $Q \cap \text{lfp}\,\phi \subseteq \text{lfp}\,\rho_n \circ \phi$):

$$T_0 = \Sigma$$
$$T_{k+1} = \text{lfp}\,\nu \circ \rho^{T_k} \circ \phi$$
$$T_\omega = \bigcap_{k<\omega} T_k \qquad \text{for all limit ordinal } \omega$$

Example 6. We continue the example (5). We have:

$$\rho^T = \lambda X.X \cap (\text{lfp}\,\lambda Y.T \cap (Q \cup \text{post}(Y \cap (A\backslash F)))).$$

Then, in the sequence (T_n), T_{n+1} is constructed by doing a forward analysis restricted to T_n, then a backward analysis restricted to the result of the forward analysis. This result is similar to the backward-forward combination used in abstract interpretation [5], even if the goal is not the same.

Remark 1. This combination which uses lower closures may seem similar to Granger's local decreasing iterations [7]. However, in Granger's iterations, lower closures are constant and applied several times. Here lower closures are modified at each iteration.

4   Abstractions of $lco\,(\wp(\Sigma))$

The examples we presented until now gives mainly already known results. To find better results, we must develop efficient abstractions of $lco\,(\wp(\Sigma))$. The first approach is to find abstractions from existing abstractions of $\wp(\Sigma)$. As an upper Moore family is an element of $\wp(\wp(\Sigma))$, this work can be related to the search of abstractions of $\wp(\wp(\Sigma))$. Following this principle, we will express the abstractions Υ as operators on the lattice of upper Moore families.

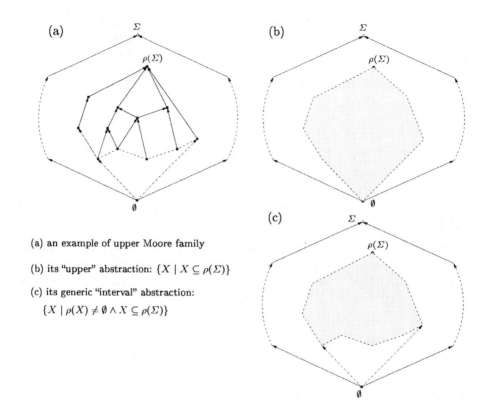

(a) an example of upper Moore family

(b) its "upper" abstraction: $\{X \mid X \subseteq \rho(\Sigma)\}$

(c) its generic "interval" abstraction:
$\{X \mid \rho(X) \neq \emptyset \wedge X \subseteq \rho(\Sigma)\}$

Fig. 3. Illustration of a lower closure operator as a Moore family (a), its generic "upper" abstraction (b) and "interval" abstraction (c).

4.1 "Upper" Abstraction

The "upper" abstraction was already given in example (5): from an abstraction $\nu \in uco\,(\wp\,(\Sigma))$, we define $\Upsilon_\nu(\rho) = \{X \mid X \subseteq \nu \circ \rho(\Sigma)\}$.

Then we can make an equivalence between the elements of Υ_ν and the elements of ν, which helps the calculus.

All these abstractions are less precise than the "generic" upper abstraction, independent of ν: $\Upsilon_0(\rho) = \{X \mid X \subseteq \rho(\Sigma)\}$ This abstraction is represented on figure (3b).

4.2 "Interval" Abstraction

The "interval" abstraction is a combination of an "upper" abstraction and a "lower" one. The "upper" abstraction was presented before. The "lower" would give properties on the lowest elements of the lower closure operator ρ. However, the lowest element of ρ is simply $\emptyset$. Thus, we will try to give properties on the "lower part" of $\rho\backslash\{\emptyset\}$. On the other hand, we forget what is between this "lower part" and the maximum $\rho(\Sigma)$: all elements are possible fixpoints.

Our "generic" abstraction is then:

$$\Upsilon_0(\rho) = \{\emptyset\} \cup \{X \mid \exists(Y,Z) \in \rho^2, Y \neq \emptyset \wedge Y \subseteq X \subseteq Z\}$$

An illustration of this abstraction is given Fig. (3c).

Described with closure operators, we see that this abstraction keeps $\rho^{-1}(\{\emptyset\})$ (i.e. $\rho^{-1}(\{\emptyset\}) = (\Upsilon_0(\rho))^{-1}(\{\emptyset\})$):

$$\Upsilon_0(\rho) = \lambda X. \begin{cases} \emptyset & \text{if } X \notin \{Y \mid \rho(Y) \neq \emptyset\} \\ X \cap \rho(\Sigma) & \text{otherwise} \end{cases}$$

With this definition, $\Upsilon_0(\rho)$ is represented by an element of $\wp(\Sigma)$ and an element of $\wp(\wp(\Sigma))$. The first one, $\rho(\Sigma)$, can be easily abstracted. However, the second one ($\{Y \mid \rho(Y) \neq \emptyset\}$) is difficult to approximate. A possible approach would be to choose a (lower) approximation of $\bigcap\{Y \mid \rho(Y) \neq \emptyset\}$. In practical cases, this approach often gives $\emptyset$. Thus, we propose another alternative, which consists in abstracting each element of the set before intersecting them in the abstract domain. The more the abstract intersection keeps informations, the better this alternative will be. Following this principle, we will use a Galois connection for this abstraction: we do not require the abstraction function to be surjective.

Starting from an abstraction of $\wp(\Sigma)$ described as a Galois connection $\wp(\Sigma) \xleftarrow{\gamma}{\alpha} \Sigma^\sharp$ ($\Sigma^\sharp$ being a complete lattice), we define $\Upsilon_{\alpha,\gamma} \in uco(lco(\wp(\Sigma)))$ as:

$$\Upsilon_{\alpha,\gamma}(\rho) = \lambda X. \begin{cases} \emptyset & \text{if } \alpha(X) \sqsubseteq^\sharp \sqcap^\sharp \{\alpha(Y) \mid Y \in \rho\} \\ X \cap \gamma \circ \alpha(\rho(\Sigma)) & \text{otherwise} \end{cases} \qquad (3)$$

We can remark that all elements of $\Upsilon_{\alpha,\gamma}$ can be represented by an element of $\Sigma^\sharp \times \Sigma^\sharp$:

Theorem 2. $\Upsilon_{\alpha,\gamma} \in uco(lco(\wp(\Sigma)))$, and $\Upsilon_{\alpha,\gamma} \sqsubseteq \Upsilon_0$. Furthermore, $\Upsilon_{\alpha,\gamma}$ is associated to the Galois connection:

$$(lco(\wp(\Sigma)), \sqsubseteq) \xleftarrow{\gamma^\bullet}{\alpha^\bullet} (\Sigma^\sharp, \sqsupseteq^\sharp) \times (\Sigma^\sharp, \sqsubseteq^\sharp)$$
$$\alpha^\bullet(\rho) = (\sqcap^\sharp \{\alpha(Y) \mid Y \in \rho\}, \alpha(\rho(\Sigma)))$$
$$\gamma^\bullet(l,u) = \{X \mid l \sqsubseteq^\sharp \alpha(X) \sqsubseteq^\sharp u\}$$

Remark 2. If ρ is generated by $\mathcal{A}$, then

$$\alpha^\bullet(\rho) = (\sqcap^\sharp \{\alpha(Y) \mid Y \in \mathcal{A}\}, \alpha(\cup\mathcal{A}))$$

Thus we do not need to compute the whole Moore family to get the abstract element.

Example 7. We choose $\Sigma = \mathbb{Z}$ and $\Sigma^\sharp = \mathbb{Z}^\infty \times \mathbb{Z}^\infty$, with $\alpha(X) = (\min X, \max X)$ and $\gamma(m, M) = \{i \mid m \leq i \leq M\}$ (this is the numerical interval domain [2], except that we do not restrict this domain to "true" intervals, where $m \leq M$).

If ρ is generated by $\{\{n, n+3\} \mid n \geq 1\}$, then $\alpha^\bullet(\rho) = ((+\infty, 4), (1, +\infty))$, and

$$\Upsilon_{\alpha,\gamma}(\rho) = \lambda X. \begin{cases} \emptyset & \text{if } \max X < 4 \\ X \cap [1, +\infty[& \text{otherwise} \end{cases}$$

We can see that this approximation is more precise than the "upper-only" abstraction used in the example (5).

Remark 3. As we can see in the example above, using a Galois connection for the abstraction of $\wp(\Sigma)$ is very important: we can use a larger abstract domain $\Sigma^\sharp$, with α non-surjective, to obtain a better precision. On the contrary, using the classical interval domain for $\Sigma^\sharp$ (where all elements (m, M) with $m > M$ are collapsed into $\bot$) would give $(\bot, (1, +\infty))$ for $\alpha^\bullet(\rho)$, which is less precise. Since all closure operators induce a surjective Galois connection, we can not use this framework here.

5   Conclusion

We have shown how lower closure operators can be used in verification in the abstract interpretation framework. Starting from a condition on the final result, we derive a new analysis which can be combined with the initial one. The news semantics is a refinement of the original one, stable for the property we want to check, so the abstract semantics will be more precise. The work of Giacobazzi and *al.* about completion of abstractions is used to get the concrete description of the new analysis and to prove its general correctness.

The main point of our contribution is the possibility of abstracting this new analysis to compute automatically an abstract lower closure operator which can be used in the original abstract analysis. Lower closure operators are needed because they can be over-approximated while keeping the correctness of the (upper) analysis, something which would not work with upper closure operators. Thus, the efficiency of this approach relies mainly on the efficiency of the abstractions on $lco(D)$.

This paper showed examples of abstractions on $lco(D)$, but many other abstractions can be developed. For example, we can construct new abstractions from existing one by using the structure of D (as a Cartesian product, or as a lattice of functions). This work is essential for the design of a real analyzer which would use this approach.

Acknowledgments. I wish to thank the anonymous referees, as well as Radhia and Patrick Cousot and Francesco Logozzo for their helpful comments and suggestions.

References

1. P. Cousot. *Méthodes itératives de construction et d'approximation de point fixes d'opérateurs monotones sur un treillis, analyse sémantique des programmes.* Thèse ès sciences mathématiques, University of Grenoble, March 1978.
2. P. Cousot and R. Cousot. Abstract interpretation: a unified lattice model for static analysis of programs by construction or approximation of fixpoints. In *Conference Record of the Fourth Annual ACM SIGPLAN-SIGACT Symposium on Principles of Programming Languages*, pages 238–252, Los Angeles, California, 1977. ACM Press, New York, NY.
3. P. Cousot and R. Cousot. Systematic design of program analysis frameworks. In *Conference Record of the Sixth Annual ACM SIGPLAN-SIGACT Symposium on Principles of Programming Languages*, pages 269–282, San Antonio, Texas, 1979. ACM Press, New York, NY.
4. P. Cousot and R. Cousot. Refining model checking by abstract interpretation. *Automated Software Engineering*, 6(1):69–95, 1999.
5. P. Cousot and R. Cousot. Software analysis and model checking. In E. Brinksma and K.G. Larsen, editors, *Proceedings of the 14th International Conference on Computer Aided Verification, CAV 2002*, Copenhagen, Denmark, LNCS 2404, pages 37–56. Springer-Verlag Berlin Heidelberg, 27–31 July 2002.
6. R. Giacobazzi, F. Ranzato, and F. Scozzari. Making abstract interpretations complete. *Journal of the ACM*, 47(2):361–416, 2000.
7. P. Granger. Improving the results of static analyses of programs by local decreasing iterations. In R. K. Shyamasundar, editor, *Foundations of Software Technology and Theoretical Computer Science, 12th conference, New Dehli, India*, volume 652 of *Lecture Notes in Computer Science*, pages 68–79. Springer-Verlag, 1992.
8. D. Massé. Combining backward and forward analyses of temporal properties. In O. Danvy and A. Filinski, editors, *Proceedings of the Second Symposium PADO'2001, Programs as Data Objects*, volume 2053 of *Lecture Notes in Computer Sciences*, pages 155–172, Århus, Denmark, 21–23 May 2001. Springer-Verlag, Berlin, Germany.
9. D. Massé. Semantics for abstract interpretation-based static analyzes of temporal properties. In M. Hermenegildo, editor, *Proceedings of the Ninth Static Analysis Symposium SAS'02*, volume 2477 of *Lecture Notes in Computer Sciences*, pages 428–443, Madrid, Spain, 17–20 September 2002. Springer-Verlag, Berlin, Germany.

Optimized Live Heap Bound Analysis

Leena Unnikrishnan, Scott D. Stoller, and Yanhong A. Liu*

Computer Science Dept., SUNY at Stony Brook, Stony Brook, NY 11794-4400 USA

Abstract. This paper describes a general approach for optimized live heap space and live heap space-bound analyses for garbage-collected languages. The approach is based on program analysis and transformations and is fully automatic. In our experience, the space-bound analysis generally produces accurate (tight) upper bounds in the presence of partially known input structures. The optimization drastically improves the analysis efficiency. The analyses have been implemented and experimental results confirm their accuracy and efficiency.

1 Introduction

Time and space analysis of computer programs is important for virtually all computer applications, especially in embedded systems, real-time systems, and interactive systems. Space analysis is becoming important due to the increasing use of high-level languages with garbage collection, such as Java, the importance of cache memories in performance [28], and the stringent space requirements of embedded applications [25]. For example, space analysis can determine exact memory needs of embedded applications; it can help determine patterns of space usage and thus help analyze cache misses or page faults; and it can determine memory allocation and garbage collection behavior.

Space analysis is also important for accurate prediction of running time [11]. For example, analysis of worst-case execution time in real-time systems often uses loop bounds or recursion depths [21,2] both of which are commonly determined by the size of the data being processed. Also, memory allocation and garbage collection, as well as cache misses and page faults, contribute directly to the running time. This is increasingly significant as the processor speed increases, leaving memory access as the performance bottleneck.

Much work on space analysis has been done in algorithm complexity analysis and systems. The former is in terms of asymptotic space complexity in closed forms [5]. The latter is mostly in the form of tracing memory behavior or analyzing cache effects at the machine level [20,28]. What has been lacking is analysis

* The authors gratefully acknowledge the support of ONR under grants N00014-99-1-0132, N00014-99-1-0358 and N00014-01-1-0109 and of NSF under grants CCR-9711253 and CCR-9876058. Authors' address: Computer Science Department, SUNY at Stony Brook, Stony Brook, NY 11794-4400 USA. Email: {leena,stoller,liu}@cs.sunysb.edu. Web: www.cs.sunysb.edu/~{leena,stoller,liu}. Phone: (631)632-1627. Fax: (631)632-8334.

L. Zuck et al. (Eds.): VMCAI 2003, LNCS 2575, pp. 70–85, 2003.

of space usage for high-level languages, in particular, automatic and accurate techniques for live heap space analysis for languages with garbage collection, such as Java, ML or Scheme.

This paper describes a general approach for automatic accurate analysis of live heap space based on program analysis and transformations. The analysis determines the maximum size of the live data on the heap during execution. This is the minimum amount of heap space needed to run the program if garbage collection is performed whenever garbage is created. This metric is useful for evaluating other garbage collection schemes, just like the performance of an optimal cache replacement algorithm is useful for evaluating other replacement algorithms. The analysis can easily be modified to determine related metrics, such as space usage when garbage collection is performed only at fixed points in the program.

Our approach starts with a program written in a high-level functional language with garbage collection. We construct (*i*) a *space function* that takes the same input as the original program and returns the amount of space used and (*ii*) a *space-bound function* that takes as input a characterization of a set of inputs of the original program and returns an upper bound on the space used by the original program on any input in that set. Finding tight space bounds is undecidable, so space-bound functions may diverge. In our experience, this is rare.

A key problem is how to characterize the input data and exploit this information in the analysis. In traditional complexity analysis, inputs are characterized by their size. Accommodating this requires manual or semi-automatic transformation of the time or space function [17,29]. The analysis is mainly asymptotic. A challenging problem that arises in this approach is optimizing the time-bound or space-bound function to a closed form in terms of the input size [17,24,7]. But closed forms are known only for subclasses of functions. Thus, such optimization can not be done automatically for analyzing general programs.

Rosendahl proposed characterizing inputs using *partially known input structures* [24]. For example, instead of replacing an input list l with its length n, we simply use as input a list of n unknown elements. A special value uk ("unknown") is introduced for this purpose. It represents unknown primitive values; if it represented constructed data, we wouldn't know how much space it used. At control points where decisions depend on unknown values, the maximum space usage of all branches is computed. Rosendahl concentrated on proving the correctness of this transformation for time-bound analysis. He relied on optimizations to obtain closed forms, but closed forms can not be obtained for all bound functions.

Our analysis and transformations are performed at source level. Our goal is a language-based analysis that abstracts from details of particular language implementations. For a particular language implementation, lower-level issues may need to be considered to determine the exact minimum heap space needed to run a given program.

Profiling, like space functions, measures the program's behavior on one input at a time; space-bound functions can efficiently analyze the program's behavior on a set of inputs at once. They can thus be used to determine worst-case space usage of a program. Alternatively, worst-case space usage may be determined by applying the space function to a worst-case input. But in general, it is non-trivial to determine such an input.

Our approach combines program analysis and model checking and is called *model analysis*.

Live heap space-bound analysis is an abstract interpretation of live heap space analysis. While the latter works in the domain of concrete heaps, the former works in the domain of abstract heaps that represent the different possible heaps at a program point. Instead of performing a fixed-point computation of the abstract function like traditional abstract interpretations, we simply execute the abstract space-bound function on a given partially known input. Our analysis could be cast as a fixed-point calculation. While this may help achieve termination, the memory needs would be far greater due to the large number of required subcomputations and the large size of abstract heaps.

Space-bound analysis may also be viewed as a specialized model checking algorithm that searches a program's state space to determine its worst-case space usage. Our analysis is similar in some ways to an explicit-state model-checker applied to a program in which primitive values have been abstracted. But there is an important difference: traditional model checkers work on unstructured transition systems and can check a large range of properties, while our analysis works directly on programs in a high-level language and incorporates optimizations that exploit program structure and are possible only because the analysis is specifically targeted to determine heap space usage. In particular, it is easy to see that the two states resulting from the two branches of a conditional in a space-bound function are the same in all ways, except for a well-delineated region of their heaps. Our analysis uses a join operation that merges such states into a single state. This reduces the number of states and the space needed to store them. It also reduces the number of transitions that need to be explored, since they may now be explored from a single merged state.

A main contribution of this paper is an extremely effective optimization in space-bound analysis that limits the state space search to paths leading to maximal heap usage. For many examples, this optimization improves the asymptotic complexity of the analysis from greater than polynomial to polynomial.

2   Language

We use a first-order, call-by-value functional language that has literal values of primitive types, structured data, operations on primitive types, testers, selectors, conditionals, bindings, and function calls. These are fundamental program constructs that have analogues in all programming languages. A program is a set of mutually recursive function definitions of the form $f(v_1, ..., v_n) = e$, where an expression e is given by the grammar in Figure 1. We sometimes use infix notation for primitive operations. A tester application $c?(v)$ returns *true* iff v has outermost constructor c. A selector application $c^{-i}(v)$ returns the i'th com-

$e ::=$	v	variable reference
	l	literal
	$c(e_1, ..., e_n)$	constructor application
	$p(e_1, ..., e_n)$	operation on primitive types
	$c?(e)$	tester application
	$c^{-i}(e)$	selector application
	if e_1 **then** e_2 **else** e_3	conditional expression
	let $v = e_1$ **in** e_2	binding expression
	$f(e_1, ..., e_n)$	function application

Fig. 1. Input language.

ponent of a data construction v with outermost constructor c. Input programs to our analysis are assumed to be purely functional, but transformed programs use arrays and imperative update. A sequential composition $e_1; e_2$ returns the value of e_2.

3   Live Heap Space Functions

To analyze the live heap space used by a program on a known input, we transform the program into one that performs all the computations of the original program and keeps track of the total amount of live data. Liveness is ascertained using reference counts. The *reference count* for a data construction v is the number of pointers to v. These may be pointers from the stack, created by **let** bindings or bindings to formal parameters of functions, or pointers from the heap, created by data constructions. Data construction v is live if its reference count is greater than 0 or if it is the result of the expression just evaluated.

A *constructor count vector* v has one element $v[i_c]$ corresponding to each data constructor c used in a given program. Let $P[i_c]$ be the size of an instance of c. Let $\cdot$ denote dot product of vectors. The maximum $\max(v_1, v_2)$ of constructor count vectors v_1 and v_2 is v_1 if $v_1 \cdot P \geq v_2 \cdot P$ and is v_2 otherwise.

The transformation $\mathcal{L}$ in Figure 2 produces live heap space functions. The transformation of testers and **let** expressions is elided for brevity. The complete transformation appears in [27]. $\mathcal{L}$ introduces two global variables, *live* and *maxlive*, that satisfy: (1) for each constructor c, $live[i_c]$ is the number of live instances of c; (2) *maxlive* is the maximum value of *live* so far during execution. The maximum live space used during evaluation of function f is at most $ml \cdot P$; ml is the value of *maxlive* after evaluation of the space or bound function for f.

Our implementation of reference counting is based on an abstract data type (ADT) called con-value ("constructed-value") that defines five functions. $new(c(x_1, \ldots, x_n))$ returns a value v representing a new data construction $c(x_1, \ldots, x_n)$, whose reference count is initialized to zero. $data(v)$ returns the data construction $c(x_1, \ldots, x_n)$. $rc(v)$ returns the reference count associated with v. $incrc(v)$ and $decrc(v)$ increment and decrement, respectively, the reference count associated with v. $incrc$ and $decrc$ are no-ops if the argument is a primitive value.

$$f_L(v_1, \ldots, v_n) = \mathcal{L}[e] \quad \text{where } e \text{ is the body of function } f, \text{ i.e., } f(v_1, \ldots, v_n) = e$$

$$\mathcal{L}[v] = v$$

$$\mathcal{L}[l] = l$$

$$\mathcal{L}[c(e1, \ldots, en)] = live[i_c]++; \textbf{ if } (P \cdot live > P \cdot maxlive)$$
$$\textbf{then for } c \in Constructors \; maxlive[i_c] := live[i_c];$$
$$\textbf{let } r_1 = \mathcal{L}[e_1], \ldots, r_n = \mathcal{L}[e_n] \textbf{ in}$$
$$incrc(r_1); \ldots; incrc(r_n); new(c(r_1, \ldots, r_n))$$

$$\mathcal{L}[p(e_1, \ldots, e_n)] = p(\mathcal{L}[e_1], \ldots, \mathcal{L}[e_n])$$

$$\mathcal{L}[c^{-i}(e)] = \textbf{let } x = \mathcal{L}[e] \textbf{ in}$$
$$\textbf{let } r = c^{-i}(data(x)) \textbf{ in}$$
$$(\textbf{if } not(isPrim(x)) \text{ and } rc(x) = 0 \textbf{ then } gcExcept(x, r)); r$$

$$\mathcal{L}[\textbf{if } e1 \textbf{ then } e2 \textbf{ else } e3] = \textbf{if } \mathcal{L}[e1] \textbf{ then } \mathcal{L}[e2] \textbf{ else } \mathcal{L}[e3]$$

$$\mathcal{L}[f(e_1, \ldots, e_n)] = \textbf{let } r_1 = \mathcal{L}[e_1], \ldots, r_n = \mathcal{L}[e_n] \textbf{ in}$$
$$incrc(r_1); \ldots; incrc(r_n);$$
$$\textbf{let } r = f_L(r_1, \ldots, r_n) \textbf{ in}$$
$$gcExcept(r_1, r); \ldots; gcExcept(r_n, r); r$$

$$gc(v) = \textbf{if } not(isPrim(v))$$
$$\textbf{then } decrc(v); \textbf{ if } rc(v) \leq 0$$
$$\textbf{then } live[conType(v)]--;$$
$$\textbf{for } i = 1..arity(v) \; gc(c^{-i}(data(v)))$$

$$gcExcept(u, v) = incrc(v); gc(u); decrc(v)$$

Fig. 2. Transformation that produces live heap space functions f_L. $isPrim(v)$ is *true* iff v is primitive. $conType(v)$ returns an integer i_c that uniquely identifies the outermost constructor c in $data(v)$. $arity(v)$ returns the arity of the outermost constructor in $data(v)$.

Updating Reference Counts. $rc(v)$ is incremented when v is bound to a variable or function parameter, or a data construction containing v as a child is created. $rc(v)$ is decremented when the scope of a **let** binding for v ends, a function call with an argument bound to v returns, or a data construction containing v as a child becomes garbage.

Updating *live* and *maxlive*. Whenever new data is constructed, *live* is incremented, and *maxlive* is recomputed. *live* is decremented by an auxiliary function gc ("garbage collect") which is called whenever data can become garbage. A data construction may become garbage (1) because of a decrement of its reference count or (2) because it is created in the argument of a selector or tester and is lost to the program after the result of the selection or test is obtained. For example, $cons(0, nil)$ is garbage after the application of $cons^{-1}$ in $cons^{-1}(cons(0, nil))$; note that its reference count is always 0. $gcExcept(u, v)$ is called when u should be garbage collected, v should not be garbage collected and v might be a descendant of u.

4   Live Heap Space Bound Functions

The transformation $\mathcal{L}_b$ in Figure 3 produces live heap space-bound functions. The transformation of certain expressions is elided for brevity; for variables, literals and constructor applications $\mathcal{L}_b$ works the same way as $\mathcal{L}$. The complete transformation appears in [27]. We sometimes refer to space-bound functions simply as bound functions. At every point during the execution of $\mathcal{L}_b\,[f]\,(x)$, the value of *live* is an upper bound on the possible values of *live* at the corresponding point in executions of $\mathcal{L}\,[f]\,(x')$, for all x' in the set represented by x. The presence of partially known inputs in bound analysis causes uncertainty. For conditionals whose tests evaluate to uk, both branches are evaluated to determine the maximum live heap space usage.

Live heap bound analysis depends on keeping track of all references and reference counts meticulously. Summarizing the results of two branches into a single partially known structure, as is done in time analysis [18], does not work for live heap bound analysis because it would be impossible to keep track of references accurately. So the result of a conditional whose test evaluates to uk is a separate entity, a join-value, that points to both results and has its own reference count.

Abstract Data Types. In addition to the con-value type, an ADT called join-value is also used. A join-value represents a set of possible results. Join-values are created by conditional expressions whose tests evaluate to uk and by selectors applied to join-values. Each join-value j has a list $branches(j)$ containing references to con-values and/or join-values. Primitive values, if any, in the set represented by j are not stored in j. Thus, if $branches(j)$ has only one element, j represents a choice between that element and some primitive value. j has an associated constructor count vector $exs(j)$. Parts of the data constructions represented by j may be live regardless of j. Of the other parts, only those occurring in a single largest branch are live in a worst case (i.e., maximal live heap space) execution of the original program. The sum of the other parts that are not in the largest branch is stored in $exs(j)$. *live* does not include $exs(j)$. When j becomes garbage, $exs(j)$ is added to *live* just before garbage collecting the branches of j. Like con-values, join-values have reference counts and related functions rc, $incrc$ and $decrc$. $newjoin(b)$ creates a join-value j with a list b of branches; $rc(j)$ is initialized to 0, and $exs(j)$ is initialized to the zero vector, denoted V_0.

Conditionals, Selectors and Testers. Consider a conditional expression $(\textbf{if } e_1 \textbf{ then } e_2 \textbf{ else } e_3)^\dagger$ whose test evaluates to uk. Suppose l_1, l_2 and l_3 are the values of *live* after evaluating e_1, $e_1; e_2$ and $e_1; e_3$, respectively. The value of *live* at $\dagger$ is set to $\max(l_2, l_3)$. The result r of the conditional is computed by

$f_{Lb}(v_1, \ldots, v_n) = \mathcal{L}_b[\![e]\!]$ where e is the body of function f, i.e., $f(v_1, \ldots, v_n) = e$

$\mathcal{L}_b[\![p(e1, \ldots, en)]\!] = p_u(\mathcal{L}_b[\![e1]\!], \ldots, \mathcal{L}_b[\![en]\!])$

$p_u(v_1, \ldots, v_n) = \textbf{if } v_1 = uk \textbf{ or } \cdots \textbf{ or } v_n = uk \textbf{ then } uk \textbf{ else } p(v_1, \ldots, v_n)$

$\mathcal{L}_b[\![c^{-i}(e)]\!] = \textbf{let } x = \mathcal{L}_b[\![e]\!] \textbf{ in}$
$\qquad\qquad \textbf{let } r = c_u^{-i}(x) \textbf{ in}$
$\qquad\qquad\quad (\textbf{if } not(isPrim(x)) \textit{ and } rc(x) = 0 \textbf{ then } gcExcept(x, r); recomputeExs(r)); r$

$c_u^{-i}(v) = \textbf{if } v = uk \textbf{ then } c^{-i}(false)$
$\qquad\quad \textbf{else if } isJoin(v)$
$\qquad\qquad\quad \textbf{then if } length(branches(v)) = 1 \textbf{ then } c^{-i}(false)$
$\qquad\qquad\qquad\quad \textbf{else } join(c_u^{-i}(first(branches(v))), c_u^{-i}(second(branches(v))))$
$\qquad\qquad \textbf{else } c^{-i}(data(v))$

$\mathcal{L}_b[\![\textbf{if } e_1 \textbf{ then } e_2 \textbf{ else } e_3]\!] =$
$\quad \textbf{let } b = \mathcal{L}_b[\![e_1]\!] \textbf{ in}$
$\quad \textbf{if } b = uk \textbf{ then let } l_1 = copy(live) \textbf{ in}$
$\qquad\qquad\qquad \textbf{let } r_2 = \mathcal{L}_b[\![e_2]\!] \textbf{ in}$
$\qquad\qquad\qquad\quad \textbf{let } l_2 = copy(live) \textbf{ in}$
$\qquad\qquad\qquad\qquad live := l_1; \textbf{let } r_3 = \mathcal{L}_b[\![e_3]\!] \textbf{ in}$
$\qquad\qquad\qquad\qquad\quad \textbf{let } l_3 = copy(live) \textbf{ in}$
$\qquad\qquad\qquad\qquad\qquad live := \max(l_2, l_3); \textbf{let } r = join(r_2, r_3) \textbf{ in}$
$\qquad\qquad\qquad\qquad\qquad\qquad setexs(r, \min(l_2 - l_1, l_3 - l_1)); r$
$\quad \textbf{else if } b \textbf{ then } \mathcal{L}_b[\![e_2]\!] \textbf{ else } \mathcal{L}_b[\![e_3]\!]$

$\mathcal{L}_b[\![f(e_1, \ldots, e_n)]\!] = \textbf{let } r_1 = \mathcal{L}_b[\![e_1]\!], \ldots, r_n = \mathcal{L}_b[\![e_n]\!] \textbf{ in}$
$\qquad\qquad\qquad\quad incrc(r_1); \ldots; incrc(r_n);$
$\qquad\qquad\qquad\quad \textbf{let } r = f_{Lb}(r_1, \ldots, r_n) \textbf{ in}$
$\qquad\qquad\qquad\qquad gcExcept(r_1, r); \ldots; gcExcept(r_n, r); recomputeExs(r); r$

$gc(v) = \textbf{if } not(isPrim(v))$
$\qquad\quad \textbf{then } decrc(v); \textbf{if } rc(v) \leq 0$
$\qquad\qquad\qquad \textbf{then if } isJoin(v)$
$\qquad\qquad\qquad\qquad \textbf{then } live = live + exs(v);$
$\qquad\qquad\qquad\qquad\qquad \textbf{for } u \textbf{ in } branches(v) \; gc(u)$
$\qquad\qquad\qquad\qquad \textbf{else } live[conType(v)]--;$
$\qquad\qquad\qquad\qquad\qquad \textbf{for } i = 1..arity(v) \; gc(c^{-i}(data(v)))$

Fig. 3. Transformation that produces live heap space-bound functions f_{Lb}. *copy* copies a vector. $+$ and $-$, when applied to vectors, denote component-wise sum and difference.

$join(r_2, r_3)$, where r_2 and r_3 are the results of e_2 and e_3, respectively. If r_2 and r_3 are primitive, then $join(r_2, r_3)$ is r_2 if $r_2 = r_3$ and uk otherwise. If r_2 and r_3 are not primitive and are the same, then $join(r_2, r_3)$ is r_2. Otherwise, $join(r_2, r_3)$ is a join-value pointing to r_2 and r_3. $exs(r)$ is set to $\min(l_2 - l_1, l_3 - l_1)$. $l_2 - l_1$ and $l_3 - l_1$ are the amounts of new data in r_2 and r_3, i.e., the amounts of data created by e_2 and e_3. r_2 and r_3 may contain old data too, i.e., data created before evaluating e_2 and e_3. Old data are live regardless of r. Between the sets of new data in r_2 and r_3, only one set is live. We keep the larger set live; the size of the other set is $exs(r)$.

Observe that in the transformation of (**if** e_1 **then** e_2 **else** e_3), we evaluate e_2 and then e_3, making copies of only *live* in between. We do not need to make copies of the heap because the source language does not contain imperative update. Thus, if h_1 is the heap after the evaluation of e_1, then e_2 and e_3 modify h_1 only by adding new con-values to it. Informally, h_2, the heap after evaluation of e_2, is $(h_1 \cup r_2)$. Similarly, h_3 is $(h_1 \cup r_3)$, h_3 having the expected meaning. In other words, the heap after evaluation of the conditional is $(h_1 \cup (r_2 \ or \ r_3))$. The choice between r_2 and r_3 is conveniently represented using a join-value that points to them both.

For join-values with two non-primitive branches, selectors and testers are first applied to the branches and the *join* of the results is returned. The *exs* field of a join-value j that is the result of applying a selector to another join-value j' is set to V_0, because when j is created, j' is live, and $exs(j')$ already takes care of any excess.

When a selector c^{-i} is applied to uk or a join-value j with a primitive branch, it simply aborts by attempting to apply the selector to an arbitrary primitive value. However, if we assume that the given program never applies selectors to primitive values, then the occurrence of $c^{-i}(j)$ in the analysis corresponds to the application of c^{-i} to the non-primitive branch of j in the original program. With this assumption, $c^{-i}(j)$ is simply the result of applying c^{-i} to the non-primitive branch. Applications of selectors to join-values with primitive branches is in fact seen in only one of our examples, namely quicksort.

Achieving Tightness. The following example illustrates why *live* may not be as tight as desired.

$$
\begin{aligned}
&\textbf{let } u = cons(1, nil) \textbf{ in}\\
&\quad \textbf{let } v = cons(2, nil) \textbf{ in}\\
&\qquad (\textbf{if } uk \textbf{ then } cons(3, v) \textbf{ else } cons(4, cons(5, u)))
\end{aligned} \tag{1}
$$

Let r be the result of the conditional. Let c_i denote the data construction with $cons^{-1}(c_i) = i$. Just after the conditional is evaluated, *live* includes the sizes of both c_1 and c_2. *live* excludes the size of c_3 because the result of the alternative branch containing c_4 and c_5 is larger; so *live* includes the latter instead of the former. Once v goes out of scope, c_2 is live only through the reference from r. At this point in any execution of the original program, either c_2 and c_3 are live or c_4 and c_5 are live; c_1 is definitely live because of the binding for u. But in the analysis, because of the reference from r, c_2 is kept live and its size is included in *live*. Thus, join-value r causes *live* to be loose by one *cons*.

In general, at any point at which all references to a data construction v are lost except for references from a join-value, there is a possibility that *live* is loose because it includes the size of v when it should not. These points arise immediately after decrements to $rc(v)$ caused by (1) a variable or parameter going out of scope or (2) parts of data becoming garbage after the application of a selector. v may then be an excess in *live* caused by a join-value j which in case (1), is in the result of a function call or **let** expression and in case (2), is in the result of the selector. The *exs* attributes of join-values in the results of function calls, **let** expressions and selectors are recomputed and the value of *live* adjusted appropriately. Observe that v may be part of a join-value j' that is not in the result of these expressions. It can be shown that loss of references to v at the completion of the expressions, has no effect on $exs(j')$ and so we do not recompute it. Note that recomputing exs is used only to obtain tighter bounds, so calling or not calling it at any point in the analysis is safe.

5 Optimizations

We use two optimizations that reduce the asymptotic complexity of live heap analysis for many programs. The first optimization avoids looking at data structures without join-value descendants when recomputing exs attributes. This is done by adding to con-values and join-values a boolean attribute that indicates the presence of join-value descendants. The second optimization is as follows: at any point p during the execution of a bound function, a join-value j with branches b_1 and b_2 and without any join-value descendants may be reduced to b_1 if b_1 leads to equal or greater live heap usage as compared to b_2. This holds with b_1 and b_2 interchanged also.

The stack and live heap can be viewed as a graph: con-values and join-values in the heap and formal parameters of functions and **let**-bound variables on the stack are vertices; references from variables, con-values and join-values to con-values and join-values are edges. The subgraph comprised of nodes and edges reachable from a node x is an edge-ordered DAG G_x rooted at x. It is acyclic because we are dealing with a first-order functional language. The ordering of fields in data constructions imposes an ordering on the out-edges from nodes. For example, if $x = cons(1, y)$ and y is not a primitive value, then G_x contains the edge $\langle x, y, 2 \rangle$. We say that a vertex u is *contained-in* a vertex v if v is an ancestor of u in every path from a node for a parameter or variable to u.

Reducibility of Join-values. $j = join(b_1, b_2)$ is reducible to b_1 at a point p_0 during execution of a bound function if at p_0

R0. j does not have any join-value descendants.
R1. G_{b_1} and G_{b_2}, the DAGs rooted at b_1 and b_2, are isomorphic. Let f be an isomorphism between G_{b_1} and G_{b_2}.
R2. Corresponding primitive values in b_1 and b_2 and their descendants are equal, taking $uk = uk$.
R3. For every node d_1 of G_{b_1}, if d_1 is not contained-in j, then d_1 and $f(d_1)$ are the same node.

R0 implies that j represents exactly two data structures: b_1 and b_2. R1 and R2 state that b_1 and b_2 have the same structure and contents. The only possible difference between b_1 and b_2 is the particular heap locations they use. No operation in our language can distinguish b_1 and b_2; recall that we don't consider eq?. Thus, R1 and R2 ensure that the program's execution is the same regardless of whether b_1 or b_2 is used, except for the heap space used by b_1 and b_2. R3 asserts that b_1 always contributes at least as much to the live heap space as b_2. For example, this happens if b_2 references data constructions that are live even without references from b_2 and the corresponding data constructions in b_1 are live only because of the references from b_1.

As an example, consider the expression below. Also shown is the abstract heap at the point just after the evaluation of the conditional. Con-values c1

let $v = cons(uk, nil)$ in
  if uk
  then $cons(uk, cons(uk, nil))$
  else $cons(uk, v)$

through c4 are numbered according to their syntactic order of appearance. The join-value result j of the conditional satisfies conditions R0 through R3, and hence may be reduced to its left branch.

Theorem 1. *If $j = join(b_1, b_2)$ is reducible to b_1 at a point p_0 during execution of a bound function, then it is safe to replace all references to j with references to b_1, i.e., space-bound analysis still returns an upper bound on live heap usage.*

Sketch of Proof: Based on the above arguments, it suffices to show that b_1 contributes at least as much to the live heap space as b_2, at p_0 and thereafter. The contribution of b_i to *live* is the amount of data contained-in j and referenced by b_i. At p_0, because of R1 and R3, for every descendant of b_2 that is contained-in j, there exists a unique descendant of b_1 that is contained-in j. So, at p_0, b_1 contributes at least as much to *live* as b_2. It can be shown that this continues to be the case after p_0. The complete proof is in [26].

6 Handling Tail Call Optimization

Tail call optimization [1] is handled in our analysis by recognizing function calls in tail position and at the sites of these calls, garbage collecting all variables in the current scope. The transformation for space functions is straightforward but that for bound functions is more involved. Consider a conditional (**if** uk **then** e_2 **else** e_3) that is in tail position. Both e_2 and e_3 need to be evaluated. Suppose both e_2 and e_3 contain tail calls. During the evaluation of e_2, all environment variables $u_1, \ldots, u_m$ are garbage collected just before the tail call. But at the start of evaluation of e_3, $u_1, \ldots, u_m$ are still live, so the effects of the earlier garbage collection have to be reversed before evaluating e_3. Also, references from the result of e_2 to $u_1, \ldots, u_m$ should not hinder their garbage collection before the tail call in e_3. Similar issues arise when only one or none of the two branches contain tail calls.

7 Experiments

We implemented the analyses and measured the results for several standard list and tree processing programs. Comparisons of results of space and bound

reversal w/append		insertion sort		selection sort		merge sort		quick sort		longest common subseq.		string edit		binary tree insert		
n	result	n	result	n	result	n	result	n	space	bound	n	result	n	result	h	n	result
100	299	100	299	100	5150	5	16	2	6	6	100	402	100	1000	2	7	33
500	1499	500	1499	500	125750	12	36	6	32	100	500	2002	500	5000	7	255	792
1000	2999	1000	2999	1000	501500	15	45	7	41	197	1000	4002	1000	10000	9	1023	3102

Fig. 4. Results of live heap space analysis. n is the input size. For binary tree insert, h is the height of the complete binary tree and n is the number of nodes in the tree.

functions show that bound functions produce exact bounds for all but one example. For most of the examples, the bound functions have the same asymptotic time complexities as the corresponding space functions. For all examples, a comparison of the running times of bound functions and the running times of space functions multiplied by the number of represented inputs showed that the bound functions are asymptotically faster than applying the corresponding space functions to all represented inputs. The non-termination issue mentioned in Section 1 is not a problem for any of these examples.

Figure 4 contains the results of live heap space analysis on some examples. For all examples except quicksort, we show only the results of bound functions on partially known inputs, because they are the same as the results of the space functions on worst-case input. Reversal using append is the standard quadratic-time version. The version of merge sort tested is the one that splits the input list into sublists containing the elements at odd and even positions. Dynamic programming algorithms [5] are used for longest common subsequence and string edit. Binary-tree insertion involves insertion of an item into a complete binary tree in which each node is a list containing an element and left and right subtrees.

The partially known inputs for the bound functions of reversal and sorting are lists of known lengths n where all elements are uk; those for longest common subsequence and string edit are two such lists of equal length n. The bound function for binary-tree insertion inserts uk into a complete binary tree of known height h with unknown elements.

The difference between the results of the space and bound functions of quicksort is due to the use of uk; every uk element of the input list is both greater and less than every other uk element. The space-bound function of quicksort terminates, while the time-bound function for quicksort in [18] diverges. This is essentially because join-values retain more information than partially known structures. See [26] for more details.

The results in Figure 4 include the space used by top-level arguments since these arguments are indeed live throughout the execution of the program. Figure 5 contains running times of live heap analysis of some examples; more results appear in [27,26]. For all examples, the live heap space function has the same asymptotic time complexity as the original function. The time complexities of the live heap bound functions of reverse using append, string edit and longest common subsequence are the same as the complexities of the corresponding original functions. The time complexities of the optimized bound functions of insertion

reversal w/append				insertion sort				selection sort				longest common subseq.			
n	S	B	Bopt	n	S	B	Bopt	n	S	B	Bopt	n	S	B	Bopt
10^1	1.0 m	0	1.0 m	10^1	1.0 m	1.0 M	9.0 m	10^1	0	37.3 s	10.0 m	10^1	10.0 m	0.8 s	44.0 m
10^2	0.1 s	0.3 s	0.1 s	10^2	0.1 s		5.1 s	10^2	0.2 s		5.0 s	10^2	6.6 s		24.0 s
10^3	10.7 s	3.5 M	11.9 s	10^3	12.8 s		1.5 H	10^3	27.3 s		1.5 H	10^3	2.0 H		7.1 H

Fig. 5. Running times of live heap space and live heap space-bound functions. Columns S, B and Bopt contain times of space, unoptimized space-bound and optimized space-bound functions, respectively. n and h are as in Figure 4. m is milliseconds, s is seconds, M is minutes and H is hours. Blank fields in B and Bopt columns indicate terminating but long analyses that were aborted after a few days.

sort and selection sort are a linear factor more than those of the original functions due to the computation involved in reducing join-values. The running time of the bound function of merge sort is more than polynomial in the size of the input. This is because the analysis examines all $(n+m)!/(n! \times m!)$ ways in which two sorted lists of sizes n and m may be merged in sorted order. The running time of the bound function of binary tree insert is polynomial in the size of the input. The first optimization in Section 5 improves the asymptotic complexity of reverse using append by a linear factor. The second optimization improves the asymptotic complexities of insertion sort, selection sort and longest common subsequence from greater than polynomial to polynomial. These speedups are shown in Figure 5.

We applied live heap space analysis handling tail call optimization to tail-recursive versions of reverse, insertion sort, selection sort and an optimized Ackermann's function. Comparing the results with those of the corresponding non-tail-recursive programs showed that tail call optimization does significantly reduce heap usage. For example, tail-recursive insertion sort uses only $O(n)$ space, while non-tail-recursive insertion sort uses $O(n^2)$ space. The optimized Ackermann's function [19] is a systematically derived program which has much better time complexity than the classical version. Let n and m be the first and second arguments to the function. The space complexity of this program was worked out by hand to be $O(n)$, but it is hard to see this because of the complicated space usage of the program. The results of our analysis for $n \in [0, 3]$, $m \in [2, 10]$ do not prove $O(n)$ space usage but helped confirm that, for a given n, the space usage is independent of m. Computing Ackermann's function for $n > 3$ is famously expensive.

We applied our analysis to a 600-line `calendar` benchmark. The partially known inputs used are partially known dates. The analysis takes only a few seconds to complete and yields tight bounds, providing preliminary evidence for the scalability of our method. We plan to analyze more benchmarks. We have also used the analysis in teaching programming languages courses.

8   Discussion

Correctness. More detailed correctness arguments appear in [26]. We are also working on more formal proofs.

Termination. The space function terminates iff the original program terminates. The bound function might not terminate, even when the original program does if the recursive structure of the original program directly or indirectly depends on unknown parts of a partially known input structure. For example, if the given partially known input structure is uk, then the bound function for any recursive program does not terminate; if such a bound function counts new space, then the original program might indeed take an unbounded amount of space. Indirect dependency on unknown data can be caused by an imprecise join operation. Making the join operation more precise might eliminate this source of non-termination. Another strategy that could be especially effective to detect non-termination of bound functions corresponding to terminating programs is as follows: for every call to a bound function, a check is made to see if the same call with equivalent arguments is on the call stack. If so, the analysis stops and reports that the bound function diverges.

Although there are other methods to deal with non-termination, incorporating such methods in our analysis could result in loose bounds on space usage, even for programs for which non-termination is not a problem. Further, non-termination is not a problem in any of the examples we analyzed.

Scalability. For large programs or programs with sophisticated control structures, the analysis is efficient if the input parameters are small, but for larger parameters, efficiency might be a challenge. One approach is to improve efficiency by memoizing calls to bound functions and reusing the memoized results wherever possible. Another strategy is to use the results of space-bound analysis on smaller inputs to semi-automatically derive closed forms and/or recurrence relations that describe the program's space usage, by fitting a given functional form to the analysis results. The closed forms or recurrence relations may then be used to determine space bounds for large inputs.

Inputs to Bound Functions. To analyze space usage with respect to some property of the input, we need to formulate sets of partially known inputs that represent all actual inputs with that characteristic, e.g., all lists with length n, all binary trees of height h or all binary trees with n nodes. As an example, $\{(uk, (uk, nil, nil), nil), (uk, nil, (uk, nil, nil)), (uk, (uk, nil, nil), (uk, nil, nil))\}$ represents all binary trees of height 1, each node being a list of the element and left and right subtrees. Often, formulating such sets of partially known inputs is straightforward but tedious for the user to do by hand. However, it is easy to write programs that generate sets of partially known inputs.

Imperative Update and Higher-Order Functions. The ideas in this paper may be combined with reference-counting garbage collection extended to handle cycles [3] or with other garbage collection algorithms, such as mark and sweep, to obtain a live heap space analysis for imperative languages. They may also be combined with techniques for analysis of higher-order functions [10].

9   Related Work

There has been much work on analyzing program cost or resource complexities, but the majority of it is on time analysis, e.g., [17,24,18]. Analysis of live heap space is different because it involves explicit analysis of the graph structure of the data.

Most of the work related to analysis of space is on analysis of cache behavior, e.g., [28,9], much of which is at a lower language level and does not consider liveness. Live heap analysis is a first step towards analysis of cache behavior in the presence of garbage collection.

Persson's work on live memory analysis [22] requires programmers to give annotations, including numerical bounds on the size of recursive data structures. His work is preliminary: the presentation is informal, and only one example, summing a list, is given. Our analysis does not require annotations.

Unlike static reference counting used for compile-time garbage collection [15], our analysis uses a reference counting method similar to that in run-time garbage collection. The former keeps track of pointers to memory cells that will be used later in the execution. Our analysis could be modified so that $decrc(v)$ is called when a parameter or **let**-variable won't be used again (instead of waiting until v goes out of scope). Our current analysis corresponds to the garbage collection behavior in, e.g., JVMs from Sun, IBM, and Transvirtual.

Several type systems [14,13,6,12] have been proposed for reasoning about space and time bounds, and some of them include implementations of type checkers [14,6]. They require programmers to annotate their programs with cost functions as types. Furthermore, some programs must be rewritten to have feasible types [14,13].

Chin and Khoo [4] propose a method for calculating sized types by inferring constraints on size and then simplifying the constraints using Omega [23]. Their analysis results do not correspond to live heap space in general. Further, Omega can only reason about constraints expressed as linear functions.

References

1. H. Abelson and G. J. Sussman. *Structure and Interpretation of Computer Programs*. MIT Press, 2 edition, 1996.
2. P. Altenbernd. On the false path problem in hard real-time programs. In *Proceedings of the 8th EuroMicro Workshop on Real-Time Systems*, pages 102–107, L'Aquila, June 1996.
3. D. Bacon, C. Attanasio, H. Lee, V. Rajan, and S. Smith. Java without the coffee breaks: A non-intrusive multiprocessor garbage collector. In *Proc. ACM SIGPLAN Conference on Programming Language Design and Implementation (PLDI)*. ACM Press, 2001.
4. W.-N. Chin and S.-C. Khoo. Calculating sized types. In *Proceedings of the ACM SIGPLAN 2000 Workshop on Partial Evaluation and Semantics-Based Program Manipulation*, pages 62–72. ACM, New York, Jan. 2000.
5. T. H. Cormen, C. E. Leiserson, and R. L. Rivest. *Introduction to Algorithms*. The MIT Press/McGraw-Hill, 1990.

6. K. Crary and S. Weirich. Resource bound certification. In *Conference Record of the 27th Annual ACM Symposium on Principles of Programming Languages*. ACM, New York, Jan. 2000.

7. P. Flajolet, B. Salvy, and P. Zimmermann. Automatic average-case analysis of algorithms. *Theoretical Computer Science, Series A*, 79(1):37–109, Feb. 1991.

8. *Proceedings of the 4th International Conference on Functional Programming Languages and Computer Architecture*. ACM, New York, Sept. 1989.

9. S. Ghosh, M. Martonosi, and S. Malik. Cache miss equations: A compiler framework for analyzing and tuning memory behavior. *ACM Trans. Program. Lang. Syst.*, 21(4):703–746, July 1999.

10. G. Gómez and Y. A. Liu. Automatic time-bound analysis for a higher-order language. In *Proceedings of the ACM SIGPLAN 2002 Workshop on Partial Evaluation and Semantics-Based Program Manipulation*, pages 75–86. ACM Press, 2002.

11. R. Henriksson. *Scheduling Garbage Collection in Embedded Systems*. PhD thesis, Department of Computer Science, Lund University, Sept. 1998.

12. M. Hofmann and S. Jost. Static prediction of heap space usage for first-order functional programs. In *Proc. ACM Symposium on Principles of Programming Languages*. ACM Press, Jan. 2003.

13. J. Hughes and L. Pareto. Recursion and dynamic data-structures in bounded space: Towards embedded ML programming. In *Proceedings of the 1999 ACM SIGPLAN International Conference on Functional Programming*, pages 70–81. ACM, New York, Sept. 1999.

14. J. Hughes, L. Pareto, and A. Sabry. Proving the correctness of reactive systems using sized types. In *Conference Record of the 23rd Annual ACM Symposium on Principles of Programming Languages*, pages 410–423. ACM, New York, Jan. 1996.

15. S. B. Jones and D. Le Métayer. Compile-time garbage collection by sharing analysis. In FPCA 1989 [8], pages 54–74.

16. *Proceedings of the ACM SIGPLAN 1999 Workshop on Languages, Compilers, and Tools for Embedded Systems*. ACM, New York, May 1999.

17. D. Le Métayer. Ace: An automatic complexity evaluator. *ACM Trans. Program. Lang. Syst.*, 10(2):248–266, Apr. 1988.

18. Y. A. Liu and G. Gómez. Automatic accurate cost-bound analysis for high-level languages. *IEEE Transactions on Computers*, 50(12):1295–1309, Dec. 2001.

19. Y. A. Liu and S. D. Stoller. Optimizing Ackermann's function by incrementalization. Technical Report DAR 01-1, Computer Science Department, SUNY Stony Brook, Jan. 2001.

20. M. Martonosi, A. Gupta, and T. Anderson. Effectiveness of trace sampling for performance debugging tools. In *Proceedings of the 1993 ACM SIGMETRICS Conference on Measurement and Modeling of Computer Systems*, pages 248–259. ACM, New York, 1992.

21. C. Y. Park. Predicting program execution times by analyzing static and dynamic program paths. *Real-Time Systems*, 5:31–62, 1993.

22. P. Persson. Live memory analysis for garbage collection in embedded systems. In LCTES 1999 [16], pages 45–54.

23. W. Pugh. The Omega Test: A fast and practical integer programming algorithm for dependence analysis. *Commun. ACM*, 31(8), Aug. 1992.

24. M. Rosendahl. Automatic complexity analysis. In FPCA 1989 [8], pages 144–156.

25. I. Ryu. Issues and challenges in developing embedded software for information appliances and telecommunication terminals. In LCTES 1999 [16], pages 104–120. Invited talk.

26. L. Unnikrishnan, S. D. Stoller, and Y. A. Liu. Optimized live heap bound analysis. Technical Report DAR 01-2, Computer Science Dept., SUNY at Stony Brook, Oct. 2001, Available at http://www.cs.sunysb.edu/~stoller/dar012.html.
27. L. Unnikrishnan, S. D. Stoller, and Y. A. Liu. Automatic accurate live memory analysis for garbage-collected languages. In *Proc. ACM SIGPLAN Workshop on Languages, Compilers, and Tools for Embedded Systems (LCTES)*, pages 102–111. ACM Press, 2001.
28. R. Wilhelm and C. Ferdinand. On predicting data cache behaviour for real-time systems. In *Proceedings of the ACM SIGPLAN 1998 Workshop on Languages, Compilers, and Tools for Embedded Systems*, volume 1474 of *Lecture Notes in Computer Science*, pages 16–30. Springer-Verlag, June 1998.
29. P. Zimmermann and W. Zimmermann. The automatic complexity analysis of divide-and-conquer algorithms. In *Computer and Information Sciences VI*. Elsevier, 1991.

Complexity of Nesting Analysis in Mobile Ambients[*]

Chiara Braghin[1], Agostino Cortesi[1], Riccardo Focardi[1],
Flaminia L. Luccio[2], and Carla Piazza[1]

[1] Dipartimento di Informatica, Università Ca' Foscari di Venezia,
{braghin,cortesi,focardi,piazza}@dsi.unive.it
[2] Dipartimento di Scienze Matematiche, Università di Trieste,
luccio@dsm.univ.trieste.it

Abstract. A new algorithm is introduced for analyzing possible nesting in Mobile Ambient calculus. It improves both time and space complexities of the technique proposed by Nielson and Seidl. The improvements are achieved by enhancing the data structure representations, and by reducing the computation to the Control Flow Analysis constraints that are effectively necessary to get to the least solution.

Keywords: Static Analysis, Ambient Calculus, Complexity.

1 Introduction

The calculus of Mobile Ambients has been introduced in [6] with the main aim of explicitly modeling mobility. In particular, ambients are arbitrarily nested boundaries which can move around through suitable capabilities. Recently, big efforts have been devoted to the study of Control Flow Analysis (CFA) of such a calculus [11,16]. In particular, some analyses have been applied to the verification of security properties [3,4,5,10,18]. The idea of [4,5,18] is to compute an over-approximation of ambient nestings that may occur during process computation, thus detecting possible intrusions and unwanted information flows.

Time and space complexities are key-issues for evaluating scalability and practical impact of any static analysis proposal. They become even more important when code mobility is possible, as low complexities would allow the very useful task of performing on the fly analysis of untrusted code migrating into a system. The computation of ambient nesting analysis, like [4,11,16], requires considerably high complexities, thus the design of efficient techniques turns out to be very important. This is the main motivation behind [19], where Nielson and Seidl reduce the worst-case time complexity of [11] from $O(N^5)$ to $O(N^3)$ steps, with N being the size of the analyzed process.

[*] Partially supported by MIUR Projects "Interpretazione Astratta, Type Systems e Analisi Control-Flow", and "Modelli formali per la sicurezza", the EU Contract IST-2001-32617 MyThs, and project "Matematica per le scienze e la tecnologia", Università di Trieste.

L. Zuck et al. (Eds.): VMCAI 2003, LNCS 2575, pp. 86–101, 2003.

The first contribution of this paper is to refine the complexity results of [19], by considering, for a given process, its number N_a of ambients, its number N_t of capabilities and the sum $N_L = N_a + N_t$. In particular, for the best algorithm proposed in [19], we find a time complexity of $O(N_a^2 \cdot N_L)$ steps and a space complexity of $O((N_a^2 \cdot N_L) \log N_L)$ bits. We also prove that this algorithm performs at least $2 \cdot N_a^2 \cdot N_L$ steps and uses at least $2 \cdot (N_a^2 \cdot N_L) \log N_L$ bits, even in the best case. This is due to the fact that it is based on a translation of the Control Flow Analysis constraints into Horn clauses, which are processed through satisfiability standard algorithms in order to compute the least analysis solution. As such algorithms always consider all the clauses corresponding to the CFA constraints, even in the best case, all the clauses need to be generated. It turns out that the number of clauses is exactly $2 \cdot N_a^2 \cdot N_L$. A similar analysis is also provided for the less efficient $O(N^4)$ algorithm of [19].

The second contribution of this paper is to propose two new algorithms that improve both time and space complexities of the ones proposed in [19].

The gist of our proposal is to face the problem by a direct operational approach (i.e., without passing through Horn formulas), and to limit the computation to the Control Flow Analysis constraints that are effectively necessary to determine the least solution. This is done in an *on the fly* (dynamic) fashion, by combining a careful choice of data representation (namely, a buffer suite) with a selection policy which identifies the constraints that are potentially activated by an element while adding such an element to the solution, so that no useless repetition occurs. We prove that our best algorithm has a worst-case time complexity of $O(N_a^2 \cdot N_L)$ steps and a space complexity of $O((N_a \cdot N_L) \log N_L)$ bits. Thus, it highly improves the space complexity of the best algorithm in [19]. More precisely, we also prove that time complexity depends on the size of the least solution and thus it may decrease down to $c \cdot N_a \cdot N_L$, for a constant c, when the solution is linear with respect to the dimension of the process. As $2 \cdot N_a^2 \cdot N_L$ steps are always performed by the best algorithm of [19], with our algorithm we also obtain a significant reduction of the average execution time.

In order to get these complexity improvements, we first apply our new technique to the less efficient $O(N^4)$ algorithm of [19]. As such an algorithm works on a simpler analysis specification, we also obtain a simpler algorithm, easier to explain and understand. We then show that all the results scale up to the more efficient $O(N^3)$ solution.

The ideas behind our new proposals are quite general. Thus, this paper may be considered as a first step towards the definition of a more general technique that could be applicable to compute Control Flow Analyses in different settings, and more abstractly, to efficiently compute the least solution of a set of Horn clauses over a finite domain, as done in [19]. This is the object of our current research.

The rest of the paper is organized as follows. In Section 2 we introduce the basic terminology of Mobile Ambient calculus and we briefly report the Control

Flow Analysis of [11]. In Section 3 we study in depth the complexity of the algorithms presented in [19]. Then, in Section 4, we present our algorithms and complexity results. Section 5 concludes the paper with final remarks.

2 Background: Mobile Ambients

The Mobile Ambient calculus has been introduced in [6] with the main aim of explicitly modeling mobility. Ambients are arbitrarily nested boundaries which can move around through suitable capabilities. The syntax of processes is given in Figure 1, where $n \in \mathbf{Amb}$ denotes an ambient name.

$$
\begin{array}{lll}
P, Q ::= & (\nu n)P & \text{restriction} \\
\mid & \mathbf{0} & \text{inactivity} \\
\mid & P \mid Q & \text{composition} \\
\mid & !P & \text{replication} \\
\mid & n^{\ell^a}[\,P\,] & \text{ambient} \\
\mid & \mathbf{in}^{\ell^t} n \,.\, P & \text{capability to enter } n \\
\mid & \mathbf{out}^{\ell^t} n \,.\, P & \text{capability to exit } n \\
\mid & \mathbf{open}^{\ell^t} n \,.\, P & \text{capability to open } n
\end{array}
$$

Fig. 1. Mobile Ambients Syntax

Intuitively, the restriction $(\nu n)P$ introduces the new name n and limits its scope to P; process $\mathbf{0}$ does nothing; $P \mid Q$ is P and Q running in parallel; replication provides recursion and iteration as $!P$ represents any number of copies of P in parallel. By $n^{\ell^a}[\,P\,]$ we denote the ambient named n with the process P running inside it. The capabilities $\mathbf{in}^{\ell^t} n$ and $\mathbf{out}^{\ell^t} n$ move their enclosing ambients in and out ambient n, respectively; the capability $\mathbf{open}^{\ell^t} n$ is used to dissolve the boundary of a sibling ambient n. The operational semantics of a process P is given through a suitable reduction relation $\rightarrow$. Intuitively, $P \rightarrow Q$ represents the possibility for P of reducing to Q through some computation (see [6] for more details).

Labels $\ell^a \in \mathbf{Lab}^a$ on ambients and labels $\ell^t \in \mathbf{Lab}^t$ on capabilities (transitions) are introduced as it is customary in static analysis to indicate "program points". They will be useful in the next sections when developing the analysis. We denote with $\mathbf{Lab}$ the set of all the labels $\mathbf{Lab}^a \cup \mathbf{Lab}^t$. We use the special label $env \in \mathbf{Lab}^a$ to denote the external environment, i.e., the environment containing the process under observation.

Given a process P, we also introduce the notation $\mathbf{Lab}^a(P)$ to denote the set of ambient labels in P plus the special label env, $\mathbf{Lab}^t(P)$ to denote the set of capability labels in P, and $\mathbf{Lab}(P)$ to denote $\mathbf{Lab}^a(P) \cup \mathbf{Lab}^t(P)$. Moreover, $N_a = |\mathbf{Lab}^a(P)|$, $N_t = |\mathbf{Lab}^t(P)|$, and $N_L = |\mathbf{Lab}(P)| = N_a + N_t$. With N we denote the global number of operator occurrences in P. Note that $N_L < N$, as there is at least one occurrence of $\mathbf{0}$ in every non-empty process.

Example 1. Process P_1 models a *cab* driving a *client* from $site_1$ to $site_2$:

$$site_1^{\ell_1^a} [\ client^{\ell_2^a} [\mathbf{in}^{\ell_3^t} cab \ . \ call^{\ell_4^a} [\mathbf{out}^{\ell_5^t} client \ . \ \mathbf{out}^{\ell_6^t} site_1 \ . \ \mathbf{in}^{\ell_7^t} site_2 \ . \ \mathbf{0}] \ ] \ | \\ cab^{\ell_8^a} [\mathbf{open}^{\ell_9^t} call \ . \ \mathbf{0}] \ ] \ | \\ site_2^{\ell_{10}^a} [\ \mathbf{0}\ ].$$

Initially, *cab* and *client* are in $site_1$, while $site_2$ is empty. The client enters the cab by applying its capability $\mathbf{in}^{\ell_3^t} cab$. Thus, process P_1 moves to:

$$site_1^{\ell_1^a} [\ cab^{\ell_8^a} [\ \mathbf{open}^{\ell_9^t} call \ . \ \mathbf{0} \ | \\ client^{\ell_2^a} [\ call^{\ell_4^a} [\mathbf{out}^{\ell_5^t} client \ . \ \mathbf{out}^{\ell_6^t} site_1 \ . \ \mathbf{in}^{\ell_7^t} site_2 \ . \ \mathbf{0}] \ ] \ ] \ ] \ | \\ site_2^{\ell_{10}^a} [\ \mathbf{0}\ ].$$

Now, the client tells the cab its destination by releasing ambient *call*, which consumes its $\mathbf{out}^{\ell_5^t} client$ capability.

$$site_1^{\ell_1^a} [\ cab^{\ell_8^a} [\mathbf{open}^{\ell_9^t} call \ . \ \mathbf{0} \ | \ call^{\ell_4^a} [\mathbf{out} \ site_1 \ . \ \mathbf{in} \ site_2 \ . \ \mathbf{0}] \ | \ client^{\ell_2^a} [\mathbf{0}] \ ] \ ] \ | \\ site_2^{\ell_{10}^a} [\mathbf{0}].$$

Then, the client request satisfaction is modeled by opening (dissolving) the client call. At this point, process P_1 has reached the state:

$$site_1^{\ell_1^a} [\ cab^{\ell_9^a} [\mathbf{out}^{\ell_6^t} site_1 \ . \ \mathbf{in}^{\ell_7^t} site_2 . \mathbf{0} \ | \ client^{\ell_2^a} [\mathbf{0}] \ ] \ ] \ | \ site_2^{\ell_{11}^a} [\mathbf{0}].$$

Then, the cab exits $site_1$ and it enters $site_2$, as expected by the client:

$$site_1^{\ell_1^a} [\mathbf{0}] \ | \ site_2^{\ell_{10}^a} [\ cab^{\ell_9^a} [\ client^{\ell_2^a} [\mathbf{0}] \ ] \ ].$$

Observe that for such a process P_1 the label sets are the following:

$$\mathsf{Lab}^a(P_1) = \{\ell_1^a, \ell_2^a, \ell_4^a, \ell_8^a, \ell_{10}^a\},$$
$$\mathsf{Lab}^t(P_1) = \{\ell_3^t, \ell_5^t, \ell_6^t, \ell_7^t, \ell_9^t\},$$
$$\mathsf{Lab}(P_1) \ = \{\ell_1^a, \ell_2^a, \ell_3^t, \ell_4^a, \ell_5^t, \ell_6^t, \ell_7^t, \ell_8^a, \ell_9^t, \ell_{10}^a\}.$$

Thus, $N_a = 5$, $N_t = 5$, $N_L = 10$, and $N = 15$ (N_L plus three $\mathbf{0}$ and two $|$). $\qquad\square$

In the rest of the paper, we assume that the ambient and capability labels occurring in a process P are all distinct. Performing the Control Flow Analysis with all distinct labels produces a more precise result that can be later approximated by equating some labels.

2.1   Control Flow Analysis

The Control Flow Analysis of a process P described in [11] aims at modeling the possible ambient nestings occurring in the execution of P. It works on pairs $(\hat{I}, \hat{H})$, where:

$$
\begin{array}{lll}
(res) & \beta_\ell^{\mathrm{CF}}((\nu n)P) & = \beta_\ell^{\mathrm{CF}}(P) \\[4pt]
(zero) & \beta_\ell^{\mathrm{CF}}(\mathbf{0}) & = (\emptyset, \emptyset) \\[4pt]
(par) & \beta_\ell^{\mathrm{CF}}(P \mid Q) & = \beta_\ell^{\mathrm{CF}}(P) \sqcup \beta_\ell^{\mathrm{CF}}(Q) \\[4pt]
(repl) & \beta_\ell^{\mathrm{CF}}(!P) & = \beta_\ell^{\mathrm{CF}}(P) \\[4pt]
(amb) & \beta_\ell^{\mathrm{CF}}(n^{\ell^a}[\,P\,]) & = \beta_{\ell^a}^{\mathrm{CF}}(P) \sqcup (\{(\ell, \ell^a)\}, \{(\ell^a, n)\}) \\[4pt]
(in) & \beta_\ell^{\mathrm{CF}}(\mathbf{in}^{\ell^t} n \,.\, P) & = \beta_\ell^{\mathrm{CF}}(P) \sqcup (\{(\ell, \ell^t)\}, \emptyset) \\[4pt]
(out) & \beta_\ell^{\mathrm{CF}}(\mathbf{out}^{\ell^t} n \,.\, P) & = \beta_\ell^{\mathrm{CF}}(P) \sqcup (\{(\ell, \ell^t)\}, \emptyset) \\[4pt]
(open) & \beta_\ell^{\mathrm{CF}}(\mathbf{open}^{\ell^t} n \,.\, P) & = \beta_\ell^{\mathrm{CF}}(P) \sqcup (\{(\ell, \ell^t)\}, \emptyset)
\end{array}
$$

Fig. 2. Representation Function for the Control Flow Analysis

- The first component $\hat{I}$ is an element of $\wp(\mathbf{Lab}^a(P) \times \mathbf{Lab}(P))$. If process P, during its execution, contains an ambient labeled ℓ^a having inside either a capability or an ambient labeled ℓ, then (ℓ^a, ℓ) is expected to belong to $\hat{I}$.
- The second component $\hat{H} \in \wp(\mathbf{Lab}^a(P) \times \mathbf{Amb})$ keeps track of the correspondence between names and labels. If process P contains an ambient labeled ℓ^a with name n, then (ℓ^a, n) is expected to belong to $\hat{H}$. [1]
- The pairs are component-wise partially ordered by set inclusion.

The analysis is defined as usual by a representation function and a specification [17]. They are recalled in Figure 2 and Figure 3, respectively, where $\sqcup$ denotes the component-wise union of the elements of the pairs.

The representation function aims at mapping concrete values to their best abstract representation. It is given in terms of a function $\beta_\ell^{\mathrm{CF}}(P)$ which maps process P into a pair $(\hat{I}, \hat{H})$ corresponding to the initial state of P, with respect to an enclosing ambient labeled with ℓ. The representation of a process P is defined as $\beta_{env}^{\mathrm{CF}}(P)$.

Example 2. Let P_2 be the process $n^{\ell_1^a}[\, m^{\ell_2^a}[\mathbf{out}^{\ell^t} n.\mathbf{0}]\,]$. The representation function of P_2 is : $\beta_{env}^{\mathrm{CF}}(P_2) = (\{(env, \ell_1^a), (\ell_1^a, \ell_2^a), (\ell_2^a, \ell^t)\}, \{(\ell_1^a, n), (\ell_2^a, m)\})$. Notice that all ambient nestings are captured by the first component $\{(env, \ell_1^a), (\ell_1^a, \ell_2^a), (\ell_2^a, \ell^t)\}$, while all the correspondences between ambients and labels of P_2 are kept by the second one, i.e., $\{(\ell_1^a, n), (\ell_2^a, m)\}$. □

The specification depicts how the process transforms one abstract representation into another one, and it mostly relies on recursive calls on subprocesses except for the three capabilities *open*, *in*, and *out*. For instance, the rule for *open*-capability states that if some ambient labeled ℓ^a has an *open*-capability ℓ^t on an ambient n, that may apply due to the presence of a sibling ambient labeled $\ell^{a'}$ whose name is n, then the result of performing that capability should also be

---

[1] We are assuming that ambient names are *stable*, i.e., n is a representative for a class of α-convertible names, following the same approach of [16]. In [11,19], an alternative treatment of α-equivalence is used, where bound names are annotated with markers, and a marker environment *me* is associated to constraints.

(res)	$(\hat{I}, \hat{H}) \models^{\mathrm{CF}} (\nu n)P$	iff $(\hat{I}, \hat{H}) \models^{\mathrm{CF}} P$
$(zero)$	$(\hat{I}, \hat{H}) \models^{\mathrm{CF}} \mathbf{0}$	always
(par)	$(\hat{I}, \hat{H}) \models^{\mathrm{CF}} P \mid Q$	iff $(\hat{I}, \hat{H}) \models^{\mathrm{CF}} P \wedge (\hat{I}, \hat{H}) \models^{\mathrm{CF}} Q$
$(repl)$	$(\hat{I}, \hat{H}) \models^{\mathrm{CF}} !P$	iff $(\hat{I}, \hat{H}) \models^{\mathrm{CF}} P$
(amb)	$(\hat{I}, \hat{H}) \models^{\mathrm{CF}} n^{\ell^a}[P]$	iff $(\hat{I}, \hat{H}) \models^{\mathrm{CF}} P$

(in) $\quad (\hat{I}, \hat{H}) \models^{\mathrm{CF}} \mathbf{in}^{\ell^t} n . P \quad$ iff $(\hat{I}, \hat{H}) \models^{\mathrm{CF}} P \wedge$
$\quad\quad \forall \ell^a, \ell^{a'}, \ell^{a''} \in \mathbf{Lab}^a(P) : ((\ell^a, \ell^t) \in \hat{I} \wedge (\ell^{a''}, \ell^a) \in \hat{I} \wedge (\ell^{a''}, \ell^{a'}) \in \hat{I}$
$\quad\quad \wedge (\ell^{a'}, n) \in \hat{H}) \implies (\ell^{a'}, \ell^a) \in \hat{I}$

(out) $\quad (\hat{I}, \hat{H}) \models^{\mathrm{CF}} \mathbf{out}^{\ell^t} n . P \quad$ iff $(\hat{I}, \hat{H}) \models^{\mathrm{CF}} P \wedge$
$\quad\quad \forall \ell^a, \ell^{a'}, \ell^{a''} \in \mathbf{Lab}^a(P) : ((\ell^a, \ell^t) \in \hat{I} \wedge (\ell^{a'}, \ell^a) \in \hat{I} \wedge (\ell^{a''}, \ell^{a'}) \in \hat{I}$
$\quad\quad \wedge (\ell^{a'}, n) \in \hat{H}) \implies (\ell^{a''}, \ell^a) \in \hat{I}$

$(open)$ $\quad (\hat{I}, \hat{H}) \models^{\mathrm{CF}} \mathbf{open}^{\ell^t} n . P$ iff $(\hat{I}, \hat{H}) \models^{\mathrm{CF}} P \wedge$
$\quad\quad \forall \ell^a, \ell^{a'} \in \mathbf{Lab}^a(P), \forall \ell' \in \mathbf{Lab}(P) : ((\ell^a, \ell^t) \in \hat{I} \wedge (\ell^a, \ell^{a'}) \in \hat{I}$
$\quad\quad \wedge (\ell^{a'}, n) \in \hat{H} \wedge (\ell^{a'}, \ell') \in \hat{I}) \implies (\ell^a, \ell') \in \hat{I}$

Fig. 3. Specification of the Control Flow Analysis

recorded in $\hat{I}$, i.e., all the ambients/capabilities nested in $\ell^{a'}$ have to be nested also in ℓ^a.

The crucial result is that whenever $(\hat{I}, \hat{H}) \models^{\mathrm{CF}} P$ and the representation of P is contained in $(\hat{I}, \hat{H})$, we are assured that every nesting of ambients and capabilities in every possible derivative of P is also captured in $(\hat{I}, \hat{H})$.

Example 3. Consider again process P_2 of Example 2. Note that it may evolve to $n^{\ell_1^a}[\mathbf{0}] \mid m^{\ell_2^a}[\mathbf{0}]$. It is easy to prove that the least solution for P_2 is $(\hat{I}, \hat{H})$, where $\hat{I} = \{(env, \ell_1^a), (env, \ell_2^a), (\ell_1^a, \ell_2^a), (\ell_2^a, \ell^t)\}$, and $\hat{H} = \{(\ell_1^a, n), (\ell_2^a, m)\}$. Notice that the analysis correctly captures through the pair (env, ℓ_2^a) the possibility for m to exit from n. $\quad\square$

3 Refining the Complexity Analysis for Nielson and Seidl Algorithms

In this section, we refine the worst case complexity results for the algorithms presented in [19] by recalculating them as functions of N_a, N_t, and N_L, instead of N. We also calculate the minimum number of steps performed by the algorithms even in the best case. The results of this section will be useful to compare the algorithms of [19] with our new ones that will be given in Section 4.

3.1 The First Algorithm of Nielson and Seidl – NS1

In the following, we will use NS1 to refer to the $O(N^4)$ algorithm for the Control Flow Analysis of Mobile Ambients presented in [19]. NS1 is based on a formulation of the analysis which is equivalent to the one presented in the previous section. The constraints in Figure 3 are rewritten as ground Horn clauses by instantiating the universally quantified variables in all possible ways. To estimate the number of these ground Horn clauses, notice that:

- the number of capabilities is obviously $O(N_t)$, since N_t is the cardinality of **Lab**$^t(P)$;
- a constraint for an *open*-capability involves two universal quantifications that range over **Lab**$^a(P)$, whose cardinality is N_a, plus another universal quantification that ranges over **Lab**(P), whose cardinality is N_L. Constraints for *in* and *out*-capabilities have three universal quantifications ranging over **Lab**$^a(P)$.

Since **Lab**$^a(P) \subseteq$ **Lab**(P), we have that the greatest number of ground Horn clauses is generated by the algorithm when all the capabilities are *open* ones. Namely, the number of generated clauses is $O(N_t \cdot N_a^2 \cdot N_L)$. Moreover, they require $O((N_t \cdot N_a^2 \cdot N_L) \log N_L)$ bits to be represented.

The next step of NS1 is to apply the algorithm presented in [9] (which represents a set of ground Horn clauses as a graph, and solves a pebbling problem on that graph) to this set, in order to find the least solution. As such algorithm uses $O(n)$ steps and $O(n \log n)$ space, where n is the size of the set of ground Horn clauses, we obtain the following (considering that the parsing of the process has already been done):

Proposition 1. *The complexity of NS1 is $O(N_t \cdot N_a^2 \cdot N_L)$ steps and $O((N_t \cdot N_a^2 \cdot N_L) \log N_L)$ bits.*

Example 4. Let P_3 be the process $n^{\ell_1^a}[\, m^{\ell_2^a}[\mathbf{open}^{\ell_1^t} n.0]\,]$. The constraint for the *open*-capability is

$$\forall \ell^a, \ell^{a'} \in \mathbf{Lab}^a(P), \forall \ell' \in \mathbf{Lab}(P):$$
$$((\ell^a, \ell^t) \in \hat{I} \,\wedge\, (\ell^a, \ell^{a'}) \in \hat{I} \,\wedge\, (\ell^{a'}, n) \in \hat{H} \,\wedge\, (\ell^{a'}, \ell') \in \hat{I}) \implies (\ell^a, \ell') \in \hat{I}.$$

In order to generate the Horn clauses ℓ^a and $\ell^{a'}$ have to be instantiated in all the possible ways in the set **Lab**$^a(P) = \{\ell_1^a, \ell_2^a\}$, whose cardinality is $N_a = 2$, and ℓ' ranges over **Lab**$(P) = \{\ell_1^a, \ell_2^a, \ell^t\}$, whose cardinality is $N_L = 3$. This introduces $N_a^2 \cdot N_L = 12$ ground Horn clauses. For instance, one of them is the one obtained by instantiating ℓ^a to ℓ_1^a, $\ell^{a'}$ to ℓ_2^a and ℓ' to ℓ_1^t, i.e.,

$$((\ell_1^a, \ell^t) \in \hat{I} \,\wedge\, (\ell_1^a, \ell_2^a) \in \hat{I} \,\wedge\, (\ell_2^a, n) \in \hat{H} \,\wedge\, (\ell_2^a, \ell_1^t) \in \hat{I}) \implies (\ell_1^a, \ell_1^t) \in \hat{I}.$$

In P there are no other capabilities, hence we obtain only these 12 ground Horn clauses. Therefore, in this case $N_t \cdot N_a^2 \cdot N_L = 12$.   □

Observe that, even in the best case (i.e., no *open* capabilities) at least $N_t \cdot N_a^3$ steps are performed to generate all the ground clauses. We obtain the following:

Corollary 1. *Algorithm NS1 performs at least $N_t \cdot N_a^3$ steps and uses at least $N_t \cdot N_a^3 \log N_L$ bits.*

3.2 The Second Algorithm of Nielson and Seidl – NS2

We now consider NS2, the cubic-time algorithm presented in [19]. It is based on an optimization of the analysis of Figure 3 reported in Figure 4 [2]. The equivalence between the analysis of Figures 3 and 4 follows from [19]. The main idea behind the optimized analysis is to reduce the number of universal quantifications in each analysis constraint. This is achieved by adding some new components that keep further information on the nestings, and that may be globally computed.

As an example, consider the *in* constraint. It requires to find three labels ℓ^a, $\ell^{a'}$, $\ell^{a''} \in \textbf{Lab}^a(P)$ such that $(\ell^a, \ell^t) \in \hat{I} \wedge (\ell^{a''}, \ell^a) \in \hat{I} \wedge (\ell^{a''}, \ell^{a'}) \in \hat{I}$. Notice that $\ell^{a''}$ is only used to check if ℓ^a and $\ell^{a'}$ are *siblings*. Thus, having a set $\hat{S} \in \wp(\textbf{Lab}^a(P) \times \textbf{Lab}^a(P))$ containing all the pairs of labels corresponding to siblings ambients, allows to limit the quantification on two labels only. In particular, it is sufficient to find two labels $\ell^a, \ell^{a'}$, such that $(\ell^a, \ell^t) \in \hat{I} \wedge (\ell^a, \ell^{a'}) \in \hat{S}$. In order to calculate set $\hat{S}$, it is now required a new global constraint (*global*, in Figure 4): $((\ell^{a''}, \ell^a) \in \hat{I} \wedge (\ell^{a''}, \ell^{a'}) \in \hat{I}) \implies (\ell^a, \ell^{a'}) \in \hat{S}$. Similar optimizations are applied to the other constraints, by introducing the components $\hat{O}, \hat{P} \in \wp(\textbf{Lab}^a(P) \times \textbf{Lab}^a(P))$, where $(\ell^{a'}, \ell^a) \in \hat{O}$ represents the fact that ℓ^a may move out of $\ell^{a'}$, and $(\ell^a, \ell^{a'}) \in \hat{P}$ indicates that $\ell^{a'}$ may be opened inside ℓ^a. Note that the rule (*global*) is applied only once during the analysis.

As for NS1, the NS2 algorithm is based on a translation of constraints into a set of ground Horn clauses, on which the algorithm in [9] is applied to compute the least solution. To estimate the size of the set of ground Horn clauses obtained by instantiating the variables in all the possible ways, notice that:

- there are N_t capabilities and all their constraints involve two universal quantifications over $\textbf{Lab}^a(P)$, whose size is N_a;
- the first two constraints in the (*global*) rule involve three universal quantifications over $\textbf{Lab}^a(P)$;
- the third constraint in the (*global*) rule involves two universal quantifications over $\textbf{Lab}^a(P)$, and one over $\textbf{Lab}(P)$, whose cardinality is N_L.

We obtain that the number of ground clauses is
$$N_t \cdot N_a^2 + N_a^3 + N_a^2 \cdot N_L = (N_t + N_a)N_a^2 + N_a^2 \cdot N_L = 2 \cdot N_a^2 \cdot N_L.$$

Proposition 2. *The complexity of the NS2 algorithm is $O(N_a^2 \cdot N_L)$ steps and $O((N_a^2 \cdot N_L) \log N_L)$ bits.*

By following the same reasoning above, it is also easy to see that:

Corollary 2. *Algorithm NS2 performs at least $2 \cdot N_a^2 \cdot N_L$ steps and uses at least $2 \cdot (N_a^2 \cdot N_L) \log N_L$ bits.*

4 The New Algorithms

In this section, we present our new algorithms for nesting analysis of Figures 3 and 4, and we compare them with the NS1 and NS2 algorithms above.

---

[2] In [19] the optimized Analysis is presented using a slightly different formalism.

$(global)$ $(\hat{I}, \hat{H}, \hat{S}, \hat{O}, \hat{P}) \models^{\mathrm{CFOpt}} P$ iff $(\hat{I}, \hat{H}, \hat{S}, \hat{O}, \hat{P}) \models^{\mathrm{Opt}} P \wedge$

$\forall \ell^a, \ell^{a'}, \ell^{a''} \in \mathbf{Lab}^a(P) : ((\ell^{a''}, \ell^a) \in \hat{I} \wedge (\ell^{a''}, \ell^{a'}) \in \hat{I})$
$\implies (\ell^a, \ell^{a'}) \in \hat{S} \wedge$

$\forall \ell^a, \ell^{a'}, \ell^{a''} \in \mathbf{Lab}^a(P) : ((\ell^{a'}, \ell^a) \in \hat{O} \wedge (\ell^{a''}, \ell^{a'}) \in \hat{I})$
$\implies (\ell^{a''}, \ell^a) \in \hat{I} \wedge$

$\forall \ell^a, \ell^{a'} \in \mathbf{Lab}^a(P), \ell' \in \mathbf{Lab}(P) : ((\ell^a, \ell^{a'}) \in \hat{P} \wedge (\ell^{a'}, \ell') \in \hat{I})$
$\implies (\ell^a, \ell') \in \hat{I}$

(res) $(\hat{I}, \hat{H}, \hat{S}, \hat{O}, \hat{P}) \models^{\mathrm{Opt}} (\nu n)P$ iff $(\hat{I}, \hat{H}, \hat{S}, \hat{O}, \hat{P}) \models^{\mathrm{Opt}} P$

$(zero)$ $(\hat{I}, \hat{H}, \hat{S}, \hat{O}, \hat{P}) \models^{\mathrm{Opt}} \mathbf{0}$ always

(par) $(\hat{I}, \hat{H}, \hat{S}, \hat{O}, \hat{P}) \models^{\mathrm{Opt}} P \mid Q$ iff $(\hat{I}, \hat{H}, \hat{S}, \hat{O}, \hat{P}) \models^{\mathrm{Opt}} P \wedge$
$(\hat{I}, \hat{H}, \hat{S}, \hat{O}, \hat{P}) \models^{\mathrm{Opt}} Q$

$(repl)$ $(\hat{I}, \hat{H}, \hat{S}, \hat{O}, \hat{P}) \models^{\mathrm{Opt}} {!}P$ iff $(\hat{I}, \hat{H}, \hat{S}, \hat{O}, \hat{P}) \models^{\mathrm{Opt}} P$

(amb) $(\hat{I}, \hat{H}, \hat{S}, \hat{O}, \hat{P}) \models^{\mathrm{Opt}} n^{\ell^a}[P]$ iff $(\hat{I}, \hat{H}, \hat{S}, \hat{O}, \hat{P}) \models^{\mathrm{Opt}} P$

(in) $(\hat{I}, \hat{H}, \hat{S}, \hat{O}, \hat{P}) \models^{\mathrm{Opt}} \mathbf{in}^{\ell^t} n \, . \, P$ iff $(\hat{I}, \hat{H}, \hat{S}, \hat{O}, \hat{P}) \models^{\mathrm{Opt}} P \wedge$

$\forall \ell^a, \ell^{a'} \in \mathbf{Lab}^a(P) : ((\ell^a, \ell^t) \in \hat{I} \wedge (\ell^a, \ell^{a'}) \in \hat{S} \wedge (\ell^{a'}, n) \in \hat{H})$
$\implies (\ell^{a'}, \ell^a) \in \hat{I}$

(out) $(\hat{I}, \hat{H}, \hat{S}, \hat{O}, \hat{P}) \models^{\mathrm{Opt}} \mathbf{out}^{\ell^t} n \, . \, P$ iff $(\hat{I}, \hat{H}, \hat{S}, \hat{O}, \hat{P}) \models^{\mathrm{Opt}} P \wedge$

$\forall \ell^a, \ell^{a'} \in \mathbf{Lab}^a(P) : ((\ell^a, \ell^t) \in \hat{I} \wedge (\ell^{a'}, \ell^a) \in \hat{I} \wedge (\ell^{a'}, n) \in \hat{H})$
$\implies (\ell^{a'}, \ell^a) \in \hat{O}$

$(open)$ $(\hat{I}, \hat{H}, \hat{S}, \hat{O}, \hat{P}) \models^{\mathrm{Opt}} \mathbf{open}^{\ell^t} n \, . \, P$ iff $(\hat{I}, \hat{H}, \hat{S}, \hat{O}, \hat{P}) \models^{\mathrm{Opt}} P \wedge$

$\forall \ell^a, \ell^{a'} \in \mathbf{Lab}^a(P) : ((\ell^a, \ell^t) \in \hat{I} \wedge (\ell^a, \ell^{a'}) \in \hat{I} \wedge (\ell^a, n) \in \hat{H})$
$\implies (\ell^a, \ell^{a'}) \in \hat{P}$

Fig. 4. The Optimized Control Flow Analysis

As highlighted in Section 3, the main idea behind NS1 and NS2 is to instantiate the analysis constraints with respect to all the possible labels in order to obtain a set of ground Horn clauses. Unfortunately, instantiating all the constraints causes that much space is used and, even in the best case, $N_t \cdot N_a^3$ and $2 \cdot N_L \cdot N_a^2$ steps are performed by NS1 and NS2, respectively (see Corollaries 1 and 2).

In order to avoid these problems, our algorithms only consider the constraints that are effectively necessary for the computation of the analysis. The algorithms take a more direct approach, in a sense that they do not translate constraints into Horn clauses and neither apply the algorithm of [9]. The algorithms start with an empty analysis $\hat{I}$ and with a buffer containing all the pairs corresponding to the initial process representation [3]. Recall that these pairs should be contained

---

[3] Indeed, our second algorithm uses a set of buffers, but this does not change the underlying ideas of the algorithm.

in the final $\hat{I}$ in order for the analysis to be correct. At each round, one pair is extracted from the buffer and it is added to the solution $\hat{I}$. Only the constraints that are potentially "activated" by the extracted pair are then considered, i.e., only the constraints that have such an element in the premise. All the pairs required by such constraints are inserted into the buffer, so that they will be eventually added to the solution. This is repeated until a fix-point is reached, i.e., until all the elements required by the constraints are in the solution. The most important ingredient in this on-the-fly generation is the use of a buffer together with a matrix which allow to use each pair of labels in the buffer *exactly once* to generate new pairs.

We show that our first algorithm has a space complexity of $O((N_a \cdot N_L) \log N_L)$ bits and a time complexity of $O(S_I^a \cdot N_t \cdot N_L + S_I^t \cdot N_a \cdot N_L)$ steps, where S_I^a (S_I^t) is the number of pairs of the form $(\ell^a, \ell^{a'})$ $((\ell^a, \ell^t)$, respectively) in the least solution. First, note that $O((N_a \cdot N_L) \log N_L)$ bits highly decreases the $O((N_t \cdot N_a^2 \cdot N_L) \log N_L)$ space complexity of NS1. Note also that the maximum size of the solution is $S_I^a = N_a^2$ and $S_I^t = N_a \cdot N_t$. Thus, only in the worst-case, our algorithm has a time complexity equal to the one of NS1. The best case is instead when the solution is linear with respect to the process dimension, i.e., $S_I^a = N_a$, $S_I^t = N_t$, thus reducing time-complexity to $c \cdot N_a \cdot N_t \cdot N_L$, where c is a suitable constant [4]. The solution cannot be less than linear as it immediately follows from the definition of the representation function.

Our second algorithm decreases with respect to NS2 space complexity to $O((N_a \cdot N_L) \log N_L)$ bits and time complexity to $O(S_I^a \cdot N_L + S_I^t \cdot N_a + S_S \cdot N_t + S_P \cdot N_L + S_O \cdot N_a)$ steps, where S_I^a and S_I^t are defined as above, and S_S, S_O, S_P are the final dimensions of $\hat{S}$, $\hat{O}$, $\hat{P}$, respectively. First, note that our space complexity $O((N_a \cdot N_L) \log N_L)$ greatly improves the $O((N_a^2 \cdot N_L) \log N_L)$ space complexity of NS2. Moreover, the maximum size of the solution is $S_I^a = S_S = S_O = S_P = N_a^2$ and $S_I^t = N_a \cdot N_t$, thus, in the worst case, time complexity becomes equal to the one of NS2. The best case is instead when the solution is linear with respect to the process dimension, thus reducing time-complexity to $c \cdot N_a \cdot N_L$ for a constant $c \leq 5$ (see Corollary 3) which is strictly better than $2 \cdot N_a^2 \cdot N_L$, i.e., the best case of NS2.

Note that, the cases in which the solutions are maximal, i.e., when our algorithms have the same time complexity of NS1 and NS2, correspond to analysis solutions that contain all the possible nestings. Such cases are either related to quite rare processes showing all possible nestings at run-time, or to excessive approximations of more common processes. We are presently trying to estimate this number of bad cases.

We now present the two algorithms in detail.

---

[4] By exploiting the same argument we used for calculating the best case of NS1, we could lower this complexity down to $c \cdot N_a^2 \cdot N_t$, for a constant c, which is strongly better (up to multiplicative constants) than $N_t \cdot N_a^3$, i.e., the best case for NS1.

Algorithm 1

Our first algorithm, called Algorithm 1, is depicted in Figure 5. We assume that the parsing of the process has already been done, producing an array cap of length N_t containing all the capabilities of the input process. For instance, cap[i] may contain "$\mathbf{in}^{\ell^t}$ n", representing an *in* capability labeled with ℓ^t and with n as target [5]. During the parsing, the representation $\beta_{env}^{CF}(P)$ is computed giving two initial sets $\hat{I}_0$ and $\hat{H}_0$ that are stored into an $N_a \times N_L$ bit matrix $B_{\hat{I}}$, and into an $N_a \times N_a$ bit matrix $M_{\hat{H}}$, respectively. By parsing P twice, we can build $B_{\hat{I}}$ in such a way that columns from 1 to N_a are indexed by ambient labels, while all the other columns by capability ones. All the pairs in $\hat{I}_0$ are also stored in a stack $\mathrm{buf}_{\hat{I}}$, on which the usual operations $\mathrm{push}_{\hat{I}}$ (1,1') and $\mathrm{pop}_{\hat{I}}$ () apply. Matrix $B_{\hat{I}}$ is used to efficiently check whether an element has ever been inserted into $\mathrm{buf}_{\hat{I}}$, thus ensuring that a pair is inserted in $\mathrm{buf}_{\hat{I}}$ at most once. In particular, the new command $\mathrm{push\_c}_{\hat{I}}$ (1,1') applies if $B_{\hat{I}}$ [1,1']=false, and it both executes $\mathrm{push}_{\hat{I}}$ (1,1') and sets $B_{\hat{I}}$ [1,1'] to true. Finally, we initialize to false another bit matrix $M_{\hat{I}}$ of size $N_a \times N_L$ that will contain the final result of the analysis. Also in $M_{\hat{I}}$ the columns from 1 to N_a are indexed by ambient labels and the ones from $N_a + 1$ to N_L by capability labels. This initialization phase requires only $O(N)$ steps, since two parsings of P are sufficient.

Example 5. Let P be the Firewall Access process of [6], where an agent crosses a firewall by means of previously arranged passwords k, k' and k'' (see [18] for a detailed analysis of the security issues related to this example):

$$P = (\nu w)\, w^{a1}[\; k^{a2}[\mathbf{out}^{t1}\, w.\mathbf{in}^{t2}\, k'.\mathbf{in}^{t3}\, w.0]\; |\; \mathbf{open}^{t4}\, k' \,.\, \mathbf{open}^{t5}\, k'' \,.\, 0]\; |$$
$$k'^{a3}[\mathbf{open}^{t6}\, k \,.\, k''^{a4}[0]\,]$$

The least solution of P, as computed using the specification of the Control Flow Analysis depicted in Figure 3, is the pair $(\hat{I}, \hat{H})$, where:

$\hat{I}=$ {$(env, a1), (env, a2), (env, a3), (a1, a1), (a1, a2), (a1, a3), (a1, a4), (a1, t1),$
$\quad (a1, t2), (a1, t3), (a1, t4), (a1, t5), (a1, t6), (a2, t1), (a2, t2), (a2, t3), (a3, a1),$
$\quad (a3, a2), (a3, a3), (a3, a4), (a3, t1), (a3, t2), (a3, t3), (a3, t6)$},
$\hat{H}=$ {$(a1, w), (a2, k), (a3, k'), (a4, k'')$}.

Let us see how Algorithm 1 applies to process P. In this case, $N_a = 5$ and $N_t = 6$, thus $B_{\hat{I}}$ and $M_{\hat{I}}$ are 5×11 bit matrices, $M_{\hat{H}}$ is a 5×5 bit matrix, and cap an array of length 6, initialized as $\langle\mathbf{out}^{t1}\, w, \mathbf{in}^{t2}\, k', \mathbf{in}^{t3}\, w, \mathbf{open}^{t4}\, k', \mathbf{open}^{t5}\, k'',$ $\mathbf{open}^{t6}\, k\rangle$. After the initial parsing, the only pairs in $M_{\hat{H}}$ which are set to true are {$(a1, w), (a2, k), (a3, k'), (a4, k'')$}, while $\mathrm{buf}_{\hat{I}}$ and $B_{\hat{I}}$ contain the pairs $\langle(env, a1), (env, a3), (a1, a2), (a3, a4), (a1, t4), (a1, t5), (a2, t1), (a2, t2), (a2, t3),$ $(a3, t6)\rangle$.

Let the pair $(env, a1)$ be the top element of $\mathrm{buf}_{\hat{I}}$. The first 6 rounds of the while-loop just move pairs from $\mathrm{buf}_{\hat{I}}$ to $M_{\hat{I}}$ (no push is performed). Then, at round 7:

---

[5] n here represents an integer $1 \leq n \leq N_a$ corresponding to the n-th ambient name. The correspondence between names and integers is kept in the symbol-table produced at the parsing-time.

```
while buf_f̂ != NIL do
  (l,l') := pop_f̂ (); M_f̂ [l,l'] := true;
  for i := 1 to N_t do
    case cap[i] of:
      in^{ℓ^t} n: if (l' ∈ Lab^t(P) and l' = l^t)
                 then for j := 1 to N_a do
                        for k := 1 to N_a do
                          if (M_f̂ [k,l] and M_f̂ [k,j] and M_Ĥ [j,n]) then push_c_f̂ (j,l)
                 else if (l' ∈ Lab^a(P) and M_f̂ [l',l^t]) then for j:= 1 to N_a do
                          if (M_f̂ [l,j] and M_Ĥ [j,n]) then push_c_f̂ (j,l');
                      if (l' ∈ Lab^a(P) and M_Ĥ [l',n]) then for j:= 1 to N_a do
                          if (M_f̂ [j,l^t] and M_f̂ [l,j]) then push_c_f̂ (l',j);
      out^{ℓ^t} n: if (l' ∈ Lab^t(P) and l' = l^t)
                  then for j := 1 to N_a do
                         for k := 1 to N_a do
                           if (M_f̂ [j,l] and M_f̂ [k,j] and M_Ĥ [j,n]) then push_c_f̂ (k,l)
                  else if (l' ∈ Lab^a(P) and M_f̂ [l',l^t] and M_Ĥ [l,n]) then for j:= 1 to N_a do
                           if M_f̂ [j,l] then push_c_f̂ (j,l');
                       if (l' ∈ Lab^a(P) and M_Ĥ [l',n]) then for j:= 1 to N_a do
                           if (M_f̂ [j,l^t] and M_f̂ [l',j]) then push_c_f̂ (l,j);
      open^{ℓ^t} n: if (l' ∈ Lab^t(P) and l' = l^t)
                   then for j := 1 to N_a do
                          for k := 1 to N_L do
                            if (M_f̂ [l,j] and M_f̂ [j,k] and M_Ĥ [j,n]) then push_c_f̂ (l,k)
                   else if (l' ∈ Lab^a(P) and M_f̂ [l,l^t] and M_Ĥ [l',n]) then for j:= 1 to N_L do
                            if M_f̂ [l',j] then push_c_f̂ (l,j);
                        if (l' ∈ Lab^a(P) and M_Ĥ [l,n]) then for j:= 1 to N_a do
                            if (M_f̂ [j,l^t] and M_f̂ [j,l]) then push_c_f̂ (j,l');
```

Fig. 5. Algorithm 1

- buf_f̂ = ⟨(a2, t1), (a2, t2), (a2, t3), (a3, t6)⟩
- M_f̂ = ⟨(env, a1), (env, a3), (a1, a2), (a3, a4), (a1, t4), (a1, t5)⟩
- B_f̂ = ⟨(env, a1), (env, a3), (a1, a2), (a3, a4), (a1, t4), (a1, t5), (a2, t1), (a2, t2), (a2, t3), (a3, t6)⟩.

We extract the top element $(a2, t1)$ of buf_f̂ , thus $l := a2$, and $l' := t1$. We show the first iteration, $i = 1$, where cap[1] is "$out^{t1} w$". Thus, we have $l' = l^t$ and $n = w$. Since $l' ∈ Lab^t(P)$ and $l' = l^t$, we are in the "then" branch. The only case that makes true the if condition is when $j = a1$ and $k = env$. Since $(a1, w) ∈ M_Ĥ$ and both $(a1, a2)$ and $(env, a1)$ are in M_f̂ , the pair $(env, a2)$ is pushed in buf_f̂ (note that it is not already in B_f̂). The algorithm ends after the 24th round, when buf_f̂ is empty.   □

We recall that S_f^a (S_f^t) is the number of pairs of the form $(ℓ^a, ℓ^{a'})$ $((ℓ^a, ℓ^t)$, respectively) in the least solution. We can prove the following result:

Theorem 1. *Algorithm 1 is correct. It has time complexity of $O(S_I^a \cdot N_t \cdot N_L + S_I^t \cdot N_a \cdot N_L)$ steps and a space complexity of $O((N_a \cdot N_L) \log N_L)$ bits.*

Sketch of the Proof. The proof mainly follows two steps. First, we show the following invariant on the outermost while−loop:

> *Let a round be one iteration of the outermost while-loop. At a generic round k: if we apply the Control Flow Analysis by considering the set $\hat{I}$ corresponding to matrix $\mathsf{M}_{\hat{I}}$, then the set of pairs (l,l') for which the analysis fails (i.e., required to be in $\hat{I}$, but such that $\mathsf{M}_{\hat{I}}$ [l,l']=false) are in $\mathsf{B}_{\hat{I}}$.*

Then we prove that the algorithm terminates when the buffer is empty, i.e., when $\mathsf{M}_{\hat{I}} = \mathsf{B}_{\hat{I}}$. The invariant proves that, in such a situation, $\mathsf{M}_{\hat{I}}$ is a correct analysis. Indeed, assume it is not correct, then all the (l,l') for which the analysis fails must be in $\mathsf{B}_{\hat{I}}$, and thus also in $\mathsf{M}_{\hat{I}}$, giving a contradiction. □

Note that the worst-case time complexity of Algorithm 1 is $O(N_t \cdot N_a^2 \cdot N_L)$, since in the worst-case $S_I^a = N_a^2$ and $S_t^I = N_a \cdot N_t$.

Algorithm 2

Time complexity of Algorithm 1 can be reduced by applying buffering techniques also to the optimized analysis of Figure 4. This leads to our second algorithm, called Algorithm 2 and depicted in Figure 6. Also in this case, we assume that the parsing of the process has already been done twice. As a result, the same data structures as in Algorithm 1 (i.e., cap, $\mathsf{buf}_{\hat{I}}$, $\mathsf{B}_{\hat{I}}$, $\mathsf{M}_{\hat{I}}$ and $\mathsf{M}_{\hat{H}}$), are initialized. In addition, we consider the additional buffers $\mathsf{buf}_{\hat{S}}$, $\mathsf{buf}_{\hat{O}}$, and $\mathsf{buf}_{\hat{P}}$, and three $N_a \times N_a$ bit matrices $\mathsf{B}_{\hat{S}}$, $\mathsf{B}_{\hat{O}}$, and $\mathsf{B}_{\hat{P}}$ set to false. These matrices have the same rôle of matrix $\mathsf{B}_{\hat{I}}$, i.e., they avoid that a pair is put twice in one of the buffers $\mathsf{buf}_{\hat{S}}$, $\mathsf{buf}_{\hat{O}}$, and $\mathsf{buf}_{\hat{P}}$. We also initialize to false the $N_a \times N_a$ bit matrices $\mathsf{M}_{\hat{S}}$, $\mathsf{M}_{\hat{O}}$, and $\mathsf{M}_{\hat{P}}$ that will contain the final result of the analysis. As for Algorithm 1, we assume that in $\mathsf{B}_{\hat{I}}$ and in $\mathsf{M}_{\hat{I}}$ columns from 1 to N_a are assigned to ambient labels and the ones from $N_a + 1$ to N_L to capability labels.

The main difference between Algorithm 1 and Algorithm 2 is the use of the data structures related to $\hat{S}$, $\hat{O}$, and $\hat{P}$, thus merging the ideas of NS2 with our on-the-fly approach. Observe that the last block of if-statements in Algorithm 2 corresponds to the *global* constraints in Figure 4.

Let S_I^a and S_I^t be as defined above, and S_S, S_O, S_P be the cardinality of $\hat{S}$, $\hat{O}$, $\hat{P}$ at the end of the execution, respectively, then we can prove the following theorem, whose proof follows the lines of Theorem 1:

Theorem 2. *Algorithm 2 is correct. It has a time complexity of $O(S_I^a \cdot N_L + S_I^t \cdot N_a + S_S \cdot N_t + S_O \cdot N_a + S_P \cdot N_L)$ steps and a worst-case space complexity of $O((N_a \cdot N_L) \log N_L)$ bits.*

Observe that these space and time complexities may boil down to quadratic and even linear size in the practice, e.g., when few nestings are actually present in the process, or when capabilities belong to few ambients.

```
while (buf_Î != NIL or buf_Ŝ != NIL or buf_Ô != NIL or buf_P̂ != NIL) do
  if buf_Î != NIL then
    (l,l') := pop_Î (); M_Î [l,l'] := true; b:= "I"
  else if buf_Ŝ != NIL then
    (l,l') := pop_Ŝ (); M_Ŝ [l,l'] := true; b:= "S"
  else if buf_Ô != NIL then
    (l,l') := pop_Ô (); M_Ô [l,l'] := true; b:= "O"
  else if buf_P̂ != NIL then
    (l,l') := pop_P̂ (); M_P̂ [l,l'] := true; b:= "P";
  if (b="I" or b="S") then for i := 1 to N_t do
  case cap[i] of:
    in^{ℓ^t} n: if (b="I" and l' ∈ Lab^t(P) and l' = l^t)
          then for j := 1 to N_a do
              if (M_Ŝ [l,j] and M_Ĥ [j,n]) then push_c_Î (j,l)
              else if (b="S" and M_Î [l,l^t] and M_Ĥ [l',n] then push_c_Î (l',l);
    out^{ℓ^t} n: if (b="I" and l' ∈ Lab^t(P) and l' = l^t)
          then for j := 1 to N_a do
              if (M_Î [j,l] and M_Ĥ [j,n]) then push_c_Ô (j,l)
              else if (b="I" and l' ∈ Lab^a(P) and M_Î [l',l^t] and M_Ĥ [l,n] then push_c_Ô (l,l');
    open^{ℓ^t} n: if (b="I" and l' ∈ Lab^t(P) and l' = l^t)
          then for j := 1 to N_a do
              if (M_Î [l,j] and M_Ĥ [j,n]) then push_c_P̂ (l,j)
              else if (b="I" and l' ∈ Lab^a(P) and M_Î [l,l^t] and M_Ĥ [l',n] then push_c_P̂ (l,l');
  if b="I" then for j:= 1 to N_a do
    if M_Î [l,j] then push_c_Ŝ (l',j);
    if M_Ô [l',j] then push_c_Î (l,j);
    if M_P̂ [j,l] then push_c_Î (j,l');
  if b="O" then for j:= 1 to N_a do
    if M_Î [j,l] then push_c_Î (j,l');
  if b="P" then for j:= 1 to N_L do
    if M_Î [l',j] then push_c_Î (l,j);
```

Fig. 6. Algorithm 2

The worst-case time complexity of Algorithm 2 is $O(N_a^2 \cdot N_L)$, since $S_I^t \leq N_a \cdot N_t$, while S_I^a, S_S, S_O, $S_P \leq N_a^2$, and $N_L = N_a + N_t$.

The following corollary further refines the result of Theorem 2, showing that the actual impact of the multiplicative constants is negligible.

Corollary 3. *Algorithm 2 has time complexity smaller than* $5 \cdot N_a^2 \cdot N_t + 3 \cdot N_a^3$ *and it requires* $N_a \cdot N_L \cdot \log N_L + 2 \cdot N_a \cdot N_L + 3 \cdot N_a^2 \cdot \log N_L + 7 \cdot N_a^2$ *bits for space complexity.*

5   Related Works and Conclusions

Complexity of static analysis is an issue that has attracted many researchers, since seminal papers like [12]. Decidability of analysis has been considered in [13], while the question why certain dataflow analysis problems can be solved efficiently, but not others, is treated in [15]. Focusing on flow-sensitive analyses, the last paper shows that analysis that requires the use of relational attributes for precision must be PSPACE-hard in general, and as soon as the language constructs are slightly strengthened to allow a computation to maintain a very limited summary of what happens along an execution path, inter-procedural analysis becomes EXPTIME-hard. On different perspectives, [14] investigates bottom-up logic programming as a formalism for expressing and analyzing static analysis, while [7,8] investigate the complexity of model checking Mobile Ambients.

As we mentioned in the introduction, [19] is the first contribution tackling the issue of estimating the complexity of Control Flow Analysis for Mobile Ambients [6], by combining a new optimization technique (sharing and tiling) with previous results on Horn clauses [9]. In [20], Nielson et al. improve on [19] by using a sparsity analysis that results in $O(N \cdot s^3)$ time complexity, where s depends on the solution size. But no improvement in space complexity is achieved. Observe that in our approach, there is no need to translate the problem into Horn clauses, neither of performing asymptotic sparsity analysis. The simplicity of our direct approach allows very easy and efficient implementations of the algorithm. We are presently working on a prototype verifier that will be soon available on-line.

The extension of our results to more general scenarios is the main topic of our current research.

References

1. C. Bodei, P. Degano, F. Nielson, and H. Riis Nielson. Static Analysis for the π-calculus with Applications to Security. *Information and Computation*, 165:68–92, 2001.
2. C. Bodei, P. Degano, F. Nielson, and H. Riis Nielson. Control Flow Analysis for the π-calculus. In D. Sangiorgi, R. de Simone, editors, *Proc. of International Conference on Concurrency Theory (CONCUR)*, LNCS 1466, pages 84–98. Springer-Verlag, 1998.
3. C. Braghin, A. Cortesi, and R. Focardi. Security Boundaries in Mobile Ambients. *Computer Languages*, Elsevier, 28(1):101–127, Nov. 2002.
4. C. Braghin, A. Cortesi, and R. Focardi. Control Flow Analysis of Mobile Ambients with Security Boundaries. In B. Jacobs and A. Rensink, editors, *Proc. of Fifth Int. Conf. on Formal Methods for Open Object-Based Distributed Systems*, pages 197–212. Kluwer Academic Publisher, 2002.
5. C. Braghin, A. Cortesi, R. Focardi, and S. van Bakel. Boundary Inference for Enforcing Security Policies in Mobile Ambients. In *Proc. of The 2nd IFIP International Conference on Theoretical Computer Science (TCS)*, Kluwer Academic Publisher, pages 383–395, 2002.

6. L. Cardelli and A.D. Gordon. Mobile Ambients. Theoretical Computer Science (TCS), 240(1):177–213, 2000.

7. W. Charatonik and J. Talbot. The Decidability of Model Checking Mobile Ambients. In L. Fribourg, editor, *Proc. of Annual Conference of the European Association for Computer Science Logic (CSL)*, LNCS 2142, pages 339–354. Springer-Verlag, 2001.

8. W. Charatonik, S. Dal Zilio, A.D. Gordon, S. Mukhopadhyay, and J. Talbot. The Complexity of Model Checking Mobile Ambients. In F. Honsell, M. Miculan, eds., *Prof. of Int. Conf. on Foundations of Software Science and Computation Structures (FoSSaCS)*, LNCS 2030, pp. 152–167. Springer, 2001.

9. W. F. Dowling and J. H. Gallier. Linear–Time Algorithms for Testing the Satisfiability of Propositional Horn Formulae. *Journal of Logic Programming*, 3:267–284, 1984.

10. P. Degano, F. Levi, and C. Bodei. Safe Ambients: Control Flow Analysis and Security. In Jifeng He and Masahiko Sato, editors, *Proc. of Advances in Computing Science - 6th Asian Computing Science Conference, Penang, Malaysia (ASIAN)*, LNCS 1961, pp. 199–214. Springer, 2000.

11. R. R. Hansen, J. G. Jensen, F. Nielson, and H. Riis Nielson. Abstract Interpretation of Mobile Ambients. In A. Cortesi and G. File', eds., *Proc. of Static Analysis Symposium (SAS)*, LNCS 1694, pp. 134–148. Springer, 1999.

12. N.D. Jones and S.S. Muchnick. Complexity of flow analysis, inductive assertion synthesis, and a language due to Dijkstra. In S.S. Muchnick and N.D. Jones, editors, *Program Flow Analysis: Theory and Applications*, chapter 12, pages 380–393. Prentice-Hall, 1981.

13. W. Landi. Undecidability of static analysis. *ACM Letters on Programming Languages and Systems*, 1(4):323–337, December 1992.

14. D.A.McAllester. On the Complexity Analysis of Static Analyses. In A. Cortesi and G. File', eds., *Proc. of Static Analysis Symposium (SAS)*, LNCS 1694, pp. 312–329. Springer, 1999.

15. R. Muth and S. K. Debray. On the Complexity of Flow-Sensitive Dataflow Analyses. In *Proc. of the ACM SIGPLAN-SIGACT Symposium on Principles of Programming Languages (POPL)*, pages 67–80. ACM Press, N.Y., U.S.A., January 2000.

16. F. Nielson, R. R. Hansen, and H. Riis Nielson. Abstract Interpretation of Mobile Ambients. *Science of Computer Programming*, Issue on Static Analysis edited by A. Cortesi and G. File', to appear, 2003.

17. F. Nielson, H. Riis Nielson, C.L. Hankin. Principles of Program Analysis. Springer, 1999.

18. F. Nielson, H. Riis Nielson, R. R. Hansen, and J. G. Jensen. Validating Firewalls in Mobile Ambients. In J.C.M. Baeten, S. Mauw, editors, *Proc. of International Conference on Concurrency Theory (CONCUR)*, LNCS 1664, pages 463–477. Springer-Verlag, 1999.

19. F. Nielson and H. Seidl. Control-flow Analysis in Cubic Time. In D. Sands, ed., *Proc. of European Symposium On Programming (ESOP)*, LNCS 2028, pp. 252–268. Springer, 2001.

20. F. Nielson, H. Riis Nielson, and H. Seidl. Automatic Complexity Analysis. In D. Le Metayer, ed.,*Proc. of European Symposium On Programming (ESOP)*, LNCS 2305, pp.243–261. Springer, 2002.

Types for Evolving Communication in Safe Ambients

Francesca Levi

Dipartimento di Informatica e Scienze dell'Informazione
Università di Genova, Italy
levifran@disi.unige.it

Abstract. We extend the evolving types of [10] to full Safe Ambients following the lines of the single-threaded types of [12] for communication. Then, we introduce more flexible evolving types which permit to define ambients, where the type of the exchanged data may vary as the internal computation proceeds or after the ambient is opened.

1 Introduction

Mobile Ambients (MA) [5] has recently emerged as a core programming language for the Web and, at the same time, as a model for reasoning about properties of mobile processes. In contrast with previous formalisms for mobile processes such as the π-calculus [14], whose computational model is based on the notion of *communication*, the MA computational model is based on the notion of *movement*. An ambient, which may be thought of as a named location, is the unit of movement. Processes within the same ambient may exchange messages; ambients may be nested, so to form a hierarchical structure. The three primitives for movement allow: an ambient to enter another ambient, an ambient to exit another ambient, a process to dissolve an ambient boundary thus obtaining access to its contents. *Safe Ambients* (SA) [12] is a modification of MA, where a movement, in or out, or an ambient dissolution can take place only if both participants agree. This is achieved by means of coactions $\overline{\text{in}}\,a$, $\overline{\text{out}}\,a$ and $\overline{\text{open}}\,a$, which complement the capabilities $\text{in}\,a$, $\text{out}\,a$ and $\text{open}\,a$, respectively. This variation does not change the expressiveness of MA[1], yet makes it easier to write programs, to define static techniques [12,3,9,8], and to formally prove their correctness, especially by using behavioural equivalences [12,13]. The types in [12] introduce basic, immobile and single-threaded (ST) ambients. Basic and immobility types simply adapt to SA the types [6,4] for MA; the ST types define ambients that, at any time, have at most one capability ready to fire. Both immobility and ST types guarantee the absence of grave interferences, which is very useful, for instance for proving the correctness of programs algebraically.

The ST types introduce an interesting feature: the type of an ambient can *evolve*, meaning that the type of its local process can be different from that of the

---

[1] There is an obvious encoding of MA into SA.

L. Zuck et al. (Eds.): VMCAI 2003, LNCS 2575, pp. 102–115, 2003.

process unleashed, when the ambient is opened. The form of evolution allowed in [12] is, however, very restrictive. For instance, the following process cannot be typed with b immobile, although a, when opened inside b, unleashes only the immobile capability $\overline{\text{out}}\, b$

$$a[\, \text{in}\, b.\, \overline{\text{open}}\, a.\, \overline{\text{out}}\, b\,] \mid b[\, \overline{\text{in}}\, b.\, \text{open}\, a.\, Q\,]. \tag{1}$$

Ambient a can be typed only ST or basic (multi-threaded), and immobile ambients cannot open ST or basic ambients; they can indeed unleash capabilities of movement. Guan et al. [10] have modified the types of [12] for a variant of SA^2 without communication. They let the thread and mobility being orthogonal concepts and, consequently, achieve more flexible types, where both the mobility and the thread rights can evolve after opening. With this modification, the problem in (1) is solved, saying that a is a ST and mobile ambient which, when opened, liberates a ST and immobile process.

Another limitation of most of the types of MA [4,7,6,15] and SA [12,3,9] is that the type of the messages exchanged inside an ambient is fixed during its lifetime and also after its dissolution. There are however cases in which the type of messages can *safely* vary as the computation proceeds. This happens, for instance, in the following processes (assuming proper types for M_1 and M_2 and $W_1 \neq W_2$)

$$a[\, \text{in}\, c.\, \langle M_1 \rangle \mid (x : W_1)\overline{\text{open}}\, a.\, \langle M_2 \rangle\,] \mid c[\, \overline{\text{in}}\, c.\, \text{open}\, a.\, (y : W_2)Q\,] \tag{2}$$

$$a[\, \langle M_1 \rangle \mid (x : W_1)(\langle M_2 \rangle \mid (y : W_2)Q)\,] \tag{3}$$

In (2) the local process of a has exchanges of type W_1 and the process unleashed, when a is opened inside c, has exchanges of type W_2. Similarly in (3) the type of the data exchanged inside a is initially W_1, and becomes W_2 after the reception of M_1.

One solution to deal with this form of *evolving communication* is to represent explicitly some causality information in the types, as suggested in [1,2]. In this paper we propose an alternative approach which uses a form of linearity inspired by the ST types of [12]. We observe that the ST types offer control on *how many* abstractions and messages are present inside an ambient, and also on *when* they are consumed. This because the ST types let the thread move between the parallel processes local to an ambient by means of open and also by means of messages. For instance, both processes (2) and (3) can be typed with a and c ST, assuming that messages carry the thread and $W_1 = W_2$. In (2) the thread over a is first held by $\text{in}\, c.\, \langle M_1 \rangle$, then it is passed to $(\overline{\text{open}}\, a.\, \langle M_2 \rangle)\{M_1/x\}$; the thread over c is first held by $\overline{\text{in}}\, c.\, \text{open}\, a.\, (y : W_2)Q$, then it is passed to the process $\langle M_2 \rangle\{M_1/x\}$ unleashed by a, and finally to $(y : W_2)Q\{M_2\{M_1/x\}/y\}$.

In cases (2) and (3), the movements of the thread, carried by messages, show that all the messages and abstractions of type W_1 have been consumed, when the message M_2 and the abstraction $(y : W_2)Q$ are ready to interact inside a or

---

[2] Where in coactions $\overline{\text{in}}\, n$ and $\overline{\text{out}}\, n$ the name n refers to the ambient that moves, and where $\overline{\text{open}}$ has no parameters.

inside c. In general, however, the conditions guaranteed by the ST types are too weak to deal with evolving communication. The problem is the limited control on the reception of messages, which carry the thread, as the following processes illustrate

$$a[\,(z : W_1)P \mid \text{in}\, c.\,\overline{\text{open}}\, a.\,\langle M_2\rangle\,]\mid c[\,\overline{\text{in}}\, c.\,\text{open}\, a.\,(y : W_2)Q\,] \qquad (4)$$

$$a[\,\langle M_1\rangle \mid (z : W_1)P \mid (x : W_1)(\langle M_2\rangle \mid (y : W_2)Q)\,]. \qquad (5)$$

Both processes can be typed with a and c ST similarly to processes (2) and (3). In (5) the thread over a is passed non-deterministically to either $(\langle M_2\rangle \mid (y : W_2)Q)\{M_1/x\}$ or to $P\{M_1/z\}$; in (4) the thread over a is held by $\text{in}\, c.\,\overline{\text{open}}\, a.\,\langle M_2\rangle$ until a is opened. The subtle difference is that processes (4) and (5) are unsafe, when $W_1 \neq W_2$, as the abstraction $(z : W_1)P$ may end up in parallel with the emission of M_2.

In Section 3 we extend the approach of [10] to full SA following the lines of [12] for communication. In this paper, we focus on the ST types; the inclusion of basic (multi-threaded) ambients is orthogonal and can be found in the complete version [11]. Then, in Section 4, we define new types for evolving communication (EC) by introducing, in ST ambients, a proper typing discipline for communication. This is obtained by imposing stronger conditions on the movements of the thread, carried by messages, according to the discussion above. With the EC types we can type ambients where the type of the exchanged data may vary when the internal computation proceeds, as in process (3), or after the ambient is opened, as in process (2).

2   Mobile Safe Ambients

We briefly recall the *Safe Ambients* ([12]) calculus. Let $\mathcal{N}$ be set of *names* (ranged over by $a, b, \ldots n, m$), $\mathcal{V}$ be set of *variables* (ranged over by $x, y, z, \ldots$) and $\mathcal{V}_R$ be a set of recursion variables (ranged over by $X, Y, Z, \ldots$). The syntax of (typed) SA processes is shown in Table 1. Standard syntactical conventions are used: trailing zeros are omitted, and parallel composition has the least syntactic precedence. Also, we may omit the type annotations in restrictions and abstractions whenever not important. The rules for the reduction relation of SA are shown in Table 2. Reductions are labelled with σ ranging over $\{\lambda, \text{com}\}$ in order to better formulate subject reduction (Theorem 1). Rule $\texttt{Struct}$ uses the auxiliary relation $\equiv$ of structural congruence to bring the participants of a potential interaction into contiguous positions; the definition of $\equiv$ is standard (we refer the reader to [11]).

3   Evolving Types for Full SA

We adapt the evolving types to the full language by integrating the approach of [10] and the typing of communication in [12]. To retain the expressive power of

Table 1. Syntax of Expressions and Processes.

$M, N ::=$		(Expressions)	$P, Q ::=$		(Processes)
	$\text{in } M$	(enter)		0	(inactivity)
	$\text{out } M$	(exit)		$(\nu a : A)\,P$	(typed restriction)
	$\text{open } M$	(open)		$P \mid Q$	(parallel composition)
	$\overline{\text{in}}\, M$	(allow enter)		$\text{rec } X.\,P$	(replication)
	$\overline{\text{out}}\, M$	(allow exit)		$a[\,P\,]$	(ambient)
	$\overline{\text{open}}\, M$	(allow open)		$M.\,P$	(prefix)
	ϵ	(empty path)		$\langle M \rangle$	(message)
	$M.\,N$	(path)		$(x : W)P$	(typed abstraction)
	x	(variable)		X	(recursion variable)
	a	(name)			

Table 2. Reduction Rules for SA.

In : $a[\,\text{in}\, b.\, P_1 \mid P_2\,] \mid b[\,\overline{\text{in}}\, b.\, Q_1 \mid Q_2\,] \longrightarrow_\lambda b[\,a[\,P_1 \mid P_2\,] \mid Q_1 \mid Q_2\,]$

Out : $b[\,a[\,\text{out}\, b.\, P_1 \mid P_2\,] \mid \overline{\text{out}}\, b.\, Q_1 \mid Q_2\,] \longrightarrow_\lambda a[\,P_1 \mid P_2\,] \mid b[\,Q_1 \mid Q_2\,]$

Open : $\text{open}\, a.\, P \mid a[\,\overline{\text{open}}\, a.\, Q_1 \mid Q_2\,] \longrightarrow_\lambda P \mid Q_1 \mid Q_2$

Com : $\langle M \rangle \mid (x : W)P \longrightarrow_{\text{com}} P\{M/x\}$

Rec : $\text{rec } X.\, P \longrightarrow_\lambda P\{\text{rec } X.\, P/X\}$ Res : $\dfrac{P \longrightarrow_\sigma P'}{(\nu n : A)\, P \longrightarrow_\sigma (\nu n : A)\, P'}$

Par : $\dfrac{P \longrightarrow_\sigma P'}{P \mid Q \longrightarrow_\sigma P' \mid Q}$ Amb : $\dfrac{P \longrightarrow_\sigma P'}{a[\,P\,] \longrightarrow_\lambda a[\,P'\,]}$

Struct : $\dfrac{P \equiv P' \quad P' \longrightarrow_\sigma P'' \quad P'' \equiv P'''}{P \longrightarrow_\sigma P'''}$

both [10] and [12], we introduce two main modifications: (i) we slightly modify the rule of parallel composition of [10]; (ii) we extend the syntax of the exchange types of [12] by letting messages carry the mobility annotation as well as the thread annotation.

The type grammar is shown in Table 3. The thread annotation can take value 0 (no thread) or 1 (thread); the mobility annotation can take value $\ominus$ (immobile) or $\uparrow$ (mobile). The intuitive meaning of the ambient types is the following:

Table 3. Type Grammar.

$$
\begin{array}{ll}
I, J := 0 \mid 1 & \textbf{(Thread Annotations)} \\
X, Y := \uparrow \mid \ominus & \textbf{(Mobility Annotations)} \\
T := {}^{I,X}W \mid \mathsf{Shh} & \textbf{(Types of Messages)} \\
E, F := T^{I,X} & \textbf{(Pre-types)} \\
S := E \mid E; J, Y & \textbf{(Simple and Evolving Pre-types)} \\
A := \mathsf{Amb}\,[S] & \textbf{(Types of Ambients)} \\
W := A \mid C & \textbf{(Types of Expressions)} \\
Z := \mathsf{Proc}\,[S] \mid \top & \textbf{(Types of Processes)} \\
C, D := \diamond \mid Z.\,C \mid (C \mid Z) & \textbf{(Capability Contexts)}
\end{array}
$$

- $\mathsf{Amb}\,[T^{I,X}]$ is the type of a *simple* (S) ambient, that cannot be opened, and inside which messages of type T can be exchanged; it has thread I and mobility X;
- $\mathsf{Amb}\,[T^{I,X}; J, Y]$ is the type of an *evolving* (E) ambient inside which messages of type T can be exchanged; it has thread I and mobility X before being opened; when opened, it unleashes a process with thread J, mobility Y, and exchanges of type T. We call $T^{I,X}$ its *current* pre-type and $T^{J,Y}$ its *future* pre-type.

Similarly, $\mathsf{Proc}\,[T^{I,X}]$ and $\mathsf{Proc}\,[T^{I,X}; J, Y]$ are the types of the processes local to a simple and evolving ambient respectively. The type of messages T can be either Shh or ${}^{I,X}W$: Shh means that there is no communication; ${}^{I,X}W$ means that data of type W are exchanged, and that I and X are the thread and mobility annotations carried by messages. The exchanged data can be either ambients or capabilities, which are represented as in [10,1] by contexts (with hole $\diamond$). The use of contexts in place of standard capability types and of the special process type $\top$, representing an error, simplifies the typing rules.

Table 4. Sub-typing.

$$
\begin{array}{ll}
\ominus \sqsubseteq \uparrow & \\
0 \sqsubseteq 1 \sqsubseteq \omega & \\
\mathsf{Shh} \sqsubseteq {}^{I,X}W & \\
T_1^{I_1, X_1} \sqsubseteq T_2^{I_2, X_2} & \text{if } I_1 \sqsubseteq I_2, X_1 \sqsubseteq X_2, T_1 \sqsubseteq T_2 \\
E_1; J_1, Y_1 \sqsubseteq E_2; J_2, Y_2 & \text{if } E_1 \sqsubseteq E_2, J_1 \sqsubseteq J_2, Y_1 \sqsubseteq Y_2 \\
\mathsf{Proc}\,[S_1] \sqsubseteq \mathsf{Proc}\,[S_2] & \text{if } S_1 \sqsubseteq S_2
\end{array}
$$

The typing rules use sub-typing and two auxiliary operators, which realize the sequential and parallel composition of process types. They are needed to derive a process type corresponding to $C[Z]$, when the hole of a context C is filled by a process type Z (specifically in the typing rules for prefixing and parallel composition of Table 6).

The relations of sub-typing, over any syntactical category, are defined as the minimal reflexive and transitive relations which satisfy the rules of Table 4. Table 5 shows the operators of parallel and sequential composition. For reasons of space, we omit the symmetric cases of | and we assume that the cases, which are not listed, are $\top$. We also use $x \sqcup y$ for the least upper bound (l.u.b.) of x and y, and we let $x \sqcup y = \top$ if the least upper bound does not exist. We assume that the effect of $\top$ is properly propagated to pre-types and process types.

Both the parallel and the sequential composition of two process types are obtained by the related composition of their pre-types.

Parallel Composition. Two S pre-types are combined by taking the l.u.b. of the message types and of the mobility annotations, and a thread annotation which is: ST only if *at most* one is ST; in particular it is no thread only if both are no thread. A E pre-type and a S pre-type are combined by composing the S pre-type with the current pre-type. In [10] a different rule is used: both the current and the future pre-type are updated reflecting the idea that any process executable in parallel with a capability $\overline{\text{open}}$ may be executed either *before* or *after* the opening. Our rule is based on the following property of ST ambients: all processes executable in parallel with a capability $\overline{\text{open}}$ have necessarily thread 0 (and are thus also immobile) so that they cannot affect the future pre-type[3]. The parallel composition of two E pre-types is not permitted as there is no control on which $\overline{\text{open}}$ may be executed first (as in [10]).

Sequential Composition. Two S pre-types are combined by taking the l.u.b. of both the types of messages, and the thread and mobility annotations. The sequential composition of a S and a E pre-type depends on which type occurs first. If the S pre-type precedes the E pre-type, it means that the simple process is executed *before* opening. Hence, we modify only the current pre-type. If the E pre-type precedes the S pre-type, it means that the simple process is executed *after* opening. We therefore require the simple pre-type to be consistent with the future pre-type.

The typing rules are shown in Table 6. A *type environment* is a finite set of assignments of types to names, variables and recursion variables.

The typing rules for expressions are similar to those in [10], and assign a proper context to any capability. These rules should be read having in mind that the hole in the context will be filled by the continuation of the capability (see rule (pref)). For capabilities the contexts are of the form $Z.C$, where Z is a process type, expressing the contribution of the capability, and C is a context, that permits to take into account the continuation. Rules (inout) and (co-inout) are analogous with the only difference that the former is mobile and the latter

---

[3] It is worth mentioning that for the calculus without communication the two rules are equivalent; our rule is however more precise in presence of abstractions and messages (see [11] for an example).

Table 5. Parallel and sequential composition of types.

$0 \mid 0 = 0, 0 \mid 1 = 1, 1 \mid 0 = 1$

$T_1^{I_1,X_1} \mid T_2^{I_2,X_2} = (T_1 \sqcup T_2)^{I_1 \mid I_2, X_1 \sqcup X_2}$

$T_1^{I_1,X_1} . T_2^{I_2,X_2} = T_1^{I_1,X_1} \sqcup T_2^{I_2,X_2}$

$E_1 \mid (E_2; J, Y) = (E_1 \mid E_2); J, Y$

$E_1 . (E_2; J, Y) = (E_1 . E_2); J, Y$

$$(T_1^{I_1,X_1}; J, Y) . T_2^{I_2,X_2} = \begin{cases} T_1^{I_1,X_1}; I_2, X_2 & \text{if } T_2^{I_2,X_2} \sqsubseteq T_1^{J,Y} \\ \top & \text{otherwise} \end{cases}$$

$\mathsf{Proc}\,[S_1] . \mathsf{Proc}\,[S_2] = \mathsf{Proc}\,[S_1 . S_2]$

$\mathsf{Proc}\,[S_1] \mid \mathsf{Proc}\,[S_2] = \mathsf{Proc}\,[S_1 \mid S_2]$

---

is immobile. In rule (open) the context shows that the process type of the continuation ends up in parallel with the future type of the opened ambient. In rule (co-open) the context shows that the capability $\overline{\mathsf{open}}\, M$ has an evolving type, dictated by the type of the evolving ambient M where it can be exercised. Rule (path) realizes context substitution.

The typing rules for processes extend those of [10] to communication. Rule (amb) says that any type can be assigned to an ambient, provided that its local process agrees with its simple or evolving pre-type. We use $S_1 \rhd S_2$ for $S_1 = S_2$. This relation is exploited to compact similar rules together and is extended in Section 4. Rule (pref) says that the context hole has to be filled with the type of the continuation. Rule (par) shows that the two types have to be combined by means of $\mid$.

The rules for communication are an adaptation of those of [12]. Rules (abs) and (e-abs) say that an abstraction, simple or evolving, has no thread and is immobile; the body of the abstraction dictates the thread and mobility annotations carried by messages. Rule (msg) shows that messages acquire the thread and mobility annotations from the message type. These typing rules guarantee that in a ST ambient, when messages carry the thread, at any moment, at most one capability or message is ready to fire. Therefore, there can be non-determinism on reception of messages but not on emission. This typing discipline for communication is too weak, when considering evolving communication, as they cannot distinguish the processes (2) and (3), (4) and (5) discussed the Introduction.

The process (1) discussed in the Introduction can instead be typed. Assume that $\Gamma \vdash a : \mathsf{Amb}\,[\mathsf{Shh}^{1,\uparrow}; 1, \ominus]$, $\Gamma \vdash b : \mathsf{Amb}\,[\mathsf{Shh}^{1,\ominus}]$, and $\Gamma \vdash Q : \mathsf{Proc}\,[\mathsf{Shh}^{0,\ominus}]$. For any type $Z \neq \top$ we have $\Gamma \vdash a[\,\mathsf{in}\, b.\, \overline{\mathsf{open}}\, a.\, \overline{\mathsf{out}}\, b\,] \mid b[\,\overline{\mathsf{in}}\, b.\, \mathsf{open}\, a.\, Q\,] : Z$.

Table 6. Typing Rules.

$$\frac{\Gamma \vdash N : A \qquad M \in \{\overline{\mathtt{in}}\, N, \overline{\mathtt{out}}\, N\}}{\Gamma \vdash M : \mathtt{Proc}\,[\mathtt{Shh}^{1,\ominus}].\diamond} \quad \text{co-inout}$$

$$\frac{\Gamma \vdash M : \mathtt{Amb}\,[T^{I,X}; J, Y]}{\Gamma \vdash \mathtt{open}\, M : \mathtt{Proc}\,[\mathtt{Shh}^{1,\ominus}].\,(\diamond \mid \mathtt{Proc}\,[T^{J,Y}])} \quad \text{open}$$

$$\frac{}{\Gamma \vdash \epsilon : \diamond} \; \epsilon \qquad \frac{\Gamma \vdash N : A \qquad M \in \{\mathtt{in}\, N, \mathtt{out}\, N\}}{\Gamma \vdash M : \mathtt{Proc}\,[\mathtt{Shh}^{1,\uparrow}].\diamond} \quad \text{inout}$$

$$\frac{\Gamma \vdash M : \mathtt{Amb}\,[T^{I,X}; J, Y]}{\Gamma \vdash \overline{\mathtt{open}}\, M : \mathtt{Proc}\,[T^{1,\ominus}; J, Y].\diamond} \quad \text{co-open} \qquad \frac{\Gamma \vdash M : C_1 \qquad \Gamma \vdash N : C_2}{\Gamma \vdash M.N : C_1\,[C_2]} \quad \text{path}$$

$$\frac{\Gamma \vdash M : \mathtt{Amb}\,[S_1] \qquad \Gamma \vdash P : \mathtt{Proc}\,[S_2] \qquad S_1 \rhd S_2}{\Gamma \vdash M[P] : Z} \quad \text{amb}$$

$$\frac{\Gamma, x : W \vdash P : \mathtt{Proc}\,[(^{I,X}W)^{I,X}]}{\Gamma \vdash (x : W)P : \mathtt{Proc}\,[(^{I,X}W)^{0,\ominus}]} \quad \text{abs}$$

$$\frac{\Gamma, x : W \vdash P : \mathtt{Proc}\,[(^{I,X}W)^{I,X}; J, Y]}{\Gamma \vdash (x : W)P : \mathtt{Proc}\,[(^{I,X}W)^{0,\ominus}; J, Y]} \quad \text{e-abs}$$

$$\frac{\Gamma \vdash M : C \qquad \Gamma \vdash P : Z}{\Gamma \vdash M.P : C[Z]} \quad \text{pref} \qquad \frac{\Gamma \vdash P_1 : Z_1 \qquad \Gamma \vdash P_2 : Z_2}{\Gamma \vdash P_1 \mid P_2 : Z_1 \mid Z_2} \quad \text{par}$$

$$\frac{\Gamma \vdash P : Z_1 \qquad Z_1 \sqsubseteq Z_2}{\Gamma \vdash P : Z_2} \quad \text{sub} \qquad \frac{\Gamma \vdash M : W}{\Gamma \vdash \langle M \rangle : \mathtt{Proc}\,[(^{I,X}W)^{I,X}]} \quad \text{msg}$$

$$\frac{}{\Gamma \vdash \mathbf{0} : Z} \; \text{nil} \qquad \frac{\Gamma, X : Z \vdash P : Z}{\Gamma \vdash \mathtt{rec}\, X.P : Z} \quad \text{rec}$$

$$\frac{\Gamma, n : A \vdash P : Z}{\Gamma \vdash (\nu n : A)P : Z} \quad \text{res} \qquad \frac{\Gamma(X) = Z}{\Gamma \vdash X : Z} \quad \text{varProc}$$

4 Evolving Communication Types

To model evolving communication we add the symbols and productions of Table 7 to the type grammar of Table 3. We introduce a new thread annotation, called $\star$, which is carried by messages similarly to the thread of Section 3. We also introduce two types of messages: (i) $\star$-messages, where $^{\star,X}W$ shows that data of type W are exchanged, and that messages carry the thread annotation

Table 7. Type Grammar for EC types

$$
\begin{aligned}
{}^{\circ}T \quad &:= \,^{\star,X}W \\
{}^{\star}T \quad &:= \,^{\star,X}W \mid \text{Shh} && (\star - \textbf{Messages}) \\
{}^{\circ}L \quad &:= {}^{\circ}T \mid^{\circ} L_1 \cdot^{\circ} L_2 \mid \text{rec} \,^{\circ}L && (\textbf{List of Messages}) \\
L \quad &:= [^{\circ}L] \mid [\text{Shh}] && (\textbf{EC Messages}) \\
{}^{\circ}E, {}^{\circ}F \quad &:= \,^{\star}T^{I,X} \mid L^{I,X} && (\star \textbf{ and EC Pre-types}) \\
E, F \quad &:= {}^{\circ}E \\
S \quad &:= {}^{\circ}E; F && (\textbf{EEC Pre-types})
\end{aligned}
$$

$\star$ and mobility annotation X; (ii) EC messages, where $[^{\circ}L]$ models evolving communication as a (possibly recursive) list of message types of the form $^{\star,X}W$. These types permit to better characterize who can pass and who can receive the thread $\star$ carried by messages. In particular, $^{\star,X}W$ is the type of a process which can pass the thread; while $[^{\circ}L]$ is the type of a process which can receive the thread. They are used precisely to impose stronger conditions on the way $\star$ can be passed, when communication evolve.

In addition, we extend the productions of pre-types S by introducing $^{\circ}E$ and $^{\circ}E; F$. The resulting new ambient types have the following intuitive meaning. $\text{Amb}\,[^{\circ}E; F]$ is the type of an evolving ambient with evolving communication, where both the thread and mobility annotations and the type of communication can change after opening; $^{\circ}E$ and F are its current and future pre-type. $\text{Amb}\,[^{\circ}E]$ is the type of a S ambient with evolving communication, whose local processes behave according to $^{\circ}E$. Similarly for the related process types.

We introduce a relation of equivalence over lists of messages $^{\circ}L$, which re-arranges lists using the associative property and realizing the fold/unfold of recursion. We define $\cong$ as the minimal transitive, reflexive and symmetric relation which satisfies the rules of Table 8. To compact similar rules together we also use

$$
\text{head}(^{\circ}L) = \begin{cases} {}^{\circ}T & \text{if } ^{\circ}L =^{\circ} T \cdot^{\circ} L_1 \text{ or } ^{\circ}L =^{\circ} T \\ \text{undefined} & \text{otherwise} \end{cases}
$$

All the notions of Section 3 (sub-typing, least upper bound, composition of types and typing rules) are valid also for the new values. We present the additional cases for sub-typing and for the operators of parallel and sequential composition in Tables 8 and 9. The rules are similar to those of Table 5. As before, the cases which are not listed correspond to $\top$ and the symmetric cases of $|$ are omitted. The main difference is due to the parallel composition of the new message types $\star$-Messages and EC messages. In particular, we permit both the sequential and parallel composition of a EC message type L only with a $\star$-message type $^{\star}T$, provided that $^{\star}T$ agrees with the first type of the list L. We forbid the parallel composition of two evolving message types L_1 and L_2, because there is no control on when they evolve. In the sequential composition

Table 8. Additional relations over EC types

$$(^\circ T \cdot^\circ L_1) \cdot^\circ L_2 \cong^\circ T \cdot (^\circ L_1 \cdot^\circ L_2)$$
$$\text{rec } ^\circ L \cong^\circ L \cdot (\text{rec } ^\circ L)$$

$^\circ L_1 \cdot^\circ L_2 \cong^\circ L_3 \cdot^\circ L_2$	if $^\circ L_1 \cong^\circ L_3$
$^\circ L_1 \cdot^\circ L_2 \cong^\circ L_1 \cdot^\circ L_3$	if $^\circ L_2 \cong^\circ L_3$
$\text{rec } ^\circ L_1 \cong \text{rec } ^\circ L_2$	if $^\circ L_1 \cong^\circ L_2$

$\text{Shh} \sqsubseteq^{\star,X} W$	
$\text{Shh} \sqsubseteq [\text{Shh}]$	
$[\text{Shh}] \sqsubseteq [L]$	
$^\circ L_1 \sqsubseteq^\circ L_1 \cdot^\circ L_2$	
$^\circ L_1 \sqsubseteq^\circ L_2$	if $^\circ L_1 \cong^\circ L_2$
$[^\circ L_1] \sqsubseteq [^\circ L_2]$	if $^\circ L_1 \sqsubseteq^\circ L_2$
$L_1^{I_1,X_1} \sqsubseteq L_2^{I_2,X_2}$	if $L_1 \sqsubseteq L_2, I_1 \sqsubseteq I_2, X_1 \sqsubseteq X_2$
$^\star T_1{}^{I_1,X_1} \sqsubseteq {}^\star T_2{}^{I_2,X_2}$	if $^\star T_1 \sqsubseteq^\star T_2, I_1 \sqsubseteq I_2, X_1 \sqsubseteq X_2$
$^\circ E_1; F_1 \sqsubseteq^\circ E_2; F_2$	if $^\circ E_1 \sqsubseteq^\circ E_2, F_1 \sqsubseteq F_2.$

$^\circ T \cdot^\circ L \rhd^\circ L$	
$^\circ L_1 \rhd^\circ L_2'$	if $^\circ L_1 \cong^\circ L_2, ^\circ L_2 \rhd^\circ L_2'$
$[^\circ L_1]^{I,X} \rhd [^\circ L_2]^{I,X}$	if $^\circ L_1 \rhd^\circ L_2$
$^\circ E_1; F \rhd^\circ E_2; F$	if $^\circ E_1 \rhd^\circ E_2$

we rule out all the other cases, as they cannot arise in the contexts modeling expressions[4].

The additional typing rules for the EC types are shown in Table 10. They include new rules only for the capabilities of opening, for messages and abstractions. For the other cases the rules of Table 6 apply. To adapt also the applicability of rule (amb) we need however to extend the relation $\rhd$. This is defined over pre-types S as the minimal reflexive and transitive relation which satisfies the rules of Table 8. The relation $\rhd$ reflects the idea that, if the type of exchanges of the local process is EC, then it may vary as the computation proceeds (as specified by Theorem 1).

Rules (ec-open) and (ec-co-open) are similar to the corresponding rules (open) and (co-open) for E ambients. Rule (ec-co-open) shows that the type of communication can vary *after* $\overline{\text{open}}\, M$, provided that the current type of messages is EC (as dictated by [Shh]). The typing rules for communication are designed to let the type of communication vary *after* a message is received.

1. Rule (ec-msg) says that, when messages carry the thread $\star$, a message can be typed only as a S process with a $\star$-message type; it has the thread and the mobility annotation carried by messages.

---

[4] There is no typing rule for expressions (in both Tables 6 and 10) where the context is $Z.C$ with $Z = \text{Proc}\,[L^{I,X}]$.

Table 9. Sequential and parallel composition of EC types

$$\star T_1{}^{I_1,X_1} \mid \star T_2{}^{I_2,X_2} = (\star T_1 \sqcup \star T_2)^{I_1|I_2,X_1\sqcup X_2}$$

$$\star T^{I_1,X_1} \mid L^{I_2,X_2} = \begin{cases} L^{I_1|I_2,X_1\sqcup X_2} & \text{if } \star T \sqsubseteq \mathbf{head}(°L), L = [°L] \\ L^{I_1|I_2,X_1\sqcup X_2} & \text{if } \star T = \mathbf{Shh}, L = [\mathbf{Shh}] \\ \top & \text{otherwise} \end{cases}$$

$$\star T_1{}^{I_1,X_1} . \star T_2{}^{I_2,X_2} = \star T_1{}^{I_1,X_1} \sqcup \star T_2{}^{I_2,X_2}$$

$$\star T^{I_1,X_1} . L^{I_2,X_2} = \begin{cases} L^{I_1\sqcup I_2,X_1\sqcup X_2} & \text{if } \star T \sqsubseteq \mathbf{head}(°L), L = [°L] \\ L^{I_1\sqcup I_2,X_1\sqcup X_2} & \text{if } \star T = \mathbf{Shh}, L = [\mathbf{Shh}] \\ \top & \text{otherwise} \end{cases}$$

$$°E_1 \mid (°E_2; F) = (°E_1 \mid° E_2); F$$
$$°E_1. (°E_2; F) = (°E_1.° E_2); F$$
$$(°E_1; F). E = \begin{cases} °E_1; E & \text{if } E \sqsubseteq F \\ \top & \text{otherwise} \end{cases}$$

2. Rules (es-abs1) and (es-abs2) say that an abstraction can be typed as a S process only with a EC message type, which is obtained by eventually appending the type of the input to the list; it has no thread and is immobile. Rules (ec-abs1) and (ec-abs2) are defined similarly for EC types.

We now discuss the typing of processes (2) and (3) shown in the Introduction. We illustrate in particular how the complementary types of communication ($\star$-Messages and EC Messages) impose stronger conditions on the way the thread $\star$ can be passed, which guarantee safe evolving communication.

Assume that $\Gamma \vdash M_1 : W_1$, $\Gamma, x : W_1 \vdash M_2 : W_2$, $\Gamma, x : W_1, y : W_2 \vdash Q : \mathtt{Proc}\,[°E]$, $\Gamma \vdash a : \mathtt{Amb}\,[L^{1,\ominus}]$, where $L = [°T_1 \cdot° T_2]$, $°E = [°T_2]^{1,\ominus}$ and $°T_i =^{\star,\ominus} W_i$ for $i \in \{1,2\}$ with $W_1 \neq W_2$. For any type $Z \neq \top$ we have $\Gamma \vdash a[\langle M_1 \rangle \mid (x : W_1)(\langle M_2 \rangle \mid (y : W_2)Q)] : Z$. The most important observation is that we can give the following type to the local process of a,

$$\mathtt{Proc}\,[°T_1{}^{1,\ominus}] \mid \mathtt{Proc}\,[[°T_1 \cdot° T_2]^{0,\ominus}] = \mathtt{Proc}\,[[°T_1 \cdot° T_2]^{1,\ominus}]$$

where $\mathtt{Proc}\,[°T_1{}^{1,\ominus}]$ is the type of the message $\langle M_1 \rangle$ and $\mathtt{Proc}\,[[°T_1 \cdot° T_2]^{0,\ominus}]$ is the type of the abstraction $(x : W_1)(\langle M_2 \rangle \mid (y : W_2)Q)$. This shows that the thread over a moves from message $\langle M_1 \rangle$ to the continuation of the abstraction $(x : W_1)(\langle M_2 \rangle \mid (y : W_2)Q)$.

By contrast the process (5) $a[\langle M_1 \rangle \mid (z : W_1)P \mid (x : W_1)(\langle M_2 \rangle \mid (y : W_2)Q)]$ cannot be typed when $W_1 \neq W_2$. There is no type for $(z : W_1)P$ which can be combined in parallel with $\mathtt{Proc}\,[L^{1,\ominus}]$ because: (i) abstractions can be given *only* EC message types (see the rules of Table 10); two EC message types cannot be combined in parallel (see Table 9). In other words $\star$ can be passed to *at most* one abstraction.

Table 10. Additional Typing Rules for EC types.

$$\frac{\Gamma \vdash M \,:\, \mathtt{Amb}\,[^{\circ}E; F]}{\Gamma \vdash \overline{\mathtt{open}}\, M \,:\, \mathtt{Proc}\,[[\mathtt{Shh}]^{1,\ominus}; F].\,\diamond} \quad \text{ec-co-open}$$

$$\frac{\Gamma \vdash M \,:\, \mathtt{Amb}\,[^{\circ}E; F]}{\Gamma \vdash \mathtt{open}\, M \,:\, \mathtt{Proc}\,[\mathtt{Shh}^{1,\ominus}]\,.\,(\diamond \mid \mathtt{Proc}\,[F])} \quad \text{ec-open}$$

$$\frac{\Gamma, x : W_1 \vdash P \,:\, \mathtt{Proc}\,[[^{\circ}L]^{1,X}; F] \qquad \mathrm{head}(^{\circ}L) \neq^{\star,X} W_1}{\Gamma \vdash (x : W_1)P \,:\, \mathtt{Proc}\,[[(\star,^{X}W_1) \cdot^{\circ} L]^{0,\ominus}; F]} \quad \text{ec-abs1}$$

$$\frac{\Gamma, x : W_1 \vdash P \,:\, \mathtt{Proc}\,[[^{\circ}L]^{1,X}] \qquad \mathrm{head}(^{\circ}L) \neq^{\star,X} W_1}{\Gamma \vdash (x : W_1)P \,:\, \mathtt{Proc}\,[[(\star,^{X}W_1) \cdot^{\circ} L]^{0,\ominus}]} \quad \text{es-abs1}$$

$$\frac{\Gamma, x : W_1 \vdash P \,:\, \mathtt{Proc}\,[[^{\circ}L]^{1,X}; F] \qquad \mathrm{head}(^{\circ}L) =^{\star,X} W_1}{\Gamma \vdash (x : W_1)P \,:\, \mathtt{Proc}\,[[^{\circ}L]^{0,\ominus}; F]} \quad \text{ec-abs2}$$

$$\frac{\Gamma, x : W_1 \vdash P \,:\, \mathtt{Proc}\,[[^{\circ}L]^{1,X}] \qquad \mathrm{head}(^{\circ}L) =^{\star,X} W_1}{\Gamma \vdash (x : W_1)P \,:\, \mathtt{Proc}\,[[^{\circ}L]^{0,\ominus}]} \quad \text{es-abs2}$$

$$\frac{\Gamma \vdash M \,:\, W}{\Gamma \vdash \langle M \rangle \,:\, \mathtt{Proc}\,[(\star,^{X}W)^{1,X}]} \quad \text{ec-msg}$$

Assume that $\Gamma \vdash M_1 : W_1$, $\Gamma, x : W_1 \vdash M_2 : W_2$, $\Gamma \vdash c : \mathtt{Amb}\,[E]$, and $\Gamma, y : W_2 \vdash Q : \mathtt{Proc}\,[E]$, $\Gamma \vdash a : \mathtt{Amb}\,[[^{\circ}T]^{1,\uparrow}; E]$, where $^{\circ}T =^{\star,\ominus} W_1$, and $E = T^{I,X}$, with $I \sqsubseteq 1$ and $T =^{I,X} W_2$. For any type $Z \neq \top$ we have (also when $W_1 \neq W_2$) $\Gamma \vdash a[\,\mathtt{in}\,c.\,\langle M_1 \rangle \mid (x : W_1)\overline{\mathtt{open}}\,a.\,\langle M_2 \rangle\,] \mid c[\,\overline{\mathtt{in}}\,c.\,\overline{\mathtt{open}}\,a.\,(y : W_2)Q\,] : Z$.

By contrast, the process (4)

$$a[\,(z : W_1)P \mid \mathtt{in}\,c.\,\overline{\mathtt{open}}\,a.\,\langle M_2 \rangle\,] \mid c[\,\overline{\mathtt{in}}\,c.\,\mathtt{open}\,a.\,(y : W_2)Q\,]$$

cannot be typed when $W_1 \neq W_2$. Process $\mathtt{in}\,c.\,\overline{\mathtt{open}}\,a.\,\langle M_2 \rangle$ has a EC process type $\mathtt{Proc}\,[[\mathtt{Shh}]^{1,\uparrow}; E]$ showing that it has the thread and that no other parallel process can receive the thread carried by messages. As above, it is not possible to type the abstraction $(z : W_1)P$.

5 Properties of the Type System

We present the fundamental properties of types[5]. Theorem 1 states subject reduction. Notice that, when the type of communication is EC and a reduction com is performed, the type can evolve as modelled by the relation $\triangleright$.

Theorem 1 (Subject Reduction). *Let $\Gamma \vdash P : \mathsf{Proc}\,[S]$.*

1. *Suppose that $S = T^{I,X}$ or $S = T^{I,X}; Y, J$. If $P \longrightarrow_\sigma P'$ then also $\Gamma \vdash P' : \mathsf{Proc}\,[S]$.*
2. *Suppose that $S =^\circ E$ or $S =^\circ E; J, Y$ or $S =^\circ E; F$. If $P \longrightarrow_\sigma P'$ with $\sigma \neq \mathsf{com}$, then also $\Gamma \vdash P' : \mathsf{Proc}\,[S]$. If $P \longrightarrow_{\mathsf{com}} P'$, then $\Gamma \vdash P' : \mathsf{Proc}\,[S']$ where $S \triangleright S'$.*

The types satisfy the same properties of the ST and immobility types in [12]. Theorem 2 shows that: (i) in a ST ambient, at any time, there is at most one capability ready to fire; (ii) in an immobile ambient, at any time, there is no capability of the form $\mathsf{in}\,a$ or $\mathsf{out}\,a$ ready to fire. Property (i) guarantees that a single-threaded ambient is willing to engage, at any time, in at most one interaction with internal or external ambients. This implies the absence of all grave interferences which is very useful, for instance for proving the correctness of programs algebraically [12].

We say that an occurrence of an expression M in a process is *unguarded* if it does appear under a prefix, an abstraction or an ambient; likewise for unguarded messages and abstractions. Also we use $\mathcal{T}$ to range over types of messages.

Theorem 2 (Single-Threaded and Immobile Ambients). *Suppose that $\Gamma \vdash P : \mathsf{Proc}\,[S]$ where $S = \mathcal{T}^{I,X}$, $S = \mathcal{T}^{I,X}; J, Y$ or $S = \mathcal{T}^{I,X}; F$. If $I = 1$ then P has at least one unguarded capability. Also, if $X = \ominus$ then P has no unguarded capabilities of the form $\mathsf{in}\,a$ and $\mathsf{out}\,a$.*

6 Conclusions

The types of Section 3 extend the approach of [10] to full SA following the lines of [12] for communication. The complete extension including also basic (multi-threaded) ambients can be found in [11]. The idea of studying types for evolving communication is not new [1,2]. The type system of [1,2] assigns to processes behaviours representing explicitly the relationship (sequential or parallel) between inputs and outputs. This approach is more general and powerful than ours. The price to pay is that it is more complex: type-checking for instance is exponential. In fact, the sub-typing relation is defined relative to the underlying trace semantics and requires to consider for the parallel composition of behaviours all traces which can be formed by arbitrary interleavings. Our types follow a different approach; they are defined as a natural extension of the ST types and capture the evolution both of thread and mobility rights and of communication without

---

[5] The proofs can be found in [11].

using any causality information. As a consequence, type-checking is polynomial. The intuition is that two EC communication types cannot be combined in parallel (see Table 9) so that there is no need to merge two EC communication types (lists of messages). Moreover, the SA processes corresponding to the MA examples of orderly-communication shown in [2] can be typed with our types. They include the processes (2) and (3) discussed in the Introduction and a protocol for routing packets that is similar. Therefore, we believe that our types provide a good compromise between accuracy and complexity.

Acknowledgments. This work has been partially supported by the project *Mefisto*.

References

1. Torben Amtoft and Assaf J. Kfoury and Santiago M. Pericas-Geertsen. What are Polymorphically-Typed Ambients? In *Proc. ESOP'01*, volume 2028 of *Lecture Notes in Computer Science*, pages 206–220. Springer Verlag, 2001.
2. Torben Amtoft and Assaf J. Kfoury and Santiago M. Pericas-Geertsen. Orderly Communication in the Ambient Calculus. To appear in *Computer Languages*.
3. M. Bugliesi and G. Castagna. Secure safe ambients. In *Proc. POPL '01*, pages 222-235. ACM Press, 2001.
4. L. Cardelli, G. Ghelli, and A.D. Gordon. Mobility types for mobile ambients. In *Proc. ICALP'99*, volume 1644 of *Lecture Notes in Computer Science*, pages 230–239. Springer Verlag, 1999.
5. L. Cardelli and A.D. Gordon. Mobile ambients. In *Proc. FoSSaCS '98*, volume 1378 of *Lecture Notes in Computer Science*, pages 140–155. Springer Verlag, 1998.
6. L. Cardelli and A.D. Gordon. Types for mobile ambients. In *Proc. POPL'99*, pages 79–92. ACM Press, 1999.
7. L. Cardelli, G. Ghelli, and A.D. Gordon. Types for ambient calculus. To apper in *Information and Computation*.
8. P. Degano, F. Levi and C. Bodei. Safe Ambients: Control Flow Analysis and Security. In *Proc. ASIAN '00*, volume 1961 of *Lecture Notes in Computer Science*, pages 199–214. Springer Verlag, 2000.
9. M. Dezani-Ciancaglini and I. Salvo. Security Types for Mobile Safe Ambients. In *Proc. ASIAN '00*, volume 1961 of *Lecture Notes in Computer Science*, pages 215–236. Springer Verlag, 2000.
10. X. Guan, Y. Yang, and J. You. Typing Evolving Ambients. *Information Processing Letters*, 80(5), 265-270, 2001.
11. F. Levi. Types for Evolving Communication in Safe Ambients (Draft). Available at http://www.di.unipi.it/~levifran/papers.html.
12. F. Levi and D. Sangiorgi. Controlling Interference in Ambients. In *Proc. POPL '00*, pages 352–364. ACM Press, 2000.
13. M. Merro and M. Hennessy. Bisimulation congruences in Safe Ambients. In *Proc. POPL '02*. ACM Press, 2002.
14. R. Milner, J. Parrow, and D. Walker. A calculus of mobile processes, (Parts I and II). *Information and Computation*, 100:1–77, 1992.
15. P. Zimmer Subtyping and typing algorithms for mobile ambients. In *Proc. FOSSACS '00*, volume 1784 of *Lecture Notes in Computer Science*, pages 375–390. Springer Verlag, 2000.

A Logical Encoding of the π-Calculus: Model Checking Mobile Processes Using Tabled Resolution*

Ping Yang, C.R. Ramakrishnan, and Scott A. Smolka

Department of Computer Science
State University of New York at Stony Brook
Stony Brook, NY, 11794-4400, USA
{pyang,cram,sas}@cs.sunysb.edu

Abstract. We present MMC, a model checker for mobile systems specified in the style of the π-calculus. MMC's development builds on our experience gained in developing XMC, a model checker for an extension of Milner's value-passing calculus implemented using the XSB tabled logic-programming system. MMC, however, is not simply an extension of XMC; rather it is virtually a complete re-implementation that addresses the salient issues that arise in the π-calculus, including scope extrusion and intrusion, and dynamic generation of new names to avoid name capture. We show that tabled logic programming is especially suitable as an efficient implementation platform for model checking π-calculus specifications, and can be used to obtain an exact encoding of the π-calculus's transitional semantics. Moreover, MMC is easily extended to handle process expressions in the spi-calculus. Our experimental data shows that MMC outperforms other known tools for model checking the π-calculus.

1   Introduction

In [26], we showed that logic programming with tabulation can be used to construct an efficient model checker for concurrent systems. In particular, we presented XMC, a model checker supporting XL (an extension of Milner's value-passing CCS [20]) as the system specification language, and the alternation-free fragment of the modal μ-calculus as the property specification language.

XMC is written in XSB Prolog, where XSB [32] is a logic-programming system that extends Prolog-style SLD resolution with *tabled resolution*. The principal merits of this extension are that XSB terminates more often than Prolog (e.g. for all datalog programs), avoids redundant sub-computations, and computes the well-founded model of normal logic programs.

XMC is written in a highly declarative fashion. The model checker is encoded in less than 200 lines of XSB Prolog using a binary predicate models/2 which

---

* This work was supported in part by NSF grants EIA-9705998, CCR-9876242, CCR-9988155, and CCR-0205376; ONR grant N000140110967; and ARO grants DAAD190110003, DAAD190110019.

L. Zuck et al. (Eds.): VMCAI 2003, LNCS 2575, pp. 116–131, 2003.

defines when an XL term satisfies a modal μ-calculus formula. This definition uses a ternary predicate `trans/3` which represents the transition relation of the labeled transition system corresponding to an XL specification.

Our experience with XMC raises the following question: Can tabled logic programming be brought to bear on the problem of verifying *mobile systems* and what new insights are required? In this paper we present *MMC*, a practical model checker for mobile systems specified in the style of the π-calculus [22].[1] The main technical difficulties that we encountered are due to the ability to express *channel passing* in the π-calculus, which give rise to a variety of issues that were not present in XMC, including scope extrusion and intrusion, and the generation of new names to avoid name capture.

Logic programming with tabulation turns out to be an ideal framework in which to implement a model checker for mobile systems. In particular, π-calculus names are represented as Prolog *variables* in MMC, which enables us to treat scope extrusion and intrusion, renaming, name restriction, etc., in a direct and efficient manner. The result is that the MMC version of the `trans` relation, when applied to a π-calculus expression p, generates the labeled transition system for p as prescribed by the π-calculus' transitional semantics [22].

By using the ability of a logic-programming engine to manipulate terms and to perform unification, we can encode monadic and polyadic versions of the π-calculus in a single framework. We can also treat the encryption/decryption constructs of the spi-calculus [3], an extension of the π-calculus for cryptographic protocols, as syntactic sugar. In fact, we can evaluate the operational semantics of spi-calculus processes without changing the `trans` relation in MMC. Thus MMC can also be viewed as a model checker for the spi-calculus.

Related work. A number of analysis techniques have been developed for the π- and spi-calculi, and many of them have been incorporated in tools. The Mobility Workbench (MWB) [31] provided the first model-checking tool for the polyadic π-calculus and the π-μ-calculus [21,10]. In addition to the model checker, MWB consists of a bisimulation checker and a prover based on sequent calculus [14]. Picasso [4] is a static analyzer for the π-calculus that focuses on checking secrecy of information such as process-level leaks and insecure communications. Cryptyc [15] uses static type checking to find security violations, such as secrecy and authenticity errors, in cryptographic protocols specified in the spi-calculus. More recently, techniques have been proposed for verifying secrecy and authenticity of cryptographic protocols specified in an extension of spi-calculus and with the intruder modeled using Prolog rules [2,7]. These techniques support the verification of an unbounded number of sessions of a protocol. In contrast, MMC can verify only a finite number of concurrent sessions, but, being a full-fledged model checker, can be used to verify other properties such as deadlock freedom and lossless transmission. Recent extensions to the Maude system [8], which uses equational and rewrite logic as a general framework for executable specifi-

---

[1] Please see [1] for MMC's source code, the source code of the examples used in this paper, and an extended version of this paper.

cations, support cryptographic protocol analysis [11], mobile computation [13], and may-testing equivalence of non-recursive π-calculus processes [29]. MMC, in contrast, is a more traditional model checker for recursive mobile processes encoded in the π-calculus. There are also some other well-known tools for analyzing security protocols without using spi-calculus, such as FDR [18] and NRL [19].

Among these approaches, MMC is most closely related to the model checker implemented in the MWB. The property logic used in MMC is an expressive subset of the π-μ-calculus that is amenable to efficient implementation. The process language used in MMC, on the other hand, is more expressive than that of MWB, and permits encoding of spi-calculus specifications. The performance of MMC is considerably better than the model checkers and equivalence checkers of MWB reported in the literature [30,6]. Moreover, MMC is even comparable to that of the first versions of XMC where, as in MMC, labeled transition systems were generated by interpreting process terms (see Section 4).

In the following, Section 2 describes the computational basis of MMC: the encoding of the operational semantics of the π-calculus as a logic program, and the implementation of a model checker for a subset of π-μ-calculus in MMC. Section 3 describes extensions to MMC to support the spi-calculus. Experimental results appear in Section 4 and our concluding remarks are given in Section 5.

2   MMC: A Model Checker for the π-Calculus

In this section, we describe our model checker (called MMC for the *Mobility Model Checker*) for the π-calculus. Processes in the π-calculus are encoded as described in Section 2.1. The operational semantics of the π-calculus is encoded as a Prolog relation `trans`, which generates symbolic transition systems from agent definitions (Section 2.2). For simplicity, we first describe the encoding for the *monadic* π-calculus. This encoding is later optimized to reduce the size of the symbolic transition system and extended to the polyadic π-calculus. Finally, the semantics of π-μ-calculus is encoded as another Prolog relation `models` which determines whether a given π-calculus expression is in the model of a given alternation-free π-μ-calculus formula (Section 2.3).

2.1   Syntax of MMC Processes

We use $\mathcal{P}$ to denote the set of all process (or agent) expressions, and $P, P_1, P_2, \ldots$ to range over individual process expressions. We use $\mathcal{V}$ to denote an enumerable set of names, and $X, X_1, X_2, \ldots$ to range over elements of $\mathcal{V}$. In MMC, names are represented by Prolog variables. We use $\mathcal{PN}$ to denote the enumerable set of process (agent) names, and $p, p_1, p_2, \ldots$ to range over process names. In MMC, process names are represented by Prolog function (i.e. data constructor) symbols. Finally, $\mathcal{D}$ is used to denote the set of process definitions. Process expressions and process definitions in the monadic π-calculus are encoded in MMC using the language described by the following grammar.

$$\mathcal{A} \;::=\; \text{in}(\mathcal{V},\mathcal{V}) \;|\; \text{out}(\mathcal{V},\mathcal{V}) \;|\; \text{outbound}(\mathcal{V},\mathcal{V}) \;|\; \text{tau}$$
$$\mathcal{P} \;::=\; \text{zero} \;|\; \text{pref}(\mathcal{A},\mathcal{P}) \;|\; \text{nu}(\mathcal{V},\mathcal{P}) \;|\; \text{par}(\mathcal{P},\mathcal{P}) \;|\; \text{choice}(\mathcal{P},\mathcal{P})$$
$$\;|\; \text{match}(\mathcal{V}{=}\mathcal{V},\mathcal{P}) \;|\; \text{proc}(\mathcal{PN}(\vec{\mathcal{V}}))$$
$$\mathcal{D} \;::=\; \text{def}(\mathcal{PN}(\vec{\mathcal{V}}),\mathcal{P})$$

Actions in, out, outbound and tau represent input, output, bound output and internal actions respectively. Among process expressions, zero is the process with no transitions; $\text{pref}(A, P)$ is the process obtained by prefixing action A to P; $\text{nu}(X, P)$ is the process obtained from P by restricting the name X; $\text{match}(X_1{=}X_2, P)$ is the process that behaves as P if the names X_1 and X_2 match, and as zero otherwise. The operators choice and par represent non-deterministic choice and parallel composition respectively. The expression $\text{proc}(p(\vec{X}))$ represents a *process invocation* where p is a process name (having a corresponding definition) and $\vec{X}$ is a comma-separated list of names that are the actual parameters of the invocation. Process invocation may be used to define recursive processes. Each process definition of the form $\text{def}(p(\vec{X}), P)$ associates a process name p and a list of formal parameters $\vec{X}$ with process expression P.

It is easy to see that MMC's syntax simply encodes the standard syntax of π-calculus expressions used in [22]. This observation is formalized below.

Definition 1 *Given a one-to-one function θ that maps names of Prolog variables to names in π-calculus expressions, the function f_θ mapping process expressions in MMC's syntax to standard π-calculus syntax is defined as follows:*

$$
\begin{aligned}
f_\theta(\text{zero}) &= 0 & f_\theta(X) &= \theta(X) \\
f_\theta(\text{match}((X_1 = X_2), P)) &= [\theta(X_1) = \theta(X_2)]f_\theta(P) & f_\theta(\text{pref}(\text{tau}, P)) &= \tau.f_\theta(P) \\
f_\theta(\text{pref}(\text{in}(X_1, X_2), P)) &= \overline{\theta(X_1)}\theta(X_2).f_\theta P & f_\theta(\text{nu}(X, P)) &= (\nu\,\theta(X))f_\theta(P) \\
f_\theta(\text{pref}(\text{out}(X_1, X_2), P)) &= \overline{\theta(X_1)}\theta(X_2).f_\theta P & f_\theta(\text{choice}(P, Q)) &= f_\theta(P) + f_\theta(Q) \\
f_\theta(\text{proc}(p(X_1, \ldots, X_n))) &= p(\theta(X_1), \ldots, \theta(X_n)) & f_\theta(\text{par}(P, Q)) &= f_\theta(P) \mid f_\theta(Q)
\end{aligned}
$$
$$f_\theta(\text{def}(p(X_1, \ldots, X_n), P)) = p(\theta(X_1), \ldots, \theta(X_n)) \overset{\text{def}}{=} f_\theta(P)$$

Definition 1 allows us to directly import the notions of bound and free names from π-calculus to our encoding. In actions of the form $\text{in}(X, Y)$, $\text{out}(X, Y)$, and $\text{outbound}(X, Y)$, the name X is said to be *free*. The name Y in the out action is also *free* while the name Y in in and outbound actions is said to be *bound*. Table 1 lists the free and bound names of process expressions (second and third column, respectively).

Note that the same name may occur both bound and free in a process expression. For instance, consider process expression pref(out(Y,X), nu(X, pref(out(Y,X), nu(X, pref(out(Y,X), zero)))))). The name X occurs both free (in the first out) and bound, and there are two distinct bound occurrences of X. Our encoding of the model checker becomes considerably simpler if we ensure that bound names are all distinct from each other and from free names. We call process expressions having this distinct-name property as *valid*. The formal definition of validity is achieved by associating with each process expression P

a set of *uniquely bound names* (denoted by $ubn(P)$), as defined in the fourth column of Table 1.

Table 1. Free, bound, and uniquely bound names of processes

Process Expression P	Free Names $fn(P)$	Bound Names $bn(P)$	Uniquely Bound Names $ubn(P)$
pref(tau, P_1)	$fn(P_1)$	$bn(P_1)$	$ubn(P_1)$
pref(in(X_1, X_2), P_1) pref(outbound(X_1, X_2), P_1)	$(fn(P_1) \cup \{X_1\})$ $-\{X_2\}$	$bn(P_1) \cup \{X_2\}$	$(ubn(P_1) \cup \{X_2\})$ $-(bn(P_1) \cap \{X_2\})$
pref(out(X_1, X_2), P_1) match(($X_1 = X_2$), P_1)	$fn(P_1) \cup \{X_1, X_2\}$	$bn(P_1)$	$ubn(P_1)$
par(P_1, P_2) choice(P_1, P_2)	$fn(P_1) \cup fn(P_2)$	$bn(P_1) \cup bn(P_2)$	$(ubn(P_1) \cup ubn(P_1))$ $-(bn(P_1) \cap bn(P_2))$
nu(X, P_1)	$fn(P_1) - \{X\}$	$bn(P_1) \cup \{X\}$	$(ubn(P_1) \cup \{X\}) - (bn(P_1) \cap \{X\})$

Definition 2 (Validity) *A process expression P is* valid *if and only if $fn(P) \cap bn(P) = \emptyset$ and $ubn(P) = bn(P)$. A process definition of the form* $\mathtt{def}(p(\vec{X}), P)$ *is valid if and only if P is valid and $bn(P) \cap \vec{X} = \emptyset$, i.e. formal parameters do not appear bound in P.*

The following property can be established based on the definition of validity:

Proposition 1 *Every subexpression of a valid process expression is also valid.*

We say that a process expression P is *closed* if and only if $fn(P) = \emptyset$. We say that a process definition of the form $\mathtt{def}(p(\vec{X}), P)$ is *closed* if and only if all free names in P occur in $\vec{X}$, i.e. $fn(P) \subseteq \vec{X}$. The encoding of the model checker described in this paper requires that all process definitions are valid and closed. Note that restricting our attention to valid definitions does not reduce expressiveness since any process expression can be converted to an equivalent valid expression by suitably renaming the bound names.

2.2   Operational Semantics of MMC

The operational semantics of π-calculus is traditionally given in terms of a symbolic transition system [16,25]. The transition relation of such a system can be derived from process definitions in MMC using the relation **trans** defined by the rules in Figure 1. The relation **trans** can be seen as a direct encoding of the symbolic semantics of [16]. At a high level, a tuple in the **trans** relation of the form $\mathtt{trans}(P_1, A, M, P_2, Nin, Nout)$ means that process expression P_1 can evolve into process expression P_2 after an A action provided equality constraints over the names in M hold. (*Nin* and *Nout* are integers used to generate new names, an implementation detail explained later.) A conjunction of equality constraints is encoded as a list in Prolog, each element in the list encoding an equality constraint over a pair of names. Each tuple in the **trans** relation corresponds to a

```
% Pref
trans(pref(A, P), A, [], P, Nin, Nout).

% Sum
trans(choice(P, Q), A, M, P1, Nin, Nout) :- trans(P, A, M, P1, Nin, Nout).
trans(choice(P, Q), A, M, Q1, Nin, Nout) :- trans(Q, A, M, Q1, Nin, Nout).

% Id
trans(proc(PN), A, M, Q, Nin, Nout) :-
        def(PN, P), trans(P, A, M, Q, Nin, Nout).

% Match
trans(match((X=Y), P), A, ML, P1, Nin, Nout) :-
        X==Y -> trans(P, A, ML, P1, Nin, Nout)
             ; trans(P, A, M, P1, Nin, Nout),
                 append([X=Y], M, ML).

% Par
trans(par(P, Q), A, M, par(P1, Q), Nin, Nout) :- trans(P, A, M, P1, Nin, Nout).
trans(par(P, Q), A, M, par(P, Q1), Nin, Nout) :- trans(Q, A, M, Q1, Nin, Nout).

% Com
trans(par(P, Q), tau, MNL, par(P1, Q1), Nin, Nout) :-
        trans(P, A, M, P1, Nin, Nout1),
        trans(Q, B, N, Q1, Nout1, Nout),
        complement(A, B, L),
        append(M, N, MN),
        append(MN, L, MNL).

% Res
trans(nu(Y, P), A, M, nu(Y, P1), Nin, Nout) :-
        gen_new_name(Y, Nin, Nout1),
        trans(P, A, M, P1, Nout1, Nout),
        not_in_action(Y, A),        % Y does not appear in action A
        not_in_constraint(Y,M).     % Y does not appear in constraint M

% Open
trans(nu(Y, P), outbound(X, Z), M, P1, Nin, Nout) :-
        gen_new_name(Y, Nin, Nout1),
        trans(P, out(X, Z), M, P1, Nout1, Nout),
        Y == Z, Y\==X,
        not_in_constraint(Y, M).

% Close
trans(par(P, Q), tau, MNL, nu(W, par(P1, Q1)), Nin, Nout) :-
        trans(P, A, M, P1, Nin, Nout1),
        trans(Q, B, M, Q1, Nout1, Nout),
        comp_bound(A, B, W, L),
        append(M, N, MN), append(MN, L, MNL).

gen_new_name(Y, Nin, Nout):-
        (var(Y) -> Nout is Nin + 1, Y = name(Nout)
                ; Nout = Nin).

complement(in(X, V), out(Y, V), L) :- X==Y -> L=[] ; L=[X=Y].
complement(out(X, V), in(Y, V), L) :- X==Y -> L=[] ; L=[X=Y].

comp_bound(outbound(X, W), in(Y, W), W, L):- X==Y -> L=[] ; L=[X=Y].
comp_bound(in(X, W), outbound(Y, W), W, L):- X==Y -> L=[] ; L=[X=Y].
```

Fig. 1. Encoding of π-calculus transition semantics.

transition in the symbolic semantics of [16] of the form $f_\theta(P_1) \overset{fc_\theta(M), f_\theta(A)}{\longrightarrow} f_\theta(P_2)$, where fc_θ is defined as follows:

Definition 3 *The following function fc_θ maps the Prolog representation of equality constraints over names to equivalent constraints over π-calculus names:*

$$fc_\theta(\texttt{[ ]}) = true$$
$$fc_\theta(\texttt{[}X_1\texttt{=}X_2\texttt{]}) = \theta(X_1) = \theta(X_2)$$
$$fc_\theta(\texttt{append}(M_1, \ M_2)) = fc_\theta(M_1) \ fc_\theta(M_2)$$

When the transitions are generated, we avoid name capture by binding each distinct instance of a restricted name to a freshly generated name drawn from an enumerable set indexed by an integer. These fresh names are represented by terms of the form $\texttt{name}(N)$. Fields Nin and $Nout$ in the $\texttt{trans}$ relation are used to maintain the index of the set of fresh names: Nin records the name with the largest index generated before a transition is generated; and $Nout$ records the same after the transition is generated.

It can be readily seen that the $\texttt{trans}$ relation preserves validity, formalized by the following proposition:

Proposition 2 *Let $\mathcal{C}$ denote the set of Prolog constants, P_1 be a valid process expression, and N_1 be larger than any N in $\texttt{name}(N)$ occurring in P_1. For any one-to-one function $\sigma : fn(P_1) \to \mathcal{C}$, if $\texttt{trans}(P_1\sigma, A, M, P_2, N_1, N_2)$ is an answer to the query $\texttt{trans}(P_1\sigma, A, M, ?, N_1, ?)$ then P_2 is also a valid process expression.*

Finally, by induction on the lengths of derivations, we can show that the transition relation computed using our encoding of Figure 1 is correct with respect to the symbolic transition semantics of [16].

Theorem 3 *Let S be the logic program encoding the symbolic semantics (given in Figure 1), and D be a set of process definitions. Let P_1 be a valid MMC process expression, N_1 be the largest N in $\texttt{name}(N)$ occurring in P_1, and $\sigma : fn(P) \to \mathcal{C}$ be a one-to-one function. Then $\texttt{trans}(P_1\sigma, A, M, P_2, N_1, N_2)$ is an answer derivable from the logic program $D \cup S$ if and only if $f_\theta(P_1) \overset{fc_\theta(M\sigma^{-1}), f_\theta(A\sigma^{-1})}{\longrightarrow} f_\theta(P_2\sigma^{-1})$ is a derivation in the symbolic semantics for the π-calculus.*

The use of structural congruence: While the encoding of the operational semantics is complete, it is not yet sufficient to build a model checker: the semantics distinguishes between process expressions based on their syntax, even if their behaviors are identical. For example, consider the following process definitions:

```
def(ser(Pc), nu(X, pref(out(Pc, X), proc(ser(Pc))))).
def(cli(Pc), pref(in(Pc, X), proc(cli(Pc)))).
def(system, nu(Pc, par(proc(ser(Pc)), proc(cli(Pc))))).
```

Process `system` consists of processes `ser(Pc)` and `cli(Pc)`. Process `ser(Pc)` repeatedly generates a new private name `X` and sends `X` to process `cli(Pc)`. Since each time this happens the name `X` is different from any other names previously generated during the computation, the state space of `system` is infinite as shown below:

```
system = nu(name(0),par(proc(ser(name(0))),proc(cli(name(0)))))
  ─τ→   nu(name(0),nu(name(1),par(proc(ser(name(0))),proc(cli(name(0))))))
  ─τ→   nu(name(0),nu(name(1),nu(name(2),par(proc(ser(name(0))),proc(cli(name(0)))))))
  ─τ→   ...
```

However, in `nu(name(1),par(proc(ser(name(0))),proc(cli(name(0)))))`, `name(1)` does not occur in `par(proc(ser(name(0))),proc(cli(name(0))))`, and hence the behavior of these two process expressions is identical. This can be formalized as the following structural-congruence rule:

$$\texttt{nu(X,P)} \equiv \texttt{P} \quad \text{if X does not occur in P.}$$

After applying this rule to modify the clauses for `Res` and `Close`, which handle restricted names, the process `system` exhibits finite behavior.

Using resolution mechanism to generate new names: Note that we have used a global counter (implemented using `Nin` and `Nout`) to generate new names when applying a restriction operator. However, using constants to generate new names in Prolog results in redundant states and transitions. For example, the two process terms `nu(name(0),pref( out(X,name(0)),zero))` and `nu(name(1),pref(out(X,name(1)),zero))` appear different, although they differ only in the bound names: `name(0)` and `name(1)`. We can exploit the fact that *variant checks*— i.e. checking if two terms are identical modulo names of variables— can be inexpensively performed in the XSB tabled logic programming system on which MMC is implemented. Instead of generating integers to index new names, we use existential logical variables in terms, and let the resolution mechanism generate a new variable every time that clause is used. This is done by discarding the arguments implementing the counter, i.e., *Nin* and *Nout*, and defining `gen_new_name` as the fact: `gen_new_name(name(_))`.

Using this mechanism, we generate `name(V0)` in the place of `name(0)`, and `name(V1)` in the place of `name(1)`. The two terms, `nu(name(V0), pref(out(X,name(V1)), zero))` and `nu(name(V1), pref(out(X,name(V1)), zero))`, now become variants of each other and MMC will treat them as the same state.

A consequence of this representation is that the equality of two names can no longer be checked by unification (=), but by the identity operator (==). For instance while the unification `name(V0)=name(V1)` will succeed after unifying `V0` and `V1`, the identity check `name(V0)==name(V1)` will fail unless `V0` and `V1` are already unified.

Another consequence of this representation is that the goal-reordering optimization, which was employed in early versions of XMC, can no longer be directly applied to our encoding. Consider the Com rule. In general, the number of solutions of complement(A, B, L) is much smaller than that of trans(Q, B, N, Q1) (note that the above optimization has discarded fields *Nout1* and *Nout*). Thus, by reordering trans(Q, B, N, Q1) and complement(A, B, L), we will compute fewer intermediate answers. This optimization can be applied using the earlier (integer) representation of names and can result in significant performance gains. However, the representation of restricted names using variables means that the program is dependent on the order in which variables are bound, and hence this optimization is not directly applicable. Hence we specialize the trans rules to two versions, the first of which is used when the action (the second argument) is known; and the second of which is used when the action is unknown. The specialization lets us change the join order appropriately without affecting the correctness.

From Monadic to Polyadic π-Calculus: The polyadic version of the π-calculus is supported in MMC by extending the above construction as follows. The syntax is extended by introducing a set $\mathcal{F}$ of tuple constructors (n-ary function symbols for $n \geq 0$) and considering the set of terms $\mathcal{T}$ built from $\mathcal{F}$ and $\mathcal{V}$. The grammar given in Section 2.1 becomes (only the changed rules are shown):

$$\mathcal{A} ::= \texttt{in}(\mathcal{V}, \mathcal{T}) \mid \texttt{out}(\mathcal{V}, \mathcal{T}) \mid \texttt{outbound}(\mathcal{V}, \vec{\mathcal{V}}, \mathcal{T})$$

$$\mathcal{P} ::= \texttt{unify}((\mathcal{V} = \mathcal{T}), P) \mid \texttt{proc}(\mathcal{PN}(\vec{\mathcal{T}}))$$

In essence, the communication actions can now be used to place names in (or extract names from) tuples and other data structures, and process invocations may contain such data structures. Note that when multiple names can be sent in a single message (e.g. when sending a tuple of names), the bound output action needs to keep track of the set of bound names (the second parameter) in the message (the third parameter). The Open and Close rules in the transition semantics for the polyadic version change correspondingly. Furthermore, we introduce an operator unify to decompose a term into subterms by pattern matching. The names in T are bound names in an expression of the form unify$((X = T), P)$. An expression unify$((X = T), P)$ behaves as P when the names in T are bound to terms over $\mathcal{F}$ and $\mathcal{V}$ such that X and T unify, and as zero if such a unifier does not exist. The modified rules can be directly encoded in Prolog as before; see [1] for details.

2.3 Model Checking in the π-μ-Calculus

A modal logic for the monadic π-calculus, the π-μ-calculus, was originally proposed in [23] and extended to the polyadic π-calculus in [21] and [10]. The π-μ-calculus has variants of the traditional box and diamond modal operators to reflect the early and late semantics of the π-calculus.

Below, we present an encoding of a model checker for an expressive subset of the π-μ-calculus which does not have explicit quantifiers ($\exists$ and $\forall$). We use the following syntax to represent formulas in our subset of the π-μ-calculus. We use

$\mathcal{F}$ to denote the set of (non fixed-point) formulas; $\mathcal{A}$ and $\mathcal{V}$ (from Section 2.1) to denote sets of actions and names; $\mathcal{Z}$ to denote formula variables in the π-μ-calculus; and $\mathcal{E}$ to denote fixed-point equations defining the formula variables.

$$\mathcal{F} ::= \text{tt} \mid \text{ff} \mid \text{pred}((\mathcal{V}, \mathcal{V}), \mathcal{F}) \mid \text{and}(\mathcal{F}, \mathcal{F}) \mid \text{or}(\mathcal{F}, \mathcal{F}) \mid \text{diam}(\mathcal{A}, \mathcal{F})$$
$$\mid \text{box}(\mathcal{A}, \mathcal{F}) \mid \text{form}(\mathcal{Z}(\overrightarrow{\mathcal{V}}))$$
$$\mathcal{E} ::= \text{fdef}(\mathcal{Z}(\overrightarrow{\mathcal{V}}), \text{lfp}(\mathcal{F})) \mid \text{fdef}(\mathcal{Z}(\overrightarrow{\mathcal{V}}), \text{gfp}(\mathcal{F}))$$

And and or are boolean connectives; diam and box are model operators; lfp and gfp represent least and greatest fixed point operators respectively; and pred is used to encode a match operation. Names in a formula definition are implicitly quantified; the quantifiers are determined as follows. Names appearing on the left hand side of a definition are called formal parameters, and the remaining names in a definition are called *local* names. For a local name X, let φ be a largest subformula of the right hand side such that $\varphi = \text{diam}(A, F)$ ($\varphi = \text{box}(A, F)$) and X occurs in A. Then X is existentially (universally) quantified, with its scope covering φ. We require that every local name in a formula be quantified in the above manner. Model checking π-μ-calculus where quanti-

Id $\quad \dfrac{}{P \vdash_\theta \text{tt}} \quad \theta \text{ is consistent}$

Pred $\quad \dfrac{P \vdash_{\theta'} F}{P \vdash_\theta \text{pred}((X{=}Y), F)} \quad \theta' = \theta \cup mgu(X, Y)$

And $\quad \dfrac{P \vdash_\theta F_1 \quad P \vdash_\theta F_2}{P \vdash_\theta \text{and}(F1, F2)}$

Not $\quad \dfrac{P \nvdash_\theta F}{P \vdash_\theta \text{not}(F)}$

Or $\quad \dfrac{P \vdash_\theta F_1}{P \vdash_\theta \text{or}(F_1, F_2)} \qquad \dfrac{P \vdash_\theta F_2}{P \vdash_\theta \text{or}(F_1, F_2)}$

Diam $\quad \dfrac{P_1 \vdash_{\theta'} F}{P \vdash_\theta \text{diam}(A, F)} \quad \text{trans}(P, A', \_, P_1), \quad \theta' = \theta \cup mgu(A, A')$

Box $\quad \dfrac{P_1 \vdash_{\theta_1} F, \dots, P_n \vdash_{\theta_n} F}{P \vdash_\theta \text{box}(A, F)} \quad \{(P_1, \theta_1), \dots, (P_n, \theta_n)\} = \{(P', mgu(A, A')) \mid \text{trans}(P, A', \_, P')\}$

Lfp $\quad \dfrac{P \vdash_\theta F[\overrightarrow{V'}/\overrightarrow{V}]}{P \vdash_\theta \text{form}(Z(\overrightarrow{V'}))} \quad \text{fdef}(Z(\overrightarrow{V}), \text{lfp}(F))$

Fig. 2. The tableau rules of the subset of π-μ-calculus

fiers are restricted as described above requires the ability to handle inequality constraints (e.g. $X \neq Y$). Inequality constraints arise even when the logic and the process specification uses only equalities, for instance, to record the substitutions under which a transition is not enabled. Equality constraints are handled by a logic programming system. In contrast, inequality constraints have to be explicitly treated: either representing them symbolically, or enumerating their consequences (i.e., $X \neq Y$ interpreted over a domain $\{a, b, c\}$ for X and Y can be enumerated as $X = a, Y = b, X = a, Y = c, \ldots$). While enumeration leads to poor performance, symbolic representation adds an additional layer of implementation (i.e. a constraint solver) with its attendant overheads. We avoid this overhead by imposing a condition that the set of constraints (the constraint store) needed while model checking is either empty or consist only of constraints over restricted names.

The semantics of this subset of π-μ-calculus can be readily derived from the semantics of the full logic given in [23]. From this semantics, we can also derive a tableau proof system for our subset given in Figure 2.3. The tableau can be shown to be sound and complete with respect to the semantics of π-μ-calculus provided all free names in the process expression and formula in original model-checking goal $P \vdash F$ are distinct. The tableau treats only least fixed point formulas but handles negation; greatest fixed point formulas are handled using their dual least fixed point forms (i.e. using the identity $\nu Z.F \equiv \neg \mu Z. \neg F[\neg Z/Z]$). The parameter θ in the tableau keeps track of the current substitution of names in the formula and names in the process expressions. A substitution θ is said to be consistent if for any name X, $X = t_1 \in \theta$ and $X = t_2 \in \theta$ then $t_1 = t_2$. In the figure, $mgu(t_1, t_2)$ denotes the most general unifier of the terms t_1 and t_2, where both terms denote actions. The logic programming encoding of the

```
Id      models(_P, tt).
Match   models(P, pred((X=Y), F))  :- X=Y, models(P, F).
And     models(P, and(F_1, F_2))   :- models(P, F_1), models(P, F_2).
Or      models(P, or(F_1, F_2))    :- models(P, F_1) ; models(P, F_2).
<A>     models(P, diam(A, F))       :- trans(P, A, _M, P1), models(P1, F).
[A]     models(P, box(A, F))        :- forall(P1, trans(P, A, _M, P1), models(P1, F)).
Neg     models(P, not(F))           :- sk_not(models(P, F)).
Lfp     models(P, form(Z))          :- fdef(Z, lfp(F)), models(P, F).
```

Fig. 3. Encoding of MMC's π-μ-calculus model checker

tableau system is given in Figure 2.3 which can be directly executed on the XSB system. In the program, sk_not(Goal) refers to the negation of Goal which treats all variables in the term Goal as existentially quantified.

The soundness and completeness of the tableau system can be proved following [28]. The following theorem states the correctness of the model checker.

Theorem 4 *Let D be a set of process and formula definitions, S be the program consisting of the clauses in Figures 1 and 2.3, P be a valid process expression, and F be a formula containing only processes and formula variables defined in D. Let σ be a one-to-one function mapping free variables in P and F to Prolog constants. Then $\mathrm{models}(P\sigma, F\sigma)$ is an answer derivable from the logic program $D \cup S$ if and only if $P \vdash F$ is a derivation in the tableau shown in Figure 2.3.*

The models predicate in MMC is an optimized version of the one shown in Figure 2.3 aimed at reducing the number of goals that will be tabled in XSB. The optimization is routine and is not shown.

3   Encoding the Spi-Calculus

The *spi-calculus* is an extension of the π-calculus with primitives for encryption and decryption to facilitate specification of cryptographic protocols [3]. Below we show that spi-calculus process expressions can be encoded in MMC using its support for the polyadic π-calculus. To express message encryption and decryption, and to represent structured messages composed of multiple segments, we use terms built from names and the two binary function symbols encrypt and mesg. The encryption and decryption primitives of the spi-calculus are encoded in MMC as follows. Encryption of a message M with a symmetric key K, denoted in the spi-calculus as $\{M\}_K$, is encoded in MMC by the term encrypt(M, K). This term can be passed as a parameter or can appear as data on an output action. Decryption is specified in the spi-calculus using a *case* expression. For example, *case L of $\{x\}_K$ in P* behaves as $P[M/x]$ if L is of the form $\{M\}_K$, and as a deadlocked process otherwise. In MMC, we use unify to look into message components and match to verify whether the encryption and decryption keys match. For instance, the above *case* expression is encoded in MMC by the expression unify$(L$ = encrypt(X, E), match$(E = K, P))$. In MMC's encoding, unify extracts the key portion of the message and match checks if the given key K matches the encryption key E.

For handling specifications that use asymmetric public/private keys, we introduce two unary function symbols priv and pub, and use priv(K) and pub(K) to denote the private and public keys of a key pair K. We also introduce a new process expression code$(Oper, P)$ where $Oper$ represents the operations written as Prolog predicate; code$(Oper, P)$ performs $Oper$ and then behaves as P. We use operation complement(K_1, K_2) to map the public key of a key pair to the corresponding private key and vice versa. For instance, complement$($pub$(K_A), K')$ binds K' to priv(K_A). Using the above representation, a message M encrypted by principal A with public key K_A^{pu} is encoded as the term t =encrypt$(M$, pub$(K_A))$. For instance, a principal B attempting to decrypt the term t with a key K will use the expression unify$(t$ = encrypt(X,K), code$($complement(K, K_1), match$(K_1$=priv(K_B), ...$)))$ which will deadlock unless K is same as priv(K_B). Similarly, a message M encrypted with a private key K_A^{pr} is encoded in MMC as encrypt$(M,$priv$(K_A))$.

Note that, as in the spi-calculus, the restriction operator nu can be used to generate fresh nonces and shared keys.

Systems with an intruder are modeled so that all communication between principals go through the intruder. We assume that there is only one intruder, and that the behavior of the intruder can be specified by a recursive process definition. When an intruder receives a message from a principal, it chooses to either transmit, intercept or fake the message transmission. The capabilities of the intruder to store and retrieve messages are encoded using a set data structure, and operations store(S, t, S') and retrieve(S, t), where S and S' are sets and t is a term. An intruder's ability to decompose or compose messages can

Table 2. Performance results of MMC on Handover, Needham-Schroeder, and Yahalom protocols.

Protocol	States	Trans	Formula	Time (sec)	Mem (MB)
Handover	137	220	deadlock	0.12	0.93
			lost data	0.40	2.68
Needham-Schroeder	59	101	deadlock	0.14	0.70
			attack	0.03	0.39
Yahalom	29133	107652	attack	0.31	1.07

Table 3. Comparative performance of XMC and MMC.

Benchmark	States	Trans	Property	Time(sec) XMC	MMC
rether	593	697	deadlock	0.47	0.57
sieve(3)	615	1423	ae_finish	0.73	1.53
sieve(5)	4023	16091	ae_finish	10.12	16.67
leader(3)	67	88	ae_leader	0.07	0.08
leader(5)	864	2687	ae_leader	2.00	2.32
leader(7)	11939	25632	ae_leader	45.83	63.12

be encoded using unify and requires no extensions. Details of the encoding of example protocols and the extensions made to MMC appear in [1].

Security properties such as authenticity can be expressed in our subset of the π-μ-calculus. For verifying authenticity properties, we use two out actions on distinguished, global channels (called send and commit below) for each pair of principals in the protocol. For instance, when principal A initiates communication with B, it does an out action on channel send_AB; similarly, when A thinks it is communicating with B, it does an out action on channel commit_AB. Authenticity is violated if a principal commits to a communication without a corresponding (preceding) initiation.

Using MMC, we can detect the violation of authenticity in the Needham-Schroeder protocol originally found by [17]. We have also verified authenticity properties of the Yahalom protocol, and the modified Needham-Schroeder protocol (see [1]).

4   Experimental Results

We implemented the MMC model checker starting from the encoding of the trans and models relations given in Section 2.3. We then applied a number of logic-programming optimizations to this encoding, including goal reordering, clause resolution factoring, and the use of resolution to generate new names. The experimental results presented in this section reflect the performance of this optimized version of MMC, and were obtained on a 1GHz Pentium III machine with 256MB memory running Linux 7.0 and XSB v2.4.

Table 2 illustrates MMC's performance on three standard benchmarks: a simplified handover procedure from [24], and the Needham-Schroeder and Yahalom cryptographic protocols. Our specifications of Needham-Schroeder and Yahalom utilize MMC's spi-calculus extensions, and contain a number of process expressions to which the restriction operator is applied. These expressions are candidates for the structural congruence rule, which ensures that MMC terminates for finite-control agents. Eliminating the application of this rule to expressions for which the scope of a restricted name does not contain recursion, led to a 3-fold improvement in model-checking execution times.

We also conducted experiments aimed at assessing both how MMC scales to large transition systems and how it compares in performance to the Mobility

Workbench. In particular, for verifying the absence of deadlocks in chains of buffers of size 4, 8, and 12, MMC's model checker takes 0.02s, 0.83s, and 25.46s, respectively. On the same formula, the MWB's model checker for the polyadic π-calculus takes 0.58s for a buffer of size 4, but does not terminate within 13 hours for a buffer of size 8. The MWB also provides a built-in "deadlock" function that uses depth-first search to detect deadlocks instead of model checking the corresponding π-μ-calculus formula. MMC's model checker outperforms MWB's deadlock function for large chain lengths (e.g. for a buffer of size 12, the MWB's deadlock function takes 139.43s); both systems show comparable performance for smaller chain lengths. The MWB also has a prototype implementation of a model prover [6] based on sequent calculus. However, at the time of this writing, the implementation appears to be in an unstable state, either looping on certain least fixed point formulas or terminating incorrectly (too early) on certain greatest fixed point formulas. Hence we were unable to get meaningful performance measurements for the MWB's prover.

Finally, Table 3 compares the performance of MMC and the initial release of XMC on several examples from the XMC benchmark suite. (The initial version of XMC did not utilize the compiler for process expressions described in [12]). MMC is slightly slower than the first version of XMC, and this is to be expected given the non-mobile nature of these benchmarks. In particular, MMC spends time checking for structural congruence, despite the optimization discussed above. Also, the Open and Close clauses in the trans relation are never used, but MMC tries (and eventually fails) to resolve using these rules. Implementing a process-expression compiler for MMC along the lines of XMC's compiler [12] will eliminate these overheads.

5   Conclusion

We presented MMC, a practical model checker for the π and spi-calculi. We are currently extending the functionality of MMC to include a symbolic bisimulation checker [5], and to handle the full π-μ-calculus, taking advantage of recent developments to add light-weight constraint processing to tabled logic programming [9]. Our results indicate that MMC's performance is comparable to that of the first versions of XMC. However, the compilation techniques incorporated into later versions of XMC have vastly improved its performance, reducing execution times by factors of 2 or more and reducing space needs by an order of magnitude [12]. A central feature of XMC's compiler is that it statically generates rules that cover all possible synchronizations between processes composed in parallel. XMC does not permit channel passing, rendering this kind of analysis possible. For the π-calculus, such static techniques appear to be infeasible. Nevertheless, we need to find mechanisms to reduce the cost of finding synchronizing transitions in order to derive model checkers for mobile processes that compete in performance with the current version of XMC. Another avenue of research is to augment MMC with program transformations (developed in [27] for combining induction-based proofs with model checking) to verify infinite families of mobile processes.

References

1. Mobility model checker for the π-calculus. Dept. of Computer Science, SUNY at Stony Brook, 2002. Available from http://www.cs.sunysb.edu/~lmc/mmc.
2. M. Abadi and B. Blanchet. Analyzing security protocols with secrecy types and logic programs. In *Proceedings of POPL'02*, pages 33–44, Jan. 2002.
3. M. Abadi and A. D. Gordon. A calculus for cryptographic protocols: The spi calculus. In *Fourth ACM Conference on CCS*, pages 36–47. ACM Press, 1997.
4. B. Aziz and G.W. Hamilton. A privacy analysis for the pi-calculus: The denotational approach. In *Proceedings of the 2nd Workshop on the Specification, Analysis and Validation for Emerging Technologies*, Copenhagen, Denmark, July 2002.
5. S. Basu, M. Mukund, C. R. Ramakrishnan, I. V. Ramakrishnan, and R. M. Verma. Local and symbolic bisimulation using tabled constraint logic programming. In *International Conference on Logic Programming*, pages 166–180, 2001.
6. F. B. Beste. The model prover - a sequent-calculus based modal μ-calculus model checker tool for finite control π-calculus agents. Technical report, Swedish Institute of Computer Science, 1998.
7. B. Blanchet. From secrecy to authenticity in security protocols. In *9th International Static Analysis Symposium*, pages 242–259, September 2002.
8. M. Clavel, F. Durán, S. Eker, P. Lincoln, N. Martí-Oliet, J. Meseguer, and J. Quesada. Maude: Specification and programming in rewriting logic. *Theoretical Computer Science*, 2001.
9. B. Cui and D. S. Warren. A system for tabled constraint logic programming. In *First International Conference on Computational Logic*, pages 478–492, 2000.
10. M. Dam. Proof systems for pi-calculus logics. *Logic for Concurrency and Synchronisation*, 2001.
11. G. Denker and J. Meseguer. Protocol specification and analysis in Maude. In *Proc. of Workshop on Formal Methods and Security Protocols*, June 1998.
12. Y. Dong and C.R. Ramakrishnan. An optimizing compiler for efficient model checking. In *Proceedings of FORTE/PSTV '99*, 1999.
13. F. Duran, S. Eker, P. Lincoln, and J. Meseguer. Principles of mobile maude. In *Proc. ASA/MA*, volume 1882, pages 73–85. Springer-Verlag, 2000.
14. T. Franzen. A theorem-proving approach to deciding properties of finite-control agents. Technical report, Swedish Institute of Computer Science, 1996.
15. A. Gordon and A.S.A.Jeffrey. Authenticity by typing for security protocols. In *IEEE Computer Security Foundations Workshop*, 2001.
16. H. Lin. Symbolic bisimulation and proof systems for the π-calculus. Technical report, School of Cognitive and Computer Science, U. of Sussex, UK, 1994.
17. G. Lowe. An attack on the Needham-Schroeder public-key authentication protocol. *Information Processing Letters*, pages 131–133, 1995.
18. G. Lowe. Breaking and fixing the Needham-Schroeder public-key protocol using FDR. *Software Concepts and Tools*, 17:93–102, 1996.
19. C. Meadows. The NRL protocol analyzer: an overview. *Journal of Logic Programming*, 26(2):113–131, 1996.
20. R. Milner. *Communication and Concurrency*. International Series in Computer Science. Prentice Hall, 1989.
21. R. Milner. The polyadic π–calculus: a tutorial. *The Proceedings of the International Summer School on Logic and Algebra of Specification*, 1991.
22. R. Milner, J. Parrow, and D. Walker. A calculus of mobile processes, Parts I and II. *Information and Computation*, 100(1):1–77, 1992.

23. R. Milner, J. Parrow, and D. Walker. Modal logics for mobile processes. *Theoretical Computer Science*, pages 149–171, 1993.

24. F. Orava and J. Parrow. An algebraic verification of a mobile network. *Formal Aspects of Computing*, 4:497–543, 1992.

25. J. Parrow. An introduction to the π-calculus. In Bergstra, Ponse, and Smolka, editors, *Handbook of Process Algebra*. Elsevier, 2001.

26. Y. S. Ramakrishna, C. R. Ramakrishnan, I. V. Ramakrishnan, S. A. Smolka, T. W. Swift, and D. S. Warren. Efficient model checking using tabled resolution. In *Proceedings of CAV '97*, Haifa, Israel, July 1997.

27. A. Roychoudhury, K. Narayan Kumar, C.R. Ramakrishnan, I.V. Ramakrishnan, and S.A. Smolka. Verification of parameterized systems using logic-program transformations. In *Proceedings of TACAS 2000*, 2000.

28. C. Stirling and D. Walker. Local model checking in the modal mu-calculus. *Theoretical Computer Science*, pages 161–177, 1991.

29. P. Thati, K. Sen, and N. Marti-oliet. An executable specification of asynchronous pi-calculus semantics and may testing in Maude 2.0. In *Intl. Workshop on Rewriting Logic and its Applications*, 2002.

30. B. Victor. The mobility workbench user's guide. Technical report, Department of Computer Systems, Uppsala University, Sweden, 1995.

31. B. Victor and F. Moller. The mobility workbench — a tool for the π-calculus. In D. Dill, editor, *Proceedings of CAV'94*. Springer-Verlag, 1994.

32. XSB. The XSB logic programming system v2.4, 2001. Available from http://xsb.sourceforge.net.

Properties of a Type Abstract Interpreter

Roberta Gori and Giorgio Levi

Dipartimento di Informatica, Università di Pisa, Pisa, Italy
{levi,gori}@di.unipi.it

Abstract. In a previous paper [7], we have developed a type abstract interpreter which was shown to be more precise then the classical ML type inference algorithm in inferring monomorphic types, represented as Herbrand terms with variables à la Hindley. In order to deal with recursive functions, we introduce a new abstract fixpoint operator which generalizes the one used in the Hindley and ML inference algorithms by performing k fixpoint computation steps (as done in [11] in the case of polymorphic types). Our abstract interpreter has many interesting properties. It is possible to reconstruct the ML result by just one fixpoint computation step ($k = 1$) and to show that for every $k \geq 1$, either we reach the least fixpoint (which is in general more precise than the ML result), or we get exactly the same result as ML. One important result is that our type interpreter turns out to correspond to a type system, which lies between monomorphism and polymorphic recursion.

1 Introduction

In a recent paper [7], we have developed a type abstract interpreter, following the methodology in [2], that is more precise than the classical ML type inference algorithm in inferring monomorphic types, represented as Herbrand terms with variables à la Hindley. The difference w.r.t. the Hindley (and ML) algorithm is related to recursive functions. We use an operator similar to the one used in the above algorithms after k fixpoint computation steps (as done in [11] in the case of polymorphic types). In this paper, we formally study the properties of our type interpreter and we show some interesting results. Namely,

- If we perform just one fixpoint computation step ($k = 1$), we get exactly the ML result.
- For every $k \geq 1$, either we reach the least fixpoint (which is in general more precise than the ML result), or we get exactly the same result as ML. Hence, unlike what is claimed in [10,11] we get an improvement in precision only if we reach the least fixpoint in k steps.
- Our type interpreter turns out to correspond to a type system, which lies between monomorphism and polymorphic recursion. The type inference algorithm is much simpler than the one for polymorphic recursion (we do not need quantification in type terms and do not perform type generalization). Yet it succeeds in typing all the programs which are used to show the power of polymorphism.

L. Zuck et al. (Eds.): VMCAI 2003, LNCS 2575, pp. 132–145, 2003.

In Sections 2.1 and 2.2 we summarize known results on monomorphic type systems (and type inference algorithms) and on abstract interpretation. In Section 3 we formalize the abstract interpreter in [7] and we prove its properties for the family of widenings. In Section 4 we compare its behavior with the ML algorithm on some examples. Finally, in Section 5, we prove that our abstract interpreter realizes a form of recursion which lies between monomorphic and polymorphic recursion.

For the sake of conciseness we have omitted the proofs. However all the lemmas and intermediate results are stated in order to help the reader to follow our reasoning.

2   Preliminaries

2.1   Monomorphic Types

The language we consider is the following version of untyped eager λ-calculus.

$x, f, \ldots \in \mathbb{X}$: program variables

$e, e_1, \ldots \in \mathbb{E}$: program expressions

$e ::= id\ x \mid \lambda x.e \mid e_1 + e_2 \mid if\ e_1\ then\ e_2\ else\ e_3 \mid int\ n \mid e_1(e_2) \mid \mu f.\lambda x.e$

$\lambda x.e$ denotes λ-abstraction and $e_1(e_2)$ denotes function application. In $\mu f.\lambda x.e$ the function f with formal parameter x is defined recursively. The guard in the conditional $if\ e_1\ then\ e_2\ else\ e_3$ is the test for zero.

In the Church/Curry monotype semantics the type of an expression e is a set of typings $< H, m >$ stating that the standard evaluation of e in an environment, where the global variables x have type $H(x)$ given by the type environment H, returns a value of type m. In the Church/Curry monotype system the type value m is a monotype, i.e.,

$m, m_1, \ldots \in \mathbb{M}^C \quad m ::= int \mid m_1 \to m_2$

The rule-based form of the Church/Curry monotype semantics allows us to *check* that a given type m is indeed the right type for the expression e, by considering $H \in \mathbb{H}^C$, where $\mathbb{H}^C$ is the domain of functions: $\mathbb{X} \to \mathbb{M}^C$.

$$H \overset{C}{\vdash} int\ n \Rightarrow int \qquad\qquad H \overset{C}{\vdash} id\ x \Rightarrow H(x)$$

$$\frac{H \overset{C}{\vdash} e_1 \Rightarrow int \quad H \overset{C}{\vdash} e_2 \Rightarrow int}{H \overset{C}{\vdash} e_1 + e_2 \Rightarrow int} \qquad \frac{H \overset{C}{\vdash} e_1 \Rightarrow int \quad H \overset{C}{\vdash} e_2 \Rightarrow m \quad H \overset{C}{\vdash} e_3 \Rightarrow m}{H \overset{C}{\vdash} if\ e_1\ then\ e_2\ else\ e_3 \Rightarrow m}$$

$$\frac{H \overset{C}{\vdash} e_1 \Rightarrow m_1 \to m_2 \quad H \overset{C}{\vdash} m_1}{H \overset{C}{\vdash} e_1(e_2) \Rightarrow m_2} \qquad \frac{H[x \leftarrow m_1] \overset{C}{\vdash} e \Rightarrow m_2}{H \overset{C}{\vdash} \lambda x.e \Rightarrow m_1 \to m_2}$$

$$\frac{H[f \leftarrow m] \overset{C}{\vdash} \lambda x.e \Rightarrow m}{H \overset{C}{\vdash} \mu f.\lambda x.e \Rightarrow m}$$

The above type rules can be used to check whether a given type is indeed the type of an expression e. However it is not possible to use directly the above rules to *infer* the right type of an expression. Hindley's algorithm [8] allows us to find the *principal* typing for the Church/Curry monotype system. A principal typing is a typing that subsumes all the others [6,9]. More generally this means that there is an exact representation for all possible typings. Hindley's algorithm uses a richer type domain, the domain of Herbrand terms, i.e., monotypes with variables. Hindley types are as follows.

$$a, \ldots \in \mathbb{V} \text{ :type variables}$$

$$\tau, \tau_1, \ldots \in \mathbb{M}_v^H \text{ :monotype with variables}$$

$$\tau ::= int \mid a \mid \tau_1 \to \tau_2$$

In this case the type environment domain $\mathbb{H}^H$ is the set of functions: $\mathbb{X} \to \mathbb{M}_v^H$.

In [2] Hindley's inference algorithm is reconstructed as an *exact* abstraction of the Church/Curry monotype semantics. This gives rise to an abstract semantics, which "implements" Hindley's inference algorithm as an abstract function $\mathcal{T}^H[\![.]\!]$, which, given a type environment $H \in \mathbb{H}^H$ returns a monotype with variables τ.

It is worth noting that the ML type inference algorithm is based on the Damas-Milner inference algorithm [6] which coincides with Hindley's inference algorithm on the language fragment (without let-polymorphism) we are considering.

The principal type computed by Hindley's inference algorithm is related to the Church/Curry monotype system by the following properties.

Theorem 1. *[2] Assume that $< H, \tau > \in \mathcal{T}^H[\![e]\!]$. Then, for all grounding substitutions $\vartheta : \mathbb{V} \to \mathbb{M}^C$, $\vartheta(H) \overset{C}{\vdash} e \Rightarrow \vartheta(\tau)$.*

Theorem 2. *[2] For all m such that $H \overset{C}{\vdash} e \Rightarrow m$, there exists a suitable $H' \in \mathbb{H}^H$ and τ such that $< H', \tau > \in \mathcal{T}^H[\![e]\!]$ and τ is the least common generalization of such m.*

2.2 Abstract Interpretation

Abstract interpretation [3,4] is a general theory for approximating the semantics of discrete dynamic systems, originally developed by Patrick and Radhia Cousot, in the late 70's. The *abstract semantics* is an approximation of the concrete one, where exact (concrete) values are replaced by (abstract) properties, modeled by an abstract domain.

In abstract interpretation based static program analysis we compute an abstract fixpoint semantics. Assume we have a semantic evaluation function $\mathcal{T}_P$ on a concrete domain $(\mathbb{C}, \sqsubseteq)$, whose least fixpoint $\text{lfp}_\mathbb{C}(\mathcal{T}_P)$ is the (concrete) semantics of the program P. The class of properties we want to consider is formalized as an abstract domain $(\mathbb{A}, \leq)$, related to $(\mathbb{C}, \sqsubseteq)$ by a Galois connection

$\alpha : \mathbb{C} \to \mathbb{A}$ and $\gamma : \mathbb{A} \to \mathbb{C}$ (abstraction and concretization functions). The corresponding *abstract semantic evaluation function* $\mathcal{T}_P^\alpha$ is systematically derived from $\mathcal{T}_P$, α and γ. The resulting abstract semantics $\mathrm{lfp}_\mathbb{A}(\mathcal{T}_P^\alpha)$ is a correct approximation of the concrete semantics by construction, i.e., $\alpha(\mathrm{lfp}_\mathbb{C}(\mathcal{T}_P)) \leq \mathrm{lfp}_\mathbb{A}(\mathcal{T}_P^\alpha)$, and no additional "correctness" theorems need to be proved. The abstract semantics $\mathrm{lfp}_\mathbb{A}(\mathcal{T}_P^\alpha)$ models a safe approximation of the property of interest: if the property is verified in $\mathrm{lfp}_\mathbb{A}(\mathcal{T}_P^\alpha)$ it will also be verified in $\mathrm{lfp}_\mathbb{C}(\mathcal{T}_P)$. An analysis method based on the computation of the abstract semantics $\mathrm{lfp}_\mathbb{A}(\mathcal{T}_P^\alpha)$ is effective only if the least fixpoint is reached in finitely many iterations, i.e., if the abstract domain is Noetherian. If this is not the case, *widening operators* can be used to ensure the termination. Widening operators [5] give an upper approximation of the least fixpoint and guarantee termination by introducing further approximation.

3   Our Type Inference Algorithm and Some of Its Properties

We have followed the general approach of [2] in using abstract interpretation theory to derive abstract type interpreters on suitable type domains. In our experiment (described in [7]) the type domain was still $\mathbb{M}_v^H$. Following the presentation of the ML type inference algorithm in [1], we have implemented the Herbrand type domain, by using (equality) constraints on type variables. Our abstract interpreter was obtained as an abstraction of the concrete denotational semantics for the untyped λ-calculus we have presented, extended with mutual recursion. We will use mutual recursion in the examples of Section 4 only, while the operational abstract semantics of this section (and the related properties) do not handle mutual recursion, for the sake of simplicity in the presentation.

The abstract semantics of an expression e in a given type environment H produces the type τ of the expression e together with some constraint γ on the type variables in H. The intuition is that the constraint γ is how H should be instantiated in order for e to have the type τ. We define $\mathbb{M}_v^N = \mathbb{M}_v^H \times (V \to \mathbb{M}_v^N)$.

$$a, \dots \in \mathbb{V} : \text{type variables}$$
$$(\tau, \gamma), (\tau_1, \gamma_1), \dots \in \mathbb{M}_v^N$$
$$\tau, \tau_1, \dots \in \mathbb{M}_v^H : \text{monotype with variables}$$
$$\tau ::= int \mid a \mid \tau_1 \to \tau_2$$
$$\gamma, \gamma_1 \in \mathbb{V} \to \mathbb{M}_v^H : \text{idempotent substitutions such that}$$
$$\gamma(\tau) = \tau.$$

In this case the type environment domain $\mathbb{H}^N$ is the set of functions: $\mathbb{X} \to \mathbb{M}_v^N$.

An abstract environment $H \in \mathbb{H}^N$ maps identifiers to abstract values. Substitutions are always restricted to the set of type variables occurring in the environment. The abstract partial order relation is defined in terms of the relations on terms and substitutions. Namely, $(\tau_1, \gamma_1) \leq (\tau_2, \gamma_2)$ if $\tau_1 \leq \tau_2$ and $\gamma_1 \leq \gamma_2$, where $\tau_1 \leq \tau_2$ if $\exists \vartheta$ such that $\vartheta(\tau_1) = \tau_2$. As usual, elements of the abstract domain are equivalence classes w.r.t. the corresponding equivalence relation. The *lub* operation can easily be defined by means of the unification algorithm. The bottom element $\perp$ is a pair consisting of a type variable and the empty substitution. The equivalence class corresponding to the top element contains all the pairs, whose first component is the distinguished term *Notype*. Note that the abstract domain is non-Noetherian since there exist infinite ascending chains.

In the following we present the rules of an abstract type interpreter on the domain $\mathbb{M}_v^N$. The inference rules are obtained systematically by abstracting the concrete semantics on the $\mathbb{M}_v^N$ type domain. We use the operators *apply* and *unify*, where $apply(\gamma, \tau) = \gamma(\tau)$ and $unify(a = b, \gamma_1, \gamma_2)$ computes the solved form of the set of equations $\{a = b, x_i^1 = t_i^1, x_i^2 = t_i^2\}$ with $x_i^1/t_i^1 \in \gamma_1$ and $x_i^2/t_i^2 \in \gamma_2$.

$$H \vdash int\ n \Rightarrow (int, \epsilon) \tag{1}$$

$$H \vdash id\ x \Rightarrow H(x) \tag{2}$$

$$\frac{\begin{array}{c} H \vdash e_1 \Rightarrow (\tau_1, \gamma_1) \quad H \vdash e_2 \Rightarrow (\tau_2, \gamma_2) \\ \gamma = unify(\{\tau_1 = int, \tau_2 = int, \gamma_1, \gamma_2\}) \end{array}}{H \vdash e_1 + e_2 \Rightarrow (apply(\gamma, \tau_1), \gamma)} \tag{3}$$

$$\frac{\begin{array}{c} H \vdash e_1 \Rightarrow (\tau_1, \gamma_1) \quad H \vdash e_2 \Rightarrow (\tau_2, \gamma_2) \quad H \vdash e_3 \Rightarrow (\tau_3, \gamma_3) \\ \gamma = unify(\{\tau_1 = int, \tau_2 = \tau_3, \gamma_1, \gamma_2, \gamma_3\}) \end{array}}{H \vdash if\ e_1\ then\ e_2\ else\ e_3 \Rightarrow (apply(\gamma, \tau_2), \gamma)} \tag{4}$$

$$\frac{\begin{array}{c} H \vdash e_1 \Rightarrow (\tau_1, \gamma_1) \quad H \vdash e_2 \Rightarrow (\tau_2, \gamma_2) \\ \gamma = unify(\{\tau_1 = f_1 \rightarrow f_2, \tau_2 = f_1, \gamma_1, \gamma_2\}) \end{array}}{H \vdash e_1 e_2 \Rightarrow (apply(\gamma, f_2), \gamma)} \tag{5}$$

$$\frac{H[x \leftarrow (f_1, \epsilon)] \vdash e \Rightarrow (\tau, \gamma) \quad \tau_1 = apply(\gamma, f_1)}{H \vdash \lambda x.e \Rightarrow ((\tau_1 \rightarrow \tau), \gamma)} \tag{6}$$

We have presented the rules for all the syntactic constructs, except recursion. If we abstract systematically the concrete semantics, the abstract semantics of recursion should be an abstract fixpoint computation. In our case we obtain the following rules.

$$\frac{H \vdash \mu f.\lambda x.e \Rightarrow_{T_P}^{n-1} (\tau_1, \gamma_1) \quad H \vdash \mu f.\lambda x.e \Rightarrow_{T_P}^{n} (\tau_2, \gamma_2)}{(\tau_1, \gamma_1) = (\tau_2, \gamma_2)} \qquad (7)$$
$$\overline{H \vdash \mu f.\lambda x.e \Rightarrow (\tau_2, \gamma_2)}$$

$$H \vdash (\mu f.\lambda x.e) \Rightarrow_{T_P}^{0} (x, \epsilon) \qquad (8)$$

$$\frac{H \vdash (\mu f.\lambda x.e) \Rightarrow_{T_P}^{n-1} (\tau_1, \gamma_1) \quad H \vdash (\mu f.\lambda x.e(\tau_1, \gamma_1)) \Rightarrow_{T_P} (\tau_2, \gamma_2)}{H \vdash (\mu f.\lambda x.e) \Rightarrow_{T_P}^{n} (\tau_2, \gamma_2)} \qquad (9)$$

$$\frac{H[f \leftarrow (\tau, \gamma)] \vdash e \Rightarrow (\tau_1, \gamma_1)}{H \vdash (\mu f.\lambda x.e, (\tau, \gamma)) \Rightarrow_{T_P} (\tau_1, \gamma_1)} \qquad (10)$$

However, our abstract domain is not Noetherian. This implies that we can have infinite ascending chains. As a consequence, we are not guaranteed to be able to find a solution to Rule 7 in a finite number of steps.

Therefore we introduce a family of widening operators. These are obtained by generalizing the operator introduced by Hindley's inference algorithm [8]. We obtain a family of widening operators simply by replacing Rule 7 (which requires the computation of the fixpoint for $\Rightarrow_{T_P}$), by the following rules.

Definition 1. *Given a k.*

$$\frac{H \vdash \mu f.\lambda x.e(\tau, \gamma) \Rightarrow_{wid}^{k} (\tau_1, \gamma_1)}{H \vdash \mu f.\lambda x.e \Rightarrow (\tau_1, \gamma_1)} \qquad (11)$$

$$\frac{H \vdash \mu f.\lambda x.e \Rightarrow_{T_P}^{k-1} (\tau_1, \gamma_1) \quad H \vdash (\mu f.\lambda x.e, (\tau_1, \gamma_1)) \Rightarrow_{T_P} (\tau_2, \gamma_2)}{(\tau_1, \gamma_1) = (\tau_2, \gamma_2)} \qquad (12)$$
$$\overline{H \vdash \mu f.\lambda x.e \Rightarrow_{wid}^{k} (\tau_1, \gamma_1)}$$

$$\frac{H \vdash \mu f.\lambda x.e \Rightarrow_{T_P}^{k-1} (\tau_1, \gamma_1) \quad H \vdash (\mu f.\lambda x.e, (\tau_1, \gamma_1)) \Rightarrow_{T_P} (\tau_2, \gamma_2)}{(\tau_1, \gamma_1) \neq (\tau_2, \gamma_2) \quad \vartheta = unify(\tau_1 \gamma_2 = \tau_2, \gamma_2)} \qquad (13)$$
$$\overline{H \vdash \mu f.\lambda x.e \Rightarrow_{wid}^{k} (apply(\vartheta, \tau_1), \vartheta)}$$

This gives us a family of widenings obtained simply by choosing a different value for k.

Consider now the Hindley type inference algorithm. We can prove that the Hindley inference algorithm can be obtained simply by choosing the widening corresponding to $k = 1$.

First we need some definitions which allow us to relate our type environments $H \in \mathbb{H}^N$ to the environment in $H \in \mathbb{H}^H$.

Definition 2. *Let $H \in \mathbb{H}^N$. Then $\tilde{H} \in \mathbb{H}^H$ is defined as follows:*

$$\tilde{H}(x) = \begin{cases} \tau & \text{if } H(x) = (\tau, \gamma) \\ \text{Undefined} & \text{otherwise} \end{cases}$$

We now define the application of a constraint γ to an environment.

Definition 3. *Let $H \in \mathbb{H}^H$. Then $\gamma(H) \in \mathbb{H}^H$ is defined as follows:*

$$\gamma(H)(x) = \begin{cases} \gamma(\tau) & \text{if } H(x) = \tau \\ \text{Undefined} & \text{otherwise} \end{cases}$$

We first prove that, if we infer (τ, γ) for the expression e, by using the widening operator with $k = 1$, then we obtain the type τ for the expression e in the environment $\gamma(H)$.

Theorem 3. *Assume that $H \vdash e \Rightarrow (\tau, \gamma)$ using Rules 11-13 with $k = 1$. Then $< \gamma(\tilde{H}), \tau >\in \mathcal{T}^H[\![e]\!]$.*

We now prove that also the opposite relation holds. We first define the most general environment $\mathcal{H} \in \mathbb{H}^N$. $\mathcal{H}$ is such that $\forall x,\ \mathcal{H}(x) = (v, \epsilon)$ where v is a variable and $\forall x, y,\ x \neq y : \mathcal{H}(x) \neq \mathcal{H}(y)$.

Theorem 4. *Assume that $< H, \tau >\in \mathcal{T}^H[\![e]\!]$ then $\mathcal{H} \vdash e \Rightarrow (\tau, \gamma)$, using Rules 11-13 with $k = 1$ and $\gamma(\mathcal{H}) = H$.*

This allows us to conclude that the Hindley inference algorithm is equivalent to our abstract semantics with the widening operator corresponding to $k = 1$.

We establish now several interesting properties of our abstract semantics.

We first formally prove that Rules 11-13 are indeed a family of widening operators, that is a correct approximation of the abstract fixpoint computation.

First we establish some elementary properties of the abstract semantics we have defined. The first properties state that starting from an environment $H \in \mathbb{N}^H$ which maps variables to abstract elements, our semantics assign to each expression an element which still belongs to the abstract domain we have defined.

Lemma 1. *If H is such that for all x, $H(x) = (\tau, \gamma)$ with $apply(\gamma, \tau) = \tau$. Then for all (τ, γ) such that $H \vdash e \Rightarrow (\tau, \gamma)$ or $H \vdash e \Rightarrow_{T_P}^n (\tau, \gamma)$ then $apply(\gamma, \tau) = \tau$.*

The next result is useful to prove Corollaries 1 and 2: the first one states that $\Rightarrow_{T_P}$ is monotone, while the latter guarantees that the computation of $\Rightarrow_{T_P}^n$, for all n leads to an ascending chain of abstract values.

Lemma 2. *For all e, if $H[f \leftarrow (\tau_0, \gamma_0)] \vdash e \Rightarrow (\tilde{\tau}_1, \tilde{\gamma}_1)$ and $H[f \leftarrow (\tau_1, \gamma_1)] \vdash e \Rightarrow (\tilde{\tau}_2, \tilde{\gamma}_2)$ with $(\tau_0, \gamma_0) \leq (\tau_1, \gamma_1)$, then $(\tilde{\tau}_1, \tilde{\gamma}_1) \leq (\tilde{\tau}_2, \tilde{\gamma}_2)$.*

Corollary 1. *Assume $(\tau_0, \gamma_0) \leq (\tau_1, \gamma_1)$. Let $(\mu f. \lambda x.e, (\tau_0, \gamma_0)) \vdash e \Rightarrow_{T_P} (\tau_2, \gamma_2)$ and $(\mu f. \lambda x.e, (\tau_1, \gamma_1)) \vdash e \Rightarrow_{T_P} (\tau_3, \gamma_3)$, then $(\tau_2, \gamma_2) \leq (\tau_3, \gamma_3)$.*

Corollary 2. *If* $(\mu f.\lambda x.e, (\tau, \gamma)) \Rightarrow_{T_P}^{n-1} (\tau_1, \gamma_1)$ *and* $(\mu f.\lambda x.e, (\tau, \gamma)) \Rightarrow_{T_P}^{n}$ (τ_2, γ_2), *then* $\tau_1 \leq \tau_2$ *and* $\gamma_1 \leq \gamma_2$.

By Tarski's theorem we know that the solution of Rule 7 consists in computing the least fixpoint of $\Rightarrow_{T_P}$, i.e., the least n such that $H \vdash \mu f.\lambda x.e \Rightarrow_{T_P}^{k-1}$ (τ_1, γ_1) $H \vdash \mu f.\lambda x.e \Rightarrow_{T_P}^{k} (\tau_2, \gamma_2)$ and $(\tau_1, \gamma_1) = (\tau_2, \gamma_2)$.

The next step is to formally prove that for each k, $\Rightarrow_{wid}^{k}$, computes a correct approximation of the least fixpoint of $\Rightarrow_{T_P}$.

We first need the following intermediate result.

Lemma 3. *Assume* e *contains* f, *then* $H[f \leftarrow (\tau, \gamma)] \vdash e \Rightarrow (\tau_1, \gamma_1)$, *then for all* ϑ, $H[f \leftarrow (\tau\gamma_1\vartheta, unify(\gamma, \gamma_1\vartheta))] \vdash e \Rightarrow (\tau_2, \gamma_2)$, *with* $\tau_2 = \tau_1\vartheta$, $\gamma_2 = \gamma_1\vartheta$.

We now prove that any abstract element (τ_k^w, γ_k^w) computed by $\Rightarrow_{wid}^{k}$ is indeed a fixpoint of $\Rightarrow_{T_P}$.

Corollary 3. *If* $H \vdash \mu f.\lambda x.e \Rightarrow_{wid}^{k} (\tau_1, \gamma_1)$ *then* $H \vdash (\mu f.\lambda x.e, (\tau_1, \gamma_1)) \Rightarrow_{T_P}$ (τ_1, γ_1).

Since the solution of Rule 7 consists in computing the least fixpoint of $\Rightarrow_{T_P}$, we can state the following.

Corollary 4. *Assume that* $H \vdash \mu f.\lambda x.e \Rightarrow (\tau_1, \gamma_1)$ *and* $H \vdash \mu f.\lambda x.e \Rightarrow_{wid}^{k}$ (τ_2, γ_2). *Then* $\tau_1 \leq \tau_2$ *and* $\gamma_1 \leq \gamma_2$.

The previous result shows that Rule13 is indeed a widening operator.

Now if we consider two widenings, different in the number of iterations (with different values of k), both terminating using Rule 13, we might wonder which is the relation among the computed abstract values. In principle, the most precise widening (the one with more iterations) might lead to a more precise result, unless we get to the fixpoint. This was claimed in [10,11] in the case of a polymorphic type system. On the contrary, the next theorem states that the result does not depend on the number of iterations.

Theorem 5. *For all* k, v, *if* $H \vdash \mu f.\lambda x.e \Rightarrow_{wid}^{k} (\tau_1^w, \gamma_1^w)$ *then* $H \vdash \mu f.e \Rightarrow_{wid}^{v}$ (τ_1^w, γ_1^w).

Theorem 5 together with Theorems 3 and 4, allows us to conclude that Hindley's inference algorithm is equivalent to our abstract semantics with the widening operator for any possible k, unless we succeed in reaching the least fixpoint.

4   Examples

In this Section we show some examples, most of which were presented in [7] as well. The theoretical results shown in the last Section allow one to better understand the experimental results. All the examples use the ML syntax for programs and type expressions.

Example 1. Consider the function (taken from [2])

```
# let rec f f1 g n x = if n=0 then g(x)
      else f(f1)(function x -> (function h -> g(h(x)))) (n-1) x f1;;
This expression has type ('a -> 'a) -> 'b but is here used with type 'b.
```

The expression cannot be typed by the ML algorithm (the underlined expression is the one to which the type error message applies, in the OCAML implementation). The expression defines the function $f\ f_1\ g\ n\ x = g(f_1^n(x))$ which has the type $(`a \to `a) \to (`a \to `b) \to int \to `a \to `b$. This type is correctly computed (by a fixpoint computation) in [2], by using a more complex type system (a polytype system à la Church-Curry). We infer the correct type, simply by using the widening corresponding to $k = 3$, because we reach the least fixpoint.

We show the sequence of abstract values (approximations for f) computed in the example.

1. step 0:
   $\tau_0 = \text{'a1}$
   $\gamma_0 = \epsilon$
2. step 1:
   $\tau_1 = \text{'a5->('a4->'a2)->int->'a4->'a2},$
   $\gamma_1 = \text{'a1} \leftarrow \text{'a5->('a3->(('a3->'a4)->'a2))->int->'a4->('a5->'a2)}\}$
3. step 2:
   $\tau_2 = \text{('a7->'a7)->('a7->'a6)->int->'a7->'a6},$
   $\gamma_2 = \{\text{'a2}\leftarrow \text{('a7->'a7)->'a6, 'a4}\leftarrow\text{'a7}\}$
4. step 3:
   $\tau_3 = \text{('a->'a) ->('a->'b)->int->'a->'b},$
   $\gamma_3 = \{\text{'a6}\leftarrow \text{('a->'a)->'b, 'a7}\leftarrow\text{'a}\}$

Note that at step 3 we reach the fixpoint since $(\tau_2, \gamma_2) = (\tau_3, \gamma_3)$ (both γ_2 and γ_3 are empty when restricted to the global environment). The sequence is obviously increasing. Looking at the sequence, we can also check the result we would obtain using a less precise widening, in particular, the ML widening ($k = 1$). In this case, we would use the Rule 13 after step 1. The computation of the $lub((apply(\gamma_1, \tau), \epsilon), (\tau_1, \gamma_1))$ would lead to the computation of the solved form of the equation

```
'a5->('a4->'a2)->int->'a4->'a2 =
'a5->('a3->(('a3->'a4)->'a2))->int->'a4->('a5->'a2).
```

The unification algorithm would generate the unsolvable equation

```
'a2=('a3->'a3)->'a2,
```

which explains the ML type error message. The result of the *lub* operation is therefore the top abstract value, i.e., the expression cannot be typed. When the widening terminates by using Rule 13 we always compute an upper approximation of the least fixpoint, i.e., a less precise type.

The next example, taken from [10], shows that ML does sometimes type a recursive function with a type which is not precise enough.

Example 2. # let rec f x = (function x -> function y -> x) 0 (f 0);;
val f : int -> int = <fun>

In the concrete semantics, f can be applied to a value of any type (not necessarily int), without causing any run time type error. If we choose $k = 2$, we reach the least fixpoint, and compute a more precise type

val f : 'a -> int = <fun>

The same type is inferred in [10], by using polymorphic recursion.

The next example, taken from [11], shows a problem similar to the one of Example 2, in an expression with mutual recursion.

Example 3. # let rec p x = if q x = q 1 then p x else p x
    and q x = p 1;;
val p : int -> 'a = <fun>
val q : int -> 'a = <fun>

If we choose $k = 3$, we reach the least fixpoint, and compute more precise types

val p : 'a -> 'b = <fun>
val q : 'a -> 'b = <fun>

The same types are inferred in [11], by using polymorphic recursion.

5   The Type System Corresponding to Our Abstract Interpreter

As we have already discussed the main difference between Hindley's monomorphic type inference algorithm and our abstract type interpreter lies in the way we deal with recursive definition. The examples presented in Section 4 show that our abstract type interpreter is more precise. Roughly speaking in a monomorphic type system each function application has to have the same type. Such a type is exactly the type of the recursive function. This is the reason why in the Hindley type inference algorithm each instantiation of the type of a recursive function produced by a function application has a direct effect in " guessing" the type of the recursive function: the instantiation produced by a function application has to produce the same instantiation on the type of the recursive function itself.

In a polymorphic type system each function application can have any type which is an instance of the recursive function type. This is the reason why in a polymorphic type inference algorithm the instantiation of the type of a recursive function in a function application does not produce the same instantiation on the type of the recursive function itself. In a polymorphic type system different function applications of a recursive function can lead to different (even *incompatible*) instantiations of the recursive function type.

Our type inference algorithm realizes a form of recursion which lies between monomorphism and polymorphic recursion. In the type system corresponding to our abstract type interpreter each function application can have any type which is an instance of the recursive function type as long as all these different instance are *compatible*. In this type system the different function applications of a recursive function can lead to different (but *compatible*) instantiations of the recursive function type. Intuitively this is due to the way we realize the computation of our abstract fixpoint. We collect all the constraints produced by the different instantiations due to different function applications in each computation step of the abstract fixpoint operator. This is the reason why such instantiations have to be *compatible* in order to produce a satisfiable constraint. On the other hand we never apply this constraint to the type of the recursive function we are trying to determine by fixpoint computation. As in a polymorphic type system, the instantiation of the type of a recursive function in a function application does not produce the same instantiation on the type of the recursive function itself. However, in our weak form of polymorphism such instantiations are checked to be *compatible*.

We now want to formally prove what we have just discussed. We first define a relation on environments in $\mathbb{H}^H$. $H, H' \in \mathbb{H}^H$ then $H \leq H'$ if $\forall x, H(x) \leq H'(x)$.

The next result guarantees us that for all the types checked by the Church/Curry monotype system there exists a principal type computed by our abstract type interpreter by using Rule 7. This result is a consequence of Theorem 2, 4 and Corollary 4.

Theorem 6. *Assume that $H \overset{C}{\vdash} e \Rightarrow m$. Then, there exists (τ, γ) such that and $\mathcal{H} \vdash e \Rightarrow (\tau, \gamma)$ with $H \geq \gamma(\tilde{\mathcal{H}})$ and $m \geq \tau$.*

On the other hand, as already shown in Section 4, there are types which can be inferred by our abstract type interpreter which can not be checked by the Church/Curry monotype system. Consider, for example, the function of Example 1.

```
# let rec f f1 g n x = if n=0 then g(x)
      else f(f1)(function x -> (function h -> g(h(x)))) (n-1) x f1;;
```

This expression cannot be typed by the ML algorithm. However, our abstract type interpreter is able to infer the type $('a \rightarrow 'a) \rightarrow ('a \rightarrow 'b) \rightarrow int \rightarrow 'a \rightarrow 'b$ for f.

The Damas-Milner-Mycroft polytype semantics associates a type to an expression e starting from a type environment which may contain universally quantified types. The quantified type $\forall a.\tau$ is used to allow one to consider any instance of τ obtained by renaming and instantiating the variable a whenever needed. This mechanism allows one to realize the recursive polymorphism since the type of a recursive function is inserted in the environment after having been generalized (i.e., all the free type variables are universally quantified). When a function application is reached, any instance obtained by a renaming of τ can be used. This allows the type τ of a recursive function to be independent from the type used in its applications.

In [2] the Damas-Milner-Mycroft polytype semantics and the corresponding type system are reconstructed on a suitable abstract domain. Let $ftv(t)$ be the set of free variables of t. Parametric/free variables (like a in $\forall b.b \rightarrow a$) are different from generic/bound type variables (like b in $\forall b.b \rightarrow a$):

$$a, \ldots \in \mathbb{V}_p : \text{parametric/free type variables}$$
$$b, \ldots \in \mathbb{V}_g : \text{generic/bound type variables}$$
$$a, b \in \mathbb{V} = \mathbb{V}_p \cup \mathbb{V}_g : \text{type variables } \mathbb{V}_p \cap \mathbb{V}_g = \emptyset$$
$$\pi \in \mathbb{P}_g^{DMM}, \quad \pi ::= \tau \mid \forall b_1 \ldots b_n.\tau \text{ where } \{b_1 \ldots b_n\} = ftv(\tau)$$

As already mentioned, our abstract domain is much simpler, i.e., it is the standard monomorphic types with variables domain without quantification. As a consequence, we do not have type generalization.

In this case the parametric type environment domain $\mathbb{H}_g^{DMM}$ is the set of functions: $\mathbb{X} \rightarrow \mathbb{P}_g^{DMM}$. The rule-based form of the Damas-Milner-Mycroft semantics allows us to *check* that a given type $\tau \in \mathbb{M}_v^H$ is indeed the right type for the expression e, by considering a given $H \in \mathbb{H}_g^{DMM}$. In this case we write $H \overset{DMM}{\vdash} e \Rightarrow \tau$.

First we need an operator which allows us to relate our type environments $H \in \mathbb{H}^N$ to the environment in $H \in \mathbb{H}_g^{DMM}$.

Definition 4. *Let $H \in \mathbb{H}^N$. Then $op(\gamma, H) \in \mathbb{H}_g^{DMM}$ is defined as follows:*

$$op(\gamma, H)(x) = \begin{cases} \gamma(\tau) & \text{if } H(x) = (\tau, \gamma') \text{ and } x \text{ is not a recursive program} \\ & \quad \text{variable} \\ gen_H(\tau) & \text{if } H(x) = (\tau, \gamma') \text{ and } x \text{ a is recursive program} \\ & \quad \text{variable} \\ Undefined & otherwise \end{cases}$$

where $gen_H(\tau)$ is a function which (universally) quantifies the free variable of τ w.r.t. the environment H.

The next result shows that any type that can be inferred with our abstract type interpreter can indeed be checked by the Damas-Milner-Mycroft polytype system.

Theorem 7. *Assume that $H \vdash e \Rightarrow (\tau, \gamma)$. Then $op(\gamma, \tilde{H}) \overset{DMM}{\vdash} e \Rightarrow \tau$.*

As already discussed at the beginning of this section polymorphic recursion is more powerful than the kind of polymorphic recursion we are able to capture with our abstract interpreter. Intuitively, the Damas-Milner-Mycroft polytype system could check an expression where the recursive function is called with two incomparable instances, for example, $int \rightarrow int$ and $bool \rightarrow int$. It is worth noting, however, that this case seems not to arise in meaningful programs. All the examples in [2,10,11,12], introduced as a motivation for the introduction of polymorphic recursion, can indeed be typed by our abstract interpreter.

6   Conclusion

We have developed an abstract interpreter on the Herbrand type domain. In this paper we show that the well known Hindley inference algorithm can be reconstructed by means of a particular widening operator on the fixpoint computation required by our abstract interpreter. We prove that all the widenings obtained as generalization of this particular operator give the same results unless the fixpoint is reached. Moreover, the type inference algorithm obtained by performing the fixpoint computation defines a new type system that we have shown to realize a form of recursion which lies between monomorphic and polymorphic recursion.

It is worth noting that our abstract domain is much simpler, i.e., it is the standard monomorphic types with variables domain without quantification. This is the reason why we do not need the type generalization. However, our abstract interpreter is able to assign the "right" type to all the examples introduced in [2,10,11,12] as a motivation for the introduction of polymorphic recursion.

One may wonder which is the type system corresponding to the inference algorithm defined by our abstract interpreter. We are currently working on its formal definition. It is worth noting that, as in the case of polymorphic recursion, not all the instances of the inferred type will be checked by the type system. This is true only for those instances which are comparable with all the function applications. In our case, since all the function applications are required to be comparable, the set of all the instances of the inferred type which can be actually checked will be finitely representable.

References

1. G. Cousineau and M. Mauny. *The Functional Approach to Programming*. Cambridge University Press, 1998.
2. P. Cousot. Types as abstract interpretations. In *Conference Record of the 24th ACM Symp. on Principles of Programming Languages*, pages 316–331. ACM Press, 1997.
3. P. Cousot and R. Cousot. Abstract Interpretation: A Unified Lattice Model for Static Analysis of Programs by Construction or Approximation of Fixpoints. In *Proceedings of Fourth ACM Symp. Principles of Programming Languages*, pages 238–252, 1977.
4. P. Cousot and R. Cousot. Systematic Design of Program Analysis Frameworks. In *Proceedings of Sixth ACM Symp. Principles of Programming Languages*, pages 269–282, 1979.
5. P. Cousot and R. Cousot. Comparing the Galois Connection and Widening/Narrowing Approaches to Abstract Interpretation. In M. Bruynooghe and M. Wirsing, editors, *Proceedings of PLILP'92*, volume 631 of *Lecture Notes in Computer Science*, pages 269–295. Springer-Verlag, 1992.
6. L. Damas and R. Milner. Principal type-schemes for functional programs. In *Proceedings of the Ninth Annual ACM Symposium on Principles of Programming Languages*, pages 207–212. ACM Press, 1982.
7. R. Gori and G. Levi. An experiment in type inference and verification by abstract interpretation. In A. Cortesi, editor, *Proc. of the VMCAI'02 workshop on Abstract Interpretaion and Model Checking*, volume 2294 of *LNCS*, pages 225–239, 2002.

8. J. R. Hindley. The principal type-scheme of an object in combinatory logic. *Transactions American Mathematical Society*, 146:29–60, 1969.

9. J. Mitchell. Type systems for programming languages. volume B of *Handbook of Theoretical Computer Science*, pages 365–458. Elsevier, 1990.

10. B. Monsuez. Polymorphic typing by abstract interpretation. In R. Shyamasundar, editor, *Proceedings of Foundation of Software Technology and Theoretical Computer Science*, volume 652 of *Lecture Notes in Computer Science*, pages 217–228. Springer-Verlag, 1992.

11. B. Monsuez. Polymorphic types and widening operators. In P. Cousot, M. Falaschi, G. Filè, and A. Rauzy, editors, *Proceedings of Static Analysis*, volume 724 of *Lecture Notes in Computer Science*, pages 224–281. Springer-Verlag, 1993.

12. A. Mycroft. Polymorphic type schemes and recursive definitions. In G. Goos and J. Hartmanis, editors, *Proceedings of the International Symposium on Programming*, volume 167 of *Lecture Notes in Computer Science*, pages 217–228. Springer-Verlag, 1984.

Domain Compression for Complete Abstractions

Roberto Giacobazzi and Isabella Mastroeni

Dipartimento di Informatica
Università di Verona
Strada Le Grazie 15, 37134 Verona (Italy)
roberto.giacobazzi@univr.it and mastroeni@sci.univr.it

Abstract. We introduce the operation of domain compression for complete refinements of finite abstract domains. This provides a systematic method for simplifying abstract domains in order to isolate the most abstract domain, when it exists, whose refinement toward completeness for a given semantic function returns a given domain. Domain compression is particularly relevant to compare abstractions in static program analysis and abstract model checking. In this latter case we consider domain compression in predicate abstraction of transition systems.

Keywords: Abstract interpretation, abstract domains, completeness, domain refinement, predicate abstraction, abstract model-checking, program analysis.

1 Introduction

A key problem in designing and implementing abstraction refinements is to have a way to control them in accuracy and costs. Automatic refinement can quickly lead to an explosion of the abstract domain, making the analysis unfeasible. This is particularly evident in completeness refinement [18], where a given sound abstraction is iteratively improved to become complete for a given semantics, providing no loss of precision in approximating semantics on the refined abstract domain. Completeness is the ideal target of most abstraction refinements. Many well known domain refinements can be viewed as making a domain complete for some given semantic function (this is the case of reduced product [7], disjunctive completion [7,21,12,16], and Heyting completion in [19]) as well as counterexamples-based abstract model checking refinement [4], provides an algorithmic account of making the abstraction complete for the transition relation of the system to analyze [14,23].

The problem. The problem of tuning refinements has been attacked from many directions: widenings [6,8], such as the oracle-guided widening [1] used to reduce the complexity of refined predicates in predicate abstraction, have been introduced to speed-up convergence in fix-point approximation. Analogously, abstract domain simplification [16,15] has been introduced as a domain-theoretic

L. Zuck et al. (Eds.): VMCAI 2003, LNCS 2575, pp. 146–160, 2003.

counterpart to reduce abstract domains in size and complexity. Intuitively a refinement is any operator improving the precision of abstract domains; while simplifications perform the dual operation of "taking out" information from domains. In this context, the notion of domain compression is particularly relevant [15,17]. The compressor is a domain simplification $\mathcal{B}$ such that if $\mathcal{R}$ is a refinement, then $\mathcal{B}(X)$ is the most abstract domain such that $\mathcal{R}(X) = \mathcal{R}(\mathcal{B}(X))$. This holds basically when the whole refined domain $\mathcal{R}(X)$ can be fully reconstructed (generated) by refinement from its *base* $\mathcal{B}(X)$ [15,17].

Related works. The notion of domain compression has been firstly introduced in abstract interpretation in [10,15], in connection with domain refinement. This provides a generalization of the operations of domain complementation [5,11] and disjunctive bases [16]. These operators are respectively the compressor associated with reduced product [7] and disjunctive completion [7], and have been used to the systematic design and optimization of abstract domains for static program analysis and in comparative semantics [21,12,16,13]. These are, to the best of our knowledge, the only known compressors introduced in the literature, even though the notion of domain compression has been studied from a general point of view. In [17] the notion of join-uniformity has been introduced to characterize domain compressors as adjoint functions of domain refinements. This notion allows the definition of a *lifted partial-order* making compressors monotone. This models the fact that compressors may take advantage of the structure of domains, leading often to non-monotone operations w.r.t. the standard inclusion order among domains. Apart from complementation and disjunctive bases, there are no systematic methods for deriving compressors from a refinement and in particular no generic pattern is known to derive compressors associated with completeness refinements.

Main results. In this paper we consider the problem of systematically deriving the compressors for the wide family of completeness refinements [18] in finite domains. We characterize when a completeness refinement has a corresponding compressor and provide an algorithm to compute the base of any domain w.r.t. the corresponding refinement. The base $\mathcal{B}(X)$ of a domain X, when it exists, includes the least amount of information needed to generate $\mathcal{R}(X)$ by refinements, i.e. it represents the least effort that a domain designer has to provide in order to have, by refinement, at least the same precision of X. This means that the family of all domains whose refinement is $\mathcal{R}(X)$ has a canonical (minimal) representative: The base $\mathcal{B}(X)$. The interest in computing $\mathcal{B}(X)$ is many-fold: (1) $\mathcal{B}(X)$ provides a minimal representation of domains. This is particularly important in designing predicate abstractions [20], where states are abstracted according to the evaluation of some predicate, and the abstract domain reflects the partition made by predicates on the space of states. In this case $\mathcal{B}(X)$ can be used to derive a core of predicates (i.e., a basic partition) which has to be included in any domain willing to achieve the precision degree of X. (2) $\mathcal{B}(X)$ can be used to compare abstractions. Indeed, if $\mathcal{B}(X) \neq \mathcal{B}(Y)$, then it is impossible to achieve the precision of $\mathcal{R}(Y)$ by refining X and the other way round. (3) $\mathcal{B}$ can be used to hide information in domains. This, combined with domain refinement $\mathcal{R}$, can be used to design optimal domains providing the way to reduce by compression irrelevant information in abstract domains. Applications of this techniques have been considered in static program analysis for the compressors of domain complementation and disjunctive base (e.g., see [15]).

2   Preliminaries

2.1   Basic Notions

Let S and C be sets. $\wp(S)$ denotes the power-set of S, $S \smallsetminus C$ denotes the set-difference between S and C, $S \subset C$ denotes strict inclusion, $|S|$ denotes the cardinality of S. Let $f : S \to C$ and $X \subseteq S$ then $f(X) \overset{\text{def}}{=} \{f(x) \mid x \in X\}$. In the following $\langle C, \leq, \vee, \wedge, \top, \bot \rangle$ ($C_{\leq}$ for short) denotes a complete lattice C, with ordering $\leq$, lub $\vee$, glb $\wedge$, greatest element (top) $\top$, and least element (bottom) $\bot$. $x \in C$ is *meet-irreducible* in C if $\forall a, b \in C$. $x = a \wedge b \Rightarrow x \in \{a, b\}$. The set of meet-irreducible elements in C is denoted $Mirr(C)$. Join-irreducibles ($Jirr(C)$) are dually defined. $\downarrow S \overset{\text{def}}{=} \{x \in C \mid \exists y \in S. \ x \leq y\}$. $\downarrow x$ is a shorthand for $\downarrow \{x\}$. The upward closure $\uparrow$ is dually defined. In the following $g \circ f$ denotes function composition, i.e., $g \circ f \overset{\text{def}}{=} \lambda x. g(f(x))$. The identity function $\lambda x. \ x : X \to X$ is denoted ι, $\cong$ denotes the isomorphism of ordered structures, and $S \longrightarrow T$ is the set of all functions from S to T ordered point-wise by $\sqsubseteq$. Let $X_{\leq}$, then $max(X) \overset{\text{def}}{=} \{\ y \in X \mid \forall x \in X . \ x \geq y \Rightarrow x = y \ \}$. *min* is dually defined.

2.2   Abstract Interpretation and Transition Systems

In the following we consider the standard Galois connection based abstract interpretation [6]. A pair of functions $f : A \to B$ and $g : B \to A$ forms an *adjunction* if $\forall x \in A. \forall y \in B. \ f(x) \leq_B y \Leftrightarrow x \leq_A g(y)$. f (g) is called the *left-(right-) adjoint* to g (f) and it is an additive (co-additive) function, i.e., f preserves lub's (glb's) of all subsets of A, empty-set included. Also, additive (co-additive) functions f admit right (resp. left) adjoint $f^{+} \overset{\text{def}}{=} \lambda x. \ \bigvee \{\ y \mid f(y) \leq x \ \}$ (resp. $f^{-} \overset{\text{def}}{=} \lambda x. \ \bigwedge \{\ y \mid x \leq f(y) \ \}$). Remember that $(f^{+})^{-} = (f^{-})^{+} = f$ [2]. A *Galois connection* (GC) is an adjunction between posets, and it is denoted (A, f, B, f^{+}). In the following we assume that the concrete domain C is a complete lattice such that (C, α, A, γ) is a GC where α and γ are respectively the abstraction and concretization. If in addition $\forall a \in A. \ \alpha(\gamma(a)) = a$, then (C, α, A, γ) is a *Galois insertion* (GI) of A in C. When (C, α, A, γ) is a GI then each value of the abstract domain A is useful in representing C, being γ 1-1 and α onto. Abstract domains can be equivalently formulated either as posets, related by a GI or as closure operators on C [7]. This second formulation has the advantage of being independent from the representation of abstract objects [7,18]. An *upper closure operator* on a poset C is an operator $\rho : C \to C$ in $uco(C)$ which is monotone, idempotent, and extensive: $\forall x \in C. \ x \leq \rho(x)$. *Lower closures* in $lco(C)$ are dually defined. Each (upper/lower) closure ρ is uniquely determined by the set of its fix-points $\rho(C)$. If C is a complete lattice then both $\langle uco(C), \sqsubseteq, \sqcup, \sqcap, \lambda x.\top, \lambda x.x \rangle$ and $\langle \rho(C), \leq, \vee_\rho, \wedge, \top, \rho(\bot) \rangle$ with $\vee_\rho X \stackrel{\text{def}}{=} \rho(\vee X)$, are complete lattices. In particular $X \subseteq C$ is the set of fix-points of an upper closure on C iff X is a *Moore-family* of C, i.e., $X = \mathcal{M}(X) \stackrel{\text{def}}{=} \{ \wedge S \mid S \subseteq X \}$ — where $\wedge \varnothing = \top \in \mathcal{M}(X)$, iff X is isomorphic to an abstract domain A in a GI (C, α, A, γ). Indeed if (C, α, A, γ) is a GI then $\gamma \circ \alpha \in uco(C)$ and if $\rho \in uco(C)$ then $(C, \rho, \rho(C), \iota)$ is a GI. For any $X \subseteq C$, $\mathcal{M}(X)$ is called the *Moore-closure* of X in C, i.e., $\mathcal{M}(X)$ is the least (w.r.t. set-inclusion) subset of C which contains X and it is a Moore-family of C. $uco(C)$ is therefore isomorphic to the so called *lattice of abstract interpretations* of C [7]. In this case $X \sqsubseteq Y$ iff $Y \subseteq X$ as Moore families of C, iff X is more concrete than Y. It turns out that an abstract domain A is always isomorphic to a complete meet subsemilattice of C, but, in general, it is not isomorphic to a complete sublattice of C, i.e., $\vee \leq \vee_{\gamma \circ \alpha}$. When $\vee = \vee_{\gamma \circ \alpha}$, viz. when γ is additive, we say that A is *disjunctive*. Let $\{A_i\}_{i \in I} \subseteq uco(C)$: $\sqcup_{i \in I} A_i$ is most concrete common abstraction of all the A_i's and $\sqcap_{i \in I} A_i$ is (isomorphic to) the well-known *reduced product*, i.e. it is the most abstract common concretization of all the A_i's. Note that $\sqcap_{i \in I} A_i = \mathcal{M}(\cup_{i \in I} A_i)$. Dual results hold for lower closures. We follow [3,7,9] in specifying a hardware or software system as a discrete transition system $\langle \Sigma, \tau \rangle$ consisting of a set Σ of *states* and a total *transition relation* $\tau \subseteq \Sigma \times \Sigma$ that is assumed to be total. We denote τ^{-1} the inverse relation of τ and τ^* its transitive and reflexive closure. Given a transition system $\langle \Sigma, \tau \rangle$ we consider two predicate transformers such that for any predicate $X \in \wp(\Sigma)$: $post[\tau](X) \stackrel{\text{def}}{=} \{ s' \in \Sigma \mid \exists s \in X.\ s\tau s' \}$ and $pre[\tau](X) \stackrel{\text{def}}{=} post[\tau^{-1}](X)$. It is well known that $pre[\tau]$ and $post[\tau]$ are additive functions on $\wp(\Sigma)$ and they both admit right adjoint functions [22]: $\widetilde{pre}[\tau](X) = \{ s \in \Sigma \mid \forall x \in \Sigma.\ s\tau x \Rightarrow x \in X \}$ and $\widetilde{post}[\tau](X) = \{ s \in \Sigma \mid \forall x \in \Sigma.\ x\tau s \Rightarrow x \in X \}$.

2.3 Completeness in Abstract Interpretation and Model Checking

Completeness in abstract interpretation formalizes the intuition that no loss of precision is accumulated by approximating concrete semantics [6]. Given a GI (C, α, A, γ), $f^\sharp$ is a *sound* abstraction of f if $\alpha \circ f \leq f^\sharp \circ \alpha$, or equivalently (by adjunction) if $f \circ \gamma \leq \gamma \circ f^\sharp$. These two definitions are not equivalent when equality is required. Indeed $\alpha \circ f = f^\sharp \circ \alpha$ means that no loss of precision is accumulated by approximating the input arguments of a given semantic function, while $f \circ \gamma = \gamma \circ f^\sharp$ means that no loss of precision is accumulated by approximating the result of computations on abstract objects. The notion of *backward* (B) and *forward* (F) completeness has been introduced in [14] to capture this difference. By generalizing the results in [18], which have been proved for backward completeness only, in [14] it has been proved that both backward and forward completeness are properties of the underlying abstract domain.

Proposition 1 ([18,14]). *Let $f : C \to C$, and (C, α, A, γ) be a Galois insertion. There exists $f^\sharp : A \to A$ such that (C, α, A, γ) and $f^\sharp$ are B-complete (F-complete) for f iff $\alpha \circ f = \alpha \circ f \circ \gamma \circ \alpha$ ($f \circ \gamma = \gamma \circ \alpha \circ f \circ \gamma$).*

Therefore, given an abstract domain $\rho \in uco(C)$ and $f : C \longrightarrow C$, we can say that ρ is B-complete (F-complete) for f if $\rho \circ f \circ \rho = \rho \circ f$ ($\rho \circ f \circ \rho = f \circ \rho$). Clearly, ρ is both backward and forward complete iff ρ is a morphism, i.e., $f \circ \rho = \rho \circ f$. As proved in [18] it is always possible to constructively refine any abstract domain ρ to make it B-complete for any (Scott-)continuous function and at the same time to find the most abstract domain for which this holds. This (least) refinement is called the B-complete shell of ρ. An analogous result has been proved in [14] characterizing the F-complete shell of ρ. Recall that, if $f : C \to C$ then $f^{-1}(y) = \{ x \mid f(x) = y \}$.

Theorem 1 ([18,14]). *Let $f : C \to C$ be continuous and $\rho \in uco(C)$. ρ is B-complete for f iff $\bigcup_{y \in \rho(C)} max(f^{-1}(\downarrow y)) \subseteq \rho(C)$. ρ is F-complete for f iff $\forall x \in \rho(C). \ f(x) \in \rho(C)$.*

Therefore, while B-complete domains are closed under (maximal) inverse image of the function f, F-complete domains are closed under direct image of f. Both B/F-complete shells can be constructively derived by minimally refining non-complete domains by adding respectively (maximal) inverse image and direct image of f. In the case where f is additive, as in the case of $pre[\tau]$ and $post[\tau]$, this can be formalized with a unique fix-point definition. Observe in fact that in this case $f^+ = \lambda x. \ max(f^{-1}(\downarrow x))$. Hence we can define a (single-step) *complete refinement* as $R_g(X) = \mathcal{M}(g(X) \cup X)$. The fix-point of $R_g(X)$ for $g \in \{f, f^+\}$ gives the corresponding complete shell. In particular, by Theorem 1, an abstract domain $X \sqsubseteq A$ is $B(F)$-complete for f iff $X = A \sqcap R_{f^+}(X)$ ($X = A \sqcap R_f(X)$). In the following we denote $\mathcal{R}_f(X) \stackrel{\text{def}}{=} gfp(\lambda X. \ A \sqcap R_f(X))$. Given $\rho \in uco(C)$ this implies that $\mathcal{R}_{f^+}(\rho)$ and $\mathcal{R}_f(\rho)$ are resp. the B- and F-complete shell of ρ.

3   Squeezing Abstract Domains

In the previous section we observed that any abstract domain refinement to achieve either B- or F-completeness, can be specified as the fix-point iteration of an abstract domain transformer which iteratively enhance domains by including the image of respectively either f^+ or f. This specifies a generic pattern for abstract domain refinement relatively to a given function: Given a concrete domain C, an abstract domain $\rho \in uco(C)$ and a monotone semantic function $f : C \to C$, the (generic) completeness refinement is defined as the limit of the sequence of abstract domains $\{X_n\}_{n \in \mathbb{N}}$ where $X_0 = \rho$ and $X_{n+1} = \mathcal{M}(f(X_n) \cup X_n)$. It is clear that $\rho = X_0 \subseteq X_1 \subseteq X_2 \ldots$ and that $\mathcal{R}_f(\rho) = \sqcap_{n \in \mathbb{N}} X_n$ [18]. In this section we consider the problem of computing the most abstract domain which is included in ρ and which provides the same refinement as ρ does. We call this domain the *base* of ρ. As observed in [10] not all refinements admit a base. Consider $Sign = \{\mathbb{Z}, +, -, \varnothing\}$, which is a closure on $\wp(\mathbb{Z})$ and the function $f = \lambda x. -x$. Note that $f^+ = f$. It is clear that $\mathcal{R}_f(\{\mathbb{Z}, +\}) = \mathcal{R}_f(\{\mathbb{Z}, -\}) = Sign$ but $\{\mathbb{Z}, +\} \cap \{\mathbb{Z}, -\} = \{\mathbb{Z}\}$ and $\mathcal{R}_f(\{\mathbb{Z}\}) = \{\mathbb{Z}\}$.

3.1   Abstract Domain Compression

Let $\mathcal{R}$ be a domain refinement, i.e., $\mathcal{R} : uco(C) \to uco(C)$ such that $\mathcal{R}(X) \sqsubseteq X$. Note that, for any monotone map $f : C \to C$, $\mathcal{R}_f \in lco(uco(C))$. Intuitively a domain compressor is an operator $\mathcal{B} : uco(C) \to uco(C)$ on abstract domains, such that $X \sqsubseteq \mathcal{B}(X)$ and $\mathcal{B}(X)$ is the most abstract domain such that $\mathcal{R}(\mathcal{B}(X)) = \mathcal{R}(X)$. This specifies $\mathcal{B}$ and $\mathcal{R}$ as a pair of inverse functions, such that $\mathcal{R}(\mathcal{B}(X)) = \mathcal{R}(X)$ and $\mathcal{B}(\mathcal{R}(X)) = \mathcal{B}(X)$. It is easy to verify that this holds (i.e. $\mathcal{B}(X)$ exists unique) iff $\mathcal{R}$ is *join-uniform* [17], i.e. iff the following equation holds: $\mathcal{R}(\bigsqcup \{\, Y \in uco(C) \,|\, \mathcal{R}(X) = \mathcal{R}(Y) \,\}) = \mathcal{R}(X)$. When this happens, we call $\mathcal{B} \stackrel{def}{=} \lambda X.\ \sqcup \{\, Y \in uco(C) \,|\, \mathcal{R}(X) = \mathcal{R}(Y) \,\}$ the *domain compressor* of $\mathcal{R}$ and, for $X \in uco(C)$, $\mathcal{B}(X)$ the *base* of X for $\mathcal{R}$. Join-uniformity is the key notion in order to let a domain refinement have a corresponding compressor as adjoint [17].

Theorem 2 ([17]). *Let $\mathcal{R}$ be a join-uniform domain refinement and for any $X, Y \in \mathrm{uco}(C)$: $X \sqsubseteq^{\mathcal{R}} Y$ iff $\mathcal{R}(X) \sqsubseteq \mathcal{R}(Y) \,\wedge\, (\mathcal{R}(X) = \mathcal{R}(Y) \;\Rightarrow\; Y \subseteq X)$. Then $(\mathrm{uco}(C)_{\sqsubseteq^{\mathcal{R}}}, \mathcal{R}, \mathrm{uco}(C)_{\sqsubseteq^{\mathcal{R}}}, \mathcal{B})$ is a GC.*

The only known examples of domain compressors are disjunctive base in [16], which is the domain compressor associated with the disjunctive completion refinement $\lambda \rho.\curlyvee(\rho) \stackrel{def}{=} \sqcup \{\, \eta \,|\, \eta \sqsubseteq \rho,\ \eta \text{ is additive} \,\}$; and domain complementation, which is the compressor of reduced product $\lambda \rho.\, \eta \sqcap \rho$ with $\eta \in uco(C)$.

Theorem 3 ([16,11]). *Let C be a complete lattice and $\rho, \eta \in \mathrm{uco}(C)$. If $C = \wp(S)$ then $\mathcal{B}_{\curlyvee}(\rho) = \mathcal{M}(Jirr(\curlyvee(\rho)))$ is the base of ρ for $\curlyvee$. If C is meet-generated by $Mirr(C)$, i.e. $C = \mathcal{M}(Mirr(C))$, then $\mathcal{B}_{\sqcap \eta}(\rho) = (\eta \sqcap \rho) \ominus \rho$ is the base of ρ for $\lambda \rho.\, \eta \sqcap \rho$, where $A \ominus B \stackrel{def}{=} \mathcal{M}(Mirr(A) \setminus B)$.*

In this paper we introduce a method for systematically derive the base of any (B or F-)complete refinements on finite lattices, when they exist. The following proposition is straightforward by the definitions given above.

Proposition 2. *Let $\mathcal{R}$ be a join-uniform refinement, $\mathcal{B}$ be the corresponding compressor and $\eta, \rho \in \mathrm{uco}(C)$. Then $\mathcal{B}(\eta) = \mathcal{B}(\rho)$ iff $\mathcal{R}(\eta) = \mathcal{R}(\rho)$.*

Therefore, domain refinements are order-embedding's on the set of corresponding bases. This means that the base provides a canonical representation of complete abstractions, which are the fix-point domains of $\mathcal{R}_f$. The following example shows a simple transition system $\langle \Sigma, \tau \rangle$ and two incomparable abstractions ρ and η, both having the same refinement.

Example 1. On the left side of Figure 1(a) we have the transition system with states $\Sigma = \{1, 2, 3, 4\}$ and transition relation τ. On the right side we have the concrete domain $\wp(\{1, 2, 3, 4\})$ including the function $f = post[\tau]$. In Figure 1(b) and (c) we consider, respectively, two different abstractions of the concrete domain and their corresponding refinements. The elements double circled are the points in the abstractions, the elements single circled are the points added by $\mathcal{R}_{post[\tau]}$. It is worth noting that both $\eta = \{\top, \{1, 4\}, \{2, 3\}, \{1\}, \bot\}$ and $\rho = \{\top, \{1, 4\}, \{2, 3\}, \{3\}, \bot\}$ have the same complete refinement: $\mathcal{R}_{post[\tau]}(\rho) = \mathcal{R}_{post[\tau]}(\eta) = \{\top, \{1, 3, 4\}, \{1, 4\}, \{2, 3\}, \{1, 3\}, \{1\}, \{3\}, \bot\}$.

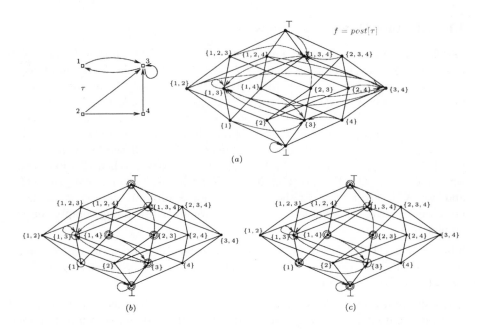

Fig. 1. A transition system, two abstractions and their complete refinements

This example shows that two incomparable abstractions may have the same completeness refinement. In this case, the base $\mathcal{B}_{post[\tau]}(\rho) = \mathcal{B}_{post[\tau]}(\eta)$, if it exists, provides the least abstraction from which we can derive, by refinement, a complete abstraction of $\langle \Sigma, \tau \rangle$ including both ρ and η. It is clear by Proposition 2, that any further abstraction of the base $\mathcal{B}_{post[\tau]}(\rho)$ cannot produce the same refinement as ρ and η do.

3.2 Reversing Abstract Domain Refinement

The key problem in designing domain compressors is to systematically derive their bases. In this section we formalize a method consisting in an algorithm for the construction of the base of any completeness refinement. By Theorem 3 it's clear that irreducible elements play a key role in designing domain compressors. This notion naturally generalizes to arbitrary functions.

Definition 1. *Given a (unary-)function* $f : C \to C$, *the set of* f-*reducible elements is* $\dot{f}(C) \overset{\text{def}}{=} \{ x \in C \mid \exists y \in C \smallsetminus \{x\} . f(y) = x \}$. $firr(C) \overset{\text{def}}{=} C \smallsetminus \dot{f}(C)$ *is the set of* f-*irreducible elements.*

The idea is that x is f-reducible if x can be generated from elements which are different from x. Consider the sequence of objects obtained by iterating a function f: $f^1(x) \overset{\text{def}}{=} f(x)$ and $f^{n+1}(x) \overset{\text{def}}{=} f(f^n(x))$. For $x \in C$ define $f^*(x) = Z \subseteq C$ if $\forall z \in Z . \exists n \in \mathbb{N} . f^n(x) = z$. The following proposition relates the lack of join-uniformity to cycles via f in C, as observed above in *Sign*.

Proposition 3. *Let C a complete lattice and let $Mirr(C) \cap \dot{f}(C) = X \neq \varnothing$. If $f : C \to C$ is a monotone map and there exists $Y \subseteq X$ and $x_1, x_2 \in X$ such that $x_1 \neq x_2$ and $f^*(x_1) = Y = f^*(x_2)$ then $\mathcal{R}_f$ is not join-uniform.*

Next example shows that, in general, the inverse of Proposition 3 doesn't hold.

Example 2. Consider the following lattice and f as drawn in the picture. Both closures, here represented with dashed and dot lines, are such that their refinements $\mathcal{R}_f$ give back the whole lattice, while their intersection $\{\top, b\}$ is still complete but different from the whole lattice. In this case $\mathcal{R}_f$ is not join-uniform and the hypotheses of Proposition 3 are not satisfied.

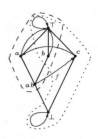

In order to model join-uniformity, we need first to model when a set of objects can be generated from a candidate base by domain refinement $\mathcal{R}_f$.

Definition 2. *Let C be a finite lattice, $X \subseteq C$, $x \in C$, and $\delta \in \text{uco}(C)$.*

$$- \ G(x) \stackrel{def}{=} min \left\{ \ Z \subseteq C \ \big| \ x \notin Z, \ (\textstyle\bigwedge Z = x \ \vee \ f(Z) = x) \ \right\};$$

$$- \ \widehat{X}(\delta) \stackrel{def}{=} \left\{ \ \bigcup_{x \in X} Y_x \ \middle| \ \begin{array}{l} ((G(x) \neq \varnothing \ \wedge \ x \notin \delta) \ \Rightarrow \ Y_x \in G(x)), \\ ((G(x) = \varnothing \ \vee \ x \in \delta) \ \Rightarrow \ Y_x = \{x\}) \end{array} \ \right\};$$

In this definition, $G(x)$ is the set of all minimal (viz., non-redundant) sets of elements that do not include x and generate x by either meet or f. $\widehat{X}(\delta)$ is the collection of all the sets that can generate X by one step of the completeness refinement assuming δ as the candidate base. This means that we have to find only the elements generating $X \smallsetminus \delta$. In order to design a method for filtering out those objects that can be generated by domain refinement, and therefore that are not in the base, we design a tree-like structure, where the descendant nodes of the tree are sets of objects from which the ancestor can be derived by refinement. Given an abstract domain $\delta \in uco(C)$, we introduce a binary relation $\to_\delta \subseteq \wp(C) \times \wp(C)$ such that $X \to_\delta Y$ if $Y \in \widehat{X}(\delta)$ (i.e. $X \subseteq \mathcal{R}_f(Y)$).

Definition 3. *Let $\delta \in \text{uco}(C)$, $x \in C$, and $\Gamma_x^n(\delta) \subseteq \wp(C)$ be the least set such that $\{x\} \in \Gamma_x^0(\delta)$ and $Y \in \Gamma_x^{n+1}(\delta)$ if $X \in \Gamma_x^n(\delta)$, $X \to_\delta Y$, $X \not\subseteq \delta$, $X \neq Y$ and $\forall m \leq n, W \in \Gamma_x^m(\delta) : W \to_\delta^* X. \ (X \smallsetminus \delta) \cap W = \varnothing$.*

In the following we denote $X \rightarrowtail Y$ if $X \to_\delta Y$, $X \in \Gamma_x^n(\delta)$ and $Y \in \Gamma_x^{n+1}(\delta)$. By construction it's clear that $\langle \bigcup_{n \in \mathbb{N}} \Gamma_x^n(\delta), \rightarrowtail \rangle$ is a tree-like poset. We abuse notation by letting $\Gamma_x(\delta)$ represent this tree. A path in the tree from the root x to X represents a sequence of different sets of objects that, by iteratively applying $\mathcal{R}_f$, may generate x. Note that X is not a leaf in the tree (i.e. $\exists Y . X \rightarrowtail Y$) if $X \not\subseteq \delta$ can be generated by $\mathcal{R}_f$ from a different set and there is no cycle w.r.t. the sets W in the path from the root to X, i.e. $(X \smallsetminus \delta) \cap W = \varnothing$.

154   R. Giacobazzi and I. Mastroeni

Remark 1. Note that if C is a finite lattice and $\rho \in uco(C)$, then for each $x \in C$ the tree $\Gamma_x(\rho)$ is finite by construction. Indeed there is a check on the existence of cycles in $\Gamma_x(\delta)$, which avoids repetitions in the tree. Moreover for each node X which is not a leaf, i.e. such that $\widehat{X}(\delta) \neq \{X\}$, $X \not\subseteq \delta$, and $\Gamma_x(\delta)$ doesn't contain a cycle, then $\widehat{X}(\delta)$ contains each possible minimal set, different from X, that can generate, by either meet or f, all the elements of X that are not in ρ.

In the following we consider finite lattices C and monotone functions $f : C \to C$. We also denote the set of leaves of $\Gamma_x(\delta)$ as $\mathcal{L}_x(\delta)$. The following proposition proves the correspondence between the tree construction and the generation of objects in the refined domain.

Proposition 4. *Let C be a finite lattice, $\delta \in uco(C)$ and $x \in C$. Then* (1) $Y \in \mathcal{L}_x(\delta) \Rightarrow x \in \mathcal{R}_f(Y)$ *and* (2) $x \in \mathcal{R}_f(\delta) \Rightarrow \exists Y \in \mathcal{L}_x(\delta) . Y \subseteq \delta$.

Example 3. Consider the concrete domains depicted below and suppose that $\rho = \iota$. Our goal is to squeeze the concrete domain C. It's clear that, in order to generate the whole concrete domain from the base, we have to generate $Mirr(\rho)$. Let's consider an example of construction of $\Gamma_x(\delta)$ where $\delta = \mathcal{M}(firr(C))$ is a possible candidate base. In the following examples f is drawn on the domain. We put an O, denoting bad leaves, under each leaf of Γ_x that contains x, and we put an X otherwise.

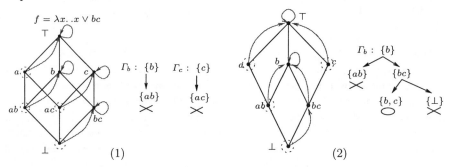

Note that in figure (1) the domain refinement $\mathcal{R}_f$ is join uniform and it is simple to verify that the base is exactly the closure $\{\top, a, ab, ac, \bot\}$. Also in figure (2) the refinement $\mathcal{R}_f$ associated with the represented function is join uniform. The candidate base $\delta = \mathcal{M}(firr(C)) = \{\top, a, c, ab, \bot\}$ is clearly too concrete: $\mathcal{R}_f(\{\top, a, c, ab, \bot\}) = C$ but also $\mathcal{R}_f(\{\top, a, c, \bot\}) = C$.

Since abstract domains are Moore families, it's clear that, if the goal is to compress the concrete domain C, then δ can be a base for $\mathcal{R}_f$ if $Mirr(C) \subseteq \mathcal{R}_f(\delta)$. Moreover if $M_f^C \stackrel{\text{def}}{=} Mirr(C) \cap \dot{f}(C)$ and $I_f(C) \stackrel{\text{def}}{=} Mirr(C) \cap firr(C)$ then since any $x \in M_f^C$ can still be generated by refinement from δ being f-reducible, δ has to include at least $I_f(C)$. Indeed, the elements in $I_f(C)$ cannot be generated neither by f nor by meet. Therefore if $\delta \in uco(C)$ is a candidate base then $I_f(C) \subseteq \delta$. In order to generalize this situation to the base of any abstraction ρ of C, we require $Mirr(\mathcal{R}_f(\rho)) \subseteq \mathcal{R}_f(\delta)$.

Lemma 1. *Let* $\rho \in uco(C)$. *Then* (1) $x \in Mirr(\mathcal{R}_f(\rho)) \cap \rho \Rightarrow x \in Mirr(\rho)$ *and* (2) $x \in Mirr(\mathcal{R}_f(\rho)) \smallsetminus \rho \Rightarrow x \in \dot{f}(C)$.

Lemma 1 says that any candidate base has to generate the following set of meet-irreducibles: $M_f^\rho \overset{\text{def}}{=} Mirr(\{x \in \dot{f}(C) \smallsetminus \rho \mid \exists L \in \mathcal{L}_x(\rho) . L \subseteq \rho\}) \cup Mirr(\rho)$. M_f^ρ is clearly redundant even though it does not require the construction of $\mathcal{R}_f(\rho)$, as specified by the following proposition (see the scenario on the side).

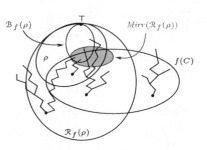

Proposition 5. *If* $\rho \in uco(C)$ *and* $\rho \sqsubseteq \delta$ *then* $M_f^\rho \subseteq \mathcal{R}_f(\delta) \Rightarrow \mathcal{R}_f(\delta) = \mathcal{R}_f(\rho)$.

The proposition above says that M_f^ρ contains all the elements of C that can be generated starting from elements in ρ and that are necessary in order to generate the whole domain $\mathcal{R}_f(\rho)$. Namely it contains the set of all the meet-irreducible elements of $\mathcal{R}_f(\rho)$ that will be generated by refinement. We use this set to derive an algorithm for computing the base of an abstract domain. Since we deal with finite domains, the algorithm gives also a method for deciding whether a refinement is join-uniform.

3.3   Computing the Base

Let $\mathcal{D}(\rho)$ be the collection of all the possible Moore families which are strictly contained in $\rho \in uco(C)$, but are still able to generate $\mathcal{R}_f(\rho)$ by refinement. They include all the elements that surely cannot be generated by refinement, i.e. $I_f(C)$: $\mathcal{D}(\rho) \overset{\text{def}}{=} \{\rho \smallsetminus \{x\} \mid x \in Mirr(\rho) \smallsetminus I_f(C)\} \subseteq uco(\rho)$. We design an algorithm for computing the base of an abstract domain ρ, w.r.t. a refinement $\mathcal{R}_f$, by induction on the construction of a sequence of sets N_n, such that:

$$\forall n \in \mathbb{N}, \ \forall \delta \in N_n : \ \rho \sqsubseteq \delta, \ \mathcal{R}_f(\delta) \sqsubseteq \rho, \text{and} \ (\sigma \in N_{n+1} \smallsetminus N_n \Rightarrow |\sigma| < |\delta|).$$

The domains $\delta \in N_n$ are the candidate bases for $\mathcal{R}_f(\rho)$ after n steps of the algorithm. The set $\mathcal{P}$ will include the minimal candidates, i.e., those domains that, by erasing any of their elements, are unable to regenerate the whole domain.

STEP 1: $\mathcal{P}(\rho) := \varnothing$. We define the following sets: $\delta_1 := \rho$ and $N_1 := \{\delta_1\}$;

STEP $n + 1$: Let $\delta_n \in N_n$. If $\mathcal{D}(\delta_n) = \varnothing$ then $\mathcal{P}(\rho) := \mathcal{P}(\rho) \cup \{\delta_n\}$ (δ_n is minimal since all the elements that can be erased are re-introduced by the Moore closure). Otherwise $\mathcal{U}_n \overset{\text{def}}{=} \{\delta \in \mathcal{D}(\delta_n) \mid \exists y \in M_f^\rho \smallsetminus \delta . \forall L \in \mathcal{L}_y(\delta) . L \not\subseteq \delta\}$. This is the set of all the candidate bases that are not able to generate all the elements in M_f^ρ. We define the set of candidate bases more abstract than δ_n, at step $n + 1$, as $N_{n+1}^{\delta_n} := \mathcal{D}(\delta_n) \smallsetminus \mathcal{U}_n$. If $N_{n+1}^{\delta_n} = \varnothing$ then δ_n is minimal and $\mathcal{P}(\rho) := \mathcal{P}(\rho) \cup \{\delta_n\}$. The set of all the candidate bases at step $n + 1$ is therefore $N_{n+1} := \bigcup_{\delta_n \in N_n} N_{n+1}^{\delta_n}$.

Because at each step n we reduce the size of the domains in N_n, and since C is finite, it is immediate to prove the following proposition.

Proposition 6. *The algorithm terminates and*

$$\mathcal{P}(\rho) = \left\{ \delta \in \mathrm{uco}(\rho) \,\middle|\, \begin{array}{l} Mirr(\delta) \smallsetminus I_f(C) = \varnothing \;\vee \\ (\forall x \in Mirr(\delta) \smallsetminus I_f(C) . \; \exists y \in M_f^\rho \smallsetminus (\delta \smallsetminus \{x\}) . \\ \qquad \forall L \in \mathcal{L}_y(\delta \smallsetminus \{x\}) . \, L \not\sqsubseteq \delta \smallsetminus \{x\}) \end{array} \right\}$$

The correctness of the algorithm is obtained by proving that $\mathcal{P}(\rho)$ contains all and only the domains whose subdomains are unable to generate ρ by refinement.

Lemma 2. *Let $\rho \in \mathrm{uco}(C)$ and $\delta \in \mathrm{uco}(\rho)$ with $\delta \neq \rho$, $\mathcal{R}_f(\delta) = \mathcal{R}_f(\rho)$, and $x \in Mirr(\delta)$ then $\mathcal{R}_f(\delta \smallsetminus \{x\}) \neq \mathcal{R}_f(\rho)$ if and only if $\delta \in \mathcal{P}(\rho)$.*

Theorem 4. *Let $\mathcal{B}_f(\rho) = \bigcap_{\delta \in \mathcal{P}(\rho)} \delta$. The completeness refinement $\mathcal{R}_f$ is join-uniform as regards $\mathcal{R}_f(\rho)$ and its base is $\mathcal{B}_f(\rho)$ if and only if $\{\mathcal{B}_f(\rho)\} = \mathcal{P}(\rho)$.*

The algorithm described above provides a systematic method for deriving the base of any F or B-completeness refinement on finite domains. The complexity of the algorithm strongly depends upon the structure of C and on how f behaves. In the worst case it may be necessary to check the whole concrete domain C, while in the best case it is sufficient to check $Mirr(C)$ whose size, in Boolean lattices, is logarithmic on the size of C.

4   An Application in Predicate Abstraction

In this section we consider two different examples of bases for predicate abstractions of transition systems $\langle \Sigma, \tau \rangle$ w.r.t F-complete refinements $\mathcal{R}_{post[\tau]}$. The idea of predicate abstraction is to choose a set of predicates φ representing sets $X \subseteq \Sigma$ of concrete states, those which satisfy φ: $X = \{ s \,|\, s \models \varphi \}$ [1,9,20]. The key point in predicate abstraction is the choice of the so called *abstract state lattice*, which is naturally induced by composing by conjunction, the chosen predicates. In this context, the abstract state lattice is a closure on $\wp(\Sigma)$. In the first example we show two different abstract state lattices with comparable but different bases, while in the second example we recall Example 1 and show different abstract state lattices sharing the same base. These examples show how bases can be useful to derive a least set of most-abstract predicates which represent the base of any given abstract state lattice. These bases can be useful both to compare abstract state lattices and to design optimal predicates for a given system. In this latter case, the predicates in the base cannot be removed without changing the way abstract state lattices can be refined. Moreover imagine the analysis of a system which is specified by a family of transition relations $\tau_1, \ldots, \tau_n$ and an abstract domain X. It is clear that if we are not interested in the precision of the analysis for τ_i, then for any $j \neq i$: $\mathcal{R}_{\widetilde{pre}[\tau_j]}(\mathcal{B}_{\widetilde{pre}[\tau_i]}(X))$ is the candidate non-redundant domain, which is backward complete for $post[\tau_j]$. In predicate abstraction, this method provides a systematic way to simplify the definition of predicates by removing all those predicates that are necessary to achieve completeness for τ_i.

Example 4. Let's consider the transition system in figure (a) below, with transition relation τ, and $f = post[\tau]$. We consider the two different abstractions represented in figure (b) and (c). As in Figure 1, we have that the points double circled are the elements of the abstractions, while the points single circled are the elements generated by the refinement. First we consider some sets of elements of C which are used by the algorithm: $M_f^C = \{\{1,2\},\{1,3\}\}$, $I_f(C) = \{\{2,3\}\}$, $\dot{f}(C) = \{\top,\{1,2\},\{1,3\}\}$. Consider the abstraction $\rho = \{\top,\{1,2\},\{2\}\}$, represented in figure (b). We note that $Mirr(\rho) = \{\{1,2\},\{2\}\}$ while $M_f^\rho = \{\{1,2\},\{2\}\}$, because the tree with root $\{1,3\}$ has no leaves in ρ.

STEP 1: $\delta_1 = \rho$ and $N_1 = \{\delta_1\}$;

STEP 2: $\mathcal{D}(\delta_1) = \{\{\top,\{1,2\}\},\{\top,\{2\}\}\}$. Moreover $\{1,2\} \in \Gamma_{\{1,2\}}(\{\top,\{1,2\}\})$ while $\{1,2\} \rightarrowtail \{2\}$ in $\Gamma_{\{1,2\}}(\{\top,\{2\}\})$, therefore both the possible successors $\{\top,\{1,2\}\}$ and $\{\top,\{2\}\}$ may generate $\{1,2\}$. Let's consider $\{2\}$. It's clear that $\{2\} \in \Gamma_{\{2\}}(\{\top,\{2\}\})$ while $\{2\} \rightarrowtail \{\{1,2\},\{2,3\}\}$ in $\Gamma_{\{2\}}(\{\top,\{1,2\}\})$, namely $\{2\}$ cannot be generated from $\{\top,\{1,2\}\}$. Hence $\mathcal{U}_2 = \{\{\top,\{1,2\}\}\}$ and $N_2 = \{\{\top,\{2\}\}\}$;

STEP 3: Let $\delta_2 \in N_2$, then $\mathcal{D}(\delta_2) = \{\top\}$, but it is clear that nothing can be generated from $\top$, therefore $\mathcal{U}_3 = \{\top\}$ and $N_3 = \varnothing$. In this way we have that $\mathcal{P} = \{\{\top,\{2\}\}\}$ and the algorithm terminates.

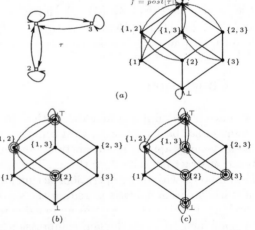

(a)

(b) (c)

It is clear that, by Theorem 4, the closure $\{\top,\{2\}\}$ is the base of $\mathcal{R}_f(\rho)$. Consider now the abstraction $\eta = \{\top,\{1,3\},\{2\},\{3\},\bot\}$, represented in figure (b).

We note that $Mirr(\eta) = \{\{1,3\},\{2\},\{3\}\}$ while it is simple to find that $M_f^\eta = \{\{1,2\},\{1,3\},\{2\},\{3\}\}$, because $\{1,2\} \rightarrowtail \{2\}$ in $\Gamma_{\{1,2\}}(\eta)$.

STEP 1: $\delta_1 = \eta$ and $N_1 = \{\delta_1\}$;

STEP 2: $\mathcal{D}(\delta_1) = \{\{\top,\{2\},\{3\},\bot\},\{\top,\{1,3\},\{2\},\bot\},\{\top,\{1,3\},\{3\},\bot\}\}$. It is clear that $\{1,2\} \rightarrowtail \{2\} \rightarrowtail \{\{1,2\},\{2,3\}\}$ in $\Gamma_{\{1,2\}}(\{\top,\{1,3\},\{3\},\bot\})$, namely $\{\top,\{1,3\},\{3\},\bot\}$ is in $\mathcal{U}_2$. Note that each other closure containing $\{2\}$ may generate $\{1,2\}$. Consider $\{3\}$, it's clear that $\{1,3\} \rightarrowtail \{3\} \rightarrowtail \{\{1,3\},\{2,3\}\}$ in $\Gamma_{\{3\}}(\{\top,\{1,3\},\{2\},\bot\})$, namely $\{\top,\{1,3\},\{2\},\bot\} \in \mathcal{U}_2$ doesn't generate $\{3\}$. Finally $\{1,3\} \rightarrowtail \{3\}$ in $\Gamma_{\{1,3\}}(\{\top,\{2\},\{3\},\bot\})$. Hence $\mathcal{U}_2 = \{\{\top,\{1,3\},\{2\},\bot\},\{\top,\{1,3\},\{3\},\bot\}\}$ and $N_2 = \{\{\top,\{2\},\{3\},\bot\}\}$;

STEP 3: Let $\delta_2 \in N_2$, then $\mathcal{D}(\delta_2) = \{\{\top,\{2\},\bot\},\{\top,\{3\},\bot\}\}$, but it is clear that, from what we saw in the previous step, $\{2\}$ and $\{3\}$ can be generated only from closures that contain respectively these two elements. Namely

$\mathcal{U}_3 = \{\{\top, \{2\}, \bot\}, \{\top, \{3\}, \bot\}\}$ and $N_3 = \varnothing$. In this way we have that $\mathcal{P} = \{\{\top, \{2\}, \{3\}, \bot\}\}$ and the algorithm terminates.

It is clear that, by Theorem 4 the closure $\{\top, \{2\}, \{3\}, \bot\}$ is the base of $\mathcal{R}_f(\eta)$. By observing $\mathcal{B}_f(\rho) \sqsupseteq \mathcal{B}_f(\eta)$ we can compare the two closures ρ and η. This implies that $\mathcal{R}_f(\rho) \sqsupseteq \mathcal{R}_f(\eta)$.

Example 5. Let's consider the transition system in Figure 1(a), with transition relation τ, and $f = post[\tau]$. Let $\rho = \{\top, \{1, 4\}, \{2, 3\}, \{3\}, \bot\}$ and $\eta = \{\top, \{1, 4\}, \{2, 3\}, \{1\}, \bot\}$, represented respectively in Figure 1(b) and (c). In this case we have that $M_f^C = \{\{1, 3, 4\}\}$, $I_f(C) = \{\{1, 2, 3\}, \{1, 2, 4\}, \{2, 3, 4\}\}$, and $\dot{f}(C) = \{\{1, 3, 4\}, \{1, 3\}, \{3, 4\}, \{3\}\}$. Note that $Mirr(\rho) = \{\{1, 4\}, \{2, 3\}, \{3\}\}$ while it is simple to verify that $M_f^\rho = \{\{1, 4\}, \{2, 3\}, \{3\}, \{1, 3\}, \{1, 3, 4\}\}$. Moreover $Mirr(\eta) = \{\{1, 4\}, \{2, 3\}, \{1\}\}$ while it is simple to verify that $M_f^\eta = \{\{1, 4\}, \{2, 3\}, \{1\}, \{1, 3\}, \{1, 3, 4\}\}$. These fact hold because the trees with root respectively $\{1, 3\}$ and $\{1, 3, 4\}$ have a leaf both in ρ and η. The algorithm terminates for both domains in 3 steps, computing the base $\mathcal{B}_f(\rho) = \mathcal{B}_f(\eta) = \{\top, \{1, 4\}, \{2, 3\}, \bot\}$. The least set of generating predicates is $\mathcal{B}_f(\rho)$. Analogously, if $\rho' = \{\top, \{1, 4\}, \{3\}, \bot\}$ and $\eta' = \{\top, \{1, 4\}, \{1\}, \bot\}$, then $\mathcal{B}_f(\rho') = \mathcal{B}_f(\eta') = \{\top, \{1, 4\}\}$. Because $\mathcal{B}_f(\rho) \sqsubset \mathcal{B}_f(\rho')$, this means that ρ and ρ' will lead to different complete domains once refined.

5   Conclusion

We have introduced a systematic method for deriving the base, when it exists, of any either backward or forward complete refinement on finite domains. This method can be applied to any abstract domain in the standard Galois connection based abstract interpretation theory. The operation of domain compression can be composed with other operations acting on domains. This can be useful both in static program analysis to reduce the size of domains and in abstract model checking. In this latter case we can imagine to improve abstract model checking by combining abstract domain compression and abstraction refinement. While soundness of abstract model checking ensures that if the abstract model $\mathbb{M}^\rho$ verifies a formula φ: $\mathbb{M}^\rho \models \varphi$, then this holds in the concrete model $\mathbb{M}$ too: $\mathbb{M} \models \varphi$, completeness ensures that if $\mathbb{M} \models \varphi$ then $\mathbb{M}^\rho \models \varphi$. This latter condition does not hold in general as the model checker may return a counterexample trace, called *spurious*, which may not correspond to any concrete trace in $\mathbb{M}$ [4]. In [14] the authors proved that spuriousness implies B-incompleteness for the abstraction w.r.t. $post[\tau]$, while [23] proved that abstractions can be made strongly preserving [22] (which again avoids spurious counterexamples) by making them B-complete w.r.t. $pre[\tau]$. Both these results imply that, by refining abstractions to become B-complete w.r.t either $post[\tau]$ or $pre[\tau]$ (or equivalently F-complete w.r.t $\widetilde{pre}[\tau]$ or $\widetilde{post}[\tau]$), we can remove spurious counterexamples from the abstract system, making abstract model checking complete. This means that the abstract model $\mathbb{M}^{\mathcal{B}_{\widetilde{pre}[\tau]}(\rho)}$ is the simplest model on which we can check a formula, yet achieving the same precision as ρ does once both are refined to avoid spurious counterexamples. Therefore, in order to design a formula-guided refinement, we can combine domain compression to reduce the size of initial abstractions and spurious counterexample refinement in [4] to refine them along only those traces that are spurious for checking φ, as shown in figure below.

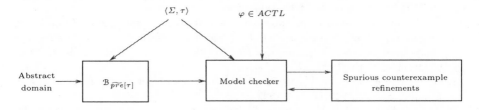

Acknowledgments. This paper has been conceived while the authors were visiting the equipe Cousot at École Polytechnique, Palaiseau, France. The authors wish to thank the École Polytechnique and Radhia Cousot for the kind hospitality.

References

1. T. Ball, A. Podelski, and S.K. Rajamani. Relative completeness of abstraction refinement for software model checking. In J.-P. Kaoen and P. Stevens, editors, *Proc. of TACAS: Tools and Algorithms for the Construction and Analysis of Systems*, volume 2280 of *Lecture Notes in Computer Science*, pages 158–172. Springer-Verlag, Berlin, 2002.
2. T.S. Blyth and M.F. Janowitz. *Residuation theory*. Pergamon Press, 1972.
3. E. M. Clarke, E. A. Emerson, and A. P. Sistla. Automatic verification of finite-state concurrent system using temporal logic specification. *ACM Trans. Program. Lang. Syst.*, 8(2):244–263, 1986.
4. E.M. Clarke, O. Grumberg, S. Jha, Y. Lu, and H. Veith. Counterexample-guided abstraction refinement. In *Proc. of the 12th Internat. Conf. on Computer Aided Verification (CAV '00)*, volume 1855 of *Lecture Notes in Computer Science*, pages 154–169. Springer-Verlag, Berlin, 2000.
5. A. Cortesi, G. Filé, R. Giacobazzi, C. Palamidessi, and F. Ranzato. Complementation in abstract interpretation. *ACM Trans. Program. Lang. Syst.*, 19(1):7–47, 1997.
6. P. Cousot and R. Cousot. Abstract interpretation: A unified lattice model for static analysis of programs by construction or approximation of fixpoints. In *Conference Record of the 4th ACM Symp. on Principles of Programming Languages (POPL '77)*, pages 238–252. ACM Press, New York, 1977.
7. P. Cousot and R. Cousot. Systematic design of program analysis frameworks. In *Conference Record of the 6th ACM Symp. on Principles of Programming Languages (POPL '79)*, pages 269–282. ACM Press, New York, 1979.
8. P. Cousot and R. Cousot. Comparing the Galois connection and widening/narrowing approaches to abstract interpretation (Invited Paper). In M. Bruynooghe and M. Wirsing, editors, *Proc. of the 4th Internat. Symp. on Programming Language Implementation and Logic Programming (PLILP '92)*, volume 631 of *Lecture Notes in Computer Science*, pages 269–295. Springer-Verlag, Berlin, 1992.

9. P. Cousot and R. Cousot. On abstraction in software verification. In D. Brinksma and K.G. Larsen, editors, *Proc. of the 14th Internat. Conf. on Computer Aided Verification (CAV '02)*, volume 2404 of *Lecture Notes in Computer Science*, pages 37–56. Springer-Verlag, Berlin, 2002.

10. G. Filé, R. Giacobazzi, and F. Ranzato. A unifying view of abstract domain design. *ACM Comput. Surv.*, 28(2):333–336, 1996.

11. G. Filé and F. Ranzato. Complementation of abstract domains made easy. In M. Maher, editor, *Proceedings of the 1996 Joint International Conference and Symposium on Logic Programming (JICSLP '96)*, pages 348–362. The MIT Press, Cambridge, Mass., 1996.

12. G. Filé and F. Ranzato. The powerset operator on abstract interpretations. *Theor. Comput. Sci*, 222(1-2):77–111, 1999.

13. R. Giacobazzi and I. Mastroeni. A characterization of symmetric semantics by domain complementation. In *Proc. of the 2nd international conference in principles and practice of declarative programming PPDP'00*, pages 115–126. ACM press, 2000.

14. R. Giacobazzi and E. Quintarelli. Incompleteness, counterexamples and refinements in abstract model-checking. In P. Cousot, editor, *Proc. of The 8th International Static Analysis Symposium, SAS'01*, volume 2126 of *Lecture Notes in Computer Science*, pages 356–373. Springer-Verlag, 2001.

15. R. Giacobazzi and F. Ranzato. Refining and compressing abstract domains. In P. Degano, R. Gorrieri, and A. Marchetti-Spaccamela, editors, *Proc. of the 24th Internat. Colloq. on Automata, Languages and Programming (ICALP '97)*, volume 1256 of *Lecture Notes in Computer Science*, pages 771–781. Springer-Verlag, Berlin, 1997.

16. R. Giacobazzi and F. Ranzato. Optimal domains for disjunctive abstract interpretation. *Sci. Comput. Program*, 32(1-3):177–210, 1998.

17. R. Giacobazzi and F. Ranzato. Uniform closures: order-theoretically reconstructing logic program semantics and abstract domain refinements. *Inform. and Comput.*, 145(2):153–190, 1998.

18. R. Giacobazzi, F. Ranzato, and F. Scozzari. Making abstract interpretations complete. *J. of the ACM.*, 47(2):361–416, 2000.

19. R. Giacobazzi and F. Scozzari. A logical model for relational abstract domains. *ACM Trans. Program. Lang. Syst.*, 20(5):1067–1109, 1998.

20. S. Graf and H. Saïdi. Construction of abstract state graphs with PVS. In *Proc. of the 9th Internat. Conf. on Computer Aided Verification (CAV '97)*, volume 1254 of *Lecture Notes in Computer Science*, pages 72–83. Springer-Verlag, Berlin, 1997.

21. T. Jensen. Disjunctive program analysis for algebraic data types. *ACM Trans. Program. Lang. Syst.*, 19(5):751–803, 1997.

22. C. Loiseaux, S. Graf, J. Sifakis, A. Bouajjani, and S. Bensalem. Property preserving abstractions for the verification of concurrent systems. *Formal Methods Syst. Des.*, 6:11–44, 1995.

23. F. Ranzato and F. Tapparo. Making abstract model checking strongly preserving. In M. Hermeneghildo and G. Puebla, editors, *Proc. of The 9th International Static Analysis Symposium, SAS'02*, volume 2477 of *Lecture Notes in Computer Science*, pages 411–427. Springer-Verlag, 2002.

Abstraction of Expectation Functions Using Gaussian Distributions

David Monniaux

LIENS
45 rue d'Ulm
75230 Paris cedex 5, France
http://www.di.ens.fr/~monniaux
David.Monniaux@ens.fr

Abstract. We consider semantics of infinite-state programs, both probabilistic and nondeterministic, as expectation functions: for any set of states A, we associate to each program point a function mapping each state to its expectation of starting a trace reaching A. We then compute a safe upper approximation of these functions using abstract interpretation. This computation takes place in an abstract domain of extended Gaussian (normal) distributions.

Category: 1 (new results)

1 Introduction

Much progress has been made recently on the model-checking of probabilistic and nondeterministic systems, considered as Markov decision processes [4,9,6]. These methods, however, consider finite-state processes. For infinite state processes, one can either approximate them using finite-state processes, or use a symbolic approximation. In this paper, we take the latter approach.

1.1 Contribution

We propose a symbolic method for computing a safe upper-bound on the probability of a certain set of events occuring in the set of traces of the analyzed program. Our analysis method is set in the general framework of abstract interpretation [3] of probabilistic programs using expectation functions [13]. This analysis method approximates expectation functions from above using Gaussian extended (n-dimensional) distributions . The kind of results that can be established using this analysis is as follows:

$$\forall x \ E_A(\boldsymbol{x}) \le \alpha \exp(-Q(\boldsymbol{x} - \boldsymbol{x}_0))$$

where $E_A(x)$ notes the expectation of reaching a state in A from an initial state x (a vector of real numbers representing the values of the various variables) and Q is a positive quadratic form. This result is achieved through an over-approximation

L. Zuck et al. (Eds.): VMCAI 2003, LNCS 2575, pp. 161–173, 2003.

of the *value iteration* sequence associated with the Markov decision process [14] using *widening operators* to force convergence [3].

This result is *sound*, meaning that the bound that is obtained is necessarily true (although not optimal in general). The algorithms used are mostly standard numerical analysis, enabling the use of standard (bi)linear algebra packages such as Matlab or libraries such as Lapack [1].

1.2   Comparison with Other Works

The field of probabilistic model checking has developed considerably during the last few years. Some tools [4] are now available; they use sophisticated algorithms on compact symbolic representations of vectors in $[0, 1]^N$ where N is the number of states. On the other hand, these tools are unable to work directly on computer programs, which have infinite or at least very large state spaces (a system with forty 32-bit variables has about 10^{384} states); they need a preliminary step of (mostly manual) abstraction into a finite model.

In an earlier paper [13], we proposed a static analysis method for probabilistic and nondeterministic programs. That method used an abstract domain of step functions, that is, linear combinations of characteristic functions of basic elements. Those basic elements are taken in an abstract domain suitable for non-probabilistic analysis. That analysis method tends to perform well on the "big mass" of distributions, but gives overly coarse approximations of the "tails" of the expectation functions: they are uniformly bounded by a constant, whereas we would like to see them bounded by some function that is negligible far away.

We also proposed a method combining Monte-Carlo sampling and non-probabilistic abstract interpretation [11]. That method considers a slightly different semantics and achieves results that are valid only up to a confidence interval; it can become prohibitively expensive if the probability to be bounded with good relative accuracy is small. It is however possible to use analyses such as the one described in this paper to fine-tune the number of samples needed in different regions by the Monte-Carlo analysis.

1.3   Structure of the Paper

In section 2, we shall explain briefly our notion of backward probabilistic abstract interpretation [11]. In section 3, we shall see the abstract domain of extended Gaussian distributions. In section 4, we shall see a few mathematical facts on second-degree polynomials and positive quadratic forms, as well as some effective algorithms.

2   Backwards Probabilistic Abstract Interpretation

With respect to probabilistic program semantics, one has the choice between forward denotational semantics [7, 8, 10], backward denotational semantics [13] and small-step operational semantics (Markov decision processes) [12, ch. 7,8]. The

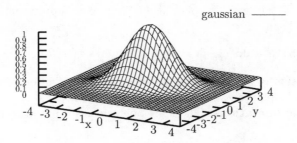

Fig. 1. An extended Gaussian distribution. Its matrix is $\left(\begin{smallmatrix} 0.6 & 0 \\ 0 & 1 \end{smallmatrix}\right)$ in the orthogonal basis $\left(\begin{smallmatrix} \cos 0.4 & -\sin 0.4 \\ \sin 0.4 & \cos 0.4 \end{smallmatrix}\right)$.

analysis method described in this paper applies both to backward denotational semantics and backward small-step operational semantics. However, for the sake of brevity, we shall explain it using denotational semantics.

2.1 Concrete Semantics

We shall begin by giving the *concrete semantics*, that is, the precise semantics of the programs to be analyzed.

In his seminal papers [7,8], Kozen introduced semantics of probabilistic programs as continuous linear operators on measure spaces. These semantics are *forward*, since they map the input probability distribution (measure) of the program to its output distribution. Using a linear duality relation, we obtained a backward probabilistic semantics operating on measurable functions [13]. This semantics is easily lifted to nondeterministic and probabilistic programs, which take choices, some of which according to a known probability distribution and the others in a certain known domain. We recall here this semantics in a compositional fashion.

$[\![H]\!]_p^*$ is the semantics of program construct H. If the environment (vector of variables, registers, heap...) before H is taken in the set X and after H taken in Y, then $[\![H]\!]_p^*$ is a function from $Y \to_{\text{measurable}} [0,1]$ to $X \to_{\text{measurable}} [0,1]$. This function is upper-continuous (the image of the limit of an ascending sequence is the limit of the images) and, when H does not include nondeterministic constructs, it is linear.

Sequence. Straightforward composition:

$$[\![e_1 \, ; e_2]\!]_p^* = [\![e_1]\!]_p^* \circ [\![e_2]\!]_p^*. \tag{1}$$

Tests. R_W is the linear operator mapping a function f to its pointwise product with the characteristic function of W. Then

$$[\![\texttt{if } c \texttt{ then } e_1 \texttt{ else } e_2]\!]_p^* = R_{\chi_{[\![c]\!]}} \circ [\![e_1]\!]_p^* + R_{\chi_{[\![c]\!]^C}} \circ [\![e_2]\!]_p^*. \tag{2}$$

Loops. lfp Ψ is the least fixpoint of Ψ. Since Ψ is upper-continuous, lfp $= \bigsqcup_n \Psi^n(0)$. Then

$$[\![\texttt{while } c \texttt{ do } e]\!]_p^*.f_0 = R_{\chi_{[\![c]\!]^C}} \cdot \text{lfp} \left(f \mapsto f_0 + R_{\chi_{[\![c]\!]}} \circ [\![e]\!]_p^*(f) \right) \qquad (3)$$

This equation is the denotational version of the definition of the value of a Markov decision process using value iteration [14, §7.2.4].

Deterministic operations. These are operations such as arithmetic, fetching data etc...

$$[\![\texttt{H}]\!]_p^*.f = f \circ [\![\texttt{H}]\!] \qquad (4)$$

where $[\![\texttt{H}]\!]$ is the denotational semantics of the deterministic operation H, mapping each input to the operation to the corresponding output.

Random generation. The operation takes an environment (vector of variables) x and appends to it a random value r taken according to the random distribution μ_R.

$$([\![\texttt{r:=random}]\!]_p^*.f)(x) = \int f(x,r) \, \mathrm{d}\mu_R(r) \qquad (5)$$

Nondeterministic generation. The operation takes an environment (vector of variables) x and appends to it a variable y nondeterministically chosen in Y.

$$([\![\texttt{r:=nondeterministic}]\!]_p^*.f)(x) = \sup_{y \in Y} f(x,y) \qquad (6)$$

2.2 Abstract Interpretation

Following [13], we associate an abstract semantics $[\![H]\!]_p^{*\sharp}$ to any program construct H. This semantics is linked to the concrete one by the *abstraction relation* :

$$\forall f, f^\sharp \ f \le f^\sharp \implies [\![H]\!]_p^*.f \le [\![H]\!]_p^{*\sharp}.f^\sharp, \qquad (7)$$

using the pointwise ordering.

We shall restrict the abstract computations to a certain family of functions taken in an *abstract domain*. We shall introduce a domain of extended Gaussian distributions in section 3.

The domain should implement some elementary abstract operations:

- abstract counterparts of the semantics of deterministic operations, nondeterministic generation, probabilistic generation
- an abstraction $+^\sharp$ of the $+$ operator
- an abstraction $R^\sharp_{[\![c]\!]}$ of $R_{[\![c]\!]}$ for any boolean condition c (such as a comparison between two variables)
- an abstraction of the $\sqcup$ (least upper bound operator):

$$f^\sharp \sqcup^\sharp g^\sharp \ge f^\sharp \qquad (8)$$
$$f^\sharp \sqcup^\sharp g^\sharp \ge g^\sharp \qquad (9)$$

  − a *widening operator* ∇:
    • for all $f^\sharp$ and $g^\sharp$, $f^\sharp \nabla g^\sharp$ is greater than $f^\sharp$ and $g^\sharp$;
    • for any sequence $v_n^\sharp$ and any $u_0^\sharp$, the sequence defined by $u_{n+1}^\sharp = u_n^\sharp \nabla v_n^\sharp$
    is ultimately stationary.

The widening operator ∇ is a kind of convergence accelerator for fixpoint iterations [3, §4.3]. Let us suppose we have a concrete function Ψ and its abstract counterpart $\Psi^\sharp$. We wish to obtain an abstraction (upper approximation) of lfp Ψ (the least fixpoint of Ψ). lfp Ψ is the limit of the sequence $(f_n)_{n \in \mathbb{N}}$ defined by $f_0 = 0$ and $f_{n+1} = \Psi f_n$. Let us now consider the sequence $f_0^\sharp = 0$ and $f_{n+1}^\sharp = f_n^\sharp \nabla \Psi^\sharp f_n^\sharp$. Obviously, $f_n \leq f_n^\sharp$ for any n. Furthermore, $f_n^\sharp$ is ultimately stationary. Its limit $L^\sharp$ is therefore an upper bound on lfp $\Psi = \lim_{n \to n} f_n^\sharp$. Let us note it lfp$^\sharp \Psi^\sharp$.

The abstract semantics is obtained by replacing each elementary operation in the definition of the concrete semantics (§2.1) by its abstract counterpart.

3   Extended Gaussian Distributions

We shall now describe the domain of extended Gaussian distributions (Fig. 1).

3.1   Construction

We shall first describe the form of the functions making up the abstract domain.

Definition 1. *Let E be a finite dimensional real vector space. Let us consider a positive quadratic form Q and a linear form L over E such that $\ker Q \subseteq \ker L$. q_0 is a real number. The function*

$$E \to \mathbb{R}_+$$
$$v \mapsto \exp(-Q(v) + L(v) + q_0)$$

is called an extended Gaussian distribution. *It shall be noted G_{Q,L,q_0}.*

Proposition 1. *Let $\phi : v \mapsto \exp(-Q(v) + Lv + q)$ be an extended Gaussian distribution over an euclidean space E. Then there exists an orthonormal basis $(v_i)_{1 \leq 1 \leq n}$, a positive real number K, coefficients $(\lambda_i)_{1 \leq 1 \leq n}$ and coordinates $(p_i)_{1 \leq 1 \leq n}$ such that*

$$\phi\left(\sum x_i v_i\right) = K \exp\left(-\sum_i \lambda_i (x_i - p_i)^2\right).$$

The point P, whose coordinates in the basis $(v_i)_{1 \leq 1 \leq n}$ are $(p_i)_{1 \leq 1 \leq n}$, is called the center *of the distribution.*

3.2   Least Upper Bound and Widening

Let (Q_1, L_1, q_1) and (Q_2, L_2, q_2) be two extended Gaussian distributions. We wish to get a common upper bound for them.

Let us note that, in general, there is no least upper bound in Gaussian distributions, even when the Gaussians are centered and unscaled: two ellipses with a common center do not necessarily have a least upper bound.

We define the extended Gaussian distribution $(Q_1, L_1, q_1) \sqcup (Q_2, L_2, q_2)$ as follows. Since Q_1 and Q_2 are positive, we diagonalize them in the same base $(v_i)_{1 \leq i \leq n}$ (theorem 2). Then $Q_1(\sum_i x_i v_i) = \sum \lambda_i x_i^2$ and $Q_2(\sum_i x_i v_i) = \sum \mu_i x_i^2$. Let us write the linear forms L_1 and L_2 in this basis: $L_1(\sum_i x_i v_i) = \sum \alpha_i x_i$ and $L_2(\sum_i x_i v_i) = \sum \beta_i x_i$.

Let σ_i and τ_i be partitions of q_1 and q_2 respectively ($\sum_i \sigma_i = q_1$ and $\sum_i \tau_i = q_2$). We can take $\sigma_i = q_1/n$ and $\tau_i = q_2/n$.

Let $a_i X^2 + b_i X + c_i = (\lambda_i X^2 + \alpha_i X + \sigma_i) \sqcap (\mu_i X^2 + \beta_i X + \tau_i)$ (as defined in §4.1).

Let $Q(\sum_i x_i v_i) = \sum_i a_i x_i^2$, $L(\sum_i x_i v_i) = \sum_i b_i x_i$ and $q = \sum_i c_i$.

Let us check that $\ker Q \subseteq \ker L$. Since $\ker Q$ is the isotropic cone of Q and the v_i form a diagonal basis for Q, it follows that a subset of the v_i form a basis of $\ker Q$. For any index i such that v_i is in that basis, $a_i = 0$; since we exclude polynomials of degree one ($\ker Q \subseteq \ker L$), b_i must also be null.

by construction, so $v_i \in \ker L$.

We define

$$(Q_1, L_1, q_1) \sqcup (Q_2, L_2, q_2) = (Q, L, q). \qquad (10)$$

Let us remark that

$$\dim \ker Q \geq \max(\dim \ker Q_1, \dim \ker Q_2) \qquad (11)$$

since for all i such that $\lambda_i = 0$ or $\mu_i = 0$, $a_i = 0$.

We define the widening operator similarly, except that this time we need to ensure convergence of the ascending sequences $u_{n+1} = u_n \nabla v_n$. We shall modify the least upper bound operator in two respects to obtain the widening operator:

1. Intuitively, when $a_i < \lambda_i$, this means that along that particular vector v_i the Gaussian gets flatter and flatter. The natural widening is to upper-approximate it by a flat line. In this case, we take $a_i' = b_i' = 0$ and

$$c_i' = \min_x (a_i x^2 + b_i x + c) = \frac{-b^2}{4a} + c. \qquad (12)$$

2. If all $a_i = 0$ and c is still decreasing, we take the last resort of removing all constraints.

The convergence of the method is ensured by the fact that whenever step 1 is applied, $\dim \ker Q$ strictly increases. Since in non-widening steps, $\dim \ker Q$ increases or stays constant, it follows that at most $\dim E$ step 1 may be applied. After this, the a_i stay constant. The only way the sequence can still go on ascending is by an increase in c. Then step 2 ensures termination.

3.3   Random Generators

Let us recall Equ. 5 the backwards operation associated with $\rho = \mathtt{random}$ where ρ is a fresh real variable

$$g = [\![\rho = \mathtt{random}]\!]_p^*.f = \boldsymbol{v} \mapsto \int_x f(\boldsymbol{v} + x\boldsymbol{e}) \, \mathrm{d}\mu_R(x) \tag{13}$$

where $\boldsymbol{e}$ is an additional basis vector corresponding to the fresh variable ρ and μ_R is the distribution of the new variable. If μ_R is given by the Gaussian $\exp(-(\lambda x^2 + c_1))$, and f is given by (Q, L, c), then

$$g(\boldsymbol{v}) = \int_{-\infty}^{+\infty} \exp\left(-(Q(\boldsymbol{v} + x\boldsymbol{e}) + L(\boldsymbol{v} + x\boldsymbol{e}) + c + \lambda x^2 + c_1)\right) \mathrm{d}x$$

$$= \exp\left(-\left(\underbrace{Q(\boldsymbol{v}) - \frac{1}{4\alpha}Q^*(\boldsymbol{v}, \boldsymbol{e})^2}_{Q'(\boldsymbol{v})} + \underbrace{L(\boldsymbol{v}) - \frac{1}{2\alpha}Q^*(\boldsymbol{v}, \boldsymbol{e})L(\boldsymbol{e})}_{L'(\boldsymbol{v})} + \underbrace{c + c_1 - \frac{L(\boldsymbol{e})^2}{4\alpha} - \frac{1}{2}\log\frac{\pi}{\alpha}}_{c'}\right)\right)$$
$$\tag{14}$$

Because of the definition of g as the integral of a bounded function versus a measure of finite total weight, g is bounded; thus Q is positive and $\ker L \subseteq \ker Q$.

3.4   Linear Operations

We shall deal here with program statements such as $v_n := \sum_i \alpha_i v_i$ and more generally any linear transformation M where the vector of variables $\boldsymbol{V}'$ after the instruction is $M.\boldsymbol{V}$ where $\boldsymbol{V}$ is the vector of variable before the instruction. Following Equ. 4,

$$[\![\boldsymbol{V} := M.\boldsymbol{V}]\!]_p^*.f = f \circ M \tag{15}$$

and thus $(Q', L', c) = ({}^tM\,QM, LM, c)$.

3.5   Other Operations

We shall approximate other operations by releasing all constraints on the variables affected by them: forgetting variable in set V is achieved as follows:

- $q'_{i,j} = q_{i,j}$ if $i \notin V$ and $j \notin V$, $q'_{i,j} = 0$ otherwise;
- $L'_i = L_i$ if $i \notin V$, $L_i = 0$.

It is quite obvious that if $f : E \mapsto E$ leaves all coordinates outside of V intact, $G_{Q,L,q_0} \circ f \leq G_{Q',L',q_0}$ point-wise.

4   Mathematical Facts

We shall see now a few mathematical points on second-degree polynomials and positive quadratic forms.

4.1 Parabolas

Let $P_1(x) = a_1x^2 + b_1x + c_1$ and $P_2(x) = a_2x^2 + b_2x + c_2$. Let us find a quadric polynomial $P_3(x) = a_3x^2 + b_3x + c_3$ less than P_1 and P_2. Obviously, a_3 must be less than both a_1 and a_2, else P_3 is above P_1 or P_2 near $\pm\infty$.

Let us first suppose that neither $P_1 \le P_2$ nor $P_2 \le P_1$ pointwise, since those cases have an obvious solution. Let us remark that this condition holds if and only if P_1 and P_2 intersect, that is, when $\operatorname{discr}(P_1 - P_2) > 0$ — $\operatorname{discr}(ax^2 + bx + c)$ is the discriminant $b^2 - 4ac$.

Let us note that there is in general no "greatest lower bound" among quadratic polynomials. The first choice, an arbitrary one, will thus be of any positive a_3 less than a_1 and a_2.

We choose P_3 to be tangent to both P_1 and P_2. This means that $P_3 - P_1$ and $P_3' - P_1'$ have a common root (resp. for $P_3 - P_2$ and $P_3' - P_2'$). This is equivalent to $P_3 - P_1$ and $P_2 - P_1$ each having a double root. That property is ensured by the conditions on the discriminants of the polynomials: $\operatorname{discr}(P_3 - P_1) = 0$ and $\operatorname{discr}(P_3 - P_2) = 0$, that is:

$$(b_3 - b_1)^2 = 4(a_3 - a_1)(c_3 - c_1) \tag{16}$$

$$(b_3 - b_2)^2 = 4(a_3 - a_2)(c_3 - c_2) \tag{17}$$

Let us suppose for now that $a_1 > a_2$. Solving this 2-unknown, 2-equation system yields:

$$b_3 = \frac{-a_2b_1 + a_3(b_1 - b_2) + a_1b_2 \pm \sqrt{\Delta}}{a_1 - a_2} \tag{18}$$

$$\Delta = (a_1 - a_3)(-a_2 + a_3)(-(b_1 - b_2)^2 + 4(a_1 - a_2)(c_1 - c_2)) \tag{19}$$

There are two solutions for this system, which means that for any choice of a_3, there are two polynomials P_3 corresponding to two parabolas tangent to both P_1 and P_2. We wish P_3 to be pointwise less than P_1 and P_2, but we would prefer it not to be too "low"; for this reason, between the two choices, we choose the one for which $\inf P_3 = -\frac{b_3}{2a_3}$ is maximal and thus b_3 is minimal. Since $a_1 > a_2$, this means that we choose

$$b_3 = \frac{-a_2b_1 + a_3(b_1 - b_2) + a_1b_2 - \sqrt{\Delta}}{a_1 - a_2} \tag{20}$$

$$c_3 = c_1 + \frac{(b_3 - b_1)^2}{4(a_3 - a_1)} \tag{21}$$

The case $a_1 < a_2$ is treated *mutatis mutandis*.

Let us now treat $a_1 = a_2$, which is a degenerate case.

$$b_3 = \frac{b1 + b2}{2} - 2\frac{(a1 - a3)(c1 - c2)}{b1 - b2} \tag{22}$$

$$c_3 = c_1 + \frac{(b_3 - b_1)^2}{4(a_3 - a_1)} \tag{23}$$

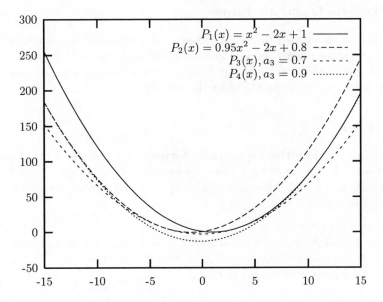

Fig. 2. An example of common lower bounds in quadratic polynomials (P_4 and P_3 for P_1 and P_2).

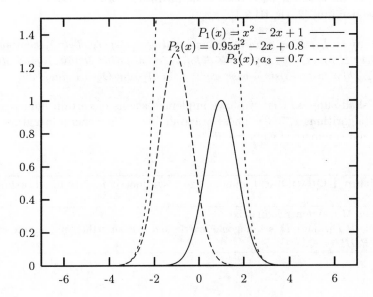

Fig. 3. The Gaussians corresponding to the preceding figure. Note that while the central part is grossly overestimated (and truncated in the figure), the tails are finely approximated.

4.2   Positive Quadratic Forms

Extended gaussian distributions are defined using positive quadratic forms. An eigenvalue of zero along an axis indicates that there is no Gaussian constraint along that axis; this is the case, for instance, if this axis corresponds to a variable chosen according to a non-Gaussian distribution.

Basic Facts

Definition 2 ((Positive) quadratic forms). *A quadratic form Q on a real vector space E is defined by a bilinear symmetric function Q^* (called its polar form) from $E \times E$ to $\mathbb{R}$. We note $Q(x) = Q^*(x, x)$. A positive quadratic form Q is such that for all x in E, $Q(x) \geq 0$.*

Lemma 1. *Let E be a vector space. Let Q be a quadratic form over E. Let F be a finite dimensional subspace of E so that $F \cap Iso\ Q = \{0\}$. Then F has an orthonormal basis with respect to Q.*

Common diagonalization. We shall often have to consider two different quadratic forms at the same time. It is then very useful to consider both of them in the same orthogonal basis. The following theorem guarantees that it is possible provided at least one of the quadratic forms is positive definite (or negative definite) [2, th. III.3.1]:

Theorem 1. *Let E be a finite dimensional vector space. Let Q_1 be a quadratic form over E and Q_2 be a positive definite (or negative definite) quadratic form over E. Then there exists a base where both Q_1 and Q_2 are diagonal.*

We shall suppose that we have implementations of certain numerical algorithms (algorithms 1, 2, 3). Those are available in the general literature as well as free and commercial software [5].

Algorithm 1 QUADDIAG0, diagonalize a symmetric matrix in an orthonormal basis

---
Require: M a symmetric matrix
Ensure: $[P, D]$ where D is a diagonal matrix and P is an orthogonal matrix such that $M = PDP^{-1}$.

Algorithm 2 ORTH, get an orthnormal basis of the image space of a matrix

---
Require: M a matrix
Ensure: B such that $Im\ B = Im\ M$ and its columns form an orthonormal free family

Algorithm 3 NULL, get an orthnormal basis of the null space of a matrix

Require: M a matrix
Ensure: B such that $\operatorname{Im} B = \ker M$ its columns form an orthonormal free family

---

Algorithm 4 QUADDIAG1, common diagonalization of a quadratic form and a positive definite quadratic form

Require: $[Q_1, Q_2]$ where Q_1 a symmetric matrix, Q_2 a positive definite symmetric matrix
Ensure: $[P, I, d, D_1]$ where P is an invertible matrix, I its inverse, $d = \det P$, D_1 is a diagonal matrices such that $Q_1 = {}^t I\, D_1 I$ and $Q_2 = {}^t I\, I$
 $\quad [P_2, D_2] \leftarrow \text{QUADDIAG0}[Q_2]$
 $\quad Z \leftarrow D_2^{-1/2}$
 $\quad H \leftarrow P_2 Z$
 $\quad G \leftarrow {}^t H\, Q_2 H$
 $\quad [P_1, D_1] \leftarrow \text{QUADDIAG0}[G]$
 $\quad I \leftarrow {}^t P_1 \sqrt{D_2}\, {}^t P_2$
 $\quad P \leftarrow P_2 Z P_1$
 $\quad d \leftarrow \det Z$

Unfortunately, in our case, we have to handle quadratic forms that have isotropic vectors. On the other hand, we only consider positive forms, and we thus have a theorem:

Theorem 2. *Let E be a finite dimensional vector space. Let n be $\dim E$. Let Q_1 and Q_2 be two positive quadratic forms over E. Then there exists a base $(e_i)_{1 \leq i \leq n}$ where both Q_1 and Q_2 are diagonal, that is, there exist two families real numbers $(\lambda_i)_{1 \leq i \leq n}$ and $(\mu_i)_{1 \leq i \leq n}$ so that*

$$Q_1\left(\sum_i \alpha_i e_i\right) = \sum_i \lambda_i \alpha_i^2 \tag{24}$$

$$Q_2\left(\sum_i \alpha_i e_i\right) = \sum_i \mu_i \alpha_i^2. \tag{25}$$

Let us now develop an effective algorithm for this theorem (Alg. 5). For effectiveness reasons, we choose F to be the orthogonal of $\ker Q_1 \cap \ker Q_2$ for the canonic dot product. Since $\ker Q_1 \cap \ker Q_2^{\perp} = \operatorname{Im} Q_1 + \operatorname{Im} Q_2$ we obtain an orthonormal basis of F by orthogonalizing a generating family of $\operatorname{Im} Q_1$ (the columns of Q_1), extending that basis to an orthonormal basis of $\operatorname{Im} Q_1 + \operatorname{Im} Q_2$ using a generating family of $\operatorname{Im} Q_2$ (the columns of Q_2). We then have an orthonormal basis of F, which can be extended to a basis B of $\mathbb{R}^n$ using a generating family of $\mathbb{R}$ (the canonical basis).

We consider both quadratic forms Q_1 and Q_2 on that basis B. Their matrices are of the form

$$Q_i = {}^t B\, Q_i B = \begin{pmatrix} Q_i' & 0 \\ 0 & 0 \end{pmatrix} \tag{26}$$

where Q_1' and Q_2' are square matrices of size $\dim F$. We diagonalize Q_1' with respect to the definite positive matrix $Q_1' + Q_2'$ and output the results with respect to the right bases.

Algorithm 5 QUADDIAG2, common diagonalization of two positive quadratic forms

---

Require: Q_1 and Q_2 two positive symmetric matrices
Ensure: $[P, I, d, D_1, D_2]$ where P is an invertible matrix, I its inverse, $d = \det P$, D_1 and D_2 two diagonal matrices such that $Q_1 = {}^t I \, D_1 I$ and $Q_2 = {}^t I \, D_2 I$

$\quad F \leftarrow \text{ORTH}\left[\left(\begin{smallmatrix} Q_1 & Q_2 \end{smallmatrix}\right)\right]$
$\quad K \leftarrow \text{NULL}\left[\left(\begin{smallmatrix} Q_1 \\ Q_2 \end{smallmatrix}\right)\right]$
$\quad [P', I', d, D_1'] \leftarrow \text{QUADDIAG1}({}^t F \, Q_1 F, \, {}^t F \, (Q_1 + Q_2)F)$
$\quad D_1 \leftarrow \begin{pmatrix} D_1' & 0 \\ 0 & 0 \end{pmatrix}$
$\quad D_2 \leftarrow \begin{pmatrix} 1 - D_1' & 0 \\ 0 & 0 \end{pmatrix}$
$\quad P \leftarrow \begin{pmatrix} F P' & K \end{pmatrix}$
$\quad I \leftarrow \begin{pmatrix} I' \, {}^t F \\ {}^t K \end{pmatrix}$

---

5   Conclusions

We presented an abstract domain for the backwards abstract interpretation of probabilistic programs, with a view to representing exactly the properties of programs using normally distributed generators.

As shown in Fig. 3, this analysis yields coarse results in the center of the functions; on the other hand, it leads to very precise results in the tails of the distribution. It therefore seems desirable to use it as a way to bound the influence of the tails of the random generators while using other methods, including abstract Monte-Carlo [11], for the center of the distribution.

The main problem with this domain is that it does not interact well with precise bounds, obtained for instance with a test with respect to an interval. A possible direction of research is an abstract domain covering both precise bounds and Gaussian bounds.

An application of this Gaussian analysis could be the study of the propagation of computational inaccuracies introduced by floating-point arithmetics, modeled by random choices.[1] We hope to contribute to that recently opened field [15] of abstract interpretation applied to round-off errors.

---

[1] This idea of modeling inaccuracies by random choices is the basis of the CESTAC method [16].

References

1. E. Anderson, Z. Bai, C. Bischof, S. Blackfordand J. Demmel, J. Dongarra, J. Du Croz, A. Greenbaum, S. Hammarling, A. McKenney, and D. Sorensen. *LAPACK Users' Guide.* SIAM, third edition, 1999. On-line extra documentation at http://www.netlib.org/lapack/.
2. J.M. Arnaudiès and H. Fraysse. *Cours de mathématiques, 4 : Algèbre bilinéaire et géométrie.* Dunod Université, 1990.
3. Patrick Cousot and Radhia Cousot. Abstract interpretation and application to logic programs. *J. Logic Prog.*, 2-3(13):103–179, 1992.
4. Luca de Alfaro, Marta Kwiatkowska, Gethin Norman, David Parker, and Roberto Segala. Symbolic model checking of probabilistic processes using MTBDDs and the kronecker representation. In *TACAS'2000*, volume 1785 of *Lecture Notes in Computer Science*. Springer-Verlag, January 2000.
5. Free Software Foundation. *GNU Octave: A high-level interactive language for numerical computations.*
6. Michael Huth and Marta Kwiatkowska. On probabilistic model checking. Technical Report CSR-96-15, University of Birmingham, School of Computer Science, August 1996.
7. D. Kozen. Semantics of probabilistic programs. In *20th Annual Symposium on Foundations of Computer Science*, pages 101–114, Long Beach, Ca., USA, October 1979. IEEE Computer Society Press.
8. D. Kozen. Semantics of probabilistic programs. *Journal of Computer and System Sciences*, 22(3):328–350, 1981.
9. Marta Z. Kwiatkowska, Gethin Norman, Roberto Segala, and Jeremy Sproston. Verifying quantitative properties of continuous probabilistic timed automata. Technical Report CSR-00-6, University of Birmingham, School of Computer Science, March 2000.
10. David Monniaux. Abstract interpretation of probabilistic semantics. In *Seventh International Static Analysis Symposium (SAS'00)*, number 1824 in Lecture Notes in Computer Science, pages 322–339. Springer-Verlag, 2000. Extended version on the author's web site.
11. David Monniaux. An abstract Monte-Carlo method for the analysis of probabilistic programs (extended abstract). In *28th Symposium on Principles of Programming Languages (POPL '01)*, pages 93–101. Association for Computer Machinery, 2001.
12. David Monniaux. *Analyse de programmes probabilistes par interprétation abstraite.* Thèse de doctorat, Université Paris IX Dauphine, 2001. Résumé étendu en français. Contents in English.
13. David Monniaux. Backwards abstract interpretation of probabilistic programs. In *European Symposium on Programming Languages and Systems (ESOP '01)*, number 2028 in Lecture Notes in Computer Science, pages 367–382. Springer-Verlag, 2001.
14. Martin L. Puterman. *Markov decision processes: discrete stochastic dynamic programming.* Wiley series in probability and mathematical statistics. John Wiley & Sons, 1994.
15. Éric Goubault. Static analyses of floating-point operations. In *Static Analysis (SAS '01)*, Lecture Notes in Computer Science. Springer-Verlag, July 2001.
16. J. Vignes and R. Alt. An efficient stochastic method for round-off error analysis. In *Accurate scientific computations (Bad Neuenahr, 1985)*, pages 183–205. Springer, Berlin, 1986.

Lifting Temporal Proofs through Abstractions

Kedar S. Namjoshi

Bell Labs, Lucent Technologies
kedar@research.bell-labs.com

Abstract. Model checking is often performed by checking a transformed property on a suitable finite-state abstraction of the source program. Examples include abstractions resulting from symmetry reduction, data independence, and predicate abstraction. The two programs are linked by a structural relationship, such as simulation or bisimulation, guaranteeing that if the transformed property holds on the abstract program, the property holds on the original program.

Recently, several algorithms have been developed to automatically generate a *deductive proof* of correctness from a model checker. A natural question, therefore, is how to 'lift' a deductive proof that is generated for an abstract program back into the original program domain. In this paper, we show how this can be done for general temporal properties, relative to several types of abstraction relationships between the two programs. We develop simplifications of the lifting scheme for common types of abstractions, such as predicate abstraction. We also show how one may generate easily checkable lifted proofs, which find use in applications such as proof-carrying code, and in the use of model checkers as decision procedures in theorem proving.

1   Introduction

Model Checking, introduced in [CE81,QS82], has enabled routine automatic verification of programs, especially in hardware and, more recently, in software. A key component of the application of model checking is the use of *abstraction* methods, which reduce the problem of checking programs with large (possibly infinite) state-spaces to checking a transformed property on a suitable small, finite-state abstraction of the original program. Typically, the two programs are related by a structural relationship, such as simulation [Mil71], or bisimulation [Par81]. This guarantees that if the transformed property holds on the abstract program, then the original property holds on the concrete program. Common examples of abstraction are those resulting from symmetry reduction [ES93, CFJ93], data independence [Wol86], and predicate abstraction [GS97].

Recently, several algorithms [RRR00,Nam01,PPZ01,TC02] have been developed that automatically generate a *deductive proof* of correctness from a model checker; such proofs have many applications, which are mentioned in these papers. In the context of model checking with abstraction, however, there remains a missing link: how to 'lift' a deductive proof generated automatically for the abstract program back to the concrete program domain. While it is well-known

L. Zuck et al. (Eds.): VMCAI 2003, LNCS 2575, pp. 174–188, 2003.

that property satisfaction can be lifted back through abstraction [HM85,BCG88], these results rely on the set-based semantics of properties, and do not indicate how to lift deductive proofs of satisfaction.

In this paper, we tackle this question for temporal properties in the Mu-calculus [Koz82], and several types of abstractions. The Mu-calculus is a very expressive temporal logic, which subsumes commonly used logics such as CTL, CTL*, and linear temporal logic. We use a deductive proof system developed in [Nam01] to represent proofs of correctness for mu-calculus properties. This proof system relies on invariant assertions (for showing safety) and rank functions (for showing progress). It is based on a direct translation of the mu-calculus to alternating tree automata [EJ91]; thus, the proof steps closely follow the syntax of the formula. We show how the invariance assertions and rank functions in a valid proof on the abstract program can be lifted to the concrete program domain to constitute a valid proof in that domain. We define how such lifting works for abstractions based on simulation (preserving universal properties), bisimulation (which preserves all properties), and abstraction with 3-valued logics (which preserves all properties, but with a potential loss of completeness).

We then explore several applications of this lifting scheme. We develop simplified versions of the scheme for common abstractions, such as the encoding of non-boolean types with bit vectors in symbolic model checkers, and predicate abstraction. We also examine the question of generating easily checkable proofs, for applications to proof-carrying code [NL96] and the addition of model checking as a trusted decision procedure to theorem provers. We show that it is possible to combine a checkable proof of the abstraction relationship and a checkable proof on the abstract program into a checkable proof showing correctness of the property on the source program.

Related Work. There is not, to the author's knowledge, an earlier systematic study of how proofs may be lifted from abstract to concrete programs, but several interesting and important instances of such lifting can be mentioned.

In [APR+01], an automatically generated invariant for a small instance of a parameterized system is heuristically (and automatically) lifted to a candidate invariant for the entire system, which is subsequently checked for validity. This check is required as it is not known in advance – unlike in our setting – whether there is an abstraction relationship between the full system and its small instances. The BLAST toolkit for verifying sequential C code [HJM+02] includes a method for lifting a checkable linear-time invariance proof through the abstraction computed by their algorithm into a checkable proof of correctness for the original program. The results in this paper apply to more general properties, including liveness and branching-time properties, and to several other types of abstractions. An alternative to proof-carrying code, called model-carrying code, is suggested in [SRRS02]. In one version, code is sent together with an abstract program and a proof of abstraction. The recipient must re-validate the property by model checking the abstract program. Our results show that it is possible to avoid this potentially expensive model checking step by combining the abstraction proof with an automatically generated deductive proof of the property.

2   Background

In this section, we define the mu-calculus and its universal fragment. For completeness' sake, we reproduce the deductive proof system from [Nam01]. In the following section, we show how to lift proofs that are developed in this system.

The mu-calculus. The mu-calculus [Koz82] is a branching time temporal logic that subsumes commonly used logics such as LTL, ω-automata, CTL, and CTL^* [EL86]. It is parameterized with respect to Σ (state labels), Γ (action labels), and V (the set of fixpoint variables). Formulas of the logic are defined using the following grammar, where l is in Σ, a is in Γ, Z is in V, and μ is the least fixpoint operator: $\Phi ::= l \mid Z \mid \langle a \rangle \Phi \mid \neg \Phi \mid \Phi \wedge \Phi \mid (\mu Z : \Phi)$.

We assume that Σ and Γ are fixed in the rest of the paper. A formula must have each variable under the scope of an even number of negation symbols. It is *closed* iff every variable is bound by a fixpoint operator. Formulas can be converted to positive normal form by introducing the operators $\Phi_1 \vee \Phi_2 ::= \neg(\neg(\Phi_1) \wedge \neg(\Phi_2))$, $[a]\Phi ::= \neg \langle a \rangle (\neg \Phi)$ and $(\nu Z : \Phi) ::= \neg(\mu Z : \neg \Phi(\neg Z))$, and using de Morgan rules to push negations inwards. The result is a formula where negations are applied only to elements of Σ. A *universal* formula is one where its positive form does not contain an $\langle a \rangle$ operator, for any a in Γ.

Formulas are evaluated over labeled transition systems (LTS's) [Kel76]. An LTS is a tuple $(S, \hat{s}, R, L)$, where S is a non-empty set of *states*, $\hat{s}$ in S is the *initial state*, $R \subseteq S \times \Gamma \times S$ is the *transition relation*, and $L : S \to \Sigma$ is a *labeling function* on states. We assume that R is *total*: i.e., for any s and a, there exists t such that $(s, a, t) \in R$. A set, I, of initial states can be accommodated by adding a dummy initial state with a transition to each state in I. The evaluation of a formula f, represented as $\|f\|_c$, is a subset of S, defined relative to a *context* c mapping variables to subsets of S. The evaluation rules are standard (see, e.g., [Sti95]) and are omitted here. A state s in the LTS *satisfies* a closed mu-calculus formula f iff $s \in \|f\|_\perp$, where $\perp$ maps every variable to the empty set. The LTS satisfies f iff the initial state $\hat{s}$ satisfies f.

Alternating Automata. The proof system we use is based on alternating automata rather than the mu-calculus. Alternating automata have a simpler structure, which results in simple proof rules. Furthermore, it is shown in [EJ91,JW95] that there is a straightforward translation from a closed mu-calculus formula to an equivalent alternating automaton: in effect, the automaton skeleton is just the parse graph of the formula (defining the acceptance condition requires an analysis of the alternation among fixpoint operators).

An *alternating automaton* is specified by a tuple $(Q, \hat{q}, \delta, F)$, where Q is a non-empty set of states, and $\hat{q} \in Q$ is the initial state. F is a partition $(F_0, F_1, \ldots, F_n)$ of Q, which defines a *parity* acceptance condition. An infinite sequence over Q satisfies F iff the *smallest* index i for which a state in F_i occurs infinitely often on the sequence is *even*. The transition function, δ, maps a pair from $Q \times \Sigma$ to a positive boolean expression formed using the operators $\wedge$, $\vee$ applied to elements of the form $true, false, q, \langle a \rangle q$ and $[a]q$, where $a \in \Gamma$, and $q \in Q$. We assume, without loss of generality, that δ is in a simple normal form where the boolean expressions have one of the following forms: $q1 \wedge q2, q1 \vee q2, \langle a \rangle q1, [a]q1, true, false$. Conversion to an equivalent, normal form automaton can be done in linear time.

The satisfaction of an automaton property by an LTS may be defined in terms of an infinite, 2-player game [EJ91] – we summarize this game here. A configuration (s, q) (s is an LTS state, q is an automaton state) is a win for player I if $\delta(q, L(s)) = true$; it is a loss if $\delta(q, L(s)) = false$. For other values of δ, player I picks the next move iff $\delta(q, L(s))$ is either $\langle a \rangle q1$ or $q1 \vee q2$. Player I picks an a-successor for s for $\langle a \rangle q1$, or the choice of disjunct. Similarly, player II picks an a-successor for s for $[a]q1$, or the choice of conjunct for $q1 \wedge q2$. A play of the game is a win for player I iff it either ends in a winning configuration, or it is infinite and the sequence of automaton states on it satisfies F. A *strategy* is a function mapping a partial play to the next move; given strategies for players I and II, one can generate the possible plays. Finally, the LTS satisfies the automaton property iff player I has a *winning* strategy (one for which every generated play is a win for player I) for the game played on the computation tree of the LTS from the initial configuration $(\hat{s}, \hat{q})$.

Deductively Verifying Mu-calculus Properties. Deductive proof systems for verifying sequential and concurrent programs rely on showing safety through invariants, and progress through a decrease of a rank function (alternative names are 'variant function', 'progress measure'). The proof system we use for verifying automaton properties (from [Nam01]) is based on the same concepts. Suppose that $M = (S, \hat{s}, R, L)$ is an LTS, and $A = (Q, \hat{q}, \delta, F)$ is a normal form automaton, where $F = (F_0, F_1, \ldots, F_{2n})$. To show that M satisfies A, one exhibits:

 - for each automaton state q, an *invariant* predicate, ϕ_q, over S, expressed in some assertion language, and
 - for each automaton state q, a partial *rank function*, ρ_q, which maps states in S to elements of a set W equipped with a well-order $\preceq$. The set W is the product, $W_1 \times \ldots \times W_n$, of well ordered sets $\{(W_i, \leq_i)\}$, and $\preceq$ is the lexicographic well-order obtained from $\{\leq_i\}$.

The invariants and rank functions must satisfy the proof obligations shown in Figure 1 (the predicate $l(s)$ is defined as $(L(s) = l)$, and the notation $[f]$ means that the formula f is valid.) For instance, the rule for a transition $\delta(q, l) = [a]q1$ asserts that for every state with label l that satisfies the invariant ϕ_q and has rank k, all of its successors must satisfy the invariant for $q1$ and change rank appropriately. To ensure progress towards termination of least fixpoints, the rank must change in a specific manner. This is given by a *rank change* relation, $\lhd_q$ (q is an automaton state), defined over $W \times W$. First, let $\prec_i$ be the restriction of $\prec$ to the first i vector components: formally, $a \prec_i b \equiv (\exists k : 1 \leq k \leq i : a[k] <_k b[k] \wedge (\forall j : 1 \leq j < k : a[j] = b[j]))$. For any a, b, and q, the relation $a \lhd_q b$ holds iff for the (unique, since F is a partition) index k such that $q \in F_k$, for some i, either $k = 2i$ and $a \preceq_i b$, or $k = 2i - 1$ and $a \prec_i b$. Informally speaking, the strict decrease of rank at odd indexed states ensures that in the game, player I can not get 'stuck' in such states, so the parity condition holds. In [Nam01], it is shown that this proof system is sound, and relatively complete.

- **Consistency:** For each $q \in Q$, $[\phi_q \Rightarrow (\exists k : (\rho_q = k))]$ (ρ_q is defined for every state in ϕ_q)
- **Initiality:** $[\phi_{\hat{q}}(\hat{s}) \equiv true]$ (the initial state satisfies the initial invariant)
- **Invariance and Progress:** For each $q \in Q$, and $l \in \Sigma$, depending on the form of $\delta(q, l)$, check the following.
  - *true*: there is nothing to check.
  - *false*: $[\phi_q \Rightarrow \neg l]$ holds,
  - $q1 \wedge q2$: $[\phi_q \wedge l \wedge (\rho_q = k) \Rightarrow (\phi_{q1} \wedge (\rho_{q1} \lhd_q k)) \wedge (\phi_{q2} \wedge (\rho_{q2} \lhd_q k))]$
  - $q1 \vee q2$: $[\phi_q \wedge l \wedge (\rho_q = k) \Rightarrow (\phi_{q1} \wedge (\rho_{q1} \lhd_q k)) \vee (\phi_{q2} \wedge (\rho_{q2} \lhd_q k))]$
  - $\langle a \rangle q1$: $[\phi_q \wedge l \wedge (\rho_q = k) \Rightarrow \langle a \rangle(\phi_{q1} \wedge (\rho_{q1} \lhd_q k))]$
  - $[a]q1$: $[\phi_q \wedge l \wedge (\rho_q = k) \Rightarrow [a](\phi_{q1} \wedge (\rho_{q1} \lhd_q k))]$

Fig. 1. A deductive proof system for verifying branching-time properties.

3   Lifting Proofs

Given a LTS N that abstracts an LTS M, we show how a proof of a property f on N can be lifted to a proof of the same property on M. We consider two common notions of abstraction: *simulation* [Mil71], which preserves only universal properties, and *bisimulation* [Par81], which preserves properties of the full mu-calculus (cf. [BCG88,Sti95]). Let M and N be LTS's, with $\Gamma_M = \Gamma_N$ and $\Sigma_M = \Sigma_N$. A relation $\xi \subseteq S_M \times S_N$ is a *simulation* from M to N if, and only if:

- The initial states of M and N are related, i.e., $\hat{s}_M \xi \hat{s}_N$, and
- For every s in S_M and t in S_N such that $s \xi t$ holds:
  - $L_M(s) = L_N(t)$, and
  - for every $a \in \Gamma_M$, and every u in S_M such that $(s, a, u) \in R_M$, there exists v in S_N such that $(t, a, v) \in R_N$ and $u \xi v$ holds.

A relation ξ is a *bisimulation* if, and only if, both ξ and its converse relation, ξ^{-1}, are simulations. We say that M is *simulated by* (*bisimilar to*) N if there exists a simulation (bisimulation) relation from M to N.

Notation. In the rest of this paper, proofs are presented in a format popularized by Dijkstra and Scholten in [DS90]. Here, individual steps of a proof are linked by a transitive connective such as $\equiv$ or $\Rightarrow$, along with a hint for why the connection holds. The notation $(Qx : r(x) : p(x))$ is used to represent an operation where x is the dummy variable, $r(x)$ is the range of x, and $p(x)$ is the term being operated on. Therefore, $(\exists x : r(x) : q(x))$ is the same as $(\exists x : r(x) \wedge q(x))$, while $(\forall x : r(x) : q(x))$ is the same as $(\forall x : r(x) \Rightarrow q(x))$.

3.1   Lifting Proofs through a Simulation

Suppose that M is simulated by N through a relation ξ, and f is a universal property. Since f is universal, the transition relation of the alternating automaton for f does not have any occurrence of $\langle a \rangle$, although any of the other connectives may occur. A proof, Π, that N satisfies f is given by the tuple (ϕ, ρ, W), where

ϕ is the invariant function, ρ is the rank function, and W is the well-ordered set of ranks. Let $\Pi' = (\phi', \rho', W')$ be defined by:

- (lifting invariants) $\phi'_q(s) \equiv (\exists t : s\xi t : \phi_q(t))$
- (lifting rank functions) $\rho'_q(s) = (\mathbf{min}\, t : s\xi t \wedge \phi_q(t) : \rho_q(t))$, where $\mathbf{min}$ is the minimum relative to $\preceq$ (the condition $\phi_q(t)$ ensures that $\rho_q(t)$ is defined.)
- (lifting rank sets) $W' = W$, $\preceq' = \preceq$

The lifted invariant is just the concretization of the abstract invariant (this is a well-known fact from abstract interpretation theory). We make frequent use of the following lemma in the subsequent proofs. It captures all of the information we need about $\lhd_q$ in order to show that the lifted proof is valid.

Lemma 1. For any a, b, c, d of equal length, and any automaton state q, if $a \preceq b, b \lhd_q c$, and $c \preceq d$, then $a \lhd_q d$.

Proof. By definition, $\lhd_q$ is $\preceq_i$ or $\prec_i$, for some i. The lemma holds as the $\preceq$ relation is stronger than $\preceq_i$, and $\preceq_i$ is transitive (it is a partial order). $\square$

Theorem 1. For a universal property f, if $\Pi = (\phi, \rho, W)$ is a valid proof that $N \models f$, and M is simulated by N through a relation ξ, then $\Pi' = (\phi', \rho', W')$, as defined above, forms a valid proof that $M \models f$.

Proof. Consider each type of proof subgoal.

(Initiality) We have to show that $[\phi'_{\hat{q}}(\hat{s}_M) \equiv true]$.

$\quad \phi'_{\hat{q}}(\hat{s}_M)$
$\equiv \quad$ (definitions)
$\quad (\exists t : \hat{s}_M \xi t : \phi_{\hat{q}}(t))$
$\Leftarrow \quad$ (logic)
$\quad \hat{s}_M \xi \hat{s}_N \wedge \phi_{\hat{q}}(\hat{s}_N)$
$\equiv \quad$ (ξ is a simulation)
$\quad \phi_{\hat{q}}(\hat{s}_N)$
$\equiv \quad$ (Initiality for the given proof)
$\quad true$

(Consistency) We have to show that, for any state s, $\phi'_q(s)$ implies that $\rho'_q(s)$ is defined. From the definition of ρ', if $\phi'_q(s)$ holds, then the range of t in $(\mathbf{min}\, t)$ is non-empty; thus, $\rho'_q(s)$ is defined.

(Invariance and Progress) Based on the form of $\delta(q, l)$:

0. $true$: nothing to check.
1. $false$: given that $[\phi_q \wedge l \Rightarrow false]$, we have to show that $[\phi'_q \wedge l \Rightarrow false]$. For any s,

$\quad \phi'_q(s) \wedge l(s)$
$\equiv \quad$ (definitions)
$\quad (\exists t : s\xi t : \phi_q(t) \wedge l(s))$
$\Rightarrow \quad$ (by simulation ξ, $l(s) \Rightarrow l(t)$)
$\quad (\exists t : s\xi t : \phi_q(t) \wedge l(t))$
$\Rightarrow \quad$ (by subgoal for N)
$\quad (\exists t : s\xi t : false)$
$\equiv \quad$ (logic)
$\quad false$

2. $q1 \wedge q2$: we have to show that $[(\phi'_q \wedge l \wedge \rho'_q = k) \Rightarrow (\phi'_{q1} \wedge \rho'_{q1} \lhd_q k) \wedge (\phi'_{q2} \wedge \rho'_{q2} \lhd_q k)]$. Consider the first consequence (the second has a symmetric proof). For any s,

$$
\begin{aligned}
&\phi'_q(s) \wedge l(s) \wedge \rho'_q(s) = k \\
\equiv\quad& (\text{ definitions }) \\
&(\exists t : s\xi t : \phi_q(t)) \wedge l(s) \wedge (\mathbf{min}\, t : s\xi t \wedge \phi_q(t) : \rho_q(t)) = k \\
\Rightarrow\quad& (\text{ definition of } \mathbf{min}\ ) \\
&(\exists t : s\xi t \wedge \phi_q(t) \wedge \rho_q(t) = k \wedge l(s)) \\
\Rightarrow\quad& (\ \xi \text{ is a simulation }) \\
&(\exists t : s\xi t \wedge \phi_q(t) \wedge \rho_q(t) = k \wedge l(t)) \\
\Rightarrow\quad& (\text{ corresponding subgoal for } N\ ) \\
&(\exists t : s\xi t \wedge \phi_{q1}(t) \wedge \rho_{q1}(t) \lhd_q k) \\
\Rightarrow\quad& (\text{ logic }) \\
&(\exists t : s\xi t \wedge \phi_{q1}(t)) \wedge (\exists t : s\xi t \wedge \phi_{q1}(t) : \rho_{q1}(t) \lhd_q k) \\
\Rightarrow\quad& (\text{ definitions, Lemma 1 }) \\
&\phi'_{q1}(s) \wedge \rho'_{q1}(s) \lhd_q k
\end{aligned}
$$

3. $q1 \vee q2$: this is similar to the previous case.

4. $[a](q1)$: we have to show that $[(\phi'_q \wedge l \wedge \rho'_q = k) \Rightarrow [a](\phi'_{q1} \wedge \rho'_{q1} \lhd_q k)]$. For any s and u,

$$
\begin{aligned}
&(\phi'_q(s) \wedge l(s) \wedge \rho'_q(s) = k) \wedge (s, a, u) \in R_M \\
\equiv\quad& (\text{ definitions }) \\
&(\exists t : s\xi t : \phi_q(t)) \wedge l(s) \wedge (\mathbf{min}\, t : s\xi t \wedge \phi_q(t) : \rho_q(t)) = k \wedge (s, a, u) \in R_M \\
\Rightarrow\quad& (\text{ definition of } \mathbf{min}\ ) \\
&(\exists t : s\xi t \wedge \phi_q(t) \wedge \rho_q(t) = k \wedge l(s) \wedge (s, a, u) \in R_M) \\
\Rightarrow\quad& (\ \xi \text{ is a simulation }) \\
&(\exists t : s\xi t \wedge \phi_q(t) \wedge \rho_q(t) = k \wedge l(t) \wedge (s, a, u) \in R_M \wedge (\exists v : (t, a, v) \in R_N : u\xi v)) \\
\equiv\quad& (\text{ rearranging }) \\
&(\exists t, v : s\xi t \wedge \phi_q(t) \wedge \rho_q(t) = k \wedge l(t) \wedge (t, a, v) \in R_N \wedge u\xi v \wedge (s, a, u) \in R_M) \\
\Rightarrow\quad& (\text{ corresponding subgoal for } N, \text{ dropping some terms }) \\
&(\exists v : \phi_{q1}(v) \wedge \rho_{q1}(v) \lhd_q k \wedge u\xi v) \\
\Rightarrow\quad& (\text{ logic }) \\
&(\exists v : u\xi v : \phi_{q1}(v)) \wedge (\exists v : u\xi v \wedge \phi_{q1}(v) : \rho_{q1}(v) \lhd_q k) \\
\Rightarrow\quad& (\text{ definitions, Lemma 1 }) \\
&\phi'_{q1}(u) \wedge \rho'_{q1}(u) \lhd_q k
\end{aligned}
$$

$\square$

3.2 Lifting Proofs through Bisimulations

Theorem 2. For any mu-calculus property f, if $\Pi = (\phi, \rho, W)$ is a valid proof that $N \models f$, and M and N are bisimilar through a relation ξ, then $\Pi' = (\phi', \rho', W')$, as defined above, forms a valid proof that $M \models f$.

Proof. Since we use the same lifted invariant and ranking function as in the simulation proof, the earlier proof claims carry over unchanged, and we only need add the proof for the $\langle\rangle$ case.

5. $\langle a\rangle q1$: We have to show that $[\phi'_q \wedge l \wedge \rho'_q = k \Rightarrow \langle a\rangle(\phi'_{q1} \wedge \rho'_{q1} \lhd_q k)]$ holds. For any s,

$$\phi_q'(s) \wedge l(s) \wedge \rho_q'(s) = k$$
$\equiv$ (definitions)
$$(\exists t : s\xi t : \phi_q(t)) \wedge l(s) \wedge (\mathbf{min}\, t : s\xi t \wedge \phi_q(t) : \rho_q(t)) = k$$
$\Rightarrow$ (definition of $\mathbf{min}$)
$$(\exists t : s\xi t \wedge \phi_q(t) \wedge \rho_q(t) = k \wedge l(s))$$
$\Rightarrow$ (ξ is a simulation)
$$(\exists t : s\xi t \wedge \phi_q(t) \wedge \rho_q(t) = k \wedge l(t))$$
$\Rightarrow$ (corresponding subgoal for N)
$$(\exists t : s\xi t \wedge (\exists v : (t,a,v) \in R_N : \phi_{q1}(v) \wedge \rho_{q1}(v) \lhd_q k))$$
$\equiv$ (rearranging)
$$(\exists t, v : s\xi t \wedge (t,a,v) \in R_N \wedge \phi_{q1}(v) \wedge \rho_{q1}(v) \lhd_q k)$$
$\Rightarrow$ (ξ is a bisimulation)
$$(\exists v : (\exists u : (s,a,u) \in R_M \wedge u\xi v) \wedge \phi_{q1}(v) \wedge \rho_{q1}(v) \lhd_q k)$$
$\equiv$ (rearranging)
$$(\exists u : (s,a,u) \in R_M : (\exists v : u\xi v \wedge \phi_{q1}(v) \wedge \rho_{q1}(v) \lhd_q k))$$
$\Rightarrow$ (logic)
$$(\exists u : (s,a,u) \in R_M : (\exists v : u\xi v \wedge \phi_{q1}(v)) \wedge (\exists v : u\xi v \wedge \phi_{q1}(v) \wedge \rho_{q1}(v) \lhd_q k))$$
$\Rightarrow$ (definitions, Lemma 1)
$$(\exists u : (s,a,u) \in R_M : \phi_{q1}'(u) \wedge \rho_{q1}'(u) \lhd_q k)$$
$\square$

3.3   Lifting Proofs through 3-Valued Refinement

A *modal* transition system (MTS) [LT88] is a tuple $(S, \hat{s}, R^{may}, R^{must}, L)$, where $S, \hat{s}$, and L are as in the LTS definition, but there are two transition relations, R^{may} (the *may*-transitions), and R^{must} (the *must* transitions), with the constraint that $R^{must} \subseteq R^{may}$. The interpretation of a mu-calculus property, f, on a MTS [HJS01] is given by inductively computing a pair, (f^{nec}, f^{pos}), with the property that $[f^{nec} \Rightarrow f^{pos}]$. The f^{nec} computation interprets $\langle a \rangle$ using R^{must}, and $[a]$ using R^{may}. Symmetrically, the f^{pos} computation uses R^{may} to interpret $\langle a \rangle$ and R^{must} to interpret $[a]$.

For MTS's M and N, N is an abstraction of M iff there exists a relation $\xi \subseteq S_M \times S_N$ such that ξ is a simulation relative to the R^{may} relations of M and N, and ξ^{-1} is a simulation relative to the R^{must} relations of N and M. Note that abstraction coincides with bisimulation and $[f^{pos} \equiv f^{nec}]$ when both MTS's are, in fact, LTS's (i.e., $R^{may} = R^{must}$).

Theorem 3. [HJS01] For MTS's M, N and a mu-calculus property f, if N abstracts M, then: (i) if $f_N^{nec}(\hat{s}_N)$, then $f_M^{nec}(\hat{s}_M)$ (success), and (ii) if $\neg f_N^{pos}(\hat{s}_N)$, then $\neg f_M^{pos}(\hat{s}_M)$ (failure).

Notice that it is not always possible to give a definite answer; there is a completeness gap. However, MTS refinement can be coarser than bisimulation, and yet be able to give a definite answer for arbitrary mu-calculus properties. It is necessary to modify our proof system slightly in order to apply it to MTS's. The proof system now checks whether f^{nec} holds: to do so, the $\langle a \rangle$ operator is interpreted using R^{must}, and the $[a]$ operator using R^{may}.

Theorem 4. Let M and N be MTS's such that N is an abstraction of M through a relation ξ, and let f be a mu-calculus property. If $\Pi = (\phi, \rho, W)$ is a valid proof that f^{nec} holds for N, then $\Pi' = (\phi', \rho', W')$, where the primed components are defined as before, is a valid proof that f^{nec} holds on M.

Proof. This follows immediately by inspecting the proofs given earlier for the validity of Π' in the simulation and bisimulation cases, substituting R^{may} for R in the $[a]$ proof, and R^{must} for R in the $\langle a \rangle$ proof. $\square$

Hence, if the success case holds, a proof of success can be lifted from N to M. By the semantics, $[\neg(f^{pos}) \equiv (\neg f)^{nec}]$. Thus, failure on N is equivalent to showing success for a negated property, so that a proof of failure becomes a proof of success of the negated property. So, on failure, we can use the previous theorem to lift the proof that $(\neg f)^{nec}$ holds from N to M.

3.4   Rank Functions and Rank Relations

A proof, as defined, is a triple (ϕ, ρ, W), where ρ is a collection of rank functions. For verifying a proof, however, we really need the rank *relations* $\rho_q(s) = k$ and $\rho_q(s) \lhd_r k$. We write the first relation as $\rho_q^=(s, k)$, and the second as $\rho_q^\lhd(r, s, k)$. We now show how to lift these relations through abstraction. For this purpose, we need a third relation, $\rho_q(s) \succeq k$, which we represent by $\rho_q^\succeq(s, k)$. The lifted relations can be calculated in terms of the original relations, as shown below.

$$\rho_q'^=(s, k)$$
$$\equiv \qquad \text{(by definition)}$$
$$(\mathbf{min}\, t : s\xi t \wedge \phi_q(t) : \rho_q(t)) = k$$
$$\equiv \qquad \text{(definition of } \mathbf{min} \text{)}$$
$$(\forall t : s\xi t \wedge \phi_q(t) : \rho_q(t) \succeq k) \wedge (\exists t : s\xi t \wedge \phi_q(t) : \rho_q(t) = k)$$
$$\equiv \qquad \text{(definitions)}$$
$$(\forall t : s\xi t \wedge \phi_q(t) : \rho_q^\succeq(t, k)) \wedge (\exists t : s\xi t \wedge \phi_q(t) : \rho_q^=(t, k))$$

$$\rho_q'^\lhd(r, s, k)$$
$$\equiv \qquad \text{(by definition)}$$
$$(\mathbf{min}\, t : s\xi t \wedge \phi_q(t) : \rho_q(t)) \lhd_r k$$
$$\equiv \qquad \text{(definition of } \mathbf{min}, \text{ Lemma 1)}$$
$$(\exists t : s\xi t \wedge \phi_q(t) : \rho_q^\lhd(r, t, k))$$

$$\rho_q'^\succeq(s, k)$$
$$\equiv \qquad \text{(by definition)}$$
$$(\mathbf{min}\, t : s\xi t \wedge \phi_q(t) : \rho_q(t)) \succeq k$$
$$\equiv \qquad \text{(definition of } \mathbf{min}, \text{ Lemma 1)}$$
$$(\forall t : s\xi t \wedge \phi_q(t) : \rho_q^\succeq(t, k))$$

Rank relations can be easier to compute than rank functions. For instance, if ξ, ϕ, and the abstract rank relations are expressed in Presburger arithmetic, the lifted relations are also expressible in Presburger arithmetic.

An alternative way of checking a proof is to fully expand the proof obligations, removing the dependence on the rank variable k through the 1-point rule. For instance, the fully expanded form of the $[a]q1$ obligation is $(\forall s : \phi_q(s) \wedge l(s) \Rightarrow$

$(\forall u : R(s,a,u) : \phi_{q1}(u) \wedge \rho_{q1}(u) \lhd_q \rho_q(s)))$. Let $\gamma(q,q1,s,u) \equiv \rho_{q1}(u) \lhd_q \rho_q(s)$. It is then desirable to lift the γ rank relation; its lifted form is $\gamma'(q,q1,s,u) \equiv (\exists v : u\xi v \wedge \phi_{q1}(v) : (\forall t : s\xi t \wedge \phi_q(t) : \rho_{q1}(v) \lhd_q \rho_q(t)))$.

4 Applications

In this section, we explore the use of proof lifting in several settings where abstraction is employed. We start with perhaps the simplest possible example: the encoding of finite types with bit-vectors in symbolic model checkers.

4.1 Symbolic Model Checking

Symbolic model checkers, such as SMV [McM93] and COSPAN [HHK96], operate on programs with finite data types. However, for the model checking computation, these programs are transformed into programs with only binary variables, by encoding variables with non-binary types with bit vectors. For instance, consider the following program, with a single action, a.

```
var x,y: [0,3]      initially (x=0) and (y=0)
a: x,y := (x+1) mod 4, (y+1) mod 4
```

To model check this program, variable x is transformed to the bit-vector (x_1,x_0), and similarly for y. This transformation induces a bisimulation between the source and result programs. Now consider the problem of lifting a proof of the bit-vector invariant, $\phi \equiv (x_0 = y_0 \wedge x_1 = y_1)$, into a proof in the original notation. The bisimulation relationship can be expressed by $(x,y)\xi((x_1,x_0),(y_1,y_0)) \equiv (x \in [0,3] \wedge y \in [0,3] \wedge x = x_0+2x_1 \wedge y = y_0+2y_1)$. Applying the lifting scheme for invariants, we get the expected result, $x = y$, as a result of Presburger simplification, which may be automated with tools such as Omega [Pug92].

$$\phi'(x,y)$$
$$\equiv \quad (\text{ definition of lifting })$$
$$(\exists x_0,x_1,y_0,y_1 : (x,y)\xi((x_1,x_0),(y_1,y_0)) : \phi(x_0,x_1,y_0,y_1))$$
$$\equiv \quad (\text{ definition of } \xi, \text{ and } \phi)$$
$$(\exists x_0,x_1,y_0,y_1 : (x \in [0,3] \wedge y \in [0,3] \wedge x = x_0+2x_1 \wedge y = y_0+2y_1) : x_0 = y_0 \wedge x_1 = y_1)$$
$$\equiv \quad (\text{ Presburger simplification })$$
$$x \in [0,3] \wedge y \in [0,3] \wedge x = y$$

4.2 Predicate Abstraction

In Predicate Abstraction [GS97], predicates of the original program are represented with boolean variables in the abstract program. For a predicate p, we let $\bar{p}$ denote its corresponding boolean variable. Let $\mathcal{P} = \{p_1,\ldots,p_n\}, (n > 0)$, denote the set of predicates. We let $s \sim_{\mathcal{P}} t$ represent the fact that concrete state s and abstract state t agree on values of the predicates in $\mathcal{P}$, up to the predicate-boolean correspondence. Formally, $s \sim_{\mathcal{P}} t \equiv (\forall i : p_i(s) \equiv \bar{p}_i(t))$. The abstract program, $\mathcal{A}$, is computed from the concrete program, $\mathcal{C}$, while satisfying the following constraints.

- The abstract initial state, $\hat{s}_{\mathcal{A}}$, is such that $\hat{s}_{\mathcal{C}} \sim_{\mathcal{P}} \hat{s}_{\mathcal{A}}$
- The abstract transition relation, $R_{\mathcal{A}}(t, a, v)$, is such that
  $(\exists s, u : s \sim_{\mathcal{P}} t \wedge u \sim_{\mathcal{P}} v : R_{\mathcal{C}}(s, a, u)) \Rightarrow R_{\mathcal{A}}(t, a, v)$

These two constraints ensure that the relation $\sim_{\mathcal{P}}$ is a simulation relation from $\mathcal{C}$ to $\mathcal{A}$, relative to the predicates in $\mathcal{P}$. Now consider a proof of a universal property on the abstract program. The lifted proof computed by the recipe of the previous section can be simplified as follows.

$$
\begin{aligned}
& \phi_q'(s) \\
\equiv \quad & \text{(by definition)} \\
& (\exists t : s \sim_{\mathcal{P}} t : \phi_q(t)) \\
\equiv \quad & \text{(by definition of } \sim_{\mathcal{P}} \text{)} \\
& (\exists t : t = (p_1(s), \ldots, p_n(s)) : \phi_q(t)) \\
\equiv \quad & \text{(1-point rule)} \\
& \phi_q(p_1(s), \ldots, p_n(s))
\end{aligned}
$$

Thus, abstract invariants can be lifted simply by substituting each boolean variable with its corresponding predicate. The rank relations can be simplified in a similar manner, to obtain the formulas below.

- $\rho_q'^{=}(s, k) \equiv (\phi_q'(s) \wedge \rho_q^{=}(p_1(s), \ldots, p_n(s), k))$
- $\rho_q'^{\triangleleft}(r, s, k) \equiv (\phi_q'(s) \wedge \rho_q^{\triangleleft}(r, p_1(s), \ldots, p_n(s), k))$
- $\rho_q'^{\succeq}(s, k) \equiv (\phi_q'(s) \Rightarrow \rho_q^{\succeq}(r, p_1(s), \ldots, p_n(s), k))$

Similar substitution-based transformations can be obtained for other types of abstraction that are (as in this case) functional in nature: i.e., $s\xi t$ if, and only if, $t = g(s)$, for a total function g. Data type reductions (e.g., reducing the integer type to $\{negative, zero, positive\}$), and symmetry reductions (reducing an equivalence class to its representative) are other examples of functional abstractions.

Example. In the self-stabilizing program below, execution of the actions $\{a, r\}$ alone maintains the invariant that $(x \bmod 3 = 0)$. However, the environment, through action e, may invalidate this property. In this case, execution of the restoration action r sufficiently many times (maximum 2) restores the invariant. This restoration property can be written in the mu-calculus as $(\nu Y : (\mu Z : (x \bmod 3 = 0) \vee [r]Z) \wedge [a, r, e]Y)$.

```
var x:integer      initially x=0
a: x := x+3
r: not(x mod 3 = 0) -> x := x+1
e: x := choose integer
```

We can verify this property through an abstraction relative to the set of predicates $\{p_i \,|\, i \in [0..2]\}$, where $p_i \equiv (x \bmod 3 = i)$. One possible abstract program is as follows.

```
var b_0,b_1,b_2: boolean     initially b_0 and not(b_1) and not(b_2)
a: b_0,b_1,b_2 := b_0,b_1,b_2
r: not(b_0) -> b_0,b_1,b_2 := b_2, b_0, b_1
e: b_0,b_1,b_2 := a_0,a_1,a_2  // the inputs {a_i} are mutually exclusive
```

The transformed property is $(\nu Y : (\mu Z : b_0 \vee [r]Z) \wedge [a, r, e]Y)$. The alternating automaton for this property (each automaton state corresponds to a sub-formula), and its correctness proof are shown in Figure 2. From this proof, one can read off the lifted correctness proof as follows (the notation $(a?b|...)$ is read as "a, if b else ...").

Invariants: $\phi_{q_3} = p_0$, all other $\phi_{q_i} = true$

Rank Functions: $\rho_{q_1} = (1?p_0|3?p_1|2); \rho_{q_4} = (0?p_0|2?p_1|1)$; and all other ranks are 0.

The set of states is $Q = \{q_0, \ldots, q_4\}$ with
initial state q_0.
The transitions are:

$\delta(q_0, true) = q_1 \wedge q_2$,

$\delta(q_2, true) = [a, r, e]q_0$,

$\delta(q_1, true) = q_3 \vee q_4$,

$\delta(q_3, b_0) = true, \delta(q_3, \neg b_0) = false$, and

$\delta(q_4, true) = [r]q_1$

The parity condition is $(Q \backslash \{q_1\}, \{q_1\})$.

Invariants: $\phi_{q_3} = b_0$, all other $\phi_{q_i} = true$

Rank Functions: $\rho_{q_1} = (1?b_0|3?b_1|2)$,

$\rho_{q_4} = (0?b_0|2?b_1|1)$,

all other ranks are 0.

Fig. 2. Alternating Automaton and the Correctness Proof

4.3   Efficiently Checkable Lifted Proofs

In several applications of automatically generated proofs discussed in [Nam01], [HJM$^+$02], it is important that the proof be efficiently checkable. For programs with bounded data types, the proof that is generated is *propositional* in nature: for instance, the invariants and rank relations may be represented by BDD's. Hence, it is possible to refine the individual validity checks of a temporal proof (which are instances of a co-NP complete problem) into proofs in a sound and complete propositional proof system (see, e.g., [Men97] for examples of such proof systems). Such a proof, for instance, in a Hilbert-style system, is easy to check in polynomial time: one need only check that each step is a proper substitution into an axiom schema, or a proper inference. The expanded proof may, of course, be exponential in the length of the original assertions.

However, abstraction often transforms a program with unbounded data types into a bounded program; thus, the lifted proof is over an unbounded data space. While it may seem that this makes it difficult to generate a checkable lifted proof, that is not necessarily the case. Suppose that M is simulated by N through a relation ξ, and that Π is the proof that $N \models f$. Let Π' be the lifted proof that $M \models f$, as defined in Section 3.1. The proof of Theorem 1 shows that each one of the conditions for Π' to be a valid proof is satisfied. Those proofs use, as sub-lemmas, the (given) facts that (i) ξ is a simulation relation, and (ii) Π forms a valid proof for the abstract program. Thus, if there are available checkable proofs of these facts, then the sub-proofs in Theorem 1 form a schema into which these can be inserted to make Π' a checkable proof.

For fixed abstraction schemes, such as reduction by symmetry, or predicate abstraction, the proof that ξ is a simulation can further be decomposed into a generic schema that any relation satisfying certain conditions (e.g., those given in Section 4.2) induces a valid abstraction relationship, and a proof that a given relationship satisfies these conditions. This further simplifies the burden of generating a checkable proof, and of checking it as well, since the generic schemas may be checked in advance.

5   Conclusions

We have shown that it is possible to lift deductive proofs, quite simply, through both simulation and bisimulation abstractions, for properties written in powerful temporal logics. We have also shown that it is possible to combine checkable proofs for the validity of an abstraction and for the temporal property on the abstract program into a checkable proof for the property on the original program. We have discussed simplifications in the lifted proof induced by the form of particular kinds of abstractions. It seems quite possible that other kinds of abstractions, such as reductions due to symmetry and data independence, will also be amenable to such simplification. Whether lifted proofs are of reasonable size in practice is still an open question, but the initial results of the BLAST project [HJM+02] are encouraging.

The lifted rank functions have the same domain as the abstract rank functions. This suggests that using the types of abstractions discussed here with finite-state abstract programs, one can only prove properties with 'bounded progress' proofs (as in the self-stabilizing example). Whether this is a limitation in practice remains to be seen. However, it is possible to abstract with unbounded progress measures, as shown in [KP00]; the extension of their results from linear time to branching time properties is the subject of ongoing work.

Acknowledgements. Thanks go to Dennis Dams, Patrice Godefroid, and the referees for a careful reading and many useful suggestions. Patrice Godefroid suggested the application to Modal Transition Systems.

References

[APR+01] T. Arons, A. Pnueli, S. Ruah, J. Xu, and L. D. Zuck. Parameterized verification with automatically computed inductive assertions. In *CAV*, volume 2102 of *LNCS*, 2001.

[BCG88]   M. Browne, E.M. Clarke, and O. Grumberg. Characterizing finite Kripke structures in propositional temporal logic. *Theoretical Computer Science*, 59, 1988.

[CE81]   E.M. Clarke and E. A. Emerson. Design and synthesis of synchronization skeletons using branching time temporal logic. In *Workshop on Logics of Programs*, volume 131 of *LNCS*. Springer-Verlag, 1981.

[CFJ93]   E. M. Clarke, T. Filkorn, and S. Jha. Exploiting symmetry in temporal logic model checking. In *CAV*, volume 697 of *LNCS*, 1993.

[DS90]   E.W. Dijkstra and C.S. Scholten. *Predicate Calculus and Program Semantics*. Springer Verlag, 1990.

[EJ91]   E.A. Emerson and C.S. Jutla. Tree automata, mu-calculus and determinacy (extended abstract). In *FOCS*, 1991.

[EL86]   E.A. and C-L. Lei. Efficient model checking in fragments of the propositional mu-calculus (extended abstract). In *LICS*, 1986.

[ES93]   E. A. Emerson and A. P. Sistla. Symmetry and model checking. In *CAV*, volume 697 of *LNCS*, 1993.

[GS97]   S. Graf and H. Saïdi. Construction of abstract state graphs with PVS. In *CAV*, volume 1254 of *LNCS*, 1997.

[HHK96]   R.H. Hardin, Z. Har'el, and R.P. Kurshan. COSPAN. In *CAV*, volume 1102 of *LNCS*, 1996.

[HJM+02] T. A. Henzinger, R. Jhala, R. Majumdar, G. C. Necula, G. Sutre, and W. Weimer. Temporal-safety proofs for systems code. In *CAV*, volume 2404 of *LNCS*, 2002.

[HJS01]   M. Huth, R. Jagadeesan, and D. Schmidt. Modal transition systems: a foundation for three-valued program analysis. In *ESOP*, number 2028 in LNCS, 2001.

[HM85]   M. Hennessy and R. Milner. Algebriac laws for nondeterminism and concurrency. *J.ACM*, 1985.

[JW95]   D. Janin and I. Walukiewicz. Automata for the modal mu-calulus and related results. In *MFCS*, volume 969 of *LNCS*, 1995.

[Kel76]   R.M. Keller. Formal verification of parallel programs. *CACM*, 1976.

[Koz82]   D. Kozen. Results on the propositional mu-calculus. In *ICALP*, volume 140 of *LNCS*, 1982.

[KP00]   Y. Kesten and A. Pnueli. Verification by augmented finitary abstraction. *Information and Computation*, 163(1), 2000.

[LT88]   K.G. Larsen and B. Thomsen. A modal process logic. In *LICS*, 1988.

[McM93]   K. L. McMillan. *Symbolic Model Checking*. Kluwer Academic Publishers, 1993.

[Men97]   E. Mendelson. *Introduction to Mathematical Logic*. Chapman and Hall (4th Edition), 1997.

[Mil71]   R. Milner. An algebraic definition of simulation between programs. In *2nd IJCAI*, 1971.

[Nam01]   K. S. Namjoshi. Certifying model checkers. In *CAV*, volume 2102 of *LNCS*, 2001.

[NL96]   G.C. Necula and P. Lee. Safe kernel extensions without run-time checking. In *OSDI*, 1996.

[Par81]   D. Park. *Concurrency and automata on infinite sequences*, volume 154 of *LNCS*. Springer Verlag, 1981.

[PPZ01]   D. Peled, A. Pnueli, and L. D. Zuck. From falsification to verification. In *FSTTCS*, volume 2245 of *LNCS*, 2001.

[Pug92]   W. Pugh. The Omega test: a fast and practical integer programming algorithm for dependence analysis. *CACM*, 35(8), 1992. web page: http://www.cs.umd.edu/projects/omega/omega.html.

[QS82]   J.P. Queille and J. Sifakis. Specification and verification of concurrent systems in CESAR. In *Proc. of the 5th International Symposium on Programming*, volume 137 of *LNCS*, 1982.

[RRR00]   A. Roychoudhury, C.R. Ramakrishnan, and I.V. Ramakrishnan. Justifying proofs using memo tables. In *PPDP*, 2000.

[SRRS02] R. Sekar, C. R. Ramakrishnan, I. V. Ramakrishnan, and S. A. Smolka. Model-carrying code (MCC): A new paradigm for mobile-code security. In *New Security Paradigms Workshop*, 2002.

[Sti95]   C. Stirling. Modal and temporal logics for processes. In *Banff Higher Order Workshop*, volume 1043 of *LNCS*. Springer Verlag, 1995.

[TC02]   L. Tan and R. Cleaveland. Evidence-based model checking. In *CAV*, volume 2404 of *LNCS*, 2002.

[Wol86]   P. Wolper. Expressing interesting properties of programs in propositional temporal logic. In *POPL*, 1986.

Efficient Verification of Timed Automata with BDD-Like Data-Structures⋆

Farn Wang

Dept. of Electrical Engineering, National Taiwan University
1, Sec. 4, Roosevelt Rd., Taipei, Taiwan 106, ROC;
+886-2-23635251 ext. 435; FAX:+886-2-23671909;
farn@cc.ee.ntu.edu.tw; http://cc.ee.ntu.edu.tw/~farn

Abstract. We investigate the efficiency of BDD-like data-structures for timed automata verification. We find that the efficiency is highly sensitive to the variable designs and canonical form definitions. We explore the two issues in details and propose to use CRD (Clock-Restriction Diagram) for timed automata state-space representation. We compare two canonical forms for zones, develop a procedure for quick zone-containment detection, and discuss the effect of variable-ordering of CRD. We implement our idea in our tool **red** 4.1 and carry out experiments to compare with other tools and **red**'s previous version in both forward and backward analysis.

Keywords: data-structures, BDD, timed automata, verification, model-checking

1 Introduction

Data-structure is the groundwork for efficient algorithms, especially for high-complexity tasks like real-time system model-checking [2]. Most modern model-checkers for real-time systems are built around symbolic manipulation procedures [10] of *zones*, which means a behaviorally equivalent convex state space of a timed automaton and is symbolically characterized by a set of difference constraints between clock pairs. DBM (difference-bounded matrix) [9] is generally considered the most efficient data-structure in representing sets of zones. But a DBM can only represent a convex state-space and DBM-technology can incur inefficiency in representing concave state-spaces.

In the last several years, people have been trying to duplicate the success of BDD techniques [4, 8] in hardware verification for the verification of timed automata [1, 7, 12, 13, 14, 15, 19]. Fully symbolic verification technologies using BDD-like structures can be efficient in both space and time complexities with

---

⋆ The work is partially supported by NSC, Taiwan, ROC under grants NSC 90-2213-E-002-131, NSC 90-2213-E-002-132
  Special thanks to Ms. Yu-Feng Chen, Mr. Geng-Dian Huang, and Mr. Fang Yu who helped collecting the huge set of experiment data.

L. Zuck et al. (Eds.): VMCAI 2003, LNCS 2575, pp. 189–205, 2003.

intensive data-sharing in the manipulation of state space representations. But so far, all BDD-like structures [1,7,12,13,14,15,19] have not performed as well as the popular DBM, which is a 2-dimensional matrix and nothing BDD-like.

After examining the previous BDD-like data-structures, we feel that the efficiencies of BDD-like data-structures are sensitive to the following two issues.

- *The design of the evaluation variables* that is, the domains and the semantics of the variables. We have identified the *representation fragmentation phenomenon*, which is caused by the semantics of variables [7], in section 5 and shown with experiments that the phenomenon can indeed affect verification performance.
- *The definition of canonical forms.* A zone can be represented by more than one sets of constraints. As being pointed out in [16,17], the more constraints are used in representing a chosen zone, the more space-complexity are incurred and the less data-sharing is possible. Moreoever, different paths in a BDD-like data-structures for dense-time systems may represent zones with intersections. It is also shown in [16,17] that too many constraints omitted in zone representations may make it difficult to efficiently decide the zone-containment relation between paths in such BDD-like data-structures. Thus it is possible that through appropriate choice of canonical forms, appropriate balance between the the width (number of paths) and depth (length of the longest path) of BDD-like data-structures can be obtained.

Without proper treatment of these two issues, we believe it is not possible to fully take advantage of the data-sharing capability of BDD-like data-structures. Straightforward adaptation from solutions for DBM, e.g. all-pair shortest-path canonical form, may result in low efficiency.

We have carried out numerous experiments with other tools [6,5] and various canonical forms with some possible canonical-form computation algorithms in order to gain better understanding of the issues. We believe the observation we have made in the experiments will be very useful for the integration of current technologies toward the construction of an efficient and practical model-checkers for timed automata. Specifically, we show how to use our new data-structure: *CRD (Clock-Restriction Diagram)* [16,17] for better efficiency. CRD shares the same shape as CDD [7] with the major difference that variable values in CDD are disjoint intervals while variable values in CRD are upperbounds, which are structurally overlapping. For example, the CRD for the union of two zones: $\{0 - x_1 \leq -3, x_1 - x_3 < -4, x_2 - x_1 < 6\}$ and $\{0 - x_2 < -1, x_2 - x_1 < 6\}$ (constraints of the form $x - x' < \infty$ are omitted) is in figure 1(a). If we change the upperbounds to interval reprsentations, we get the structure in figure 1(b), which is very like CDD but still different in that the interval labels from the root are not disjoint. The equivalent CDD for the same state-space, in figure 1(c), has both greater depth and greater width than figures 1(a) and (b).

We have also compared two canonical forms for zones. Interestingly, with DBM, these two canonical forms do not incur any difference in space-complexity. But with CRD, they incur great differences in representation and manipulation

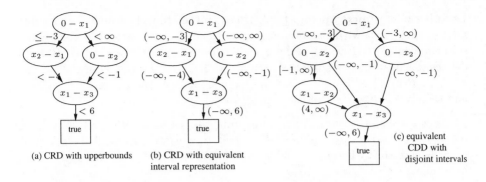

(a) CRD with upperbounds

(b) CRD with equivalent
interval representation

(c) equivalent
CDD with
disjoint intervals

Fig. 1. Differences between CRD and CDD

complexities. Finally, we also compare three evaluation ordering schemes and report their performances.

In sections 2 and 3, we shall first define the basic concepts of timed automata verification and zones. In section 4, we restate the definition of CRD [16, 17] and its basic manipulations for the benefit of readers unfamiliar with CRD. In section 5, we shall examine the effect of data-structure designs on complexity. Especially, the section also serves as a short survey to compare with previous data-structures. In section 6, we report our implementations. In section 7, we report our experiments to compare

- various canonical forms, in both forward and backward analysis, and also with other tools;
- CRD's performance w.r.t. input timing constant magnitudes; and
- CDD and CRD's representation complexity in several benchmarks.
- CRD's performance w.r.t. three variable-ordering.

2   Timed Automata Verification

We use the widely accepted model of *timed automata* [2]. We assume familiarity with this model and will not go into much detail due to the page-limit. A *timed automaton* is a finite-state automaton equipped with a finite set of clocks which can hold nonnegative real-values. At any moment, the timed automaton can stay in only one *mode* (or *control location*). In its operation, one of the transitions can be triggered when the corresponding triggering condition is satisfied. Upon being triggered, the automaton instantaneously transits from one mode to another and resets some clocks to zero. In between transitions, all clocks increase their readings at a uniform rate.

For convenience, given a set Q of modes and a set X of clocks, we use $B(Q, X)$ as the set of all Boolean combinations of inequalities of the forms $\texttt{mode} = q$ and $x - x' \sim c$, where $\texttt{mode}$ is a special auxiliary variable, $q \in Q$, $x, x' \in X \cup \{0\}$, "$\sim$" is one of $\leq, <, =, >, \geq$, and c is an integer constant.

Definition 1. timed automata A timed automaton A is given as a tuple $\langle X, Q, I, \mu, T, \tau, \pi \rangle$ with the following restrictions. X is the set of clocks. Q is the set of modes. $I \in B(Q, X)$ is the initial condition on clocks. $\mu : Q \mapsto B(\emptyset, X)$ defines the invariance condition of each mode. $T \subseteq Q \times Q$ is the set of transitions. $\tau : T \mapsto B(\emptyset, X)$ and $\pi : T \mapsto 2^X$ respectively defines the triggering condition and the clock set to reset of each transition. ‖

A *valuation* of a set is a mapping from the set to another set. Given an $\eta \in B(Q, X)$ and a valuation ν of X, we say ν *satisfies* η, in symbols $\nu \models \eta$, iff it is the case that when the variables in η are interpreted according to ν, η will be evaluated *true*.

Definition 2. states A state ν of $A = \langle X, Q, I, \mu, T, \tau, \pi \rangle$ is a valuation of $X \cup \{\texttt{mode}\}$ such that
- $\nu(\texttt{mode}) \in Q$ is the mode of A in ν; and
- for each $x \in X$, $\nu(x) \in \mathcal{R}^+$ such that $\mathcal{R}^+$ is the set of nonnegative real numbers and $\nu \models \mu(\nu(\texttt{mode}))$. ‖

For any $t \in \mathcal{R}^+$, $\nu + t$ is a state identical to ν except that for every clock $x \in X$, $\nu(x) + t = (\nu + t)(x)$. Given $\bar{X} \subseteq X$, $\nu\bar{X}$ is a new state identical to ν except that for every $x \in \bar{X}$, $\nu\bar{X}(x) = 0$.

Definition 3. runs Given a timed automaton $A = \langle X, Q, I, \mu, T, \tau, \pi \rangle$, a *run* is an infinite sequence of state-time pair $(\nu_0, t_0)(\nu_1, t_1) \ldots (\nu_k, t_k) \ldots \ldots$ such that $\nu_0 \models I$ and $t_0 t_1 \ldots t_k \ldots \ldots$ is a monotonically increasing real-number (time) divergent sequence, and for all $k \geq 0$,
- for all $t \in [0, t_{k+1} - t_k]$, $\nu_k + t \models \mu(\nu_k(\texttt{mode}))$; and
- either $\nu_k(\texttt{mode}) = \nu_{k+1}(\texttt{mode})$ and $\nu_k + (t_{k+1} - t_k) = \nu_{k+1}$; or
  - $(\nu_k(\texttt{mode}), \nu_{k+1}(\texttt{mode})) \in T$ and
  - $\nu_k + (t_{k+1} - t_k) \models \tau(\nu_k(\texttt{mode}), \nu_{k+1}(\texttt{mode}))$ and
  - $(\nu_k + (t_{k+1} - t_k))\pi(\nu_k(\texttt{mode}), \nu_{k+1}(\texttt{mode})) = \nu_{k+1}$. ‖

We can define the TCTL model-checking problem of timed automata as our verification framework. Due to page-limit, we here adopt the safety-analysis problem as our verification framework for simplicity. A safety analysis problem instance, $SA(A, \eta)$ in notations, consists of a timed automata A and a safety state-predicate $\eta \in B(Q, X)$. A is *safe* w.r.t. η, in symbols $A \models \eta$, iff for all runs $(\nu_0, t_0)(\nu_1, t_1) \ldots (\nu_k, t_k) \ldots \ldots$, for all $k \geq 0$, and for all $t \in [0, t_{k+1} - t_k]$, $\nu_k + t \models \eta$, i.e., the safety requirement is guaranteed.

3 Zones, Closure Form, Reduced Form, and Cascade Form

A *zone* is symbolically represented by a set of difference constraints between clock pairs and means a behaviorally equivalent state subspace of a timed automaton. For convenience, let $\mathcal{Z}$ be the set of integers. Given $c \geq 0$ and $c \in \mathcal{Z}$, let $\mathcal{I}_c$ be $\{\infty\} \cup \{d \mid d \in \mathcal{Z}; -c \leq d \leq c\}$. Also for any $d \in \mathcal{Z}$, $d + \infty = \infty + d = \infty$.

Given an SA(A,η) with biggest timing constant C_A used in A and η, a zone is a set of constraints like $x - x' \sim d$, with $x, x' \in X \cup \{0\}$, $\sim \in \{\text{"}\leq\text{"}, \text{"}<\text{"}\}$, and $d \in \mathcal{I}_{C_A}$, such that when $d = \infty$, $\sim$ must be "<". For convenience, let $\mathcal{B}_c = \{(\sim, d) \mid \sim \in \{\text{"}\leq\text{"}, \text{"}<\text{"}\}; d \in \mathcal{I}_c; d = \infty \Rightarrow \sim = \text{"}<\text{"}\}$. With respect to given X and C_A, the set of all zones is finite. Formally, a zone ζ can be defined as a mapping $(X \cup \{0\})^2 \mapsto \mathcal{B}_{C_A}$. Alternatively, we may also represent a zone ζ as the set $\{x - x' \sim d \mid \zeta(x, x') = (\sim, d)\}$. We shall use the two equivalent notations flexibly as we see fit.

There can be many zones representing the same convex subspace. A straight-forward *canonical* representation of a zone-characterizable convex subspace is its zone in *closure form* (called shortest-path closure in [11]). A zone ζ is in closure form if and only if all its constraint bounds are tight, i.e., for any sequence of elements $x_1, \ldots, x_k \in X \cup \{0\}$, with $x_1 - x_k \sim d \in \zeta$ and $\forall 1 \leq i < k (x_i - x_{i+1} \sim_i d_i \in \zeta)$, either $d < \sum_{1 \leq i < k} d_i$ or $(d = \sum_{1 \leq i < k} d_i \wedge (\sim = \text{"}\leq\text{"} \Rightarrow \bigwedge_{1 \leq i < k} \sim_i = \text{"}\leq\text{"}))$. We can artificially designate the closure form of each zone as our canonical form. For convenience, given a zone ζ, we let ζ^C be the notation for its closure form.

Another candidate for the canonical representation of zones is the *reduced form* (called shortest-path reduction in [11]) which records only minimum number of constraints for each zone according to some policy. We refer interested readers to [11,16] for explanation how to convert a given zone ζ to its zone in reduced form, in symbols ζ^R, according to certain policy. It is shown in [11] that $\zeta^C = (\zeta^R)^C$ and DBM with zones in reduced form can be used as a canonical representation of timed automaton convex states-spaces and can significantly save space in verification.

In [16,17], another canonical form called *cascade form* is proposed and used in red 3.1. It is identical to reduced form except that more constraints are added among clocks with equivalence relations for efficient detection of zone-containment relation.

4   Clock Restriction Diagram

4.1   Definitions

CRD [16,17] is not a decision diagram for state space membership. Instead it is like a decision diagram for zone set membership. Each *evaluation variable* in a CRD is of the form $x - x'$, where x, x' are zeros or clocks, and the values of such variables range over $\mathcal{B}_{C_A}$, where C_A is the bound used in DBM for a given safety-analysis problem instance. Thus a value, say $(\leq, 5)$, of evaluation variable $x - x'$ describes the constraint of half-space $x - x' \leq 5$. A path from root to the only leaf node *true* in CRD represents a zone.

By fixing an evaluation ordering, we can construct a CRD just as BDD, CDD, or RED. In CRD, a missing constraint on the difference of a clock pair, say x, x', is interpreted as $x - x' < \infty$. Thus in the root node in figure 1(a), even no constraint is on $0 - x_1$ in zone of the right path, we still construct an arc with $0 - x_1 < \infty$ from the root node.

Given a set V of evaluation variables with $true \in V$, an *evaluation index* Ω over V is a 1-to-1 onto mapping from V to $\{0, 1, \ldots, |V| - 1\}$ such that $\Omega(true) = |V| - 1$. For all $v, v' \in V$, we shall write $v \prec_\Omega v'$ iff $\Omega(v) < \Omega(v')$.

Definition 4. *Clock Restriction Diagram (CRD)* Given a set of variables $V = \{x - x' \mid x, x' \in X \cup \{0\}\} \cup \{true\}$, an evaluation index Ω over V, and a timing constant C_A, a CRD over V, Ω, and C_A is a tuple $D = (v, (\beta_1, D_1), \ldots, (\beta_n, D_n))$ with $n \geq 0$ and $v \in V$ such that

- $v = true$ iff $n = 0$;
- if $v \neq true$, then for all $1 \leq i \leq n$, $\beta_i \in \mathcal{B}_{C_A}$ and D_i is a CRD, say $(v_i, (\beta_{i,1}, D_{i,1}), \ldots, (\beta_{i,m}, D_{i,m}))$, over V, Ω, and C_A with $v \prec_\Omega v_i$;
- if $v \neq true$, then for all $1 \leq i < j \leq n$, $\beta_i \neq \beta_j$; and
- if $v \neq true$ and $n = 1$, then $\beta_1 \neq (<, \infty)$.   ‖

4.2   Basic Set-Oriented Manipulations on CRD

For convenience of discussion, given a CRD, we may just represent it as the set of zones recorded in it. Definitions of set-union ($\cup$), set-intersection ($\cap$), and set-exclusion ($-$) of two zone sets respectively represented by two CRDs are straightforward. For example, given CRDs $D_1 : \{\zeta_1, \zeta_2\}$ and $D_2 : \{\zeta_2, \zeta_3\}$, $D_1 \cap D_2$ is the CRD for $\{\zeta_2\}$; $D_1 \cup D_2$ is for $\{\zeta_1, \zeta_2, \zeta_3\}$; and $D_1 - D_2$ is for $\{\zeta_1\}$. The complexities of the three manipulations are all $O(|D_1| \cdot |D_2|)$.

We need the following notation to conveniently define CRD manipulations. Given $(\sim_1, d_1), (\sim_2, d_2) \in \mathcal{B}_{C_A}$, we say $(\sim_1, d_1)$ is *stricter* than $(\sim_2, d_2)$, in symbols $(\sim_1, d_1) \sqsubseteq (\sim_2, d_2)$, iff $d_1 < d_2 \vee (d_1 = d_2 \wedge (\sim_2 = \text{``}<\text{''} \Rightarrow \sim_1 = \text{``}<\text{''}))$. The following convenient notations are also adopted: $(\sim_1, d_1) \sqsubset (\sim_2, d_2) \equiv (\sim_1, d_1) \sqsubseteq (\sim_2, d_2) \wedge (\sim_2, d_2) \not\sqsubseteq (\sim_1, d_1)$, $(\sim_1, d_1) \sqsupset (\sim_2, d_2) \equiv (\sim_2, d_2) \sqsubset (\sim_1, d_1)$, and $(\sim_1, d_1) \sqsupseteq (\sim_2, d_2) \equiv (\sim_2, d_2) \sqsubseteq (\sim_1, d_1)$.

Given two zones ζ_1 and ζ_2, $\zeta_1 \sqcap \zeta_2$ is a new zone representing the space-intersection of ζ_1 and ζ_2. Formally speaking, for every x, x', $\zeta_1 \sqcap \zeta_2(x, x') = \zeta_1(x, x')$ if $\zeta_1(x, x') \sqsubseteq \zeta_2(x, x')$; or $\zeta_2(x, x')$ otherwise. Space-intersection ($\sqcap$) of two CRDs D_1 and D_2, in symbols $D_1 \sqcap D_2$, is a new CRD for $\{\zeta_1 \sqcap \zeta_2 \mid \zeta_1 \in D_1; \zeta_2 \in D_2\}$.

4.3   Two Zone Canonical Forms

We have come up with various canonical forms for CRDs. Each canonical form demonstrates a different space-complexity and time-complexity in the representation and manipulation. Due to page-limit, in this manuscript, we only discuss two canonical forms: *Closure form* and *difference-reduced closure (DRC) form*, which have shown better performance than the others. We adopt the tradition that a CRD is in its closure form if all its zones are in closure form (check section 3). Same tradition will be honored with other canonical forms. *Closure form* [7,9] is discussed in this paper because it has been a popular choice for DBM and used for many BDD-like data-structures.

A clock constraint $x - x' \sim c$ is a *difference constraint* if neither x or x' is clock zero, i.e. the constant of zero. Difference-reduced closure (DRC) form is basically identical to closure form except that a difference constraint is omitted from a zone representation if the difference constraint can be derived from two non-difference constraints in the same zone. With DRC form, we may have less constraints along each root-terminal path in CRDs than with closure form.

4.4   CRD+BDD

It is possible to combine CRD and BDD into one data-structure for fully symbolic manipulation. Since CRD only has one sink node: *true*, it is more compatible with BDD without FALSE terminal node which is more space-efficient than ordinary BDD. There are two things we need to take care of in this combination. The first is about the interpretation of default values of variables. In BDD, when we find a variable is missing during valuating variables along a path, the variable's value can be interpreted as either TRUE or FALSE. But in CRD, when we find a variable for constraint $x - x'$ is missing along a path, then the constraint is interpreted as $x - x' < \infty$.

The second is about the interpretation of CRD manipulations to BDD variables. Straightforwardly, "$\cup$" and "$\cap$" on Boolean variables are respectively interpreted as "$\vee$" and "$\wedge$" on Boolean variables. $D_1 - D_2$ on Boolean variables is interpreted as $D_1 \wedge \neg D_2$ when the root variable of either D_1 or D_2 is Boolean. For $D_1 \sqcap D_2$, the manipulation acts as "$\wedge$" when either of the root variables are Boolean. Due to page-limit, we shall omit the proof for the soundness of such interpretation. From now on, we shall call it CRD+BDD a combination structure of CRD and BDD.

4.5   Variable Ordering in CRD+BDD

The manipulation efficiency of BDD-like data-structure is strongly related to the variable evaluation ordering. Traditional wisdom is that we should place two strongly related variables close to each other in the ordering. We consider three variable-orderings to test how CRD+BDD reacts to variable orderings.

- **N**, with no interleaving between discrete variables and clock constraints in the ordering.
- **H**, only with interleaving between discrete variables and non-difference clock constraints, and
- **F**, with full interleaving between discrete variables and clock constraints.

Due to page-limit, we shall omit the detailed definitions. When interleaving is implemented, we consider the precedence of process identifiers and variable declaration ordering to define the interleaving ordering. Our experiments in subsection 7.4 show performance data very compatible with the traditional wisdom. That is, **F** is more efficient than **H**, which is in turn more efficient than **N**.

4.6   Reachable State-Space Representation Computation with CRD

We need two basic procedures, one for the computation of weakest precodition of transitions and the other for that of backward time-progression. Various presentations of the two procedures can be found in [10, 14, 15, 16, 17, 18]. Given a state-space representation η and an transiton (q, q'), the first procedure, $\texttt{xtion\_bck}(\eta, (q, q'))$, computes the weakest precondition

• in which, every state satisfies the invariance condition imposed by μ; and
• from which we can transit to states in η through (q, q').

The second procedure, $\texttt{time\_bck}(\eta)$, computes the space reprsentation of states

• from which we can go to states in η simply by time-passage; and
• states in the time-passage satisfy the invariance condition imposed by μ.

Due to page-limit, we shall omit the presentation of the two procedures.

With the two basic procedures, we can construct a symbolic backward reachability procedure as in [10, 14, 15, 16, 17, 18]. Computationally, this backward reachable state-space can be defined as the solution Y to the following least fixpoint of equation: $Y = \eta_2 \vee \texttt{time\_bck}(\bigvee_{(q,q')\in T} \texttt{xtion\_bck}(Y, (q, q')))$, i.e., $\texttt{lfp}Y. \left(\eta_2 \vee \texttt{time\_bck}(\bigvee_{(q,q')\in T} \texttt{xtion\_bck}(Y, (q, q')))\right)$. Due to page-limit, we shall omit the detailed presentation.

5   Design of Data-Structures

In the design of BDD-like data-structures, two aspects need to be considered, i.e. the domain of variables and semantics of variable values. Since BDD-like data-structures exhibit exponential blowup w.r.t. the size of variable domain, in general it is good to keep the variable domain small. The semantics of variable values is about how we should interpret the values of variables and has a much subtle effect on space-complexity. We feel that it will help the readers understand this issue if we compare CRD with the previous data-structures. DBM-technology generally handles the complexity of timing constant magnitude very well. Since a DBM can only represent conjunctive relations and there is no data-sharing among DBMs, when the number of clocks increases, its performance may degrade rapidly.

NDD [1] uses binary encoding for discrete clock readings and its performance is very sensitive to timing-constant magnitude.

DDD [12,13] uses Boolean variables like $x - y \sim d$ to encode representations for dense-time state-spaces. The approach is very similar to Wang et al's work [19] and the size of variable domain is propotional to the timing constants and thus exponential to the input size.

RED [14, 15] encodes the ordering of fractional parts of clock readings in the variable ordering and has achieved very high space-efficiency for symmetric systems with large number of clocks and small timing constants. RED is indeed a canonical representation of timed automaton state subspaces. But for large timing constants, RED's performance degrades rapidly.

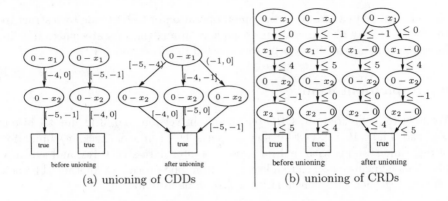

(a) unioning of CDDs   (b) unioning of CRDs

Fig. 2. Comparison between variable semantics of CDD and CRD

Finally, we want to compare our CRD with CDD [7], which is a decision diagram for state-space membership and has a very similar structure to CRD. The major difference between CRD and CDD is that the arcs from a node in CDD are labeled with "DISJOINT" intervals while those from a node in CRD are labeled with upperbounds, which are structurally overlapping. Due to this little difference, for some state-spaces, CDD may demand exponential size of memory. For example, we have the following state-space for n clocks:

$$\bigvee_{1\leq i\leq n} \bigwedge_{1\leq j\leq n}((i+j)\%n) \leq x_j \leq 2n + ((i+j)\%n) \tag{1}$$

Here "%" represents the modulo operator. When clock count n is 2, the compositions of the state-spaces in CDD and in CRD are in figure 2 (a) and (b) respectively. As can be seen, the CDD union operation will produce a CDD of three paths out of two zones while the CRD union operation will basically maintain the structures of the component zones. In fact, our experiment shows that the state-space of (1) exhibits an exponential blow up in CDD representation with respect to clock counts in the following table.

clock counts		2	3	4	5	6	7	9	11	13	15
CDD	node counts	4	12	31	73	162	346	1479	6064	24469	98166
	arc counts	6	23	78	238	663	1721	10056	52427	256674	1210285
CRD	node counts	7	16	29	46	67	92	154	232	326	436
	arc counts	8	18	32	50	72	98	162	242	338	450

Such exponential blowup, we believe, is due to the "DISJOINT" requirements of CDD on intervals. The requirement, although makes sense in mathematics, but actually contradicts the characteristics of zones which are noncanonical representations of convex state-spaces and may intersect with one another. Thus when union operation is performed, intervals will intersect each other into fragments. Such fragmentation phenomenon not only blows up the memory space requirement, but also destroys the manipulation results on zones. Such manipulation results can be generated from closure form computation or from zone-containment reduction. Since the union operation of CDD tends to restructure the zones, it may likely make previous effort in analysis of state-spaces in vain. More experiments in this aspect are reported in subsection 7.3.

6   Implementation

We have implemented our CRD-technology in versions 3.0, 3.1, and 4.1 of our tool red [14,15,16,17]. red 4.1 now supports TCTL model-checking/simulation of real-time systems with multiprocesses, pointer data-structures, and synchronizations (synchronous send and receive) from one process to another. The new version, together with benchmarks, will soon be available at:

    http://cc.ee.ntu.edu.tw/~val/red

Each process can use *global* and *local* variables of type *clock*, *discrete*, and *pointer*. Pointer variables either contain value NULL or the identifiers of processes. Thus in the models input to red, we allow complicate dynamic networks to be constructed with pointers.

At this moment, red runs with backward reachability analysis, evaluation ordering **F**, DRC form, and contained-zone elimination by default. It supports options for forward reachability analysis, deadlock detection, GUI, and counter-example generation. We have also implemented the reduction by elimination of inactive variables [18], which is always executed. A variable is *inactive* in a state iff it is not read in any computation from the state before its content is overwritten. Contents of inactive variables can be omitted from state information without any effect on the computations.

7   Experiments

We carried out four experiments to see in reality how combinations of techniques for CRD perform compared to other tools. We choose the following three previous tools for comparison.

- *Kronos* [5] (version 2.4 release 5), which supports forward and backward model-checking of TCTL [2].
- *UPPAAL2k* [6] (version 3.2.4), which supports on-the-fly forward reachability analysis with reduced zone representations and various searching and reduction strategies.
- red 3.1: This is bascially CRD in cascade form [16] with backward analysis and evaluation ordering **F**.

Kronos and UPPAAL2k are perhaps the two best-known model-checkers for real-time systems with DBM-technology. We choose UPPAAL2k and Kronos because first, DBM is now generally considered as the best data-structure for timed automata verification, and second, these two tools are mature and have been very successful. Also comparison with these two tools also gives us some rough feeling about how well CRD-technology performs against DBM-technology with both forward analysis (i.e. UPPAAL2k), and backward analysis (i.e. Kronos).

We also make comparison among various combinations of verification strategies in red 4.1. The following shorthands refer to these strategies.

- *Fw*: forward reachability analysis,
- *Bk*: backward reachability analysis (by default),
- **N**, **H**, **F**: as defined in subsection 4.5.

We use six benchmarks to compare the performance.

- *Fischer's timed mutual exclusion algorithm* [3, 18, 14]: The algorithm relies on a global lock and a local clock per process to control access to the critical section. Two timing constants used are 10 and 19. The property to be verified is that at any moment, no more than two processes are in the critical section.
- *CSMA/CD benchmark* [20]: Basically, this is the ethernet bus arbitration protocol with the idea of collision-and-retry. The timing constants used are 26, 52, and 808. We want to verify that at any moment, at most one process is in the transmission mode for no less than 52 time units.
- *FDDI token-ring mutual exclusion protocol* [5]: We need one process to model the network and the other processes to model the stations. For each station process, two local clocks are needed. Each station process can use the token to transmit message in mandatory synchronous mode and optional asynchronous mode. The biggest timing constant used is $50*m+20$, where m is the number of stations. We want to verify that at any moment, at most one stations is holding the token.
- *Scheduling problem of real-time operating system (PATHOS)* [3]: In the system, each process runs with a distinct priority in a period equal to the number of processes. Priority among processes must be observed by the scheduling policy. We want to verify that no deadlines will be missed.
- *Safeness of a leader-election algorithm (leader)*: Each process has a local pointer parent and a local clock. All processes initially come with its parent = NULL. Then a process with its parent = NULL may broadcast its request to be adopted by a parent. Another process with its parent = NULL may respond. Then the process with smaller identifier will become the parent of the other process in the requester-responder pair. The biggest timing constant used is 2. We want to verify that at any moment, there is at least a process who is a child to no other processes.
- *Bounded liveness of a leader-election algorithm (lbound)*: It is the same systems used in the fifth benchmark. But we assume that a process with parent = NULL will finish an iteration of the algorithm in 2 time units. We want to verify that after $2\lceil \log_2 m \rceil$ time units, where m is the number of processes, the algorithm will finish.

In subsection 7.1, we report the performances of some targets w.r.t. to the number of clocks. In subsections 7.2, we report the performances of Kronos, UPPAAL2k, red 3.1, and red 4.1 w.r.t. timing constant magnitudes. In section 7.3, we report our experiment to observe the effect of representation fragmentation. In section 7.4, we report the experiment with different variable orderings. All data are collected on an Intel Pentium IV 1.7GHz with 256MB memory running LINUX. In the table, only execution times are collected for Kronos and

UPPAAL2k while both times and memory (for data-structure) are collected for red. "s" means seconds of CPU time, "k" means kilobytes for memory space, "M" means megabytes, "O/M" means "out-of-memory" while "N/A" means "not available."

7.1 Performance w.r.t. Number of Clocks

The first experiment compares the performace, w.r.t. number of clcoks, of the following eight targets: Kronos 2.4.5, UPPAAL2k 3.2.4, red 3.1, and red 4.1 with Fw+Closure, with Fw+DRC, with Bk+Closure, and with Bk+Drc. Both red 3.1 and red 4.1 run with variable-ordering **F**. Table 1 shows performance data. Except for the FDDI benchmark, UPPAAL2k is invoked with forward analysis and options "-aSOWD." For the FDDI benchmark, UPPAAL2k is invoked with options "-SOTDda." Kronos is invoked with backward analysis.

Discussion The performance data shows that CRD-technologies are more space-efficient and scales better w.r.t. number of clocks than the DBM-technologies. For time complexities, Bk+DRC is only outperformed by the following case.

- *DBM-technologies with small number of clocks.* This shows that DBM-technology generally have good time complexities for small systems with its cubic complexity all-pair shortest-path algorithm on matrices.

But for systems with high concurrency, Bk+DRC outperforms the other targets. This can be attributed to the following two facts.

- In many of these benchmarks, backward reachability analysis leads to less total-ordering enumeration among clock values and thus less constraints in the zone-representations.
- When there are less constraints in zone-representations, according to the observation in [16, 17], higher data-sharing in CRD can be achieved.

Thus the reasoning behind the design of CRD seems justified.

Also, for forward analysis, in general, CRD-technology shows greater space-efficiency than DBM-technology with forward analysis as represented by UP-PAAL2k. But in time-complexity, DBM-technology performs better. According to our experience, BDD-like data-structures can create a lot of intermediate data-structures only to be garbage-collected. For example, in our CSMA/CD benchmark, we usually observed that the maximum memory consumption in the model-checking process is one hundred times the memory requirement for the final reachable state-space representation. This may imply that with better garbage-collection techniques, we can further improve the performance of CRD-technology. On the other hand, DBM manipulation usually does not incur any intermediate space-consumption. You basically just work on the same two-dimensional matrix.

7.2 Performance w.r.t. Timing Constant Magnitude Complexity

The performance of some previous technologies, e.g. NDD and RED, does not scale very well to the magnitude of timing constant. The data in table 2 is collected by runnning Kronos, UPPAAL2k, red 3.1, and red 4.1 with Bk+DRC+**F**.

Table 1. Performance data of scalability w.r.t. number of processes

benchmarks	m	Kronos 2.4.5	UPPAAL 3.2.4	red 3.1	red 4.1			
					Fw+Closure	Fw+DRC	Bk+Closure	Bk+DRC
Fischer's	3	0.02s	0.01s	0.66s/47k	0.17s/25k	0.17s/22k	0.16s/16k	0.15s/15k
mutual	4	0.15s	0.09s	3.87s/166k	0.95s/111k	0.86s/87k	0.79s/41k	0.71s/34k
exclusion	5	0.95s	2.97s	18.84s/467k	8.65s/582k	6.37s/417k	3.06s/87k	2.49s/70k
(m	6	O/M	292.56s	74.12s/1.2M	112.2s/3.3Mk	86.09s/2.2M	9.71s/187k	7.35s/127k
processes)	7	O/M	O/M	251.0s/2.6M	1224s/21.3M	910.1s/13.5M	27.96s/393k	18.09s/206k
	8	O/M	O/M	783.0s/5.3M	O/M	1150s/97.1M	81.7s/823k	40.07s/313k
	9	O/M	O/M	O/M	O/M	O/M	217.4/1.8M	88.58s/445k
	10	O/M	O/M	O/M	O/M	O/M	560.7s/3.8M	184.8s/610k
	11	O/M	O/M	O/M	O/M	O/M	1141s/8.8M	366.9s/1.2M
	12	O/M	O/M	O/M	O/M	O/M	3580s/20.5M	722.3s/2.5M
	13	O/M	O/M	O/M	O/M	O/M	9279s/47.0M	1324s/5.2M
CSMA/CD	3	0.01s	0.01s	0.43s/103k	0.30s/77k	0.27s/74k	0.08s/50k	0.08s/50k
(1 bus+	4	0.04s	0.04s	1.33s/181k	2.38s/371k	2.11s/344k	0.19s/82k	0.17s/82k
m senders)	5	0.26s	0.46s	4.05s/292k	31.57s/2.5M	25.43s/1.9M	0.43s/167k	0.40s/167k
	6	1.91s	13.87s	14.54s/470k	417.3s/16.8M	321.5s/10.9M	0.98s/313k	0.89s/313k
	7	O/M	752.42s	50.14s/974k	6728s/125M	4962s/68.3M	2.34s/617k	2.00s/617k
	8	O/M	O/M	158.7s/2.1M	O/M	O/M	5.77s/1.5M	4.51s/1.5M
	9	O/M	O/M	466.5s/4.4M	O/M	O/M	14.98s/3.3M	10.86s/3.3M
	10	O/M	O/M	1325s/9.3M	O/M	O/M	37.14s/7.5M	25.36s/7.5M
	11	O/M	O/M	3679s/19.9M	O/M	O/M	99.54s/17.0M	67.86s/17.0M
	12	O/M	O/M	10108s/42.6M	O/M	O/M	289.8s/38.2M	205.9s/38.2M
	13	O/M	O/M	28039s/91.1M	O/M	O/M	961.1s/85.3M	755.0s/85.3M
FDDI	11	72.61s	30.96s	1.22s/345k	0.36s/136k	0.38s/136k	0.24s/85k	0.18s/85k
token-ring	12	O/M	118.35s	1.85s/456k	0.52s/140k	0.56s/140k	0.33s/140k	0.29s/140k
passing	20	O/M	O/M	16.88s/1.4M	1.97s/504k	1.90s/504k	0.67s/259k	0.65s/259k
(1 ring+	30	O/M	O/M	81.37s/2.9M	6.96s/1.4M	6.91s/1.4M	1.91s/618k	1.93s/618k
m	40	O/M	O/M	266.0s/6.0M	17.52s/1.8M	17.62s/1.8M	15.34s/1.8M	15.36s/1.8M
stations)	50	O/M	O/M	O/M	36.10s/3.0M	35.48s/3.0M	37.70s/3.0M	37.43s/3.0M
	60	O/M	O/M	O/M	65.31s/4.6M	64.49s/4.6M	79.49s/4.6M	80.23s/4.6M
	70	O/M	O/M	O/M	109.68s/6.6M	107.9s/6.6M	153.9s/6.6M	154.8s/6.6M
pathos	3	0.0s	0.01s	0.45s/44k	0.28s/83k	0.27s/61k	0.05s/17k	0.05s/17k
(m	4	O/M	0.11s	4.28s/113k	5.78s/464k	5.15s/449k	0.18s/36k	0.14s/36k
processes)	5	O/M	8.02s	49.55s/299k	175.4s/5.3M	158.1s/5.2M	0.65s/75k	0.53s/75k
	6	O/M	O/M	718.5s/1.2M	5890s/83.4M	5385s/81.8M	2.82s/224k	1.94s/134k
	7	O/M	O/M	O/M	O/M	O/M	16.14s/711k	9.52s/375k
	8	O/M	O/M	O/M	O/M	O/M	93.48s/2.4M	50.59s/1.2M
	9	O/M	O/M	O/M	O/M	O/M	493.8s/7.5M	259.4s/3.4M
	10	O/M	O/M	O/M	O/M	O/M	2473s/23.9M	1261s/10.3M
	11	O/M	O/M	O/M	O/M	O/M	12998s/76.0M	6039s/31.2M
leader	3	0.13s	0.00s	0.05s/46k	0.04s/22k	0.04s/22k	0.04s/32k	0.05s/32k
(m	4	4.88s	0.01s	0.15s/94k	0.08s/38k	0.09s/38k	0.15s/72k	0.14s/72k
processes)	5	O/M	0.09s	0.40s/165k	0.22s/55k	0.19s/55k	0.51s/140k	0.49s/140k
	6	O/M	0.74s	1.21s/263k	0.40s/74k	0.41s/74k	1.69s/244k	1.60s/244k
	7	O/M	3.34s	3.47s/479k	0.73s/93k	0.75s/93k	5.47s/396k	5.51s/396k
	8	O/M	O/M	8.67s/819k	1.39s/123k	1.40s/123k	19.30s/606k	18.66s/606k
	9	O/M	O/M	19.07s/1.4M	2.22s/164k	2.20s/164k	50.87s/891k	50.80s/891k
	10	O/M	O/M	38.01s/2.2M	3.47s/213k	3.50s/213k	120.4s/1.3M	120.5s/1.3M
	11	O/M	O/M	69.84s/3.3M	5.25s/270k	5.30s/270k	262.7s/1.8M	262.6s/1.8M
	12	O/M	O/M	122.8s/4.9M	7.61s/340k	7.67s/340k	530.3s/2.9M	530.5s/2.9M
	13	O/M	O/M	206.9s/7.0M	10.98s/421k	11.00s/421k	1008s/4.8M	1007s/4.8M
	14	O/M	O/M	N/A	15.23s/514k	15.49s/514k	1854s/8.0M	1858s/8.0M
lbound	3	0.13s	0.00s	1.08s/75k	0.20s/105k	0.19s/105k	0.17s/45k	0.14s/39k
(m	4	4.88s	0.02s	15.21s/313k	1.47s/161k	1.42s/157k	1.47s/151k	0.99s/103k
processes)	5	O/M	0.08s	237.8s/1.8M	13.08s/541k	10.83s/465k	16.32s/562k	6.36s/308k
	6	O/M	0.65s	2188s/6.7M	100.19s/2.0M	79.26s/1.5M	144.8s/2.0M	44.16s/933k
	7	O/M	3.14s	19081s/21.8M	625.8s/7.2M	474.6s/5.4M	933.8s/6.0M	230.6s/2.8M
	8	O/M	O/M	O/M	4094s/29.0M	2984s/17.8M	5017s/17.2M	1016s/7.6M
	9	O/M	O/M	O/M	O/M	19275s/72.2M	24856s/47.8M	4247s/20.5M

against Fischers' mutual exclusion algorithm with various timing constant magnitudes. The table shows that CRD is at least as good as DBM technology as

Table 2. Performance data of scalability w.r.t. timing-constant magnitude

Tools	# proc	$C_A = 38$	$C_A = 76$	$C_A = 152$	$C_A = 304$	$C_A = 608$	$C_A = 1216$
Kronos	3	0.04s	0.03s	0.03s	0.03s	0.03s	0.04s
	4	0.21s	0.20s	0.20s	0.21s	0.21s	0.21s
UPPAAL2k	3	0.01s	0.01s	0.01s	0.01s	0.01s	0.01s
	4	0.09s	0.09s	0.09s	0.09s	0.09s	0.09s
red 3.1	3	0.65s/46k	0.69s/46k	0.67s/46k	0.67s/46k	0.66s/46k	0.68s/46k
	4	3.89s/166k	3.89s/166k	3.86s/166k	3.96s/166k	3.92s/166k	3.91s/166k
red 4.1	3	0.16s/16k	0.16s/16k	0.16s/16k	0.14s/16k	0.16s/16k	0.15s/16k
	4	0.77s/41k	0.79s/41k	0.78s/41k	0.78s/41k	0.77s/41k	0.78s/41k

long as performance scalability with respect to timing constant complexity is concerned.

7.3   Performance with Representation Fragmentation

To observe the effect of representation fragmentation phenomenon of CDD, we have endeavored to implement some CDD manipulation routines. This enables us to collect data, in table 3, of sizes of reachable state-space representations in CDD and CRD for the six benchmarks used in subsection 7.1. The state-space representation of benchmarks leader election safeness and liveness are very similar except that one more global clock is used for the liveness benchmark. From the table, we observe that CDD demonstrates exponential blow-up for two of the benchmarks (Fischer's, pathos) in comparison with CRD. For benchmark FDDI, it seems a blow-up is ongoing. For the other three benchmarks (CSMA/CD, leader election safeness, liveness), CDD performs better than CRD with a nearly constant factor. This is understandable because in CDD, both lowerbound and upperbound are specified with the same CDD variable while in CRD, two separate variables have to be used. For instance, the constraint of $3 < x_1 - x_2 < 5$ can be specified with one variable in CDD. But in CRD, it is specified with two variables as $x_1 - x_2 < 5 \wedge x_2 - x_1 < -3$. This explains why when CDD performs better, it does by a constant factor.

7.4   Performance w.r.t. Variable-Ordering

We compare the performance of red 4.1 w.r.t. the three variable-ordering discussed in section 4.5. The performance data is in table 4 and is very compatible with the traditional experience about BDD-like data-structures. That is, variables with strong relation should be placed near to each other.

8   Conclusion

To efficiently model-check timed automata, it takes deep understanding of the subtle interaction between data-structures and algorithms. We feel that previous

Table 3. Representation complexity of reachable state-spaces in CDD and CRD

benchmarks	concurrency	CDD			CRD			Size Ratio
		#nodes	#arcs	size	#nodes	#arcs	size	CDD/CRD
Fischer's	3 processes	69	131	200	86	147	233	0.858
mutual	4 processes	170	333	503	202	350	552	0.911
exclusion	5 processes	388	782	1170	398	677	1075	1.088
	6 processes	953	2019	2972	727	1209	1936	1.535
	7 processes	2669	5941	8610	1308	2121	3429	2.511
	8 processes	8296	19101	27397	2392	3780	6172	4.439
	9 processes	27235	63888	91123	4510	6959	11469	7.945
	10 processes	91279	216111	307390	8785	13287	22072	13.927
CSMA/CD	bus+3 senders	63	81	144	99	110	209	0.689
	bus+4 senders	127	162	289	195	218	413	0.700
	bus+5 senders	262	331	593	399	446	845	0.702
	bus+6 senders	546	683	1229	831	926	1757	0.699
	bus+7 senders	1142	1415	2557	1743	1934	3677	0.695
	bus+8 senders	2390	2935	5325	3663	4046	7709	0.691
	bus+9 senders	4998	6087	11085	7695	8462	16157	0.686
	bus+10 senders	10438	12615	23053	16143	17678	33821	0.682
FDDI	3 stations	37	45	82	46	54	100	0.82
token-ring	4 stations	57	68	152	69	80	149	0.839
passing	5 stations	81	105	186	92	106	198	0.939
	6 stations	109	141	250	122	139	261	0.958
	7 stations	141	182	323	156	176	332	0.973
	8 stations	177	228	405	194	217	411	0.985
pathos	3 processes	31	40	71	33	38	71	1.000
scheduliblity	4 processes	117	175	292	120	143	263	1.11
	5 processes	399	676	1075	376	446	822	1.308
	6 processes	1427	2689	4116	1160	1361	2521	1.633
	7 processes	5571	11424	16995	3587	4163	7750	2.193
	8 processes	23692	51833	75525	11106	12768	23874	3.163
	9 processes	110038	253020	363058	34353	39179	73532	4.937
leader	3 processes	93	116	209	118	141	259	0.807
election	4 processes	198	253	451	255	310	565	0.798
safeness	5 processes	352	454	806	457	559	1016	0.793
	6 processes	564	731	1295	736	903	1639	0.790
	7 processes	843	1096	1939	1104	1357	2461	0.788
	8 processes	1410	1775	3185	1785	2150	3935	0.809
	9 processes	1949	2451	4400	2466	2968	5434	0.810
leader	3 processes	199	222	421	255	277	532	0.791
election	4 processes	785	910	1695	1021	1121	2142	0.791
bounded	5 processes	2810	3297	6107	3667	3978	7645	0.799
liveness	6 processes	8962	10631	19593	11922	12948	24870	0.788
	7 processes	25389	29986	55375	34285	37263	71548	0.774
	8 processes	65500	76914	142414	89198	96914	186112	0.765
	9 processes	162306	189300	351606	222382	240776	463158	0.759

#node: number of nodes; #arcs: number of arcs; sizes = #node + #arcs;

BDD-like data-structures did not perform as well as DBM because such subtlety has not been paid proper attention. We have identified some of the issues in the design of efficient BDD-like data-structures and manipulation algorithms for timed automata state-spaces. We have carried out extensive experiments to justify our arguments. We have also developed techniques for DRC form. We believe the experience reported in this manuscript will be very valuable toward the implementation of industry-usable model-checkers for real-time systems.

Table 4. Performance data w.r.t. variable-ordering

benchmarks	concurrency	N	H	F
Fischer's mutual exclusion	3 processes	0.15s/16k	0.15s/15k	0.15s/15k
	4 processes	0.80s/41k	0.74s/34k	0.71s/34k
	5 processes	3.47s/111k	2.60s/70k	2.49s/70k
	6 processes	14.68s/289k	7.55s/127k	7.35s/127k
	7 processes	67.70s/719k	19.76s/243k	18.09s/206k
	8 processes	287.70s/1745k	47.85s/521k	40.07s/313k
	9 processes	1072.26s/4213k	111.75s/1129k	88.58s/445k
	10 processes	3713.66s/10192k	250.16s/2447k	184.77s/610k
	11 processes	13028.59s/24967k	549.04s/5326k	366.94s/1171k
	12 processes	N/A	N/A	722.29s/2443k
CSMA/CD	bus+3 senders	0.07s/53k	0.08s/50k	0.08s/50k
	bus+4 senders	0.23s/156k	0.20s/95k	0.19s/82k
	bus+5 senders	0.78s/444k	0.55s/267k	0.43s/167k
	bus+6 senders	2.87s/1178k	1.50s/766k	0.98s/313k
	bus+7 senders	10.64s/3040k	4.40s/2168k	2.34s/617k
	bus+8 senders	33.17s/7696k	13.11s/5986k	5.77s/1424k
	bus+9 senders	105.70s/19069k	41.76s/16146k	14.98s/3282k
	bus+10 senders	314.23s/41433k	154.38s/42607k	37.14s/7489k
	bus+11 senders	1044.05s/103226k	783.77s/110384k	99.54s/16958k
	bus+12 senders	N/A	N/A	289.81s/38192k
	bus+13 senders	N/A	N/A	961.06s/85265k
FDDI token-ring passing	11 stations	73.97s/52397k	0.17s/85k	0.38s/136k
	12 stations	O/M	0.30s/140k	0.56s/140k
	20 stations	O/M	0.65s/259k	1.90s/504k
	30 stations	O/M	1.88s/618k	6.91s/1317k
	40 stations	O/M	15.25s/1746k	17.62s/1746k
	50 stations	O/M	37.09s/2935k	35.48s/2935k
	60 stations	O/M	78.36s/4539k	64.49s/4539k
pathos	3 processes	0.05s/17k	0.04s/17k	0.05s/17k
	4 processes	0.15s/37k	0.16s/36k	0.14s/36k
	5 processes	0.52s/96k	0.58s/71k	0.53s/71k
	6 processes	2.32s/215k	2.23s/180k	1.94s/134k
	7 processes	13.79s/517k	13.30s/576k	9.52s/375k
	8 processes	78.39s/1361k	81.33s/2033k	50.59s/1111k
	9 processes	404.04s/4358k	469.20s/7431k	259.37s/3366k
	10 processes	1969.21s/14178k	2704.75s/26921k	1260.65s/10237k
	11 processes	N/A	N/A	6039.40s/31185k
leader	3 processes	0.05s/35k	0.05s/32k	0.05s/32k
	4 processes	0.16s/82k	0.17s/72k	0.14s/72k
	5 processes	0.59s/171k	0.51s/140k	0.49s/140k
	6 processes	3.84s/376k	1.56s/244k	1.60s/244k
	7 processes	21.65s/931k	5.64s/396k	5.51s/396k
	8 processes	97.30s/238k	18.77s/606k	18.66s/606k
	9 processes	389.76s/5954k	51.36s/891k	50.80s/891k
	10 processes	1486.50s/14874k	120.96s/1261k	120.46s/1261k
	11 processes	N/A	N/A	262.59s/1761k
	12 processes	N/A	N/A	530.46s/2814k
	13 processes	N/A	N/A	1006.48s/4733k
	14 processes	N/A	N/A	1857.20s/7925k
lbound	3 processes	0.13s/38k	0.15s/42k	0.14s/39k
	4 processes	0.92s/117k	1.13s/134k	0.99s/103k
	5 processes	7.98s/401k	8.78s/554k	6.36s/308k
	6 processes	63.95s/1382k	67.75s/2341k	44.16s/933k
	7 processes	368.03s/4520k	399.00s/8951k	230.56s/2710k
	8 processes	1812.74s/14102k	2229.66s/31537k	1015.59s/7589k
	9 processes	8506.04s/42120k	N/A	4246.73s/20491k

References

1. Asaraain, Bozga, Kerbrat, Maler, Pnueli, Rasse. Data-Structures for the Verification of Timed Automata. Proceedings, HART'97, LNCS 1201.
2. R. Alur, C. Courcoubetis, D.L. Dill. Model Checking for Real-Time Systems. IEEE LICS, 1990.
3. F. Balarin. Approximate Reachability Analysis of Timed Automata. IEEE RTSS, 1996.
4. J.R. Burch, E.M. Clarke, K.L. McMillan, D.L.Dill, L.J. Hwang. Symbolic Model Checking: 10^{20} States and Beyond. IEEE LICS, 1990.
5. M. Bozga, C. Daws. O. Maler. Kronos: A model-checking tool for real-time systems. 10th CAV, June/July 1998, LNCS 1427, Springer-Verlag.
6. J. Bengtsson, K. Larsen, F. Larsson, P. Pettersson, Wang Yi. UPPAAL - a Tool Suite for Automatic Verification of Real-Time Systems. Hybrid Control System Symposium, 1996, LNCS, Springer-Verlag.
7. G. Behrmann, K.G. Larsen, J. Pearson, C. Weise, Wang Yi. Efficient Timed Reachability Analysis Using Clock Difference Diagrams. CAV'99, July, Trento, Italy, LNCS 1633, Springer-Verlag.
8. R.E. Bryant. Graph-based Algorithms for Boolean Function Manipulation, IEEE Trans. Comput., C-35(8), 1986.
9. D.L. Dill. Timing Assumptions and Verification of Finite-state Concurrent Systems. CAV'89, LNCS 407, Springer-Verlag.
10. T.A. Henzinger, X. Nicollin, J. Sifakis, S. Yovine. Symbolic Model Checking for Real-Time Systems. IEEE LICS 1992.
11. K.G. Larsen, F. Larsson, P. Pettersson, Y. Wang. Efficient Verification of Real-Time Systems: Compact Data-Structure and State-Space Reduction. IEEE RTSS, 1998.
12. J. Moller, J. Lichtenberg, H.R. Andersen, H. Hulgaard. Difference Decision Diagrams. In proceedings of Annual Conference of the European Association for Computer Science Logic (CSL), Sept. 1999, Madrid, Spain.
13. J. Moller, J. Lichtenberg, H.R. Andersen, H. Hulgaard. Fully Symbolic Model-Checking of Timed Systems using Difference Decision Diagrams, In proceedings of Workshop on Symbolic Model-Checking (SMC), July 1999, Trento, Italy.
14. F. Wang. Efficient Data-Structure for Fully Symbolic Verification of Real-Time Software Systems. TACAS'2000, March, Berlin, Germany; LNCS 1785, Springer-Verlag.
15. F. Wang. Region Encoding Diagram for Fully Symbolic Verification of Real-Time Systems. The 24th COMPSAC, Oct. 2000, Taipei, Taiwan, ROC, IEEE press.
16. F. Wang. RED: Model-checker for Timed Automata with Clock-Restriction Diagram. Workshop on Real-Time Tools, Aug. 2001, Technical Report 2001-014, ISSN 1404-3203, Dept. of Information Technology, Uppsala University.
17. F. Wang. Symbolic Verification of Complex Real-Time Systems with Clock-Restriction Diagram. In proceedings of FORTE'2001, Kluwer; August 2001, Cheju Island, Korea.
18. F. Wang, P.-A. Hsiung. Efficient and User-Friendly Verification. IEEE Transactions on Computers, Jan. 2002.
19. F. Wang, A. Mok, E.A. Emerson. Symbolic Model-Checking for Distributed Real-Time Systems. In proceedings of 1st FME, April 1993, Denmark; LNCS 670, Springer-Verlag.
20. S. Yovine. Kronos: A Verification Tool for Real-Time Systems. International Journal of Software Tools for Technology Transfer, Vol. 1, Nr. 1/2, October 1997.

On the Expressiveness of 3-Valued Models

Patrice Godefroid[1] and Radha Jagadeesan[*][2]

[1] Bell Laboratories, Lucent Technologies, god@bell-labs.com
[2] DePaul University, rjagadeesan@cs.depaul.edu

Abstract. Three-valued models and logics have been recently advocated as being more suitable to reason about automatically-generated abstractions of reactive systems than traditional "2-valued" models such as standard Kripke structures or Labeled Transition Systems. Indeed, abstractions specified in 3-valued models are able to distinguish properties that are true, false and unknown of the concrete system, and hence their analysis can yield correctness proofs and counter-examples that can be both guaranteed to be sound. In this paper, we study several 3-valued modeling formalisms proposed in the literature and show that they have the same expressiveness, in the sense that any model specified in any of these formalisms can be translated into a model specified in any other. We also show that the complexity of the model checking and generalized model checking problems does not change from one formalism to the other.

1 Introduction

Program verification via automatic abstraction and model checking is currently an active area of research (e.g., [BPR01,DDP99,HJMS02]). This approach consists of automatically extracting a model out of a program by statically analyzing its code, and then of analyzing this model using model-checking techniques. If the model-checking results are inconclusive due to too much information being lost in the current abstraction, the model can then be automatically refined into a more detailed one provided the abstraction process can be parameterized and adjusted dynamically guided by the verification needs, as is the case with predicate abstraction [GS97] for instance. Current frameworks and tools that follow the above paradigm (e.g., [BR01,HJMS02]) typically use traditional formalisms (such as Kripke structures or Labeled Transition Systems) for representing models, while the soundness of their analysis is based on using a simulation relation for relating the abstract model to the concrete program being analyzed. Two well-known drawbacks of these design choices are that the scope of verification is then limited to universal properties, and that counter-examples are generally unsound since abstraction usually introduces unrealistic behaviors that may yield spurious errors being reported when analyzing the model.

Recently [GJ02,GHJ01,HJS01,BG00,BG99], it was shown how automatic abstraction can be performed to verify arbitrary formulas of the propositional μ-calculus [Koz83] in such a way that both correctness proofs and counter-examples

[*] Supported in part by NSF grants CCR 99010171 and CCR 02030716.

are guaranteed to be sound. The key to make this possible is to represent abstract systems using richer models that distinguish properties that are true, false and unknown of the concrete system. Examples of such richer modeling formalisms are partial Kripke structures [BG99] and Modal Transition Systems [LT88]. Reasoning about such systems requires 3-valued temporal logics [BG99], i.e., temporal logics whose formulas may evaluate to *true, false* or $\perp$ ("unknown") on a given model. Then, by using an automatic abstraction process that generates by construction an abstract model which is less complete than the concrete system with respect to a completeness preorder logically characterized by 3-valued temporal logic, every temporal property ϕ that evaluates to *true* (resp. *false*) on the abstract model automatically holds (resp. does not hold) of the concrete system, hence guaranteeing soundness of both proofs and counter-examples. In case ϕ evaluates to $\perp$ on the model, *generalized model checking* [BG00,GJ02] can be used to check whether there exist concretizations of the abstract model that satisfies ϕ or violates ϕ; if a negative answer is obtained in either one of these two tests, ϕ does not hold (resp. holds) of the concrete system. Otherwise, the analysis is still inconclusive and a more complete (i.e., less abstract) model is then necessary to provide a definite answer concerning this property of the concrete system. This approach is applicable to check arbitrary formulas of the propositional μ-calculus (thus including negation and arbitrarily nested path quantifiers), not just universal properties as with a traditional "conservative" abstraction that merely simulates the concrete system. It is shown in [GHJ01] that building a 3-valued abstraction can be done using existing abstraction techniques at the same computational cost as building a conservative abstraction. See [GJ02] for examples of programs and properties that cannot be verified using traditional conservation abstraction.

In this paper, we study and compare several 3-valued modeling formalisms that have been proposed in the literature, namely partial Kripke structures [BG99], Modal Transition Systems [LT88], and Kripke Modal Transition Systems [HJS01]. We define procedures for translating models specified in any of these formalisms into models specified in any other. As a corollary of these translations, we show that these modeling formalisms have the same expressiveness. We also study properties of these translations, and show that the model checking and generalized model checking problems can be both reduced from one formalism to any other. We then conclude by discussing applications and consequences of these results, as well as why these formalisms complement each other.

2   Background: 3-Valued Modeling Formalisms

In this section we recall the definitions of several 3-valued models used in the literature, as well as of temporal logics interpreted over them.

2.1   Partial Kripke Structures

The first 3-valued model we review is the *partial Kripke structure* as defined in [BG99,BG00]. A partial Kripke structure is simply a Kripke structure whose atomic propositions can have a third truth value $\perp$, which means "unknown whether true or false". Formally, we have the following.

Definition 1. *A partial Kripke structure (PKS) M is a tuple $(S, P, \rightarrow, L)$, where S is a set of states, P is a set of atomic propositions, $\rightarrow \subseteq S \times S$ is a transition relation on S, and $L : S \times P \rightarrow \{true, \perp, false\}$ is an interpretation that associates a truth value in $\{true, \perp, false\}$ with each atomic proposition in P for each state in S.*

A standard Kripke structure is a special case of partial Kripke structure. We sometimes refer to standard Kripke structures as *complete* Kripke structures to emphasize that no propositions within them take value $\perp$. In what follows, we often write $s \rightarrow s'$ as shorthand for $(s, s') \in \rightarrow$.

Propositional operators are interpreted on PKSs using Kleene's strong 3-valued propositional logic [Kle87]. Conjunction $\wedge$ in this logic is defined as the function that returns *true* if both of its arguments are *true*, *false* if either argument is *false*, and $\perp$ otherwise. We define negation $\neg$ using the function 'comp' that maps *true* to *false*, *false* to *true*, and $\perp$ to $\perp$. Disjunction $\vee$ is defined as usual using De Morgan's laws: $p \vee q = \neg(\neg p \wedge \neg q)$. Note that these functions give the usual meaning of the propositional operators when applied to values *true* and *false*.

Propositional modal logic (PML) is propositional logic extended with the modal operator AX (which is read "for all immediate successors"). Formulas of PML have the following abstract syntax: $\phi ::= p \mid \neg\phi \mid \phi_1 \wedge \phi_2 \mid AX\phi$, where p ranges over P. The following 3-valued semantics generalizes the traditional 2-valued semantics for PML.

Definition 2. *The value of a formula ϕ of 3-valued PML in a state s of a PKS $M = (S, P, \rightarrow, L)$, written $[(M, s) \models \phi]$, is defined inductively as follows:*

$$[(M, s) \models p] = L(s, p)$$
$$[(M, s) \models \neg\phi] = comp([(M, s) \models \phi])$$
$$[(M, s) \models \phi_1 \wedge \phi_2] = [(M, s) \models \phi_1] \wedge [(M, s) \models \phi_2]$$
$$[(M, s) \models AX\phi] = \bigwedge_{s \rightarrow s'} [(M, s') \models \phi].$$

This 3-valued logic can be used to define a preorder on KMTSs that reflects their degree of completeness. Let $\leq$ be the *information ordering* on truth values, in which $\perp \leq true$, $\perp \leq false$, $x \leq x$ (for all $x \in \{true, \perp, false\}$), and $x \not\leq y$ otherwise.

Definition 3. *Let $M_1 = (S_1, P, \rightarrow_1, L_1)$ and $M_2 = (S_2, P, \rightarrow_2, L_2)$ be partial Kripke structures. The completeness preorder $\preceq$ is the greatest relation $\mathcal{B} \subseteq S_1 \times S_2$ such that $(s_1, s_2) \in \mathcal{B}$ implies the following:*

- $\forall p \in P : L_1(s_1, p) \leq L_2(s_2, p),$
- if $s_1 \rightarrow s_1'$ then there is some $s_2' \in S_2$ such that $s_2 \rightarrow s_2'$ and $(s_1', s_2') \in \mathcal{B},$
- if $s_2 \rightarrow s_2'$ then there is some $s_1' \in S_1$ such that $s_1 \rightarrow s_1'$ and $(s_1', s_2') \in \mathcal{B}.$

Intuitively, $s_1 \preceq s_2$ means that s_1 and s_2 are "nearly bisimilar" except that the atomic propositions in state s_1 may be less defined than in state s_2. The following theorem states that 3-valued PML logically characterizes the completeness preorder on PKSs [BG99].

Theorem 1. *Let* $M_1 = (S_1, P, \rightarrow_1, L_1)$ *and* $M_2 = (S_2, P, \rightarrow_2, L_2)$ *be partial Kripke structures such that* $s_1 \in S_1$ *and* $s_2 \in S_2$, *and let* Φ *be the set of all formulas of 3-valued PML. Then*

$$s_1 \preceq s_2 \text{ iff } (\forall \phi \in \Phi : [(M_1, s_1) \models \phi] \leq [(M_2, s_2) \models \phi]).$$

In other words, partial Kripke structures that are "more complete" with respect to $\preceq$ have more definite properties with respect to $\leq$, i.e., have more properties that are either *true* or *false*. Moreover, any formula ϕ of 3-valued PML that evaluates to *true* or *false* on a partial Kripke structure has the same truth value when evaluated on any more complete structure. This result also holds for PML extended with fixpoint operators [BG00], also known as the propositional μ-calculus [Koz83].

2.2 Modal Transition Systems

Modal Transitions Systems are a generalization of Labeled Transition Systems introduced in [LT88,Lar89].

Definition 4. *A* Modal Transition System *(MTS) M is a tuple* $(S, \Sigma, \overset{must}{\longrightarrow}, \overset{may}{\longrightarrow})$, *where* S *is a set of* states, Σ *is a set of* action symbols, $\overset{must}{\longrightarrow} \subseteq S \times \Sigma \times S$ *and* $\overset{may}{\longrightarrow} \subseteq S \times \Sigma \times S$ *are transition relations such that* $\overset{must}{\longrightarrow} \subseteq \overset{may}{\longrightarrow}$.

An MTS is thus a Labeled Transition System (LTS) with two types of transitions, *must* and *may* transitions, with the additional constraint that every *must*-transition is also a *may*-transition. Reasoning about the existence of transitions of MTSs can be viewed as reasoning with a three-valued logic: transitions that are necessarily true are *true*, transitions that are possibly true but not necessarily true are $\perp$, and transitions that are not possibly true are *false*. Formally, we can define a 3-valued PML on MTSs, let us denote it PML^{Act}, whose abstract syntax is defined recursively as follows: $\phi ::= \text{tt} \mid \neg\phi \mid \phi_1 \wedge \phi_2 \mid (\forall a)\phi$, where a ranges over Σ. The semantics of these operators can be defined as follows.

Definition 5. *The value of a formula* ϕ *of 3-valued PML^{Act} in a state* s *of an MTS* $M = (S, \Sigma, \overset{must}{\longrightarrow}, \overset{may}{\longrightarrow})$, *written* $[(M, s) \models \phi]$, *is defined inductively as follows:*

$$[(M, s) \models \texttt{tt}] = \textit{true}$$

$$[(M, s) \models \neg \phi] = comp([(M, s) \models \phi])$$

$$[(M, s) \models \phi_1 \wedge \phi_2] = [(M, s) \models \phi_1] \wedge [(M, s) \models \phi_2]$$

$$[(M, s) \models (\forall a)\phi] = \begin{cases} \textit{true if } \forall (s, a, s') \in \xrightarrow{may}: [(M, s') \models \phi] = \textit{true} \\ \textit{false if } \exists (s, a, s') \in \xrightarrow{must}: [(M, s') \models \phi] = \textit{false} \\ \bot \quad \textit{otherwise} \end{cases}$$

The above semantics is equivalent to the one that appeared in [HJS01,GHJ01]. We use this alternate form to facilitate the comparison with other models in later sections.

The degree of completeness of MTSs can be measured by the following completeness preorder (whose inverse is called "refinement preorder" [LT88]).

Definition 6. *Let* $M_1 = (S_1, \Sigma, \xrightarrow{must}_1, \xrightarrow{may}_1)$ *and* $M_2 = (S_2, \Sigma, \xrightarrow{must}_2, \xrightarrow{may}_2)$ *be MTSs. The* completeness preorder $\preceq$ *is the greatest relation* $\mathcal{B} \subseteq S_1 \times S_2$ *such that* $(s_1, s_2) \in \mathcal{B}$ *implies the following:*

- *if* $(s_1, a, s_1') \in \xrightarrow{must}_1$, *there is some* $s_2' \in S_2$ *such that* $(s_2, a, s_2') \in \xrightarrow{must}_2$ *and* $(s_1', s_2') \in \mathcal{B}$,
- *if* $(s_2, a, s_2') \in \xrightarrow{may}_2$, *there is some* $s_1' \in S_1$ *such that* $(s_1, a, s_1') \in \xrightarrow{may}_1$ *and* $(s_1', s_2') \in \mathcal{B}$.

Again, $s_1 \preceq s_2$ means that s_1 is more abstract (i.e., less complete) than s_2. This definition allows to abstract a system M_2 by a more abstract system M_1 by letting *must*-transitions of M_2 become *may*-transitions in M_1, but all *may*-transitions of M_2 must be preserved in M_1. It can be shown that this completeness preorder is logically characterized by 3-valued PML [HJS01,GHJ01].

Theorem 2. *Let* $M_1 = (S_1, \Sigma, \xrightarrow{must}_1, \xrightarrow{may}_1)$ *and* $M_2 = (S_2, \Sigma, \xrightarrow{must}_2, \xrightarrow{may}_2)$ *be MTSs such that* $s_1 \in S_1$ *and* $s_2 \in S_2$, *and let* Φ *be the set of all formulas of 3-valued PML$^{\texttt{Act}}$. Then,*

$$s_1 \preceq s_2 \textit{ iff } (\forall \phi \in \Phi : [(M_1, s_1) \models \phi] \leq [(M_2, s_2) \models \phi]).$$

2.3   Kripke Modal Transition Systems

A third model we consider here is (a simplified version of) the Kripke Modal Transition Systems introduced in [HJS01]. This model combines features of both PKSs and MTSs, although it does not increase their expressiveness as will be shown later in this paper. Precisely, we define a Kripke Modal Transition System as follows [GJ02].

Definition 7. *A* Kripke Modal Transition System *(KMTS)* M *is a tuple* $(S, P, \xrightarrow{must}, \xrightarrow{may}, L)$, *where* S *is a nonempty finite set of states,* P *is a finite set of atomic propositions,* $\xrightarrow{may} \subseteq S \times S$ *and* $\xrightarrow{must} \subseteq S \times S$ *are transition relations such that* $\xrightarrow{must} \subseteq \xrightarrow{may}$, *and* $L : S \times P \to \{true, \bot, false\}$ *is an interpretation that associates a truth value in* $\{true, \bot, false\}$ *with each atomic proposition in* P *for each state in* S.

Clearly, KMTSs generalize PKSs since a PKS is a KMTS where $\stackrel{must}{\longrightarrow} = \stackrel{may}{\longrightarrow}$. Reasoning about KMTSs can be done using the same 3-valued PML defined as for PKSs provided that we modify the semantics of the AX operator to account for the presence of *must* and *may* transitions as follows:

Definition 8. *The value of a formula ϕ of 3-valued PML in a state s of a KMTS $M = (S, P, \stackrel{must}{\longrightarrow}, \stackrel{may}{\longrightarrow}, L)$, written $[(M, s) \models \phi]$, is defined inductively as follows:*

$$[(M, s) \models p] = L(s, p)$$
$$[(M, s) \models \neg\phi] = comp([(M, s) \models \phi])$$
$$[(M, s) \models \phi_1 \wedge \phi_2] = [(M, s) \models \phi_1] \wedge [(M, s) \models \phi_2]$$
$$[(M, s) \models AX\phi] = \begin{cases} true & if \ \forall s' : s \stackrel{may}{\longrightarrow} s' \Rightarrow [(M, s') \models \phi] = true \\ false & if \ \exists s' : s \stackrel{must}{\longrightarrow} s' \wedge [(M, s') \models \phi] = false \\ \bot & otherwise \end{cases}$$

The completeness preorder on KMTSs is then the following.

Definition 9. *Let $M_1 = (S_1, P, \stackrel{must}{\longrightarrow}_1, \stackrel{may}{\longrightarrow}_1, L_1)$ and $M_2 = (S_2, P, \stackrel{must}{\longrightarrow}_2, \stackrel{may}{\longrightarrow}_2, L_2)$ be KMTSs. The* completeness preorder $\preceq$ *is the greatest relation $\mathcal{B} \subseteq S_1 \times S_2$ such that $(s_1, s_2) \in \mathcal{B}$ implies the following:*

- $\forall p \in P : L_1(s_1, p) \leq L_2(s_2, p)$,
- *if $s_1 \stackrel{must}{\longrightarrow}_1 s_1'$, there is some $s_2' \in S_2$ such that $s_2 \stackrel{must}{\longrightarrow}_2 s_2'$ and $(s_1', s_2') \in \mathcal{B}$,*
- *if $s_2 \stackrel{may}{\longrightarrow}_2 s_2'$, there is some $s_1' \in S_1$ such that $s_1 \stackrel{may}{\longrightarrow}_1 s_1'$ and $(s_1', s_2') \in \mathcal{B}$.*

Thus, the completeness preorder on KMTSs also generalizes the completeness preorder on PKSs. It can be shown that this completeness preorder is logically characterized by 3-valued PML as defined above [GJ02].

Theorem 3. *Let $M_1 = (S_1, P, \stackrel{must}{\longrightarrow}_1, \stackrel{may}{\longrightarrow}_1), L_1$ and $M_2 = (S_2, P, \stackrel{must}{\longrightarrow}_2, \stackrel{may}{\longrightarrow}_2, L_2)$ be KMTSs such that $s_1 \in S_1$ and $s_2 \in S_2$, and let Φ be the set of all formulas of 3-valued PML. Then,*

$$s_1 \preceq s_2 \ iff \ (\forall \phi \in \Phi : [(M_1, s_1) \models \phi] \leq [(M_2, s_2) \models \phi]).$$

2.4   Model Checking and Generalized Model Checking

Computing the value of $[(M, s) \models \phi]$ is referred to as the *model checking* problem in what follows. As argued in [BG00], the semantics of $[(M, s) \models \phi]$ returns $\bot$ more often that it should. For instance, consider a KMTS M with two states s_0 and s_1 such that $p = q = true$ in s_0 and $p = q = false$ in s_1, and with a *may*-transition from s_0 to s_1. The formula $AXp \wedge \neg AXq$ (which is neither a tautology nor unsatisfiable) is $\bot$ at s_0, yet in all complete structures more complete than (M', s_0) the formula is *false*. This observation is used in [BG00] to define an alternative 3-valued semantics for modal logics called the *thorough* semantics since it does more than the other semantics to discover whether enough information is present in a model to give a definite answer. Let the *completions* $\mathcal{C}(M, s)$ of a state s of a model M be the set of all states s' of complete models M' such that $s \preceq s'$.

Definition 10. *Let ϕ be a formula of any two-valued logic for which a satisfaction relation $\models$ is defined on complete models. The truth value of ϕ in a state s of a model M under the* thorough *interpretation, written $[(M,s) \models \phi]_t$, is defined as follows:*

$$[(M,s) \models \phi]_t = \begin{cases} true & if\ (M',s') \models \phi\ for\ all\ (M',s')\ in\ C(M,s) \\ false & if\ (M',s') \not\models \phi\ for\ all\ (M',s')\ in\ C(M,s) \\ \bot & otherwise \end{cases}$$

By definition, we always have $[(M,s) \models \phi] \leq [(M,s) \models \phi]_t$. In general, interpreting a formula according to the thorough three-valued semantics is equivalent to solving two instances of the generalized model-checking problem [BG00].

Definition 11 (Generalized Model-Checking Problem). *Given a state s of a model M and a formula ϕ of a (two-valued) temporal logic L, does there exist a state s' of a complete model M' such that $s \preceq s'$ and $(M',s') \models \phi$?*

In other words, generalized model checking means checking whether there exists a completion of an abstraction that satisfies a temporal logic formula. This problem is called generalized model checking since it generalizes both model checking and satisfiability checking: at one extreme, when M is completely unknown (i.e., unconstrained), all complete models are more complete than M and the problem reduces to the satisfiability problem; at the other extreme, when M is complete, only a single structure needs to be checked and the problem reduces to model checking. Model checking and generalized model checking are the two main types of analyses of 3-valued models we consider in what follows.

3   Translation from PKS to MTS

We start by showing how to translate PKSs to MTSs. This can simply be done as follows.

Definition 12. *For any PKS $M = (S, P, \rightarrow, L)$, we define an equivalent MTS $M' = (S', \Sigma, \xrightarrow{must}, \xrightarrow{may})$ such that*

- $S' = S \cup \{s_{new}\}$,
- $\Sigma = P \cup \{x\}$,
- $\xrightarrow{must} = \{(s,p,s_{new})|L(s,p) = true\} \cup \{(s,x,s')|s \rightarrow s'\}$, and
- $\xrightarrow{may} = \{(s,p,s_{new})|L(s,p) \in \{true, \bot\}\} \cup \{(s,x,s')|s \rightarrow s'\}$.

Note that the previous definition does indeed generate an MTS since we always have $\xrightarrow{must} \subseteq \xrightarrow{may}$ by construction. Given an input PKS M of size $O(|\rightarrow|+|S|\cdot|P|)$, the size of the output MTS M' produced by Definition 12 is $O(|\xrightarrow{must}|+|\xrightarrow{may}|)$ $= O(|\rightarrow|+|S|\cdot|P|)$, i.e., linear in the size of the input. We can show that the above translation preserves the completeness preorder.

Theorem 4. *Given any two PKSs (M, s_m) and (N, s_n), let M' and N' denote the corresponding MTSs obtained by applying Definition 12. Then, we have*

$$(M, s_m) \preceq (N, s_n) \text{ iff } (M', s_m) \preceq (N', s_n).$$

Proof. (Sketch)[1] Assuming $(M, s_m) \preceq (N, s_n)$, we define a binary relation R on the states of M' and N' such that sRt if $s \preceq t$ or $s = t = s_{new}$; then we show that R satisfies the conditions of Definition 6. Conversely, assuming $(M', s_m) \preceq (N', s_n)$, we define a binary relation R on the states of M and N such that sRt if $s \preceq t$ with $s, t \neq s_{new}$; it can be shown that R satisfies the conditions of Definition 3.

We can also prove the following.

Lemma 1. *Let M be a PKS and M' be the corresponding MTS obtained by applying Definition 12. If there exists an MTS Q such that $(M', s_m) \preceq (Q, s_q)$, then there exists a PKS N such that $(N', s_n) \preceq (Q, s_q)$ and $(Q, s_q) \preceq (N', s_n)$, where N' denotes the translation of N by Definition 12.*

Proof. (Sketch) Let $Q = (S, \Sigma, \overset{must}{\longrightarrow}, \overset{may}{\longrightarrow})$, let s_{new} denote the state of M' defined as in Definition 12, and let $S_{new} = \{s \in S | s_{new} \preceq s\}$. Then we define a PKS $N = (S', P, \rightarrow, L)$ from Q as follows: $S' = S \setminus S_{new}$, $P = \Sigma \setminus \{x\}$, $\rightarrow = \{(s, s') \in (S \setminus S_{new}) \times (S \setminus S_{new}) | (s, x, s') \in \overset{must}{\longrightarrow}\}$, and $L(s, p) = true$ if $\exists s' \in S_{new} :$ $(s, p, s') \in \overset{must}{\longrightarrow}$, or $L(s, p) = false$ if $\forall s' \in S_{new} : (s, p, s') \notin \overset{may}{\longrightarrow}$, or $L(s, p) = \bot$ otherwise. It is then easy to show that $(N', s_n) \preceq (Q, s_q)$ and $(Q, s_q) \preceq (N', s_n)$.

PML temporal-logic formulas defined on PKSs can be translated into PML^{Act} formulas defined on MTSs as follows.

Definition 13. *Given any PML formula ϕ defined on PKSs with a set P of atomic propositions, we define an equivalent PML^{Act} formula $T(\phi)$ defined on MTSs with action alphabet $\Sigma = P \cup \{x\}$ by applying recursively the following rewrite rules:*

- *for all $p \in P$, $T(p) = (\exists p)\mathsf{tt} = \neg(\forall p)\neg\mathsf{tt}$,*
- *$T(\neg\phi) = \neg T(\phi)$,*
- *$T(\phi_1 \wedge \phi_2) = T(\phi_1) \wedge T(\phi_2)$,*
- *$T(AX\phi) = (\forall x)T(\phi)$.*

The next theorem states that the model and formula translations of Definitions 12 and 13 can be used to reduce (in linear time and logarithmic space) the model checking and generalized model checking problems from PKSs to MTSs.

Theorem 5. *Given any PKS M and formula ϕ defined on PKSs, let M' denote the MTS obtained by applying Definition 12 and let $T(\phi)$ denote the translated formula obtained by applying Definition 13. Then, we have the following:*

1. *$[(M, s) \models \phi] = [(M', s) \models T(\phi)]$*
2. *$[(M, s) \models \phi]_t = [(M', s) \models T(\phi)]_t$*

Proof. (Sketch) (1) is proved by induction on the length of ϕ. (2) is proved as follows: if $[(M, s) \models \phi]_t = true$, i.e., if there exists $s' \in N$ such that $s \preceq s'$ and $[(N, s') \models \phi] = true$, then $(M', s) \preceq (N', s')$ by Theorem 4 and we have $[(N', s') \models T(\phi)] = true$ by (1), hence $[(M', s) \models T(\phi)]_t = true$; conversely, if

---

[1] Complete proofs are omitted in this extended abstract due to space limitations.

$[(M', s) \models T(\phi)]_t = true$, i.e., there exists $s' \in Q$ such that $(M', s) \preceq (Q, s')$ and $[(Q, s') \models T(\phi)] = true$, then there exists N such that $N' \preceq Q$ and $Q \preceq N'$ by Lemma 1 and we also have $(M, s) \preceq (N, s')$ by Theorem 4 and $[(N, s') \models \phi] = true$ by (1), hence $[(M, s) \models \phi]_t = true$. The case where $[(M, s) \models \phi]_t = false$ is similar.

4   Translation from MTS to KMTS

The second translation we consider is from MTSs to KMTSs. We present in this section results of the same nature as those of the previous section. A translation from MTSs to KMTSs that preserves the completeness preorder can be defined as follows.

Definition 14. *For any MTS $M = (S, \Sigma, \overset{must}{\longrightarrow}, \overset{may}{\longrightarrow})$, we define an equivalent KMTS $M' = (S', P, \overset{must'}{\longrightarrow}, \overset{may'}{\longrightarrow}, L)$ such that*

- $S' = S \times \Sigma$,
- $P = \Sigma$,
- $\overset{must'}{\longrightarrow} = \{((s, a), (s', a')) | (s, a', s') \in \overset{must}{\longrightarrow}\}$,
- $\overset{may'}{\longrightarrow} = \{((s, a), (s', a')) | (s, a', s') \in \overset{may}{\longrightarrow}\}$, *and*
- $\forall(s, a) \in S' : \forall p \in P : L((s, a), p) = true$ *if $p = a$ or $L((s, a), p) = false$ otherwise.*

The previous definition thus simply replaces transition labels by state labels. Given an MTS with $|S|$ states and an action set Σ, the number of states in the translated KMTS M' defined by Definition 14 is at most $|S| \cdot |\Sigma|$. In other words, each state of M can be copied at most $|\Sigma|$ times in M'. For a fixed action set Σ, the number of states and transitions in M' is nevertheless linear in the number of states and transitions, respectively, in M.

Note that the above translation only uses atomic propositions $p \in P$ whose truth value is always defined as either *true* or *false*. However, it does not seem possible to improve this translation by using the third unused value $\perp$. Indeed, in the particular case of a MTS which is completely defined, i.e., such that $\overset{must}{\longrightarrow} = \overset{may}{\longrightarrow}$, the above translation then becomes the traditional translation from LTSs to Kripke structures whose states are pairs of states and actions of the LTS [MSS99], the latter translation being also similar to the classic translation from Mealy automata to Moore automata [HU79].

The translation above preserves the completeness preorder.

Theorem 6. *Given any two MTSs (M, s_m) and (N, s_n), let M' and N' denote the corresponding KMTSs obtained by applying Definition 14. Then, for all $a \in \Sigma$, we have*

$$(M, s_m) \preceq (N, s_n) \text{ iff } (M', (s_m, a)) \preceq (N', (s_n, a)).$$

Proof. (Sketch) Given $(M, s_m) \preceq (N, s_n)$, we define a binary relation R on the states of M' and N' such that $(s, a)R(t, b)$ if $s \preceq t$ and $a = b$; then we show that

R satisfies the conditions of Definition 9. Conversely, assuming $(M', (s_m, a)) \preceq (N', (s_n, a))$, we define a binary relation R on the states of M and N such that sRt if $(s, a) \preceq (t, a)$ with $s, t \in S$; R can be shown to satisfy the conditions of Definition 6.

We also have the following.

Lemma 2. *Let M be a MTS and M' be the corresponding KMTS obtained by applying Definition 14. If there exists a KMTS Q such that $(M', s_m) \preceq (Q, s_q)$, then there exists a MTS N such that $N' = Q$, where N' denotes the translation of N by Definition 14.*

Proof. (Sketch) Let $Q = (S, P, \overset{must}{\longrightarrow}, \overset{may}{\longrightarrow}, L)$. Since $(M', s_m) \preceq (Q, s_q)$, we know that, in every state $s \in S$, there is exactly one proposition p in P that is *true* in s while all other propositions in P are then *false* in s. We define an MTS $N = (S, P, \overset{must'}{\longrightarrow}, \overset{may'}{\longrightarrow})$ from the KMTS Q as follows: $\overset{must'}{\longrightarrow} = \{(s, p, s')|(s, s') \in \overset{must}{\longrightarrow}$ and $L(s', p) = true\}$, and $\overset{may'}{\longrightarrow} = \{(s, a, s')|(s, s') \in \overset{may}{\longrightarrow}$ and $L(s', p) = true\}$. Clearly, $N' = Q$.

PML^{Act} formulas can be translated into PML formulas as follows.

Definition 15. *Given any formula ϕ defined on MTSs with an action set Σ, we define an equivalent formula $T(\phi)$ defined on KMTSs with a set $P' = \Sigma$ of atomic propositions by applying recursively the following rewrite rules:*

- $T(\text{tt}) = true,$
- $T(\neg\phi) = \neg T(\phi),$
- $T(\phi_1 \wedge \phi_2) = T(\phi_1) \wedge T(\phi_2),$
- $T((\forall a)\phi) = AX((\neg a) \vee T(\phi)).$

The right term of the last rule is thus equivalent to $AX(a \Rightarrow T(\phi))$ where $\Rightarrow$ denotes logical implication. The correctness of this formula translation is again defined by showing a reduction of the model checking and generalized model checking problems on MTSs to KMTSs.

Theorem 7. *Given any MTS M and formula ϕ defined on MTSs, let M' denote the KMTS obtained by applying Definition 14 and let $T(\phi)$ denote the translated formula obtained by applying Definition 15. Then, for any $a \in \Sigma$, we have the following:*

1. $[(M, s) \models \phi] = [(M', (s, a)) \models T(\phi)]$
2. $[(M, s) \models \phi]_t = [(M', (s, a)) \models T(\phi)]_t$

Proof. Similar to the proof of Theorem 5.

5 Translation from KMTS to PKS

The third and last translation we discuss is from KMTSs to PKSs. This translation is more elaborate than the two previous ones. We start by showing how to translate a KMTS to a PKS with the goal of reducing model checking and generalized model checking from KMTSs to PKSs.

Definition 16. *For any KMTS $M = (S, P, \overset{must}{\longrightarrow}, \overset{may}{\longrightarrow}, L)$, we define an equivalent PKS $M' = (S', P', \rightarrow', L')$ such that*

- $S' = S \times \{must, may\}$,
- $P' = P \cup \{p_{must}\}$,
- $\rightarrow' = \{((s, x), (s', x')) | (s, s') \in \overset{may}{\longrightarrow}, x' = must$ *if* $(s, s') \in \overset{must}{\longrightarrow}$ *or* $x' = may$ *otherwise*$\}$,
- $\forall (s, x) \in S' : \forall p \in P : L'((s, x), p) = L(s, p)$, *and* $L'((s, x), p_{must}) = true$ *if* $x = must$ *or* $L'((s, x), p_{must}) = \bot$ *otherwise.*

Two examples of KMTSs M and N and their PKS translations M' and N' with the previous definition are shown in Figure 1. These KMTSs have a single atomic proposition p whose value is defined in each state as indicated in the figure. The dotted transition in M is a *may*-transition that is not a *must*-transition.

We now define a translation of temporal-logic formulas on KMTSs to formulas on PKSs.

Definition 17. *Given any formula ϕ defined on KMTSs with a set P of atomic propositions, we define an equivalent formula $T(\phi)$ defined on PKSs with a set $P' = P \cup \{p_{must}\}$ of atomic propositions by applying recursively the following rewrite rules:*

- *for all $p \in P$, $T(p) = p$,*
- $T(\neg\phi) = \neg T(\phi)$,
- $T(\phi_1 \wedge \phi_2) = T(\phi_1) \wedge T(\phi_2)$,
- $T(AX\phi) = AX(p_{must} \Rightarrow T(\phi)) = AX((\neg p_{must}) \vee T(\phi))$.

The next theorem states that model checking and generalized model checking can be reduced (in linear time and logarithmic space) from KMTSs to PKSs.

Theorem 8. *Given any KMTS M and formula ϕ defined on KMTSs, let M' denote the PKS obtained by applying Definition 16 and let $T(\phi)$ denote the translated formula obtained by applying Definition 17. Then, we have the following:*

1. $[(M, s) \models \phi] = [(M', (s, must)) \models T(\phi)]$
2. $[(M, s) \models \phi]_t = [(M', (s, must)) \models T(\phi)]_t$

Proof. (Sketch) The proof of (1) is by induction on the length of the formula. To prove (2), we show that, if (N, t) is a complete KMTS such that $(M, s) \preceq (N, t)$, then there exists a PKS M'' such that $(M', (s, must)) \preceq (M'', r)$ and $[(M'', r) \models T(\phi)] = [(N', (t, must)) \models T(\phi)] = [(N, t) \models \phi]$. Next we show that, if (Q, r) is a complete PKS such that $(M', (s, must)) \preceq (Q, r)$, then there exists a complete KMTS (N, t) such that the translation N' of N by Definition 16 is equal to the part of Q containing all the states where $p_{must} = true$; we finally show that $(M, s) \preceq (N, t)$ and that $[(N, t) \models \phi] = [(N', (t', must)) \models T(\phi)] = [(Q, r) \models T(\phi)]$.

In other words, the model and formula translations of Definitions 16 and 17 can be used to reduce (in linear time and logarithmic space) the model checking and generalized model checking problems from KMTSs to PKSs.

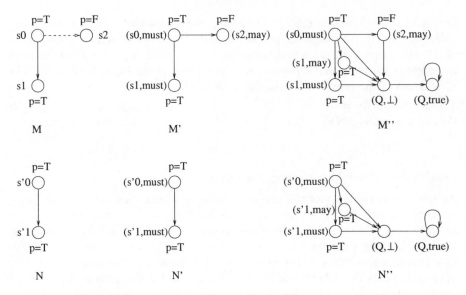

Fig. 1. Examples of KMTSs and of their translations. KMTSs M and N (left) are translated into PKSs M' and N' (middle) using Definition 16, and into PKSs M'' and N'' (right) using Definition 18.

It is worth noticing that the translation from KMTS to PKS of Definition 16 does not preserve the completeness preorder: for any two KMTSs M and N and their respective PKS translations M' and N' obtained by applying the construction of Definition 16, $M \preceq N$ does not necessarily imply that $M' \preceq N'$. For instance, consider the KMTSs M and N of Figure 1. Clearly, $(M, s_0) \preceq (N, s'_0)$ but $(M', (s_0, must)) \npreceq (N', (s'_0, must))$ since the second condition of Definition 3 is not satisfied for transition $((s_0, must), (s_2, may))$ of M' which cannot be matched in N'.

However, it is possible to design a translation from KMTS to PKS that does preserve the completeness preorder. Such a translation is now presented.

Definition 18. *For any KMTS* $M = (S, P, \overset{must}{\longrightarrow}, \overset{may}{\longrightarrow}, L)$, *we define an equivalent PKS* $M' = (S', P', \rightarrow', L')$ *such that*

- $S' = S \times \{must, may\} \cup \{(q, \bot), (q, true) | q \in 2^P\}$,
- $P' = P \cup \{p_{must}, p_{dummy}\}$,
- $\rightarrow' = \{((s, x), (s', may)) | (s, s') \in \overset{may}{\longrightarrow}\} \cup \{((s, x), (s', must)) | (s, s') \in \overset{must}{\longrightarrow}\} \cup \{((s, x), (q, \bot)) | (s, x) \in S \times \{must, may\} \text{ and } q \in 2^P\} \cup \{((q, \bot), (q', true)), ((q, true), (q', true)) | q, q' \in 2^P\}$,
- $\forall (s, x) \in S \times \{must, may\}, \forall p \in P : L'((s, x), p) = L(s, p),$ $L'((s, x), p_{dummy}) = \bot, L'((s, x), p_{must}) = true \text{ if } x = must \text{ or }$ $L'((s, x), p_{must}) = \bot \text{ otherwise}; \forall q \in 2^P, x \in \{\bot, true\}, L'((q, x), p_{dummy}) = true, L'((q, x), p_{must}) = x \text{ and } \forall p \in P : L'((q, true), p) = true \text{ if } p \in q \text{ or }$ $L'((q, true), p) = false \text{ otherwise}.$

Considering again the KMTSs M and N of Figure 1, the previous definition generates the PKSs M'' and N'' respectively, where (Q, x) denotes the whole cluster of states $\{(q, x) | q \in 2^P\}$. The reader can check that $(M'', (s_0, must)) \preceq$ $(N'', (s_0', must))$. Although the number of states of the form (q, x) is exponential in $|P|$, the number of states and transitions in the resulting PKS M' is linear in the number of states and transitions, respectively, of the input KMTS M. The correctness of the previous translation is defined as follows.

Theorem 9. *Given any two KMTSs (M, s_m) and (N, s_n), let M' and N' denote the corresponding PKSs obtained by applying Definition 18. Then, we have*

$$(M, s_m) \preceq (N, s_n) \text{ iff } (M', (s_m, must)) \preceq (N', (s_n, must)).$$

Proof. Omitted here due to space limitations.

An interesting corollary of the previous theorem is that checking whether $M' \preceq N'$ between two PKSs M' and N' is as hard as checking whether $M \preceq N$ between two KMTSs. Since the latter problem is itself in general at least as hard as checking for a simulation relation between M and N (since $\preceq$ reduces to a simulation relation in the case of KMTSs with no *must*-transitions), this implies that checking whether $M' \preceq N'$ between two PKSs can be as expensive as checking the existence of a simulation between them, which may not be obvious when looking at Definition 3.

Finally, note that this second more elaborate translation can also be used to reduce model checking and generalized model checking from KMTSs to PKSs provided another, more complicated, formula translation $T(\phi)$ (not presented here due to space constraints) is used.

6   Applications, Discussion, and Other Related Work

The translations and theorems of the previous sections make it possible to derive several new results concerning the expressiveness and conciseness of the 3-valued models considered, as well as the complexity of model checking and generalized model checking for these models.

The first result we obtain is that *Partial Kripke Structures, Modal Transition Systems and Kripke Model Transition Systems are all equally expressive.* In other words, any PKS, MTS or KMTS can be translated into any other of these formalisms using the translations defined in Sections 3 to 5, or any combination of these translations. In what follows, let us denote by "3-valued formalism" either a PKS, MTS or KMTS.

Second, following Theorems 5 and 7 and 8, any model checking or generalized model checking problem defined on any 3-valued formalism can be reduced to a model checking or generalized model checking problem, respectively, on any other of these formalisms. These results hold not only for PML, but also for PML extended with fixpoint operators, i.e., the propositional μ-calculus [Koz83], and hence all of its fragments (such as LTL, CTL and CTL*). This extension to the μ-calculus follows immediately from the facts that the completeness preorder is logically characterized by both PML and the μ-calculus (exactly as bisimulation is logically characterized by both PML and the μ-calculus in the 2-valued case), and that fixpoint operators are left unchanged when translating μ-calculus formulas from one formalism to another (formula translation essentially affects modal operators only).

Third, since the translations of the previous sections require only linear time and logarithmic space in the size of their inputs and can be applied to translate any 3-valued formalism into any other in both directions, both upper and lower complexity bounds for problems defined on any of these formalisms carry over to the other formalisms. In particular, the algorithms and complexity bounds for the model checking and generalized model checking problems obtained with PKSs in [BG00] and with KMTSs in [GJ02] apply equally to all three formalisms.

Specifically, these translations extend the scope of the results of [BG00] and formally prove that, for any 3-valued formalism, 3-valued model checking for any temporal logic L has the same time and space complexity, both in the size of the model and of the formula, as traditional 2-valued model checking for the logic L. This new result subsumes the direct model-checking procedures of [GHJ01] for MTSs and of [Hut02a] for KMTSs.

Concerning the complexity of generalized model checking in the size of the formula, a similar extension of the results of [BG00] is possible thanks to the translations: for any 3-valued formalism, in the case of a branching-time temporal logic L (such as CTL, CTL*, the mu-calculus, PML and also propositional logic), generalized model checking for L has the same complexity in the size of the formula as satisfiability checking for L, while in the case of linear-time temporal logic (LTL), generalized model checking is EXPTIME-complete in the size of the formula, i.e., harder than both satisfiability and model checking (which are both PSPACE-complete for LTL).

Regarding the complexity of generalized model checking in the size of the model, we note that the formula translations of Sections 3 to 5 preserve the co-Büchi recognizability of formulas: if a property represented by a temporal formula ϕ is recognizable by an automaton (on infinite trees or words, depending if ϕ is a branching or linear property, respectively) with a co-Büchi acceptance condition, then the property represented by the temporal property $T(\phi)$ is also recognizable by an automaton with a co-Büchi acceptance condition. Therefore, the complexity results of [GJ02] can be extended to cover any 3-valued formalism: the worst-case runtime complexity of generalized model checking for the temporal logics LTL and CTL can be quadratic in the size of the model for any 3-valued formalism, but generalized model checking can be solved in time linear in the size of the model in the case of persistence properties, i.e., properties recognizable by co-Büchi automata.

Notice that one could think at first sight that generalized model checking for KMTSs and MTSs is exponential in the size of the KMTS/MTS M since the number of possible completions of a set N of *may*-transitions from any given state is $2^{|N|}$. Instead, our linear translation from KMTSs to PKSs presented in the previous section proves that considering one-by-one the exponentially-many subsets of N is not necessary, and that generalized model checking can be done in polynomial time (linear or quadratic) in $|N|$.

Since PKSs, MTSs and KMTSs are all equally expressive, one can wonder why three different yet equivalent models have been proposed in the literature. Let us first observe that the equivalence of their expressiveness is not as straight-

forward as one might think (see the results of the previous sections). More importantly, these different formalisms are useful to facilitate abstraction of different
aspects of reactive systems. PKSs generalize Kripke structures which model state
changes of reactive systems, while MTSs generalize LTSs which model the external behavior of a system (i.e., sequences of actions the system can perform).
Although equivalent themselves, Kripke structures and LTSs provide complementary views for reasoning about reactive systems, and PKS versus MTS is just
an extension of this duality. Indeed, PKSs conveniently model state abstractions
while MTSs are a natural formalism for representing transition abstractions.

The third 3-valued formalism, KMTSs, was created with the purpose of unifying both views by combining features of both PKSs and MTSs [HJS01], although
without increasing expressiveness as demonstrated by the results of the present
paper. The "syntactic sugaring" provided by KMTSs enables a more nimble
representation of abstractions of reactive systems. We illustrate this claim with
two examples of applications where the use of KMTSs is convenient: predicate
abstraction and shape analysis.

Predicate abstraction (e.g, [GS97]) abstracts a program using a set $\Psi =
\{\psi_1, \ldots, \psi_n\}$ of n predicates, each of which is typically represented by a
quantifier-free formula of first-order logic (such as $(x == y + 1) \vee (x < y - 5)$)
(e.g., [DDP99]). An abstract state is defined as a vector of n truth-values, which
identifies all concrete states that satisfy the same set of predicates in Ψ. Typically,
consistency of states is checked using theorem-proving techniques for quantifier-
free first-order logic. The resulting abstract transition system can conveniently
be represented by a KMTS: propositions at abstract states corresponding to
the predicates in Ψ can be 3-valued, with the third value $\perp$ modeling a loss of
information due to abstraction or the potential incompleteness of the auxiliary
theorem prover; similarly, the transition relation is also 3-valued, where *may*-
only transitions can be used to model transitions from a conditional node (such
as program statements of the form `if-then-else`) whose guard's evaluation is
unknown (e.g., [GHJ01]).

Shape analysis (e.g., [CWZ90]) is a form of pointer analysis where the contents of heap storage is approximated by a graph, whose nodes denote objects
and whose arcs denote the values of the objects' fields. Local-variable points-to
information can be represented using unary predicates (e.g., $x(u_0)$ is true at an
object u_0 if variable x points to object u_0) and binary predicates ($next(u_0, u_1)$
is true if the *next* field of object u_0 points to object u_1) (e.g., [SRW99]). Again,
KMTSs can conveniently encode such abstractions: a proposition x can be associated with each unary predicate $x(u_0)$ at every node of the graph in such a way
that proposition x has $\perp$ for value at object (node) u_0 if it is possible but not
guaranteed for variable x to point to object u_0 in the current heap; similarly,
binary predicates can be modeled as a 3-valued transition relation, where the
arc with label *next* from u_0 to u_1 is a *may*-only transition if there is a possibility
but no guarantee for the *next* field of object u_0 to point to u_1 (e.g., [HJS01]).

We conclude by mentioning a few other modeling formalisms closely related
to those considered in this paper. Variants of KMTSs with labeled transitions
and two interpretation functions L^{may} and L^{must} are defined in [HJS01]; it
is straightforward to show by using the translation techniques of our paper

that these simple extensions do not increase expressiveness over the defini-tion of KMTS considered in Section 2. Extended transition systems [Mil81] can be viewed as a particular class of MTSs [HJS01,BG99]. Mixed transition sys-tems [Dam96] are MTSs where the constraint $\xrightarrow{must} \subseteq \xrightarrow{may}$ is removed; eliminating this constraint makes it possible to specify inconsistent models, i.e., models that cannot be refined by any complete systems [HJS02], and hence increases expres-siveness compared to the modeling formalisms considered in this paper. Recent work on 3-valued models for probabilistic systems can be found in [Hut02b].

References

[BG99]   G. Bruns and P. Godefroid. Model Checking Partial State Spaces with 3-Valued Temporal Logics. In *Proceedings of the 11th Conference on Com-puter Aided Verification*, volume 1633 of *Lecture Notes in Computer Sci-ence*, pages 274–287, Trento, July 1999. Springer-Verlag.

[BG00]   G. Bruns and P. Godefroid. Generalized Model Checking: Reasoning about Partial State Spaces. In *Proceedings of CONCUR'2000 (11th International Conference on Concurrency Theory)*, volume 1877 of *Lecture Notes in Computer Science*, pages 168–182, University Park, August 2000. Springer-Verlag.

[BPR01]   T. Ball, A. Podelski, and S. K. Rajamani. Boolean and Cartesian Ab-straction for Model Checking C Programs. In *Proceedings of TACAS'2001 (Tools and Algorithms for the Construction and Analysis of Systems)*, vol-ume 2031 of *Lecture Notes in Computer Science*. Springer-Verlag, April 2001.

[BR01]   T. Ball and S. Rajamani. The SLAM Toolkit. In *Proceedings of CAV'2001 (13th Conference on Computer Aided Verification)*, volume 2102 of *Lecture Notes in Computer Science*, pages 260–264, Paris, July 2001. Springer-Verlag.

[CWZ90]   D.R. Chase, M. Wegman, and F.K. Zadeck. Analysis of pointers and struc-tures. In *Proccedings of Conference on Programming Language Design and Implementation*, pages 296–310, June 1990.

[Dam96]   D. Dams. *Abstract interpretation and partition refinement for model check-ing*. PhD thesis, Technische Universiteit Eindhoven, The Netherlands, 1996.

[DDP99]   S. Das, D. L. Dill, and S. Park. Experience with Predicate Astraction. In *Proc. of the 11th International Conference on Computer-Aided Verification*, Lecture Notes in Computer Science, pages 160–172, Trento, July 1999. Springer Verlag.

[GHJ01]   P. Godefroid, M. Huth, and R. Jagadeesan. Abstraction-based Model Checking using Modal Transition Systems. In *Proceedings of CON-CUR'2001 (12th International Conference on Concurrency Theory)*, vol-ume 2154 of *Lecture Notes in Computer Science*, pages 426–440, Aalborg, August 2001. Springer-Verlag.

[GJ02]   P. Godefroid and R. Jagadeesan. Automatic Abstraction Using General-ized Model Checking. In *Proceedings of CAV'2002 (14th Conference on Computer Aided Verification)*, volume 2404 of *Lecture Notes in Computer Science*, pages 137–150, Copenhagen, July 2002. Springer-Verlag.

[GS97]   S. Graf and H. Saidi. Construction of Abstract State Graphs with PVS. In *Proceedings of the 9th International Conference on Computer Aided Verification*, volume 1254 of *Lecture Notes in Computer Science*, pages 72–83, Haifa, June 1997. Springer-Verlag.

[HJMS02]   T. Henzinger, R. Jhala, R. Majumdar, and G. Sutre. Lazy Abstraction. In *Proceedings of the 29th ACM Symposium on Principles of Programming Languages*, pages 58–70, Portland, January 2002.

[HJS01]   M. Huth, R. Jagadeesan, and D. Schmidt. Modal Transition Systems: a Foundation for Three-Valued Program Analysis. In *Proceedings of the European Symposium on Programming (ESOP'2001)*, volume 2028 of *Lecture Notes in Computer Science*. Springer-Verlag, April 2001.

[HJS02]   M. Huth, R. Jagadeesan, and D. Schmidt. A Domain Equation for Refinement of Partial Systems. Submitted to Mathematical Structures in Computer Science, 2002.

[HU79]   J. Hopcroft and J. Ullman. *Introduction to Automata Theory, Languages and Computation*. Addison-Wesley, 1979.

[Hut02a]   M. Huth. Model Checking Modal Transition Systems using Kripke Structures. In *Proceedings of the Third International Workshop on Verification, Model Checking and Abstract Interpretation (VMCAI'2002)*, volume 2294 of *Lecture Notes in Computer Science*, pages 302–316, Venice, January 2002. Springer-Verlag.

[Hut02b]   M. Huth. Possibilistic and Probabilistic Abstraction-based Model Checking. In *Proceedings of the PAPM-Probmiv 2002 Workshop*, volume 2329 of *Lecture Notes in Computer Science*, pages 115–134, Copenhagen, July 2002. Springer-Verlag.

[Kle87]   S. C. Kleene. *Introduction to Metamathematics*. North Holland, 1987.

[Koz83]   D. Kozen. Results on the Propositional Mu-Calculus. *Theoretical Computer Science*, 27:333–354, 1983.

[Lar89]   K. G. Larsen. Modal Specifications. In J. Sifakis, editor, *Workshop on Automatic Verification Methods for Finite-State Systems*, volume 407 of *Lecture Notes in Computer Science*, pages 232–246. Springer-Verlag, June 1989. International Workshop, Grenoble, France.

[LT88]   K. G. Larsen and B. Thomsen. A Modal Process Logic. In *Proceedings of Third Annual Symposium on Logic in Computer Science*, pages 203–210. IEEE Computer Society Press, 1988.

[Mil81]   R. Milner. A Modal Characterization of Observable Machine Behavior. In *Proc. CAAP'81*, volume 112 of *Lecture Notes in Computer Science*, pages 25–34. Springer-Verlag, 1981.

[MSS99]   M. Muller-Olm, D. Schmidt, and B. Steffen. Model Checking: A Tutorial Introduction. In *Proceedings of the 6th International Static Analysis Symposium (SAS'99)*, volume 1694 of *Lecture Notes in Computer Science*, pages 331–354, Berlin, September 1999. Springer-Verlag.

[SRW99]   M. Sagiv, T. Reps, and R. Wilhelm. Parametric Shape Analysis Via 3-Valued Logic. In *Proceedings of the 26th ACM Symposium on Principles of Programming Languages*, January 1999.

Bisimulation and Unwinding for Verifying Possibilistic Security Properties*

Annalisa Bossi, Riccardo Focardi, Carla Piazza, and Sabina Rossi

Dipartimento di Informatica, Università Ca' Foscari di Venezia
{bossi,focardi,piazza,srossi}@dsi.unive.it

Abstract. We study bisimulation-based information flow security properties which are *persistent*, in the sense that if a system is secure, then
all states reachable from it are secure too. We show that such properties
can be characterized in terms of *bisimulation-like equivalence relations*
between the system and the system itself prevented from performing confidential actions. Moreover, we provide a characterization of such properties in terms of *unwinding conditions* which demand properties of individual actions. These two different characterizations naturally lead to
efficient methods for the verification and construction of secure systems.
We also prove several *compositionality* results and discuss a sufficient
condition to define *refinement* operators preserving security.

1 Introduction

Non-interference was introduced by Goguen and Meseguer [11,12] as a concept
for formalizing security within deterministic systems. Given a system in which
confidential (i.e., high level) and *public* (i.e., low level) information may coexist,
non-interference requires that confidential inputs never affect the output on the
public interface of the system, i.e., never interfere with the low level users. If such
a property holds, one can conclude that no information flow is ever possible from
high to low level.

A possibilistic security property can be regarded as an extension of non-
interference to non-deterministic systems. Starting with Sutherland [34], various
such extensions have been proposed, e.g., [4,9,16,21,22,23,24,28,33,35]. Most of
these properties are based on *traces*, i.e., the behavior of a system that may
possibly be observed is the set of its execution sequences. Examples are non-
inference [28], generalized non-interference [21], restrictiveness [21], and the per-
fect security property [35].

In [4], Focardi and Gorrieri express the concept of non-interference in the
Security Process Algebra (*SPA*, for short) language in terms of bisimulation
semantics. In particular, they introduce the notion of *Bisimulation-based non
Deducibility on Compositions* (*BNDC*, for short): a system E is *BNDC* if what

---

* This work has been partially supported by MURST projects "Interpretazione
astratta, type systems e analisi control-flow" and "Modelli formali per la sicurezza"
and the EU project MyThS (IST-2001-32617).

a low level user sees of the system is not modified (in the sense of the bisimulation semantics) by composing any high level process Π with E. The main advantage of $BNDC$ with respect to trace-based properties is that it is powerful enough to detect information flows due to the possibility for a high level malicious process to block or unblock a system (see [4,6] for more detail). As a matter of fact, although Martinelli [20] has shown that $BNDC$ is decidable over finite state processes, the problem of verifying $BNDC$ is still open. The main difficulty consists of getting rid of the universal quantification on high level processes Π. A way to overcome this problems is to adopt sufficient conditions for $BNDC$. We recall from [6,8] two of them, named *Strong BNDC* (*SBNDC*, for short) and *Persistent_BNDC* (*P_BNDC*, for short) [1]. In particular, *P_BNDC* has been shown to be suitable for analysing systems in dynamic contexts [8].

In this paper we consider *P_BNDC* and *SBNDC* and for both these properties we study two different characterizations that allow to exploit different verification techniques. The first kind of characterization is based on *bisimulation-like equivalence relation* between the system E to be analysed and the low level view of the system itself, denoted by $E \setminus H$ (the system E prevented from performing confidential actions). These bisimulation-based characterizations allow to exploit very efficient techniques for verifying the properties over finite-state processes using existing algorithms for the verification of strong bisimulation. The second kind of characterization is given in terms of *unwinding conditions* which demand properties of individual actions. Unwinding conditions aim at "distilling" the local effect of performing high level actions and are useful to define both proof systems (see, e.g., [2]) and *refinement* operators that preserve security properties, as done in [17]. Proof systems allow to incrementally build systems which are secure by construction. Similarly refinement operators are useful in a stepwise development process as properties which have been already investigated in some phase need not to be re-investigated in later phases.

In particular, we start by considering the two characterizations above, given in [2] for *P_BNDC* . By studying the relation between such two characterizations, we are able to give a new bisimulation-based characterization for *SBNDC*, which was originally defined through unwinding conditions. As a next step we investigate the compositionality of *P_BNDC* and *SBNDC*. Compositionality is useful for both verification and synthesis: if a property is preserved when systems are composed, then the analysis may be performed on subsystems and, in case of success, the system as a whole can be proved to satisfy the desired property. We notice that both *P_BNDC* and *SBNDC* are compositional with respect to the parallel operator, but they are not *fully* compositional, since they are not compositional with respect to the non-deterministic choice operator, which allows us to built a system that may choose to behave as one of two specified subsystems. It would be intuitive to require that a choice between two secure processes is still secure as observed in [10]. To this aim we introduce a new security property, named *Compositional P_BNDC* (*CP_BNDC*, for short), properly included in *P_BNDC*, which is fully compositional, i.e., it is compositional also with re-

---

[1] In [8], *P_BNDC* has been shown to be equivalent to the *SBSNNI* property of [6].

spect to the non-deterministic choice. *CP_BNDC* can be equivalently expressed through both a bisimulation-like equivalence and unwinding conditions.

We show that the bisimulation-based characterizations of our persistent security properties allow us to perform the verification task for finite state processes in polynomial time with respect to the number of states of the system, also improving on the polynomial time complexity required by the Compositional Security Checker Cosec presented in [5]. Finally, we provide a sufficient condition to define refinement operators preserving all our security properties.

The paper is organized as follows. In Section 2 we introduce some basic notions on the *SPA* language and the security properties *BNDC* and *P_BNDC*. In Section 3 we study the property *SBNDC* and provide a bisimulation-based characterization of it. In Section 4 we introduce the class of *CP_BNDC* processes and prove that it is fully compositional. Section 5 is devoted to complexity results for the bisimulation-based characterizations of the three properties. In Section 6 we propose a sufficient condition to define refinement operators for SPA processes preserving security. Finally, in Section 7 we discuss related works and draw some conclusions. All the proofs of propositions and theorems can be found in [1].

2   Basic Notions

In this section we report the syntax and semantics of the *Security Process Algebra* (*SPA*, for short) [6] and the definition of the security properties *BNDC* [4] and *P_BNDC* [8] together with some main results [2].

The SPA Language. The *Security Process Algebra* [6] is a variation of Milner's CCS [27], where the set of visible actions is partitioned into high level actions and low level ones in order to specify multilevel systems. SPA syntax is based on the same elements as CCS that is: a set $\mathcal{L}$ of *visible* actions such that $\mathcal{L} = I \cup O$ where $I = \{a, b, \ldots\}$ is a set of *input* actions and $O = \{\bar{a}, \bar{b}, \ldots\}$ is a set of *output* actions; a special action τ which models internal computations, i.e., not visible outside the system; a complementation function $\bar{\cdot} : \mathcal{L} \to \mathcal{L}$, such that $\bar{\bar{a}} = a$, for all $a \in \mathcal{L}$. Function $\bar{\cdot}$ is extended to *Act* by defining $\bar{\tau} = \tau$. $Act = \mathcal{L} \cup \{\tau\}$ is the set of all *actions*. The set of visible actions is partitioned into two sets, H and L, of high and low actions such that $\overline{H} = H$ and $\overline{L} = L$. The syntax of SPA *terms* (or *processes*) is defined as follows:

$$E ::= \mathbf{0} \mid a.E \mid E + E \mid E|E \mid E \setminus v \mid E[f] \mid Z$$

where $a \in Act$, $v \subseteq \mathcal{L}$, $f : Act \to Act$ is such that $f(\bar{\alpha}) = \overline{f(\alpha)}$, $f(\tau) = \tau$, $f(H) \subseteq H \cup \{\tau\}$, and $f(L) \subseteq L \cup \{\tau\}$, and Z is a constant that must be associated with a definition $Z \stackrel{\text{def}}{=} E$.

We denote by $\mathcal{E}$ the set of all SPA processes and by $\mathcal{E}_H$ the set of all high level processes, i.e., those constructed only using actions in $H \cup \{\tau\}$. The operational semantics of SPA agents is given in terms of *Labelled Transition Systems* (*LTS*, for short) as defined in [6].

The concept of *observation equivalence* is used to establish equalities among processes and it is based on the idea that two systems have the same semantics if and only if they cannot be distinguished by an external observer. This is obtained by defining an equivalence relation over $\mathcal{E}$. The *weak bisimulation* relation [27] equates two processes if they are able to mutually simulate their behavior step by step. Weak bisimulation does not care about internal τ actions.

We will use the following auxiliary notations. If $t = a_1 \cdots a_n \in Act^*$ and $E \xrightarrow{a_1} \cdots \xrightarrow{a_n} E'$, then we write $E \xrightarrow{t} E'$. We also write $E \stackrel{t}{\Longrightarrow} E'$ if $E(\xrightarrow{\tau})^* \xrightarrow{a_1} (\xrightarrow{\tau})^* \cdots (\xrightarrow{\tau})^* \xrightarrow{a_n} (\xrightarrow{\tau})^* E'$ where $(\xrightarrow{\tau})^*$ denotes a (possibly empty) sequence of τ labelled transitions. If $t \in Act^*$, then $\hat{t} \in \mathcal{L}^*$ is the sequence gained by deleting all occurrences of τ from t. As a consequence, $E \stackrel{\hat{a}}{\Longrightarrow} E'$ stands for $E \stackrel{a}{\Longrightarrow} E'$ if $a \in \mathcal{L}$, and for $E(\xrightarrow{\tau})^* E'$ if $a = \tau$ (note that $\stackrel{\tau}{\Longrightarrow}$ requires at least one τ labelled transition while $\stackrel{\hat{\tau}}{\Longrightarrow}$ means zero or more τ labelled transitions).

Definition 1 (Weak Bisimulation). *A binary relation* $\mathcal{R} \subseteq \mathcal{E} \times \mathcal{E}$ *over agents is a* weak bisimulation *if* $(E, F) \in \mathcal{R}$ *implies, for all* $a \in Act$,

- *if* $E \xrightarrow{a} E'$, *then there exists* F' *such that* $F \stackrel{\hat{a}}{\Longrightarrow} F'$ *and* $(E', F') \in \mathcal{R}$;
- *if* $F \xrightarrow{a} F'$, *then there exists* E' *such that* $E \stackrel{\hat{a}}{\Longrightarrow} E'$ *and* $(E', F') \in \mathcal{R}$.

Two agents $E, F \in \mathcal{E}$ *are* weakly bisimilar, *denoted by* $E \approx F$, *if there exists a weak bisimulation* $\mathcal{R}$ *containing the pair* (E, F).

The relation $\approx$ is the largest weak bisimulation and is an equivalence relation [27].

Security Properties. The *BNDC* [4] security property aims at guaranteeing that no information flow from the high to the low level is possible, even in the presence of malicious processes. The main motivation is to protect a system also from internal attacks, which could be performed by the so called *Trojan Horse* programs, i.e., programs that are apparently honest but hide inside some malicious code. Property *BNDC* is based on the idea of checking the system against all high level potential interactions, representing every possible high level malicious program. In particular, a system E is *BNDC* if for every high level process Π a low level user cannot distinguish E from $(E|\Pi)$, i.e., if Π cannot interfere with the low level execution of the system E.

Definition 2 (BNDC). *Let* $E \in \mathcal{E}$.

$$E \in BNDC \quad \textit{iff} \quad \forall \, \Pi \in \mathcal{E}_H, \ E \setminus H \approx (E|\Pi) \setminus H.$$

Example 1. The *BNDC* property is powerful enough to detect information flows due to the possibility for a high level malicious process to block or unblock a system. Let $H = \{h\}$, $L = \{l, j\}$ and $E_1 = l.h.j.\mathbf{0} + l.j.\mathbf{0}$. Consider the process $\Pi = \bar{h}.\mathbf{0}$. We have that $(E_1|\Pi) \setminus H \approx l.j.\mathbf{0}$, while $E_1 \setminus H \approx l.\mathbf{0} + l.j.\mathbf{0}$. Note that the latter may (nondeterministically) block after the l input. Having many instances of this process, a low level user could deduce if $\bar{h}$ is executed by observing whether the system always performs j or not. Process E_1 may be "repaired", by including the possibility of choosing to execute j or not inside the process. Indeed, process $E_2 = l.h.j.\mathbf{0} + l.(\tau.j.\mathbf{0} + \tau.\mathbf{0})$ is *BNDC*.

In [8], it is introduced a security property called *Persistent_BNDC* (*P_BNDC*, for short), which is suitable for analysing systems in dynamic execution environments. Intuitively, a system E is *P_BNDC* if it never reaches insecure states.

Definition 3 (P_BNDC). *Let* $E \in \mathcal{E}$.

$$E \in P\_BNDC \quad iff \quad \forall \ E' \ reachable \ from \ E, \ E' \in BNDC.$$

Example 2. Consider the process E_2 of Example 1, i.e., $E_2 = l.h.j.\mathbf{0} + l.(\tau.j.\mathbf{0} + \tau.\mathbf{0})$ where $l, j \in L$ and $h \in H$. Suppose now that E_2 is moved in the middle of a computation. This might happen when it find itself in the state $h.j.\mathbf{0}$ (after the first l is executed). Now it is clear that this process is not secure, as a direct causality between h and j is present. In particular $h.j.\mathbf{0}$ is not *BNDC* and this gives evidence that E_2 is not *P_BNDC*. The process may be "repaired" as follows: $E_3 = l.(h.j.\mathbf{0} + \tau.j.\mathbf{0} + \tau.\mathbf{0}) + l.(\tau.j.\mathbf{0} + \tau.\mathbf{0})$. It may be proved that E_3 is *P_BNDC*. Note that, from this example it follows that $P\_BNDC \subset BNDC$.

In [8] it has been shown that even if the definition of *P_BNDC* introduces an universal quantification over all the possible reachable states, this can be avoided by including the idea of "being secure in every state" inside the bisimulation equivalence notion. This is done by defining an equivalence notion which just focus on observable actions which do not belong to H. More in details, it is defined an observation equivalence, named *weak bisimulation up to H* where actions from H are allowed to be ignored, i.e., they are allowed to be matched by zero or more τ actions. To this aim, the following transition relation is used.

Definition 4. *Let* $a \in Act$. *We define the transition relation* $\overset{\hat{a}}{\Longrightarrow}_{\backslash H}$ *as follows:*

$$\overset{\hat{a}}{\Longrightarrow}_{\backslash H} = \begin{cases} \overset{\hat{a}}{\Longrightarrow} & if \ a \notin H \\ \overset{a}{\Longrightarrow} \ or \ \overset{\hat{\tau}}{\Longrightarrow} & if \ a \in H \end{cases}$$

Note that the relation $\overset{\hat{a}}{\Longrightarrow}_{\backslash H}$ is a generalization of the relation $\overset{\hat{a}}{\Longrightarrow}$ used in the definition of weak bisimulation [27]. In fact, if $H = \emptyset$, then for all $a \in Act$, $E \overset{\hat{a}}{\Longrightarrow}_{\backslash H} E'$ coincides with $E \overset{\hat{a}}{\Longrightarrow} E'$.

Definition 5 (Weak Bisimulation up to H). *A binary relation* $\mathcal{R} \subseteq \mathcal{E} \times \mathcal{E}$ *over agents is a* weak bisimulation up to H *if* $(E, F) \in \mathcal{R}$ *implies, for all* $a \in Act$,

- *if* $E \overset{a}{\to} E'$, *then there exists* F' *such that* $F \overset{\hat{a}}{\Longrightarrow}_{\backslash H} F'$ *and* $(E', F') \in \mathcal{R}$;
- *if* $F \overset{a}{\to} F'$, *then there exists* E' *such that* $E \overset{\hat{a}}{\Longrightarrow}_{\backslash H} E'$ *and* $(E', F') \in \mathcal{R}$.

Two agents $E, F \in \mathcal{E}$ *are* weakly bisimilar up to H, *written* $E \approx_{\backslash H} F$, *if* $(E, F) \in \mathcal{R}$ *for some weak bisimulation* $\mathcal{R}$ *up to H.*

The relation $\approx_{\backslash H}$ is the largest weak bisimulation up to H and it is an equivalence relation. In [8] *P_BNDC* has been characterized in terms of $\approx_{\backslash H}$.

Theorem 1 (P_BNDC - Bisimulation). *Let* $E \in \mathcal{E}$. $E \in P\_BNDC$ *iff* $E \approx_{\backslash H} E \setminus H$.

In [2] we give a further characterization of *P_BNDC* processes in terms of *unwinding conditions*. This new characterization provides a better understanding of the operational semantics of *P_BNDC* processes. In practice, whenever a state E' of a *P_BNDC* process may execute a high level action moving to a state E'', then E' should be also able to simulate such high move through a τ sequence moving to a state E''' which is equivalent to E'' for a low level user.

Theorem 2 (P_BNDC - Unwinding). *Let* $E \in \mathcal{E}$ *be a process.* $E \in P\_BNDC$ *iff for all* E' *reachable from* E, *if* $E' \xrightarrow{h} E''$, *then* $E' \xLongrightarrow{\hat{\tau}} E'''$ *and* $E'' \setminus H \approx E''' \setminus H$.

Here we observe that there is a strict relation between the bisimulation-based characterization of *P_BNDC* given in Theorem 1 and the unwinding condition of Theorem 2: the equivalence $\approx_{\setminus H}$ between E and $E \setminus H$ in Theorem 1 states that high level actions of E are simulated by zero or more τ actions of $E \setminus H$, while the unwinding condition in Theorem 2 say that for every high level action there must exists a path of zero or more τ actions leading to equivalent states from the low level view. This suggests us that consistent changes in the way of dealing with high level actions in $\approx_{\setminus H}$ and in the corresponding unwinding condition, may lead to different bisimulation-like and unwinding characterizations of novel information flow security properties.

This idea will be exploited in the next sections when we study the properties *SBNDC* and *CP_BNDC*.

In [8] it is also proved that *P_BNDC* is compositional with respect to the parallel composition, restriction and low level prefix operators. Unfortunately, *P_BNDC* is not compositional with respect to the nondeterministic choice operator as illustrated in Example 4 in the next section.

3 Strong BNDC

The property *Strong BNDC* (*SBNDC*, for short) has been introduced in [4] as a sufficient condition for verifying *BNDC*. It just requires that before and after every high step, the system appears to be the same, from a low level perspective. It has been defined through unwinding conditions as follows.

Definition 6 (SBNDC - Unwinding). *Let* $E \in \mathcal{E}$. $E \in SBNDC$ *iff for all* E' *reachable from* E, *if* $E' \xrightarrow{h} E''$, *then* $E' \setminus H \approx E'' \setminus H$.

SBNDC is *persistent* in the sense that if a process E is *SBNDC* then all processes E' reachable from E are *SBNDC*, i.e., every state reachable from a secure system is still secure. From Theorem 2 it is easy to prove the following:

Corollary 1. $SBNDC \subseteq P\_BNDC \subseteq BNDC$.

By exploiting the relationships between the unwinding and the bisimulation characterizations discussed for the property *P_BNDC* in the previous section, we show that we can avoid the universal quantification over all the possible reachable states in the definition of *SBNDC* by defining a suitable bisimulation equivalence notion. Note that Definition 6 requires that high level actions of E are simulated by no moves, i.e. by zero τ actions, thus we define an observation equivalence, named *weak bisimulation up to H with zero τ*, where actions from H are allowed to be totally ignored, i.e., they are allowed to be matched by zero actions. To this aim, we use the following transition relation which does not take care of internal actions and may totally ignore actions from H.

Definition 7. *Let $a \in Act$. We define the transition relation $\overset{\hat{a}}{\Longrightarrow}{}^{0}_{\backslash H}$ as follows:*

$$\overset{\hat{a}}{\Longrightarrow}{}^{0}_{\backslash H} = \begin{cases} \overset{\hat{a}}{\Longrightarrow} & \text{if } a \notin H \\ \overset{a}{\Longrightarrow} \text{ or } \overset{\cdot}{\rightarrow} & \text{if } a \in H \end{cases}$$

where $\overset{\cdot}{\rightarrow}$ denotes a sequence of zero actions [2].

Note that relation $\overset{\hat{a}}{\Longrightarrow}{}^{0}_{\backslash H}$ is included into $\overset{\hat{a}}{\Longrightarrow}_{\backslash H}$, introduced in Definition 4, since the empty sequence is a particular sequence of τ actions.

The concept of *weak bisimulation up to H with zero τ* is defined as follows.

Definition 8 (Weak Bisimulation up to H with zero τ). *A weak bisimulation up to H with zero τ is a weak bisimulation where the transition relation $\overset{\hat{a}}{\Longrightarrow}$ is replaced by $\overset{\hat{a}}{\Longrightarrow}{}^{0}_{\backslash H}$. Two agents $E, F \in \mathcal{E}$ are weakly bisimilar up to H with zero τ, written $E \approx^{0}_{\backslash H} F$, if $(E, F) \in \mathcal{R}$ for some weak bisimulation $\mathcal{R}$ up to H with zero τ.*

The relation $\approx^{0}_{\backslash H}$ is the largest weak bisimulation up to H with zero τ and it is an equivalence relation.

SBNDC processes can be characterized in terms of $\approx^{0}_{\backslash H}$ as follows.

Theorem 3 (SBNDC - Bisimulation). *Let $E \in \mathcal{E}$. $E \in SBNDC$ iff $E \approx^{0}_{\backslash H} E \setminus H$.*

Example 3. Let us consider the process depicted below, modelling the use of a shared resource by a low level *producer* and an high level *consumer*, i.e., *produce* $\in L$ and *consume* $\in H$.

$$R_0 = produce.R_1$$
$$R_i = produce.R_{i+1} + \overline{consume}.R_{i-1} \quad \text{for } i \in [1, n-1]$$
$$R_n = produce.R_n + \overline{consume}.R_{n-1}$$

Note that the resource has a maximum capacity of n and the low level *produce* action is ignored when such a limit is reached. This non-intuitive behavior is needed in order to avoid a potential flow from high to low level. In particular, if the low level producer could observe when the resource is full, this will be exploited to deduce how many high level *consume* actions have been performed.

It is easy to see that this process is *SBNDC* by directly applying Definition 6. In fact all the R_j states are equivalent when restricted on high level actions, as they may only perform a *produce* action moving to another restricted $R_{j'}$.

---

[2] If $E \overset{\cdot}{\rightarrow} E'$ then E coincides with E'.

In [6] (see Theorem 4) it is proved that *SBNDC* is compositional with respect to the parallel and restriction operators. It is easy to extend the compositionality result by showing that *SBNDC* is also compositional with respect to low level prefix and relabelling.

Proposition 1. *Let $E, F \in \mathcal{E}$. If $E, F \in SBNDC$, then*

- $a.E \in SBNDC$, *for all* $a \in L \cup \{\tau\}$;
- $(E|F) \in SBNDC$;
- $E \setminus v \in SBNDC$, *for all* $v \subseteq \mathcal{L}$;
- $E[f] \in SBNDC$.

As *P_BNDC* also *SBNDC* is not compositional with respect to the nondeterministic choice operator. The following example concerns *SBNDC*, but a similar reasoning can be done for *P_BNDC*.

Example 4. Consider the processes $E_4 = h.0$ with $h \in H$ and $E_5 = l.0$ with $l \in L$. It is easy to see that both E_4 and E_5 are *SBNDC* but $E_4 + E_5$ is not *SBNDC*. In fact $E_4 + E_5 \xrightarrow{h} 0$ while $E_4 + E_5 \xrightarrow{\cdot} E_4 + E_5 = h.0 + l.0$, but $(h.0 + l.0) \setminus H \not\approx 0$. The problem lies in the fact that while the high level action in E_4 is safely simulated by a sequence of zero τ in $E_4 \setminus H$, the same high level action in $E_4 + E_5$ is not safely simulated by a sequence of zero τ in $(E_4 + E_5) \setminus H$ due to the presence of the additional component E_5. This problem would not arise if h were be simulated by at least one τ action. This observation will be exploited in the next section to define a fully compositional security property.

4   Compositional P_BNDC

It is well-known that security properties are, in general, not preserved under composition [21]. We have seen in the previous sections that *P_BNDC* and *SB-NDC* are both non-compositional with respect to the nondeterministic choice operator. However, compositionality results are crucial for making the development of large and complex systems feasible [23,25,19]. In this section we show how the notion of *P_BNDC* can be slightly restricted in order to obtain a class of processes which is *fully compositional* (i.e., it is compositional also with respect to the nondeterministic choice). We call such a class *Compositional P_BNDC* (*CP_BNDC*, for short). We also show that this class can be equivalently characterized in terms of a bisimulation-like relation and unwinding conditions.

We start by modifying the way of dealing with high level actions in the first characterization of *P_BNDC* given in terms of $\approx_{\setminus H}$. The idea is that of defining an observation equivalence, named *weak bisimulation up to H with at least one* τ, where actions from H are allowed to be matched by one or more τ actions, but not zero τ. To this aim, we use the following transition relation which generalizes the relation $\stackrel{\hat{a}}{\Longrightarrow}$. As in Definition 4, a high level move can be simulated by a sequence of τ moves, but now we require that the sequence is not empty.

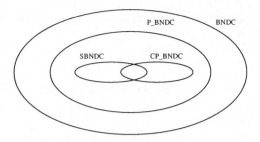

Fig. 1. Security Properties.

Definition 9. *Let $a \in Act$. We define the transition relation $\xRightarrow{\hat{a}}{}^+_{\backslash H}$ as follows:*

$$\xRightarrow{\hat{a}}{}^+_{\backslash H} = \begin{cases} \xRightarrow{\hat{a}} & \text{if } a \notin H \\ \xRightarrow{a} \text{ or } \xRightarrow{\tau} & \text{if } a \in H \end{cases}$$

The concept of *weak bisimulation up to H with at least one τ* is as follows.

Definition 10 (Weak Bisimulation up to H with at least one τ). *A weak bisimulation up to H with zero τ is a weak bisimulation where the transition relation $\xRightarrow{\hat{a}}$ is replaced by $\xRightarrow{\hat{a}}{}^+_{\backslash H}$. Two agents $E, F \in \mathcal{E}$ are weakly bisimilar up to H with at least one τ, written $E \approx^+_{\backslash H} F$, if $(E, F) \in \mathcal{R}$ for some weak bisimulation $\mathcal{R}$ up to H with at least one τ.*

The relation $\approx^+_{\backslash H}$ is the largest weak bisimulation up to H with at least one τ and it is an equivalence relation. The relation $\xRightarrow{\hat{a}}{}^+_{\backslash H}$ is included in $\xRightarrow{\hat{a}}_{\backslash H}$.

The class of *CP_BNDC* processes is defined in terms of $\approx^+_{\backslash H}$ as follows.

Definition 11 (CP_BNDC - Bisimulation). *Let $E \in \mathcal{E}$.*

$$E \in CP\_BNDC \quad \text{iff} \quad E \approx^+_{\backslash H} E \setminus H.$$

CP_BNDC can be characterized in terms of unwinding conditions.

Theorem 4 (CP_BNDC - Unwinding). *Let $E \in \mathcal{E}$. $E \in CP\_BNDC$ iff for all E' reachable from E, if $E' \xrightarrow{h} E''$ then $E' \xRightarrow{\tau} E'''$ and $E'' \setminus H \approx E''' \setminus H$.*

Corollary 2. *CP_BNDC $\subseteq$ P_BNDC $\subseteq$ BNDC.*

Notice that neither *SBNDC* implies *CP_BNDC* nor *CP_BNDC* implies *SB-NDC*. For example, process $h.0$ is *SBNDC* but it is not *CP_BNDC*, as no τ transitions simulate the high level h. On the other side, process $h.0 + l.0 + \tau.0$ is *CP_BNDC* but not *SBNDC*, as, after performing h, the low level action l is no longer executable. However, there are processes which are both *SBNDC* and *CP_BNDC*, e.g., processes which perform only low level actions. The situation is summarized in Fig. 1. Notice that all the inclusions are strict.

Example 5. Consider the process C (channel) described through a value-passing extension of SPA by:

$$C = in(x).(\overline{out}(x).C + \tau.C).$$

C may accept a value x at the left-hand port, labelled in. When it holds a value, it either delivers it at the right-hand port, labelled $\overline{out}$, or resets itself performing an internal transition.

If the domain of x is $\{0,1\}$, then the channel C can be translated into SPA in a standard way by following [27] as:

$$C = in_0.(\overline{out}_0.C + \tau.C) + in_1.(\overline{out}_1.C + \tau.C).$$

Let us assume that C is used as communication channel from low to high level. This can be expressed as $in_0, in_1 \in L$ and $\overline{out}_0, \overline{out}_1 \in H$. Since, in correspondence of each high level action $(\overline{out}_0, \overline{out}_1)$ there is a τ transition leading to the same state, by Theorem 4 we can conclude that C is *CP_BNDC*. The τ transitions basically makes the channel a lossy one, as high level outputs may be non-deterministically lost. However, note that non-determinism is used to abstract away implementation details. For example, such τ's could correspond, at implementation time, to time-outs for the high level output actions, i.e., events that empty the channel and allow a new low level input, whenever high outputs are not accepted within a certain amount of time. Analogously, it is possible to see that C is also *SBNDC*. Note that process $C' = in(x).\overline{out}(x).C'$ with no τ's is neither *CP_BNDC* nor *SBNDC*. Indeed, a high level user may block and unblock C' in order to transmit information to low level user.   □

Exploiting the unwinding characterization we are now ready to prove that *CP_BNDC* is compositional with respect to the nondeterministic choice operator.

Proposition 2. *Let $E, F \in \mathcal{E}$. If $E, F \in CP\_BNDC$, then*

- $a.E \in CP\_BNDC$, for all $a \in L \cup \{\tau\}$;
- $(E + F) \in CP\_BNDC$;
- $(E|F) \in CP\_BNDC$;
- $E \setminus v \in P\_BNDC$, for all $v \subseteq \mathcal{L}$;
- $E[f] \in CP\_BNDC$.

5   Verification Complexity

Let us denote with $\approx^*_{\backslash H}$ the relation $\approx_{\backslash H}$. By adopting this notation we have that a process E is *P_BNDC*, *SBNDC*, and *CP_BNDC* if and only if $E \approx^s_{\backslash H} E \backslash H$ for $s = *$, $s = 0$ and $s = +$, respectively.

The characterizations of properties in terms of bisimulation equivalences allow us to efficiently verify them. Let $n = |S_E|$ be the number of states in $LTS(E)$, for each $a \in Act$, let m_a be the number of $\xrightarrow{a}$ transitions in $LTS(E)$, and $m = \sum_{a \in Act} m_a$. Similarly, let $\hat{m}_a$ be the number of $\xRightarrow[\backslash H]{\hat{a}}{}^{s}$ transitions, and $\hat{m} = \sum_{a \in Act} \hat{m}_a$.

Theorem 5. *Let $s \in \{0, *, +\}$. The test $E \approx^s_{\backslash H} E \backslash H$ can be performed in time $O(n\hat{m}_\tau + n^w + \hat{m} \log n)$ and space $O(n^2)$, where w denotes the exponent in the running time of the matrix multiplication algorithm used.*[3]

The proof of this complexity result follows exactly the lines of the proof presented in the case of *P_BNDC* in [7] paying some attention to modify the third point of the algorithm. In particular the time complexity depends on the fact that in all the cases it is necessary to compute the transitive closure of the τ-transitions. Notice that in the complexity result $\hat{m} \log n$ comes from the fact that we use the algorithm by Paige and Tarjan ([30]) to compute the maximum bisimulation.

6   Preserving Security under Refinement

In a stepwise development process, one usually starts with a very abstract specification of the desired system. The specification is then refined and decomposed until one arrives at a concrete specification that can be directly implemented. Naturally, one expects that a system which is formally developed in this way satisfies all properties that are satisfied by the abstract specification (plus possibly additional ones). While this holds for safety and liveness properties, it is not true for most information flow properties. This problem has been widely discussed in [14] and some progress toward a solution has been made in [13,29, 31,18]. In particular, in [18] Mantel shows how from unwinding conditions one can easily define refinement operators which preserve security.

A refinement for a process is defined in terms of a basic refinement operator $ref : \mathcal{E} \rightarrow \mathcal{E}$ that, given a process E, returns a process $ref(E)$ which is a refinement of E.

Following [18], we identify a sufficient condition to be satisfied by basic refinement operators in order to preserve the bisimulation-based possibilistic security properties studied in this paper.

Definition 12. *A basic refinement operator ref preserves the low level observations if for all $E, F \in \mathcal{E}$ if $E \backslash H \approx F \backslash H$, then $ref(E) \backslash H \approx ref(F) \backslash H$.*

Example 6. Let $v \subseteq \mathcal{L}$. The restriction operator $\backslash v$ is a basic refinement operator which preserves the low level observations. In fact, if $E \backslash H \approx F \backslash H$ then it is easy to prove that $(E \backslash v) \backslash H \approx (E \backslash v) \backslash H$.

Given a basic refinement operator *ref*, a refinement *refine(E, ref, S)* for a complex system E is the process obtained by applying *ref* to all $E' \in S$ reachable from E. If E satisfies *P_BNDC* (or *CP_BNDC* or *SBNDC*) then we would like that also the resulting system satisfies it. However, by simply applying the *ref* operator to all the processes in S one may obtain a system which does not satisfy the desired property.

---

[3] In the algorithm in [3], which is at the moment the fastest in literature, we have that $w = 2.376$.

Example 7. Consider the process $E_6 = E_7 + h.E_8$, where $E_7 = l.h.\mathbf{0}$ and $E_8 = l.\mathbf{0}$, with $h \in H$ and $l \in L$. The process E_6 is *SBNDC*. If we consider the basic refinement operator $\backslash\{l\}$ and the set $S = \{E_8\}$ we obtain that $refine(E_6, ref, S) = l.h.\mathbf{0} + h.\mathbf{0}$ which is not *SBNDC*. The problem is due to the fact that by refining E_8 we loose the unwinding property: $refine(E_6, ref, S)$ does not contain any subprocess E' reachable with zero τ actions and such that $E' \backslash H \approx ref(E_8) \backslash H$. On the other hand, $refine(E_6, ref, \{E_7, E_8\}) = h.\mathbf{0}$ is *SBNDC*.

The above example suggests how to guarantee the unwinding conditions, and then our security properties, in refining a process: when we refine a subprocess E' we have to refine also all the subprocesses E'' such that $E' \backslash H \approx E'' \backslash H$.

Theorem 6. *Let $E \in \mathcal{E}$, ref be a basic refinement operator which preserves the low level observations. Let S be a set of states such that for all E', E'' reachable from E if $E' \in S$ and $E' \backslash H \approx E'' \backslash H$ then $E'' \in S$ too.*
If E satisfies P_BNDC (CP_BNDC, SBNDC) then $refine(E, ref, S)$ satisfies P_BNDC (CP_BNDC, SBNDC, respectively).

Proof. Immediate by the unwinding Theorems 2 and 4, and Definition 6.

Given an intended refinement $refine(E, ref, S)$ which does not satisfy the hypothesis on S of the above theorem, there are two natural ways for obtaining an approximation of it which preserves our security properties. We denote them by $refine^+(E, ref, S)$ and $refine^-(E, ref, S)$. While $refine^+(E, ref, S)$ refines through ref all the states which are in S (plus possibly states not in S), $refine^-(E, ref, S)$ only refines through ref states which are in S (but possibly not all states in S). The formal definition of $refine^+(E, ref, S)$ and $refine^-(E, ref, S)$ are as follows.

Definition 13 (*$refine^+$ and $refine^-$*). *Let $E \in \mathcal{E}$, let ref be a basic refinement operator which preserves the low level observations and let S be a set of states reachable from E.*
$refine^+(E, ref, S) = refine(E, ref, S \cup S')$ *where*
$\qquad\qquad S' = \{E'' \text{ reachable from } E \mid \exists E' \in S \text{ and } E' \backslash H \approx E'' \backslash H\}$
$refine^-(E, ref, S) = refine(E, ref, S')$ *where*
$\qquad\qquad S' \text{ is the greatest subset of } S \text{ such that if } E' \in S' \text{ and } E'' \text{ is}$
$\qquad\qquad reachable \text{ from } E \text{ and } E' \backslash H \approx E'' \backslash H \text{ then } E'' \in S.$

If a state $E' \in S$ is refined through ref then $refine^+(E, ref, S)$ refines also all states E'' which are equivalent to E' from the low level view. On the other hand, $refine^-(E, ref, S)$ refines through ref a state $E' \in S$ only if all states E'' which are equivalent to E' from the low level view belong to S.

Corollary 3. *Let $E \in \mathcal{E}$, ref be a basic refinement operator which preserves the low level observations, and S be a set of states reachable from E. If E satisfies P_BNDC (CP_BNDC, SBNDC) then $refine^+(E, ref, S)$ and $refine^-(E, ref, S)$ both satisfy P_BNDC (CP_BNDC, SBNDC, respectively).*

7   Related Works and Conclusions

In this paper we study three persistent information flow security properties based on the bisimulation semantics model. For these properties we provide two characterizations: one in terms of a bisimulation-like equivalence relation and another one in terms of unwinding conditions.

The first characterization allows us to perform the verification of the properties for finite state processes in polynomial time with respect to the number of states of the system, also improving on the polynomial time complexity required by the Compositional Security Checker Cosec presented in [5].

The second characterization is based on unwinding conditions. This kind of conditions for possibilistic security properties have been previously proposed in many papers, see, e.g., [13,32,26,17]. All such conditions have been proposed for traces-based models and are, in most cases, only sufficient for the respective security properties. Here we propose new necessary and sufficient unwinding conditions for bisimulation-based properties.

In [2] we show how unwinding conditions can be exploited for defining a proof system which provides a very efficient technique for the verification and the development of *P_BNDC* secure processes. Indeed, the proof system allows us to verify whether a process is secure just by inspecting its syntax, and thus avoiding the state-explosion problem. In particular, it allows us to deal with recursive processes which may perform unbounded sequences of actions, possibly reaching an infinite number of states. Moreover, the system offers a mean to built processes which are *P_BNDC* by construction in an incremental way. Such a proof system could be easily adapted to deal with the *CP_BNDC* and *SBNDC* properties studied in this paper.

We show that *P_BNDC* and *SBNDC* are compositional with respect to all the operators of SPA, except the non-deterministic choice. Moreover, we prove that the new property named *CP_BNDC* is fully compositional. Compositionality of possibilistic security properties has been widely studied in the literature. There are several information flow properties based on the traces model which have been proved to be fully compositional like, e.g., restrictiveness [21], forward correctability [15] or separability [23]. In [23,25] it has been studied how to restrict composition in order to preserve certain security properties which are not preserved by (more general) composition. To the best of our knowledge, *CP_BNDC* is the only bisimulation-based security property in literature which is fully compositional.

Finally, we provide a sufficient condition to define refinement operators preserving our persistent security properties. The problem of finding refinements under which security is preserved has been widely discussed in [14] and some progress toward a solution has been made in [13,29,31,18]. In particular, in [18] Mantel shows how one can easily define refinement operators which preserve security, starting from unwinding conditions. The approach we follow in this paper is indeed inspired by that work.

References

1. A. Bossi, R. Focardi, C. Piazza, and S. Rossi.   Bisimulation and unwinding for verifying possibilistic security properties.   Technical Report CS-2002-15, Dipartimento di Informatica, Università Ca' Foscari di Venezia, Italy, 2002. http://www.dsi.unive.it/ricerca/TR/index.htm.

2. A. Bossi, R. Focardi, C. Piazza, and S. Rossi. A Proof System for Information Flow Security. In M. Leuschel, editor, *Proc. of Int. Workshop on Logic Based Program Development and Transformation*, LNCS. Springer-Verlag, 2002. To appear.

3. D. Coppersmith and S. Winograd. Matrix multiplication via arithmetic progression. In *Proc. of the 19th Symposium on Theory of Computing*, pages 1–6, 1987.

4. R. Focardi and R. Gorrieri.   A Classification of Security Properties for Process Algebras. *Journal of Computer Security*, 3(1):5–33, 1994/1995.

5. R. Focardi and R. Gorrieri. The Compositional Security Checker: A Tool for the Verification of Information Flow Security Properties. *IEEE Transactions on Software Engineering*, 23(9):550–571, 1997.

6. R. Focardi and R. Gorrieri. Classification of Security Properties (Part I: Information Flow). In R. Focardi and R. Gorrieri, editors, *Foundations of Security Analysis and Design*, volume 2171 of *LNCS*. Springer-Verlag, 2001.

7. R. Focardi, C. Piazza, and S. Rossi. Proof Methods for Bisimulation based Information Flow Security. In A. Cortesi, editor, *Proc. of Int. Workshop on Verification, Model Checking and Abstract Interpretation*, volume 2294 of *LNCS*, pages 16–31. Springer-Verlag, 2002.

8. R. Focardi and S. Rossi.   Information Flow Security in Dynamic Contexts.   In *Proc. of the IEEE Computer Security Foundations Workshop*, pages 307–319. IEEE Computer Society Press, 2002.

9. S. N. Foley. A Universal Theory of Information Flow. In *Proc. of the IEEE Symposium on Security and Privacy*, pages 116–122. IEEE Computer Society Press, 1987.

10. R. Forster. *Non-Interference Properties for Nondeterministic Processes*. PhD thesis, Oxford University Computing Laboratory, 1999.

11. J. A. Goguen and J. Meseguer. Security Policies and Security Models. In *Proc. of the IEEE Symposium on Security and Privacy*, pages 11–20. IEEE Computer Society Press, 1982.

12. J. A. Goguen and J. Meseguer. Inference Control and Unwinding. In *Proc. of the IEEE Symposium on Security and Privacy*, pages 75–86. IEEE Computer Society Press, 1984.

13. J. Graham-Cumming and J. W. Sanders. On the Refinement of Non-Interference. In *Proc. of the IEEE Computer Security Foundations Workshop*, pages 35–42. IEEE Computer Society Press, 1991.

14. J. Jacob. On the Derivation of Secure Components. In *Proc. of the IEEE Symposium on Security and Privacy*, pages 242–247. IEEE Computer Society Press, 1989.

15. D. M. Johnson and F. J. Thayer. Security and the Composition of Machines. In *Proc. of of the IEEE Computer Security Foundations Workshop*, pages 72–89. IEEE Computer Society Press, 1988.

16. H. Mantel. Possibilistic Definitions of Security - An Assebly Kit -. In *Proc. of the IEEE Symposium on Security and Privacy*, pages 185–199. IEEE Computer Society Press, 2000.

17. H. Mantel. Unwinding Possibilistic Security Properties. In *Proc. of the European Symposium on Research in Computer Security*, volume 2895 of *LNCS*, pages 238–254. Springer-Verlag, 2000.

18. H. Mantel. Preserving Information Flow Properties under Refinement. In *Proc. of the IEEE Symposium on Security and Privacy*, pages 78–91. IEEE Computer Society Press, 2001.

19. H. Mantel. On the Composition of Secure Systems. In *Proc. of the IEEE Symposium on Security and Privacy*, pages 88–101. IEEE Computer Society Press, 2002.

20. F. Martinelli. Partial Model Checking and Theorem Proving for Ensuring Security Properties. In *Proc. of the IEEE Computer Security Foundations Workshop*, pages 44–52. IEEE Computer Society Press, 1998.

21. D. McCullough. Specifications for Multi-Level Security and a Hook-Up Property. In *Proc. of the IEEE Symposium on Security and Privacy*, pages 161–166. IEEE Computer Society Press, 1987.

22. J. McLean. Security Models and Information Flow. In *Proc. of the IEEE Symposium on Security and Privacy*, pages 180–187. IEEE Computer Society Press, 1990.

23. J. McLean. A General Theory of Composition for Trace Sets Closed under Selective Interleaving Functions. In *Proc. of the IEEE Symposium on Security and Privacy*, pages 79–93. IEEE Computer Society Press, 1994.

24. J. McLean. Security Models. *Encyclopedia of Software Engineering*, 1994.

25. J. McLean. A General Theory of Composition for a Class of "Possibilistic" Security Properties. *IEEE Trabsactions on Software Engineering*, 22(1):53–67, 1996.

26. J. K. Millen. Unwinding Forward Correctability. In *Proc. of the IEEE Computer Security Foundations Workshop*, pages 2–10. IEEE Computer Society Press, 1994.

27. R. Milner. *Communication and Concurrency*. Prentice-Hall, 1989.

28. C. O'Halloran. A Calculus of Information Flow. In *Proc. of the European Symposium on Research in Security and Privacy*, pages 180–187. AFCET, 1990.

29. C. O'Halloran. Refinement and Confidentiality. In *Proc. of the 5th Refinement Workshop*, pages 119–139, 1992.

30. R. Paige and R. E. Tarjan. Three partition refinement algorithms. *SIAM Journal on Computing*, 16(6):973–989, 1987.

31. A. W. Roscoe, J. C. P. Woodcock, and L. Wulf. Non-Interference through Determinism. In *Proc. of the European Symposium on Research in Computer Security*, volume 875 of *LNCS*, pages 33–53. Springer-Verlag, 1994.

32. P. Y. A. Ryan. A CSP Formulation of Non-Interference and Unwinding. *Cipher*, pages 19–27, 1991.

33. S. Schneider. May Testing, Non-Interference, and Compositionality. *Electronic Notes in Theoretical Computer Science*, 40, 2000.

34. D. Sutherland. A Model of Information. In *Proc. of the 9th National Computer Security Conference*, pages 175–183, 1986.

35. A. Zakinthinos and E. S. Lee. A General Theory of Security Properties. In *Proc. of the IEEE Symposium on Security and Privacy*, pages 74–102. IEEE Computer Society Press, 1997.

Formal Verification of the Horn-Preneel Micropayment Protocol

Kazuhiro Ogata[1,2] and Kokichi Futatsugi[2]

[1] NEC Software Hokuriku, Ltd.
ogatak@acm.org
[2] Japan Advanced Institute of Science and Technology (JAIST)
kokichi@jaist.ac.jp

Abstract. We have formally verified that the Horn-Preneel micropayment protocol possesses an important safety property. The property, called non-overcharge property in this paper, is that a payee cannot be credited amount more than what a payer intends to pay by the broker. The verification has been done by modeling the protocol as an observational transition system considering malicious principals, describing the model in CafeOBJ, writing proof scripts showing that the protocol possesses the property in CafeOBJ, and executing the proof scripts with the CafeOBJ system. We describe the modeling of the protocol and the verification in this paper.

1 Introduction

Commercial transactions are being performed actively over the Internet, and they are supposed to be getting much more active in the near future. Thus the importance of electronic payment protocols has been increasing more and more. Several electronic payment protocols have been proposed. Those protocols are largely classified into two categories: macropayment protocols and micropayment protocols. The former[1,2] are often based on existing credit card payment organizations. There are payments of small amounts each of which makes the transaction cost relatively too much to use credit cards. Processing a credit card transaction costs about 25 cents today, while a typical micropayment may be worth one cent[3]. Applications of micropayments include paying for each web page visited, and for each minute of music or video as it is streamed to the user. Micropayment protocols[4,5] try to aggregate many small payments into fewer, larger payments, which processing costs are relatively small.

As those electronic payment protocols have been increasingly used and have been getting more and more important, the technology with which we can verify that the protocols are really secure is getting more and more significant because security protocols among electronic payment protocols are subject to subtle errors that are especially difficult to reveal by traditional testing methods and usual operations. Actually it has been found that a lot of security protocols such as the NSPK authentication protocol[6] have serious security flaws even if cryptosystems used are unbreakable.

L. Zuck et al. (Eds.): VMCAI 2003, LNCS 2575, pp. 238–252, 2003.

We have formally verified that the Horn-Preneel micropayment protocol[4] possesses an important safety property. The property is that a payee cannot be credited amount more than what a payer intends to pay by the broker. The property is called *non-overcharge property* in this paper. The verification has been done with CafeOBJ[7,8]. CafeOBJ is an algebraic specification language in which abstract machines as well as abstract data types can be described. The verification process is roughly as follows. First we abstract the protocol by hiding quantities that are irrelevant to the property and model the abstract protocol as an observational transition system (OTS)[9]. When modeling the abstract protocol, we have to consider malicious principals who try to confuse the protocol and/or to make profits illegally. Next the OTS is described in CafeOBJ. Then proof scripts to show that the abstract protocol possesses the property are written in CafeOBJ and get executed by the CafeOBJ system.

2 Preliminaries

2.1 CafeOBJ in a Nutshell

CafeOBJ[7,8] is mainly based on two logical foundations: *initial* and *hidden* algebra. Initial algebra is used to specify abstract data types, and hidden algebra[10] to specify abstract machines. There are two kinds of sorts (corresponding to types in programming languages) in CafeOBJ: *visible* and *hidden* sorts. A visible sort represents an abstract data type, and a hidden sort the state space of an abstract machine. There are basically two kinds of operations to hidden sorts: *action* and *observation* operations. An action operation can change a state of an abstract machine. Only observation operations can be used to observe the inside of an abstract machine. An action operation is basically specified with equations by describing how the value of each observation operation changes. Declarations of observation and action operations start with bop or bops, and those of other operations with op or ops. Declarations of equations start with eq, and those of conditional ones with ceq. The CafeOBJ system, an implementation of CafeOBJ, rewrites a given term by regarding equations as left-to-right rewrite rules. This executability makes it possible to simulate described systems and to verify that they possess some desired properties.

2.2 Observational Transition Systems (OTSs)

We assume that there exists a universal state space called Υ. A system is modeled by observing only quantities that are relevant to the system and that interest us and how to change the quantities by state transition from the outside of each state of Υ. An OTS[9] can be used to model a system in this way. UNITY[11] is an ancestor of OTS's, which are reformalized by adopting the concept of hidden algebra[10]. An OTS $\mathcal{S} = \langle \mathcal{O}, \mathcal{I}, \mathcal{T} \rangle$ consists of:

- $\mathcal{O}$: A set of observations. Each observation $o \in \mathcal{O}$ is a function $o : \Upsilon \to D$, where D is a data type and may be different for each observation. The value returned by an observation (in a state) is called the value of it (in the state).

Given an OTS S and two states $v_1, v_2 \in \varUpsilon$, the equality between two states, denoted by $v_1 =_S v_2$, with respect to S is defined as follows:

$$v_1 =_S v_2 \text{ iff } \forall o \in \mathcal{O}.o(v_1) = o(v_2),$$

where '=' in $o(v_1) = o(v_2)$ is supposed to be well defined.

- $\mathcal{I}$: The initial condition. This condition specifies the initial value of each observation that defines initial states of the OTS.
- $\mathcal{T}$: A set of conditional transition rules. Each transition rule $\tau \in \mathcal{T}$ is a function $\tau : \varUpsilon/=_S \to \varUpsilon/=_S$ on equivalent classes of $\varUpsilon$ with respect to $=_S$. Let $\tau(v)$ be the representative element of $\tau([v])$ for each $v \in \varUpsilon$ and it is called *the successor state* of v with respect to τ.
  The condition c_τ for a transition rule $\tau \in \mathcal{T}$, which is a predicate of states, is called *the effective condition*. Given a state $v \in \varUpsilon$, c_τ is true in v, namely τ is *effective* in v, iff $v \neq_S \tau(v)$.

An OTS is described in CafeOBJ[9]. Observations are denoted by CafeOBJ observation operations, and transition rules by CafeOBJ action operations.

Given an OTS, a set of infinite sequences of states is obtained. The infinite sequence of states is called an execution of the OTS. More specifically, an execution of an OTS S is an infinite sequence $v_0, v_1, \ldots$ of states satisfying:

- *Initiation*: For each $o \in \mathcal{O}$, $o(v_0)$ satisfies $\mathcal{I}$.
- *Consecution*: For each $i \in \{0, 1, \ldots\}$, $v_{i+1} =_S \tau(v_i)$ for some $\tau \in \mathcal{T}$.

A state is called *reachable* with respect to S iff it appears in an execution of S.

All properties considered in this paper are safety properties. *Safety properties* are defined as follows: a predicate $p : \varUpsilon \to \{\text{true}, \text{false}\}$ is a safety property with respect to S iff $p(v)$ holds for every reachable $v \in \varUpsilon$ with respect to S. We prove that an OTS S has a safety property p mainly by induction on the number of transition rules applied (executed) as follows:

- Base case: For any state $v \in \varUpsilon$ in which each observation $o \in \mathcal{O}$ satisfies $\mathcal{I}$, we show that $p(v)$ holds.
- Inductive step: Given any reachable state $v \in \varUpsilon$ with respect to S such that $p(v)$ holds, we show that, for any transition rule $\tau \in \mathcal{T}$, $p(\tau(v))$ also holds.

3   The Horn-Preneel Micropayment Protocol

Günther Horn and Bart Preneel have proposed an electronic micropayment protocol suited for the third generation mobile system UMTS (Universal Mobile Telecommunications System) in 1998[4]. The protocol is called the Horn-Preneel micropayment protocol or the HPMP in this paper. The HPMP makes use of the Pedersen's tick payment scheme[12] that is an application of the Lamport's one-time password scheme[13] to encode amounts in payments. It takes advantage of elliptic-curve cryptosystems so that cryptographic operations can be efficiently executed and resulted messages can be compact compared to use of other public-key cryptosystems.

The protocol involves three parties: users, VASPs (value-added service providers) and brokers. We assume that there exists one and only (legitimate) broker in this paper that is denoted by B. We also use U and V for a user and a VASP respectively. First U and V authenticate each other in the early phase of the protocol. After the mutual authentication, V asks U to pay for services given by V multiple times and U pays for each of the requests. At the end of the protocol, V is credited the total amount by B.

Since the HPMP should have other properties than non-overcharge property, messages exchanged between principals include information that is not directly needed to possess the property. The focus of the paper is to describe the verification that the HPMP possesses the property. Hence we abstract the protocol by hiding quantities that are irrelevant to the property. The abstract version of the protocol, called the abstract HPMP or the AHPMP, is described in this paper.

The cryptographic primitives used in the protocol are as follows:

- $\{\cdot\}_k$: A symmetric encryption function with a symmetric key k.
- $\mathrm{Sig}_P(\cdot)$: A digital signature computed with principal P's private key.
- $h1(\cdot)$, $h2(\cdot)$, $h3(\cdot)$: One-way hash functions.
- $F(\cdot)$: A length-preserving one-way function on T-th iterates[12], where T is a natural number giving the maximum number of ticks (the currency unit) to which U can commit himself/herself by one signature.

Quantities occurring in the protocol are as follows:

- g : A generator for the multiplicative group of a finite field or a subgroup of an elliptic curve in which the discrete logarithm problem is hard.
- u, v : U's private key, V's private key.
- g^p : Principal P's public key, where p is P's private key.
- r : A random number generated by V.
- K : A symmetric key computed by $K = h1(\langle (g^u)^v, r \rangle)$.
- K_V : A symmetric key shared with V and B.
- α_x : $\alpha_x = F^x(\alpha_0)$, the result of applying F to α_0 x times, where α_0 is a random number and x is a natural number. Since preimages of α_x are valuable, α_x is called e-cash in this paper.
- d_i $(i = 1 \ldots n)$: natural numbers, which are called ticks in this paper.

The protocol flows can be described in Fig.1, where $\langle x_1, \ldots, x_m \rangle$ denotes an m-tuple consisting of $x_1, \ldots, x_m$. We name messages exchanged such as Init, Resp, etc. for the sake of convenience. Note that Clear messages are not explicitly described in the original paper[4], and the symmetric key K_V is not used.

At the start of the protocol, U sends his/her public key to V as an Init message.

On receipt of the Init message from U, V generates r and computes $K = h1(\langle (g^u)^v, r \rangle)$. He/She computes $h2(\langle K, r, V \rangle)$ to show knowledge of K, and sends r and $h2(\langle K, r, V \rangle)$ to U as a Resp message.

On receipt of the Resp message from V, U retrieves r and a hash value h_1. U obtains g^v from a key server or something, and computes $K = h1(\langle (g^v)^u, r \rangle)$

Init: $U \longrightarrow V : g^u$
Resp: $V \longrightarrow U : \langle r, h2(\langle K, r, V \rangle) \rangle$
Ack: $U \longrightarrow V : \{\langle \mathrm{Sig}_U(h3(\langle g^u, g^v, r, V, \alpha_T \rangle)), \alpha_T \rangle\}_K$
Bill: $V \longrightarrow U : d_1$
Pay: $U \longrightarrow V : \alpha_{T-d_1}$

$\vdots$

Bill: $V \longrightarrow U : d_n$
Pay: $U \longrightarrow V : \alpha_{T-(d_1+\cdots+d_n)}$
Clear: $V \longrightarrow B : \{\langle \alpha_{T-(d_1+\cdots+d_n)}, U, \mathrm{Sig}_U(h3(\langle g^u, g^v, r, V, \alpha_T \rangle)), \alpha_T, r \rangle\}_{K_V}$

Fig. 1. The abstract Horn-Preneel micropayment protocol

and $h2(\langle K, r, V \rangle)$. He/She checks if the hash value matches h_1, which makes him/her assured that V is his/her intended principal. He/She then generates α_0 to compute $\alpha_T = F^T(\alpha_0)$, computes $h3(\langle g^u, g^v, r, V, \alpha_T, \rangle)$ and signs it with his/her private key. Finally he/she encrypts the signature and α_T with K, and sends the cipher to V as an Ack message.

On receipt of the Ack message, V decrypts the cipher with K, and obtains a signature and α_T. He/She computes $h3(\langle g^u, g^v, r, V, \alpha_T \rangle)$ and verifies the signature with U's public key, which authenticates U to V .

These three message exchanges establish mutual authentication between U and V and initialize the payment to V by U.

After the mutual authentication, V asks U to pay some amount, say d_i ($i = 1, \ldots, n$), by sending Bill messages to U. On receipt of each Bill message containing d_i, U sends the preimage $\alpha_{T-(d_1+\ldots+d_i)}$ of α_T to V as a Pay message.

At the end of the protocol, V encrypts $\alpha_{T-(d_1+\ldots+d_n)}$, U, the U's signature, α_T and r with K_V and sends the cipher to B as a Clear message. On receipt of it, B decrypts the cipher with K_V, gets α_x, U, a signature, α_T and r, computes $h3(\langle g^u, g^v, r, V, \alpha_T \rangle)$ and verifies the signature with U's public key. He/She finally checks $\alpha_x = \alpha_{T-(d_1+\ldots+d_n)}$ and credits the amount $d_1 + \ldots + d_n$ to V.

4   Non-overcharge Property

There are several properties that the HPMP should possess. In this paper, we consider the following one: *a VASP cannot be credited amount more than what a user intends to pay by the broker.* That the broker credits some amount to a VASP and debits the amount against a user implies that the broker has received a valid Clear message stating that the user intends to pay the VASP the amount, and that a user intends to pay a VASP some amount implies that the user sends the VASP a Pay message including α_{T-d} where d denotes the amount. Consequently the property can be restated in a more specific way to the HPMP as follows: *if the broker receives a valid Clear message saying that a user pays the amount d ticks to a VASP (namely that the valid Clear message includes α_{T-d}), no matter who has sent the valid Clear message, then the user has always sent a*

Pay *message including* $\alpha_{T-d'}$ *where* $d \leq d'$ *to the VASP.* This property is called *non-overcharge property* in this paper.

In this paper, we formally verify that the AHPMP possesses this property provided that the cryptosystems used cannot be broken.

5   Modeling the Abstract HPMP

5.1   Modeling Outline

We suppose that there exists one and only legitimate broker as stated earlier. We also suppose that there not only exist multiple trustable users and VASPs but also multiple malicious (untrustable) users and VASPs. Trustable users and VASPs exactly follow the protocol, while malicious users and VASPs may do something against the protocol as well, namely intercepting and/or faking messages so as to attack the protocol. Generally speaking, we cannot predict what exactly those malicious principals do and how many they are. Therefore, instead of describing each of the malicious users and VASPs, the combination and cooperation of the malicious users and VASPs is modeled as the most general intruder à la Dolev and Yao[14]. The intruder can do the following:

- Eavesdrop any message flowing in the network.
- Glean any quantity from the message; however the intruder can decrypt a cipher text only if he/she knows the key to decrypt, and cannot compute preimages of a hash value if he/she does not know the preimages.
- Fake and send messages based on the gleaned information; however the intruder can encrypt and/or sign something only if he/she knows the key to encrypt and/or sign.

Accordingly we can regard the network as part of the intruder or the storage that the intruder can use[15,16].

5.2   Formalization of Messages

There are six kinds of messages that are Init, Resp, Ack, Bill, Pay and Clear messages. Data constructors for those messages are im, rm, am, bm, pm and cm, respectively, which are declared in module MSG as follows:

```
op im : User User Vasp   Pub      -> Msg
op rm : Vasp Vasp User   Re       -> Msg
op am : User User Vasp   Cipher1  -> Msg
op bm : Vasp Vasp User   Tick     -> Msg
op pm : User User Vasp   Ecash    -> Msg
op cm : Vasp Vasp Broker Cipher2  -> Msg
```

Msg, User, Vasp, Broker, Pub, Re, Cipher1, Tick, Ecach and Cipher2 are visible sorts for messages, users, VASPs, brokers, public keys, pairs of random numbers (r's) and hash values computed with $h2$, cipher texts encrypted with symmetric keys (K's), ticks, e-cash and cipher texts with symmetric keys (K_V's), respectively.

The first, second and third arguments of each constructor mean the actual generator or sender, the source and the destination of the corresponding message. The first argument is meta-information that is only available to the outside observer and that cannot be forged by the intruder, while the remaining arguments may be forged by the intruder. Therefore, suppose that there exists a message which first argument is a principal in the network. It is true that the principal has sent the message. If the principal is trustable, we can also deduce that the second argument is the principal and the principal has sent the message to a principal denoted by the third argument. On the other hand, if the principal is the intruder, the second argument may not be the principal, which means that the intruder has faked the message.

5.3   Formalization of the Network

The network is modeled as a bag (multiset) of messages, which is used as the storage that the intruder can use. Any message that has been sent or put once into the network is supposed to be never deleted from the network because the intruder can replay the message repeatedly. Consequently, the emptiness of the network means that no messages have sent.

The intruder can obtain 11 kinds of quantities from the network, namely the bag of messages. The 11 kinds of quantities are private keys of users and VASPs, random numbers (r's) generated by VASPs, symmetric keys (K_V's) shared with VASPs and the broker, random numbers (α_0's) for e-cash, e-cash, hash values (K's) computed with $h1$, hash values with $h2$, hash values with $h3$, digital signatures signed with users' private keys, cipher texts encrypted with symmetric keys (K's) and cipher texts with symmetric keys (K_V's).

Those quantities are denoted by CafeOBJ operators `csecret`, `crand`, `clkey`, `cecrand`, `cecash`, `chash1`, `chash2`, `chash3`, `csig`, `cci1` and `cci2`, respectively, which are declared in module `Network` as follows:

```
op csecret : Network -> ColSecret      op crand   : Network -> ColRand
op clkey   : Network -> ColLkey        op cecrand : Network -> ColECRand
op cecash  : Network -> ColEcash       op chash1  : Network -> ColHash1
op chash2  : Network -> ColHash2       op chash3  : Network -> ColHash3
op csig    : Network -> ColSig         op cci1    : Network -> ColCipher1
op cci2    : Network -> ColCipher2
```

`Network` is a visible sort for the network. `ColX` (X = `Secret`, `Rand`, `Lkey`, `ECRand`, `Ecash`, `Hash1`, `Hash2`, `Hash3`, `Sig`, `Cipher1`, `Cipher2`) are visible sorts for collections of those quantities, where X's are visible sorts for the quantities.

The quantities gleaned by the intruder are defined with equations. For example, `csig` is defined as follows:

```
eq  G \in csig(void) = false .
ceq G \in csig(M,NW) = true if am?(M) and G = g(c1(M)) and k(c1(M)) \in chash1(M,NW) .
ceq G \in csig(M,NW) = true if cm?(M) and G = g(c2(M)) and k(c2(M)) \in clkey(M,NW) .
ceq G \in csig(M,NW) = G \in csig(NW)
    if not(am?(M) and G = g(c1(M)) and k(c1(M)) \in chash1(M,NW)) and
       not(cm?(M) and G = g(c2(M)) and k(c2(M)) \in clkey(M,NW)) .
```

`G`, `M` and `NW` are CafeOBJ variables for visible sorts `Sig`, `Msg` and `Network`, and constant `void` denotes the empty bag. Comma ',' is the data constructor of bags, and the term `M,NW` denotes the bag obtained by putting `M` into `NW`. `am?`

and cm? are predicates checking if a given message is Ack and Clear. c1 and c2 return cipher texts in Ack and Clear messages. g and k return the signature in a cipher text and the key used for the cipher text.

The equations mean the following. There is no signature available to the intruder if the network is empty. The intruder can glean the signature in the message if and only if there exists an Ack or Clear message in the network and the key to use for encryption is available to the intruder. The other operators are defined in the same way.

5.4   Formalization of Trustable Principals

Before modeling the behavior of trustable principals, we describe the values observable from the outside of the protocol. We suppose that the following are observable: the network, the used random numbers generated by VASPs, the used random numbers for e-cash, the amount that a VASP has charged a user and the amount that a user has paid a VASP. Those observable values are denoted by CafeOBJ observation operators nw, ur, uecrv, bill and ec, respectively, which are declared in the main module as follows:

```
bop nw    : Protocol            -> Network
bop ur    : Protocol            -> URand    bop uecrv : Protocol            -> UECRandValue
bop bill  : Protocol Vasp User -> Tick      bop ec    : Protocol User Vasp -> Ecash
```

URand and UECRandValue are visible sorts for sets of random values generated by VASPs and random values for e-cash respectively. Given a state p, a VASP v and a user u, the terms $nw(p)$, $ur(p)$, $uecrv(p)$, $bill(p,v,u)$ and $ec(p,u,v)$ denote the network, the used random numbers generated by VASPs, the used random numbers for e-cash, the amount that v has charged u and the amount that u has paid v, respectively, in state p.

The behavior of trustable principals is modeled by six kinds of transition rules that correspond to sending the six kinds of messages. The six kinds of transition rules are denoted by CafeOBJ action operators sdim, sdrm, sdam, sdbm, sdpm and sdcm, which are declared in the main module as follows:

```
bop sdim : Protocol User Vasp                 -> Protocol
bop sdrm : Protocol Vasp Rand       Msg       -> Protocol
bop sdam : Protocol User ECRandValue Msg Msg  -> Protocol
bop sdbm : Protocol Vasp Tick       Msg Msg   -> Protocol
bop sdpm : Protocol User Rand       Msg Msg   -> Protocol
bop sdcm : Protocol Vasp Rand       Msg Msg   -> Protocol
```

Protocol is a hidden sort denoting the state space and ECRandValue is a visible sort denoting random values for e-cash.

Given a user and a VASP, sdim corresponds to that the user sends an Init message to the VASP. The effective condition is always true.

Given a VASP, a random value and a message, sdrm corresponds to that the VASP sends a Resp message to a user if there exists the message in the network, the message is Init which source and destination (namely the second and third arguments) are the user and the VASP respectively, and the random number is really fresh. The first two conditions mean that the VASP receives an Init message from the user, although the user may not be the actual sender of the message (namely that the first argument of the message may be the intruder).

Given a user, a random value for e-cash and two messages $m1, m2$, sdam corresponds to that the user sends an Ack message to a VASP if the following hold: the random value is really fresh, there exist the two messages in the network, $m1$ is Init sent by the user to the VASP, and $m2$ is Resp seemingly sent by the VASP to the user in response to $m1$.

Given a VASP, a tick and two messages $m1, m2$, sdbm corresponds to that the VASP sends a Bill message to a user if the following hold: there exist the two messages in the network, $m1$ is Resp sent by the VASP to the user, and $m2$ is Ack seemingly sent by the user to the VASP in response to $m1$.

Given a user, a random number and two messages $m1, m2$, sdpm corresponds to that the user sends a Pay message to a VASP if the following hold: there exist the two messages in the network, $m1$ is Ack sent by the user to the VASP, $m2$ is Bill seemingly sent by the VASP to the user in response to $m1$, and the random number is used in $m1$.

Given a VASP, a random number and two messages $m1, m2$, sdcm corresponds to that the VASP sends a Clear message to the broker if the following hold: there exist the two messages in the network, $m1$ is Ack sent to the VASP, $m2$ is Pay sent to the VASP, the sources of the both messages are the same, the random number is used in $m1$, the signature in $m1$ is valid, and the e-cash in $m2$ is a preimage of the e-cash in $m1$.

The CafeOBJ action operators are defined with equations by describing how the observable values change if the corresponding transition rules are executed. For example, sdcm is defined as follows:

```
op c-sdcm : Protocol Vasp Rand Msg Msg -> Bool
eq c-sdcm(P,V,R,M1,M2)
   = M1 \in nw(P) and M2 \in nw(P) and am?(M1) and pm?(M2) and V = ad(M1) and
     V = pd(M2) and as(M1) = ps(M2) and k(c1(M1)) = h1(comp(pub(s(ps(M2))),s(V)),R) and
     g(c1(M1)) = sig(s(ps(M2)),h3(pub(s(ps(M2))),pub(s(V)),R,V,ec(c1(M1)))) and
     ec(c1(M1)) = f(ecr(ec(M2)),t(ec(M2)) + bill(P,V,ps(M2))) .
eq bill(sdcm(P,V,R,M1,M2),V1,U1) = bill(P,V1,U1) .
eq ec(sdcm(P,V,R,M1,M2),U1,V1)   = ec(P,U1,V1) .
eq ur(sdcm(P,V,R,M1,M2))         = ur(P) .
eq uecrv(sdcm(P,V,R,M1,M2))      = uecrv(P) .
ceq nw(sdcm(P,V,R,M1,M2))
    = cm(V,V,broker,enc(k(V),ec(M2),ps(M2),g(c1(M1)),ec(c1(M1)),R)) , nw(P)
    if c-sdcm(P,V,R,M1,M2) .
ceq sdcm(P,V,R,M1,M2)            = P if not c-sdcm(P,V,R,M1,M2) .
```

P, V, R, M1, M2 are CafeOBJ variables for the intended sorts. broker denotes the legitimate broker. sdcm(P,V,R,M1,M2) denotes the successor state. pm? checks if a message is Pay. as and ad return the source and destination of an Ack message, and ps and pd return those of a Pay message. s, pub, comp, sig and enc are data constructors for private keys, public keys, their compositions such as $(g^u)^v$, users' signatures and cipher texts, respectively. The first arguments of sig and enc are private keys and symmetric keys. ec returns e-cash in a cipher text or a Pay message. f denotes F, and ecr and t return α_0 and x of $F^x(\alpha_0)$. Operator c-sdcm denotes effective conditions of transition rules corresponding to sdcm. If a transition rule corresponding to sdcm is executed in a state in which the effective condition is true, a Clear message is put into the network in the successor state. The other action operators are defined in the same way.

5.5 Formalization of the Intruder

Part of the intruder has been modeled as the network. We have defined what information the intruder can glean from the network. We describe what messages the intruder fakes based on the gleaned information in this subsection.

The transition rules corresponding to the intruder's faking messages are divided into six classes, each of which fakes each type of messages. The effective condition of these transition rules are that the intruder can take advantage of the necessary information to fake messages.

The CafeOBJ action operator corresponding to transition rules faking Init messages is declared in the main module as follows:

```
bop fkim1 : Protocol User Vasp        -> Protocol
```

The CafeOBJ action operators corresponding to transition rules faking Resp messages are declared in the main module as follows:

```
bop fkrm1 : Protocol Vasp User Rand Hash2 -> Protocol
bop fkrm2 : Protocol Vasp User Rand Hash1 -> Protocol
bop fkrm3 : Protocol Vasp User Rand Secret -> Protocol
bop fkrm4 : Protocol Vasp User Rand Secret -> Protocol
```

The CafeOBJ action operators corresponding to transition rules faking Ack messages are declared in the main module as follows:

```
bop fkam1 : Protocol User Vasp Cipher1                -> Protocol
bop fkam2 : Protocol User Vasp Hash1   Sig   Ecash    -> Protocol
bop fkam3 : Protocol User Vasp Rand    Secret Sig   Ecash -> Protocol
bop fkam4 : Protocol User Vasp Rand    Secret Ecash   -> Protocol
```

The CafeOBJ action operator corresponding to transition rules faking Bill messages is declared in the main module as follows:

```
bop fkbm1 : Protocol Vasp User Tick -> Protocol
```

The CafeOBJ action operators corresponding to transition rules faking Pay messages are declared in the main module as follows:

```
bop fkpm1 : Protocol User Vasp Ecash  Tick -> Protocol
bop fkpm2 : Protocol User Vasp ECRand Tick -> Protocol
```

The CafeOBJ action operators corresponding to transition rules faking Clear messages are declared in the main module as follows:

```
bop fkcm1 : Protocol Vasp Cipher2                      -> Protocol
bop fkcm2 : Protocol Vasp User Lkey Ecash Sig   Ecash Rand -> Protocol
bop fkcm3 : Protocol Vasp User Lkey Ecash Secret Ecash Rand -> Protocol
```

Those CafeOBJ action operators are defined with equations. For example, fkcm1 is defined as follows:

```
eq  bill(fkcm1(P,V,C2),V1,U1) = bill(P,V1,U1) .
eq  ec(fkcm1(P,V,C2),U1,V1)   = ec(P,U1,V1) .
eq  ur(fkcm1(P,V,C2))         = ur(P) .
eq  uecrv(fkcm1(P,V,C2))      = uecrv(P) .
ceq nw(fkcm1(P,V,C2))         = cm(iv,V,broker,C2) , nw(P) if C2 \in cci2(nw(P)) .
ceq fkcm1(P,V,C2)             = P                          if not(C2 \in cci2(nw(P))) .
```

Given a VASP and a cipher text encrypted with one of K_V's, fkcm1 corresponds to that the intruder fakes a Clear message containing the cipher text that is seemingly sent by the VASP to the broker if the cipher text is available to the intruder. The other action operators are defined in the same way.

6   Verification

6.1   Formalization of Property to Verify

According to the way of modeling the protocol, that the broker receives a valid Clear message implies that there exists the valid Clear message in the network, and that there exists a Pay message in the network implies that the user denoted by the first argument of the message has sent the Pay message. Consequently, non-overcharge property can be restated as follows: *if there exists a valid* Clear *message stating that a user pays the amount d ticks to a VASP, no matter who has sent the valid* Clear *message (namely that the first and second argument may be different), then there always exists a* Pay *message which first and second arguments are the user, which third argument is the VASP and that includes* $\alpha_{T-d'}$ *where* $d \leq d'$, which is described in CafeOBJ as follows:

Claim 0. *For any reachable* p : Protocol, *any* v1 v2 v3 : Vasp, *any* u1 u2 : User, *any* r1 : Rand, *any* ecrv1 : ECRandValue, *any* t1 t2 : Tick, *and some* t3 : Tick,

```
not(v1 = iv and u1 = iu) and
cm(v3,v1,broker,enc(k(v1),f(ecr(u2,v2,ecrv1),t1),u1,
                     sig(s(u1),h3(pub(s(u1)),pub(s(v1)),r1,v1,f(ecr(u2,v2,ecrv1),t2))),
                     f(ecr(u2,v2,ecrv1),t2),r1)) \in nw(p)
implies pm(u1,u1,v1,f(ecr(u2,v2,ecrv1),t3)) \in nw(p) and t3 =< t1
```

iv and iu denote the intruder as a VASP and a user. If the protocol is performed by broker, iv and iu, namely the legitimate broker and the intruder, then it is clear that this setting breaks the property concerned because the intruder can fake any Clear message stating that iu pays any amount to iv. That is why the first conjunct of the premise of the property is added.

6.2   Verification Outline

Claim 0 and a few necessary lemmas are proved by simple case analysis only, and the remaining lemmas by induction described in Sect. 2.2. In any case, we write proof scripts in CafeOBJ. In this subsection, we outline how to write proof scripts in CafeOBJ if we prove a claim by induction.

Suppose that we prove that the protocol possesses a property denoted by $PROP(P, X)$ where P is a state of the protocol and X is any other parameters. We first write a module in which the property is declared. In the module called PRED, a constant x denoting arbitrary value corresponding to X is declared. The operator prop denoting the property and the equation defining it are also declared as follows:

```
op prop : Protocol SortX -> Bool
eq prop(P,X) = PROP(P,X) .
```

Let init denote any initial state of the protocol. To show that the property holds in any initial state, the following proof script is written:

```
open PRED
 red prop(init,x) .
close
```

CafeOBJ command `red` reduces a given term by regarding declared equations as left-to-right rewrite rules.

We next write a module in which the predicate to prove in each inductive step is declared. In the module called `ISTEP`, two constants `p` and `p'` are declared, denoting any (reachable) state and the successor state after executing a transition rule in `p`. The predicate to prove in each inductive step and the equation defining it are also declared as follows:

```
op istep : SortX -> Bool
eq istep(X) = prop(p,X) implies prop(p',X) .
```

In each inductive step, we usually split the state space into multiple sub-spaces, namely doing case analysis, and in each case we write a proof script that looks like the following:

```
open ISTEP
  Declare constants denoting arbitrary objects.
  Declare equations denoting the case or assumption.
  Declare equations denoting facts (e.g. from lemmas) if necessary.
  eq p' = action(p,...) .
  red istep(x) .
close
```

6.3   Verification of Claims

To prove Claim 0, we need 23 more claims as lemmas. The lemmas directly needed to prove Claim 0 are the following two:

Claim 13. *For any reachable* p : Protocol, *any* v1 v2 : Vasp, *any* u1 : User, *any* ec1 ec2 : Ecash, *any* r1 : Rand,

```
cm(v2,v1,broker,
    enc(k(v1),ec1,u1,sig(s(u1),h3(pub(s(u1)),pub(s(v1)),r1,v1,ec2)),ec2,r1)) \in nw(p)
implies
cm(v1,v1,broker,
    enc(k(v1),ec1,u1,sig(s(u1),h3(pub(s(u1)),pub(s(v1)),r1,v1,ec2)),ec2,r1)) \in nw(p)
```

Claim 23. *For any reachable* p : Protocol, *any* v1 v2 : Vasp, *any* u1 u2 : User, *any* r1 : Rand, *any* ecrv1 : ECRandValue, *any* t1 t2 : Tick, *and some* t3 : Tick,

```
not(v1 = iv and u1 = iu) and
cm(v1,v1,broker,enc(k(v1),f(ecr(u2,v2,ecrv1),t1),u1,
                    sig(s(u1),h3(pub(s(u1)),pub(s(v1)),r1,v1,f(ecr(u2,v2,ecrv1),t2))),
                    f(ecr(u2,v2,ecrv1),t2),r1)) \in nw(p)
implies pm(u1,u1,v1,f(ecr(u2,v2,ecrv1),t3)) \in nw(p) and t3 =< t1
```

In this subsection, we describe part of the proof of Claim 23 using the following claim as lemma:

Claim 21. *For any reachable* p : Protocol, *any* u1 : User, *any* v1 : Vasp, *any* ec1 : Ecash,

```
pm(u1,iu,v1,ec1) \in nw(p) implies u1 = iu
```

The claim says that if there exists a Pay message which second argument is the intruder, then the first argument is always the intruder, namely that the message has always been sent by the intruder.

Proof of Claim 23. We first write a module in which the property to prove is declared. In the module called PRED0, nine constants (v1, v2, u1, u2, r1, ecrv1, t1, t2, t3) denoting any objects with the intended sorts are declared. The operator p23 denoting the property and the corresponding equation are also declared as follows:

```
op p23 : Protocol Vasp Vasp User User Rand ECRandValue Tick Tick Tick -> Bool
eq p23(P,V1,V2,U1,U2,R1,ECRV1,T1,T2,T3)
   = not(V1 = iv and U1 = iu) and
   cm(V1,V1,broker,enc(k(V1),f(ecr(U2,V2,ECRV1),T1)),U1,
       sig(s(U1),h3(pub(s(U1)),pub(s(V1))),R1,V1,f(ecr(U2,V2,ECRV1),T2))),
       f(ecr(U2,V2,ECRV1),T2),R1)) \in nw(P)
   implies  pm(U1,U1,V1,f(ecr(U2,V2,ECRV1),T3)) \in nw(P) and T3 =< T1 .
```

where P, V1, V2, U1, U2, R1, ECRV1, T1, T2 and T3 are CafeOBJ variables.

Base Case. In any initial state init, to show that the property holds, the following proof script is described and executed by the CafeOBJ system:

```
open PRED0
  red p23(init,v1,v2,u1,u2,r1,ecrv1,t1,t2,t3) .
close
```

Inductive Step. The predicate to prove in each inductive step is defined in module ISTEP23, in which two constants (p, p') are declared. The predicate and the corresponding equation are declared as follows:

```
op istep23 : Vasp Vasp User User Rand ECRandValue Tick Tick Tick -> Bool
eq istep23(V1,V2,U1,U2,R1,ECRV1,T1,T2,T3)
   = p23(p,V1,V2,U1,U2,R1,ECRV1,T1,T2,T3)
     implies
     p23(p',V1,V2,U1,U2,R1,ECRV1,T1,T2,T3) .
```

All we have to do is to show istep23(v1,v2,u1,u2,r1,ecrv1,t1,t2,t3) for every transition rule. In this paper, we describe proof scripts showing that any transition rule denoted by sdcm preserves property p23. For the proof that sdcm preserves p23, the state space is split into five cases basically according to the effective condition and a new message added into the network as follows:

1		u1 = iu	clear1 = clear2
2	c-sdcm(p,v10,r10,m10,m20)		not(clear1 = clear2)
3		not(u1 = iu)	clear1 = clear2
4			not(clear1 = clear2)
5	not c-sdcm(p,v10,r10,m10,m20)		

clear1 and clear2 are supposed to be the following:

```
clear1 = cm(v1,v1,broker,enc(k(v1),f(ecr(u2,v2,ecrv1),t1)),u1,
            sig(s(u1),h3(pub(s(u1)),pub(s(v1))),r1,v1,f(ecr(u2,v2,ecrv1),t2))),
            f(ecr(u2,v2,ecrv1),t2),r1))
clear2 = cm(v10,v10,broker,enc(k(v10),ec(m20),as(m10),
            sig(s(as(m10)),h3(pub(s(as(m10)))),
                pub(s(v10)),r10,v10,f(ecr(ec(m20)),t(ec(m20)) + bill(p,v10,as(m10)))))),
            f(ecr(ec(m20)),t(ec(m20)) + bill(p,v10,as(m10))),r10))
```

Each case is denoted by the predicate obtained by connecting ones appearing in the row with conjunction. For example, case 1 means any state satisfying c-sdcm(p,v10,r10,m10,m20) and u1 = iu and clear1 = clear2.

In this paper, we show the proof script for case 1 as follows:

```
open ISTEP23
-- arbitrary objects
  op v10 : -> Vasp . op r10 : -> Rand . ops m10 m20 : -> Msg . op nw10 : -> Network .
-- assumptions
  -- c-sdcm(p,v10,r10,m10,m20)
  eq nw(p) = m10 , m20 , nw10 . eq am?(m10) = true . eq pm?(m20) = true .
  eq ad(m10) = v10 . eq pd(m20) = v10 . eq ps(m20) = as(m10) .
  eq k(c1(m10)) = h1(comp(pub(s(ps(m20))),s(v10)),r10) .
  eq g(c1(m10)) = sig(s(ps(m20)),h3(pub(s(ps(m20))),pub(s(v10)),r10,v10,ec(c1(m10)))) .
  eq ec(c1(m10)) = f(ecr(ec(m20)),t(ec(m20)) + bill(p,v10,ps(m20))) .
  --
  eq u1 = iu .
  -- clear1 = clear2
  eq f(ecr(u2,v2,ecrv1),t1) = ec(m20) . eq as(m10) = iu . eq r1 = r10 . eq v1 = v10 .
  eq ecr(ec(m20)) = ecr(u2,v2,ecrv1) . eq t2 = (t(ec(m20)) + bill(p,v10,as(m10))) .
-- facts
  eq pc(m20) = iu . -- from Claim 21 (due to pm(pc(m20),iu,v10,ec(m20)) \in nw(p))
-- successor state
  eq p' = sdcm(p,v10,r10,m10,m20) .
-- check if the property is also true in p'.
  eq t3 = t1 . -- for some t3
  red istep23(v1,v2,u1,u2,r1,ecrv1,t1,t2,t3) .
close
```

In the proof script, constants are first declared, which denote any objects with the intended sorts. Equations are next declared, which define assumptions for each case. Claim 21 is used as lemma. The equation which left-hand side is p' defines that constant p' denotes the successor state.

The size of all the proof scripts is approximately of 22,000 lines. It took about 5 minutes to have the CafeOBJ system execute the proof scripts on a laptop with 850MHz Pentium III processor and 512MB memory.

7   Concluding Remarks

Several methods of formally analyzing security protocols have been proposed. But most of them focus on authentication protocols. There are few case studies reported that formally analyze payment protocols, especially micropayment protocols. To the best of our knowledge, we are the first to analyze the Horn-Preneel micropayment protocol formally.

Our approach is similar to Paulson's Inductive Method[15] supported by the theorem prover Isabelle/HOL. The main difference is that our approach uses rewriting only to prove a security protocol safe and does not use any heavy and slow operations such as (higher-order) unification.

The mutual authentication between a user and a VASP relies on K. We have verified as lemma that the intruder cannot glean any K shared with a trustable user and a trustable VASP, which assures that the intruder cannot impersonate a trustable user or VASP to authenticate him/her to a trustable VASP or user.

The lessons learned through the case study are as follows:

- The formalization of messages such that the actual sender of each message is included in the message as meta-information is useful to formulate and verify properties such as the one concerned in this paper.
- Algebraic specification languages can be used to appropriately describe (models of) security protocols because various data structures such as bags can be defined adequately and abstract machines can be defined as well.

- Writing middle-sized proof scripts in an algebraic specification language is manageable, although some kind of tool-support should be useful such as automatic generation of outline of proof scripts and/or (semi-)automatic case analysis.
- The performance of the CafeOBJ system is quite well.

In this case study, a micropayment protocol has been analyzed with respect to only one property, although a few dozens of properties have been verified as lemmas. We will identify and formulate what properties a micropayment protocol should possess and verify that the Horn-Preneel micropayment protocol possesses the properties.

References

1. Bellare, M., Garay, J.A., Hauser, R., Herzberg, A., Krawczyk, H., Steiner, M., Tsudik, G., Herreweghen, E.V., Waidner, M.: Design, implementation and deployment of the iKP secure electronic payment system. IEEE Journal of Selected Areas in Communications **18** (2000) 611–627
2. MasterCard/Visa: SET secure electronic transactions protocol. Book One: Business Specifications, Book Two: Technical Specification, Book Three: Formal Protocol Definition (http://www.setco.org/set_specifications.html) (1997)
3. Micali, S., Rivest, R.L.: Micropayments revisited. In: Progress in Cryptology – CT-RSA 2002. LNCS 2271, Springer (2002) 149–163
4. Horn, G., Preneel, B.: Authentication and payment in future mobile systems. In: Computer Security – ESORICS 98. LNCS 1485, Springer-Verlag (1998) 277–293
5. Hauser, R., Steiner, M., Waidner, M.: Micro-payments based on iKP. In: 14th Worldwide Congress on Computer and Communications Security Protection. (1996) 67–82
6. Lowe, G.: An attack on the Needham-Schroeder public-key authentication protocol. Inf. Process. Lett. **56** (1995) 131–133
7. CafeOBJ: CafeOBJ web page. http://www.ldl.jaist.ac.jp/cafeobj/ (2001)
8. Diaconescu, R., Futatsugi, K.: CafeOBJ report. AMAST Series in Computing, 6. World Scientific, Singapore (1998)
9. Ogata, K., Futatsugi, K.: Rewriting-based verification of authentication protocols. In: WRLA '02. Volume 71 of ENTCS., Elsevier Science Publishers (2002)
10. Goguen, J., Malcolm, G.: A hidden agenda. Theor. Comput. Sci. **245** (2000) 55–101
11. Chandy, K.M., Misra, J.: Parallel program design: a foundation. Addison-Wesley, Reading, MA (1988)
12. Pedersen, T.P.: Electronic payments of small amounts. In: Security Protocols. LNCS 1189, Springer-Verlag (1996) 59–68
13. Lamport, L.: Passward authentication with insecure communications. Comm. ACM **24** (1981) 770–772
14. Dolev, D., Yao, A.C.: On the security of public key protocols. IEEE Trans. Inform. Theory **IT-29** (1983) 198–208
15. Paulson, L.C.: The inductive approach to verifying cryptographic protocols. J. Comput. Security **6** (1998) 85–128
16. Schneider, S.: Verifying authentication protocols in CSP. IEEE Trans. Softw. Eng. **24** (1998) 741–758

Action Refinement from a Logical Point of View

Mila Majster-Cederbaum, Naijun Zhan, and Harald Fecher

Lehrstuhl für Praktische Informatik II,
Fakultät für Mathematik und Informatik,
Mannheim Universität,
D7,27, 68163, Mannheim, Deutschland
{mcb,zhan,hfecher}@pi2.informatik.uni-mannheim.de

Abstract. Action refinement provides a mechanism to design a complex reactive system hierarchically. This paper is devoted to action refinement from a logical point of view, and to combining the hierarchical implementation of a complex system with the hierarchical specification of the system in order to verify it in an easy way. To this end, we use a TCSP-like language with an action refinement operator as a modeling language, and an extension of the modal μ-calculus, called FLC (Fixpoint Logic with Chop) [18], as a specification language. Specifications in FLC can be refined via a mapping that takes as arguments an abstract specification ϕ for the process P, an action a of P and a specification ψ for the process Q that may refine a and produces a refined specification. We prove under some syntactical conditions: if $Q \models \psi$ then $P \models \phi$ iff $P[a \rightsquigarrow Q]$ satisfies the refined specification. Therefore our approach supports 'a priori' verification in system design and can be used to decrease substantially the complexity of verification.

Keywords: action refinement, modal logics, specification, verification, reactive systems

1 Introduction

Generally speaking, it is not easy, even impossible to capture a complex system at the beginning. *The hierarchical development methodology* is useful to understand a complex system. It has made a great success in sequential programming, and is known as *top-down system specification and analysis technique.* [3,9,20] introduced this method into process algebraic settings, called *action refinement*, that provides a mechanism to hierarchically develop concurrent systems. In this method, how to relate a hierarchical specification of a complex system with its hierarchical implementation (abstraction) in order to simplify verification is a challenging problem. In the literature, some first attempts to solve this problem are given, for example in [12,14,15].

The main results obtained in [12,14,15] are as follows: A model of a system is represented by processes or synchronization structures, and a specification of a system is given in terms of modal logic formulae. Then define action refinement both for the model and specification by refinement of a primitive of the abstract

L. Zuck et al. (Eds.): VMCAI 2003, LNCS 2575, pp. 253–267, 2003.
© Springer-Verlag Berlin Heidelberg 2003

model. [12] coped with action refinement for models from a semantic point of view, whereas [14,15] dealt with it from a syntactic point of view, but they both considered *action refinement for the specification* as a form of *syntactical transformation*. In detail, let P stand for a high level system, ϕ for its specification, Q for the refinement of an abstract action a in P, $\rightsquigarrow$ for refinement relations both for the model and the specification. Then the main result of [12,14,15] can be re-illustrated as follows:

$$
\begin{array}{ccc}
P & \models & \phi \\
& \updownarrow & \\
P[a \rightsquigarrow Q] & \models & \phi[a \rightsquigarrow Q]
\end{array}
$$

where $\phi[a \rightsquigarrow Q]$ stands for substituting $\langle a \rangle$ and $[a]$ in ϕ by some formulae of forms $\langle a_1 \rangle \langle a_2 \rangle \ldots \langle a_n \rangle$ and $[a_1][a_2] \ldots [a_n]$ respectively, where $a_1 a_2 \ldots a_n$ is a run of Q. These results support 'a priori' verification in the following sense: Assume that $P \models \phi$ has been established and ϕ is refined to $\phi[a \rightsquigarrow Q]$ then we automatically obtain a process satisfying $\phi[a \rightsquigarrow Q]$. The analogous remark is true when we refine P to $P[a \rightsquigarrow Q]$. Then we obtain automatically a refined formula that is satisfied by the refined process.

In both approaches, the refinements of the specification are explicitly built on the structure of Q. This restricts the refinement step in two ways: firstly, there are properties of the refined system that cannot be deduced in the setting of [12, 14]. For example, let $P = a; b+a; c$, $\phi = \langle a \rangle$, $Q = a'; (c'; b'; d'+c'; b')$. It's obvious that $P \models \phi$ and $Q \models \langle a' \rangle [c'] \langle b' \rangle$. It is expected that $P[a \rightsquigarrow Q] \models \langle a' \rangle [c'] \langle b' \rangle$. But it cannot be derived using the approaches of [12,14]. Secondly, the refinement step is restricted to one choice of Q for refining an action a, which appears both in the refined process and the refined specification explicitly. In contrast to this we allow action a in P, where $P \models \phi$, to be refined by any process Q that satisfies a specification ψ and show that the refined system $P[a \rightsquigarrow Q]$ satisfies the refined specification under some conditions.

In this paper, we propose a general approach to construct a specification of a low-level complex reactive system based on a higher-level specification and the properties of the refinement of an abstract action. To this end, we also model processes by a TCSP-like language and use FLC as a specification language. The basic idea of our work is to define a refinement mapping Ω which maps a high-level specification ϕ and the properties ψ of the refinement of an abstract action a to a lower-level specification by substituting ψ for $\langle a \rangle$ and $[a]$ in ϕ. For example, in the above example, we can get $\Omega(\phi, \langle a' \rangle [c'] \langle b' \rangle, a) = \langle a' \rangle [c'] \langle b' \rangle$ which is exactly what we expect.

A safety property stipulates that some 'bad thing' does not happen during execution, whereas *a liveness property* stipulates that a 'good thing' eventually happens during execution. Therefore safety properties are completely different from liveness properties. [4] proved that every property can be represented as the conjunction of a safety property and a liveness property in linear models, a similar result for tree models was shown in [5]. On the other hand, the properties of a system also can be classified into *universal* and *existential*. So by our intuition, a refinement mapping should be property-preserving, i.e. a safety property should be refined to a safety property and similarly for the other properties.

We can show the following theorem, called Refinement Theorem, that says: If $Q \models \psi$ and some other conditions hold then

$$P \qquad \models \qquad \phi$$
$$\Updownarrow$$
$$P[a \rightsquigarrow Q] \qquad \models \qquad \Omega(\phi, \psi, a)$$

To achieve the intended result, two tasks have to be done: the first one is to select a specification language in which we can implement our idea of refinement. The suitable candidate could be the μ-calculus since most modal and temporal logics that are used as specification languages for concurrent systems can be reduced to it. Unfortunately, the μ-calculus is not suitable for such a task. For example, suppose that $P \models \langle a \rangle \phi_1$, and there is no occurrence of $\langle a \rangle$ or $[a]$ in ϕ_1, and that $Q \models \psi$. After refining a by Q in P, a specification for the refined system that one expects should be naturally $\psi(\phi_1)$ which means that the behavior of the system can be divided into two successive segments such that the former satisfies ψ and the second one meets ϕ_1. But this is no longer a formula of the μ-calculus. Therefore, here we use an extension of the μ-calculus, FLC [18] as a specification language. FLC has a sequential composition operator, called '*chop*' operator (denoted by $\diamondsuit$). Informally, $P \models \phi \diamondsuit \psi$ means that there exists a behaviour of P which can be divided into two successive segments such that the first satisfies ϕ and the second meets ψ. Therefore, the idea of refinement can be implemented as syntactical substitution in this logic. In the above example, if $\langle a \rangle \diamondsuit \phi_1$ is a formula FLC, after substituting ψ for $\langle a \rangle$, the refined formula $\psi \diamondsuit \phi_1$ is still a formula of FLC. Furthermore, the refined formula expresses the expected meaning. In FLC, a safety property can be represented in the form $\nu X.([b] \diamondsuit false) \wedge ([a] \diamondsuit X)$ and a liveness property can be expressed in the form $\mu X.(\langle a \rangle \diamondsuit true) \vee (\langle b \rangle \diamondsuit X)$ (See [23]).

A second issue is the atomicity of action refinement for models. One of our aims in this work is to establish a correspondence between hierarchical implementations and hierarchical specifications, but if we allow that the refining process can be interleaved with others problems will arise. E.g. $(a \parallel_{\{\}} b)[a \rightsquigarrow a_1; a_2]$ means the parallel executions of a and b in which a is refined by $a_1; a_2$. It's obvious that $a \parallel_{\{\}} b$ satisfies $\langle a \rangle$, and $a_1; a_2$ satisfies $\langle a_1 \rangle \diamondsuit (\langle a_2 \rangle \wedge [b] \diamondsuit false)$ which means that $a_1; a_2$ firstly performs a_1, then follows a_2 but cannot perform b. We expect that $a \parallel_{\{\}} b$ meets $\langle a_1 \rangle \diamondsuit (\langle a_2 \rangle \wedge [b] \diamondsuit false)$ after refining a by $a_1; a_2$. This is not true in the case of non-atomic action refinement since b can be performed between the execution of a_1 and a_2, but it is valid if we assume that action refinement is atomic [6,8]. So, in the sequel, we discuss action refinement for models under the assumption of atomicity.

Due to the limitation of space, we will omit all proofs for the theorems and lemmas in this paper. The detailed proofs can be found in [16].

The remainder of this paper is organized as follows: A modeling language is defined in Section 2; Section 3 briefly reviews FLC. A refinement mapping for specifications is given in Section 4. The correspondence between the hierarchical specification and the hierarchical implementation of a complex system is shown in Section 5. Finally, a brief conclusion is given in Section 6.

2   Modeling Language – A TCSP-Like Process Algebra

2.1   Syntax

As in [14], we use a TCSP-like process algebra in combination with an action refinement operator as a modeling language. We use Act (ranged over by $a, b, c, \ldots$) to stand for an infinite set of (atomic) actions, $\sqrt{}$ for a special terminating action that only can be performed by the terminated process, A for a subset of Act. $Act \cup \{\sqrt{}\}$ is ranged over by $\gamma, \ldots$. Let $\mathcal{X}$ be a set of process variables (ranged over by $x, y, z, \ldots$).

We consider to refine an action by a finite process. Furthermore, it is prohibited to refine an action by a terminated process, which is not only counter-intuitive but also technically difficult, as discussed, e.g. in [21]. Therefore, we define two classes of process expressions. The first are finite and are used as refining processes, the other represent processes that may be refined.

Definition 1. *Let $\mathcal{F}$ be the set of finite processes (ranged by $Q, Q', Q_1, \ldots$) generated by the following grammar:*

$$Q ::= a \mid (Q_1 + Q_2) \mid (Q; Q) \mid Q[a \rightsquigarrow Q'].$$

$\mathcal{P}$ be the set of all closed terms generated by the following grammar:

$$P ::= \delta \mid nil \mid a \mid x \mid P_1; P_2 \mid P_1 + P_2 \mid P_1 \parallel_A P_2 \mid rec\ x.P \mid P[a \rightsquigarrow Q]$$

where $Q \in \mathcal{F}$.

An occurrence of a process variable $x \in \mathcal{X}$ is called *bound* in a process expression P iff it does occur within a suberm of the form $rec\ x.P'$, otherwise called *free*. A process expression P is called *closed* iff all occurrences of all variables occuring in it are bound, otherwise it is called *open*.

Intuitively, $P[a \rightsquigarrow Q]$ means that the system replaces the execution of an action a by the execution of the subsystem Q every time when the subsystem P performs a. This operator provides a mechanism to hierarchically design reactive systems. The other expressions of $\mathcal{P}$ can be understood as usual.

Sometimes, we abuse $Act(P)$ to stand for the set of actions which occur in P. We use $F_{act}(P)$ to stand for the set of actions that is possibly performed by P immediately, i.e. $F_{act}(nil) = F_{act}(\delta) = F_{act}(x) = \emptyset$; $F_{act}(a) = \{a\}$; $F_{act}(P_1; P_2) =$ if $F_{act}(P_1) \neq \emptyset$ or $P_1 \equiv \delta$ then $F_{act}(P_1)$ else $F_{act}(P_2)$; $F_{act}(P_1 + P_2) = F_{act}(P_1 \parallel_A P_2) = F_{act}(P_1) \cup F_{act}(P_2)$; $F_{act}(rex\ x.P) = F_{act}(P)$; $F_{act}(P[a \rightsquigarrow Q]) =$ if $a \notin F_{act}(P)$ then $F_{act}(P)$ else $F_{act}(P) \cup F_{act}(Q) - \{a\}$.

Traces and runs of a process P are defined as in [11]. For example, the traces of the process $a; b + a; c$ are $\varepsilon, a, a; b$ and $a; c$, whereas its runs are $a; b$ and $a; c$, where ε stands for empty trace. We use $Tr(P)$ to denote the set of traces of P, and $Run(P)$ the set of its runs. The standard operators on traces and runs of processes will be used, e.g. $\frown$ for catenation, $\upharpoonright$ for restriction.

2.2   Operational Semantics

A transition system is a triple $\mathcal{T} = (S, A, \rightarrow)$ where S is a set of states or processes, A is a set of labels, and $\rightarrow \subseteq S \times A \times S$. Sometimes we use transition systems with initial states, $(S, A, \rightarrow, P_0)$, where $P_0 \in S$.

Here we define the operational semantics of the language by labeled transition systems where $\sqrt{}$-labeled transitions are deterministic and final. The meaning of the constructs can be defined in the standard way except for the refinement operator. In order to guarantee the atomicity of the refinement, the basic idea is to define a transition system for the process that maybe be refined, then replace all transitions labeled by the action to be refined by the transition system for the refinement.

Similar to [10], the above idea can be implemented by introducing an auxiliary operator $*$ to indicate that a process prefixed with it is the remainder of some process, which has the highest execution precedence and must be executed atomically. The operator is used to guarantee the atomicity of refinements of actions. The intermediate language, denoted by $\mathcal{P}^*$, ranged over by $s, \ldots$, is given by:

$$s \quad ::= nil \mid \delta \mid a \mid x \mid *s \mid s; s \mid P + P \mid s \parallel_A s \mid s[a \rightsquigarrow Q] \mid rec\ x.P$$

where $P \in \mathcal{P}, Q \in \mathcal{F}$.

Definition 2. *Let $\sqrt{}$ and* **ab** *be the minimal relations on $\mathcal{P}^*$ which satisfy the following rules respectively:*

$\dfrac{}{\sqrt{(nil)}}$ $\quad \dfrac{\sqrt{(s)}}{\sqrt{(*s)}}$ $\quad \dfrac{\sqrt{(s_1)}\ \sqrt{(s_2)}}{\sqrt{(s_1 \parallel_A s_2)}}$ $\dfrac{}{\sqrt{(rec\ x.s)}}$ $\quad \dfrac{}{\sqrt{(s_1; s_2)}}$ $\dfrac{}{\sqrt{(s[a \rightsquigarrow Q])}}$	$\dfrac{\sqrt{(s)}}{\textbf{ab}(s)}$ $\quad \dfrac{\textbf{ab}(s_1)\ \textbf{ab}(s_2)}{\textbf{ab}(s_1; s_2)}$ $\quad \dfrac{\textbf{ab}(s)}{\textbf{ab}(s[a \rightsquigarrow Q])}$ $\textbf{ab}(\delta)$ $\quad \textbf{ab}(s_1 + s_2)$ $\quad \textbf{ab}(rec\ x.s)$ $\textbf{ab}(a)$ $\quad \textbf{ab}(s_1 \parallel_A s_2)$ $\textbf{ab}(x)$ $where\ Q \in \mathcal{F}.$
Definition of $\sqrt{}$	*Definition of* **ab**

Note that $\sqrt{(s)}$ means that s terminates after executing the terminated action $\sqrt{}$; $\textbf{ab}(s)$ means that s is in the $*$-free fragment of $\mathcal{P}^*$.

A process s is called *abstract* if $\textbf{ab}(s)$, otherwise, called *concrete* . For technical reason, as in [10], we require the following well-formedness conditions on $\mathcal{P}^*, \mathcal{P}$ and $\mathcal{F}$: None of operands of $+$ meets the predicate $\sqrt{}$; Furthermore, recursion is allowed on guardedness in the presence of ; only. $*s$ behaves like s except that the execution of $*s$ can not be interleaved with others and it is to be executed before abstract processes.

An operational semantics of the process algebra is given by the following inference rules:

Nil $nil \xrightarrow{\surd} \delta$ Act $a \xrightarrow{a} nil$

Nd $\dfrac{s_1 \xrightarrow{a} s_1'}{s_1+s_2 \xrightarrow{a} s_1' \text{ and } s_2+s_1 \xrightarrow{a} s_1'}$ Seq-1 $\dfrac{s_1 \xrightarrow{a} s_1'}{s_1;s_2 \xrightarrow{a} s_1';s_2}$

Seq-2 $\dfrac{s_1 \xrightarrow{\surd} s_1' \quad s_2 \xrightarrow{a} s_2'}{s_1;s_2 \xrightarrow{a} s_2'}$ Ref-1 $\dfrac{s \xrightarrow{b} s'}{s[a \leadsto Q] \xrightarrow{b} s'[a \leadsto Q]} \quad a \neq b$

Ref-2 $\dfrac{s \xrightarrow{a} s' \quad Q \xrightarrow{a'} Q'}{s[a \leadsto Q] \xrightarrow{a'} (*Q');s'[a \leadsto Q]}$ Rec $\dfrac{s_1[rec\ x.s_1/x] \xrightarrow{a} s_1'}{rex\ x.s_1 \xrightarrow{a} s_1'}$

S-1 $\dfrac{s \xrightarrow{a} s'}{*s \xrightarrow{a} *s'}$ Syn1 $\dfrac{s_1 \xrightarrow{\surd} s_1' \text{ and } s_2 \xrightarrow{\surd} s_2'}{s_1 \|_A s_2 \xrightarrow{\surd} s_1' \| s_2'}$

S-2 $\dfrac{s_1 \xrightarrow{a} s_1'}{s_1 \|_A s_2 \xrightarrow{a} s_1' \|_A s_2 \text{ and } s_2 \|_A s_1 \xrightarrow{a} s_2 \|_A s_1'} \quad a \notin A \wedge \mathbf{ab}(s_2)$

Syn2 $\dfrac{s_1 \xrightarrow{a} s_1' \quad s_2 \xrightarrow{a} s_2'}{s_1 \|_A s_2 \xrightarrow{a} s_1' \|_A s_2' \text{ and } s_2 \|_A s_1 \xrightarrow{a} s_2' \|_A s_1'} \quad a \in A \wedge (\mathbf{ab}(s_1) \wedge \mathbf{ab}(s_2))$

Syn3 $\dfrac{s_1 \xrightarrow{a} s_1' \quad s_2 \xrightarrow{a} s_2'}{s_1 \|_A s_2 \xrightarrow{a} s_1' \|_A s_2' \text{ and } s_2 \|_A s_1 \xrightarrow{a} s_2' \|_A s_1'} \quad a \in A \wedge (\neg\mathbf{ab}(s_1) \wedge \neg\mathbf{ab}(s_2))$

Definition 3. – *A binary symmetric relation R over the closed terms of $\mathcal{P}^*$ is a strong bisimulation if for all $(s_1, s_2) \in R$ and $s_1 \xrightarrow{\gamma} s_1'$, there exists s_2' such that $s_2 \xrightarrow{\gamma} s_2'$ and $(s_1', s_2') \in R$.*
– *s_1 and s_2 are strong bisimilar, denoted by $s_1 \cong s_2$, if and only if there exists a strong bisimulation R such that $(s_1, s_2) \in R$.*

According to the above semantics, it is easy to show that

Lemma 1. *For any closed term $s \in \mathcal{P}^*$, $s \cong *s$.*

Since a concrete process can not communicate with an abstract process, so $\cong$ is not preserved by $\|_A$ in $\mathcal{P}^*$. Even more $\cong$ is not a congruence relation over the language $\mathcal{P}$. For example, $a_1; a_2 \cong a[a \leadsto a_1; a_2]$, but $(a_1; a_2) \|_{\{\}} b \not\cong a[a \leadsto a_1; a_2] \|_{\{\}} b$. However, once we strengthen Definition 3 by adding the following condition:

– If $\mathbf{ab}(s_1)$ then $\mathbf{ab}(s_2)$

then the resulting largest bisimulation, denoted by $\cong_{\mathbf{ab}}$, is a congruence relation over $\mathcal{P}^*$. Besides, obviously, $\cong_{\mathbf{ab}}$ is a proper subset of $\cong$. That is,

Lemma 2. $\cong_{\mathbf{ab}} \subset \cong$.

Theorem 1. $\cong_{\mathbf{ab}}$ *is a congruence over $\mathcal{P}^*$.*

3   Specification Language – FLC

3.1   Syntax and Semantics of FLC

Let $X, Y, Z, \ldots$ range over an infinite set Var of *variables*, $p, q, r, \ldots$ over an assumed finite set $Prop$ of *atomic propositions*, that contains *true* and *false*.

The formulae of FLC are generated according to the following grammar:

$$\phi ::= p \mid term \mid X \mid [a] \mid \langle a \rangle \mid \phi \wedge \phi \mid \phi \vee \phi \mid \phi \Diamond \phi \mid \mu X.\phi \mid \nu X.\phi,$$

where $p \in Prop, X \in Var$ and $a \in Act$.

In the later, $\boxed{a}$ stands for $\langle a \rangle$ or $[a]$, op for $\wedge$ or $\vee$, and σ for μ or ν.

As in the modal μ-calculus, the two *fixpoint operators* μX and νX bind the respective variable X and we will apply the usual terminology of *free* and *bound* variables in a formula, *closed* and *open* formulae etc. $term, p, \langle a \rangle$ and $[a]$ are called *atomic formulae*. We say that X is guarded in ϕ if each occurrence of X is within some sub-formula $\boxed{a}\Diamond\psi$. $\mu X.X$ is equivalent to *false* and $\nu X.X$ is equivalent to *true*. It is easy to show that every closed formula is equivalent to a formula in which all variables are guarded.

The FLC is interpreted over a given labeled transition system $T = (S, Act, \rightarrow)$. Furthermore, an *interpretation* $\mathcal{I} \in (Prop \mapsto 2^S)$ is assumed, which assigns to each atomic proposition the set of states for which it is valid, and satisfies that $\mathcal{I}(false) = \emptyset$ and $\mathcal{I}(true) = S$. The meaning of variables is given by an *environment* $\varrho : Var \mapsto (2^S \mapsto 2^S)$ that maps variables to monotonic functions from sets to sets. $\varrho[X \mapsto f]$ agrees with ϱ except for associating f with X. The formulae of FLC are interpreted as *monotonic predicate transformers* that are simply mappings $f : 2^S \mapsto 2^S$ which are monotonic w.r.t. the inclusion ordering on 2^S. We use MPT_T to represent all these monotonic predicate transformers over S. MPT_T together with the inclusion ordering defined by $f \subseteq f'$ iff $f(A) \subseteq f'(A)$ for all $A \subseteq S$ forms a complete lattice. We denote the join and meet operators by $\sqcup$ and $\sqcap$. By Tarski-Knaster Theorem [24], the least and greatest fixed points of monotonic functions: $(2^S \mapsto 2^S) \mapsto (2^S \mapsto 2^S)$ exist. They are used to interpret the fixed point formulae.

The predicate transformer assigned to an formula ϕ, denoted by $\mathcal{C}_T^{\mathcal{I}}(\phi)(\varrho)$, is inductively constructed as follows:

$$
\begin{aligned}
\mathcal{C}_T^{\mathcal{I}}(p)(\varrho)(E) &= \mathcal{I}(p) \\
\mathcal{C}_T^{\mathcal{I}}([a])(\varrho)(E) &= \{s \mid \forall s' : s \xrightarrow{a} s' \Rightarrow s' \in E\} \\
\mathcal{C}_T^{\mathcal{I}}(\langle a \rangle)(\varrho)(E) &= \{s \mid \exists s' : s \xrightarrow{a} s' \wedge s' \in E\} \\
\mathcal{C}_T^{\mathcal{I}}(\phi_1 \wedge \phi_2)(\varrho)(E) &= \mathcal{C}_T^{\mathcal{I}}(\phi_1)(\varrho)(E) \cap \mathcal{C}_T^{\mathcal{I}}(\phi_2)(\varrho)(E) \\
\mathcal{C}_T^{\mathcal{I}}(\phi_1 \vee \phi_2)(\varrho)(E) &= \mathcal{C}_T^{\mathcal{I}}(\phi_1)(\varrho)(E) \cup \mathcal{C}_T^{\mathcal{I}}(\phi_2)(\varrho)(E) \\
\mathcal{C}_T^{\mathcal{I}}(X)(\varrho) &= \varrho(X) \\
\mathcal{C}_T^{\mathcal{I}}(\mu X.\phi)(\varrho) &= \sqcap\{f \in MPF_T \mid \mathcal{C}_T^{\mathcal{I}}(\phi)(\varrho[X \rightsquigarrow f]) \subseteq f\} \\
\mathcal{C}_T^{\mathcal{I}}(\nu X.\phi)(\varrho) &= \sqcup\{f \in MPF_T \mid \mathcal{C}_T^{\mathcal{I}}(\phi)(\varrho[X \rightsquigarrow f]) \supseteq f\} \\
\mathcal{C}_T^{\mathcal{I}}(term)(\varrho)(E) &= E \\
\mathcal{C}_T^{\mathcal{I}}(\phi_1 \Diamond \phi_2)(\varrho) &= \mathcal{C}_T^{\mathcal{I}}(\phi_1)(\varrho) \cdot \mathcal{C}_T^{\mathcal{I}}(\phi_2)(\varrho)
\end{aligned}
$$

where $\cdot$ stands for the compositional operator over functions, $\setminus$ for the complementary operator over sets.

The set of processes *satisfying* a given closed formula ϕ is $\phi(S)$. A process P with associated rooted transition system $((S_P, Act(P), \rightarrow_P), P)$, where S_P

stands for the set of states in the transition system, is said to satisfy ϕ iff $P \in \mathcal{C}_T^{\mathcal{I}}(\phi)(\varrho)(S_P)$ for some interpretation $\mathcal{I}$ and environment ϱ, denoted by $P \models \phi$. $\phi \Leftrightarrow \psi$ denotes that for any process P with associated rooted transition system $T = ((S_P, Act(P), \rightarrow_P), P)$, $\mathcal{C}_T^{\mathcal{I}}(\phi)(\varrho)(E) = \mathcal{C}_T^{\mathcal{I}}(\psi)(\varrho)(E)$ for any $E \subset S_P$, interpretation $\mathcal{I}$, and environment ϱ. The other notations can be defined in a standard way.

[18] proved that FLC is strictly more expressive than the μ-calculus since context-free processes can be characterized in it; FLC is decidable for finite-state processes, undecidable for context-free processes, satisfiability and validity of it are undecidable; And FLC does not enjoy the finite-model property. [13] presented a model-checking algorithm of FLC for finite-state processes.

For the sake of proving technique, we introduce approximants of fixed point formulae. Let $\alpha, \beta, \lambda \in \mathcal{O}n$, the ordinals, there λ is a limit ordinal. Then $\mu^0 X.\phi_1 = false$, $\mu^{\alpha+1} X.\phi_1 = \phi_1\{\mu^\alpha X.\phi_1/X\}$, $\mu^\lambda X.\phi_1 = \bigvee_{\alpha < \lambda} \mu^\alpha X.\phi_1$. $\nu^0 X.\phi_1 = true$, $\nu^{\alpha+1} X.\phi_1 = \phi_1\{\nu^\alpha X.\phi_1/X\}$, $\nu^\lambda X.\phi_1 = \bigwedge_{\alpha < \lambda} \nu^\alpha X.\phi_1$. Note that by Tarski and Knaster's Theorem, $\mu X.\phi \Leftrightarrow \bigvee_{\alpha \in \mathcal{O}n} \mu^\alpha X.\phi$ and $\nu X.\phi \Leftrightarrow \bigwedge_{\alpha \in \mathcal{O}n} \nu^\alpha X.\phi$. If only finite state processes are considered $\mathcal{O}n$ can be replaced by ω, moreover, if P is a finite-state process then $P \models \sigma X.\phi$ iff $P \models \sigma^k X.\phi$ where $\sigma \in \{\nu, \mu\}$, and k is the number of the states or processes of the rooted transition system associating with P. As shown in [7], we can show that $\mathcal{O}n$ can be replaced by ω_1, where ω_1 stands for the first uncountable limit ordinal.

Convention: In the sequel, we assume that the unary operators have the highest precedence, $\Diamond$ has a priority to other binary operators, $\vee$ and $\wedge$ have the same precedence too, but they have a priority over $\Rightarrow$ and $\Leftrightarrow$ in order to avoid the excessive use of brackets and improve the readability.

3.2   Normal Form

In this subsection, we define a special subset of FLC, called *normal form formulae (nff for short)*. Intuitively, a normal form formula exactly corresponds to a formula of the μ-calculus if we omit *term* and the 'chop' operator occurring in it. [18] pointed out that the modal μ-calculus can be encoded into FLC straightforwardly by replacing $\langle a \rangle \Diamond \phi$ and $[a] \Diamond \phi$ for $\langle a \rangle \phi$ and $[a]\phi$ respectively. This implies that the expressiveness of the subset is at least as powerful as the modal μ-calculus.

Definition 4. *Given a formula $\phi \in FLC$, we define its* runs *as follows:*

$$Run(\phi) \triangleq \begin{cases} \{\varepsilon\} & \text{if } \phi = p, term, \text{ or } X \\ \{a\} & \text{if } \phi = \boxed{a} \\ Run(\phi_1) \cup Run(\phi_2) & \text{if } \phi = \phi_1 \, op \, \phi_2 \\ \{s^\frown t \mid s \in Run(\phi_1) \wedge t \in Run(\phi_2)\} & \text{if } \phi = \phi_1 \Diamond \phi_2 \\ \bigcup_{\alpha < \mathcal{O}n} Run(\sigma^\alpha X.\phi_1) & \text{if } \phi = \sigma X.\phi_1 \end{cases}$$

where ε stands for the empty run that has the property $s\widehat{\ }\varepsilon = s = \varepsilon\widehat{\ }s$ for any run s. The set of traces of ϕ is defined as $Tr(\phi)\widehat{=}\{s \mid s \in Run(\phi) \vee \exists s'.s\widehat{\ }s' \in Run(\phi)\}$.

Definition 5. *A formula which is of the following form is called* normal form:

$$\psi ::= p \mid X \mid term \mid \boxed{a} \mid \boxed{a}\Diamond\psi \mid \psi\, op\, \psi \mid \sigma X.\psi.$$

The set of nffs is denoted by $\mathcal{NF}$. For simplicity, we use cnff *for closed normal form formula.*

Definition 6. *Given a nff ϕ, we define its first non-trivial atomic sub-formula as follows:*

$$FSub(\phi) \widehat{=} \begin{cases} \{\} & \text{if } \phi = p, X, \text{ or term} \\ \{\langle a\rangle\} & \text{if } \phi = \langle a\rangle \text{ or } \langle a\rangle\Diamond\phi_1 \\ \{[a]\} & \text{if } \phi = [a] \text{ or } [a]\Diamond\phi_1 \\ FSub(\phi_1) \cup FSub(\phi_2) & \text{if } \phi = \phi_1\, op\, \phi_2 \\ FSub(\phi_1) & \text{if } \phi = \sigma X.\phi_1 \end{cases}$$

The set of first actions of ϕ is defined as: $F_{act}(\phi)\widehat{=}\{a \mid \boxed{a} \in FSub(\phi)\}$. The set of key actions of ϕ w.r.t. P, denoted by $K_{act}(\phi, P)$, is defined as: $K_{act}(\phi, P)\widehat{=}\{a \mid \exists s \in Tr(\phi).s \in Run(P) \wedge s\widehat{\ }a \notin Run(P) \wedge s\widehat{\ }a \in Tr(\phi)\}$.

Example 1. Given a formula $\phi\widehat{=}\langle a\rangle\Diamond\langle b\rangle \wedge [c]\Diamond\langle e\rangle\Diamond[f]$, $FSub(\phi) = \{\langle a\rangle, [c]\}$, the set of its first actions is $\{a, c\}$, and the set of its key actions w.r.t. $P\widehat{=}a; b+c; (e+d)$ is $\{f\}$.

Remark 1. The intention of key actions is to avoid the case that $P \models \phi$ and $Q \models \psi$, but $P;Q \not\models \phi\Diamond\psi$, because ϕ concerned some execution of Q. For instance, in the above example, let $Q\widehat{=}f;g$ and $\psi\widehat{=}\langle f\rangle\Diamond\langle g\rangle$. It's obvious that $P \models \phi$ and $Q \models \psi$, but $P;Q \not\models \phi\Diamond\psi$ since $K_{act}(\phi, P) \cap F_{act}(Q) \neq \emptyset$.

Definition 7. *A formula $\phi \in \mathcal{NF}$ is called* existential formula *if $\forall a \in Act.[a] \notin FSub(\phi)$. We use $\mathcal{ENF}$ to stand for the set of existential formulae. Dually, a formula $\phi \in \mathcal{NF}$ is called* universal formula *if $\forall a \in Act.\langle a\rangle \notin FSub(\phi)$. We use $\mathcal{UNF}$ to stand for the set of universal formulae. For technical reasons, we stipulate term $\notin \mathcal{UNF}$. A formula is called* property formula *if $\phi \Leftrightarrow \phi_1 \wedge \phi_2$, where $\phi_1 \in \mathcal{ENF}$ and $\phi_2 \in \mathcal{UNF}$. The set of property formulae is denoted by $\mathcal{PNF}$. A formula ϕ is called* pure path formula *if all variables occurring in it are guarded and no propositional letter occurs in it.*

For $\mathcal{NF}, \mathcal{ENF}, \mathcal{UNF}$, we have

Theorem 2. $\mathcal{NF}, \mathcal{ENF}, \mathcal{UNF}$ *are closed under all operators of the logic. I.e., there exists a $\psi \in \mathcal{NF}(\mathcal{ENF},\mathcal{UNF})$ which is equivalent to $\phi\, op\, \varphi$ or $\sigma X.\phi$ for any closed ϕ and φ, if $\phi, \varphi \in \mathcal{NF}(\mathcal{ENF},\mathcal{UNF})$ where $op \in \{\vee, \wedge, \Diamond\}$.*

FLC does not have finite model property [18], i.e., not all of satisfiable formulae of FLC have a finite model, but [13] showed that it has the tree model property, that is

Theorem 3. *If $s_1 \cong s_2$, then for any closed formula ϕ, $s_1 \models \phi$ iff $s_2 \models \phi$.*

4   Hierarchically Specifying Complex Reactive Systems

As the complexity of reactive system designs becomes overwhelming very quickly, methods which allow to develop designs in a hierarchical fashion must be supported by the design formalisms employed. Such methods allow to develop a design on different levels of abstraction thereby making the development procedure more transparent and thus tractable: Most likely, a developer first divides the intended (complex) design into various "sub-designs" to capture the abstract overall structure of the complete design. Subsequently, the sub-designs will be developed by enriching them step by step with details. This is the design technique usually encountered in practice, see e.g. in [22]. In the algebraic settings, action refinement as introduced in Section 2 supports the hierarchical design. In this section we investigate how to provide such technique in a logical framework.

To this end, we define a refining mapping which substitutes the properties of the refinement of an abstract action for the ones of the abstract action in a high-level specification and produces a lower-level specification. In a logical framework, actions are addressed as modalities and descriptions of systems are represented by formulae. In most modal logics, there are two kinds of modalities, i.e. $\langle a \rangle$ and $[a]$ which are used to express existential and universal properties respectively. By our intuition, a refinement mapping should be property-preserving, i.e. an existential property should be refined to an existential property and similarly for the other properties. Otherwise, the mapping is meaningless since it's impossible to establish a correspondence between action refinement for models and action refinement for specifications. For example, $P \hat{=} a; b + a; c \models \langle a \rangle \Diamond \langle b \rangle$, $a_1; a_2 \models [a_1] \Diamond \langle a_2 \rangle$, but $P[a \rightsquigarrow a_1; a_2] \not\models ([a_1] \Diamond \langle a_2 \rangle) \Diamond \langle b \rangle$, since in the high-level specification, $\langle a \rangle \Diamond \langle b \rangle$ is an existential liveness property, however its refinement becomes a universal liveness property.

To ensure the mapping is property-preserving, we partition the property ψ of the refinement of a into two parts: existential property ψ_1 and universal property ψ_2 i.e. $\psi \in \mathcal{PNF}$. $[a]$ will be replaced by ψ_2, and $\langle a \rangle$ will be replaced by ψ_1. This is justified by the result shown in [5] that any property can be expressed as the intersection of a liveness property and a safety property in branching temporal logics. So, $\mathcal{PNF}$ is powerful enough to define the properties of reactive systems.

Therefore, we define the refinement mapping as follows:

Definition 8. *Suppose $\phi \in \mathcal{NF}$ is a high-level specification, a is an abstract action to be refined, $\psi \Leftrightarrow \psi_1 \wedge \psi_2 \in \mathcal{PNF}$ is the description of the refinement of a where $\psi_1 \in \mathcal{ENF}$ and $\psi_2 \in \mathcal{UNF}$. We define the refinement mapping, denoted by $\Omega(\phi, \psi, a)$, as $\phi\{\psi_1/\langle a \rangle, \psi_2/[a]\}$.*

According to the above definition, we have the following results.

Lemma 3. *Suppose X does not occur in ψ. Then*

$$\Omega(\phi_1\{\phi_2/X\}, \psi, a) \Leftrightarrow \Omega(\phi_1, \psi, a)\{\Omega(\phi_2, \psi, a,)/X\}.$$

Lemma 4. *If $\phi \Leftrightarrow \phi'$ then $\Omega(\phi, \psi, a) \Leftrightarrow \Omega(\phi', \psi, a)$.*

Theorem 4 (Applicability). *If $\phi \in \mathcal{NF}$ and $\psi \in \mathcal{PNF}$, then $\Omega(\phi, \psi, a) \in \mathcal{NF}$; If $\phi, \psi \in \mathcal{PNF}$, then $\Omega(\phi, \psi, a) \in \mathcal{PNF}$.*

We give the following example which is firstly given in [8] to demonstrate how to use our approach to hierarchically specify a complex systems.

Example 2. Suppose that a salesman has to go by car from his office in Paris to another office in London and work there for some time, and then has to go back to Paris repeatedly. He takes a hovercraft to cross the Channel.

At the beginning, we can specify the system as:

$$\phi \hat{=} \nu X. \begin{pmatrix} \langle leave\_Paris \rangle \Diamond [fr\_through\_the\_Channel] \\ \Diamond \langle arrive\_in\_London \rangle \Diamond \langle work \rangle \Diamond \langle leave\_London \rangle \\ \Diamond [gb\_through\_the\_Channel] \Diamond \langle arrive\_in\_Paris \rangle \Diamond X \end{pmatrix}.$$

Then, we can refine $x\_through\_the\_Channel$ by a process with the property

$$\psi_x \hat{=} \begin{pmatrix} [x\_load] \Diamond [x\_departure] \Diamond \langle cross\_the\_Channel \rangle \\ \Diamond \langle \overline{x}\_arrival \rangle \Diamond \langle \overline{x}\_unload \rangle \wedge true \end{pmatrix}.$$

Further, we can refine $x\_departure$ by a process with the property

$$\psi_2 \hat{=} [finish\_loading] \Diamond \langle engine\_on \rangle \Diamond \langle bye - bye \rangle \wedge true$$

where $finish\_loading$ signals the end of loading, and $cross\_the\_Channel$ by a process with the property

$$\psi_3 \hat{=} \langle sit\_down \rangle \Diamond (\begin{matrix} \langle newspaper \rangle \Diamond (\langle tea \rangle \vee \langle coffee \rangle) \\ \vee (\langle tea \rangle \vee \langle coffee \rangle) \Diamond \langle newspaper \rangle \end{matrix}) \Diamond \langle stand\_up \rangle \wedge true.$$

Hence, the final system should satisfy the specification given by

$$\Omega(\phi, \Omega(\Omega(\psi_1, \psi_2, x\_departure), \psi_3, cross\_the\_Channel), x\_through\_the\_Channel).$$

Where $x \in \{fr, gb\}$, and if $x = fr$ then $\overline{x} = gb$ else $\overline{x} = fr$.

5   Hierarchically Verifying Complex Reactive Systems

In this section we establish a correspondence presented by the Refinement Theorem below between action refinement for models and action refinement for specification. It states that if $Q \models \psi$ then under certain syntactical conditions $P \models \phi$ iff $P[a \rightsquigarrow Q] \models \Omega(\phi, \psi, a)$. This result supports 'a priori' verification. In the development process we start with $P \models \phi$ and either refine P and obtain automatically a (relevant) formula that is satisfied by $P[a \rightsquigarrow Q]$. Or, we refine ϕ using $\Omega(\phi, \psi, a)$ and obtain automatically a refined process $P[a \rightsquigarrow Q]$ that satisfies the refined specification. Of course such refinement steps may be iterated.

It's possible that ψ only describes the partial execution of Q, so the semantic model of the refined specification cannot be simulated by the refined system.

Therefore, $P \models \phi$ and $Q \models \psi$, but $P[a \rightsquigarrow Q] \not\models \Omega(\phi, \psi, a)$. For example, it's obvious that $a; b + a; c \models \phi \hat{=} \langle a \rangle \Diamond \langle b \rangle$ and $a_1; a_2 \models \psi \hat{=} \langle a_1 \rangle$, but $(a; b + a; c)[a \rightsquigarrow a_1; a_2] \not\models \langle a_1 \rangle \Diamond \langle b \rangle$. In order to solve such a problem, we define a bridging formula $Br(\psi, Q)$ which depends on Q and ψ and will be appended to ψ such that $\psi \Diamond Br(\psi, Q)$ describes the full execution of Q, as follows:

Definition 9. *Given a sequence of actions s and a set of sequences of actions D, we define the distance from s to D, denoted by $d(s, D)$, as $d(s, D) = $ if $s \in D$ or $\exists s_1, s_2.s = s_1\hat{\ }s_2 \wedge s_1 \in D$ or $D = \emptyset$ then 0 else $min\ \{|s_2| \mid s_1\hat{\ }s_2 \in D \wedge \forall 1 \leq i \leq |s_1|.s(i) = s_1(i) \wedge |s| > |s_1| \Rightarrow s_2(1) \neq s(|s_1| + 1)\}$, where $|s|$ stands for the length of s, $s(i)$ for the ith element of sequence s. Suppose B is another set of sequences of actions, we define $d(B, A) = max\ \{d(s, A) \mid s \in B\} \cup \{0\}$.*

Definition 10. *Given a process P and a formula ϕ, we define a bridging formula as follows: $Br(\phi, P) \hat{=} term \vee \mu^{d(Run(\phi), Run(P))+1} X.(term \vee (\bigvee_{a \in Act(P)} \langle a \rangle) \Diamond X)$. For example, in the above example, $Br(\langle a_1 \rangle, a_1; a_2) = term \vee \langle a_1 \rangle \vee \langle a_2 \rangle$. It is easy to show that $(a; b + a; c)[a \rightsquigarrow a_1; a_2] \models (\langle a_1 \rangle \Diamond Br(\langle a_1 \rangle, a_1; a_2)) \Diamond \langle b \rangle$.*

Lemma 5. $P \models \phi$ *iff* $P \models \phi \Diamond Br(\phi, P)$.

In the following Refinement Theorem, $Act(P) \cap Act(Q) = \emptyset$ ensures that no deadlock will be introduced or removed by action refinement.

For the first part of the theorem, it is possible that ψ describes some properties concerning some partial or full executions of $P'[a \rightsquigarrow Q]$, $Q; P'[a \rightsquigarrow Q]$ or $Q; Q$ but it is not satisfied by them, where P' is P itself or one of its derivatives. For instance, let $P \hat{=} a; b; c$, $\phi \hat{=} \langle a \rangle \Diamond \langle b \rangle$, $Q \hat{=} a_1$, and $\psi \hat{=} \langle a_1 \rangle \Diamond [b] \Diamond \langle d \rangle$. It is obvious that $P \models \phi$ and $Q \models \psi$ but $P[a \rightsquigarrow Q] \not\models \Omega(\phi, \psi \Diamond Br(\psi, Q), a)$. Therefore, we stipulate that $K_{act}(\psi, Q) \cap (Act(P) \cup F_{act}(Q)) = \emptyset$ and $F_{act}(\psi) \cap Act(P) = \emptyset$ in order to avoid such case.

For the second part of the theorem, it must be ensured that P performs the action a according to ϕ iff $P[a \rightsquigarrow Q]$ performs some actions of Q according to ψ in $\Omega(\phi, \psi, a)$. Otherwise, the converse is not true. For instance, let $P \hat{=} a; b; c$, $\phi \hat{=} [a] \Diamond \langle c \rangle$, $Q \hat{=} d; e$, $\psi \hat{=} true$. It's obvious that $P[a \rightsquigarrow Q] \models \Omega(\phi, \psi, a)$, but $P \not\models \phi$. So we require $Run(\psi) \subseteq Tr(Q) \upharpoonright_{Act}$ and ψ is a pure path formula.

Theorem 5 (Refinement Theorem).
If $Q \models \psi$ and $Act(P) \cap Act(Q) = \emptyset$ then

- *if $K_{act}(\psi, Q) \cap (Act(P) \cup F_{act}(Q)) = \emptyset$ and $F_{act}(\psi) \cap Act(P) = \emptyset$, then $P \models \phi$ implies $P[a \rightsquigarrow Q] \models \Omega(\phi, \psi \Diamond Br(\psi, Q), a)$;*
- *if $Run(\psi) \subseteq Tr(Q) \upharpoonright_{Act}$, and ψ is a pure path formula then $P[a \rightsquigarrow Q] \models \Omega(\phi, \psi, a)$ implies $P \models \phi$.*

Where $\psi \in \mathcal{PNF}, \phi \in \mathcal{NF}$.

Remark 2. Assume the number of actions and conbinators occuring in Q and P are n and m respectively, the number of atomic formulae and connectives occuring in ψ is l. Then the complexity of checking the syntactical constraints is in $\mathcal{O}(ln^2(m + n))$. On the other hand, FLC model checking is in EXPTIME

(See [13]). Therefore, using the above theorem, model-checking for a complex reactive system will be reduced to model-checking of its simple abstraction and the refinement of a primitive of the system, and this will indeed decrease the complexity of verification of the system.

We will continue Example 2 to show how to apply the Refinement Theorem to verify a complex system hierarchically.

Example 3. At the beginning, we can implement the system as

$$Sys \triangleq fr\_Channel\|_{\{fr\_through\_the\_Channel\}} salesman$$
$$\|_{\{gb\_through\_the\_Channel\}} gb\_Channel.$$

Where

$$x\_Channel \triangleq rec\, y.x\_through\_the\_Channel; y,$$

and

$$salesman \triangleq rec\, x.leave\_Paris;\, fr\_through\_the\_Channel;\, arrive\_in\_London;$$
$$work;\, leave\_London;\, gb\_through\_the\_Channel;\, arrive\_in\_Paris;\, x.$$

It's obviously, $Sys \models \phi$.

Then, $x\_through\_the\_Channel$ is implemented by

$$subsys_x \triangleq x\_load\|_{\{x\_load\}} Channel$$

where

$$Channel \triangleq fr\_platform\|_{\{fr\_arrival, fr\_departure\}} hovercraft$$
$$\|_{\{gb\_arrival, gb\_departure\}} gb\_platform\,,\ \text{where}$$
$$hovercraft \triangleq fr\_departure;\, cross\_the\_Channel;\, gb\_arrival+$$
$$gb\_departure;\, cross\_the\_Channel;\, fr\_arrival,$$
$$x\_platform \triangleq x\_load;\, x\_departure + x\_arrival;\, x\_unload.$$

It's easy to show that $subsys_x \models \psi_x$.

Further, we can refine $x\_departure$ by $subsys_2$ and $cross\_the\_Channel$ by $subsys_3$, where,

$$subsys_2 \triangleq finishing\_loading;\, engine\_on;\, bye - bye,$$
$$subsys_3 \triangleq sit\_down;\, ((coffee + tea)\|_{\{\}} newspaper);\, stand\_up.$$

Certainly, $subsys_2 \models \psi_2$ and $subsys_3 \models \psi_3$.

The final system is obtained as:

$$Sys[x\_through\_the\_Channel \rightsquigarrow subsys_x \begin{bmatrix} x\_departure \rightsquigarrow subsys_2, \\ cross\_the\_Channel \rightsquigarrow subsys_3 \end{bmatrix}].$$

Where $x \in \{fr, gb\}$. According to the Refinement Theorem, the final system satisfies the final specification.

6   Concluding Remarks

In this paper, we present an approach to refine an abstract specification by defining a refinement mapping from a high-level specification and the properties of the refined lower-level component to a lower-level specification. Furthermore, we show $P \models \phi$ iff $P[a \rightsquigarrow Q] \models \Omega(\phi, \psi, a)$ provided $Q \models \psi$ and some syntactical conditions hold.

Similar results are shown in [12,14,15], but in their approaches, a refined specification is obtained from the original specification and the refinement Q. Therefore, some interesting expected properties of the refined system cannot be derived using their approaches. Besides, we can show that their approaches can be seen as a special case of our method presented in this paper from a constructing specification point of view. [2] discussed composing, refining specifications of reactive systems as some sound rules of a logic. [1] considered the problem given a low-level specification and a higher-level specification, how to construct a mapping from the former to the latter in order to guarantee the former implements the latter. Our refinement mapping Ω maps the abstract specification to the detailed specification, i.e. we go the converse direction.

In our framework, composing specifications also can be dealt with, for example, supposing $P \models \phi$ and $Q \models \psi$, we can get a composite specification like $\phi \diamond Br(\phi, P) \diamond \psi$ for $P; Q$. We would like to leave more detailed discussion related to this topic for the full version of this paper.

In this paper, we used the standard interleaving setting, so we only consider the case of atomic action refinement. In fact, we believe our approach can be applied to the case of non-atomic action refinement, too, if a suitable specification language is available. For example, we can extend νTrPTL [19] with 'chop' and its duality as a specification language.

References

1. M. Abadi and L. Lamport. The existence of refinement mappings. *Theoretical Computer Science*, 82:253–284, 1991.
2. M. Abadi and G. Plotkin. A logical view of composition and refinement. *Theoretical Computer Science*, 114:3–30, 1993.
3. Aceto L. and Hennessy. M, Towards action refinement in process algebra. Proc. LICS'89, 138–145,1989.
4. Bowen Alpern and Fred B. Schneider. Defining liveness. *Information Processing Letters*, 21:191–185, 1995.
5. A. Bouajjani, J.C. Fernandez, S. Graf, C. Rodriguez, and J. Sifakis. Safety for branching time semantics. 18th ICALP,July 1991, LNCS 510, pp. 76–92.
6. G. Boudol. Atomic actions. *Bull. European Assoc. The. Com. Sci.* 38:136–144.
7. J.C. Bradfield. *Verifying Temporal Properties of Systems*. Birkhäuser Boston, Mass.
8. P. Degano and R. Gorrieri, Atomic Refinement in Process Description Languages. TR 17–91 HP Pisa Center, 1991.
9. R.J. van Glabbeek and F.W. Vaandrager. Petri nets models for algebraic theories of concurrency. Proc. PARLE conference, Eindhoven, The Netherlands 1987, Vol. II (Parallel Languages), LNCS 259, pp. 224–242.
10. R. Gorrieri and A. Rensink. Action refinement. *Handbook of Process Algebra*, Elsevier Science, 1047–1147. 2001.
11. C.A.R. Hoare. *Communicating Sequential Processes*, Prentice-Hall, 1985.
12. Michaela Huhn. Action refinement and properties inheritance in systems of sequential agents. CONCUR'96, LNCS 1119, pp. 263–277.

13. Martin Lange and Colin Stirling. Model checking fixed point logic with chop. FOSSACS 2002, LNCS 2303, pp. 250–263.
14. Mila Majster-Cederbaum and Frank Salger. Correctness by construction: towards verification in in hierarchical system development. SPIN 2000, LNCS 1885, pp. 163–180.
15. Mila Majster-Cederbaum and Frank Salger. A priori verification of reactive systems. In Eds T. Bolognesi, D. Latella: Formal Methods for Distributed System Development. pp.35–50. Kluwer Publishers, 2000.
16. Mila Majster-Cederbaum, Naijun Zhan and Harald Fecher. Action refinement from a logical point view. To appear as a research report.
17. R. Milner. Communication and Concurrency. Prentice Hall, 1989.
18. Markus Müller-Olm. A Modal Fixpoint Logic with Chop. STACS'99, LNCS 1563, pp. 510–520.
19. Peter Niebert. A ν-calculus with local views for systems of sequential agents. MFCS'95, LNCS 969, pp.563–573.
20. M. Nielsen, U. Engberg and K.S. Larsen. Fully abstract models for a process language with refinement. Proc. REX School on Linear Time, Branching Time and Partial Order in Logics and Models for Concurrency, 1989, LNCS 354, pp. 523–548.
21. A. Rensink. *Models and Methods for Action Refinement*. PhD thesis, University of Twente, Enschede, Netherlands, Aug. 1993.
22. J. Sifakis. Research directions for concurrency. *ACM Computing Surveys*, 28(4es):55. 1996.
23. C. Stirling. Modal and temporal logics for processes, Banff Higher Order Workshop 1995, LNCS 1043, pp. 149–237.
24. A. Tarski. A lattice-theoretical fixpoint theorem and its application. *Pacific J. Math.*, 5:285–309, 1955.

Reasoning about Layered Message Passing Systems

B. Meenakshi and R. Ramanujam

The Institute of Mathematical Sciences
Chennai 600113, India.
{bmeena,jam}@imsc.res.in

Abstract. Lamport diagrams are partial orders which depict computations of message passing systems. It is natural to consider generalizations of linear time temporal logics over such diagrams. In [MR00], we presented a decidable temporal logic with local temporal modalities and a global 'previous' modality to talk of message receipts. It seems reasonable to extend the logic with a global 'next' modality as well, so that sending of messages may also be easily specified, but this (or other similar attempts) lead to undecidability. Hence we consider ways of restricting the models so as to obtain decidability, while retaining the expressiveness of global 'next' and global 'previous' modalities. For this, we consider Lamport diagrams presented as a sequence of *layers*. The layers themselves describe finite communication patterns and a diagram is obtained by sequential composition of such parallel processes. The logic is defined appropriately, with layer formulas describing processes within a layer, and temporal formulas describing the sequence of layers in the computation. When the number of events in layers is uniformly bounded and each layer is communication closed, we get decidability. Alternatively, a stronger uniform bound on what we term channel capacity also yields decidability. We present an example of system specification in the logic.

1 Summary

Consider a distributed protocol which consists of a fixed finite set of agents, which are sequential programs themselves and which exchange messages between each other. A computation of such a protocol can be depicted as a diagram, where the events of each agent in the computation are given in a line, and the sending and receipt of messages between agents are depicted by arrows between the lines. What the diagram represents is a partial order on the set of events that occur during the computation, with their projection for each agent forming a linear order. The ordering relation captures the causal dependence of events that constitute receipt of messages on their corresponding send events. We refer to such partial orders as Lamport Diagrams (LDs)([La78]). What would be an appropriate temporal logic to reason about systems whose behaviours are Lamport diagrams ? One option is to consider the set of all sequentializations of all the behaviours, so that standard linear time temporal logics (LTL) may be

L. Zuck et al. (Eds.): VMCAI 2003, LNCS 2575, pp. 268–282, 2003.

employed. There are many drawbacks to such an approach. For one, it is very easy to come up with diagrams whose sequentializations constitute non-regular languages.[1] Since LTL cannot express such languages, the diagrams specified would have to then exclude such behaviour. (For instance consider the producer — consumer example depicted in Figure 1; considering only finite behaviours, its sequentializations give us the language with all sequences over a's and b's, with every prefix having at least as many a's as b's, a context-free language.) The other drawback is that such a logic specifies how the global histories of the system may evolve; we would like to specify the effect of message passing in the systems described, and this is more naturally done using local histories of agents in the system rather than using the global histories of the system.

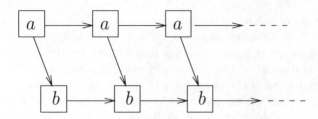

Fig. 1. Lamport diagram of the producer — consumer problem

Another option is to interpret the logic directly over Lamport Diagrams themselves, in the spirit of **locally based linear time logics** ([Thi94], [APP95], [Ra96], [Pe00]). In these logics, the formulas are interpreted on events in the partial order, and the modalities constrain the causal ordering appropriately. This approach directly addresses the second issue, in the sense that prime configurations of diagrams (on which formulas are interpreted) represent local histories and the modalities describing the covering relation of the partial order may be used to specify the effect of message passing. Coming to the technical issue of expressiveness, we then are faced with the question of whether formulas of such a logic describe regular sets of diagrams. This is the central issue addressed in this paper.

Thus, what we seek is a temporal logic where the behaviour of a distributed system may be specified structurally for each agent in the system. For each agent, we would like to specify conditions on when that agent may send a message, and what the agent would do on receipt of a message. Further, a sender (receiver) may specify what information is conveyed through the message it sends (receives). It is easy to define a logic which is essentially an indexed version of LTL for each agent, with two additional modalities: $\mathbf{X}\alpha$, asserted by the sender of a message,

---

[1] In itself, this may not be a problem, as a reviewer points out; however, the associated language inclusion problem (typically) tends to be undecidable.

that α holds on receipt, and $\mathbf{Y}\alpha$, asserted by the receiver of a message, that α held at the time of sending the message.

In [MR00] we studied m-LTL, a local temporal logic on Lamport diagrams. This logic is essentially like the one described above, except that it only has a modality analogous to the $\mathbf{Y}\alpha$ described above, and without the $\mathbf{X}\alpha$. It was shown that the logic was decidable. The omission of the $\mathbf{X}$ modality was justified on essentially philosophical grounds (that a sender of a message cannot hope to have any certain knowledge of the state of the receiver at the time of receipt). As it turns out, this was a happy choice, since the logic with both of these modalities is undecidable, as we show here. On the other hand, [Pe00] considers a logic which (with some work) may be seen as a similar logic with the $\mathbf{X}$ modality and without the $\mathbf{Y}$ modality, which is again decidable.

Given that the logic with both $\mathbf{X}$ and $\mathbf{Y}$ modalities is undecidable and that we may get decidability retaining only one of them, we may look for logics 'in between'. Note that the requirement that we be able to specify conditions on when an agent may send a message may be met by including special 'send' propositions in the logic, as the decision is local. Similarly, what the agent would (locally) do on receipt of a message, may be specified (less naturally) using special 'receive' propositions. So we may consider a combination of the $\mathbf{Y}$ modality with special send propositions, or the $\mathbf{X}$ modality with special receive propositions. Both these logics turn out to be undecidable as well. (We could consider a locally based logic with neither $\mathbf{X}$ nor $\mathbf{Y}$ modalities but with only the special send and receive propositions; this would specify "pure" signalling systems rather than message passing systems. This may be of independent interest, but not relevant to the discussion in this paper.)

Faced with such undecidability, we turn our attention to the models, and look for what constraints may be placed on the Lamport diagrams so that decidability obtains. The first observation is that the undecidability results hold for models based on *finite* diagrams, and hence we need to somehow place bounds on the size of diagrams. We are therefore led to the consideration of Lamport diagrams that are obtained by concatenating bounded diagrams. Following this intuition, we define here a class of **Layered Lamport Diagrams** (LLDs), in such a way that every (countable) LD can be thought of as a (countable) concatenation of finite layers. Bounded LLDs are those where all layers are uniformly bounded.

Such a definition of layering allows very general ways of structuring distributed protocols in an *episodic* manner. The protocol itself is described using several possible episodes, each of which may be a pattern of communications with a bound on the number of messages used within the episode. The episode may be *communication closed*, or there may be *delays*, whereby messages sent during one episode may be received later, in another episode. Communication closed layering of systems is a concept that has been studied at length in the context of process algebra ([PZ92]). On the other hand, it is interesting to consider LLDs where the layers need not be communication closed. In such diagrams, the receipt of a message maybe delayed unboundedly, and a natural condition is to insist that this be bounded as well. Diagrams with uniformly bounded delays correspond to systems with bounded channel capacities, a class commonly studied in distributed computing.

The layering of Lamport diagrams suggests a similar structuring of specifications as well. We have layer formulas that come from a standard modal logic on finite partial orders, and temporal formulas which are built from these using the usual linear time connectives. In such a logic we can describe many interesting properties of LLDs. Specifications in this logic describe a sequential composition of parallel processes, rather than the other way around (in the sense of [AY99]).

Now we can show that undecidability obtains even when we restrict the size of layers to be uniformly bounded. However, imposing either of the restrictions, that the diagrams be communication closed, or that channel capacity be bounded along with a uniform bound on the size of the layers, leads to elementary decidability of the logic, though the complexity is high when layers are not communication closed. We also provide an example of system specification in the logic.

Lamport Diagrams bear a close resemblance to **Message Sequence Charts** (MSCs), a standard notation in the formal specification of communication protocols ([RGG96], [ITU97]). In fact, LDs can be seen as the partial orders generated by MSCs (in the obvious manner; for instance, see [AHP96]). Thus, LDs describe causality rather than messages as in MSCs; rather MSCs are intended as another specification language (like the temporal logics here) whose meanings may be given using semantic structures such as LDs. With such an understanding, layered diagrams with bounded and communication closed layers may be seen to correspond to the class of Message Sequence Graphs (MSGs) which are finite state automata with their nodes labelled by MSCs. Bounded LLDs which are not communication closed, but where delay is bounded, correspond to the class of Compositional Message Sequence Graphs (CMSGs) introduced by [GMP01].

We remark that the logics studied here are structural (in the sense of [Ma01]) rather than one defined on linearizations. Thus it is closer to TLC^- defined by [Pe00], rather than [AY99] who study MSCs in terms of their linearizations. As we have already remarked, many protocols (for example, the producer — consumer protocol) can be described by using bounded communication closed diagrams, though the associated set of linearizations is not a regular MSC language ([HMNT00]). [BL01] study Lamport diagrams with bounded channel capacity using a related logic which they call $LTML^-$, but again in terms of linearizations.

2   A Logic on Lamport Diagrams

Throughout the paper, we fix $n > 0$, and study distributed systems of n agents. We will follow the linguistic convention that the term 'system' will refer to composite distributed systems, and 'agent' to component processes in the system. We will refer to the agents by the indices i, $1 \leq i \leq n$. We will use the notation $[n]$ to denote the set $\{1, 2, \ldots, n\}$. We will denote the set of natural numbers by $\mathbb{N}$ and the natural ordering on them by $\leq_\mathbb{N}$.

2.1 Lamport Diagrams

Definition 2.1 *A **Lamport diagram** is a tuple $D = (E, \leq, \phi)$ where*

- *E is an at most countable set of* events.
- *$\leq \subseteq (E \times E)$ is a partial order called the* causality relation *such that for every $e \in E$, $\downarrow e \stackrel{\text{def}}{=} \{e' \in E \mid e' \leq e\}$ is finite.*
- *$\phi : E \to [n]$ is a* labelling *function which satisfies the following condition: Let $E_i \stackrel{\text{def}}{=} \{e \in E \mid \phi(e) = i\}$ and $\leq_i \stackrel{\text{def}}{=} \leq \cap (E_i \times E_i)$. Then, for every $i \in [n]$, $\leq_i$ is a total order on E_i.*

Since for all $e \in E$, $\downarrow e$ is finite, $\leq$ must be discrete. Hence there exists $\lessdot \subset \leq$, the *immediate causality relation*, which generates the causality relation; that is: for all e, e', e'', if $e \lessdot e'$ and $e \leq e'' \leq e'$ then $e'' \in \{e, e'\}$. We have: $\leq = (\lessdot)^*$. For $e, e' \in E$, define $e <_c e'$ iff $e \in E_i$, $e' \in E_j$, $i \neq j$ and $e \lessdot e'$. In this case, we interpret e as the sending of a message by agent i and e' as its corresponding receipt by j. Accordingly, if $e <_c e'$ then, e will be referred to as a **send** event and e' will be its corresponding **receive** event. An event e will be interpreted as a **local** event if there exists no e' such that $e <_c e'$ or $e' <_c e$.

Given a Lamport diagram $D = (E, \leq, \phi)$ and $E' \subseteq E$, the Lamport diagram induced by E' is defined as $D_{E'} = (E', \leq \cap (E' \times E'), \phi \restriction E')$ where $\phi \restriction E'$ denotes the projection of ϕ on E'.

2.2 Logic

Fix countable sets of *propositional letters* $(P_1, P_2, \ldots P_n)$ where P_i consists of atomic local properties of agent i. We assume that $P_i \cap P_j = \emptyset$ for $i \neq j$. Let $P \stackrel{\text{def}}{=} \cup_i P_i$. The set of i-local propositions P_i also includes a special *type proposition* τ_i which is true exactly at all the events of agent i.

We first consider a modal logic LD_0, whose syntax is given below:

$$LD_0 ::= p \in P \mid \neg\alpha \mid \alpha_1 \vee \alpha_2 \mid \mathbf{X}\,\alpha \mid \mathbf{Y}\,\alpha \mid \mathbf{F}\,\alpha \mid \mathbf{P}\,\alpha$$

The logic is a standard propositional modal logic over any labelled partial order. The $\mathbf{X}$ modality refers to a successor event and the $\mathbf{Y}$ modality refers to a predecessor event. $\mathbf{F}$ stands for 'future' and $\mathbf{P}$ for 'past' respectively. We will use indexed modalities as abbreviations: for instance, $\mathbf{X}_i\alpha$ denotes the formula $\mathbf{X}(\tau_i \wedge \alpha)$; the other abbreviations are defined similarly. The dual of $\mathbf{F}$ is denoted $\mathbf{G}$ and the dual of $\mathbf{P}$ is denoted $\mathbf{H}$. $\overline{\mathbf{X}}$ and $\overline{\mathbf{Y}}$ denote, respectively, the duals of $\mathbf{X}$ and $\mathbf{Y}$. (Note that the abbreviations denote implications for the dual modalities; for instance $\mathbf{G}_i\alpha$ denotes $\mathbf{G}(\tau_i \supset \alpha)$).

The formulas are interpreted on Lamport diagrams. We will denote models by $M = (D, V_E)$ where $D = (E, \leq, \phi)$ is a Lamport diagram, $V_E : E \to 2^P$ is a valuation function such that $V_E(E_i) \subseteq P_i$ for all $i \in [n]$, and for all $e \in E$, $\tau_i \in V_E(e)$ iff $e \in E_i$.

Let $\alpha \in LD_0$ and $e \in E$. The notion that α holds at e in M is denoted $M, e \models \alpha$ and is defined inductively as follows:

- $M, e \models p$ iff $p \in V_E(e)$.
- $M, e \models \neg\alpha$ iff $M, e \not\models \alpha$.
- $M, e \models \alpha \vee \beta$ iff $M, e \models \alpha$ or $M, e \models \beta$.
- $M, e \models \mathbf{X}\alpha$ iff there exists $e' \in E$ such that $e \lessdot e'$ and $M, e' \models \alpha$.
- $M, e \models \mathbf{F}\alpha$ iff there exists e' such that $e \leq e'$ and $M, e' \models \alpha$.
- $M, e \models \mathbf{Y}\alpha$ iff there exists $e' \in E$ such that $e' \lessdot e$ and $M, e' \models \alpha$.
- $M, e \models \mathbf{P}\alpha$ iff there exists e' such that $e' \leq e$ and $M, e' \models \alpha$.

For a model M, $i \in [n]$ and $\alpha \in LD_0$, we say that $M, i \models \alpha$ iff $M, e_{min} \models \alpha$ where e_{min} is the i-minimal element of D (with respect to $\leq$). α is *satisfiable* iff there exists a model M and $i \in [n]$ such that $M, i \models \alpha$. α is *finitely satisfiable* iff there exists a *finite* model M such that $M, i \models \alpha$ for some $i \in [n]$. α is *b-satisfiable* iff there exists a model $M = (D, V_E)$ where $D = (E, \leq, \phi)$, $| E | \leq b$ and $M, i \models \alpha$, for some $i \in [n]$.

Theorem 2.2 *The (finite) satisfiability problem for LD_0 is undecidable.*

The negative result here mainly stems from the fact that instances of the Post Correspondence Problem (PCP) can be described easily using Lamport diagrams. An *instance* of PCP is a tuple $\Delta = (\Pi, x_1, \ldots, x_k, y_1, \ldots, y_m)$, where Π is a finite alphabet, $0 < k \leq m$ and $x_1, \ldots, x_k, y_1, \ldots, y_m \in \Pi^*$. A *solution* to PCP is a sequence of indices $i_1, \ldots, i_l$, $1 \leq i_j \leq m$ for all $j \in \{1, \ldots, l\}$ such that $x_1 \cdot x_{i_1} \cdot \ldots \cdot x_{i_l} = y_1 \cdot y_{i_1} \cdot \ldots \cdot y_{i_l}$. PCP is undecidable.

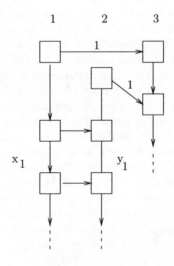

Fig. 2. The PCP language of LLDs

Given any instance Δ of PCP, we first define a 3-agent Lamport diagram that 'describes' a solution of Δ.[2] The diagram is depicted in Figure 2: agent

---

[2] Such a coding, attributed to P. S. Thiagarajan, is used in [MM01].

1 keeps choosing an index from 1 to k, say i and then sending the word x_i to agent 2. The latter does a similar thing, choosing indices j from 1 to m and then generating the word y_j; however it checks, every time, whether a letter received from 1 is the same as one that it has locally generated. Both these agents, as soon as they start on a new word, send a message to agent 3, announcing the index of the new word. Agent 3 receives an index from agent 1 followed by the same index from agent 2. Thus, while 1 and 2 together ensure that the same word is generated by both, 3 makes sure that the same sequence of indices is generated.

We now show that such a diagram can be described by a formula of the logic. That is, we define a formula α_Δ such that α_Δ is finitely satisfiable iff the instance Δ of PCP has a solution, thus proving the undecidability of finite satisfiability. We write formulas using local modalities to assert that agents 1 and 2 generate indices and send them to 3 after which they generate words accordingly, with 1 sending a message to 2 every time it generates a letter. Both the global modalities $\mathbf{X}$ and $\mathbf{Y}$ are used by 2 and 3 respectively, the former asserting that the letter it generates is the same as the one generated by 1, and the latter asserting that 1 and 2 generate the same sequences of indices.

2.3   Variations on the Theme

We first note that the modality $\mathbf{P}$ is not needed in the coding of PCP above. Secondly, the future modality is needed only in the form $\tau_i \wedge \mathbf{G}_i$, and hence a more restricted logic with *local* $\mathbf{G}$ and $\mathbf{H}$ modalities would be undecidable as well. That brings us to the use of the $\mathbf{X}$ and $\mathbf{Y}$ modalities. Both are crucially needed in the coding above, and as 'global' modalities. That is, if the logic were to be restricted to have only local modalities for the covering relation, such a coding would not obtain; on the other hand, such a logic would not be able to enforce communications in the models and hence would be uninteresting.

This leads us to the consideration of combinations where one of these two modalities is local and the other global. For instance, consider a logic where the $\mathbf{X}$ modality is local and the $\mathbf{Y}$ modality is global. When we now examine the coding above, we see two uses for these modalities: for instance, say the agent 1 generates a sequence ab. With the $\mathbf{Y}_1$ modality, agent 2 can assert only that the 1-events seen by 2 constitute the sequence ab. In between, agent 1 may generate other letters, and the logic cannot force agent 1 to send messages to 2 every time it generates a letter. But then, while the $\mathbf{X}_2$ modality is useful for such forcing, it is not necessary; a special proposition of the form s_2 would do the job as well.

Consider the logic LD_1 defined as follows. Let s_i^j, $i, j \in [n]$, $i \neq j$, be special propositions in P_i. $M, e \models s_i^j$ iff $e \in E_i$ and there exists $e' \in E_j$ such that $e \lessdot e'$. Now the formula $\tau_1 \wedge \mathbf{G}_1((a, 1) \equiv s_1^2)$ ensures that agent 1 sends a message to 2 exactly when it generates a letter. Similarly the formulas $\tau_1 \wedge \mathbf{G}_1((i, 1) \equiv s_1^3)$ and $\tau_2 \wedge \mathbf{G}_2((i, 2) \equiv s_2^3)$ ensure that agents 1 and 2 inform agent 3 of an index when they choose one. It should be clear that the rest of the coding works as above.

Theorem 2.3 *The (finite) satisfiability problem for LD_1 is undecidable.*

In [MR00], we had conjectured that m-LTL enriched with special send propositions is decidable; this theorem shows that the conjecture is false. Though the semantics of m-LTL is slightly different, the argument is very similar.

We can now consider the logic LD_2, a symmetric variation on LD_1, with a global $\mathbf{X}$ modality, local $\mathbf{Y}$ modality and special receive propositions. It is easy to see that a similar exercise as above shows undecidability of LD_2 as well.

On the other hand, it is easy to see that these logics are decidable over bounded-size models. The decidability result for logic LD_0 given below suggests how the argument goes for the other logics mentioned above as well.

Theorem 2.4 *The satisfiability of a formula of length m in LD_0 over b-bounded diagrams is decidable in time $m \cdot 2^{O(b^2)}$.*

3   Layered Lamport Diagrams

As explained earlier, we now turn our attention to restricted classes of models. For this, we define a notion of layering on Lamport diagrams.

Definition 3.1 *A* **layered Lamport diagram** *is a tuple $D = (E, \leq, \phi, \lambda)$ where $(E, \leq, \phi)$ is a Lamport diagram and $\lambda : E \to \mathbb{N}$ is a* layering *function which satisfies the following conditions:*

- *for every k, $\lambda^{-1}(k)$ is finite.*
- *for every k, if $\lambda^{-1}(k) \neq \emptyset$, then for all $i \in [n]$, $(\lambda^{-1}(k) \cap E_i) \neq \emptyset$.*
- *for $e, e' \in E$, $e \leq e'$ implies $\lambda(e) \leq_{\mathbb{N}} \lambda(e')$.*

Thus a layer is a finite set of events that includes at least one event of each agent, and the layering respects the causality relation.

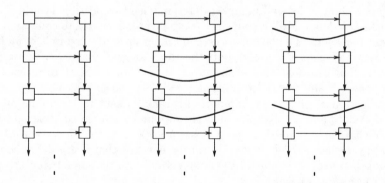

A Lamport diagram   A bounded layering   An unbounded layering

Fig. 3. A layered Lamport diagram

Given a layered Lamport diagram $D = (E, \leq, \phi, \lambda)$, $\lambda(E)$ is an infinite set and can be denoted by an increasing (infinite) sequence of natural numbers.

More precisely, let ν_D denote the sequence of natural numbers $k_1, k_2, \ldots$ such that $\lambda(E) = \{k_1, k_2, \ldots\}$ and $k_1 <_\mathbb{N} k_2 <_\mathbb{N} \ldots$. For $k \in \lambda(E)$, $\lambda^{-1}(k)$ induces a (finite) Lamport diagram which we call a layer of D and denote by D_k.

We now consider natural conditions that can be imposed on layers of an LLD. Consider a layered Lamport diagram $D = (E, \leq, \phi, \lambda)$. Let $delay_D = \{\lambda(e') - \lambda(e) \mid e <_c e'\}$ denote the set of *communication delays* associated with D.

Definition 3.2   *1. D is said to be* **communication closed** *if for every $e, e' \in E$ such that $e <_c e'$, $\lambda(e) = \lambda(e')$.*

2. *Let $b > 0$. D is said to be b-bounded, if for all $k \in \lambda(E)$, $|\lambda^{-1}(k)| \leq b$. D is said to be* **bounded** *if there exists $b \in \mathbb{N}$ such that D is b-bounded.*

3. *Let $b > 0$. D is said to be* **delay b-bounded**, *if D is b-bounded and for all $k \in delay_D$, $k \leq b$.*

4. *Let ν' be a finite prefix of ν_D ending in k_m; let $F_{\nu'} = \cup_{l \leq m} \lambda^{-1}(l)$; for $i, j \in [n]$, define $F_{\nu'}(i, j) = |\{e \in F_{\nu'} \cap E_i \mid$ for some $e' \in (E_j - \overline{F_{\nu'}}), e <_c e'\}|$. We say that D is* **channel b-bounded**, *if D is b-bounded and for all prefixes ν' of ν_D and $i, j \in [n]$, $F_{\nu'}(i, j) \leq b$.*

Thus, a communication closed LLD is one in which a send event and its corresponding receive event belong to the same layer. In a delay b-bounded LLD, the number of layers between a send event and its corresponding receive event can be at most b in addition to the size of each layer being bounded by b. Finally, in a channel b-bounded LLD, for every pair of agents i, j such that $i \neq j$, at any layer, the number of send-events from i to j until this layer, for which corresponding receive-events by j have not been included yet, can be at most b.

Figure 3 shows a layered Lamport diagram with two possible layerings. Note that when D is b-bounded, $b \geq n$, since every layer is assumed to contain at least one event per agent. The layering in second diagram in the figure is bounded as every layer has exactly 2 events but, the third diagram has two events in the first layer, four events in the second layer, six events in the third layer and so on and hence, is an unbounded layering.

A collection $\mathcal{L}$ of layered Lamport diagrams is said to be communication closed if every Lamport diagram in $\mathcal{L}$ is communication closed. $\mathcal{L}$ is said to be (delay / channel) bounded if there exists $b \in \mathbb{N}$ such that for every $D \in \mathcal{L}$, D is (delay / channel) b-bounded. It can be checked that every delay bounded LLD is also a channel bounded LLD (though not with the same bound), but the converse need not hold.

Let $\mathcal{B}$ denote the class of all bounded LLDs, $\mathcal{S}_b$ the class of channel b-bounded LLDs and $\mathcal{C}_b$ the class of LLDs which are both b-bounded and communication closed. These classes will be of importance when we study decidability issues below. The results proved for channel bounded LLDs are similarly proved for delay bounded LLDs, so we do not formally consider the latter class.

When D is communication closed, the sequence of layers $D_{k_1}, D_{k_2}, \ldots$, where $\nu_D = k_1, k_2 \ldots$, completely specifies the diagram D. However, in the case of diagrams which are not communication closed, a layer D_k is typically *incomplete*.

'Communication edges' across layers in the Hasse diagram of D are missing in the diagram given by ν_D.

Reconstructing D from ν_D for general diagrams is more work. Define a **labelled fragment** to be a tuple $F = (E, \leq, \phi, A, \eta)$ where $(E, \leq, \phi)$ is a Lamport diagram, A is some (abstract) alphabet of labels, and η is a map that demarcates "hanging" sends and receives as follows. Let $T = (\{r, s\} \times [n] \times A)$. Elements of T represent 'tags'; for instance, the tag (s, i, a) denotes a hanging send to i labelled a, and similarly (r, j, a') is a hanging receive from j labelled a'. $\eta : E \longrightarrow (A \times 2^T)$ associates with each event, a set of tags, subject to the following condition: if $\eta(e) = (a, X)$, then $(s, i, a') \in X$ implies that $e \notin E_i$ and there does not exist $e' \in E_i$ such that $e <_c e'$, and $(r, j, a') \in X$ implies that $e \notin E_j$ and there does not exist $e' \in E_j$ such that $e' <_c e$.

With this preparation, we can see the relationship between D and ν_D. Given D, there exists an alphabet A such that the sequence $\nu_D = k_1, k_2 \ldots$ associates a sequence of fragments $F_{k_1}, F_{k_2}, \ldots$, such that: for any k_j, if there exists $e \in F_{k_j}$ such that $\eta(e) = (a, X)$ and $(s, i, a') \in X$, then there exists $e' \in D$ such that $e' \in E_i$, $e <_c e'$ and there exists $k_\ell > k_j$ such that $e' \in F_{k_\ell}$, and $\eta(e') = (a', Y)$ and $(r, j, a) \in Y$ where $e \in E_j$; and a similar condition holds for tags of the form (r, j, a'). (Strictly speaking, labels are not necessary for describing this correspondence, but we need them later on.) In the case of b-bounded diagrams, a finite alphabet suffices above.

In the definition of layers, we have assumed that every layer includes at least one event of every agent. We can define *weak layering* maps which do not satisfy this condition. Weakly layered and communication closed diagrams were introduced by [EF82] and extensively developed by [PZ92] and others. For technical reasons, we have preferred to study layered diagrams rather than weakly layered ones; for instance, a layering with exactly one event in every layer is a weak layering. Similarly, one where every layer is either an internal event or a pair of events representing a communication, is a layering that is weak and communication closed. As we will see, the technical results obtained do not depend crucially on whether we use weak layerings or not.

4   The Temporal Logic

We fix a finite set of *layer names*, Γ. Formulas of our logic, which we call λ-**LTL**, are defined using a two-level syntax. We first define *layer formulas* which will be interpreted at a particular layer of an LLD . We use *temporal formulas* to talk about sequences of layers that make up an LLD. The syntax of layer formulas is given as in LD_0:

$$\Phi_l ::= p \in P \mid \neg \alpha \mid \alpha_1 \vee \alpha_2 \mid \mathbf{X}\,\alpha \mid \mathbf{Y}\,\alpha \mid \mathbf{F}\,\alpha \mid \mathbf{P}\,\alpha$$

Temporal formulas are given by the following syntax:

$$\Psi ::= \alpha@i, \ \alpha \in \Phi_l, \ i \in [n] \mid a \in \Gamma \mid \neg \varphi \mid \varphi_1 \vee \varphi_2 \mid \bigcirc \varphi \mid \varphi_1 \,\mathbf{U}\, \varphi_2$$

This is the same as the standard propositional temporal logic of linear time, but built up from layer formulas and layer names. The propositional connectives $(\wedge, \supset, \equiv)$ and the derived temporal modalities $(\Box, \Diamond)$ are defined as usual.

The formulas are interpreted on *countable* layered Lamport diagrams. Formally, models are layered Lamport diagrams equipped with two valuation functions; one maps the events to a subset of propositions and the other maps a particular layer to some layer name from Γ. We will denote models by $M = (D, V_E, V_\lambda)$ where $D = (E, \leq, \phi, \lambda)$ is a countable layered Lamport diagram, $V_E : E \to 2^P$ and $V_\lambda : \lambda(E) \to \Gamma$.

We will first define the semantics of layer formulas, over the layers of a given model. For this, it matters crucially whether the layer is communication closed or not, since the $\mathbf{X}$ and $\mathbf{Y}$ modalities are constrained to be satisfied within the layer or not, appropriately. For technical convenience, we always interpret $\mathbf{F}$ and $\mathbf{P}$ modalities within layers, and locally for every agent. As we will see later, this suffices for many interesting specifications of message behaviours.

Let $\alpha \in \Phi_l$ and $e \in E$. We define two notions below: the first notion that α holds at e in M is denoted $M, e \models_l \alpha$ and is defined inductively as before; we list only the changed definitions below.

- $M, e \models_l \mathbf{F}\alpha$ iff there exists e' such that $e \leq e'$, $\phi(e) = \phi(e')$, $\lambda(e) = \lambda(e')$ and $M, e' \models_l \alpha$.
- $M, e \models_l \mathbf{P}\alpha$ iff there exists e' such that $e' \leq e$, $\phi(e) = \phi(e')$, $\lambda(e) = \lambda(e')$ and $M, e' \models_l \alpha$.

The second notion is defined on communication closed layers. Let M be a model based on a communication closed LLD. The notion that α holds at e in M is denoted $M, e \models_{cl} \alpha$ and is defined inductively as above. The only changes are:

- $M, e \models_{cl} \mathbf{X}\alpha$ iff there exists $e' \in E$ such that $e \lessdot e'$, $\lambda(e) = \lambda(e')$ and $M, e' \models_{cl} \alpha$.
- $M, e \models_{cl} \mathbf{Y}\alpha$ iff there exists $e' \in E$ such that $e' \lessdot e$, $\lambda(e) = \lambda(e')$ and $M, e' \models_{cl} \alpha$.

Temporal formulas are interpreted at layers of a layered Lamport diagram. Given a model $M = (D, V_E, V_\lambda)$ and $\varphi \in \Psi$, the notion that φ holds in the layer k of D is denoted $M, k \models \varphi$ and is defined inductively as follows:

- $M, k \models \alpha@i$ iff $M, e \models_l \alpha$ where e is the i-minimum event of D_k.
- $M, k \models a$, $a \in \Gamma$, iff $V_\lambda(k) = a$.
- $M, k \models \neg\varphi$ iff $M, k \not\models \varphi$.
- $M, k \models \varphi \vee \psi$ iff $M, k \models \varphi$ or $M, k \models \psi$.
- $M, k \models \bigcirc\varphi$ iff $M, k' \models \varphi$ where k' is the successor of k in ν_D.
- $M, k \models \varphi\mathbf{U}\psi$ iff there exists $k' \in \lambda(E): k \leq_{\mathbb{N}} k', M, k' \models \psi$ and for all $k'' \in \lambda(E) : k \leq_{\mathbb{N}} k'' <_{\mathbb{N}} k' : M, k'' \models \varphi$.

When M is a model based on a communication closed LLD, we define $M, k \models_c \varphi$ exactly as above, except for the base case: $M, k \models_c \alpha@i$ iff $M, e \models_{cl} \alpha$ where e is the i-minimum event of D_k.

For a model M and $\varphi \in \Psi$, we say that $M \models \varphi$ iff $M, k_{min} \models \varphi$ where k_{min} denotes the first element in the sequence ν_D. The notion $M \models_c \varphi$ is defined similarly when M is a model based on a communication closed LLD. φ is *satisfiable* iff there exists a model M such that $M \models \varphi$. φ being C-satisfiable is defined similarly.

We will be interested in other restricted satisfiability notions as well. Say φ is *B-satisfiable* if there exists a model M based on a bounded LLD such that $M \models \varphi$. The notion of S_b-satisfiability is defined similarly using a model based on a channel b-bounded LLD, and C_b-satisfiability using a model based on an LLD that is both communication closed and b-bounded.

Theorem 4.1 *B-satisfiability and C-satisfiability are undecidable.*

The result is proved in the same way as we did in the previous section. Of course, the diagram constructed there was a finite diagram, whereas we need countable diagrams as models. This is easily achieved by appending an infinite sequence of dummy local events to each agent. Moreover, we wish to layer the diagram, with at least one event of each agent in every layer, so we add dummy local events to agent 3 in the PCP part of the diagram.

We first show that B-satisfiability is undecidable. Consider the following layering, which picks exactly one event from each agent for a layer. Clearly this is a bounded layering, but it is not channel bounded nor is it communication closed. We can now show that such a layering as well as the diagram itself can be described by a formula of the logic, proceeding along the same lines as before.

Now consider the entire PCP part of the diagram as one layer, and each subsequent layer as above. This is a communication closed (but unbounded) layering, and can easily be specified using a formula as well. This shows that C-satisfiability is also undecidable.

5 Decidability

The decision procedures are automata theoretic in the sense that they rely on associating a nondeterministic Büchi automaton with every formula such that the language accepted by the automaton is exactly the set of models of the formula. The construction of such an automaton is more straightforward for C_b-satisfiability than for S_b-satisfiability. Since models are b-bounded layered Lamport diagrams, the automata defined here run on such diagrams, with transitions labelled by b-bounded layers. Let $\mathcal{LC}_b$ denote the set of b-bounded communication closed layers; it is clearly a finite set.

A **Diagram automaton** is given by a tuple $\mathcal{A} = (Q, \mathcal{D}, \rightarrow, I, G)$ where Q is a finite set of states, $\mathcal{D} \subseteq \mathcal{LC}_b$, $I \subseteq Q$ is the set of initial states, $G \subseteq Q$ is the set of good states and $\rightarrow \subseteq (Q \times \mathcal{D} \times Q)$ is the transition relation. That is, a diagram automaton is just a Büchi automaton whose alphabet is a finite set of b-bounded Lamport diagrams.

Consider a sequence of states of $\mathcal{A}$, $\rho = q_0, q_1, \ldots$ such that $q_0 \in I$ and $q_i \overset{D_i}{\rightarrow} q_{i+1}$ for all $i \geq 0$. Let D be the b-bounded communication closed LLD defined by the sequence $D_0, D_1, \ldots$. We say that ρ is a run of $\mathcal{A}$ on D. ρ is said to be accepting if $inf(\rho) \cap G \neq \emptyset$, where $inf(\rho) = \{q \mid q = q_i$ for infinitely many $i\}$. The language of b-bounded communication closed LLDs accepted by $\mathcal{A}$ is denoted by $L_C^b(\mathcal{A})$ and is defined as $L_C^b(\mathcal{A}) = \{D \mid$ there exists an accepting run of $\mathcal{A}$ on $D\}$.

Lemma 5.1 *Given a diagram automaton* $\mathcal{A} = (Q, \mathcal{D}, \rightarrow, I, G)$, *the problem of checking if* $L_C^b(\mathcal{A}) \neq \emptyset$ *is decidable in time* $O(|Q|^2)$.

We can similarly define automata with fragments, rather than diagrams as input. Fix a finite alphabet A and let $\mathcal{LF}_b(A)$ denote the set of b-bounded A-labelled fragments; it is again a finite set.

A **Fragment automaton** is given by a tuple $\mathcal{B} = (Q, A, \mathcal{F}, \rightarrow, I, G)$ where A is a finite alphabet, $\mathcal{F} \subseteq \mathcal{LF}_b(A)$, and $Q, \rightarrow, I, G$ are defined appropriately as above. Now consider a run of $\mathcal{B}$, $\rho = q_0, q_1, \ldots$ such that $q_0 \in I$ and $q_i \xrightarrow{F_i} q_{i+1}$ for all $i \geq 0$. We say that ρ is a run of $\mathcal{B}$ on a channel b-bounded diagram D if the sequence of fragments $F_0, F_1, \ldots$ *matches* D. ρ is said to be accepting if $inf(\rho) \cap G \neq \emptyset$, where $inf(\rho)$ is as defined above. The language of channel b-bounded LLDs accepted by $\mathcal{B}$ is denoted by $L_S^b(\mathcal{B})$ and is defined as $L_S^b(\mathcal{B}) = \{D \mid$ there exists an accepting run of $\mathcal{B}$ on $D\}$.

Lemma 5.2 *Given a fragment automaton* $\mathcal{B} = (Q, A, \mathcal{F}, \rightarrow, I, G)$, *the problem of checking if* $L_S^b(\mathcal{B}) \neq \emptyset$ *is decidable in time* $O(|Q|^2 \times k^{b^2})$, *where* $k = |A|$.

Emptiness checking is no longer a simple search for a connected component containing a good state. We need to check in addition that every pending 'send' is matched with a 'hanging receive' with labels appropriately matched.

Theorem 5.3 *Given a temporal formula* φ_0 *of length* m, *the satisfiability of* φ_0 *over* b-bounded communication closed diagrams can be checked in time $2^{O(m+b^2)}$.

This theorem is proved by associating a diagram automaton $\mathcal{A}_0$ with φ_0 such that $L_C^b(\mathcal{A}_0) = \{M \mid M$ is a model of φ_0 based on a b-bounded communication closed LLD $\}$. Hence, φ_0 is satisfiable iff $L_C^b(\mathcal{A}_0) \neq \emptyset$, thus giving decidability. Note that the states and transitions are the same as what we would use for LTL; we only need to decide the diagram alphabet carefully, and this relies on decidability of the logic LD_0 over b-bounded diagrams (Theorem 2.4).

Theorem 5.4 *Given a temporal formula* φ_0 *of length* m, *the satisfiability of* φ_0 *over channel* b-bounded diagrams can be checked in time $2^{O(m+2^{b^2})}$.

We associate a fragment automaton with every formula. Once again, defining the set of fragments on which the automaton runs is the only important detail; the rest of the construction is standard. For this, we construct pseudo-models of layer formulas in which $\mathbf{X}$ and $\mathbf{Y}$ requirements may not be met. But this is where labels come useful; we not only label every event in the pseudo-model with a layer atom, but also add a 'send' or 'receive' tag with a semantically matching atom as the label in the tag, for such unfulfilled requirements. Since accepting runs match labels successfully, all requirements are fulfilled in the associated model. (The proofs of these theorems can be found in [MR02].)

Note that the theorems above suggest that we can consider systems presented as diagram automata or fragment automata and define appropriate model checking problems which are thus proved decidable.

For instance, consider the system in Figure 4 representing the communication scenario of an Automatic Teller Machine (ATM), which can be viewed as a diagram automaton. There are three agents—User, Bank and the ATM. The ATM provides options for the user to check the balance in his/her account and to withdraw cash after validating the balance. Note that each state is labelled by a layer name, associated with which is a communication closed finite Lamport diagram. (The layer *Get Option* in this system is weak, but may be enriched with a local dummy event for *Bank* if necessary.)

The following are some properties of this system that can be written using λ-**LTL**.

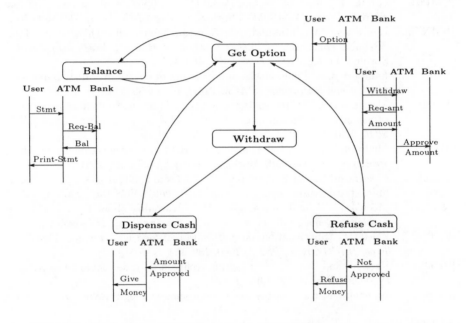

Fig. 4. A system representing an ATM scenario

- ATM accepts options to either check balance or to withdraw cash.
  $\Box(((option \land \tau_{ATM})@ATM) \supset$
  $\bigcirc((\tau_{user} \land stmt)@user \lor (\tau_{user} \land withdraw)@user))$
- Every request for withdrawal from the user is approved or rejected by the ATM depending on whether the bank approves or rejects the amount.
  $\Box((\mathbf{P}(\tau_{user} \land withdraw)@ATM) \supset$
  $\bigcirc((\mathbf{Y}(\tau_{bank} \land \neg approve) \supset \mathbf{X}(Refuse)@ATM)$
  $\lor (\mathbf{Y}(\tau_{bank} \land approve) \supset \mathbf{X}(Givecash)@ATM)))$

References

[AHP96]   Alur, R., Holzmann, G. J. and Peled, D., "An analyzer for message sequence charts", *Software Concepts and Tools*, 17(2), 1996, 70–77.

[APP95]   Alur, R., Peled, D. and Penczek, W., "Model checking of causality properties", *Proc. LICS*, 1995, 90–100.

[AY99]   Alur, R. and Yannakakis, M., "Model checking of message sequence charts", *Proc. CONCUR 1999*, Springer-Verlag *LNCS 1664*, 1999, 114–129.

[BL01]   Bollig, B. and Leucker, M., "Modelling, specifying and verifying message passing systems", *Proc. TIME 2001*, 2001, 240–247.

[EF82]   Elrad, T. and Francez, N., "Decomposition of distributed programs into communication closed layers", *Science of Computer Programming, 2*, 1982, 155–173.

[GMP01]   Gunter, E., Muscholl, A. and Peled, D., "Compositional message sequence charts", *Proc. TACAS 2001*, Springer-Verlag *LNCS 2031*, 2001, 496–511.

[HMNT00] Henriksen, J.G., Mukund, M., Narayan Kumar and Thiagarajan, P.S., "Regular collections of message sequence charts", *Proc. MFCS 2000*, Springer-Verlag *LNCS 1893*, 2000, 405–414.

[La78]   Lamport, L., "Time, clocks and ordering of events in a distributed system", *Communications of ACM 21(7)*, 1978, 558–565.

[Ma01]   Madhusudan, P., "Reasoning about sequential and branching behaviours of message sequence graphs", *Proc. ICALP 2001*, Springer-Verlag *LNCS 2076*, 2001, 396–407.

[MM01]   Madhusudan, P. and Meenakshi, B., "Beyond message sequence graphs", *Proc. FST & TCS 2001*, Springer-Verlag *LNCS 2245*, 2001, 256–267.

[MR00]   Meenakshi, B. and Ramanujam, R., "Reasoning about message passing in finite state environments", *Proc. ICALP 2000*, *LNCS 1853*, 2000, 487–498.

[MR02]   Meenakshi, B. and Ramanujam, R., "Reasoning about layered message passing systems", full version, http://www.imsc.res.in/~bmeena.

[Pe00]   Peled, D., "Specification and verification of message sequence charts", *In Proc. IFIP FORTE/PSTV*, 2000, 139–154.

[PZ92]   Poel, M. and Zwiers, J., "Layering techniques for development of parallel systems", *Proc. CAV*, 1992, 16–29.

[Ra96]   Ramanujam, R., "Locally linear time temporal logic", *Proc. LICS*, 1996, 118–127.

[RGG96]   Rudolph, E., Graubmann, P. and Grabowski, J., "Tutorial on message sequence charts", *Computer Networks and ISDN Systems—SDL and MSC, Vol. 28*, 1996, 1629–1641.

[Thi94]   Thiagarajan, P.S., "A trace based extension of propositional linear time temporal logic", *Proc. LICS*, 1994, 438–447.

[ITU97]   *ITU-TS Recommendation Z.120—Message sequence chart*, ITU-TS, 1997.

Using Simulated Execution in Verifying Distributed Algorithms

Toh Ne Win, Michael D. Ernst, Stephen J. Garland,
Dilsun Kırlı, and Nancy A. Lynch

MIT Laboratory for Computer Science
{tohn,mernst,garland,dilsun,lynch}@lcs.mit.edu

Abstract. This paper presents a methodology for proving properties of distributed systems in which simulated execution assists and enhances formal proofs. It is well known that techniques such as testing can increase confidence in an implementation, but cannot by themselves demonstrate correctness. In addition to detecting simple errors quickly and to providing intuition about behavior, execution-based techniques can also reveal unexpected properties, suggest necessary lemmas, and provide information to structure proofs. This paper also describes the use of these techniques in a machine-checked proof of correctness of the Paxos algorithm for distributed consensus.

1   Introduction

Traditionally, execution serves as a prelude to formal verification. Testing reveals departures from desired behavior that are corrected (either in the code or in the specification of its behavior) before attempting to prove code correct. Testing via simulated execution can do the same even in the absence of a complete implementation. This paper discusses additional ways execution or simulated execution can assist in formal verification, and describes their use in producing a machine-checked proof of a distributed algorithm.

First, execution can serve in a more powerful way as a prelude to formal verification. Tools for dynamic program analysis can extract descriptions of program behavior from executions, and programmers can match the extracted descriptions against their expectations. Unlike the traditional use of execution to test behavior, this use can reveal unexpected behaviors, not just departures from anticipated behaviors.

Second, execution can help produce the lemmas required for successful proofs of correctness. Unlike human proofs, which are peppered with phrases like "it is obvious that," machine-checked proofs often require many explicit lemmas. To avoid the tedium of enumerating these lemmas by hand, verifiers can discover them by using execution and dynamic program analysis.

Third, information that directs simulated execution to examine interesting aspects of a program's behavior can also be used to direct a proof of correctness. For example, programmers may ensure that executions cover the entire range of

L. Zuck et al. (Eds.): VMCAI 2003, LNCS 2575, pp. 283–297, 2003.

expected behaviors by formulating case splits that distinguish between normal and unusual behaviors; these same case splits can also provide helpful ways of organizing a proof.

We illustrate these uses of execution in constructing a formal proof of correctness for Paxos, a distributed algorithm for consensus [Lam98,PLL00]. This paper is concerned primarily with a general methodology for verifying distributed algorithms — and with the role execution and automated tools play in that methodology — and not with the details of the Paxos algorithm itself. Our methodology is based on the input/output (I/O) automaton framework [LT89] for modeling and verifying distributed algorithms, in which each component of a system is represented as an automaton whose external behavior is defined by a simple mathematical object called a trace.

This paper is organized as follows. Section 2 introduces the I/O automaton model, discusses the IOA language and toolkit, which support use of this model, and contrasts the toolkit with related tools that use run-time techniques to aid formal verification. The remainder of the paper presents our execution-based methodology in more detail, using a proof of the Paxos algorithm as a running example. Section 3 formulates specifications and implementations as I/O automata, Section 4 describes how these automata are executed, and Section 5 shows how dynamically detected invariants reveal properties of an automaton. Section 6 describes how two automata, one a specification and one an implementation, can be executed in lock-step, and Section 7 shows how this paired execution can be used to construct a machine-verified proof.

2   Preliminaries

Our methodology uses the I/O automaton model, the IOA language, and three tools in the IOA toolkit [GL98]: the IOA interpreter, the LP theorem-prover, and the Daikon dynamic invariant detector.

2.1   I/O Automata and the IOA Language

An I/O automaton is a simple state machine in which transitions between states are associated with named *actions*, which are classified as either *input, output,* or *internal.* The inputs and outputs are external actions used for communication with the automaton's environment; internal actions are visible only to the automaton itself. An automaton controls which output and internal actions it performs, but input actions are not under its control. An I/O automaton consists of its *signature*, which lists its actions; a set of *states*, some of which are distinguished as start states; a *state-transition relation*, which contains triples of the form (state, action, state); and an optional set of *tasks* (not considered in this paper).

Action π is *enabled* in state s if there is a state s' such that (s, π, s') is a transition of the automaton. Input actions are enabled in every state. The operation of an I/O automaton is described by its *executions* $s_0, \pi_1, s_1, \ldots$, which are alternating sequences of states and actions, and by its *traces*, which are the externally visible behavior occurring in executions. One automaton *implements* another if all its traces are also traces of the other.

Definition 1 (Forward simulation). *A forward simulation from automaton A to automaton B is a relation f on states(A) × states(B) with the following two properties. (1) For every start state a of A, there is a start state b of B such that f(a,b). (2) If a is a reachable state of A, b is a reachable state of B such that f(a,b), and a $\xrightarrow{\pi}$ a′, then there is a state b′ of B such that f(a′,b′) and an execution fragment β of B such that b $\xrightarrow{\beta}$ b′ and trace(π) = trace(β).*

Theorem 1. *If there is a forward simulation relation from A to B, then every trace of A is a trace of B [Lyn96].*

The IOA language provides notations for describing I/O automata and for stating their properties; it uses Larch Shared Language [GHG+93] specifications to axiomatize the semantics of I/O automata and the data types used to describe algorithms. In IOA, transition relations are defined in terms of preconditions and effects. These can be written either in an imperative style (as a sequence of assignment, conditional, and loop statements), or in declarative style (as a predicate relating state variables in the pre- and post-states, transition parameters, and other nondeterministically chosen parameters). It is also possible to use a combination of these two styles. Nondeterminism appears in IOA in two ways: *explicitly*, in the form of **choose** constructs in state variable initializations and the effects of the transition definitions, and *implicitly*, in the form of action scheduling uncertainty.

Nondeterminism allows systems to be described in their most general forms and to be verified considering all possible behaviors without being tied to a particular implementation of a system design.

The sample programs in this paper do not exploit the full generality of the language. They all define primitive (i.e., not composite) automata in an imperative style with no explicit nondeterminism.

2.2 Tools Used in the IOA Toolkit

The IOA interpreter. The IOA interpreter [KCD+02a,KCD+02b] assists users in formulating and checking properties of automata. The interpreter can simulate execution either of a single automaton in isolation (checking stated assertions and displaying or logging the automaton's execution) or of two automata running in lockstep. In the latter case, a user presents the interpreter with two automata, a candidate simulation relation, and a mapping, called a step correspondence, from the actions of the lower-level automaton to sequences of actions of the higher-level one. The interpreter simulates execution of the low-level automaton, generates a simulated execution of the high-level automaton induced by the step correspondence, checks that the two executions have the same trace, and checks that the candidate simulation relation holds throughout the executions. The IOA interpreter is also known as the "IOA Simulator," but is called the interpreter in this paper to avoid confusion with the notions of forward and backward simulation.

The Larch Prover. The Larch Prover [GG91] (LP) is an interactive theorem proving system for multisorted first-order logic. It admits specifications of theories in the Larch Shared Language (LSL). The IOA toolkit includes a tool called ioa2lsl [Bog01], which translates IOA definitions of automata into LSL theories that describe the operation of the automaton. It also generates proof obligations for the invariants and simulation relations of the automaton.

The Daikon invariant detector. The Daikon invariant detector [ECGN01] proposes program properties that are likely to be true. It operates dynamically, by examining values computed during execution, postulating and checking properties, and reporting those that pass a battery of statistical and other tests. The technique is unsound, because there is no guarantee that the test suite fully characterizes the execution environment. However, the reported properties are often true and generally helpful in explicating the system under test and/or its test suite. We achieve soundness by using LP to check proofs.

2.3   Related Work

Other toolkits, such as AsmL [GSV01], Mocha [AHM+98], SMV [McM], and TLC [LY01], support execution or verification of concurrent and distributed systems. The execution is used mainly for debugging and understanding the behavior of a system. The IOA toolkit uses execution not only for these purposes, but also for automatically discovering program properties that can be used as lemmas in formal proofs. Moreover, the facility for executing of pairs of automata together, matching actions of one against those of the other, helps users in organizing formal proofs of correctness based on simulation relations.

Mocha, SMV and TLC use model checking as the verification method. Model checking is attractive because it requires relatively less expertise than theorem-proving and it provides counter-examples to falsified properties. However, model checkers provide no intuition about true properties and can analyze only a finite state space; theorem-provers apply to finite and infinite systems alike.

The "invisible invariants" method [PRZ01] facilitates automated verification of parameterized, finite-state systems. This method uses model-checking techniques for calculating candidate invariants, for checking their inductiveness, and for proving the verification conditions generated by the standard invariance rule of deductive verification. A key characteristic of this method is that invariants can be proved automatically and they need not be shown to a human. By contrast, we regard invariants as a means to inform users about interesting program properties they might have overlooked. Invariants detected by Daikon are intended to be simple and easily readable properties. Additionally, our methodology is not limited to finite-state systems or inductively provable properties.

```
type Node = tuple of location: Int
type Value = tuple of value: Int

automaton Cons
signature
  input fail(i: Node), init(i: Node, v: Value)
  output decide(i: Node, v: Value)
  internal chooseVal(v: Value)
states
  initiated: Set[Node] := {},    proposed: Set[Value] := {},
  chosen: Set[Value]    := {},    decided: Set[Node]    := {},
  failed: Set[Node]     := {}
transitions
  input init(i, v)
    eff if ¬(i ∈ failed) ∧ ¬(i ∈ initiated) then
              initiated := initiated ∪ {i};
              proposed := proposed ∪ {v}
        fi
  internal chooseVal(v)
    pre v ∈ proposed ∧ chosen = {}
    eff chosen := {v};
  output decide(i, v)
    pre i ∈ initiated ∧ ¬(i ∈ decided) ∧
            ¬(i ∈ failed) ∧ v ∈ chosen
    eff decided := decided ∪ {i}
  input fail(i)
    eff failed := failed ∪ {i}
```

Fig. 1. Specification of consensus in IOA

---

3   Specifying Automata in IOA

The first step in verifying that an implementation is correct with respect to a specification is to define the specification and implementation automata in IOA. The I/O automaton version of Paxos defines a hierarchy of four automata for achieving consensus. The highest-level automaton, Cons, provides a specification for consensus. The lowest-level automaton, Paxos, provides a distributed implementation. An intermediate-level automaton, Global1, although non-distributed, captures how Paxos uses ballots and quorums to achieve consensus. The correctness proof involves showing the existence of a series of forward simulations, between each pair of successive levels in the hierarchy. Our case study examines the forward simulation between Cons and Global1.

3.1   Specification Automaton

Paxos implements distributed consensus in an asynchronous system in which individual processes can fail. Suppose that I is a finite set of nodes representing the processes in the system and V is the set of possible consensus values. Processes in I may propose values in V. The consensus service is allowed to return decisions to processes that have proposed values. It must satisfy two conditions: all nodes must receive the same value ("agreement") and that value must have been proposed by some process ("validity").

The signature of the specification automaton Cons (Figure 1) contains an input action init(i,v), representing the proposal of value v by process i, an

```
type Ballot = tuple of ordering: Int

automaton Global1
signature
   input fail(i: Node), init(i: Node, v: Value)
   output decide(i: Node, v: Value)
   internal start(theNodes: Set[Node]), makeBallot(b: Ballot),
            abstain(i: Node, B: Set[Ballot]), assignVal(b: Ballot, v:Value),
            vote(i: Node, b: Ballot), internalDecide(b: Ballot)
states
   initiated: Set[Node] := {},    proposed: Set[Value]    := {},
   decided: Set[Node]    := {},    failed: Set[Node]       := {},
   ballots: Set[Ballot] := {},    succeeded: Set[Ballot] := {},
   val: Array[Ballot, Null[Value]]        := constant(nil),
   voted: Array[Node, Set[Ballot]]        := constant({}),
   abstained: Array[Node, Set[Ballot]] := constant({})
   quorums: Set[Node],
   dead: Set[Ballot] := {}

transitions
   internal start(theNodes)
      eff quorums := delete([1], theNodes);
         for i: Node in theNodes do voted[i] := {};
                                    abstained[i] := {} od;
   input init(i, v)
   input fail (i)
      eff failed := failed ∪ {i}
   internal makeBallot(b)
      pre ¬ (b ∈ ballots);
      eff ballots := ballots ∪ {b};
   internal assignVal(b, v)
      pre b ∈ ballots ∧ val[b] = nil ∧ v ∈ proposed
         ∧ ∀ b':Ballot (b'.ordering < b.ordering ⇒
                                    val[b'] = embed(v) ∨ b' ∈ dead)
      eff val[b] := embed(v)
   internal vote(i, b)
      pre i ∈ initiated ∧ ¬(i ∈ failed) ∧ b ∈ ballots ∧ ¬(b ∈ abstained[i])
      eff voted[i] := voted[i] ∪ {b}
   internal abstain(i, B)
      pre i ∈ initiated ∧ ¬(i ∈ failed) ∧ voted[i] ∩ B = {}
      eff abstained[i] := abstained[i] ∪ B;
         for aBallot:Ballot in B do
            if ∀ aNode:Node (aNode ∈ quorums ⇒ aBallot ∈  abstained[aNode])
               then dead := insert (aBallot, dead);
            fi ;
         od;
   internal internalDecide(b)
      pre b ∈ ballots ∧ ∀ j:Node (j ∈ quorums ⇒ b ∈ voted[j])
      eff succeeded := succeeded ∪ {b}
   output decide(i, v)
      pre i ∈ initiated ∧ ¬(i ∈ decided) ∧  ¬(i ∈ failed)
         ∧ ∃ b:Ballot (b ∈ succeeded ∧ embed(v) = val[b])
      eff decided := decided ∪ {i}
```

Fig. 2. A ballot-based implementation of consensus in IOA

internal action chooseVal(v), representing the choice of a consensus value v, an output action decide(i,v), representing the report of the consensus value to process i, and an input action fail(i), representing the failure of process i. The automaton provides the required agreement and validity guarantees: only a single consensus value can be chosen, and that value must have been previously proposed.

3.2   Implementation Automaton

The automaton Global1 (Figure 2) specifies an algorithm that implements consensus in a non-distributed setting. This automaton uses a totally ordered set of ballots for values, one of which may eventually be chosen as the consensus value if sufficient approval is collected from the processes in the system.

In addition to the external actions of the automaton Cons, the signature of Global1 includes internal actions for making ballots, assigning them values, and voting for or abstaining from ballots. The automaton Global1 determines the fate of a ballot by considering the actions of quorums, which are finite subsets of I, on that ballot. Global1 allows a ballot to succeed only if every node in a quorum has voted for it.

4   Simulating Execution of an Automaton with the IOA Toolkit

The second step in verifying the correctness of an implementation using the IOA toolkit is to test its behavior by simulating its execution. The IOA interpreter simulates execution of an I/O automaton on a single machine, allowing the user to help select the executions and to propose invariants for the interpreter to check.

The interpreter requires that IOA programs be transformed into a form suitable for execution. For example, quorums in Paxos have to be initialized operationally, whereas they were specified declaratively in the original I/O automaton model. Aside from such bookkeeping issues, the crucial problem in this transformation is resolving nondeterminism. The IOA interpreter solves this problem by requiring the user to supply a program, called an *NDR program*, to each source of nondeterminism in an automaton [KCD+02a,KCD+02b].

In our case study, we wrote several NDR programs to execute Global1 with different interleavings of actions, causing some nodes to fail and some to abstain from a ballot. For example, the NDR program statement

```
fire output decide([4], [1]);
```

causes the IOA interpreter to execute the decide action with the given arguments. We did not use structured test generation methods (e.g., code coverage) to produce the NDR programs; instead, we simply selected executions that exhibited what we felt was the normal behavior of the automaton (and that exercised every action). In our experience, such an intuitive scheduling is adequate for the purpose of dynamic invariant detection. However, as noted in Section 5.2, a preliminary test run reported an unexpected invariant, which indicated a (subsequently corrected) deficiency in the test data. In another case study, involving the Peterson mutual exclusion algorithm, use of the IOA simulator uncovered a bug in the IOA transcription of the implementation.

5   Dynamically Detecting Likely Invariants

A proof of a simulation relation often depends on invariants and on auxiliary lemmas; machine verification requires that such bookkeeping details be made explicit. These parts of the proof are usually not the most interesting parts and also tend to be relatively simple; thus, automating them holds promise. We attempt to automatically generate invariants and lemmas by use of dynamic invariant detection.

The Daikon invariant detector is a run-time tool that proposes invariants based on program executions [ECGN01]. It examines the values that a program computes, generalizes over them, and reports the generalizations in the form of IOA invariants. Daikon's heuristics and analyses result in output in the form of a formal specification that often matches what a human would have written [NE02]. Three potential problems with the technique are that it is unsound, that it is incomplete, and that the reported properties are not guaranteed to be useful. We discuss Daikon's output and how to cope with the potential problems.

5.1   Daikon Results for the Case Study

For Paxos, Daikon analysis produced 23 invariants, four of which were helpful in the simulation relation proof in Section 7. The four were:

```
Inv1:  ∀ anIndex:Node (size(voted[anIndex] ∩ abstained[anIndex]) = 0)
Inv2:  val.values.val(nonNull) ⊆ proposed
Inv3:  size(succeeded ∩ dead) = 0
Inv5:  succeeded ⊆ ballots
```

We have added the names Inv$i$ for convenience in this presentation.

A full proof of the Paxos simulation relation required six invariants: five for the simulation relation proper, and one more for one of the invariants. The two missing invariants were:

```
Inv4:  ∀ b:Ballot ∀ b':Ballot
         (val[b] ≠ nil ∧ b' < b ⇒ val[b'] = val[b] ∨ b' ∈ dead(abstained))
Inv6:  ∀ b_Inv6:Ballot
         (b_Inv6 ∈ succeeded ⇒ ∃ q_Inv6:Set[Node] ∀ n_Inv6:Node
           (q_Inv6 ∈ wquorums ∧ (n_Inv6 ∈ q_Inv6 ⇒ b_Inv6 ∈ voted[n_Inv6])))
```

These two invariants are outside Daikon's grammar, so it neither checked nor reported them. (Daikon does not report invariants with existential quantifiers, nor does it report those with more than a given number of subterms.)

5.2   Discussion of Dynamically Detected Invariants

We now discuss how to cope with potential problems in the invariant detector output.

First, dynamic invariant detection is unsound: reported properties are true over the test suite, but, as with all execution-based techniques, there is no guarantee that the test suite fully characterizes the execution environment of the program. This does not hinder us for two reasons. First, we use Daikon's output to help in proposing, understanding, and verifying program properties, but soundness is provided by the theorem prover. Second, most of the output in our case study was correct. Most false facts Daikon produced were easily-corrected artifacts of the test suite (execution scheduling). For example, in one set of executions, Daikon reported that the size of the `failed` variable was a constant. We corrected this by randomizing failures in our NDR program, thereby improving the quality of the test suite for its use in Section 6. In the general, however, simply covering every action seems to be adequate.

Second, dynamic invariant detection is incomplete: the proposed invariants may be insufficient for verification, because some true invariants are not reported. Daikon restricts the set of invariants it checks for two reasons: to conserve runtime and to reduce the number of false positives that it reports (the more properties it checks, the larger the number of false properties it will report). In our case study, we had to add `Inv4` and `Inv6` to the set proposed by Daikon. We did not find this a hindrance because our methodology does not aim for completely automatic verification. Rather, we aim to reduce human effort — particularly non-imaginative effort. Qualitatively, we believe the output did so, by providing four of the six required invariants. Some assistance was better than none, even though work remained.

It is notable that `Inv3`, while true and necessary for the proof, was not provable in isolation: establishing it required use of `Inv6`. In other words, Daikon was able to postulate a simple property with a complicated proof, prompting a user to find that proof. In addition to nicely decomposing the proof into parts, this demonstrates a strength of our technique: it is easy to dynamically check properties that may have quite complicated static proofs and thus are likely to be beyond the capabilities of static tools.

Third, some reported properties may be true but not useful. As an example, Daikon reported `decided` $\subseteq$ `initiated` (and a number of other properties), but we did not use that fact in the proof. Daikon uses heuristics to prune useless facts, for instance, by limiting output based on variable types. However, it is impossible for a tool to know what a human will find desirable in a given situation. We found that although there were over a dozen true but irrelevant invariants, it was easy to pass over the uninteresting ones — and examining them helped us solidify our understanding of the algorithm and the implementation. Thus, a moderate amount of extra information does not distract or disable users.

Finally, the reported properties may be more than are needed for a proof: a proof accepted by a theorem-prover may use more invariants than are strictly necessary, thus obscuring the essential argument. We believe it is better to first obtain a working, machine-verified proof, and then to reduce it after the fact. Automating this task (possibly following Rintanen [Rin00]) is future work. We did not have to perform such a reduction in our case study.

6 Paired Execution

As noted in Section 2.2, users can also exploit the IOA interpreter in formulating and checking the validity of a forward simulation relation, as they work

```
forward simulation from Global1 to Cons:
    Cons.initiated = Global1.initiated ∧
    Cons.proposed  = Global1.proposed ∧
    Cons.decided   = Global1.decided ∧
    Cons.failed    = Global1.failed  ∧
    ∀ v: Value (v ∈ Cons.chosen ⇔
            ∃ b: Ballot (b ∈ Global1.succeeded ∧ Global1.val[b] = embed(v) ))
proof
initially Cons = [{}, {}, {}, {}, {}]
for internal start(S: Set[Node], B: Set[Ballot]) ignore
for input init(i: Node, v: Value) do fire input init(i, v) od
for input fail(i: Node) do fire input fail(i) od
for output decide(i: Node, v: Value) do fire output decide(i, v) od
for internal makeBallot(b: Ballot) ignore
for internal abstain(i: Node, B: Set[Ballot]) ignore
for internal vote(i: Node, b: Ballot) ignore
for internal assignVal(b: Ballot, v: Value) do
 if ¬(b ∈ Global1.succeeded) then ignore
 elseif ∃ b:Ballot (b ∈ Global1.succeeded ∧ Global1.val[b] ≠ nil) then ignore
 else fire internal chooseVal(v)
 fi od
for internal internalDecide(b: Ballot) do
 if (b ∈ Global1.succeeded) then ignore
 elseif (Global1.val[b] = nil) then ignore
 elseif ∃ b:Ballot (b ∈ Global1.succeeded ∧ Global1.val[b] ≠ nil) then ignore
 else fire internal chooseVal(Global1.val[b].val)
 fi od
```

Fig. 3. Forward simulation relation and step correspondence (**proof** block) from Global1 to Cons

toward the goal of proving the correctness of an implementation with respect to a specification.

A forward simulation relation is a predicate that relates the states of two automata (see Definition 1). Figure 3 contains a candidate forward simulation relation from Global1 to Cons. The simulation relation is just a predicate relating the states of the two automata. It does not specify how each step in the implementation Global1 corresponds to a sequence of steps in the specification Cons. In general, there might be multiple step correspondences that preserve the simulation relation; even if there is only one, it can be difficult to find it. Hence Figure 3 also contains a "proof block," which describes a step correspondence for use as an "attempted proof" of the simulation relation. With this proof block, the paired interpreter can execute the specification automaton in lockstep with the implementation automaton.

The proof block contains two sub-blocks, corresponding to the two properties needed to show a simulation relation (Definition 1). The first sub-block, started by **initially**, shows how to start the specification automaton[1]. The second sub-block contains an entry for each action of the low-level automaton; this entry provides an algorithm for producing a high-level execution fragment. A **proof**

[1] The set of legal start states of the specification automaton is determined by the **states** block in its code as usual; the **initially** block picks a particular start state, which may depend on the start state of the implementing automaton.

section may also contain a third sub-block that declares auxiliary variables used by the step correspondence.

In Figure 3, the proposed simulation relation is the identity on all state variables of Cons except chosen, which is not a state variable of Global1. The simulation relation defines chosen in Cons to contain a value v if and only if there is a successful ballot in Global1 with value v. The proof block is straightforward for the start state and for the external actions: each external action in the low-level execution is matched by the action with the same name in the high-level automaton. The internal actions start, makeBallot, abstain, and vote are matched by an empty execution sequence of the automaton Cons.

The IOA interpreter reveals the need for the careful treatment of the internal actions assignVal and internalDecide in Figure 3. Given a naive treatment

```
for internal assignVal(b: Ballot, v: Value) ignore
for internal internalDecide(b: Ballot)
    do fire internal chooseVal(Global1.val[b].val) od
```

for these actions in the proof block, the interpreter catches two problems with the purported step correspondence. First, given a (legal) schedule that executes internalDecide twice in Global1, the interpreter discovers that the precondition for chooseVal fails the second time it is executed in the lockstep execution of Cons. Second, assignVal needs to fire chooseVal if a ballot has been decided internally but does not yet have a value assigned; hence we must fire chooseVal when firing assignVal, but only if no other ballot in Global1.succeeded has a non-nil value.

Most of the above case analysis is necessary because Global1 allows ballots to be voted on (and to succeed) before they are assigned values. This nondeterminism makes the algorithm more flexible, but the proof a bit longer.

7 Verifying a Simulation Relation in LP

Since a paired execution provides only empirical evidence for the correctness of a simulation relation, it is desirable to supplement this evidence with a proof — ideally, a proof checked by an automated tool such as LP. The uses of simulated executions described in Sections 5 and 6 assist the LP user in constructing such a proof that the purported forward simulation relation in Figure 3 has the required properties. First, the proof block of the paired execution provides an outline for the proof. Second, invariants suggested by Daikon provide insight and can save the user time in finding auxiliary invariants needed for verification.

The LP proof that the purported simulation relation satisfies property (1) of Definition 1 is straightforward. The only interaction required from the user is to supply the start state of Cons specified in the **initially** section of Figure 3 as a "witness" for an existential quantifier:

```
prove start(a:States[Global1]) ⇒ ∃ b:States[Cons] (start(b) ∧ F(a, b)) by ⇒
    resume by specializing b to [{}, {}, {}, {}, {}]
```

Given this witness, LP automatically rewrites the conjecture and finds that start(b) and F(a, b) are both true, thereby completing the proof.

The LP proof that the purported simulation relation satisfies property (2) of Definition 1, being lengthier, benefits to a greater extent from the results in earlier sections. This proof proceeds by cases, one for each action of the implementation automaton Global1. In each case, the user must supply an execution fragment β of Cons, which is readily available from the **for** statements in the proof block in Figure 3: each action referred to in a **fire** statement is just an element of the witness execution, while the ignore statement represents the null execution. For the init, fail, makeBallot, abstain, and vote actions, the user need supply nothing more: LP finishes the proof automatically. For example, to guide the proof for the init action, it suffices to type

```
resume by specializing beta to init(n, v) * {}
```

Only a trivial amount of additional guidance (telling LP to work harder) is needed for the decide action.

The cases for the assignVal and internalDecide actions are themselves further divided into subcases, in accordance with the **for** statements for those actions in the proof block. In addition, the proof in these cases uses invariants Inv1 through Inv5. Invariant Inv2 is used when ChooseVal is the witness execution for InternalDecide to show that the value being chosen belongs to Cons.proposed. The other four, which show that all ballots not in Global1.dead have identical or nil values, help show that changes to Global1.succeeded and Global1.val preserve the simulation relation.

Of course, the invariants used to establish the simulation relation must be verified themselves. Here too, the interpreter and Daikon provide help. First, invariants sometimes require other invariants in their proofs. In the case study, only Inv3 required auxiliary invariants: Inv1 and Inv6. Daikon detected one of these. Second, the statement of complicated invariants such as Inv6 can be tested via simulated execution; once stated properly, the proof of this invariant was rather simple.

Our techniques do not completely eliminate the need for human guidance in proving invariants and simulation relations. They can automatically discover, and prove with little human assistance, invariants such as Inv1, Inv2, and Inv5. They cannot yet discover invariants such as Inv4 and Inv6, even though their proofs are simple. And although they discover invariant Inv3, which is simple, the proof of this invariant using LP requires moderate human guidance.

8   Conclusion

Theorem provers are the only tools that can soundly reason about general infinite state systems, leading to guarantees of correctness or other properties. A machine-checked proof provides more assurance than a hand proof, but it also carries a cost in terms of human interaction. We propose a methodology that reduces but does not eliminate the human effort required for formally proving properties of programs. In particular, the methodology partially automates some of the tedious, low-level aspects of using a theorem prover, freeing the user to focus on the proof itself.

The methodology integrates simulated execution — running a distributed algorithm over a test suite on a uniprocessor — with theorem proving. Exploratory analysis by experimenting with a system is a well-known technique for building intuition and performing inexpensive sanity checks. We extend the use of run-time techniques in two ways.

First, we use a dynamic invariant detector to generalize over observed executions, reporting logical properties that are likely to be true of the implementation. This technique reifies properties that would otherwise have to be synthesized by a person. These properties can reveal unexpected properties of the implementation, can buttress understanding more effectively than merely examining execution traces, and can provide invariants and lemmas that simplify proofs and reduce theorem-proving effort.

Second, we observe that the effort to build good test suites can be re-used in theorem-prover scripts: the proof scripts often mirror the form of the scripts for driving paired executions, and it pays to get these scripts right before investing effort in attempting a formal proof.

We have illustrated the use of the methodology, and of a toolset that supports the methodology, by means of a case study that formally proves the correctness of an implementation of consensus based on Lamport's Paxos protocol.

References

[AHM+98]   Rajeev Alur, Thomas A. Henzinger, F.Y.C. Mang, Shaz Qadeer, Sriram K. Rajamani, and Serdar Tasiran. Mocha: Exploiting modularity in model checking. In *Proceedings of the Tenth International Conference on Computer-aided Verification*, volume 1427 of *Lecture Notes in Computer Science 1427*, pages 521–525, 1998.

[Bog01]   Andrej Bogdanov. Formal verification of simulations between I/O automata. Master's thesis, Department of Electrical Engineering and Computer Science, Massachusetts Institute of Technology, Cambridge, MA, 2001.

[ECGN01]   Michael Ernst, Jake Cokrell, William G. Grisworld, and David Notkin. Dynamically discovering likely program invariants to support program evolution. *IEEE Transactions on Software Engineering*, 27(2):1–25, 2001.

[GG91]   Stephen Garland and John Guttag. *A guide to LP, the Larch Prover*. Technical report, DEC Systems Research Center, 1991. Updated version avaliable at URL http://nms.lcs.mit.edu/Larch/LP.

[GHG+93]   John V. Guttag, James J. Horning, S. J. Garland, K. D. Jones, A. Modet, and J. M. Wing. *Larch: Languages and Tools for Formal Specification*. Texts and Monographs in Computer Science. Springer-Verlag, New York, 1993.

[GL98]   Stephen J. Garland and Nancy A. Lynch. The IOA language and toolset: Support for designing, analyzing, and building distributed systems. Technical Report MIT/LCS/TR-762, Laboratory for Computer Science, Massachusetts Institute of Technology, Cambridge, MA, August 1998. URL http://theory.lcs.mit.edu/tds/papers/Lynch/IOA-TR-762.ps.

[GSV01]   Yuri Gurevich, Wolfram Schulte, and Margus Veanes. Toward industrial
            strength abstract state machines. Technical Report MSR-TR-2001-98,
            Microsoft Research, 2001. URL for software
            http://www.research.microsoft.com/foundations/asml/.

[KCD⁺02a]   Dilsun Kırlı, Anna Chefter, Laura Dean, Stephen J. Garland, Nancy A.
            Lynch, Toh Ne Win, and Antonio Ramirez-Robredo. The IOA simula-
            tor. Technical Report MIT-LCS-TR-843, MIT Laboratory for Computer
            Science, July 2002.

[KCD⁺02b]   Dilsun Kırlı, Anna Chefter, Laura Dean, Stephen J. Garland, Nancy A.
            Lynch, Toh Ne Win, and Antonio Ramirez-Robredo. Simulating nonde-
            terministic systems at multiple levels of abstraction. In *Proceedings of
            Tools Day 2002*, pages 44–59, Brno, Czech Republic, August 2002. Also
            available as Masaryk University Technical Report FI MU-RS-2002-05.

[Lam98]   Leslie Lamport. The part-time parliament. *ACM Transactions on Com-
            puter Systems*, 16(2):133–169, May 1998.

[LT89]   Nancy A. Lynch and Mark R. Tuttle. An introduction to Input/Output
            automata. *CWI-Quarterly*, 2(3):219–246, September 1989.

[LY01]   Leslie Lamport and Yuan Yu. *TLC – The TLA+ Model Checker*. Compaq
            Systems Research Center, Palo Alto, California, 2001. URL
            http://research.microsoft.com/users/lamport/tla/tlc.html.

[Lyn96]   Nancy Lynch. *Distributed Algorithms*. Morgan Kaufmann Publishers,
            Inc., San Mateo, CA, March 1996.

[McM]   Kenneth L. McMillan. *The SMV Language*. Cadence Berkeley Labs, 2001
            Addison Street, Berkeley, CA 94 704, USA.
            URL http://www.cis.ksu.edu/santos/smv-doc/.

[NE02]   Jeremy W. Nimmer and Michael D. Ernst. Automatic generation of pro-
            gram specifications. In *Proceedings of the 2002 International Symposium
            on Software Testing and Analysis (ISSTA)*, pages 232–242, Rome, Italy,
            July 22–24, 2002.

[PLL00]   Roberto De Prisco, Butler Lampson, and Nancy Lynch. Fundamental
            study: Revisiting the Paxos algorithm. *Theoretical Computer Science*,
            243:35–91, 2000.

[PRZ01]   Amir Pnueli, Sitvanit Ruah, and Lenore Zuck. Automatic deductive ver-
            ification with invisible invariants. In *Tools and Algorithms for the Analy-
            sis and Construction of Systems (TACAS)*, volume 2031 of *LNCS*, pages
            82–97, Genova, Italy, April 2–6, 2001.

[Rin00]   Jussi Rintanen. An iterative algorithm for synthesizing invariants. In
            *Proceedings of the Seventeenth National Conference on Artificial Intel-
            ligence and Twelfth Conference on Innovative Applications of Artificial
            Intelligence*, pages 806–811, Austin, TX, July 30–August 3, 2000.

A   A Schedule Block for Executing `Global1`

Following is a sample schedule block for `Global1`, which produces the output
in Appendix B. The full test suite, used for our runtime analysis with Daikon,
employs more sophisticated constructs, such as loops and conditionals, along
with randomized ballot creation. We omit it here to conserve space.

```
schedule
states
  theNodes: Set[Node] := insert([0], insert([1], insert([2], {}))) ∪
                         insert([3], insert([4], insert([5], {})))

do
  fire internal start(theNodes);
  fire input init([0], [1]);
  fire input init([1], [2]);
  fire input fail([5]);
  fire internal makeBallot([0]);
  fire input init([2], [1]);
  fire input init([4], [3]);
  fire internal assignVal([0], [1]);
  fire internal vote([0], [0]);
  fire internal vote([1], [0]);
  fire internal vote([2], [0]);
  fire internal vote([4], [0]);
  fire input init([3], [2]);
  fire internal makeBallot([1]);
  fire internal abstain([3], {[0]});
  fire internal assignVal([1], [1]);
  fire internal makeBallot([2]);
  fire internal abstain([0], {[1]});
  fire internal abstain([1], {[1]});
  fire internal abstain([2], {[1]});
  fire internal abstain([3], {[1]});
  fire internal assignVal([2], [1]);
  fire internal vote([0], [2]);
  fire internal vote([1], [2]);
  fire internal vote([2], [2]);
  fire internal vote([3], [2]);
  fire input fail([0]);
  fire internal internalDecide([2]);
  fire output decide([1], [1]);
  fire output decide([4], [1]);
od
```

B Paired Interpreter Output for Global1

Following is the beginning of the output of a paired execution of Global1 and
Cons, in which execution of Global1 is driven by the schedule block shown in
Exhibit A and execution of Cons is driven by the **proof** block of the forward
simulation relation.

```
1: internal start((([0] [1] [2] [3] [4] [5])) in automaton Global1
2: input init([0], [1]) in automaton Global1
2: input init([0], [1]) in automaton Cons
3: input init([1], [2]) in automaton Global1
3: input init([1], [2]) in automaton Cons
4: input fail([5]) in automaton Global1
4: input fail([5]) in automaton Cons
5: internal makeBallot([0]) in automaton Global1
6: input init([2], [1]) in automaton Global1
6: input init([2], [1]) in automaton Cons
```

Efficient Computation of Recurrence Diameters[*]

Daniel Kroening and Ofer Strichman

Computer Science, Carnegie Mellon University, Pittsburgh, PA
{kroening|ofers}@cs.cmu.edu

Abstract. SAT based Bounded Model Checking (BMC) is an efficient method for detecting logical errors in finite-state transition systems. Given a transition system, an LTL property, and a user defined bound k, a bounded model checker generates a propositional formula that is satisfiable if and only if a counterexample to the property of length up to k exists. Standard SAT checkers can be used to check this formula. BMC is complete if k is larger than some pre-computed threshold. It is still unknown how to compute this threshold for general properties. We show that the longest initialized loop-free path in the state graph, also known as the *recurrence diameter*, is sufficient for $\mathbf{F}p$ properties. The recurrence diameter is also a known over-approximation for the threshold of simple safety properties ($\mathbf{G}p$). We discuss various techniques to compute the recurrence diameter efficiently and provide experimental results that demonstrate the benefits of using the new approach.

1 Introduction

SAT-based Bounded Model Checking (BMC)[1] was introduced several years ago as a complementary technique for the more traditional BDD-based symbolic model checking [2]. The basic idea of BMC is to search for a counterexample in traces whose length is bounded by some integer k. If no bug is found then the bound k is increased until either a bug is found, the problem becomes intractable, or some pre-computed *Completeness Threshold* $\mathcal{CT}$ is reached[1]. If the completeness threshold is reached without finding a bug, it is implied that the property holds in the given model. The BMC problem can be efficiently reduced to a propositional satisfiability problem, and can therefore be solved by standard SAT methods.

Knowing the completeness threshold $\mathcal{CT}$ is essential for making BMC complete. Without it, there is no way of knowing whether the property holds or rather the bound is not sufficiently high. The value of $\mathcal{CT}$ depends on the model M, the temporal property p,

---

[*] This research was sponsored by the Semiconductor Research Corporation (SRC) under contract no. 99-TJ-684, the National Science Foundation (NSF) under grant no. CCR-9803774, the Office of Naval Research (ONR), and the Naval Research Laboratory (NRL) under contract no. N00014-01-1-0796. The views and conclusions contained in this document are those of the author and should not be interpreted as representing the official policies, either expressed or implied, of SRC, NSF, ONR, NRL, the U.S. government or any other entity.

[1] In all previous publications on this matter, the term 'diameter' was used to denote what we refer to as the completeness threshold. Since the term diameter has a specific meaning in graph theory that coincides with the completeness threshold only for some properties (as we explain later), it is unsuitable for describing the general case.

L. Zuck et al. (Eds.): VMCAI 2003, LNCS 2575, pp. 298–309, 2003.
© Springer-Verlag Berlin Heidelberg 2003

and the exact translation scheme used for obtaining the SAT instances. In this paper we refer to the original LTL translation of Biere et al.[3]. For this translation and $\mathbf{G}p$ (where p is a non-temporal expression) formulas, they show that $\mathcal{CT}$ is equal to d, the longest shortest-path from the initial state (the 'diameter', or, because the path has to start from an initial state, the 'radius' of the model [4]). For a given model and a number k, finding whether $d > k$ can be done by solving a Quantified Boolean Formula (QBF). Thus, finding d amounts to solving a sequence of QBF formulas with increasing k, which is computationally very expansive.

There are several approaches for making this process more efficient. Baumgartner et al. [5] perform an analysis of the circuit structure on the netlist level and identify frequently occurring components with pre-known diameters. The overall diameter of the circuit is then defined recursively over its individual components. With this analysis they found a large number of cases were the diameter can be computed in a short amount of time, and, more importantly, the diameter itself is relatively very small (less than 20 in many cases). Mneimneh and Sakallh[6] suggest a method for simplifying the QBF formulas: while normally one has to check whether each state that is reachable in k steps can be reached sooner, they observe that it is sufficient to check whether it can be reached within $k - 1$ steps, if the initial state has a self loop (such a loop can always be added without affecting the value of the diameter). In [3], Biere et al. suggest to over-approximate the diameter with the *recurrence diameter* r, which is the longest loop-free path between two states. Since every shortest-path is a loop-free path, then obviously $d \leq r$. The recurrence diameter can be computed by solving a series of SAT instances, rather than QBF instances, and it is therefore typically easier to compute. The recurrence diameter is important not only as an over-approximation of d, but also because r characterizes the completeness threshold for $\mathbf{F}p$ properties.

In section 2 we suggest several refinements to the original definition of r that result in shorter paths that are still larger or equal than $\mathcal{CT}$. In section 4.1 we present an efficient way of computing r, based on *sorting networks*. While the currently known technique for computing it requires solving a SAT instance of size quadratic in k, our method requires solving a formula of size $O(k \log k)$. With these improvements we were able to compute the recurrence diameter in several cases that were otherwise impossible to compute with the original method. We provide experimental results to quantify the performance impact of our method.

2 The Completeness Threshold for Simple Properties

We begin with some notation and definitions:

1. A finite transition system $M = \langle \mathcal{S}, I, T \rangle$ is defined by a finite set of states $\mathcal{S}$, an initial-state predicate I, and a transition relation T. States are defined by valuations of the state variables st and input variables in. For simplicity we assume that these are the only type of variables in M.
2. Given a finite transition system M and an LTL property p, we write $M \models p$ if p holds for M, and $M \models_k p$ if p holds for M up to cycle k. Each 'cycle' corresponds to a single application of the transition function, or, in other words, an exploration of the immediate successor states.

3. The predicate $R(t, n)$, $t \in S, n \in \mathbb{N}$, is true if and only if t is reachable within n steps from an initial state:

$$R(t, n) \overset{\text{def}}{=} \exists s_0 \ldots s_n. \, I(s_0) \wedge \bigwedge_{i=0}^{n-1} T(s_i, s_{i+1}) \wedge s_n = t$$

4. The predicate $R_o(t, n)$ denotes that a state t is reachable in n steps from an initial state and cannot be reached via a shorter path.

$$R_o(t, n) \overset{\text{def}}{=} R(t, n) \wedge \not\exists m, m < n. \, R(t, m)$$

5. The predicate $R(t)$, $t \in S$, is true if and only if t is reachable from an initial state:

$$R(t) \overset{\text{def}}{=} \exists n. \, R(t, n)$$

We use this terminology in our definition of the completeness threshold CT with respect to a model M and an LTL formula φ:

Definition 1 (Completeness threshold). *The* completeness threshold *of a finite transition system M and a property φ, denoted by $CT(M, \varphi)$ is the minimal number such that if φ holds up to cycle $CT(M, \varphi)$, it holds globally. Formally:*

$$CT(M, \varphi) \overset{\text{def}}{=} \min\{i \mid M \models_i \varphi \rightarrow M \models \varphi\} \tag{1}$$

Note that $CT(M, \varphi)$ can be arbitrarily large, because φ can specify an arbitrarily long path. The most widely used properties in practice are unnested formulas like $\mathbf{G}p$ and $\mathbf{F}p$, where p is a non-temporal expression (most safety properties can be reduced to $\mathbf{G}p$). This is the only type of formula for which a method for computing $CT(M, \varphi)$ is currently known. The completeness threshold for $\mathbf{G}p$ formulas is the *reachability diameter*[2]:

Definition 2 (Reachability Diameter). *The reachability diameter $rd(M)$ is the minimal number of steps required for reaching all reachable states:*

$$rd(M) \overset{\text{def}}{=} \min\{i \mid \forall t, t \in S. \, \exists j, j \leq i. \, R(t) \rightarrow R(t, j)\} \tag{2}$$

It is easy to see why the reachability diameter is sufficient for $\mathbf{G}p$ formulas. A counterexample to $\mathbf{G}p$ is a path to a state that contradicts p. Since all states can be reached through paths of length $rd(M)$ or less, checking paths whose length is bounded by $rd(M)$ is sufficient for finding all reachable states that contradict p. On the other hand, the reachability diameter is not sufficient for finding all counterexamples to $\mathbf{F}p$ formulas. A counterexample for such a formula is a path ending in a back-loop, where all the states on the path satisfy $\neg p$. Figure 2 demonstrates such a path. While the top path is the shortest counterexample (of length four), all states are reachable through paths of length two or less (i.e. $rd(M) = 2$).

Thus, in order to find a counterexample to $\mathbf{F}p$ it is not sufficient to check all paths of length smaller or equal to $rd(M)$. For this type of formulas we need to look for the longest loop-free path from an initial state, or, in other words, for the reachability recurrence diameter [1], which is defined as follows:

---

[2] This definition is equivalent to the 'radius' in [4].

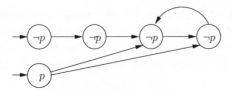

Fig. 1. While the reachability diameter $rd(M)$ in this model is equal to two, the shortest counterexample to the property $\mathbf{F}p$ is of length four.

Definition 3 (Reachability Recurrence Diameter). *The Reachability Recurrence Diameter with respect to a model M, denoted by $rrd(M)$, is the longest loop-free path in M starting from an initial state:*

$$rrd(M) \stackrel{def}{=} max\{i|\; \exists s_0 \ldots s_i.\; I(s_0) \wedge \bigwedge_{j=0}^{i-1} T(s_j, s_{j+1}) \wedge \bigwedge_{j=0}^{i-1} \bigwedge_{k=j+1}^{i} s_j \neq s_k\} \quad (3)$$

The difference between $rd(M)$ and $rrd(M)$ is demonstrated in the drawing below. It shows a structure in which the reachability diameter $rd(M)$ is three, because all states are reachable from the initial state through paths of length three, while $rrd(M)$, the maximal loop-free path starting from an initial state, is equal to four.

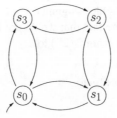

The recurrence diameter was originally suggested in [1] as an over-approximation to the completeness threshold of $\mathbf{G}p$ formulas. The reachability diameter, which is smaller but sufficient for this type of formulas, is too hard to compute because it is a QBF, as was mentioned in the introduction. Restricting the first state to an initial state, as definition 3 requires, is still conservative with respect to $\mathbf{G}p$, because clearly any shortest path to a $\neg p$ state is a loop-free path starting from an initial state. Thus, to summarize this section, the reachability recurrence diameter $rrd(M)$ is useful for both computing the completeness threshold for $\mathbf{F}p$ and for over-approximating it in the case of $\mathbf{G}p$ formulas.

From now on we will only refer to formulas of the form $\mathbf{G}p$ and $\mathbf{F}p$, and therefore, for conciseness, omit the word 'reachability'.

3   A Shorter Recurrence Diameter

Definitions 1–3 refer to states without explicitly saying by which variables these states are defined. Normally a state is defined to be the product of the valuation of all variables.

In subsections 3.1 and 3.2 we show that by ignoring the input variables and variables that are not in the bounded cone of influence of the property, we can find shorter thresholds. Although we prove the correctness of these improvements with respect to the recurrence diameter, they apply to the reachability diameter as well. We will use the following additional notation:

1. The value of a variable v in a state $s \in S$ is denoted by $s(v)$.
2. Let $\hat{s}$ be the set of variables that define the state s. Given a set of variables v, s^v is the projection of s to variables that appear both in v and $\hat{s}$, i.e., if $\{v_1 \ldots v_p\} \subseteq v \cap \hat{s}$, $s^v = (s(v_1), ..., s(v_p))$.
3. If v is some subset of $\hat{s}$, then we denote the recurrence diameter for reachability (as defined in equation 3) by $rrd(M, v)$, when the states are restricted to s^v. Thus, $rrd(M)$ of equation 3 can be written as $rrd(M, \hat{s})$.
4. We use superscripts for cycle numbers and subscripts for variable indices. For example, $in_0^k \ldots in_n^k$ can represent $n + 1$ input variables in cycle k.

3.1   Ignoring the Inputs

In this section we show that there is no need to consider input variables when comparing states, and, consequently, that it is possible to find smaller completeness thresholds. In other words, when computing the recurrence diameter, we will treat all states that are equal modulo their input variables as a single state. Consider, for example, the transition system in Fig. 2. The system has one state variable x and n inputs. If we consider the inputs, from the right state ($x = 1$) we can progress to a $2^n - 1$ long loop-free path while maintaining $x = 1$ (all possible assignments to the input variables, except the one that assigns them all 0). Thus, the fact that we do not distinguish between these states shortens the recurrence diameter from $O(2^n)$ to 2.

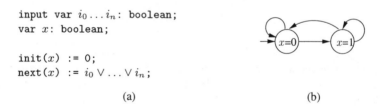

```
input var i₀...iₙ: boolean;
var x: boolean;

init(x)  := 0;
next(x)  := i₀ ∨ ... ∨ iₙ;
```

(a)   (b)

Fig. 2. A transition system (a) and its corresponding Kripke structure (b). When considering inputs, the calculated recurrence diameter of this system is $O(2^n)$ long.

Definition 4 (State variables recurrence diameter). *The state variables recurrence diameter with respect to a model M, denoted by $rrd(M, st)$, is the longest loop-free path in M starting from an initial state, where two states are considered as equal if their state variables have the same value:*

$$rrd(M, st) \overset{def}{=} max\{i|\ \exists s_0 \ldots s_i.\ I(s_0) \wedge \bigwedge_{j=0}^{i-1} T(s_j, s_{j+1}) \wedge \bigwedge_{j=0}^{i-1} \bigwedge_{k=j+1}^{i} s_j^{st} \neq s_k^{st}\} \quad (4)$$

Note that other than the way that states are compared to one another, $rrd(M, st)$ is defined exactly as the recurrence diameter $rrd(M)$.

It is not obvious that inputs can be ignored when computing $\mathcal{CT}$, because the property may refer to inputs. Thus, two states that can only be distinguished by their input variables are not equivalent with respect to a counterexample trace. The following lemma states that nevertheless, ignoring the inputs is safe:

Lemma 1. *If there exists a counterexample to* **F**p *of length greater than* $rrd(M, st)$ *(where the length is defined by the number of distinct states in the path), then there exists another counterexample to* **F**p *of length smaller or equal to* $rrd(M, st)$.

Proof. Assume that there exists a path π ending with a back-loop s.t. $|\pi| > rrd(M, st)$ and every state in π satisfies $\neg p$. Further, assume that π is the shortest path with this property. π must have at least two states that are equal in all state bits. Let s_l, s_r be such two states, where s_l is the state on the left (closer to the initial state). Given an assignment α that satisfies this path, we construct a new assignment α' as follows. First, α' is equal to α in all states to the left of s_l, and equal to α in s_l itself with respect to the state variables. Second, α' assigns the inputs of s_l the same values that α assigns to the inputs of s_r. Now α' satisfies $\alpha'(s_l) = \alpha(s_r)$, and we can therefore proceed from s_l to s_{r+1}. Thus, the third stage of the construction shifts the assignment of α to states $s_{r+1} \ldots s_{|\pi|}$ to states $s_{l+1} \ldots s_{|\pi|-(r-l)}$. Now α' corresponds to a path shorter than π that satisfies $\neg p$ in all of its states. The existence of such a path contradicts our assumption.   □

Although Lemma 1 refers explicitly to **F**p formulas, it is clear that inputs can be ignored also when computing an over-approximation to **G**p formulas. Baumgartner et al. [5] ignore the inputs as well when they compute the reachability diameter.

3.2   Ignoring Variables That Do Not Affect the Property

It was observed in [5] that the reachability diameter should be computed while considering only the cone of influence of the property. We now show that this observation can be extended to the *bounded* cone of influence. Bounded cone of influence (BCOI) [7] is a reduction method that operates in two stages. First, it identifies the variables that affect the property at (or up to) the cycle bounding the search; second, it simplifies the formula by assuming an arbitrary value for the rest of the variables. For example, in the following transition system, the value of the state variables x_1 and x_2 affect the property with a delay of one and two cycles, respectively.

```
var x_0, x_1, x_2: boolean;
init(x_0) = 0; init(x_1) = 0; init(x_2) = 0;
next(x_2) := !x_2;
next(x_1) := x_2
next(x_0) := x_1
SPEC AG(! x_0)
```

Consequently, when checking the property at cycle k, we can ignore the value of x_2 in cycles k and $k-1$, and ignore the value of x_1 in cycle k. The same idea can be used for finding a smaller completeness threshold.

Let $B^k(i)$, $i \le k$ be the set of variables such that their value in cycle i affect the property at cycle k. Since $B^k(i)$ can include different variables for each cycle i, we need to redefine 'comparison' between two states. We define two states $s_i, s_j, j > i$ to be equal if and only if they are equal in all variables in $B^k(j)$, i.e., $\forall v \in B^k(j), s_i(v) = s_j(v)$. Given this definition, we now redefine the recurrence diameter:

$$rrdb(M) \overset{\text{def}}{=} max\{i| \; \exists s_0 \ldots s_i. \; I(s_0) \wedge \bigwedge_{j=0}^{i-1} T(s_j, s_{j+1}) \wedge \bigwedge_{j=0}^{i-1} \bigwedge_{k=j+1}^{i} s_j^{B^i(j)} \neq s_k^{B^i(k)}\}$$

(5)

To combine the improvement of section 3.1 with this definition, we can restrict the comparison further to state variables only (that is, each state s_j is restricted to $B^i(j) \cap st$), and denote the result of this restriction by $rrdb(M, st)$. For simplicity, however, we assume from here on that all variables in the bounded cone of influence are state variables.

Lemma 2. *If there exists a state t_1 that contradicts the property such that $R_o(t_1, n_1)$, $n_1 > rrdb(M)$, then there exists a state t_2 that contradicts the property as well and $R_o(t_2, n_2)$, $n_2 \le rrdb(M)$.*

Proof. Assume the contrary. By Equation 5 and Lemma 1, this implies that in the path to t_1 there exists two states, say s_i and $s_j, j > i$, that are equal in their $B^{n_1}(j)$ variables but different in at least one other variable. A state equal to s_{j+1} in all $B^{n_1}(j+1)$ variables can be reached in one step from s_i. Let s_{i+1} denote this state. Then, a state equal to s_{j+2} in all $B^{n_1}(j+2)$ can be reached from s_{i+1}, and so forth. Thus, a sequence of states which is equivalent to the path from s_j to t_1 in all variables relevant to the property can be reached in one step from s_i, which means that we can reach a state contradicting the property in less than n_1 steps. This contradicts our assumption.   □

As an example of where the restriction to BCOI variables can shorten the computed recurrence diameter, consider the diagram in Fig. 3, and a property $\mathbf{G}p$. The states in this diagram are defined by two state variables, say v_1 and v_2. The variables that affect p in cycle 4 (according to a BCOI analysis) are underlined. The states s_1 and s_2 are considered different if we consider all variables, but equal if we consider only variables that affect the property. Taking the second option implies that $s_0 \to s_1 \to s_3$ is the longest loop free path, and hence the threshold is reduced from four to three. Note that the path from s_2 to a state that contradicts p implies that there must exist such a state that can be reached in one step from s_1, possibly s_3 itself. This is because the value of p depends only on v_1, and we know that this variable has the same value in s_1 and s_2.

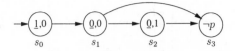

Fig. 3. Two possible paths, where the variables affecting the property p are underlined.

4   Finding the Recurrence Diameter with Sorting Networks

4.1   Sorting Networks for Loop Detection

The currently used technique [1] for computing the recurrence diameter (either $rrd(M)$ or $rrd(M, st)$) compares all pairs of states, as implied by Equations 3 and 4. The size of the resulting formula is therefore quadratic in the length of the path k.

We propose the following alternative: first, we generate an equation that represents the same set of states but in a sorted order; second, we compare the neighbors in the sorted sequence. Since we have to generate the equation without any actual knowledge of the states, the sequence of comparisons performed must be the same for all possible states. This is known as the Bose-Nelson sorting problem. A circuit that solves this problem is called a *sorting network* (see Knuth [8] for a survey).

Ajtai, Kolmós, Szemerédi [9] show that sorting networks for n inputs can be built with size $O(n \log n)$. However, there is a very high constant (several thousands) hidden in this complexity result that makes it impractical for our purpose. We therefore use a variant of a *bitonic sorting network* as described by Batcher [10], which has an asymptotic size of $O(n \log^2 n)$. Bitonic sorting networks have a recursive structure (see Fig. 4). The inputs are split into two parts that are sorted independently and then merged. This means that the sorting blocks can be replaced by any other sorting network. While for an arbitrary input size the minimal size of the sorting network is unknown, for small numbers there are known optimal or near optimal solutions. For these cases, we replace the bitonic sorting network with these known small sorting networks. Figure 5 shows a simple sorting network for three input states.

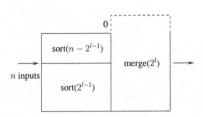

Fig. 4. Block diagram for a bitonic sorting network with n inputs and $l = \lceil \log_2 n \rceil$. If n is not a power of two, the smallest element (denoted by 0) is used for merging.

Let $s_0 \ldots s_{n-1}$ denote the n states of the path. Using the sorting network, we obtain an ordered permutation of these states $s'_0 \geq s'_1 \ldots \geq s'_{n-1}$. It is obvious that a sequence

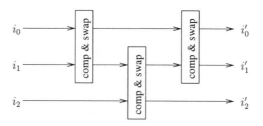

Fig. 5. Sorting network for three inputs. $i_0..i_2$ are the input unsorted states, and $i'_0..i'_2$ are the output sorted states.

of states contains two equal states if and only if its corresponding sorted sequence contains two equal neighboring states, or, formally:

$$\exists i : s'_i = s'_{i+1} \iff \exists l, j : l \neq j \wedge s_l = s_j \tag{6}$$

Thus, we now only have to compare all neighbors in this sequence. This can be done with $n - 1$ comparisons.

4.2 Ordering and Swapping

All sorting networks require a *compare* and *swap* operation. Two elements a and b are compared and, if $a > b$, are swapped. We implement the ordering operator by computing the last carry bit of the sum $a + (-b)$. Let a denote a bit vector of length β, and let a_i, $0 \leq i < \beta$ denote the i-th component of a. Let $\bar{b}$ denote the inverted vector b. Since $\bar{b} + 1$ is equal to $-b$, we can compute $a + (-b)$ by computing $a + \bar{b} + 1$. The first carry bit c_0 of this sum is:

$$c_0 := a_0 \vee \bar{b_0} \tag{7}$$

The i-th carry bit of this sum with $i \geq 1$ is:

$$c_i := (a_i \wedge \bar{b_i}) \vee (a_i \wedge c_{i-1}) \vee (\bar{b_i} \wedge c_{i-1}) \tag{8}$$

The value of the last carry bit $c_{\beta-1}$ determines whether we swap a and b. Let b' denote the new value (after swapping) of b. The equation for a' follows the same pattern.

$$b'_i = a_i \wedge c_{\beta-1} \vee b_i \wedge \overline{c_{\beta-1}} \tag{9}$$

Equation 7 is transformed into CNF using 1 new literal and 3 clauses, equation 8 requires 1 new literal and 6 clauses, and equation 9 requires 1 new literal and 4 clauses. The swapping has to be done for both a and b. Thus, the total cost of one compare/swap operation with β bits is 4β literals and 17β clauses.

5   Experimental Results

We experimented with several circuits from the ISCAS'89 benchmark netlists. First, we checked the influence of considering only state variables when comparing states. We were able to compute $rrd(M, st)$ (the reachability recurrence diameter of state variables) of 6 out of the 35 instances in the benchmark (see top 6 circuits in figure 6). On the other hand we could not compute $rrd(M)$ for any of them using a one hour time limit[3].

We also tried several other circuits. The recurrence diameter for the arithmetic circuits div8 and mult8, and the serial bus controller circuit IIC is computed easily (see the bottom part of figure 6).

Circuit	$rrd(M, st)$	time $(rrd(M, st))$ (SAT)	time$(rrd(M, st) + 1)$ (UNSAT)	$rrd(M)$	time$(rrd(M))$ (SAT)
s27	5	< 1s.	< 1s.	?	*
s386	11	< 1s.	< 1s.	?	*
s510	46	< 1s.	< 1s.	?	*
s832	17	< 1s.	1 s.	?	*
s820	17	< 1s.	< 1s.	?	*
s208.1	255	2.58 s.	3.35 s.	?	*
div8	11	< 1s.	2.28 s	?	*
mult8	9	< 1s.	< 1s	?	*
IIC	31	< 1s.	< 1s	?	*

Fig. 6. Ignoring the inputs while comparing states shortens the diameter, and hence makes it easier to compute.

To check the efficiency of sorting networks versus the previously known all-pair method, we generated the CNF files of the s27 benchmark circuit with both methods for an increasing bound k. Figure 7 depicts our results. It shows that for k larger than about 50, the CNF file that is generated with sorting networks is smaller, both with respect to the number of variables, and the the number of clauses (the break-even point depends on the number of state-bits. This point is smaller if there are less state bits). Although the size of the CNF does not directly predict the time it takes to solve it, it does give some estimation of how hard the problem is, especially when the difference in size is significant.

6   Conclusions and Directions for Future Work

Finding the recurrence diameter of designs with respect to a given property is important for achieving completeness in Bounded Model Checking. We have presented several techniques for making this calculation easier than previously known techniques. Since

---

[3] We reached $k = 300$ with most of these files, but the recurrence diameter is apparently much higher.

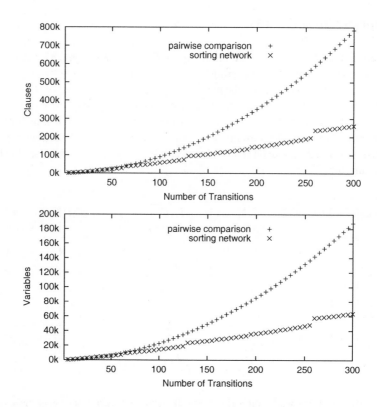

Fig. 7. Comparison of the CNF size (number of literals and clauses) with pairwise comparison and with sorting network

the recurrence diameter is typically very high (it can be exponential in the number of state variables), in many cases it is still impractical to find, let alone perform bounded model checking with such a high bound. Thus, finding more efficient ways to calculate the recurrence diameter is still an important research topic. The question of how to find the completeness threshold for a general LTL property is still open.

References

1. A. Biere, A. Cimatti, E. Clarke, and Y. Zhu. Symbolic model checking without BDDs. In *Tools and Algorithms for Construction and Analysis of Systems*, pages 193–207, 1999.
2. E.M.Clarke, O.Grumberg, and D.Peled. *Model Checking*. MIT Press, Cambridge, MA, 1999.
3. A. Biere, A. Cimatti, E. M. Clarke, M. Fujita, , and Y. Zhu. Symbolic model checking using SAT procedures instead of BDDs. In *Design Automation Conference (DAC'99)*, 1999.
4. A. Biere, C. Artho, and V. Schuppan. Liveness checking as safety checking. In *FMICS workshop 2002*, 2002.
5. J. Baumgartner, A. Kuehlmann, and J. Abraham. Property checking via structural analysis. In *Proc. 14th Intl. Conference on Computer Aided Verification (CAV'02)*, 2002.

6. M. Mneimneh and K. Sakallah. SAT-based sequential depth computation. In *Constraints in formal verification workshop*, Cornell University, Ithaca, New York, Sep 2002.
7. A. Biere, E. Clarke, R. Raimi, and Y. Zhu. Verifying safety properties of a PowerPC^{TM} microprocessor using symbolic model checking without bdds. In N. Halbwachs and D. Peled, editors, *Proc. 11th Intl. Conference on Computer Aided Verification (CAV'99)*, LNCS. Springer-Verlag, 1999.
8. D.E. Knuth. *The Art of Computer Programming, volume 3: Sorting and Searching*. Addison Wesley, 1973.
9. M. Ajtai, J. Komlós, and S. Szemerédi. An $O(N \log N)$ sorting network. In *Proceedings of the 25th ACM Symposium on Theory of Computing*, pages 1–9, 1983.
10. K.E. Batcher. Sorting networks and their applications. In *Proc. AFIPS Spring Joint Comput. Conf.*, volume 32, pages 307–314, 1968.

Shape Analysis through Predicate Abstraction and Model Checking

Dennis Dams and Kedar S. Namjoshi

Bell Labs, Lucent Technologies, 600 Mountain Ave., Murray Hill, NJ 07974.
{dennis,kedar}@research.bell-labs.com

Abstract. We propose a new framework, based on predicate abstraction and model checking, for *shape analysis* of programs. Shape analysis is used to statically collect information — such as possible reachability and sharing — about program stores. Rather than use a specialized abstract interpretation based on shape graphs, we instantiate a generic and automated abstraction procedure with shape predicates from a correctness property. This results in a predicate-discovery procedure that identifies predicates relevant for correctness, using an analysis based on weakest preconditions, and creates a finite state abstract program. The correctness property is then checked on the abstraction with a model checking tool. To enable this process, we calculate weakest preconditions for common shape properties, and present heuristics for accelerating convergence. Exploring abstract state spaces with model checkers enables one to tap into a wealth of techniques and highly optimized implementations for state space exploration, and to analyze properties that go beyond invariances. We illustrate this simple and flexible framework with the analysis of some "classical" list manipulation programs, using our implementation of the abstraction algorithm, and the SPIN and COSPAN model checkers for state space exploration.

1 Introduction

Shape analysis is used to statically determine global properties of the program heap. Examples of such properties are "points-to" reachability between objects, the existence of cycles, or sharing within the heap. Typically, such analyses are based on abstract interpretations [7] of heaps with various kinds of *shape graphs*. This paper presents a new framework for shape analysis, which is based on Schmidt and Steffen's observation that static analysis is model checking of an abstract interpretation [30]. The exploitation of this paradigm renders our framework different in several key ways.

A major difference is the way in which abstract interpretation is performed. We use a *generic* abstraction algorithm to calculate an abstraction of the program, relative to a given shape property. Starting with the shape predicates in the property, the algorithm iteratively, and in a goal-directed manner, discovers other predicates that are relevant to the property, by computing weakest preconditions (wp) [12]. It also constructs an abstraction where these predicates

L. Zuck et al. (Eds.): VMCAI 2003, LNCS 2575, pp. 310–323, 2003.
© Springer-Verlag Berlin Heidelberg 2003

are represented with boolean variables: the process is an instance of *predicate abstraction* [14]. The correctness of the abstract interpretation is guaranteed by the algorithm. An advantage is that non-shape predicates (such as arithmetic inequalities), which improve the precision of abstraction, are included in a straightforward manner. One of the main contributions of this paper is the calculation of weakest preconditions for second-order shape predicates like reachability, the identification of other predicates that arise in this process, and the calculation of their *wp*'s. We have implemented a weakest precondition calculator for shape predicates relative to C-like program constructs, including heuristics to accelerate convergence.

The abstract program computed by this algorithm is analyzed with a *generic* model checker. This enables one to tap into a wealth of techniques and highly optimized implementations for state space exploration. Furthermore, one can check for temporal properties that go beyond invariances. Our calculator generates the abstracted program in formats that are accepted by the explicit state model checker SPIN [18] and the BDD-based model checker COSPAN [16]. We demonstrate our approach on a "classical" list reversal program. A detailed description of the experiments, including input and result files, can be found at [32].

```
typedef struct node
   {struct node *n; int data;} Node;
typedef Node *List;

List insert(List x, int a)
{
List t;
n1: t=(List) malloc(sizeof(Node));
n2: t->data=a;
n3: t->n=x;
n4: x=t;
ne: return x;
}
```

```
n1: {reach[;n](x,k), false}
    t=(List) malloc (sizeof(Node));
n2: {reach[&(t->n);n](x,k), (t==k)}
    t->data=a;
n3: {reach[&(t->n);n](x,k)\/(t==k)}
    t->n=x;
n4: {reach[;n](t,k)}
    x=t;
ne: {reach[;n](x,k)}
    return x;
```

Fig. 1. List insertion procedure (left) and *wp* calculations (right)

Overview. We introduce our framework through the analysis of a C program for inserting an element at the head of a list, shown in Figure 1. We are interested in checking the property that the insertion process does not, inadvertently, make one of the existing list members unreachable from x. Define the predicate $reach[A;F](i,j)@l$ to be true of those program states where control is at location l and, in the heap, it is possible to reach address j from address i, following only those fields in F and avoiding all addresses in set A. We write $reach[;F](i,j)$ if A is empty, and when $F = \{n\}$ it is written as n. The above property can then be expressed formally by the linear temporal logic formula $(\forall k : \mathsf{G}(reach[;n](x,k)@n1 \Rightarrow \mathsf{G}(true@ne \Rightarrow reach[;n](x,k)@ne)))$.

The predicate $reach[; n](x, k)$ holds at ne iff its *weakest precondition (wp)* [12] holds at $n4$. While weakest preconditions for simple constructs can be computed by syntactic substitution, this is not true for second order predicates like reachability. We show in Section 3 how to compute wp for reachability: for the present discussion, it suffices to know that the wp for this predicate simplifies to the expected value: $reach[; n](t, k)$. The abstraction algorithm (Section 2) computes wp's for individual predicates in this goal-directed, "backward" manner until the initial location $n1$ is reached. The results are shown enclosed in $\{\ldots\}$ in Figure 1 (right) with wp's for predicates at $n3$ separated by a comma at $n2$. The key point to note is how the wp calculations identify further predicates that are relevant to the correctness property.

```
b0 <-> reach[;n](x,k)
b1 <-> reach[;n](t,k)
b2 <-> reach[&(t->n);n](x,k)
b3 <-> (t==k)
```

```
n1: b2 := b0, b3 := false;
n2: b2 := b2, b3 := b3;
n3: b1 := b2 \/ b3;
n4: b0 := b1;
ne:
```

Fig. 2. Predicate-boolean correspondence (left) and abstract program (right)

The abstract program, and the predicate-boolean correspondence, is shown in Figure 2. The abstract actions are calculated by substituting boolean variables for predicates in the results of the wp calculations. For instance, the update for $b1$ on edge $n3$ to $n4$ is given by $b2 \lor b3$, which is the result of substitution on the wp for its corresponding predicate $reach[; n](t, k)$. Note that booleans are only guaranteed to have correct values where it matters — e.g. $b1$ may have the (clearly wrong) value *true* at $n2$, but it is set to its correct value at location $n3$, just before it is used to calculate $b0$. The abstraction algorithm ensures this property which, in turn, ensures the correctness of the abstraction.

The adjusted correctness property for the abstract program, $G(b0@n1 \Rightarrow G(true@ne \Rightarrow b0@ne))$ can be established using a model checker. For this example, the property can be established directly from the wp calculations; however, this is difficult to do for the analysis of programs with loops. In general, the wp calculations serve to transform the program *locally*, while the model checking determines *global* properties. As the abstraction is always *conservative* in nature, a property that holds of the abstraction also holds of the source program. Hence, the source program is also correct.

The various components of the framework are described in detail in subsequent sections.

2   Abstraction by Iterated Weakest Preconditions

In Predicate Abstraction [14], the abstract program is defined over a set of boolean variables which represent source program predicates. Determining a set of predicates relevant to showing a correctness property is undecidable in general

[17]; however, several (semi-) algorithms exist [26,6,3,22]. We use a modified form of the algorithm from [26]. This algorithm *simultaneously* derives a set of relevant predicates and computes the abstract actions, through an iterated weakest precondition calculation.

The original algorithm operates on programs modeled by a set of actions defined as guarded commands. A sequential procedure body can be easily translated to this notation by using a variable, say "pc", to represent the control location. With this encoding, however, the scheme in [26] examines every action at each iteration, resulting in several unnecessary calculations. Thus, we encode the control transition in the action name itself, and tailor the algorithm to only inspect relevant actions. A control flow edge from location m to n labeled with *guard g* and *update a* is turned into the action $s_{m,n} : g \to a$ (note that a is deterministic). For an update $s : g \to a$, $wp(s,p) \equiv g \land wp(a,p)$[1]. The other major difference is that we allow for user guidance of the abstraction in the form of abstraction hints.

Our modified algorithm is presented in Figure 3. The algorithm iteratively computes a set of pairs (p, n), where p is a predicate and n is a control location. The pair (p, n) asserts that predicate p holds at location n. The data structures used are a set of pairs, S, and a set of newly generated pairs, N. The parameters to the algorithm are: (a) a correctness property, written in a universal temporal logic such as LTL or ACTL*, (b) an iteration bound k, and (c) a set of *approximation hints*.

In the main loop (step 2), the algorithm processes unmarked pairs in a breadth-first manner. For each unmarked pair (p, n), and every action $s_{m,n}$, the algorithm computes $wp(s_{m,n}, p)$. By the semantics of wp, the truth of predicate p at node n after executing statement $s_{m,n}$ is given by the value of $wp(s_{m,n}, p)$ at node m. This, in turn, is determined by the values of its constituent predicates at node m. These predicates are extracted, and processed in the next iteration. From the undecidability result, there can be no termination guarantee in general, so a user-supplied bound k is used to limit the number of iterations. The approximation hints are used to introduce new predicates that may accelerate the termination of the loop – an example is provided in Section 5. Every predicate p generated during the algorithm has a corresponding boolean variable, called b_p. The substitution of predicates in a formula f with their corresponding booleans results in a formula $\bar{f}$ – as a general rule, we represent the abstract version of a concrete object o by $\bar{o}$. *Simplification* is used in step 2 to reduce the number of newly generated pairs for faster termination: correctness does not depend on the power, but only on the soundness of the simplifier.

We now examine some other issues that arise in applying this algorithm. An *initial condition*, *init*, can be encoded by introducing a new transition $s_{n0,n1} : init \to skip$, between a new initial location ($n0$) and the old one ($n1$). An abstraction computed without hints can be used only to prove properties that depend solely on predicates generated by the iterated wp calculations. While this

---

[1] This reflects the semantics that an action is executed at a state only if its guard holds at that state.

1. Initially, S contains all pairs from the correctness property, together with (q, m), for each predicate q that occurs in the guard of some action $s_{m,n} : g \to a$. Initially, the abstract actions are defined as $\overline{s}_{m,n} : \overline{g} \to skip$. All pairs in S are unmarked, and N is empty.

2. At each iteration, as long as there is an unmarked pair in S, and the iteration bound k is not reached, do the following.
   a) For each unmarked pair (p, n), mark it as examined, and:
      i. if there is an approximation hint mapping (p, n) to an expression h, then add the equivalence $b_p \equiv \overline{h}$ at node n and insert $\{(q, n) \mid q \in pred(h)\}$ into N.
      ii. else, consider action $s_{m,n} : g \to a$, for each m, and:
         A. compute $wp(s_{m,n}, p)$, and *simplify* it to obtain a formula f.
         B. for each q in $pred(f)$, add (q, m) to the set N.
         C. add $b_p := \overline{f}$ to the update of abstract action $\overline{s}_{m,n}$.
   b) Add all pairs in N to S.

3. After step 2 has terminated, *over-approximate* the booleans corresponding to any unmarked predicates, using either an approximation hint, or non-determinism ($\{false, true\}$), or $\top$.

Fig. 3. The predicate abstraction algorithm

may be sufficient in some cases (e.g., list insertion) it is necessary, in general, to use hints. The approximation hint for $p@n$ can be any expression h that is "more abstract" than p. This is formalized as $p \preceq_3 h$, where $\preceq_3$ is the "abstraction order" relation of 3-valued logic[2]. For instance, $(x > 3)$ may be approximated by *if* $(x \le 0)$ *then false else* $\top$.

The algorithm always computes a conservative approximation to the source program, where a program state (s, n) is related to an abstract state (s', n') if, and only if, the control locations n, n' are identical, and for every predicate p such that the pair (p, n) is considered during abstraction, $p(s) \preceq_3 b_p(s')$. This algorithm is also complete in the sense shown in [26,2].

As stated, this algorithm is intra-procedural. It can be extended to handle procedure calls by the process described in [1]. For example, $wp(x := F(y), p(x))$ can be calculated by determining $wp(body(F), p(r))(y)$, where r is the return value of the body of F. This introduces additional predicates within the body of F. The call to F is then replaced by a call to the abstract version of F, i.e., $b_p := \overline{F}(\{b_q \mid q \in pred(wp(body(F), p(r)))\})$.

3 Weakest Preconditions for Shape Analysis

To utilize the above abstraction algorithm for shape analysis, we need to calculate weakest preconditions for common shape properties such as *reachability*, *cyclicity*, and *sharing*. The definitions of these properties, and their weakest precondition calculations, are both based on a *memory model*.

---

[2] $x \preceq_3 x$ for all x, and $x \preceq_3 \top$, for all x. $\top$ and $\{false, true\}$ are identified for this purpose.

3.1   Memory Model

Heap and stack contents are modeled by an unbounded array M, indexed by the integers, together with a finite subset of the integers, called *alloc*, which records the allocated addresses. A structure field name, such as n, is represented with a function, called $\hat{n}$, which maps the address of the structure to the address where field n is 'stored' – we assume field names are globally distinct. An expression e has two attributes relative to M: its *address*, denoted by $addr_M(e)$, and its *value*, denoted by $val_M(e)$. The rules for calculating these attributes, and the interpretations of basic program statements, are given in Figure 4. In these rules, attributes are written as a pair (address,value), $\perp$ represents an undefined result, and we have simplified matters by having *malloc* allocate a single memory location.

Program variable x: $(\alpha(x), M[\alpha(x)])$, where α maps program variables to addresses
Structure access $e.n$: $(\hat{n}(addr_M(e)), M[\hat{n}(addr_M(e))])$
Address expression $\&e$: $(\perp, addr_M(e))$
Dereference $*e$: $(val_M(e), M[val_M(e)])$, if $val_M(e) \in alloc$, else error
Numeric constant c: $(\perp, c)$
Arithmetic operation $op(e1, \ldots, en)$: $(\perp, op(val_M(e1), \ldots, val_M(en)))$
Pointer addition $e + i$: $(\perp, val_M(e) + i)$

Guard g: $val_M(g)$
Ordinary assignment $e1 := e2$: $M[addr_M(e1)] := val_M(e2)$
Memory allocation $e := malloc$: $M[addr_M(e)] := a; alloc := alloc \cup \{a\}$,
    for some $a \notin alloc$
Memory de-allocation $free(e)$: $alloc := alloc \setminus \{val_M(e)\}$

Fig. 4. The memory model

The *wp* of a predicate p relative to a statement s is computed by translating both p and s in terms of M, calculating *wp* in the standard way for array updates[3] [15], and translating the result back to the syntax of program expressions (see e.g. [5]). For example, consider the predicate $p \equiv (x = 0)$, for a program variable x, and statement $s : *u := 10$. The assignment is interpreted as a memory update resulting in $M' \equiv M[val_M(u) \leftarrow 10]$, and $wp(s, p)$ is given by $(val_M(x') = 0)$. Distributing M' into *val* results in *(if* $(val_M(u) = \alpha(x))$ *then* 10 *else* $val_M(x)) = 0$, which simplifies to $(val_M(u) \neq \alpha(x)) \wedge (val_M(x) = 0)$. Translating back to program syntax gives $(u \neq \&x) \wedge (x = 0)$ as the weakest precondition. This process of translating back and forth from M thus correctly takes into account *aliasing* effects. It is tedious to carry out such calculations by hand, but they are easily automated, as described in the following section.

---

[3] $wp(M[a] := v, p(M))$ is given by $p(M')$, where $M'[i] = M[i]$ for $i \neq a$, and $M'[a] = v$, denoted by $M' = M[a \leftarrow v]$. Distributing M' into p results in an expression in terms of M.

3.2   Weakest Preconditions for Shape Predicates

We have, so far, considered wp calculations for simple kinds of predicates, albeit taking into account complex aliasing effects. We are primarily interested in more global, second-order shape properties. The key property is $reach[A; F](i, j, M)$. Informally, this says that there is a sequence of steps in M from address i to address j, which avoids all addresses in A, and uses only the fields in F. We define this precisely below as a least fixpoint. A *step* refers to a memory dereference. For example, if z is a variable of type Node (see Figure 1), the location where the address of the next node is stored is $\hat{n}(\alpha(z))$ (the value of $\&((*z).n)$). But the address of the next element itself is given by $M[\hat{n}(\alpha(z))]$, which results from a memory dereference.

For a set F of field names, let $F^*(w, y, A)$ hold iff y is reachable from w using only field accesses from F (e.g. $x.a.b.c$), while avoiding addresses in A. This is defined as follows:

$$F^*(w, y, A) \equiv alloc(y) \wedge$$
$$(\mu Z, x : alloc(x) \wedge (x = y \vee (\neg A(x) \wedge (\exists a : a \in F : Z(\hat{a}(x))))))(w)$$

We can then define *reach* by

$$reach[A; F](w, b, M) \equiv$$
$$(\mu Z, x : alloc(x) \wedge (\exists k : F^*(x, k, A) : (k = b \vee (\neg A(k) \wedge Z(M[k]))))))(w)$$

Note the explicit dereferencing step $M[k]$ in this definition.

The wp for *reach* is calculated for an update $M' = M[i \leftarrow c]$ by substituting M' for M in this fixpoint expression, and simplifying the result. For the other predicates, which are defined in terms of *reach*, their wp's are calculated using the wp for *reach*. The definitions of these predicates and their wp's are shown in Figure 5; their derivations are available at [32]. Informally, the wp for reachability says that it is possible to reach b from x after an update $M' = M[i \leftarrow c]$ provided that, in the previous state, either: (i) it is possible to reach b from x avoiding addresses in $A \cup \{i\}$, or (ii) i is not in A, and there are paths from x to i, and from c to b that avoid A. In the first case, the memory update does not invalidate the path and, in the second case, the memory update serves to link two paths into the desired path from x to b. The other wp expressions have similar informal readings.

A remarkable feature one may observe is a kind of *closure* property, in that the wp for a shape predicate is expressible in terms of other shape predicates— of course, with differences in the arguments. Closure ensures that only these types of shape predicates arise during the iterations of the abstraction algorithm, making it possible to spot patterns that indicate where approximation is needed. An example of such a pattern is given in the analysis of a list reversal program in Section 5.

We use predicates with the same names to state program properties: e.g., $reach[A; F](e1, e2)$, where A is a set of program expressions, and $e1, e2$ are program expressions. The translation of the predicate into the memory model as

- $reach[A; F](x, b, M)$: it is possible to reach address b from address x in 0 or more steps. The wp is given by

$$reach[Ai; F](x, b, M) \lor (\neg A(i) \land reach[Ai; F](x, i, M) \land reach[Ai; F](c, b, M))$$

- $reachp[A; F](x, b, M)$: it is possible to reach address b from address x in 1 or more steps. This is defined by $alloc(x) \land (\exists k : F^*(x, k, A) : \neg A(k) \land reach[A; F](M(k), b, M))$, with wp:

$$reachp[Ai; F](x, b, M) \lor (reach[Ai; F](c, b, M) \land \neg A(i) \land reach[Ai, F](x, i, M))$$

- $dshared[A; F](x, y, M)$: there exists a non-null node reachable from both x and y. This is defined by $(\exists v : v \neq \mathsf{NULL} : reach[A; F](x, v, M) \land reach[A; F](y, v, M))$, with wp:

$$dshared[Ai; F](x, y, M) \lor$$
$$(\neg A(i) \land reach[Ai; F](x, i, M) \land dshared[Ai; F](y, c, M)) \lor$$
$$(\neg A(i) \land reach[Ai; F](y, i, M) \land dshared[Ai; F](x, c, M)) \lor$$
$$(\neg A(i) \land (c \neq \mathsf{NULL}) \land reach[Ai; F](x, i, M) \land reach[Ai; F](y, i, M))$$

- $cyclic[A; F](x, M)$: x reaches a node that is involved in a cycle. This is defined by $(\exists v : reach[A; F](x, v, M) \land reachp[A; F](v, v, M))$, with wp:

$$cyclic[Ai; F](x, M) \lor$$
$$(\neg A(i) \land reach[Ai; F](x, i, M) \land cyclic[Ai; F](c, M)) \lor$$
$$(\neg A(i) \land reach[Ai; F](x, i, M) \land reach[Ai; F](c, i, M))$$

Fig. 5. Weakest preconditions for shape predicates for $M' = M[i \leftarrow c]$. In these formulas, we use Ai to represent $A \cup \{i\}$

a prelude to computing wp is given by $reach[val_M(A); F](val_M(e1), val_M(e2), M)$.

As an example, in the program from Section 1, consider the predicate $reach[; n](x, k)$, and the assignment $x := t$, where t and x are of type List. The translated predicate is given by $reach[; n](val_M(x), val_M(k), M)$, while the assignment results in the memory update $M' = M[\alpha(x) \leftarrow val_M(t)]$. Substituting M' for M gives $reach[; n](val_{M'}(x), val_{M'}(k), M'))$. This simplifies, using the wp for $reach$, to $reach[\alpha(x); n](val_M(t), val_M(k), M) \lor (true \land reach[; n](val_M(t), \alpha(x), M) \land reach[; n](val_M(t), val_M(k), M))$. From the definition of type List, it is clear that t can never reach the address of x. Thus, the underlined term simplifies to *false*, and the result is: $reach[\alpha(x); n](val_M(t), val_M(k), M)$. The avoiding address $\alpha(x)$ is superfluous for the same reason, so it can be removed, giving the result (in program syntax) as $reach[; n](t, k)$.

4   A Predicate Calculator for Shape Analysis

We have implemented a prototype predicate abstractor for shape analysis, based on the set of predicates discussed above, in OCaml. The input to this tool consists of a flow-chart program with C-style instructions and variable types including all basic types as well as struct and pointer types. Nested structs, unions, and array types are not currently accepted by the tool but their inclusion poses no technical difficulties. The tool does not yet handle procedure calls. Along with the program, a set of predicate-location pairs is given, as e.g. extracted from the property to be checked. These serve as the starting point for the wp calculations. Finally, an iteration bound and a (possibly empty) collection of approximation hints are given as input.

The tool's main challenge is in simplifying the "raw" formulas that are obtained as wp's. These may be large due to case distinctions for aliasing. By rewriting newly generated predicates to simpler ones, semantical equivalence with already-computed predicates can often be detected. This reduces the overall number of generated predicates, which is essential in a practical application of the algorithm. Also, it renders the predicates more readable, which facilitates the identification of good approximations. We have implemented a variety of rules that aim to simplify individual predicates like $reach$ and their arguments, and pointer (in)equalities. For example, $reach[A;F](null,e)$ rewrites to $false$ regardless of A, F, and e; in $reach[A;F](e_1,e_2)$, e_2 can be removed from the avoid set A; and $\&(x \to n) \neq \&y$ is true when y is a variable. Another essential class of rewrite rules is formed by *type reasoning*, further discussed below. Furthermore, we apply several standard rules, including the Davis-Putnam-Logemann-Loveland procedure [11], to simplify boolean expressions. The tool includes automatic conversion of abstract programs to S/R or Promela format, the resp. input formalisms for the model checkers COSPAN and SPIN. The correctness property to be verified can be added to the abstract program by using assertions or temporal logic.

4.1   Type Reasoning

Suppose that x and y are program variables of the *List* type from our examples. A typical predicate that may occur during the manipulation of wp's is $reach[A;n](x,\&y)$. Regardless of the avoid set, this predicate is false, as can be seen by reasoning about types, as follows. Variable x itself is of type *List*. By dereferencing x, we get an object of struct-type *Node*, in which selection of the n field yields a *List* again. So the only types that are reachable from *List* are *List* and *Node*. The type of $\&y$ however is pointer to *List*. So $\&y$ cannot be reachable from x.

Reachability between types is formalized by a predicate *typreach*. For a set F of field names, $typreach[F](t_1,t_2)$ expresses that from an object of address type t_1 it is possible to reach an object of address type t_2 if only selection of fields from F is allowed. It is possible to prove the key correctness property that if $reach[A;F](e_1,e_2)$, then $typreach[F](t_1,t_2)$ for any address expressions e_1

and e_2 with types t_1 and t_2 resp. This property allows the simplifier to replace a predicate of the form $reach[A; F](e_1, e_2)$by *false* if $typreach[F](t_1, t_2)$ fails to hold. (Otherwise, nothing is replaced.) Type reasoning is also used to simplify equalities; e.g. $(x == y)$ is false if the types of x and y differ.

5   An Example

We illustrate our approach on a program for in-place reversal of singly-linked lists, also considered in e.g. [4,24,33,28,29]. The core of the program is given in Figure 6.

```
List x, y, t;   /* x is an acyclic list */

n1: y = NULL;
n2: while (x != NULL) {
n3:    t = y;
n4:    y = x;
n5:    x = x->n;
n6:    y->n = NULL;
n7:    y->n = t; };
n8:
```

Fig. 6. The list reversal program

Initially, x is the list to be reversed. It is traversed head to tail, reversing the next-pointers (n) one by one. At the start of every iteration of the while loop, x is the rest of the list to be reversed and y is the initial segment that has been reversed so far. Variable t is auxiliary; at any point during the reversal, it points to one of the first two nodes of the already-reversed segment. Using shape analysis, we want to verify that y is an acyclic list after the reversal (using the negation of predicate $p_1 = cyclic[; n]y@n8$), given the precondition that x is acyclic ($p_2 = cyclic[; n]x@n1$).

We run our tool on (the flow-chart description of) the program together with predicates p_1 and p_2, but without any approximation. By choosing a relatively large iteration bound, predicates are generated that occur in wp's obtained by propagating p_1 backwards through the sequence of statements of the while loop for a several iterations (p_2, being at $n1$, does not generate any new predicates). By manually inspecting these predicates, we can get an idea of the appropriate approximations to be applied. Setting the iteration bound to 30, 185 predicate/location pairs are calculated corresponding to about 3 backward iterations through the while loop. All predicates are of type *cyclic*, *reach*, or *equality*; they differ in their arguments. The following is an excerpt from the tool's output, showing some predicates relevant at location $n5$.

```
n5: reach[(&(y->n),&(*(x).n->n));n](t,*(x).n)
n5: reach[(&(y->n),&(*(x).n->n),&(*(*(x).n).n->n));n](t,*(x).n)
n5: reach[(&(y->n),&(*(x).n->n),&(*(*(x).n).n->n));n](t,*(*(x).n).n)
```

The difference between these instantiations of the *reach* predicate is in the number of "$\rightarrow n$ dereferences" of x. Clearly, the predicates will keep growing along this pattern for every next iteration of *wp*'s around the while loop, due to the assignment $x = x \rightarrow n$ after $n5$. An approximation that weeds out this growth is found by observing that the union of all these predicates implies that *from t, an address can be reached that can also be reached by following k n-fields starting from $*(x).n$, for some k*. A similar property can be expressed by a single *dshared* predicate — hence we use that as an approximation. If *dshared*$[;n](t,x)$ is false, then so is every of the predicates above. So we will try to cut off the growth pattern by approximating the first of those predicates, *reach*$[(&(y \rightarrow n), &(*(x).n \rightarrow n)); n](t, *(x).n)$ at $n5$, by "if $\neg dshared[;n](t,x)$ then *false* else $\top$".

This is the only pattern that occurs in the list of predicates, and indeed several other predicates at $n5$ can be approximated in terms of *dshared*$[;n](t,x)$ as well. The pattern also occurs in a sequence of equality predicates. At $n5$ these equations are in terms of y and x, and it is not immediately clear how to approximate them. But if we consider the same pattern at $n4$, where the y's get replaced by x's due to the *wp* over the assignment $y = x$, it shows up as follows.

```
n4: (x==*(x).n)
n4: (x==*(*(x).n).n)
n4: (x==*(*(*(x).n).n).n)
```

It is clear that none of the predicates can be true under the given precondition that x is not cyclic. So here we bring in the predicate *cyclic*$[;n]x$ by approximating $x = (*(x).n)$ by "if $\neg cyclic[;n]x$ then *false* else $\top$".

Having added 5 approximations, introducing the two new predicates mentioned above, we rerun the tool. We choose a larger iteration bound (40) so that not only all points will be reached where the approximations apply, but also the two new predicates introduced by them are propagated backwards far enough so that any patterns that they themselves may generate become apparent. This time, the pattern (the same as before: growing $\rightarrow n$-dereferences) occurs in 3 new predicates. One of them is a *dshared* predicate and can be approximated, at $n5$, in terms of the predicate *dshared*$[;n](t,x)$ from above. The other 2 stem from the predicate *cyclic*$[;n]x$ and can be approximated by that same predicate, at $n4$.

The third run of the tool, although started with iteration bound 40 again, converges after 29 iterations with the message that no predicates remain to be examined. A total number of 33 relevant predicates have been found at that point, 3 of which are suggested by the approximations, of which there are 8 altogether. Each run of the tool takes about 1 second.

Another way to identify suitable predicates for approximation is through the analysis of counter-examples that are produced by the model checkers in case the current abstraction is too coarse. Error-trace analysis boils down to solving satisfiability questions over predicate formulae, and thus we might benefit here from work on *decidable* logics to reason about heaps or arrays [4,19,21,31].

Model checking. Next, we instruct the tool to produce the corresponding abstracted list reversal program in both S/R and Promela formats, and use the COSPAN and SPIN model checkers to independently verify the original cyclicity property. In both cases, the checking is done in the order of hundredths of a second, within minimal amounts of memory (0.1MB with SPIN and less with COSPAN[4]). The Promela version has 34 reachable states, each 48 bytes in size. For the S/R version, 32 states are reached[5] and the constructed BDD's have 2454 nodes. Both verifications confirm that the property holds. Removing the precondition that x is acyclic results in failure, showing that it is necessary.

In case of the list-insertion example from the Introduction, the tool converges after 4 iterations without the need for any approximations. So in this case the abstraction is fully automatic. The resulting S/R and Promela models have 12 and 7 reachable states resp., and verification is again done in a fraction of a second with minimal amounts of memory in both cases.

6   Related Work and Conclusions

A synthesis and generalization of several existing algorithms for shape analysis is presented in [29]. Their algorithm constructs a shape graph invariant, expressed in 3-valued logic, by an abstract interpretation of program actions. The invariant is based on two core predicates: $x(v)$ (the node for variable x) and $n(v1, v2)$ (a link from $v1$ to $v2$ via field n). To improve precision, user-supplied instrumentation predicates have to be used, including shape predicates and also non-shape predicates such as $\leq$. Precision can also be improved by a *focus* operation that turns undefined values into non-determinism, or by *materializing* new elements (e.g., to distinguish between reachability in 0, 1, or more steps). A *coerce* operation eliminates inconsistent parts of an invariant. The implementation (TVLA) [24] includes a *blur* operation, which weakens an invariant.

Although the exact relationship between our algorithms is—as yet—unclear, some general comments can be made. First, the abstraction computed by our algorithm can be used to construct shape graph invariants—this is done implicitly by the model checking procedure—but also to check non-invariance properties. Secondly, operations similar to focus, coerce, and blur, all of which have to do with the precision of the reachability computation, are implemented in model checkers. Determining how well these generic techniques work for the particular problem of shape analysis is an intriguing question for future work but, in the examples we have considered, the model checking was not an issue.

One of the chief differences is the backward, goal-directed nature of our abstraction method, and the corresponding lack of distinction between core and instrumentation predicates. In fact, the iterated *wp* calculations, starting with predicates from the property, naturally identify other relevant predicates, including all of the needed instrumentation predicates. On the other hand, the TVLA tool analyzes the list reversal example fully automatically, in contrast to our use of user-supplied approximation hints. However, we believe that it is possible

---

[4] SPIN always seems to take at least 0.1MB due to overhead or a built-in lower bound.
[5] The difference in the number of reachable states is due to different ways of modeling.

to automate the heuristics we have used for identifying approximations, so that programs such as this are handled fully automatically.

In [25,27], *wp* for reachability is calculated, but no other shape predicates are considered. Predicate abstraction, combined with model checking, has been used in analyses of some heap properties: points-to analysis [1], correctness of concurrent garbage collectors [10,9], and loop invariants [13]. These papers, however, do not handle shape properties.

In conclusion, we believe that the separation of concerns between abstraction and state space exploration that is proposed in the new framework opens up several possibilities. The abstraction method serves to discover the predicates that are relevant for proving a given property. The *wp* calculations perform abstraction *locally*, leaving the *global* state space exploration to a model checker. One can thus take advantage of highly optimized model checking implementations, and the wide variety of logics and system models to which they apply. Our initial experience has, we hope, demonstrated the promise of this method, while raising several interesting questions for theoretical investigations and experimental improvements.

Our ongoing efforts are focused on mechanizing the heuristics for approximations. As the verification problem for shape properties is undecidable, we cannot hope for a fully automated procedure that works on all instances. However, there have been successful attempts [23] to automate similar approximation heuristics using recognition of pattern growth in (regular) expressions, based on the framework of *widening* [7,8]. Also, we can potentially benefit from the design of theorem proving tools, such as ACL2 [20], which successfully recognize induction patterns in many cases.

References

1. T. Ball, R. Majumdar, T.D. Millstein, and S.K. Rajamani. Automatic predicate abstraction of C programs. In *PLDI*, 2001.
2. T. Ball, A. Podelski, and S. Rajamani. Relative completeness of abstraction refinement for software model checking. In *TACAS*, volume 2280 of *LNCS*, 2002.
3. T. Ball and S. Rajamani. The SLAM toolkit. In *CAV*, volume 2102 of *LNCS*, 2001.
4. M. Benedikt, T. Reps, and M. Sagiv. A decidable logic for describing linked data structures. In *ESOP*, volume 1576 of *LNCS*, pages 2–19, 1999.
5. R. Bornat. Proving pointer programs in Hoare logic. In *Mathematics of Program Construction*, volume 1837 of *LNCS*, pages 102–126, 2000.
6. E.M. Clarke, O. Grumberg, S. Jha, Y. Lu, and H. Veith. Counterexample-guided abstraction refinement. In *CAV*, volume 1855 of *LNCS*, 2000.
7. P. Cousot and R. Cousot. Abstract interpretation: A unified lattice model for static analysis of programs by construction or approximation of fixpoints. In *POPL*, pages 238–252, 1977.
8. Patrick Cousot and Radhia Cousot. Comparing the Galois connection and widening/narrowing approaches to abstract interpretation. In M. Bruynooghe and M. Wirsing, editors, *Programming Language Implementation and Logic Programming*, volume 631 of *LNCS*, pages 269–295, 1992.

9. S. Das and D. Dill. Successive approximation of abstract transition relations. In *LICS*, 2001.
10. S. Das, D. Dill, and S. Park. Experience with predicate abstraction. In *CAV*, volume 1633 of *LNCS*, 1999.
11. M. Davis and H. Putnam. A computing procedure for quantification theory. *J. Assoc. Computing Machinery*, 7:201–215, 1960.
12. E.W. Dijkstra. Guarded commands, nondeterminacy, and formal derivation of programs. *C.ACM*, 18, 1975.
13. C. Flanagan and S. Qadeer. Predicate abstraction for software verification. In *POPL*, 2002.
14. S. Graf and H. Saïdi. Construction of abstract state graphs with PVS. In *CAV*, volume 1254 of *LNCS*, 1997.
15. D. Gries. *The Science Of Programming*. Springer-Verlag, 1981.
16. R.H. Hardin, Z. Har'el, and R.P. Kurshan. COSPAN. In *CAV*, volume 1102 of *LNCS*, 1996.
17. T.A. Henzinger, R. Jhala, R. Majumdar, and G. Sutre. Lazy abstraction. In *POPL*, 2002.
18. G. Holzmann. The SPIN model checker. *IEEE Transactions on Software Engineering*, 23(5), May 1997.
19. J.L. Jensen, M.E. Jørgensen, N. Klarlund, and M.I. Schwartzbach. Automatic verification of pointer programs using monadic second-order logic. In *SIGPLAN Conference on Programming Language Design and Implementation*, pages 226–236, 1997.
20. M. Kaufmann, P. Manolios, and J.S. Moore. *Computer-Aided Reasoning: An Approach*. Kluwer Academic Publishers, 2000.
21. N. Klarlund and M.I. Schwartzbach. Graphs and decidable transductions based on edge constraints (extended abstract). In *Colloquium on Trees in Algebra and Programming*, pages 187–201, 1994.
22. Y. Lakhnech, S. Bensalem, S. Berezin, and S. Owre. Incremental verification by abstraction. In *TACAS*, volume 2031 of *LNCS*, 2001.
23. D. Lesens, N. Halbwachs, and P. Raymond. Automatic verification of parameterized networks of processes. *Theoretical Computer Science*, 256:113–144, 2001.
24. T. Lev-Ami and M. Sagiv. TVLA: A system for implementing static analyses. In *SAS*, volume 1824 of *LNCS*, 2000.
25. J. Morris. (1) A general axiom of assignment (2) Assignment and linked data structures. In M. Broy and G. Schmidt, editors, *Theoretical Foundations of Programming Methodology*, 1981.
26. K.S. Namjoshi and R.P. Kurshan. Syntactic program transformations for automatic abstraction. In *CAV*, volume 1855 of *LNCS*, 2000.
27. G. Nelson. Verifying reachability invariants of linked structures. In *POPL*, 1983.
28. N. Rinetzky and S. Sagiv. Interprocedural shape analysis for recursive programs. In *Computational Complexity*, pages 133–149, 2001.
29. M. Sagiv, T. Reps, and R. Wilhelm. Parametric shape analysis via 3-valued logic. *TOPLAS*, 24(3):217–298, 2002.
30. D.A. Schmidt and B. Steffen. Program analysis *as* model checking of abstract interpretations. In *SAS*, volume 1503 of *LNCS*, 1998.
31. A. Stump, C.W. Barrett, D.L. Dill, and J.R. Levitt. A decision procedure for an extensional theory of arrays. In *LICS*, pages 29–37, 2001.
32. http://www.cs.bell-labs.com/~kedar/shape_analysis.html.
33. E. Yahav. Verifying safety properties of concurrent Java programs using 3-valued logic. In *POPL*, pages 27–40, 2001.

Author Index

Lecture Notes in Computer Science

For information about Vols. 1–2476

please contact your bookseller or Springer-Verlag

Vol. 2516: A. Wespi, G. Vigna, L. Deri (Eds.), Recent Advances in Intrusion Detection. Proceedings, 2002. X, 327 pages. 2002.

Vol. 2517: M.D. Aagaard, J.W. O'Leary (Eds.), Formal Methods in Computer-Aided Design. Proceedings, 2002. XI, 399 pages. 2002.

Vol. 2518: P. Bose, P. Morin (Eds.), Algorithms and Computation. Proceedings, 2002. XIII, 656 pages. 2002.

Vol. 2519: R. Meersman, Z. Tari, et al. (Eds.), On the Move to Meaningful Internet Systems 2002: CoopIS, DOA, and ODBASE. Proceedings, 2002. XXIII, 1367 pages. 2002.

Vol. 2521: A. Karmouch, T. Magedanz, J. Delgado (Eds.), Mobile Agents for Telecommunication Applications. Proceedings, 2002. XII, 317 pages. 2002.

Vol. 2522: T. Andreasen, A. Motro, H. Christiansen, H. Legind Larsen (Eds.), Flexible Query Answering. Proceedings, 2002. XI, 386 pages. 2002. (Subseries LNAI).

Vol. 2525: H.H. Bülthoff, S.-Whan Lee, T.A. Poggio, C. Wallraven (Eds.), Biologically Motivated Computer Vision. Proceedings, 2002. XIV, 662 pages. 2002.

Vol. 2526: A. Colosimo, A. Giuliani, P. Sirabella (Eds.), Medical Data Analysis. Proceedings, 2002. IX, 222 pages. 2002.

Vol. 2527: F.J. Garijo, J.C. Riquelme, M. Toro (Eds.), Advances in Artificial Intelligence – IBERAMIA 2002. Proceedings, 2002. XVIII, 955 pages. 2002. (Subseries LNAI).

Vol. 2528: M.T. Goodrich, S.G. Kobourov (Eds.), Graph Drawing. Proceedings, 2002. XIII, 384 pages. 2002.

Vol. 2529: D.A. Peled, M.Y. Vardi (Eds.), Formal Techniques for Networked and Distributed Sytems – FORTE 2002. Proceedings, 2002. XI, 371 pages. 2002.

Vol. 2531: J. Padget, O. Shehory, D. Parkes, N. Sadeh, W.E. Walsh (Eds.), Agent-Mediated Electronic Commerce IV. Proceedings, 2002. XVII, 341 pages. 2002. (Subseries LNAI).

Vol. 2532: Y.-C. Chen, L.-W. Chang, C.-T. Hsu (Eds.), Advances in Multimedia Information Processing – PCM 2002. Proceedings, 2002. XXI, 1255 pages. 2002.

Vol. 2533: N. Cesa-Bianchi, M. Numao, R. Reischuk (Eds.), Algorithmic Learning Theory. Proceedings, 2002. XI, 415 pages. 2002. (Subseries LNAI).

Vol. 2534: S. Lange, K. Satoh, C.H. Smith (Ed.), Discovery Science. Proceedings, 2002. XIII, 464 pages. 2002.

Vol. 2535: N. Suri (Ed.), Mobile Agents. Proceedings, 2002. X, 203 pages. 2002.

Vol. 2536: M. Parashar (Ed.), Grid Computing – GRID 2002. Proceedings, 2002. XI, 318 pages. 2002.

Vol. 2537: D.G. Feitelson, L. Rudolph, U. Schwiegelshohn (Eds.), Job Scheduling Strategies for Parallel Processing. Proceedings, 2002. VII, 237 pages. 2002.

Vol. 2538: B. König-Ries, K. Makki, S.A.M. Makki, N. Pissinou, P. Scheuermann (Eds.), Developing an Infrastructure for Mobile and Wireless Systems. Proceedings 2001. X, 183 pages. 2002.

Vol. 2539: K. Börner, C. Chen (Eds.), Visual Interfaces to Digital Libraries. X, 233 pages. 2002.

Vol. 2540: W.I. Grosky, F. Plášil (Eds.), SOFSEM 2002: Theory and Practice of Informatics. Proceedings, 2002. X, 289 pages. 2002.

Vol. 2541: T. Barkowsky, Mental Representation and Processing of Geographic Knowledge. X, 174 pages. 2002. (Subseries LNAI).

Vol. 2544: S. Bhalla (Ed.), Databases in Networked Information Systems. Proceedings 2002. X, 285 pages. 2002.

Vol. 2545: P. Forbrig, Q, Limbourg, B. Urban, J. Vanderdonckt (Eds.), Interactive Systems. Proceedings 2002. X, 269 pages. 2002.

Vol. 2546: J. Sterbenz, O. Takada, C. Tschudin, B. Plattner (Eds.), Active Networks. Proceedings, 2002. XIV, 267 pages. 2002.

Vol. 2548: J. Hernández, Ana Moreira (Eds.), Object-Oriented Technology. Proceedings, 2002. VIII, 223 pages. 2002.

Vol. 2549: J. Cortadella, A. Yakovlev, G. Rozenberg (Eds.), Concurrency and Hardware Design. XI, 345 pages. 2002.

Vol. 2550: A. Jean-Marie (Ed.), Advances in Computing Science – ASIAN 2002. Proceedings, 2002. X, 233 pages. 2002.

Vol. 2551: A. Menezes, P. Sarkar (Eds.), Progress in Cryptology – INDOCRYPT 2002. Proceedings, 2002. XI, 437 pages. 2002.

Vol. 2552: S. Sahni, V.K. Prasanna, U. Shukla (Eds.), High Performance Computing – HiPC 2002. Proceedings, 2002. XXI, 735 pages. 2002.

Vol. 2553: B. Andersson, M. Bergholtz, P. Johannesson (Eds.), Natural Language Processing and Information Systems. Proceedings, 2002. X, 241 pages. 2002.

Vol. 2554: M. Beetz, Plan-Based Control of Robotic Agents. XI, 191 pages. 2002. (Subseries LNAI).

Vol. 2555: E.-P. Lim, S. Foo, C. Khoo, H. Chen, E. Fox, S. Urs, T. Costantino (Eds.), Digital Libraries: People, Knowledge, and Technology. Proceedings, 2002. XVII, 535 pages. 2002.

Vol. 2556: M. Agrawal, A. Seth (Eds.), FST TCS 2002: Foundations of Software Technology and Theoretical Computer Science. Proceedings, 2002. XI, 361 pages. 2002.

Vol. 2557: B. McKay, J. Slaney (Eds.), AI 2002: Advances in Artificial Intelligence. Proceedings, 2002. XV, 730 pages. 2002. (Subseries LNAI).

Vol. 2558: P. Perner, Data Mining on Multimedia Data. X, 131 pages. 2002.

Vol. 2559: M. Oivo, S. Komi-Sirviö (Eds.), Product Focused Software Process Improvement. Proceedings, 2002. XV, 646 pages. 2002.

Vol. 2560: S. Goronzy, Robust Adaptation to Non-Native Accents in Automatic Speech Recognition. Proceedings, 2002. XI, 144 pages. 2002. (Subseries LNAI).

Vol. 2561: H.C.M. de Swart (Ed.), Relational Methods in Computer Science. Proceedings, 2001. X, 315 pages. 2002.

Vol. 2566: T.Æ. Mogensen, D.A. Schmidt, I.H. Sudborough (Eds.), The Essence of Computation. XIV, 473 pages. 2002.

Vol. 2567: Y.G. Desmedt (Ed.), Public Key Cryptography – PKC 2003. Proceedings, 2003. XI, 365 pages. 2002.

Vol. 2569: D. Gollmann, G. Karjoth, M. Waidner (Eds.), Computer Security – ESORICS 2002. Proceedings, 2002. XIII, 648 pages. 2002. (Subseries LNAI).

Vol. 2572: D. Calvanese, M. Lenzerini, R. Motwani (Eds.), Database Theory – ICDT 2003. Proceedings, 2003. XI, 455 pages. 2002.

Vol. 2575: L.D. Zuck, P.C. Attie, A. Cortesi, S. Mukhopadhyay (Eds.), Verification, Model Checking, and Abstract Interpretation. Proceedings, 2003. XI, 325 pages. 2003.